FORTEAN TIMES 26—30
SEEING OUT THE SEVENTIES

Robert Rankin

1990

FORTEAN TIMES 26–30
SEEING OUT THE SEVENTIES

Edited for volume publication by
PAUL SIEVEKING.

FORTEAN TOMES
LONDON, 1990.

Published for Fortean Times
by Fortean Tomes, 1 Shoebury Road, East Ham. London E6 2AQ.

Cover painting by **Una Woodruff** for Fortean Times 30.

WARNING
The magazines in this volume are reproduced facsimile.
Please remember that addresses and prices quoted may very well be out of date, so check them out before ordering books and magazines.

The editorial address for Fortean Times is
96 Mansfield Road, London NW3 2HX.

Subscription inquiries – or requests for a sample recent issue of *Fortean Times* at a special price of £2.00 each (overseas by airmail for £3.00 or US$5.00) – to:
SKS (FT), 20 Paul Street, Frome, Somerset BA11 1DX.

British Library Cataloguing in Publication data:

Fortean Times 26–30: Seeing out the Seventies.
1. Mysteries
I. Sieveking, Paul, *1949–* II. Fortean Times, ISSN 0308–5899.
001.94

ISBN   1 870021 20 7

1 3 5 7 9 10 8 6 4 2

Printed in Great Britain by
Bookcraft (Bath) Ltd., Midsomer Norton, Avon.

PREFACE

The five issues of *Fortean Times* reprinted in this book were out of print by 1983. The first three were still largely bashed out on Bob Rickard's typewriter. I was introduced to Bob in 1978 by our mutual friend, the perpetual traveller and fortune-teller Ion Will, and joined the FT team as associate editor. The Forteans used to meet every Tuesday afternoon above the science-fiction bookshop *Dark They Were And Golden-Eyed* in Soho (thanks to the kindness of proprietor Derek Stokes), where they would open the post, chortle over the latest japes of fate, and receive visiting monster-hunters and weird-watchers. My first contributions appeared in FT28, which was printed by an Israeli entrepreneur in northern Greece and shipped to London in the boot of a tourist bus.

FT29, with full typesetting and an A4 format, was our first attempt to "go public". We had a limited distribution through W.H. Smiths. Sales were quite encouraging, but for financial and personal reasons we couldn't sustain a regular newsstand distribution at that time. FT30 appeared at the very end of the decade, and established our familiar, nameless, format (230mm x 165mm, derived by random attrition from folded American foolscap). Now, ten years later, Bob and I plan to put a lot more time and effort into *Fortean Times.* Our first priority will be to publish the mag on a regular schedule so that it ceases to be a sporadical.

The magazines in this volume are reproduced facsimile, except for new running heads, the improvement of some pictures and the correction of 655 errors. I have made the contents as detailed as possible, as compensation for the lack of an index. We are planning a comprehensive index to all the magazines published so far, but the task of compilation is daunting.

Paul Sieveking
April 1990

ARTICLES

ILLUSTRATORS

Hunt Emerson has done dozens of wonderful drawings which occur throughout these magazines. The other illustrators are: **Mitch Davies** FT29 p47;   **Albrecht Dürer** FT26 cover;   **John Ellis** FT30 p38;   **Honeysett** FT29 p13 + FT30 p11;   **A. Krauze** FT30 p44;   **Steve Moore** FT28 p35 + FT29 p17;   **Pokkettz** FT30 p42;   **Bill Sanderson** FT29 p34;   **Ralph Steadman** FT29 p33;   **J.H. Szostek** FT30 p31;   **Bill Tidy** FT27 p14; **Peter Till** FT30 p53;   **Una Woodruff** FT30 cover.

FORTEAN TIMES 26-30 (1978-1979)
FULL CONTENTS

FORTEAN TIMES 26

FORTEAN TIMES 27

FORTEAN TIMES 28

FORTEAN TIMES 29

FORTEAN TIMES 30

THE SUBSCRIBERS TO THIS VOLUME

Mrs Sandra Amiss
Alan Lance Anderson
Jack Arnell
K.C. Austin
Andy Ayres
Sherry Baker
John Ball
Gary P.B. Baptiste
Ed Baxter
Miss Marsali Baxter
Peter Bayliss
K.A. Beer
Rodd Bench
Colin Bennett
Paul H. Birch
Gordon Black
Michael R. Blair
Ian Blake
Claire Blamey
C.J. Bond
Janet & Colin Bord
J.R. Bowcott
Richard Bowden
P. Braithwaite
G. Bromley
Mrs E. Brook
Paul Brough
Linda Brown
Mark Brown
David J. Burns
K.L.M. Butterfield
Mrs M. Callaghan
Christopher Cameron
Ken Campbell
Andrew Carter
Rachel Carthy
Brian Chapman
Dag Christiansen
Peter Christie
D.A. Clark
Nigel Clark
Loren Coleman
the Viscount
    Combermere
John Cooms
David T. Cooper

Les Cornwell
Mat Coward
Mrs K. Criddle
A.S. Crisp
Jim Darroch
Colin Dascombe
Mike Dash
Robert Dehon
Stephen H. Dickens
Joseph M. DiGiacomo
Mrs E.C. Donkin
Michael Eaton
Mark Ellis
A.S. Evans
Bob Everett
Harold Faretto
David Farrance
George R. Featherston
Jon Felix
The Folklore Society
Robert Friede
Jon Paul Fry
Brian Funnell
Richard Furlong
Rob Gandy
Dr T.J. Gaynard
Mr G.S. Gildersleeve
R.R. Gordon
Tarquin Rees Gore
Paul Green
Mr A.J. Greenhalgh
Mr M.K. Griffiths
David Grimbleby
Hans-Ake Gustavsson
J.A. Hall
Lucy Hall
John Halliday
Kim Möller Hansen
Mr B.D. Harder
Mr P. Harmson
M.J.C. Harpur
Mr M.K. Harris
Jim Haslam
Jeffrey Helfont
Mr A.H. Henshall
Stuart A. Herkes

Jenny Hierons
Anthony Holt
D. Howard
Dean Howard
Ralph O. Howard Jr
A.J. Howell
Graham Jacobs
Oli James
Karl Jeffery
Jason John
I.K. Johnson
Peter Kels
Jake Kirkwood
Daniel Kleinman
W.A. Knight
Andrew Knowles
Walter Krieger
Curt A. Krumpe
C.H. Lambert
J.G. Lane
Walter J. Langbein
John H. Lawson
Stuart Leadbetter
Ronald Lee
Harold L. Lesser
Phil Lord
Peter J. Luce
Mr M. Luke
Alexis Lykiard
Colin Mackereth
Ulrich Magin
Christopher Makepiece
John Macmillan
Nick Maloret
K.C. Mann
Vladimir Markotic
Jeff Marriott
Eileen Marshall
Jeremy Marston
Otto Martinussen
Chris Matheson
Marcus J. Matthews
Colin McKay
Gordon McLennan
Jim McLennan
William McPhail

J.C. Mentes
Mike Merrington
John Michell
Mr R.W. Mills
Barbara Millspaw
P.R. Missin
Robert Mitchell Jr
John Mollett
Steve Moore
Mr J.R. Munns
Raymond Nelke
David Norman
Ralph Noyes
John S. Oney
Michael Orson
Peter Overton
Chris Owen
R.H. Partridge
Dr Audrey Patrick
Gordon Perkins
Tom Perrott
Mrs J. Petrie
Hugh Pincott
Stephen Plant
Ian Pollard
Ronald D. Polton
Colin Potter
Larry Potter
Linda Price
Michael Prime
Pasi Punnonen
Carolyn Pyla
Terry Pyle
Simon A. Queen

Robin & Luc
    Pascoe van der Raaij
Mr F.W.G. Rau
Kurt Reimel
Samuel Renshaw
Barry Reynolds
Jonathan P. Roberts
Perry Roberts
Roy Robinson
Conrad C. Romo
Alan J. Rooke
Sven Rosén
Tom Rosenbloom
David Rossiter
Steve Roud
John Rowe
Mike Rowe
Rick Sanders
Craig Saunders
Mr Genya Savin
Jeff Saward
Ronnie Scott
Stephen Scott
Dr Keith Seddon
Robin Shelley
Ian Simmons
Bruce A.S. Skeer
Gordon Skinner
Ian Skinner
A.C. Moody-Smith
Miss M. Stacey
P. Stallard
Paul R. Standing
Mark W. Stephenson

Hugh N. Stiles
Akio Stribling
R.D. Summers
Henry Tenhovaara
S.R. Thackery
Mark Tinkler
Anthony Tocker
Mr W.J. Toombs
Lars Thomas
Andreas Trottmann
Dennis Turner
George Ventura
Col. Leen Verhoeff
Roger Waddington
James Wallis
Wendell Wagner Jr
David Wallechinsky
G.E. Wallwork
Geoffrey Wareing
Nigel Watson
Arthur Waugh
Theo de Weert
Christine R. Weiner
Robert Wellington
S.P. Whatley
Owen Whiteoak
J. Wiesen
Terry Wilkin
Gene Wolfe
Jeane Worthington
E. van Wouwe
C.E. Wren
Jon Wright
Chris Xenis
Mr T. Young
Myron Zamoznyj.

Fortean Times

Christ´s Face at Shamokin 33

75p:$1·50

UK ISSN 0308-5899

FORTEAN TIMES

A Contemporary Record of Strange Phenomena

FORTEAN TIMES ℅ Dark They Were & Golden Eyed,
9-12 St Annes Court, London, W1, England

FORTEAN TIMES is a non profitmaking quarterly miscellany of news, notes and references on current and historical strange phenomena, related subjects and philosophies. Formerly 'The News'. Affiliated to the International Fortean Organisation (INFO), and the Society for the Investigation of The Unknown (SITU), and other Fortean journals in continuing the work of Charles Fort (1874-1932).

Edited and published by Robert JM Rickard.
Contributing editors: Phil Ledger, Steve Moore,
Paul J Willis. Heading art by Hunt Emerson.

SUBSCRIPTION information and details of other deals can be found on the back page.

CONTRIBUTIONS of articles, artwork, notes and letters-of-comment on related subjects are always welcome. YOU CAN HELP by sending us a copy or clipping of any item you think will interest FT readers – just add a note of the DATE, the SOURCE and your NAME (for the credit). All clippings go on file to be published in due course. Please don't assume we must know about it already – there are surprisingly few duplications.
The editor regrets that it is not always possible to reply to all correspondence. Acknowledgements of money received will be sent via the following issue of FT.

FORTEAN PICTURE LIBRARY – We are laying the foundations for a long-needed pictorial archive to satisfy both research and commercial needs for the preservation and supply of visual material on Fortean subjects. Interested parties (users or those with material) can contact us via FT's editorial address.

Printed by Windhorse Press at Sukhavati,
51 Roman Rd, London E2

Projects

Your editor's article, last issue, about the great Fortean computer project erred on the side of enthusiasm in some respects. It seems that the great amount of groundwork that must be done is ill-suited to a committee-type administration, and apologies are offered for giving the impression that a team has been assembled, or will be assembled in future. The work will continue as it has done to date, most efficiently on a private, small and personal level until the parties involved decide on another approach. In the article your editor was partly trying to plead the case for computer-assisted filing and indexing of Fortean data, and partly trying to locate any UK Forteans with computer experience, with whom he could chew over some preliminary ideas and perhaps alleviate his abysmal ignorance in these matters. It's going to take longer than I imagined, but I'm undaunted – the goal and the material demand that we get matters right, and in the right order.

Our other projects continue apace. The Fortean Picture Library has acquired the Doc Shiels Nessie pictures, and some sales are lining up. As soon as our descriptive material is printed up we'll be trying to acquire much more.

Plans are already in motion for the launching, next year, of a special series of 'Occasional Papers' in Fortean subjects, under the general editorship of our able friend and scholar Steve Moore. They will cover all manner of Forteana and related material, and range from wholly new papers of detailed research, to reprinted reference material sorely needed but long out-of-print or otherwise unobtainable. Some titles will be announced early next year.

TRUSS FUND...

...in which we acknowledge the generous donations of the following: Richard King, Ray Manners, SN Morgan, Keith Raison, Dwight Whalen – and the member of the Three-legged Toad Cabal (who wishes to remain anonymous) who has enabled Ion Will, Steve Moore and your editor to attend this year's Fortfest in Washington. Many thanks !

cont on p50...

WHAT D'YOU THINK, MARV?

I REALLY DO GENE

A fairly random round-up of some of the curiosities swelling the file...first some interesting finds...

Remains of hitherto unknown temple beside the great Artemis Temple, at Ephesus, Turkey, dating to 6-700BC. Bombay Sunday Standard 18 Sept 1977 (Cr: Ion Will.) A temple of King Ptolemy VI, who ruled Egypt from 181-145BC, discovered at Luxor in Upper Egypt, and inside a temple to the Goddess Mot. A number of other relics, including 2 statues of Rameses III (1193-1166BC). Calcutta Statesman 5 Oct 1977 (Cr: Ion Will.)

A life-size statue of the Roman goddess Minerva, in terracotta, regarded as one of the most important finds in recent years, was dug out, with fragments of 50 broken statues, of a cave in the region known as the Sacred City of Lavinium, 18 miles south of Rome, and just a few 100yds from the tomb of Aeneas, who fled from Troy to Carthage and whose ancestors, legend has it, founded Rome. St Louis Globe-Democrat 25 Nov 1977 (Cr: Lou Farish.) An intact head of the goddess Athena, in marble, found at Beit Shean, the first of its kind to be found in Israel. It is a helmeted design, copied from the Greek model, dating to 2nd C, and was part of a statue 3 meters high. NY Herald Tribune 6 Jan 1978 (Cr: Ion Will.) A mystery find of a statue of a bare-breasted woman wearing pearls, thought to be Indonesian, was found by workers on 27 Jan in a false ceiling during demolition of a house in Bracknell, formerly used as the offices of a German pharmaceutical chemist. The antique figure, 7½" high and made of ivory, has baffled the police in their attempts to find out how it got there...they think it might be part of an antique robbery ...but we remember the Chinese seals found in Ireland! Reading Evening Post 1 Feb 1978.

An oldie but unrecorded here - the tomb of a pair of giants was found by Soviet archeologists in the northern Caucasus, and may date back 5000yrs. The tomb is made from highly polished slabs of volcanic rock each weighing up to a ton, and was furnished in gold, with household articles and gold ornaments. The male and female occupants measured 7ft 2" tall. Voice of the Nation (Bangkok) 29 March 1976, Pretoria News 31 March 1976 (Cr: I Will, C Holtzhausen.) An ancient smelting furnace, and an intact temple complete with tower, found at Mokhrablur Hill excavations, Ararat Valley, in south Caucasus, provides wealth of new knowledge about early civilisation there. Soviet Union no335, 1978 (Cr: I Will.) Clay and stone chess pieces, some with carved faces were found in a stone-age settlement at Gadyme-Depe, Soviet Turkmenia. They date back 8000yrs. Herald Tribune 13 July 1978 (Cr: Ion Will.)

A tomb containing a 700yr-old male was uncovered in Kiangsu province, China London Evening Standard 13 Sept 1977 (Cr: Ian Lawes.) We wonder if this is an erroneous account of the 2100yr-old tomb, containing 1000 burial objects, unearthed in Kwangsi, told of in the Guardian 16 Aug 1977. A stone-age site, dated back 10,000yrs, found on bank of Heilung river in northeastern Heilungkiang province, China. London Evening Standard 26 Jan 1978. 40 tombs dating back 2000yrs, found in eastern Sinkiang province. It is apparently the cemetary of a rich family from the Warring States period, and contains meat offerings and many relics. Daily Telegraph 5 June 1978.

Rare copper plates engraved with the edicts of the 4th Buddhist Council held in Kashmir in the 2nd C, found 65km SW of Srinagar. The plates bearing 6.6 million words were buried under stone "which cannot be found outside Egypt" says Kashmir archeologist Mohammad Amin. Amrita Bazar (Calcutta) 9 Oct 1977 (Cr: Ion Will.) A tomb filled with artifacts dating to 350-320BC has been claimed "without a doubt that this is King Philip's tomb." The remains of a man in a solid gold chest, and 5 carved ivory busts of Philip, his wife Olympiada, and his son Alexander the Great, prove this is the tomb of Philip of Macedon, claims Manolis Andronikos of Salonica University, Greece, who organised the excavations deep below a narrow street in the village of Virgina. The chest was in a marble sarcophagus in a chamber said to be the first Macedonian tomb found intact, and containing priceless relics, carvings, gold armor and weapons. St Louis Globe-Democrat 25 Nov 1977 (Cr: Lou Farish.)

Electricity company workers digging below the busy streets near Mexico City's main square, on the site of the ancient Aztec city of Tenochtitlan, struck solid rock - it proves to be a 20 ton ceremonial monolith, elaborately carved with the image of Coyolxauhqui, the Aztec moon goddess. Hailed as the find of 2 centuries almost unanimously by all Mexican archeologists, it has led to the extraordinary call from top archeologists to level all the buildings in the square to allow the whole site to be exposed. Claudia Jonguitud voiced the opinion of many: "What's underneath means more to Mexicans than what's above," which includes the cathedral, national palace and post office. Inscriptions on the stone give information about the Aztec religious beliefs destroyed by the Spanish conquest. The stone dates from 1480 and was part of the great pyramid to the sun god, destroyed by the Spaniads in 1521. The stone is also thought to contain a tomb. Guardian 28 Feb 1978, London Evening News 13 March, Dallas Times Herald 15 March, Daily Telegraph 5 June 1978 (Cr: Phil Ledger, Tom Adams.)

A new policy on archeology by the Saudi Arabia government has invited solutions to the 'Mystery of the Rings,' enigmatic circular stone-wall formations found scattered in remote areas on hilltops as well as in valleys. The 1-2ft high walls form circles of 5-100yds in diameter, and have been likened to the Nazca formations, and cluster in an area 30 miles north of Jædda. As part of a programme "to learn more about the country's ancient history", the Saudis plan to publish an archeological journal, establish museums, and tackle other mysteries, and shed new light on the ancient Romans, Nabataeans, Lihyanites, and the Queen of Sheba's Sabaeans. Minneapolis Star 29 Dec 1977, Arkansas Gazette 1 Jan 1978, St Louis Post-Dispatch 3 Jan 1978 (Cr: Lou Farish, Mark Hall.)

Traces of an ancient civilisation pre-dating by 3 centuries the fabulous finds of the cities at Harappa and Moenjodaro in the Indus valley, have excited archeologists in Pakistan. Pictographs on pottery and other relics indicate that written language was in use in the area well over 5000yrs ago. The site, at Rehman Dheri, in the North West Frontier province, some 200 miles south of Peshawar, is being excavated by Peshawar University. The National Echo (Malaysia) 10 Aug 1977 (Cr: Ion Will.) US archeologists using electronic detection equipment have located evidence of a lost city beneath the sands of the Nile delta. Pottery fragments and coins date the site to 400BC. London Evening Standard.

VON DANIKEN BARGIN BASEMENT

200 natural caves in Mexico's Baja California region have been discovered bearing strange drawings, in reds, yellows and blues...and among more recognizable representations of animals are unidentifiable "devices" and strange creatures. In a curious reversal of the usual roles, it is Mexico's minister of tourism, and not a journalist, who is waving the flag for ET intervention. Guillermo Rossell de la Lama says: "You get the impression the devices may be spaceships or a helicopter...You must think they are from outer space." Some drawings are "three dimensional" and stretch "up to 24ft off the ground." Harry Crosby, a Californian journalist and archeologist, who has studied the caves since 1967, said they "had been known to Western man since Jesuit missionaries visited the area in the 1700s. A Frenchman 'rediscovered' them in the 1890s, and they were even mentioned in a book on Baja by the late Erle Stanley Gardner." Crosby added: "It is certainly one of the world's major group of aboriginal cavepaintings...but (de la Lama) is trying to make a romance. The style is highly realistic, with certain artistic conventions suggesting they are the work of a single culture. The size of the paintings clearly point to the use of scaffolding or ladders. Hartlepool Mail 19 April, Phoenix Gazette (Az) 20 April 1977 (Cr: Paul Screeton, Mark Hall.)

Three large mysterious discs, each "exactly 1.4 meters in diameter, 46cm high at the center, and perfectly circular", were found in an open-cast coal mine at Leigh Creek, South Australia. At first they were thought to be fossil sea shells, but an Adelaide marine expert, Michael Lawrie, said: "I've never seen anything like these objects. They appear to be rusty on the outer casing and are believed to be millions of years old. One thing is certain - they are not fossilised shells." Shirley Kemp, of the Australian UFO Research Society, said the discs, one of which is broken, could be the find of the century. "Scientists believe the coalfield was burned out by a blazing meteor thousands of years ago. But aboriginal folklore tells of a giant craft that came from the heavens many years ago and landed in the area. Then the men on board lit a huge fire to signal their arrival." Anyone heard any more about this intriguing story? New Zealand Herald 25 June, Sunday Express 26 June 1977 (Cr: Mrs PD Dixon, Ann Williams, Valerie Martin.)

AND SPEAKING OF ABOS...
The 'Rainbow Serpent' rides again... it seems that the Western gift of dispossession, demoralisation, alcoholism, handouts, disease, and even ruthless extinction of whole tribes, is about to take an unexpected and grim turn for the worse. It was not until as shamefully late as 1976 that the Australian government awarded their aborigines the rights to their tribal lands, but all kinds of strings were attached that now look like being pulled. East of Darwin, between the South and East Alligator Rivers lies an undisturbed land of alligator swamps, wild buffalo and waterfalls, which was seen as fairly useless and so generously handed back to the original incumbents. For the 1000 or so Abos there it is the landscape of their "dreamtime heroes". Now it seems they are to be cheated once again, like abos everywhere, as gold and a lode of uranium has been discovered there. In the smallprint of the legislation the government can sell off mining rights to whomever and whenever they please. So far the Abos' committees have successfully delayed any attempt to disturb the resting place of the 'Rainbow Serpent'...but when up against callous government and big business how long can they hold out. Somehow they must, and must be given support and encouragement. Our hearts go out to them. London Evening Standard 4 June 1978.

Similarly, millions of tons of coal have been found below the Crow Indian reservation in Montana. As the pressure on the US for energy conservation increases, the value of this powersource in their backyard is incalculable, and you can understand the pressure in turn on the 'Crow Coal Authority', who not only wish to avoid being cheated all over again, but have no wish to see their hard-won homelands scarred by

pits and black-slag heaps. Understandably they want a fair price on today's values, and control of the exploitation - but every underhand trick in the legal and economic book will inevitably be brought into play by the 'government' "for the greater good." Our hearts go out to the Crow too - unfortunately they must be ever vigilant. London Evening Standard 30 May 1978. RJMR

Further to our section on feral children last issue (FT25pp8-10), we have a few additions to make with new data to hand.

BEAR BOY
Firstly our account of the boy was badly told; and the source Universe, is not Indian, but the well-known (to all but me!) Catholic newspaper printed in London; so we'll start again. The boy, aged about 8yrs, was brought to the Sisters of Charity in Lucknow by a priest of a nearby region, Father Michael John, who had kept him for a few days after discovering the boy in a cage in the village of Sultanpur. It seems that a year earlier, a hunter from the village was following bear tracks, and came upon the boy in the cave. Once back at the village, the caged boy was fed on berries, roots and snails. The nuns claim that already they have weaned him onto curry and rice after refusing their food for a while. Sister Antonia, in charge of him, said: "He certainly doesn't talk like a human being, but only mews to show when he is pleased. A doctor said: "All his gestures are those of an animal. But he can learn to walk on his feet and be taught to speak. But we don't want to rush things. The check-up showed he lived like an animal and survived on whatever the mother-bear brought him. Police were trying to trace the boy's parents in the villages around Sultanpur. Additional sources: News of the

World 14 May, <u>Daily Express</u> 18 April, Pretoria News (South Africa) 21 April 1978 (Cr: Colin Mather, Paul Screeton, Chris Holtzhausen.)

FERAL GIRL - SUMATRA

More often than not, feral children are reckoned to have been abandoned because they were physically deformed or mentally retarded. The following story offers an interesting alternative in this one case. Two rattan harvesters, in the seemingly inhospitable dense rain forest of Aceh, in northern Sumatra, suddenly came upon a girl in the jungle, and took her back to Beutong village at the jungle's edge. She was aged about 27, completely naked, her hair long and matted, her teeth yellow with neglect and her skin scaly and covered with scabs. It was not too hard to discover where she had come from as many villagers remembered the story of a 13yr-old girl called Rusdah who ran off into the jungle after her parents' greed ruined her chance of a happy marriage. The girl was sent to stay with an uncle because her parents were too embarrassed to have her back. Rusdah wanted to marry a local boy she loved, but her father regretted his consent and upped the dowry. Unable to meet the new demands the boy's family called the marriage off. Fearing the girl would elope, her father tied her to a post. Her cries filled the village with pity and a sister helped her escape into the jungle. A search party called off their unsuccessful week's search, and that was the last anyone heard of Rusdah - openly.

In her uncle's home, Rusdah has gradually readjusted to the food, clothes, and ways she left behind her 14 years ago - and has relearned her dialect enough to confirm the story of her disappearance - and here it gets interesting for me. She tells a story of strange friendly beings and animals who brought her consolation and relief from lonliness in her long exile. Apparently tigers and elephants had become her friends, and she never feared the wild animals in her jungle. She says she met about a 100 mysterious people, who came from time to time to see if she was all right. She added that she survived on rice brought to her regularly by some mysterious being she never saw - that and whatever the jungle provided. Nothing is said about whether her parents had set their grudge aside, or whatever happened to the boy she wanted to marry. <u>South China Morning Post</u> 8 Jan 1978 (Cr: Colin Johnson.)

SIBERIAN WILDMAN

A widely reported Tass release gave details of a wildman that roamed the Yakutia region of Verkhoyansk, about 400 miles north of Yakutsk city - but a bit belatedly it seems; since the last known sighting was in the 1950s, it was feared the breed had died out. Almost universally billed as 'Yetski' or Russia's answer to Bigfoot and the Abominable Snowman, Dr Semyon Nikolaev, of the Institute of Language, Literature and History, in the Yakut Branch of the Academy of Sciences, saw it more in terms of a survival from the earliest inhabitants of the region, possibly the last survivor of a remnant group of the aboriginal population, ousted from the more habitable areas by the ancestors of the present occupiers. Supporting this notion, he says, is that the name for the creature, 'Chuchunaa', also means 'fugitive' or 'outcast' in the Yakut dialect. Witnesses say the being reaches 6ft 6inches high, thin, with long arms to below the knees; its face looks human, but darker, and has a low protruding forehead; its chin is big and broad, and it runs in quick leaps. It has shaggy hair, and has a tendancy to shrill shrieks. It favours the dawn or late evenings for sneaking up to dwellings and stealing anything edible. Interestingly, this release came not long after details of the monster sighting at Lake Kok Kol (yet to be given in <u>FT</u>), and investigations by Soviet scientists into the Bermuda Triangle - are Soviet scientists becoming more interested in Fortean phenomena, or is it a cover for more political oneupmanship? <u>Guardian</u>, <u>Worthington Globe</u> (Minneapolis, <u>Calgory Herald</u> (Alberta), <u>Sacramento Bee</u> (Calif.), <u>San Francisco Chronicle</u> (Cal.) all 4 Feb 1978; <u>South China Morning Post</u>, <u>International Herald Tribune</u>, <u>The Herald</u> (New Zealand) all 6 Feb 1978; <u>Nature</u> 271:603 (Cr: Peter Roberts, Mark Hall, John Chalke, Dr EC Krupp, Colin Johnson, Ion Will, Mrs PD Dixon, Kurt Lothmann, D Robbins).
RJMR

Axemen/ cont from p8
was to terrorize the smaller gang and the Wo Shing Wo men left a number of shocked and wounded victims, including a man out back with his hand nearly severed.   RJMR

*** Next time we run this column, we'll have a more palatable derangement or two, like hat-snatchers, skirt-slashers, spectacle-swipers, pin-jabbers, and folks who hide out in car boots!

COMPULSIONS

Compulsions – our new file – covers the
gamut of strange behaviour from vampirism (of which we have much) to the berserk killers; the weak souls drowning
in floods of terrible urges, the mad
cultists, the desperate...Sometimes it
seems spontaneous:

When a loony's gotta do
What the Voices tell him to;
but if you look through the file, very
often there are clumpings. Consider:
within 3 weeks of mid-June this year
there were 3 self-immolations of the
'human torch' kind (we'll detail them
in our next 'Fires' section). What do
we mean by 'spontaneous' when we're ignorant of the myriad currents flowing
through any given nexus in time or
space? All we can do is chart the phenomena and learn the patterns... Some
events seem part of no pattern – like
the man who called at a service station
in Missouri, about 10am on 25 Aug last
year, demanded $5's worth of small
change, walked over to the water fountain, and gulped the money down with
mouthfuls of water, then said 'Thank
you," as he left. St Louis Post-Dispatch
26 Aug 1977 (Cr: J Peldyak, MJ Kautz-
man) – and others...well, we have so
many accounts of berserkers – it's an
affliction that fattens files – so for
this first sampler we'll look at mad
hacksmiths.

BURYING THE HATCHET
15 Nov 1975 – a Chinese woman goes
berserk in an unexplained incident in
Sutton-in-Ashfield, Notts, killing 2
young boys and seriously injuring 2
others in a house shared by 2 Chinese
families – the children's parents were
out working. Sunday Post 16 Nov 1975.
10 Jan 1976 – things get too much
for author Kudno Mojesic. He was arrested in the street outside his Belgrade,
Yugoslavia home, attacking cars with an
axe, yelling: "Away with all cars –
they are the Devil's work." Sunday Mirror 11 Jan 1976.
22 June 1976 – pedestrians in central Johannesburg scream and flee wildly
as an unnamed African strolled through
the crowd chopping at random. He hacked
4 whites before he was shot twice by a
policeman. At the policestation, he managed to summon the energy to escape and
jump from a 4th floor window – but he
survived even this and was in hospital
critically ill. An Indian flower-seller
said: "The axeman didn't even run. He
just walked along chopping out at whites
and shouting that he was doing it for
the children dying in Soweto." London
Evening News 22 June 1976.
15 June 1977 – peaceful scene, a tug
chugging down the River Thames. Suddenly a man with an axe goes bananas in
the cabin below then charges up to the
bridge and starts laying about him. The
skipper and four crewmen jump overboard
in terror, and for two miles the tug
veered crazily as police launches followed it, warning all shipping to stay
clear. Finally police boarded it and
disarmed the man as he was trying to
ram a fireboat at Greenwich. Daily
Mirror 16 June 1977.
4 July 1977 – like a suicidal finish
to a kung-fu film a young coloured youth
ran along Rye Lane, Peckham slashing
out with a knife in each fist. It was
10am – an elderly man died and 3 others
were seriously wounded before he was
cornered and disarmed by 2 policemen.
One shopkeeper said: "The man was carrying 2 long-bladed knives, running up
the street, shouting: 'I'm being treated as a slave in this country.' About
300yds from my shop he attacked an elderly man of about 70 who was walking
along the pavement and stabbed him once
in the stomach." I've a feeling that
the US TV-film 'Roots' was showing
about this time. London Evening News
4 July, The Sun & Daily Mirror 5 July
1977 (Cr: Anon.)
18 Sept 1977 – Richard Talmadge, in
Peking with actor William Holden and
actress Stephanie Powers as guests of
the government, was suddenly attacked
by a man with a knife, as he and Ms

Powers were strolling in a boulevard. It was said: "The reason for the attack was a mystery." A similar attack on an Australian woman teacher occurred "earlier this year", but we have no note of it. Daily Mail, Daily Mirror, Daily Express 19 Sept 1977.

15 Nov 1977 - a man wielding a knife went berserk on a tube train between Bayswater and Earls Court, London. Two girls were treated for cuts, bruises, and shock - the man got away. London Evening News 15 Nov 1977.

Now we come to an interesting grouping. On 12 June, David Berkowitz was sentenced to 315 years for his 6 murders and 7 woundings. There is much that is interesting about his case, not the least being the compulsive voices ordering him to commit these acts, which, according to Beserkowitz himself came from 'Sam' a millennia-old demon currently inhabiting the body of a neighbour's dog. After blessed absence of axemen in the first half of the year, it seemed as if the sentencing of 'Son of Sam' unloosed living nightmare, preceded by this little but grim joke:

10 June 1978 - a man brandishing a chain saw sent a screaming audience into utter panic as he charged through a packed cinema in Toronto - the 'Texas Chainsaw Massacre' was showing. Guardian 12 June 1978 (Cr: Paul Screeton.)

27 June 1978 - without warning, a "hefty, crazed" Russian went berserk with an axe at the entrance of Moscow's Intourist Hotel, killing 2 elderly Swedish tourists, and injuring a third. It is said that suddenly he "flung" himself at a group as they left the hotel and began hacking wildly at them. One reporter said that as police recovered from their shock and jumped him, there was blood and bits of flesh everywhere, one body beheaded and the axe still buried in the head of the other. Russia has publicly prided itself on not suffering the "senseless" crimes that plague the West, but as the Telegraph points out, the preceding month saw a public shoot-out between police and a hijacker who had seized Finnish hostages...and a prison guard shot 3 KGB men. The Telegraph's columnist 'Peterborough' adds that in 1976 a 'Jack the Ripper' murdered 9 women dressed in red and carrying shopping bags - and in another case a mad axeman, posing as a gas-inspector, killed 7 before being arrested, in the meantime gas-inspectors were being assaulted. Neither case was reported in the Soviet Press at the time. Daily Tele-

graph 28 June 1978.

7 July 1978 - 2 men, believed to be alcoholics, were found hacked to death on an abandoned car lot in Brooklyn. A note beside them read: "Two down, and nine to go." London Evening Standard 7 July 1978.

7 July 1978 - in the quiet Somerset village of North Petherton, the afternoon was shattered when a man burst into a cottage. The occupant, village postmistress, Margaret Majors, fled but she was hacked at and killed from behind and fell among her roses. A second woman was hurt trying to rescue Mrs Majors. Then the man battered on the front door of a nearby cottage, and when the door opened hit a third woman on the head - the two women were recovering in hospital. A retired policeman, Nelson Bidgway, heard the screams and rushed to the scene. "I saw the man with an axe and shouted to him. He was demented. He dropped his head and charged at me like a bull. I picked up a broom and hit him in the face with it as hard as I could." The man dropped his axe and Bidgway tied him up. It seems the man had just been released from hospital after being found running in a road a fortnight previously wearing only his shirt. It was also revealed that the police had responded to a call to the man's house earlier that day when his sons took refuge with neighbours saying their father had gone berserk. Mrs Majors was one of the few people to befriend him in the village. The Sun 8 July 1978. NB: This incident took place on the same day as the double axe death in Brooklyn, above.

10 July 1978 - after a near collision on a Birmingham main road a man was taken to hospital after the other driver fractured his skull with an axe, then drove off. Daily Telegraph 11 July 1978.

13 July 1978 - an elderly woman in Bethnal Green, London, was seriously ill after she was attacked in her own home by a man with a meat cleaver, inexplicably. Despite serious facial injuries and a skull split in 2 places she crawled for help - her crippled brother was treated for shock. Daily Telegraph 14 July 1978. The same edition of the paper gives the verdict on 3 Chinese Wo Shing Wo Triad members who, together with 14 others all armed with razor-sharp knives, choppers and a sword, attacked members of the rival Shui Fong Triad in a Bayswater restaurant, earlier this year. The purpose

cont on p6

We blithely went ahead typing up this section on teratology and genetic hankypanky, and just a few days away from pasting-up found we hadn't asked our intrepid and loony artist, Hunt Emerson, for a suitable heading...so please bear with us for lumping this very mixed bag under one of his recent efforts, which has come in..er..handy!

The controversy over David Rorvik's book, alleging the successful cloning of a mysterious American millionaire, continues with the disclosure of an interview with Rorvik, back in 1970, in which he says he was writing a pornographic novel about cloning. As we type, Dr JD Broomhall, the Oxford geneticist, has begun his suit against Rorvik's publishers, JP Lippincott, claiming that Rorvik had tricked out of him a detailed description of the most advanced techniques of genetic engineering that he has pioneered, and consequently damaged his own reputation - see Sunday Times 23 April 1978 and other sources. That same month saw a story that the Anderson Hospital and Tumor Institute, in Houston, Texas, has a clone zoo on ice, with cells of 300 animals stored in liquid nitrogen against the day of perfected technique - Russellville, Ark, Daily Courier-Democrat 11 April 1978 (Cr: Tom Adams). The inevitable comic-relief (or bad taste, depending on your views) has been injected by a US national weekly offering a reward for the location and identification of Elvis Presley's clone! So much for privacy!

So we thought the time was as right as it ever would be to tip out our genetic freaks, sports and mutations file, and type some up before the little buggers scuttle for cover!

FEAR & LOATHING IN THE FOREST...
Michael King, a forestry worker at Drigg, Cumbria, told an astonishing story to the Daily Express 30 June 1978.

In a clearing in the forest at Drigg, he stumbled upon giant spiders "very brightly coloured - blue, red and yellow", which spin webs "like steel. You could feel them pull tight against your body. You had to force your way through them. The spiders were over half an inch across their bodies." The area was formerly used as a dump for low-level radioactive waste from Windscale. King added there were "brambles the size of golf balls" (!) and that "All the vegetation was very lush and quick growing. I felt the whole area and its insect life was being mutated by the presence of radioactive waste." The nuclear complex at Windscale is currently at the center of much controversy about the future of the British energy programme (Did someone at the back cry "What programme?"?) - see recent issues of Undercurrents et al - and the sceptic in me nags that such a lurid story is not beyond the imagination, or motives, of the new breed of brilliant young journalists in the 'ecology' and 'radical technology' movements. But we wonder... King claims that he is "not against Windscale" nor a member of any environment pressure group, but he was "alarmed and worried by what I saw at Drigg.". A spokesman for British Nuclear Fuels admitted that waste was buried at Drigg, but dismissed King's claims as "ludicrous!" Beyond that single word pregnant with pomposity, there has been no news at all - not even an inquiry and a public reassurance - and I find that more disturbing than giant spiders in Cumbria.

... AND ON THE SEA BED.
In an earlier issue of FT, we mentioned briefly the reports of giant sponges found growing on and around barrels in an off-shore atomic waste graveyard, near San Francisco, California. Recently, the US Environmental Protection Agency decided to inspect the dumping ground, 3000ft down near the Farallon Islands, and found some containers had cracked, possibly on original impact, and others, with the giant sponge in residence, could have been cracked by the grip of the sponge itself. In an attempt to capture one of these 4ft tall new-comers - apparently they have never been seen in the area before - an oceanographer, Robert Dyer, was sent down in a minisub, but the wily vegetable or whatever it is proved too clever for him, eluding his mechanical grasp, slipping away appar-

ently to be "eaten by sharks." Despite Dyer's statement - "There is no reason to believe the sponge is a mutant", against which at least two of our clipsters had scrawled "Ha!" - the sponge was new to the area, or a new species altogether, and it's "snowflake-like body" drew some interest. UPI 31 October 1977, South China Morning Post 23 April 1978 (Cr: Colin Johnson, Larry Arnold, Tom Adams.)

A VERY PECULIAR PROCESSION

The following mutant march-past, like the unfortunate sports themselves, is quite mixed-up...

Cats: A ginger stray has been found in Nottingham with 6 claws on each paw. Daily Mirror, Daily Telegraph 3 July 1978. Interestingly, there had been a correspondence on 6-toed cats just 5 months previously, in the letter column of the Daily Mirror. On 1 Feb, Jennifer Wellstead, of Penzance, Cornwall, asked if any others had a cat with 6 toes on each paw. On 15 Feb, Mrs 'I', of Kettering, Northants, pointed out that 6-toed cats were favored as the familiars of witches; and Mrs M Farley, of Havant, Hants, said she had 6 cats, 3 of them with 6 toes, and 2 with 4 toes on each foot in place of the 'normal' 5. A recent litter, she says, produced 1 with 7 toes, 4 with 6 and 2 normal toed cats. Must be more widespread than people had thought!

Another old note comes from the ever industrious burrowings, by Nigel Watson, in the backfiles of the Gainsborough News - in the edition for 4 April 1947, quoting from an earlier edition of the paper for 31 March 1922, is a mention of a cat that lived for only an hour after being born with 8 legs and 2 heads.

Chickens: Perhaps this should go under 'Coincidences'...SF Christian, of Cambridge, wrote to the Daily Mirror 8 June 1978, to say that for the past eight weeks she has bought the same brand of frozen chicken, and that 7 of the birds had two necks and no livers!

Make of that what you will, but Ivan Bunn, editor of Lantern, sends us an old note from the Lowestoft Journal 7 June 1890, saying that a 2-headed chicken with 4 wings, 4 legs and 2 bodies (being joined at the heads) was hatched out in the town the previous week, and was now on view at Mr Howard Bunn's, Naturalist, in the town's High Street. Another coincidence?

We have quite a few notes on 'green gulls' and multiple-yolked eggs etc but we'll keep these for a more detailed 'Bird Curiosities' section.

Crustaceans: Fishermen, at Montevideo, Uruguay, pulled some kind of "sea monster" out of the Rio De La Plata. It was fantailed, had a tortoise-like shell 6ft in diameter and huge fins, weighed about a ton, and was dying as it was brought ashore. Prof Victor Bertullo, of Uruguay's Institute of Fish Research, admitted the identification of the creature confounded him, as it "was not to be found in any book." St Louis Globe-Democrat 13 May 1978, South China Morning Post 13 May 1978 (Cr: William Zeiser, Colin Johnson.)

The photo below, from The News, Portsmouth, 25 April 1977, shows a three-clawed lobster, caught earlier that week by lobster fisherman Eric McLeod, who said he'd seen nothing like it during his nine years of fishing from Portsmouth's Camber Docks. Mr McLeod is the one wearing the pullover! (Cr: Nick Maloret.)

Cattle: In 1952, a 3-legged calf was born on Harry Barber's Scunthorpe farm, surviving well into adulthood. A photo of it appeared in the Scunthorpe Star 7 August 1954 (Cr: Nigel Watson.)

Another thriving calf, this time with 5 legs, was born on a farm near Oimer, Nova Bystrice, in Czechoslovakia. Lincoln Star, Nebraska, 19 Sept 1974 (Cr: Joe Swatek.)

Horned animals have a special fascination. If you'll bear with the inclusion here of an elk, we'll tell of a female elk found with male antlers, not unheard of but exceedingly rare, in the world's largest elk herd at the National Elk Refuge, Jackson, Wyoming. Paris News, Texas, 17 Jan 1978 (Cr: Tom Adams.) The picture below, from The Times, Laredo, Texas, 15 Jan 1976, shows a unique one-horned steer, owned by George Magonical, of Lincoln, California, who crossed a Hereford with a shorthorn. The 7yr-old animal began with normal horns which were cut - then its singular protruberance sprouted. (Cr: Mark Hall.)

January this year saw several other cattle prodigies, as well as the elk (above). According to the Sunday Express 1 Jan 1978, thousands of people in northern Sri Lanka, were flocking to the village of Kanderodai to see a calf born with 2 heads and 3 eyes. (Cr: Paul Pinn). Later the same month a UPI release dated 30 Jan, tells of hundreds of Israelis trekking to the village of Zlafon, near Jerusalem, to see a calf born with 3 mouths, each

with lips, teeth and a tongue. According to our day-log, another miracle of 3 happened about the same time, just across the river into Jordan - see the story of the icon of the BVM in our 'Images' section this issue. This calf story was clipped from International Herald Tribune 31 Jan 1978 (Cr: I Will).

Sheep: 2 notes of 2-headed lambs... One, born on the farm of HD Addey, Claythorpe, Alford, Lincs, had 2 heads and necks. Gainsborough News 24 April 1925. The other, again with 2 distinct heads was born with another lamb, on the farm of Ernest Heffield, Donington, Lincs. Lincoln Leader 1 May 1909 (Cr: both to Nigel Watson.)

More happy is the story of the 3-legged lamb, born with a twin from crossing a Masham ewe with a Suffolk ram on the farm of Frank Craggs, at Sedgefield, Co Durham - it appears to have skipped around with its friends none the worse for not having a leg to stand on. Darlington & Stockton Times 29 March 1975 (Cr: Paul Screeton.)

A rather back-to-front piggy is remembered in the Cornish & Devon Post 26 Oct 1974, from its edition of 22 Oct 1904; it had one tail in the usual place and another between its ears! (Cr: Nigel Watson.)

Heaven only knows how we classify the following monstrosity, still-born from a goat in southern India on 24 June. Villagers claimed the 2 kilo freak was half-human in form, with a human face and stunted legs and hands! South China Morning Post 27 June 1978 (Cr: Colin Johnson.) Which brings us to

Humans: Sextuplets born at Leyden University Hospital, Holland, on 18 Sept, Daily Telegraph 19 Sept 1977 (Cr: Valerie Martin). Japanese mother gives birth to 2 sets of twin boys in succession, London Evening Standard 7 Feb 1978 (Cr: Ion Will.) Unprecedented legel wrangle caused by the paternity suits of a West German mother, who apparently ovulated twice in one day having made love to a white German and a black American soldier on the same day. She gave birth to twins, one black and the other white! Daily Mirror 29 May , Sunday Times 30 April 1978. Three sets of triplets born in the same ward at Merritt Hospital, Oakland, California within 10 weeks, claimed as 3 in a million odds, International Herald Tribune 10 July 1978 (Cr: Ion Will).

Siamese twins have also featured in 1977 . Two girls, joined at the torso sharing a pelvis and one pair of legs, but having separate spines, lungs hearts, heads etc, were separated in a drastic 10hr operation, on 23 June, at Children's Hospital, Washington, Miami Herald 9 July 1977. Another pair of girls were successfully separated at North Shore University Hospital, Long Island, on 26 Sept. In a 5hr operation 20 surgeons separated their livers and the 8½" tissue tube that linked their abdomens. Newport News, Va, Daily Press, and Daily Telegraph 29 Sept 1977 (Cr: Gary Abbott, Valerie Martin). At the University of Arkansas Medical Center, a 3wk-old girl died during the operation to separate her from her twin with whom she shared a trunk, their hearts conjoined. The surviving twin was still critically ill a week later. They were born on 14 Sept at El Dorado. Newport News, Va, Daily Press 6,7,9 & 16 Oct 1977 (Cr: Gary Abbott).

India seems to generate an unusual number of freaks -- An otherwise normal boy, aged 14, was found at Bastar, in Central India, with a 4½" tail, Omaha World Herald, Nebraska, 13 Jan 1969 (Cr: Joe Swatek). At King George Hospital, New Delhi, the lifeless foetus twin of an 11mth-old boy was removed from his abdomen in a 3hr operation, The Eagle, Texas, 14 Sept 1978 (Cr: Tom Adams). A baby consisting of an ill-formed double-trunk with 2 heads, 4 arms and 4 legs, died shortly after birth in the Government hospital at Nemara on 11 Dec. Amrita Bazar 12 Dec 1977 (Cr: Ion Will).

At Children's Hospital, Philadelphia, a baby boy was born with its heart throbbing away outside its chest. It was immediately rushed into a 2½hr operation to replace the heart inside the chest, on 31 Mar . Using techniques that improved upon a similar operation there, on 10 Aug 1975, doctors have paralyzed the baby for several days to prevent him opening the sutures in his chest. A note in the report said this condition had only been noted 200 times since the first recorded case in 1671. Florida Times-Union 2 April 1977 (Cr: Gary Abbott). 13yr-old Doug Pitchard was astonished as the doctors to learn that he had a tooth growing in his foot. Dr Amar Bouraouie, of Lenoir, N Carolina, who removed it, said it was perfectly formed down to its roots. Dallas Morning News 22 Jan 1978, Moneysworth May 1978 (Cr: Tom Adams, Larry Arnold.)

Two remaining miscellaneous items of varying degrees of grimmo — A Coroner's raid on a "ghoulish" carnival sideshow at the Lake County Fair at Grayslake, Illinois, revealed that the exhibits labelled 'Cyclops', 'Froggirl' and 'Elephant-nosed Baby' etc, were not in fact made of plastic or rubber. The exhibitor, Chris Christ, was charged with the illegal disposition of bodies, and illegal possession of human remains. Santa Fe New Mexican 3 Aug 1977 (Cr: Tom Adams.) And more recently, from the Federal News Service of the Austrian Government announced a disturbing discovery: "...recent serial observation has shown that the shape of the head in the Austrian population is turning ever more into a round and spherical form." Scientific research, they add has been unable to ascertain the reason for this headchange! Guardian 18 May 1978 (Cr: Ion Will).

SOME CROSS-BREEDS
Mary Jackson was puzzled when, over a year, her guineapig had four litters - and the only other occupant of the hutch was a rabbit, who wasn't telling! Her claims that the rabbit had fathered the furry enigmas on the guineapig were swiftly scorned by experts at the Kessingland Wildlife Park - interspecies fertility, they roared, was "genetically impossible". They said that the first litter could be explained if Mrs Jackson, of Lowestoft, had bought the animal while it was pregnant; and the others might have been caused by one of the mother's own darlings, who, it seems, are quite prepared to keep certain things in the family! But it seems that Mrs Jackson may have given the litters away before they reached sexual maturity. The last we heard was that guineapig and rabbit were again closetted under the beady eyes of the experts who awaited further developments. Eastern Daily Press 8 Feb 1974 (Cr: RTA Hill). In our phenomenal universe pomposity precipitates many a good joke. While the experts of Kessingland peered through a hutch's keyhole, a 'bunny-pig' resulting from the mating of a rabbit and a guineapig was born at Knaresborough Zoo, Sun 5June 1974, just a few months later!

Another curious double phenomenon played out last year with the appearance in two places of a curiously formed cat whose hindquarters resembled that of a rabbit. The first account of the "cabbit" was its exhibition in Los Angeles by Val Chapman, who found it in New Mexico. The cabbit, claims Chapman, is the result of breeding a cat with a

rabbit - plainly impossible said Los Angeles Zoo-ologists. Judging from the photos in Dallas Morning News, Houston Chronicle, and Santa Fe New Mexican all of 11 July 1977, the animal looked more like it had a deformed pelvis forcing its legs out and back! (Cr: Tom Adams, Mark Hall.) The same term, cabbit, was being applied, just 2 months later, to the pet of Marian Pitcher, of Greenfield, Indiana. She too believed she had the product of a cat-rabbit mating. Zoo officials laughed when she rang to tell them of her cabbit purring at one end and hopping at the other. In contrast to the opinion of his colleagues, however, it seems that Dr David Osgood, prof of vertebrate anatomy at Butler University, Indianapolis, declared that it would not be impossible for a cat and rabbit to produce offspring, but "It's almost beyond comprehension for a biologist to imagine that it could happen." Hops and squirms - the motions respectively of cabbits and experts!

San Angelo, Tx, Standard-Times 18 Sept 1977 (Cr: Tom Adams.) Several days later another cabbit turned up in Pennsylvania, owned by Harry Goodwin, of Lower Swatara Township...only he'd always thought the peculiar animal was a Manx cat (even the local vet didn't seem too sure what a Manx looked like!) Goodwin's cat had ears slightly larger than a domestic cat, and longer whiskers, but its rear end had rabbit-like legs and heavy mottled fur. Goodwin said he used to keep a tame rabbit and remembered that a cat used to "play around" with it. "Some people say there is no way a cat and a rabbit can cross," Goodwin said,"but I say look at it and be your own judge. It hops like a rabbit, looks like a rabbit, and has fur like a rabbit." Harrisburg, Pa, Patriot 15 July 1977 (Cr: Larry Arnold.)

Knaresborough Zoo also figures in a story of an alligator kept there alone for 7 yrs, which suddenly produced a handful of little ones - parthogenesis? Roger Broadie heard this on BBC radio sometime around the early part of Oct 1975, and we have nothing else on it.

Farmer Dick Lanyon, near Melbourne, Australia, put a billygoat among his sheep to scare off foxes during lambing. Now, he says, he has dozens of 'lambs', half-sheep half-goat, and more are arriving every day. Last we heard: scientists examining the new animals, and Billy is locked up doubtless wishing these situations were reversed. Daily Mirror 17 Sept 1969 (Cr: Anthony Smith.)

A tigress sharing a cage with a lion at a zoo in Osaka, Japan, gave birth to 3 cubs with tiger's heads and lion's body. Alas - 2 died and the remaining one very poorly, Sunday Telegraph 14 Sept 1975 (Cr: Peter Hope-Evans.)

At Prospect Park Zoo, New York, a donkey was pregnant by a zebra, Sun 26 Oct 1973 (Cr: Anthony Smith). Whether it was ever born or not, we have no record - but one was certainly born in Christmas week of 1975 at Colchester Zoo, the third foal successfully born of mating a donkey with different male zebras. Previous attempts at crossbreeding zebras with horses and donkeys had failed to produce surviving foals, let alone the hoped for disease-resistant work-horse for Africa. Colchester Zoo believe success lies with their use of an Arabian donkey (not tried before), and even hold out a hope that these hybrids might viably breed (normally hybrids are sterile). Sunday Express 11 April 1976, Weekend 30 June 1976 (Cr: Anthony Smith.)

RJMR

Species Metapsychology UFOs and Cattle Mutilations

by Tom Bearden

*The following portion of a book by Marshal Grechko
was deleted from its English translation, at the request
of the Soviet Union: 'Of particular importance is basic
research aimed at discovering still unknown attributes
of matter for their study and use to reinforce the state's
defense capabilities.'*

FOREWORD

For some years it has been increasingly apparent that
UFO phenomena can be explained as temporarily
materialized archetypes from the collective human
unconscious; archetypes which are overlaid, filtered,
modulated, altered, and shaped by the shallower
levels of unconsciousness above the collective species
unconscious. These shallower layers must be travers-
ed by the archetypal form on its way to physical
materialization and conscious observation. A UFO
event involves one or more archetypes which are
triggered into full or partial materialization, but
whose reality formats appearing in the final
materialization are determined by the shallower
layers of unconsciousness's 'plumbing' through
which it passes.

E.g., it is well known in parapsychology that the
personal unconscious of an individual can sometimes
exert appreciable physical effects on the physical
world; the poltergeist phenomenon is one direct
example. Since the collective species unconscious
is vastly more powerful than a single personal unconscious layer of itself, the effect it can exert on
the physical world must be very powerful indeed.
So from what we already know in parapsychology,
it would appear possible for the collective unconscious to powerfully affect physical reality, even to
the point of materializing thought forms into actual
living existence, and possibly even to the point of
materializing living beings. But since no physics to
describe mind has existed, then no physical theory
to describe such drastic interaction of the collective
mind upon matter has existed.

However, the researcher has devoted considerable
effort over the last 13 years to model mind and

matter and the entire process of their interactions
in terms of a new physics. Some success has been
achieved, and within the last six years, a series of
papers sketching out the model and the physics to
describe it have been published.

But if this new model is valid, then one ought to
be able to directly psychoanalyse the UFO phenomena and gain a deep insight, and the process should
be very similar to dream interpretation routinely
accomplished by psychotherapists. However, just as
the 'dream popouts' from an individual's personal
unconscious into his conscious awareness symbolically reveal the pressure and conflict within that
personal unconscious, then the tulpoid materialization phenomena generated by the collective species
unconscious should reveal the pressure and conflict
within that collective species unconscious. So a parapsychological extension of Jungian psychology is
directly indicated. Were we a wiser and more
enlightened nation, we would already have established and developed such a metapsychology/meta-
psychiatry to assist us in our dealings with other
nations.

At any rate, since none of the new metapsycholo-
gists/metapsychiatrists seem to have developed, then
perhaps an amateur effort is warranted to indicate
the new path, its direction, and its usefulness. This
author — admittedly an amateur in psychology —
has made such an effort, and this paper represents a
brief condensation of the quite startling results
obtained.

In preparing the reader for the drastic nature of
those results, it must be emphasized that the major
pressure exerted on the human species since WWII
has been due to the conflict between the Western-
aligned nations and the Soviet Bloc. So in the meta-
psychiatry of the collective species unconscious, the
tulpoid materialization phenomena must directly
exhibit strong symbolic aspects of this present 'cold
war' mental and emotional conflict of the species as
a dominating effect, and so in fact it does. In
particular, each major UFO wave must be directly

connected with a peaking of the cold war pressure in the collective unconscious, and it is.

One of the most bizarre and unexpected aspects which emerges is a startling but quite specific explanation for the cattle mutilations that have occurred across the US in the last several years. Even more horrifyingly, a direct prediction is indicated from the analysis: That prediction is that the Soviet Union is preparing to attack the West and China in the near future, and the last metapsychiatric symptom or indicator to be expected prior to that attack is a series of paranormal mutilations of human females in the U.S. and perhaps in a few associated countries as well.

As these words are written, a candidate for the first such female mutilation may already have occurred near Boston, Massachusetts in May 1977. If indeed so, then the moment of truth for the West is imminent, and more such appalling cases are to appear in the immediate future.

In science, a researcher strives to remain unemotionally involved, unattached, and unbiased. But in any research directly involving human beings, there is always a point at which scientific detachment must yield to human consideration, and this metapsychiatric analysis is such a point, beyond all question, for this researcher. The pen, the heart, and the hand that write these words are deeply shaken. For the first time in 13 years of unrelenting effort, I fervently pray that my insights and analyses might be proved totally in error.

* *

There is a distinct possibility that this author may have solved the UFO phenomena, and in fact Fortean phenomena and paranormal phenomena of all types as well. The key, however, has been found in a most unexpected place: It is necessary to make a formal change (an addition) to Aristotle's three laws of logical thought, and then the solution can proceed. [1]. Further, it turns out that the entire matter can be fitted onto a perfectly good, albeit fantastically strange, physics written by Everett at Princeton University under John Wheeler in 1957. [2]. And that makes it totally consistent with the entire experimental basis of present physics.

From this approach, the solutions to the problem of mind and the classic mind/body problem emerge. A mind can be modelled as a physical 4-space which shares the same time dimension as the laboratory 4-space, but one whose 3-dimensional spatial frame is three or more orthogonal turns away from the laboratory 3-dimensional spatial frame, in n-dimensional space. I.e., in an infinite set of orthogonal 3-spaces which all share the same time dimension in common, all 3-space frames three or more orthoturns away from the lab 3-space are mindframes or mind worlds. In this model, a thought form is physically real, but just in a separate world three

or more orthogonal rotations away from this physical world. The thought form is absolutely concrete in its own realm. This includes any thought form, whether of an inert object, a living biological system, or an abstract structure. Tulpas — thought forms which can under certain circumstances orthorotate several times and appear or 'materialize' in the ordinary laboratory 3-space — thus encompasses anything at all than can be thought — dragons, fairies, Sasquatches, Nessies, inert objects, ships, craft, Virgin Marys, demons,   gods, angels, UFOS, monsters etc.

Now a tiny amount of crosstalk exists among all the orthogonal worlds sharing a common time axis. Further, the time 'axis' is really more of an oscillating wave [3], and from the laboratory observer's viewpoint, the other orthogonal worlds exist merely as a tiny, tiny jitter on his time wave carrier. [4] I.e., these orthogonal realities are tiny modulations riding on the time dimensional carrier wave. Normally the magnitude of these modulations is so small as to fall below the quantum threshold of measurable/detectable change, so the orthogonal realities are virtual with respect to the laboratory observer.

However, if ordinary time coherence to one of the orthogonal forms is established in a large number of coherent stages in the laboratory frame, then the virtual phases for that coherent form increase (multiply) as an exponential function of the number of stages cohered [5]. If this is done for a sufficient number of stages, then the virtual coherent forms which are exponentially superposing reach and breach the quantum threshold, turning into observable change and 'materializing', i.e., quite automatic orthorotation back toward this physical frame ensues whenever sufficient multistaged coherence is established to a thought form in one of the orthogonal worlds. If there are sufficient tuning stages (these stages may be either mental or physical), the superposing form or tulpa rotates all the way back to the laboratory frame, and appears there in physically materialized reality.

If there is only sufficient tuning stages to rotate it to within one orthogonal turn away, that is the 'electromagnetic field' frame and the tulpa is seen as just a glowing light form. When the tuning starts becoming unstable, the tulpa starts turning away or dematerializing.

So all sorts of phenomena result: fairies (to a culture which soaks a belief in fairies down into enough unconsciousnesses) devils, imps, angels, godforms, sasquatches, skunkmen, Nessies, etc. In a previous dark age, when everyone believed in devils, occasionally one was met. When Satanic possession was widely believed in, it sometimes happened (this type of tuned reality is not quite yet vanished). The persons in the Dark Ages who feared witchcraft and demons had something behind their fears — they unconsciously were evoking the realities they feared. When the ancient Jewish tribes believed in a strong Father/King type of male god, one that was spiteful, vengeful, jealous, and which must be continually placated with sacrifice, pleading, and whining — then that is the type of god-figure they evoked. Similarly with other religions and beliefs.

An example of a tulpa which is being tuned in more and more frequently is Nessie, the Loch Ness monster. The more intense interest there is, the more photos that are taken, and the more investigation that is done, the easier it is to find evidence of Nessie, because the additional infiltration of the material and the thought form into more and more unconscious-nesses provides more and more tuning stages, and tuning stabilization of a materialized tulpa is an exponential function of the number of tuning stages and the degree of coherence (sameness) attained by the stages. It appears that Nessie is on the way to being permanently tuned in; a family of pleiosaurs is going to wind up living in Loch Ness, whether or not there is enough fish in the loch to support them — the past will just be changed to accommodate it accordingly.

All possible realities exist and are concretely real, but are just normally compressed to the virtual state by successive orthogonal rotation away from the laboratory 3-space. From the number of 'states' of the future, one can be selectively 'tuned in' if enough coherent minds (or physical stages) are involved. Any future at all — even the wildest and most implausible and least possible — can be tuned in. And the tuning effect increases exponentially, not linearly, as a function of the number of tuners. [5].

The same mechanism is what causes or initiates the radioactive decay of a specific nucleus [6]. Thus the frequent association of geiger counter activity with Fortean phenomena or UFO phenomena. Further, rotation toward the laboratory frame causes the tulpa to pass first into and through the world frame that is just one turn away. That is the electromagnetic field when approaching the lab frame from one direction; it is a sort of 'negative electromagnetic field' when approaching the lab frame from the other direction. Coming in from one direction, one thus gets glowing light forms and electromagnetic radiation, and then finally the 'light object' solidifies into a three-dimensional physical object. Then as the turn away from the lab worldframe is made, the object first turns into glowing light (one turn away) and then disappears (two or more turns away). On the other hand, turn-ing away from the lab worldframe in the other direction results in a 'dark object' or 'dark-ringed' object', then disappearance. Further, when a turn past the first orthoturn is being made, the 'light object' or 'dark object' generates DeBroglie waves (i.e., it is turning into pure DeBroglie waves). This DeBroglie turning backwards turning away from the electromagentic field frame (from the frame one orthoturn away from the laboratory worldframe) constitutes a 'wipe out' of the electromagnetic field, including the virtual photons that generate the actual charge of an electron flowing free in an electromagnetic circuit [*]. Hence the associa-tion of the phenomena with the conking out of electrical/electromagnetic equipment (auto lights, communications, etc) without really doing

[*] which converts the electron to a neutrino .

permanent damage — all that happens is that essentially the electrons flowing in the circuitry have their 'charge' directly dissolved, and magnetic fields get 'cancelled'. When the tulpoid rotates on through the second orthogonal turn, the effect is gone, electrons resume flowing in the circuits, magnetic fields resume, and everything is back to normal again.

The same effect is evidenced on the human body, where the 'current quenching' effect affects the electrical functioning of the nervous system. I.e., if one gets a little bit of the 'current quenching' effect, it is rather like a mild whiff of anaesthesia, and one has a very unreal, dreamy feeling, but is still conscious   and still mobile. It one gets a heavier whiff, then one has a heavily unreal, hypnogogic feeling, and the single channel nervous functions are electrically disrupted (circuit currents blanked) so that the individual is paralysed (the single channel system is primarily the nervous system controlling the voluntary muscular system). Get a heavier dose yet, and the multichannel systems start to go — here consciousness is lost. The autonomic nervous system, however, is manag-ing to function with difficulty, so the individual is still gaspingly breathing and his heart is still beating with difficulty. Get a stronger dose even yet, and everything blanks out electrically, and death ensues.

Since UFO phenomena are unconscious mental forms which are materializing to reality, one can directly 'psychoanalyse' the phenomena, if one is careful to add in the greater effects which are involved at the various levels of unconsciousness and pressing on them. So let us examine the phemenona from that aspect.

During World War II, Stalin laid plans to attack the West within about two years after the end of the war. He knew that, when the war was finished, the 'decadent capitalists' would immediately beat their swords into plowshares and disman and dis-arm, for they had always done so after each war. All he had to do was hold his forces ready and wait for this to occur, then take Europe in six weeks. However the advent of the atomic bomb frustrated this plan. He could no longer mass his forces, for American bombers loaded with atomic bombs could have simply obliterated them. Consequently, he had to change the plan and the time schedule. During 1946-7 the Communists were intensively revising the master plan and hatching the plans for a global cold war, reschedul-ing an eventual attack and takeover within a long-range, worldwide, strategic plan. So during this time, a great deal of threat stress — quite heavy pressure — was pressing down into the unconscious-ness of a large number of Soviet Communists. This constituted a heavy pressure on the collective unconscious of all humanity at a deeper level yet, and so in the other parts of the collective uncon-scious, popouts (tulpoid forms, i.e. archetypes) start pressing up through the successive layers of unconsciousness above the species unconscious — the racial unconscious, the national/cultural unconscious, large subgroup unconscious, group unconscious, personal unconscious, etc. These successive layers modulate and shape the pattern of reality that is pushing up, much like the different frequencies add together in Fourier analysis to compose the final form that emerges. Let us pause a moment to analyse some factors bearing on these reality modulations/shapings that are occurring.

The human unconscious is deepest ingrained with the experience of the ancient jungle days of millions of years ago, not recent history. In the human 'old experience' that is in our genes, the male went where the threat/action was, while the female stayed behind in the cave/fortress with the children, protected. Also, in the primates, the erect penis is a sign of domination, i.e., dominant monkeys 'erect and mount' other male monkeys to show dominance. The erect midfinger is still a hostile gesture, and one of domination. Further, fire is a power symbol to the collective unconscious; fire was power over animal adversaries, for it kept the tigers at bay.

So all the 'threat saturation' by the Soviets in 1946-47 ought to give a male penis symbol, include the fire symbol, etc., in adjacent areas. Power and domination. Further, into the unconsciousnesses of many persons (cultural and national unconsciousness) had seeped deeply the German use of rockets — male penis/fire domination/power symbols — in WWII. Use of these weapons had fired the imagination of the free world.

So in 1946-47 the erect penis/fire symbol — for dominance, threat, and power — ought to pop out where the action is, i.e, closest to the threat of 'war threatening' agent or zone. Bingo! Ghost rockets in the countries next to the Soviet Union — Norway, Sweden, Denmark, etc.

But the U.S. is a natural fortress, or so it had always been — two great ocean barriers east and west and no strong enemy north or south. That corresponds to the 'cave/fortress' protected place, and thus a 'female symbol' should result there. Bingo! Kenneth Arnold, flying over Washington state — the closest state at the time to the Soviet Union — in 1947 sees flying saucers, which are simply female mandalas modulated by our scifi/ Buck Rogers/flying aircraft national/cultural unconsciousness. Arnold's personal unconscious, the last modulation and shaper of the reality format that emerged, is that of a pilot. So flying saucers are what appeared over the U.S.

In 1973 the Yom Kippur War occurred. That was the Soviet's 'Spanish Civil War', where the final tactics and equipment for antitank and antiaircraft weaponry were tested. The effect on the U.S. and NATO of the cutoff of Arab oil was tested. Further, when the Israelis at one point succeeded in cutting off an Egyptian army, Brezhnev telephoned the U.S. president and informed him that the Soviets were going in; the U.S. could do whatever it pleased. The Soviets had seven airborne divisions ready to send in, and the U.S. had its single airborne division on full alert, ready for insertion. So the world teetered on the brink of direct confrontation between the Soviet Union and the U.S. with all its possible consequences. And 'confrontation' is after all another word for **contact**.

Now UFO 'contactee' cases involve **confrontation**. In **the very** month — October — that the Yom Kippur War erupted, the greatest wave of UFO contactee cases in history broke out in the U.S. Further, in the shallower unconscious levels above the collective species unconscious which were modulating and molding the reality format, the imagination of the world had been captured by the spacesuited astronauts who had walked on the moon. So most U.S. contactee cases involved spacesuited beings, conditioned into that framework by the national/cultural modulation. Some of the contactee cases involved robots or metallic men, analogous to the mechanista and robotry of the U.S. space program. And here in the U.S., the fortress, the female-mandala craft symbol was generally maintained.

Within the last several years, a rather fantastic number of paranormal cattle mutilations have occurred across the midsection of the U.S. A peak has apparently been centred in and around Colorado — the home of Cheyenne Mountain, in whose bosom the 'heart' or control center for the strategic retaliatory forces of the U.S. is nestled. That is significant, for it is the 'heart' of the U.S. which is to be slashed and eviscerated, in the Soviet plan. But to explain the cattle mutilations, some additional factors must be developed.

When checked in his plan to attack by the advent of the atomic bomb at the close of WWII, Stalin called in his scientists and told them the destiny of Communism had been frustrated by this great U.S. technical breakthrough. Further, this would not be the last great breakthrough. However, he informed them in no uncertain terms that the next great breakthrough of that magnitude had better be Soviet in origin. Thus they were to follow every field of human knowledge, no matter how strange or unorthodox, and intensely search for such another field of breakthrough. No stone was to be left unturned in this search. Once the field was discovered, they would intensely develop superweapons in secret — just as the U.S. had done — and spring them by surprise on the West — just as the U.S. had done on Japan. Ironically, we had showed Stalin the scenario by means of which the West could eventually be overcome.

In the interim, the guerrilla tactics of terrorism and insurgency, and unrelenting pressure, that had proven so successful in the Russian Revolution,were to be launched around the world on an international scale. In all the continents, small conventional wars would 'bleed the U.S. dragon' and weaken it. The Soviet Union would also embark on a massive crash program to establish defenses weapons and jet aircraft the Germans had so brilliantly demonstrated in WWII. So in 1947 the cold war was launched, and the Soviet path to eventual world domination was clearly spelled out. The reader is assumed to be familiar with the major events of the cold war since then; and it is stressed that, since about 1972, the Soviets have greatly accelerated their procurement and stockage of new arms and equipment, and Soviet production of war material has risen to feverish levels not reached by any other nation since Adolf Hitler's production peak just prior to his initiation of World War II.

In 1957 Everett's many-worlds interpretation of quantum mechanics was published by Princeton University. If one meticulously examines this theory, and if one regards a mental object as just an ordinary physical object whose time dimension is synonymous with the time dimension of ordinary physical objects, but whose spatial dimensions do not intersect spatially with the spatial dimensions of ordinary objects; then one realizes that minds are just ordinary physical worlds three or more orthogonal spatial turns away from the ordinary laboratory 3-space, and cotemporal with it — i.e., sharing the same time dimension. This is particularly likely to be noticed if one has the dialectical method (a slightly confused way of stating the author's fourth law of logic [1]), deeply ingrained in his thinking. Bingo! The Soviet theoreticians made the connection. So in 1960 Khruschev, speaking to the Presidium — to the leaders of the Communist Party, not for propaganda — stated at the conclusion of his report that the Soviet Union had a new weapon, just within the portfolio of the scientists, which was so powerful that, if unrestrainedly used, it could wipe out all life on earth. I.e., intensive psychotronic/psycho-energetic weapon development was underway in the Soviet Union [7] .

At about the same time, complex, weak micro-wave radiation of the U.S. Embassy in Moscow began. The purpose was to modulate psychotronic signals onto weak RF carriers [8], and hit a high level U.S. target, the U.S. Ambassador to the Soviet Union. This would guarantee the personal attention of the U.S. President, CIA, DIA, NSA, State Department, National Security Council, etc. A few blood changes and diseases would be introduced as a Red Herring [9]. By the U.S's response to the radiation stimulus, the state of U.S. knowledge of the new breakthrough area — psychotronics — could be positively ascertained, because the decision for the response would come from the highest levels in the U.S. Government. If the U.S. reacted only to the electromagnetic component, it would show with 100% certainty that the U.S. knew nothing of psychotronics, and hence had not developed psychotronic superweapons in secret. If the U.S. reacted to the psychotronic modulation, it would show that the U.S. possessed a knowledge of psychotronics — and the specific type of reaction would indicate the sophistication of that knowledge, hence the probable nature of weaponry they might have developed. Since the beginning of this radiation of the U.S. Embassy, we have been reassuring the Soviets we know nothing about the mechanism for their new superweapons. Just how vital this strange intelligence probe is to the Soviet Union can be ascertained from the fact that three American presidents have asked them to stop the radiation, but they have not done so, merely reducing the power level to a seemingly insignificant level [10] .

Khruschev, ever the ebullient peasant, quickly attempted to move strategic rocket weapons into Cuba and immediately change the balance of power, before his new superweapons were operationally deployed. The 1962 Cuban missile crisis thus caught him without his new superweapons and with his missiles in woeful operational shape. Hence he simply had to back down. About 1963, the first Soviet superweapons became operational. Today third generation superweapons are probably deployed and ready.

Ironically, in psychotronic devices the flow (background) of orthorotational flux in which coherence is multistagedly established must be relatively uniform for the coherence to be maintained: i.e. in weapons this is necessary for the superweapons to work. Occasionally, for random intervals of from 15 minutes or so to a day or two, turbulent flux is encountered. All of a given type case work simultaneously, and all resume again together — something totally different from any normal weapon system failure mode. Hence the superweapons cannot be absolutely depended upon for the primary effectors, but are best used as a backup, with mind-stunning shock and devastation, just as the U.S. used its two atomic bombs on Japan in WWII.

So for that reason the Soviet buildup in conventional and nuclear arms has aimed at overwhelming strength in those categories, even though the superweapons exist and are deployed and ready. The greatest armada of weaponry in history has continued to steadily be built up by the Soviet Union. The attack operation is poised and ready. A lightning blow of unprecedented ferocity and speed — followed by a massive, mind-paralyzing, awesome demonstration of devastation by the superweapons — is imminent.

The plan is simple and three-phased: 1) Secure the Eurasian continent by defeating NATO and annihilating Red China, ejecting the U.S. presence, and taking over Europe. This requires three to six days. In the process, just as the U.S. President is contemplating full nuclear strategic retaliation — say, after 50% casualties in NATO in the first three days, a ground advance of 250 kilometres, seizure of total air superiority in the first several hours, and unrelenting and merciless air attack has devastated critical installations, supplies, centres, and forces throughout the NATO rear — the psychotronic weapons will be unleashed in a mindbending, terrible demonstration that will totally paralyse the West, just as the two atomic bombs on Hiroshima and Nagasaki paralysed a fanatical Japan in WWII. [11] 2) Split the American continent in two, seizing South America and the Panama Canal. The Cubans are the stars of this show. That is why they have been involved in about 11 or so countries to gain experience. Angola was the dress rehearsal for the Cuban forces. 3) After the U.S. has collapsed in total chaos and economic destitution, Soviet forces simply march in to restore order.

Now if all this unbelievable scenario has any validity, then after the final rehearsal — i.e., after the 1973 MidEast War — one ought to see an increase in the Tulpoid phenomena of a sharply symbolic nature which can be appropriately psychoanalysed. And so it has happened, and so one can.

The cow is in the Western female symbol par excellence; Western children nurse on cow's milk. So if the fortress is going to be violated, then one ought to see the female symbol being violated. So cattle mutilations of a mysterious, paranormal nature have been occurring all across the U.S. — from the East coast out through Colorado, Utah, and Montana — about two thousand or so by now. The U.S's lifeblood is going to be drained — and **totally**. Thus all the blood is drained from the cattle. The Soviet operation will be launched with blinding speed and surgical precision — and so the mutilation of the cattle is as if surgically performed. The children of the West shall be cut off from their sustenance — and so teats are removed. The armed forces (males) confronting the Soviet forces will be devastated — i.e., the 'fruit of the womb' will be devastated — so the sexual organs of the cows are excised. Free speech and freedom to hear will be excised, so the lips, tongues, and ears are excised. A very high technology will play a role, but one which will limit the resistance. — so the cut edges are as if made by pinking shears and then precisely burned with a laser (laser being highly symbolic of new, strange technology/ weaponry almost incomprehensible to the average person). In at least one case a horse was the victim — a young horse, symbolic of the young soldier. It was castrated — i.e., the dominance of the Western soldier will be excised surgically. Castration of the male symbolizes the total loss of power and the infliction of absolute impotency. There is even more meaning available to be read in the animal mutilations, but this sampling should suffice to give a bloodcurdling example of the metapsychiatric analysis results.

But yet a final shock awaits us. Just prior to the actual Soviet attack against NATO, the tulpoid symbology should be raised to the highest possible degree. And there would seem to be only one additional degree higher than the mutilation of the cow: that is the sexual mutilation of the human female. So in horror one realizes that the model predicts the raising of the cattle mutilation symbology to a rash or wave of human female mutilations. The first such incident may already have occurred. In May 1977 a strange, horrible, sexual mutilation of a human female occurred in the Greater Boston area.

In paranormal phenomena, the inadvertent or forced raising of the kundalini often evokes a paroxysm of insanity. The raising of the kundalini of the entire human species seems now to be underway, and a drastic forcing of it seems to be at hand.

The final agony of the birth of Man — or of his death — is begun.

Tom Bearden — 25 May 1977

NOTES AND REFERENCES

1. For development and discussion of the fourth law of logic, see Thomas E. Bearden, *An Approach to Understanding Psychotronics,* Defense Documentation Center (DDC), June 1976, AD-A027866; *Writing the Observer Back Into the Equation,* DDC, June 1976, AD-A027867; and *Solution of the Fundamental Problem of Quantum Mechanics,* DDC, January 3, 1977, AD-A034237.

2. See *The Many-Worlds Interpretation of Quantum Mechanics,* A Fundamental Exposition by Hugh Everett, III, with papers by J.A. Wheeler, B.S. DeWitt, L.N. Cooper and D. Van Vechten, and N. Graham; eds. Bryce S. DeWitt and Neill Graham, Princeton Series In Physics, Princeton University Press, 1973.

3. For a brief description of how and why the time 'dimension' is actually an oscillatory wave, see Thomas E. Bearden, *Photon Quenching of the Paranormal (Time) Channel: A Breif Note,* DDC, April 20, 1977, AD-A038588.

4. With the possible exception of Kozyrev -- whose more technical works on time remain undisclosed to open science -- no other person known to this author seems to have grasped the implications of a dynamic structure of time as deeply and penetratingly as has Charles Muses. E.g., see Muses foreword to Jerome Rothstein, *Communication, Organization, and Science,* The Falcon's Wing Press, Indian Hills, Colarado, 1958, pp. vii-xcvi. Western scientists have not grasped the engineering implications of Muses work -- matter materialization, dematerialization, and consciousness processing -- on time and his brilliant work on hypernumbers. It is little short of astonishing that the genesis point for a totally new science and technology has been shelved since 1957-58 in the works of Everett and Muses, and that even today Western scientists continue to ignore works of such fundamental importance. The referenced Foreword by Muses is a remarkable document which analyses the structure of time itself, and on p. lxii, Muses pointed out that the celebrated wave-particle paradox remains a paradox only so long as the chronotopological phases of the phenomena are left unrealized in the analysis. Thus in 1958 Muses had already pointed out that the structure of time held the key to all of quantum mechanics, a conclusion reached independently by this present author in 1977 (see reference 2 above). This author also pointed out that the photon interaction was the key to the creaton of 'objectivity', and this observation appears to be the final factor necessary to solving the two-slit experiiment (see references 2 and 3 above).

5. For the amplification mechanism and its theory, see Thomas E. Bearden, *The One Human Problem, Its Solution, and Its Relation to UFO Phenomena,* DDC, January 3, 1977, AD-A034236, Appendix I: The Holographic Hyperchannel Effect. While the mechanism is developed for linked brain stages, it also applies to certain types of multistaged amplifiers, and to 'mental' forms coherently existing in more than one human mind.

6. The so-called 'collapse of the wave function' is simply the result of the coherent time superposition of virtual subquanta of action — in all $\Delta T \Delta E$ quanta of which the ΔT's are of identical magnitude — reaching and breaching the quantum threshold given by $\Delta E \Delta T = h/4\pi$ **and** turning into observable change. The mechanism for this direct amplification of the virtual state is referenced in reference 5 above. Mass itself is simply the localized

totality of such 'switching' from the virtual state to the objective state; see Thomas E. Bearden, *Quiton/Perceptron Physics: A Theory of Existence, Perception, and Physical Phenomena, DDC, March 1973, AD 7632 10* for the defining equation of mass in this respect. The 'switching' from virtual state to observable state actually involves orthorotation from other orthogonal spatial frames into the laboratory spatial frame, among and in an infinite set of orthogonal 4 -spaces which share in common a single time dimension. If, in addition to its 'switching circulation' flux into and out of the laboratory 3-space (which constitutes mass), the area or locality of laboratory 3-space also contains a 'switching circulation' flux into and out of an orthogonal 3-space that is one orthogonal turn away from the laboratory frame, then that orthogonal flux is virtual --i.e., the flux may be said to consist of 'virtual photons,' and that arrangement constitutes *charge* since the first ortho-frame constitutes the electric field (see the first reference listed in Note 1 above).

7. The words 'psychoenergetic' and 'psychotronics' in fact imply the interaction of 'mind' and matter and the processing of these interactions by physical devices. In an infinite set of time clustered, spatially orthogonal frames which all share in common a single time dimension, all frames three or more orthogonal spatial turns away from the laboratory frame are *minds* or *mindworlds*. The 'thought forms' in each mindworld are actually concrete, physical objects *in that frame.* The Soviet term *psychoenergetics* and the Czechoslovakian term psychotronics are thus quite appropriate indeed. Peter Kapitsa, the renowned physicist and freethinker, informed Kruschev that if a means of total neutralization of foreign missiles was to be found, it could only come from a group of new principles in physics called 'energetics'. It was at this time that the Soviets began a massive research program in energetics. It would also appear from this nomenclature that the Soviet choice of the term 'psychoenergetics' for what the West calls 'parapsychology' is particularly significant.

8. To prevent the time-squelching effect of the photon interaction in the visible light spectrum, psychotronic signals may be modulated upon RF carrier waves, I.e., each 'RF photon' carries a vibratory bit of time carrier wave along with it, and the psychotronic pattern may quite comfortably ride along in that bit of oscillatory time as a modulation upon it, and thus ride right through visible light photons without interaction.

9. For extremely significant Soviet work on the transmission of death and disease patterns from one cell culture to another in a very unusual manner, see V.P. Kaznacheyev et al, 'Distant Intercellular Interactions in a System of Two Tissue Cultures,' *Psychoenergetic Systems,* Vol. 1, No. 3, March 1976, pp. 141-142. See also V.P. Kaznacheyev et al, 'Apparent Information Transfer Between Two Groups of Cells'. *Psychoenergetic Systems,* Vol. 1, No.1, December 1974, p.37. (Tom Bearden's article carried a few supplementary references to the microwave bombardment of the US Embassy in Moscow from early 1976. Although lack of space forbids their inclusion here, we summarise a few recent reports, including the emergence of a strange blood disorder among Embassy staff, in the section on 'Electromagnetic Curiosities' elsewhere in this issue - Ed.)

10. With the 'kindling effect' recently discovered in brain research related to epilepsy, repetition of even an extremely weak signal is sufficient. All that is necessary is to insure the survival of the psychotronic pattern through the squelching effect of the visible light spectrum. That is easily done by modulating it onto an RF carrier wave. See 'Kindling, Once Epilepsy Model, May Relate to Kundalini' *Brain/Mind Bulletin* Vol. 2, No. 7, Feb. 21, 1977, pp. 2-3.

11. And to make the U.S. President's decision not to use or attempt to use strategic nuclear weapons easier the wily opponent will probably offer a 'Dunkirk,' i.e., to stop the victorious Soviet field forces in position and allow the battered remnants of the U.S. forces in the European Theater to withdraw. Congress particularly would find that appealing; the world would not get blown up, the troops would be allowed to survive and return home, and the terrible fear of the fantastic new weaponry unveiled by the adversary might be assuaged. Congress pressure on the President in such a case would be formidable, to say the least! And after all, would not the Soviets be merely imposing their own 'Monroe Doctrine' in their own hemisphere, just as we had once done in ours?

OUR COVER

To herald our selection of 'Holygrams (see p33 and pp36-40) we chose this magnificent woodcut, by Albrecht Dürer, from the Nuremburg Prayer Book, 1503. It depicts St Veronica holding the famous veil with which she wiped Christ's face when he stumbled on the Via Dolorosa, and which came thereby to be imprinted with his image. Although there is no evidence at all to support the original existence of such a woman - whose name is derived from 'vera-icon' (true image) - a cloth said to be St Veronica's Veil has been kept in a secret reliquary in St Peter's at Rome, since the 8th century.

NEXT ISSUE

Next issue will carry an article by Paul Begg debunking the legend of the UFO kidnapping of the Norfolk 'regiment'; Bob Skinner analyses the methods by which the damned data of Forteanism are defused by the ignorant, the blind the fearful and the stupid; plus notes (we hope) on fires, ball lightnings, ice-falls, spoon-benders, and we hope to have a listing of some of the 'superlative' weather and quake events of the last couple of years; plus another episode of 'Fortean Funnies'.

ℛEVIEW ℨUPPLEMENT

We welcome books and journals for review or ex
change on all topics of related interest. The details and
contents of journals are given in the next issue after
receipt, and the return favour in their pages would be
appreciated.

hardbacks

Encyclopedia of Occultism and Parapsychology: edited by Leslie Shepard (Gale Research, Book Tower, Detroit, MI 48226, USA., 1978; $48.00;
2 vols, pp1084, 10 indexes) -- I'm
sure that many of you interested in subjects in or overlapping the general
fields of the Occult ('hidden') and psychic phenomena of all kinds, at some
time or another, have keenly felt the
need for an authoritative reference work
in the form of an encyclopedia for quick
references and explanations on obscure,
long defunct, or unfamiliar terms, topics or societies; or on encountering
references to one of the myriad forms
of the unknown you have wished for a
good, quick and knowledgable scene-set-
ting encapsulation of the subject and
its implication. If you were lucky, rich
or a book-collector, you could probably
turn to Lewis Spence's Encyclopedia of
the Occult (1920), or Dr Nandor Fodor's
Encyclopedia of Psychic Science (1934),
both sadly neglected masterpieces of
their time and compilers' skill and unrivalled knowledge, the former long out
of print and quite rare, the latter hard
to find outside the USA where it had
1966 and 1974 reprintings (both thanks
to Leslie Shepard). Beyond these sources
the average inquirer would find very
little of help - the new edition of the
Encyclopedia Britanica is of little help
with unorthodox subjectmatter, and the
otherwise splendid Man, Myth & Magic
has the limitation of being too general
in many important areas.
      Leslie Shepard conceived the idea

of combining the encyclopedias of Spence
and Fodor, a useful enough project on
its own, but taking some pains to go
further. Shepard, who has a considerable
reputation as a scholar himself, edited
the 1966 University Books edition of
Fodor, bringing many entries up to date
and adding a very few tantalising but
essential new entries. This was reprinted by Citadel in 1974, but clearly was
inadequate in view of the amount of new
material (and historical insight) accre-
ting to nearly every topic every year,
as well as the wholly new topics arising
out of modern parapsychological studies
etc etc. It was clear that an extensive
revision and expansion was needed beyond
the straightforward correlation of the
two encyclopedias. And so, after several
years in the making, we at last have one
of the most valuable and practical works
one can imagine or want. Shepard adds
nearly 2000 new entries to the 3000 or
so of Fodor and Spence, collated into a
single edition spanning 2 volumes, covering every conceivable phenomenon, cult,
society, personality, periodical, topic
and issue in the field. It must be especially commended for the nine cross-
referenced special subject indexes on
animals, demons, gems, places, gods,
phenomena, periodicals, plants, and societies. The phenomena index is further
subdivided into 50 topics ranging from
apparitions, eyeless sight and levitation, to stigmata and teleportation. The
whole is topped by a cross-referenced
42 page general index.
      In a work of this scope there are
inevitable errors and omissions - and
sometimes the lack of signposts in the
layout make it difficult to know where
you are without flicking back and forth
for the nearest heading...but these niggles can be forgiven when you hold the
2 volumes - their weight and the patient
work in just getting this far are truly

impressive. If the measure of an encyclopedia lies in its usefulness then this one justifies itself easily. Already in the short time I've had the review copy it has proved invaluable, saving me considerable time and effort in looking for essential cases and quotes, compiling short bibliographies on a number of phenomenal themes, and in explaining to me some spiritualist and occult-philosophy terms that were new to me - it also helped locate a starting point for a colleague's research into the origin of certain geomantic themes in the various Indian religions. This is a good omen for a long life of continuous use.

As if all this wasn't enough, Gale Research and Shepard plan the irregular publication of four supplements of corrections, updates and new material in the coming years to keep it even more current. This highly laudable project, called Occultism Update, will be available at the subscription of $30.00 for the four issues. Perhaps, sometime in the future, Gale could be persuaded to compound the superlatives by bringing out a new edition with the new material, this time with the benefit of illustrations.

In the meantime I have no hesitation in urging you all to get this Encyclopedia - the effort that's gone into it it worthy of the fullest support of Forteans and other researchers. It should be on the reference shelves of every library, public, personal, university and school libraries. Without a doubt it is one of the most important reference works of its type to be published, and its consultation will be mandatory for a long long time. RJMR

Hauntings by Peter Underwood (JM Dent, 1977; £5.95; pp256, photos, bib, index) -- The subtitle reads 'New Light on the Greatest True Ghost Stories of the World', but it would have been more accurate (though less appealing) to have said: 'A Glimmer of New Light on Some of the Most Often Retold, Possibly True, Ghose Cases of Britain, Canada and France'. The cases dealt with in Underwood's new book, are: Hampton Court, the Drummer of Tedworth, the Wesley poltergeist, the Hinton Ampner poltergeist, Glamis Castle, the Amherst (Nova Scotia) poltergeist, Berkeley Square (London), Cheltenham, Versailles and Borley Rectory. In each chapter we are given a description of the events and the research done over the years, followed by any new evidence unearthed by Underwood, and his conclusions. These are never (except in one instance

I'll come to) as revolutionary as the subtitle leads us to believe. For example, he seems to accept that there are ghosts at Hampton Court, and Borley, which we already know, but is less accommodating about the poltergeist cases.

Although he gives the Wesley poltergeist of 1716, and the Hinton Ampner poltergeist of mid-18th century, the thumbs up, he dismisses the Tedworth poltergeist of the 1660s: "This particular classic case of haunting falls apart when subjected to scrutiny and would appear on present day re-examination to be the result of exaggeration, conscious fraud and inexact and biased reporting." (p56) 300 years later we cannot know for sure. He is also unhappy about the Amherst case of 100 years ago: "On reflection it must seem probable that the 'Great Amherst Mystery' can be answered in terms of psychosomatic disturbance and inaccurate or exaggerated reporting of incidents that took place in the vicinity of the unfortunate and unhappy Esther Cox." (p153) But I feel he writes the case off too easily; many of the events sound like classic poltergeist effects, not easily hoaxed. An example of his dismissal which I cannot accept appears on p141: "The Rev RA Temple, their own minister, said he was witness to a particularly curious incident when a bucket of cold water, standing on the kitchen table, became agitated as though boiling, although the water remained cold. Esther was present but nowhere near the bucket at the time. It is an effect that could have been produced in a number of ways and it is perhaps the first incident in the house of mystery that smacks of conscious fraud." Unfortunately Underwood does not enlarge on this and fails to tell the reader of any way in which this effect could be faked.

The ghosts of Berkeley Square are difficult to track down with the lack of first-hand reports, and I agree in this case that it is "impossible to sort fact from fiction". Also the paranormal nature of the 1901 Versailles experience of the Misses Moberly and Jourdain is, I agree, suspect. But I have saved till last the chapter that most surprised me - the chapter in which Underwood lets his imagination run away with his reason - on the Cheltenham ghost of 1882-6. This impressive case concerns a large house haunted by a woman thought to be one of the previous tennants; the chief witness being a daughter of the house, Rosina Despard, who later became a doctor. She took a great interest in the ghost which was also seen by other members of the family but not by her father - and Underwood thinks it strange she did not mention the ghost to him for over 2 years. This isn't so strange - my father isn't the sort of person to tell such things to either! Underwood acknowledges that a strange woman was seen in the house, but doubts she was a ghost - he suggests she was "an illicit lodger", installed by Captain Despard whose wife was an invalid. The mind boggles! This might account in part for the figure being seen at night; but she was also seen once in the daytime, downstairs, and when cornered by the curious Rosina, she disappeared. Some lodger! Underwood does not attempt to explain away such features of the case. There are other criticisms: the 'lodger' was never seen going to the bathroom; and what about her meals? How could she walk through strings fixed over the stairs? What about the independent testimony of the charwoman who saw the ghost vanish? So many flaws spring to mind that I wonder if Underwood can be serious in his suggestion, or whether he is desperate to find any explanation for a case which has implications he is unwilling to accept. Despite this, it is an interesting book for the newcomer to ghost-lore, but may be found repetitive by those well versed in it.

Janet Bord

Sea Serpents, Sailors & Sceptics by Graham J McEwan (RKP, 1978; £4.50; pp133, photos, illus, chron table, bib) -- Taking the works of Tim Dinsdale and Bernard Heuvelmans as his main sources, Graham McEwan has produced a succinctly informative introduction to the subject of the Great Sea Serpent. He covers all the important nineteenth and twentieth century sightings, from the 1817 appearances of a monster in Gloucester Bay, Massachusetts to my own close encounter with Morgawr the Cornish 'Sea Giant', in November 1976.

Like Oudemans, Heuvelmans and Costello before him, Graham McEwan seems keen to promote the hypothetical long-necked pinniped as a likely candidate for the subject of most reported sightings. He classifies Morgawr under this heading - maybe he's right...maybe not. Disappointingly, he avoids any discussion of sea serpents as phenomenal entities, planting his feet firmly in the flesh-and-blood-physical camp - eg a mermaid, captured, and described in great detail, by a group of 19th C

Shetland fishermen, is dismissed as "too improbable"...whatever that may mean! The section on Morgawr steers clear of any reference to the coincidental appearances, in 1976, of the Mawnan Owlman and a flurry of UFOs over Cornwall (maybe long-necked pinnipeds are attracted by such things?)

The book is illustrated with drawings and photographs...and I was interested to note the probably quite insignificant fact that, of the 10 silhouettes of monsters, 9 depict the beasts moving from left to right. The 10th, a plan view of the Mackintosh Bell beastie, is obviously upside down! I wish it had been stated clearly that Mary F took two photos, and I took three, showing the monster in varying positions - these were all reproduced in Bob Rickard's article on Morgawr in the Oct 1977 issue of Fate - Graham uses just one of each.

Having got those minor criticisms off my chest, I must say that SSS&S is efficiently written and nicely produced, aimed at the general reader, not the specialist. Graham's next book, I'm told, will be on the subject of UFOs. Perhaps his researches will encourage him, eventually, to regard the sea serpent from a phenomenalist point of view.

Doc Shiels

Divining the Primary Sense: Unfamiliar Radiation in Nature, Art and Science, by Herbert Weaver (RKP 1978; £4.75; pp140, photos, diagrams, notes index) -- Using a device called a Revealer Field Detector, and a technique similar to that employed in dowsing, Herbert Weaver claims to have discovered natural radiations which the animal kingdom can sense, but man no longer can. He also believes that certain patterns can suppress the radiations, and that many living creatures employ this system of suppression as a protection against predators. Further, he finds such symbols in man's art and architecture throughout his evolution. If all the examples given in this book have been checked by experimentation then the author has undertaken a prodigious amount of work. The author is obviously deeply involved in his work with the Revealer - but as dowsing can sometimes show a subjective influence, the author 's work ought (and deserves) to be checked and double-checked independently. The author has applied his interpretations to several wide fields, and appears widely read, yet it not said how his work relates to or agrees with the findings of other dowsers, ley and

earth current researchers, and astro-archeologists. This omission suggests Weaver is not aware of the findings and methods of people like TC Lethbridge and Guy Underwood for example, or prefers to ignore them - odd to say the least. One gets the feeling he has worked in a vacuum, isolated from the developments in closely related fields. His work may be valid and valuable, an important contribution to the present upsurge of interest   in natural currents and radiations - but it is difficult to tell, because it is not easy to read or understand.
Janet Bord

Sun, Moon and Standing Stones by John Edwin Wood (Oxford University Press, 1973; £6.95; pp218, photos, figs) -- Dr Wood (Deputy Director of the Admiralty Surface Weapons Establishment) considers the evidence for and against the recent geometrical and astronomical interpretations of Neolithic and Early Bronze Age architecture in the British Isles. This is a useful book for those who want a down-to-earth account of 'new wave' prehistory - but Forteans beware! Dr Wood is not on our side'. On p131, after the expected dismissal of leys, he also disposes of 'magic , dowsing, ESP and the occult, and indeed...almost anything with an air of mystery about it, whether the Loch Ness Monster or previous visitations from outer space." Archeologists are boringly consistent in their attitude to the "lunatic fringe" (a phrase used yet again, in this book), and in their refusal to even consider any alternative approach to their subject. To quote Dr Wood again: "Unfortunately those ideas go largely unchallenged, because scientists are reluctant to divert their attention from productive work to what they see as sterile argument, unlikely to lead to any useful conclusion." But on the next page he tells us about the breakdown of the diffusionist theory, which was literally the cornerstone of British and European prehistory until radiocarbon dating showed it to be totally inaccurate. With the diffusionist theory "no longer tenable" and new ideas having to be worked out to take its place, how can Dr Wood be so sure that research into leys etc is "unlikely to lead to any useful conclusion"? It is really sad that archeologists and others are so cut off from the exciting discoveries being made in ley and Fortean research. But perhaps, beneath their outward disdain, they are afraid to face

the extraordinary phenomena of this earth. Bones and pottery are more familiar and predictable.
Janet Bord

In Search of Ancient Astronomies, EC Krupp (ed)(Doubleday, 1978;$10.00; pp300, photos, diagrams, bib, index) -- In contrast to Dr Wood (above) Dr Krupp is virtually a model of flexibility in an establishment figure (he is Director of the Griffith Observatory, Los Angeles) who has found the time to critically examine many of the fields that are beneath Dr Wood's outraged dignity. Through his long association with top researchers he has assembled this timely collection of detailed articles on 'archeoastronomy', the new study of the astronomies of ancient and prehistoric times. Seven chapters by five authors cover different aspects of archeoastronomy worldwide, including Neolithic ring and menhir geometry (by the Thoms); Stonehenge; cliffs, mounds and medicine wheels of North America; Meso-America (Maya and Aztec); Egypt and the pyramids; some guidelines and principles of astronomy that would be practical for the megalith-builders; and a final chapter which "contrasts" the earlier subject matter with the theses of Velikovsky, Von Daniken, the Glastonbury Zodiac and the Sirius mystery. This last task is handled by Krupp himself (with some style), his main attack being "not their ideas but the way in which their ideas are defended", in particular the usual appeal to science, in which case the evidence should be presented and judged according to accepted scientific standards of criticism. Where this breaks down, of course, is when intractable and pompous scientists, no less than the crank, applies one law to himself and another to those he sees threatening him.
    This is a thorough and readable book, a useful reference with a comprehensive bibliography, and heavily illustrated (though some of the site photos could have been better printed).
RJMR/JB

Stone Circles of the Peak by John Barnatt (Turnstone Books, 1978; £4.95; pp208, maps, diagrams, index, bib) -- John Barnatt has combined his interest in Thom's work on the geometry of stone circles with his obvious love of the Derbyshire Peak District, and the result is a thorough study of the prehistoric sites of that small area of Britain. Introductory text on the Peak, its landscape, history and prehistory, is followed research into geometry and measurement, astronomy, relationships to the landscape and macrocosmic geometry. Itineraries for the visitor are given, then detailed descriptions and interpretations of the sites themselves. Illustrations consist mainly of site plans, area maps and diagrams of the astronomical geometry of the stones in their landscape. This book will be of great value to researchers engaged in similar work, to show them what can be done and how to go about it; and visitors to the sites, who have an interest in astroarcheology, will surely find it will enhance their appreciation of the Peak stone circles.

Janet Bord.

Shakespeare's Use of Dream & Vision by John Arthos (Bowes & Bowes; £5.00; £5.00; pp208, index, notes) -- Precisely what the title says it is. Although primarily a literary analysis of dreams, ghosts and apparitions in Shakespeare's plays and poems, Arthos does relate this on the one hand to the audience's need for wonder (then as now), and on the other Shakespeare 's own fascination with the visionary as a character of complex tragedy and comedy - perhaps one of the most consistent themes throughout his work.

Arthos disdains the intellectual sport of spotting the Bard's sources, but does enlarge on what Shakespeare's use of ghosts and portents tells us about the beliefs of the audience, and about his own learning. On either point the material is intelligently discussed and provides diverting reading for the Fortean who would like to know what a poetic genius thought and felt about the Forteana of earlier days.

RJMR

Zen and Confucius in the art of Swordsmanship by Reinhard Kammer (RKP 1978; £3.95; pp 118; bib, notes, illos) - The Buddhist Writings of Lafcadio Hearn (Ross-Erikson, Santa Barbara, 1977; $; pp330; bib, illos) We have met the Tengu, the winged mountain demons of Japan, before in these pages (FT 17/20) where their mastery of illusion was discussed. They were also considered masters of the art of swordsmanship, and the bulk of Kammer's slim book, apart from some additional material on the history and schools of Japanese swordskill, is taken up by a translation of 'Tengu Geijutsu Ron', the Discourse on the art of the

Tengu', written in 1728 by Chozan Shissai. Put into the mouths of the Tengu, this a philosophical treatise on the mystical and essential features of swordsmanship as a 'way', similar to Zen archery; though from a viewpoint that is almost entirely neo-Confucian, despite the title. Hearn, who died in 1904, was an admirable prose stylist who devoted his latter years to presenting Japan, its legends and folklore to the West. This collection, introduced by Kenneth Rexroth, deals more with popular belief than Buddhism's philosophical aspects and, even if more interesting Fortean material (including tales of the Tengu) is to be found in his many other works, it makes an excellent introduction to the work of a brilliant and neglected writer.

SM

Supernatural England by Eric Maple (Robert Hale, 1977; £4.50; pp208; photos, bib, index) -- Several recent books have made use of Britain's rich store of folklore, ghostlore, magic and witchcraft. Maple's is no better and no worse than its predecessors, but an interesting read for anyone new to this kind of material. Each chapter is devoted to a geographical region, and the result is somewhat list-like. The book adds nothing to present research and it is a pity that sources are not given. There are a meagre 12 photos of sites, and an unnecessarily lurid dust-jacket.

JB

Haunted Ireland: Her Romantic and Mysterious Ghosts, by John J Dunne (Appletree Press, Belfast, 1977; £4.50; pp109 - also in paper, price unknown) -- An odd book, not because of the text (52 short accounts of ghosts of all kinds, traditional and vague) but because the accompanying B&W photos, although evoking the period, have little or no connection with the text, as indicated by the often irrelevant and annoying captions. The text itself is rather dull, written with little comprehension of the subject matter - but does contain some useful fragments, eg some Black Dog accounts, and a recent (1966) case where a girl saw "a huge horse with a man's face and horrible bulging eyes". I eagerly looked up p40, 'The Tragic Bride of Charles Fort', only to discover that 'he' is an old garrison near Kinsale, Co Cork!; and on "the grey ramparts of historic Charles Fort,

her graceful wraith still walks..." The
3 blank pages at the end could have use-
fully been filled by an index.
                                    JB

paperbacks

Sky Creatures: Living UFOs by Trevor
James Constable (Pocket Books, NY,
1978; $1.95; pp252) -- Ovoid mica-
like plasmatic unicellular amoeba-type
life-forms, ranging from the size of
"a coin to a half mile" - these are the
critters, the name given by Constable to
the sky creatures that "live invisibly
like fish in the ocean of atmosphere."
These organisms are wholly external to
the biological classification of Earth's
biota, and thus pose a stunning and un-
suspected challenge to exobiologists
whose attentions are focused hypotheti-
cally in far-away galaxies while super-
massive alien beasties roam through our
stratosphere...and lower!
    The first widespread mention of the
flourishing Sky Creatures was postulated
in 1955 by John Bessor, who asked: "If
the seas of our earth are swarming with
varieties of living things, both great
and small, is it not logical to assume
that the 'sea' of our sky abounds with
sundry forms of living things...adapt-
able to their celestial environment?"
    Now, almost a quarter of a century
later, confirmation of Bessor's speculation abounds in Sky Creatures. These
critters, though normally vibrating in
the infrared spectrum (to which the
human eye is ocularly insensitive),can
nevertheless be photographed! The required investment is far less than the
millions of dollars the professional
exobiologists demand of taxpayers for
their flights of fancy. Constable shows
how, for about $25, anyone can begin
his own -potentially rewarding - search
for these aerial creatures that assail
Biology's tenets,about what life is and
where it can be, as well as Newtonian
optics and Einsteinean physics!
    Needless to say, metallic-like discs
travelling at many hundreds of MPH only
to disappear on radar scopes are apt to
be labelled as UFOs (which is strictly
correct, of course!) Constable argues
for the mandatory consideration that
"Many UFOs are living organisms...nat-
ive to our atmosphere that have been
living with us, side by side, unnoticed,
since the begining of time." Not completely unnoticed, though! A few dramatic
visual sightings of luminous living
aeroforms are described - eg the mysterious "Meteor Procession" of 1913.

Even a USAF report issued in 1949 (!)
commented that many so-called UFOs "acted more like animals than anything else."
Constable has even photographed USAF
jets vainly trying to "chase down" a
critter as it soared above the Mojave
Desert! (Wonder what the Condon Committee would have said about that!)
    Sky Creatures, and its unabridged
classic predecessor, The Cosmic Pulse of
Life (1976), sound the death knell for
the view that all intelligently maneuv-
ering inexplicable aerial displays must
be alien spaceships - though Constable's
investigations of etherean physics do
reveal clues about the propulsion of
mechanical UFOs. Besides UFOs and alien
creatures, other subjects of Fortean
interest include the work of Dr Wilhelm
Reich and others into alternative energies; models of reality; expanded consciousness; bioenergies...and life...
The scope is clearly broad - the ramif-
ications immense - and the synthesizing
bold, incisive and provocative. Constable says: "Because of my faith in
the new humanity coming to earth...I
now hand you the results of my labor
and urge you to press on." Where might
it lead?
                            Larry Arnold

Creatures of the Outer Edge by Loren
Coleman & Jerome Clark (Warner, NY,
$?; NEL, London, 1978; 85p; pp239,
bib) -- To anyone who has followed
the UFO and Fortean journals over the
last few years, the subject of mystery
animals that look like animals but
which the evidence (or lack of it) suggests were not animals as we know them,
will not be an unfamiliar one. We have
seen them populate the undergrowth of
UFOs, Bigfoot, leys, fairylore, folklore and witchcraft, and they have materialised in other Fortean fields. Although this book was largely written 2
years ago (and unaccountably delayed)
there has until now been no serious
study of what we might call 'phenomenal
zoology'. The writings and researches
of Clark and Coleman, together and separately, have usually included references to the other-world or dream-like
aura attatched to mystery animal sightings, and this timely book presents
their collected considerations, with an
epilogue bringing the subject up to
date (ie 1977).
    Despite the railings against the lim-
itations of scientists, Forteans suffer
from specialisation too - for example
the ETH nuts-and-bolts school of ufology
and the flesh-and-blood camp of Bigfoot
hunters both refuse to acknowledge cases

or details in cases which seem to be descriptions of paraphysical or parapsychological phenomena. In the case of UFOs there have been a number of books dealing with associated paranormal phenomena, and two journals of discussion (the excellent MUFOB, and FSR)...but the equivalent attention to the paranormal side of mystery animals is fairly lacking outside the book by Slate & Berry, and occasional articles. Yet the subject bears considerable depth, and sketchy though the historical material is in this book, it does convey the antiquity and high strangeness of mystery animal phenomena. What are we to make of animals which seem real but leave no tracks, kills or lairs? Or their phenomenal opposites, the phantoms that do leave tracks and kills? And what about the demonstrable UFO link: some MAs seem to be occupants, others merely appear in a flap-area, during before or after the flap? And what about the extremely puzzling paranormal factor: animals that dematerialise, or generally behave like UFOs and their occupants themselves, giving witnesses paralysing psychic shock, or premonitions, and even a classic case of post-encounter personality-change?

The answers to these questions are complex and far-reaching - and with the best will in the world Clark and Coleman have only room enough here to set the scene for the questions. The anwers are not given (wisely) but hinted. No one really knows, but intelligent conclusions can be tentatively drawn from a cool consideration of the data, and this means (the authors plead) the inclusion of psychological, mythological and sociological factors also. If there is one thing to learn it is the folly of seeing single facets of the phenomenon in isolation, both from parts of the account distasteful to the investigator, and from the cultural context.

Structurally, the authors divide their chapters among MAs generally, Bigfeet, Manimals, Phantom Cats and Dogs, and Winged Creatures - they omit aquatic monsters for several reasons, I feel: their personal experience and expertise covers all the above, but not sea and lake monster research; the inclusion would make the present study large and unmanageable in this format; and time forced them to draw a line conveniently between land and water monsters...but the present work does not suffer for the

lack, in fact to the contrary it has
sharpened the authors' concentration.
By comparing cases in all categories
they arrive at the conclusion that
is a consistent morphology, a pattern
of events that repeats in all times and
places (with variations) and across the
categories. Because of this they cannot
agree with those who say MAs are 'created' by UFOs, but that UFOs, MAs and even
ghosts and other paranormal phenomena
seem to be but different and interrelat-
ed expressions of the same pattern or
organising force. MAs, like poltergests, UFOs and their occupants, make,
similar sounds, noises, similarly leave
ambiguous evidence, contradict 'natural'
laws, have a psychic component, cause
power-drains and stop cars, and appear
to have meaningful actions and details.

Where then should we look for answers? Perhaps the most encouraging direction is also the most obscure - and
certainly the one many people regard
with foreboding (is that itself a clue?)
The phenomena may be symbols evoked
through the very processes which define
for us reality and fantasy. This thesis
notes that the 'animal' has always been
a symbol for the archaic nature of the
human psyche, and that an alienated
symbol (or a symbol of an alienated
psychic process) would appear in its
negative aspect - baffling, alien, dark,
menacing, violent and disruptive - though these qualities are dangers real
enough to a beleaguered mind they become more sinister as the product of
denial and repression of our archaic
and instinctive natures. The UFO is more
than a symbol of psychic unity, it has
become corrupted by an overlay symbol
of the 'Deux ex machina', the salvation
from ourselves, from outside the planet,
conceived of in terms of a space-age
'cargo cult'. Small wonder then that in
its negative mode the UFO aligns itself
with other alienated phenomena and processes, and becomes the agent (and its
occupants, the angels) of possession
and menace, not of salvation. Like poltergeists, witches and evil abducting
entities, the MAs tell us more about
ourselves than they reveal about themselves - which is all a symbol should
be. What is most disturbing is what
they are reflecting, about our spirit
and our long suffering Mother planet.

This book deserves your attention,
as the quality of the writing, research
and discussions therein come from two
of the world's top Forteans - besides
it's damned good! Perhaps NEL will take
a hint and bring out the authors' previous, and to date unrivalled, book,
The Unidentified, in this country.
RJMR

Jesus Died in Kashmir by A Faber-
Kaiser (Abacus, 1978; £1.25; pp184,
maps, photos, bib, index) -- Jesus,
it seems, made an extensive tour of
India during his early life, visiting
shrines and gurus and developing his
doctrine of equality of all men. He
returned to Palestine in his 29th year
and met the same stiff reaction to his
socially unacceptable doctrine in his
own land as he had among the venerable
Brahmins - and was crucified. The Turin
Shroud stains prove - since blood does
not flow from a dead body - that he was
alive when taken down from the Cross.
He recovered and returned, together
with his mother and St Thomas, to India
to preach to the Lost Tribes of Israel,
his last hope. He married and lived
long - a photo of a direct lineal des-
cendant, is shown - and is buried in
Kashmir. His tomb can be visited ((and
among the list of those who have made
the pilgrimage, we find the name of Von
Daniken! - Ed.))

The evidence is pretty convincing
that a holy man did become venerated by
Jewish Kashmiris, who still live in the
area, and that he could have been called Jesus or one of its variants. There
is some interesting speculation on a
possible wholesale mutual borrowing of
Christian and Buddhist doctrine and
mythology - as well as the obligatory
ancient book in an isolated Tibetan
monastery. Whether this proves that the
Nazarene did all this is another matter.
Given the habit of events tending to
occur in clumps and remembering the rumours of a contemporaneous 'Jesus' among
the Indians of New Mexico, perhaps there
were several Jesuses, and the one who
got busted got all the publicity.

Well written, and not at all a mystical argument.
Ion Will

Weird America: A Guide to Places of
Mystery in the United States, by Jim
Brandon (EP Dutton, NY, 1978; $4.95;
pp244) -- A lovely book to dip into!
Jim Brandon presents all manner of phenomena - UFOs, falls, archeological enigmas, Indian mysteries, petrifactions,
errant crocodiles, water monsters, Bigfeet, curios gravestones etc - in a
state-by-state tabulation, beginning
with sites in Alabama and working through to Wisconsin (including Hawaii, but
not Alaska, Puerto Rico or Virgin Islands). Most entries begin with a brief
location detail for the benefit of the

traveller - then follow the unadorned facts. By this I mean that Brandon does not adopt a flowery style which so many guidebook writers feel is 'literary', but presents the information in a refreshingly succinct and straightforward manner that still manages to be enthusiastic - Brandon is obviously a discriminating lover of Forteana.

We recommend the book to FT readers, wherever they may be, for the Fortean information it contains transcends any national boundary or purely local interest - although there is a growing tourist market for curiosa. For the researcher, though, an index would have been a very worthwhile addition, or at the very least a short index of phenomena types - as it is, the book's importance will drive many Forteans to compile their own or face the alternative of much time-consuming page-flicking for that fascinating case you know is in there somewhere. Some sources are given in the text, but a source list or bibliography would have been nice too!

Despite these criticisms, this is definitely a book to get.

RJMR/JB

Beyond the Body: The Human Double, by Benjamin Walker (RKP, 1977; £1.95; pp224, bib, index) -- A new paperback edition of a book first published in 1974, and a welcome reissue. All aspects of out-of-the-body experiences are described and analysed, including the act of projection and the various methods claimed to achieve this. Here also are psychological, metaphysical and scientific insights, plus data from folklore, anthropology, occultism and psychic research. The result is a complete view of the out-of-the-body problem (sometimes called 'Astral Projection'). An especially good introduction to a fascinating subject.

JB

Compassion Yoga: The Mystical Cult of Kuan Yin, by John Blofeld (Unwin Paperbacks, 1977; £1.95; pp158) -- John Blofeld has a wide following for his perceptive and evocative writings about Chinese Buddhism and Taoism - and this compact offering about the thoroughly neglected cult of the Goddess/Bodhisatva Kuan Yin, does some small justice in helping Westerners understand one of the most universally respected religious and mystical images of the Chinese, Japanese and Tibetan world. In the inimatable oriental fashion the image of Kuan Yin is a complex mixture of popular Taoism, abstract occult philosophy, Buddhist metaphysics, and local legends of a compassionate Queen of Heaven in lands from Tibet to Japan. Blofeld here makes a plea for a return to a devotional religious stance in personal life, and outlines meditational practices centered on this extremely attractive and moving symbol of the positive, intuitive, emotional, compassionate feminine principle, so sadly exiled from this world that values the opposites of these qualities. As usual, Blofeld illustrates his exposition with accounts of his early travels in China and his conversations and lessons at the hands (and feet) of scholars, hermits, priests and ordinary folk. For me these glimpses into a world banished by time and history are worth the price of the book alone, fragments of a worldview we are just begining to recognise that is quite different, but in no way inferior, to our own way of interpreting both the everyday and the special wonders that surround us.

RJMR

Man into Wolf: An Anthropological Interpretation of Sadism, Masochism and Lycanthropy, by Robert Eisler (Ross-Erikson, Santa Barbara, Ca, 1978; $3.95; pp263, index) -- What an astonishing and awesome piece of research and writing! The centerpiece is an extremely compact paper on the cultural and psychological significance and role of violence, pain and bizarre behaviour - a model of exposition which condenses views of evolution, history, culture, and psychology, both normal and abnormal, into a mere 30 pages. Then follow nearly 200 pages of notes which boggle the mind with their range and depth, with full references. The book closes with five equally valuable appendices: on Jung's archetypes and Neo-Lamarckism; the woman-beating cult-ritual of ancient Rome, and its modern equivalents; flagellation in the Dionysian mysteries; the vampirism of John George Haigh; and on berserk-rage (which includes the type of behaviour described in our 'Compulsions' section on p7 this issue). One of the main threads in Eisler's argument relates to the pan-cultural traditions of berserkers, vampires, werewolves, ghouls, 'mass-murderers' and other extremes of behaviour which have always been extra-ordinary enough to be considered outside normal considerations of morality and behaviour and more in the realm of divine or demonic possession and madness. An introduction by Donald Lathrop puts this study in a direct relationship with contemporary behaviour curiosities and an up-to-date social context. For the insights into curiosities of human behaviour and what Fort might have called were-humans, and its implications for some strange phenomena and folklore, this book cannot be recommended too highly to all scholars.

RJMR

The Lambton Worm, by Paul Screeton (Zodiac House, 7 Hugon Rd, Fulham, London SW6 3EL, 1978; £2.10; pp72, bib) - Woven around the full text of 'The Lambton Worm' - a folkpoem celebrating a famous local dragon - Paul Screeton tells of the many Northumberland dragon legends and the local dragon-slayers, themes that abound in British folklore. He also includes a useful chapter on possible origins and influences on the symbol of the dragon and its death at the hands of a solar hero. A valuable study, nice to read and a pleasure to have to hand.

God's Weapon, by David Medina (Privately published at: 6 Grant Court, 18 Spencer Hill, London SW19 4NY, 1978; £1.00; pp80, bib, index) - a study of the manufacture, use and history of the 'Ark of the Covenant' in some detail. Medina argues that the Ark gave off radiation and electrical discharges, the plans for which seem to have originated off this planet! An interesting and still enigmatic story.

USEFUL REISSUES IN PAPERBACK
The Ancient Mysteries Reader, by Peter Haining (Sphere, 1978; 2 vols, 85p each; pp220 & 176) -- famous short stories on the phenomenal themes of Hollow Earth, lost races, lost continents, ancient sites, gods from the skies, etc. A good read.
The Sufis, by Idries Shah (Star, 1977; £1.95; pp404, notes)-- Shah's great classic on Sufi teachings, about enlightenment and their view of cosmology and phenomenology; plus descriptions of the Sufi orders, methods and teachers.
A Field Guide to the Little People, by Nancy Arrowsmith and George Moorse (Pan, 1978; 95p; pp297, notes, index, bib, drawings) -- more whimsical than Katherine Briggs' Dictionary of Fairies but still a useful introduction and guide to the varieties of 'Gentry' in most European countries.
The Undiscovered Country, by Stephen Jenkins (Abacus, 1978; £1.75; pp269, index, notes) -- a fascinating overview of Forteana, UFOs, fairies, monsters etc by a historian, who has 3 oriental languages, received Buddhist instruction

in Mongolia, and puts in much intelligent synthesis.
Circles & Standing Stones, by Evan Hadingham (Abacus, 1978; £1.95; pp268, notes, illus, photos, gazeteer, index) -- one of the first of the better reviews of 'alternative archeology', the mysteries of the megalithic ruins, astroarcheology, 'earth mysteries' and leys. A good book to start interest.
Children of the Universe, by H von Ditfurth (Futura 1977; £1.25; pp301, photos, illos) - translated from German, subtitled 'The Tale of our Existence' and considered "enthralling reading" by von Daniken. You have been warned.
The Key, by John P Cohane (Fontana, 1977; 80p; pp224, bib, index photos) - covers von Daniken-type material but from a novel and illuminating angle - the key of the title is etymology and language - scattering fascinating asides in the journey through the world's antiquities and ancient cultures. Recommended.
The Secret of the Gods by ET Stringer (Abacus, 1976; £1.25; pp264, notes, bib, index, photos, illus)- a reknowned biologist and climatologist expounds his view of the way life functions on every level from the tiniest element up to the all-inclusive universal total, in a fascinating fusion of the sciences with fringe and Fortean concepts.

journals

Pursuit 42 (Spring 1978): articles on settlement in space, skyquakes, quake-lights; 'Witchcraft & Weather modification' pt1, by George M Eberhart; 'The Concept of Simultaneity', plus some 'synchronicity' experiments you can do while listening to radio or reading a book!; frozen mammoths; 'The Transformist Myth', a critique of Darwinism; critique of Berlitz's Without a Trace, and his reply; brief notes. Pursuit has become both progressive and impressive over the last few issues, and is very worthwhile. For details write to SITU, Membership Services, RFD 5, Gales Ferry, CT 06335, USA.

Lantern 21 (Spring 1978): Bee-lore; 2 'fire-balls' from 1890, and one from 1977; UFO reports; more by editor Ivan

Bunn on his Black Dog research; news &
reviews. Lantern 22 (Summer 1978): East
Anglian field names; the Secret Tunnels
of Norfolk & Suffolk; UFO reports, notes
and reviews. Lantern is the organ of
the Borderline Science Investigation
Group of East Anglia covering UFOs,
Forteana and folklore etc locally. UK
sub: 85p/year - Overseas rates available. Write: Lantern, 3 Dunwich Way,
Oulton Broad, Lowestoft, Suffolk NR32
4RZ.

Page Research - not only have they
changed their name to UFO Information
Network (UFOIN, not to be confused with
the British group of the same initials),
but I must apologise to them for the
inconvenience caused by getting their
details horribly wrong. Their Newsletter
on Forteana and UFOs is $6.00 for six
issues; and catalogues of news and used
books on UFO and Fortean topics come
with the Newsletter or with book orders.
UK readers will find UFOIN an invaluable
source for US material and even some
rare and out-of-print material. Send
$6.00 to UFOIN: Box 5012, Rome, Ohio
44085, USA.

Specula 1:2 (Mar/June 1978): if you
are interested in the sort of material
and approach discussed in Tom Bearden's
article this issue (p14), then you'll
be doubly interested in Specula, the
journal of the new Assoc. of Meta-Science, formed by Tom and others. It contains news and notes on this distinctive approach to subjects from psychic
healing and UFOs to Bigfeet and Life
energies...has a big article by Tom on
psychotronic weapons. For details write:
AAMS, Box 1182, Huntsville, AL 35801,
USA.

Journal of Occult Studies 1:2 (Spring 1978): This astonishinly valuable
journal has established a quality reputation, in only 2 issues, for practical
research and theory monographs. This
issue contains 'Systematic Investigation of Allegedly Haunted House with
Infrared Documentation'; psychokinetic
experiments; thumb-size and palm-lines
in relation to dominant personality
characteristics; personality tests cor-
related with astrology; analysis of
the Aletti psychic photograph; Tom
Bearden with more on what he calls
'Species meta-psychology'; report of
a parapsychology conference with Matthew Manning. JOS is $8.50/yr for USA,
overseas $12.00/yr. JOS, Occult Studies
Foundation, Box 32, Kingston, Rhode
Island 02881, USA.

Journal of Meteorology 3:39 (May/
June 1978): indispensable to the serious Fortean as a monthly record of weather and climatic freaks - this issue
includes a listing of disasters for
March 1978, mystery noises, tornadoes,
and other notes. For details write:
JMet, Cockhill House, Trowbridge BA14
9BG.

Nessletter 27 (April 1978), a monthly newsletter from the Ness Information
Service, with latest details of expeditions, discoveries, sightings and personalities. $7.00/£1.75/yr. From: Rip
Hepple, Huntshieldford, St Johns Chapel,
Bishop Aukland, Co Durham.

Res Bureaux Bulletin conducted tri-
weekly by Mr X. One of the best Fortean
newsletters around - but not for mass
circulation. Mr X will exchange for
journals or material. RBB: Box 1598,
Kingston, Ontario, Canada K7L 5C8.

Forteana 5: a Danish Fortean newspaper-format quarterly covering all
topics of Forteana, plus reviews - in
Danish. Write Scanfo: Classensgade 8,
Dk 2100 Kobenhaven Ø, Denmark.

Kadath - a glossy, impressive, serious journal on 'forgotten' civilisat-
ions and their artifacts. Bimonthly, in
French. Write for details to: Kadath,
6 Blvd Saint-Michel, B-1150 Bruxelles,
Belgium.

Looking Glass - an intriguing consp-
iracy/symbolism/synchronicity/word-game
newsletter, eruditely edited by Michael
A Hoffman. He asks for an SASE from US
readers - but interested UK & other
readers had better inquire first. From
Michael A Hoffman, Box 343, Geneva,
NY 14456, USA.

Energy Unlimited - the flyer announcing this new mag mentions all kinds of
Fortean topics, including Tesla res
earch, UFO propulsion systems, psychotronics, alchemy, holography etc etc.
Sounds fascinating. Quarterly; $15.00
for 4 issues, plus $2.50 surface post,
or $6.00 airmail. EU, Dept MBRB, 3562
Moore St, Los Angeles, CA 90066, USA.

Unusual News - a newspaper-format
round-up of recent Forteana. Write for
details: UN, c/o L Syrinda Kaplan, Box
12181, Cincinnati, OH 45212, USA.

The Ley Hunter 80: the essential
magazine for those interested in Earth
Mysteries and study of archeoastronomy,

leys etc. This issue is a special on 'ancient America' with contributions from John Michell, 'Prehistoric Earth Sculpture'; Dr EC Krupp on 'Uxmal Alignments'; Francis Hitching on 'Megalithic America'; plus pieces on US forms of leys, earth-forces, dragons and of course Mystery Hill, from Hoult, Lonegren, Pettis, Ross and Rothovius. A splendid issue on a neglected area of collective discussion. Bimonthly: £2.70 in UK & Europe; £4.00/$8.00 overseas airmail. TLH: Box 152, London N10 1EP. For the convenience of FT readers, TLH may be ordered via us.

Ancient Skills & Wisdom Review - a quarterly journal and book review newsletter on Fortean, UFO and Earth Mystery subjects: £2.00/yr. From Paul Screeton, 5 Egton Drive, Seaton Carew, Hartlepool, Cleveland TS25 2AT.

Paranormal & Psychic Australian 3:6 (June 1978): We have discovered this excellent and recommended review of Australian Forteana, UFOs and psychic phenomena rather late, but now that we have established links you should be hearing more of P&PA. Monthly, Austral ian $12.00/yr. This issue contains: 'Strange Aboriginal Beings'; living globes of UFO light; 'I met a Min-Min globe', a curious 'ball-light' encounter in which the figure of a small humanoid materialised or coalesced; plus many illustrated notes and news. P&PA: Box 19, Spit Junction, NSW 2088, Australia.

FSR 23:6 (April 1978): the Stonehenge incident; encounter at Rainford; humanoids at Stack Rock, Pembs; 'Man-in-Black Syndrome'; and pts 1&2 of one of the most astonishing cases in recent years, right here on the outskirts of London, the 'Aveley Abduction'. 24:1 (June 1974): pt3 of the amazing abduction case at Aveley; 'Boxcar' over Preston; encounters on a Yorks moor; landings in Estonia; 'Did humanoids kill these men?'; 'Bent Spoons or Bent Reality?'; and more. FSR: West Malling, Maidstone, Kent.

MUFOB ns10 (Spring 1978): continues to make direct contibutions to the reformation of UFO studies. This issue has a fundamentally important article by Donald Johnson on the approach to nonphysical UFO evidence; Nigel Watson on the 'Cigar Ship' of 1909; Roger Sandell 'Challenging the Chariots'; plus a review by the editors, on their 10th anni-

versary, of the changes (or lack of) in ufology in that period; plus notes, reviews and pt15 of Peter Rogerson's catalogue of 'type 1' UFO records. Quarterly, £1.25/$3.00 (air). MUFOB: 11 Beverley Rd, New Malden, Surrey.

Our sincere congratulations to the editors of MUFOB (John Rimmer, Peter Rogerson, Roger Sandell & John Harney) for their consistent pioneering more inclusive approaches to UFO phenomena over their 10 years; and we look forward to another 10, or more!

Watsup Journal - Wessex UFOs and more. No8 has articles on 'The Philadelphia Experiment'; humanoids,from the future?; pt3 of Bermuda Triangle analysis; catalogue of haunted sites in Hampshire pt3; reports, sightings etc. £2.00/yr. WATSUP: 10 Westwood Rd, Southampton.

Earthlink (Spring 1978) journal of Essex UFO Study Group (retitled) - with local sightings, articles etc. EUFOSG: 16 Raydons Rd, Dagenham, Essex RM9 5JR.

Northern UFO News - journal of the Northern UFO Investigators Network, one of the most active of UK groups, which tends to break stories before anyone else. Write to Jenny Randles: 23 Sunningdale Drive, Irlam, Salford M30 6NJ.

Les Extraterrestres - French glossy UFO coverage - big story on UN debate on UFOs. France 10Frs/ other countries 15Frs. LE: Saint-Denis-les-Rebais, 77510 Rebais, France.

CHAOS: A Review of the Damned
Once again we urge support of Mr X's project to publish Fort's sources and studies of classical Fortean data in a bimonthly serialcalled Chaos. He needs at least 250 subscribers to cover his costs, and surely there must be that many if not seriously interested, then interested enough in the field generally to support a genuine scholarly project?

Subscription details: Full subs - Canada $15.00; USA $13.50; UK £7.00; all other nations remit at the Canadian rate. Annual airmail subs will cost an additional $4.00 (USA); £2.50 (UK); and all other nations Canada $2.50. Single copies - Canada $2.00; USA $2.00; UK £1.00; all other nations Canada $2.00.

Send to: Mr X, Box 1598, Kingston, Ontario K7L 5C8, Canada; or write for more information.

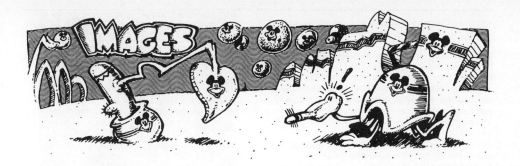

THE SHAMOKIN IMAGE

Largely ignored by the British press, an image of a face, said by many to be the face of Christ seen on an altar cloth, has been drawing attention and pilgrims to the town of Shamokin, Pennsylvania, for over a year.

It was first noticed by Rev Frank Knutti, rector of the Holy Trinity Episcopal Church, in Shamokin, who said he became aware of an "unusual presence" in the sanctuary as he read his Breviary, around midnight on Maundy Thursday 1977, which that year fell on 7th April. He says, in the first local reports of the event (1): "The church was empty – the last watchers before the Altar of Repose had left – but I felt a strong certainty I was not alone. I glanced around the church but saw nothing unusual until I turned toward the altar. There on the linen cloth surrounding the ciborium containing the Blessed Sacrament, I beheld the face of Jesus." He called his wife and daughter and they too saw the image, and for the next week or so "many of our members and a few non-members have witnessed this miraculous vision."

One of these members, Mrs Marvin Beck, said that while she was engaged in private prayer before the altar, she noticed "a very bright light" around the ciborium. "As the light changed, I could clearly see the figure of the Lord, both kneeling and standing. I could see his long hair and the wound in the palm of His hand. It was a beautiful sight." (1)

Looking at the handful of clippings in front of me now, it's interesting to see how quickly the myth-making processes began, and the events which have already become legend. I have here a clipping from just before Easter this year, ie nearly a year after the first appearance of the image. In it, apart from the news that the image appears as strong as (some insist stronger than) before, the image was said to have vanished from Good Friday (8th) until the Wednesday after Easter (13th), and that according to the testimony of Mrs Helen Keiser, she and other parishioners were with Knutti, that Maundy night, when the face first appeared. For several days, she says, they kept their thoughts to themselves for fear of being branded religious fanatics. (6) I suppose such a divergence from the first account (quoted above) is to be expected after a year...and I rather think Mrs Keiser's recollection must have been from the early part of the hiatus, which in turn could be seen as a time in which the witnesses were quietly thinking over what they had seen.

Whatever, the first of the subsequent viewings by thousands of people since, occurred on that Wednesday after Easter, the 13th April, when, in the grand tradition of the Emperor's Clothes, a child dared to say aloud what many found hard to acknowledge even in their hearts. Iris Reigle, aged 9, in the church with her grandmother, Mrs Clarence Fegley, tugged at her grandmother's dress to "come and see God's face." Mrs Fegley said: "At first I couldn't see anything except the altar, the flowers and the tabernacle. Then, as I looked more closely at the veil, I too could plainly see...the face of Jesus." (1) Iris was quickly sent to fetch her parents and others from the Parish House where they were gathering after that evenings prayers, "and each of them saw the face on the veil covering the tabernacle. With one accord," adds Mrs Fegley, "we knelt in prayer and wonderment...to see this miraculous revelation." (1) The next day, at Mass, the whole congregation saw the face – some saw a full figure – on the cloth though apparently "less distinct." The news spread rapidly far and wide, attracting the curious, the TV and press crews, and in their wake, the bus-loads of pilgrims. Rev Knutti started to hold regular healing services – and although he must be under much strain from callers at all hours of the night, a church so perpetually crammed with lookers that it can't be cleaned properly and help is needed to herd the crowd out to close the doors at night, and the darker side with the inevitable souvenir-snatchers and commercial hustlers, the gallant reverend "seems to radiate a strong inner peace that wasn't evident before." (6)

Thinking further about the Rev Knutti's and other statements about the first sightings, we note something he said in another interview (5)...that he saw the image for the first time on the Thursday midnight, but that he was unable to see it again until the child, Iris, saw after the following Wednesday's service. Our source (6) in describing the girl's vision (in error, they say she was calling her mother) use the telling words: "It was the voice of a young child which finally brought the image into focus." Of course it may be that Rev Knutti himself is psychic, for in his original statement about his midnight sighting he hints that he had seen something like this image before: "He was facing me - just as He did at the same time and in the same place two years ago." (1)

The Church, contrary to popular belief, measures a 'miracle', not so much by the number of natural laws it confounds, but by the way it reinforces the fundamental dogma and kindles faith. This is certainly happening in Shamokin. Knutti says his congregation has burgeoned from a mere 60, to a good portion of the quarter of a million who have visited the church in the last year, many from overseas, in what he calls "a world-wide parish". The event, too, has unified the local congregation - previously they squabbled like anyone else. There have been healings, and many have written to Knutti to say how their lives have changed for the better. One man, deaf for years, attended only to accompany his wife. He remained in a pew while she knelt at the altar. Suddenly he felt an "inner explosion" in his ears, and heard a buzzing. With awe he realized the sound was people talking. (6)

As in previous cases of spontaneous images (see FT7p11 (the Castelnau-de-Guers face-of-Christ, also on a ciborium napkin), FT10pp5-10, and FT18pp3-5) we note the curious detail that different folk are seeing different images...in this case a full face and both kneeling and full figures. One visitor - a rel-

igious scholar - said the face resembled that of the Turin Shroud. We present here the best photos we have - not very good at all - with a detail of the Turin face for comparison. Although I cannot see any organising pattern that might be a face in these photos, the testimony of thousands cannot be dismissed, even if they seem to be discribing different images. In this context we include the following statement from Fortean researcher Larry Arnold, who went to Shamokin to join the queue to see what he would see.

"Most visitors reported seeing the face of Jesus full-front (head-on). This view we also discerned - but there was more. We perceived two profiles: one looking to the right and upwards; the other, cranium draped in a shawl, was facing left and looking downwards. Both these images were superimposed on the 'normal' face reported by others. We asked one of the church's deacons if anyone else had reported this multiple-image effect and he said the left-facing (profile) had been mentioned by a few, but no-one else had reported the right-facing figure. Additionally, we noted a feminine figure that can best be described by alluding to the standard representation of the Blessed Virgin Mary. Again, this figure was draped in a shawl (which seemed blue) and manifested the most plaintive expression of sorrow with an offering of compassion. Two companions, as well as ourself, also commented on the reddish-orange glow sporadically discernable near the center of the altar cloth. It was quite apparent that the 3 of us were seeing things not discerned by most of the 100-or-so observers at Holy Trinity Episcopal Church that Sunday afternoon. We wonder of course whether others had seen even more than we, and not reported it...
Larry E Arnold."

Of course, there's a joker in every pack - at Shamokin, up popped a character calling himself Abbot David Schott, of an "independent Catholic" community at St Jude's Abbey, Delmar, Maryland. Schott claimed to have reproduced an identical image by using lights and shadows in the altar cloth. He was even able to turn it into an image of the Virgin Mary "and an alligator." (huh?) On the pretext of sounding a warning to many people not to spend their savings in the expectation of a miracle healing or whatever, he felt he had to urge caution. "There's nothing to say it is a miracle," he said, and as if it were a spell to ward off sudden lynching, he quickly added, "...and nothing to say it isn't." He went to see Bishop Stevenson, of the Central Pennsylvania Diocese to get an official bucket of cold water put on the affair, but the Bishop refused, saying he had no evidence of trickery at all. Schott complained that Knutti refused to allow him near the cloth, or to conduct a blessing service (both of which he was perfectly entitled to do in his own church). Schott and a few "colleagues" hung about for a few days trying to get evidence of trickery - first he alleged that altar cloths imprinted with an image of Christ could be purchased from church supply catalogues (not true, said the Bishop); then he alleged that a light to one side

of the church was not turned on because, he said, it would "erase" the image if it were (Mrs Pat Knutti, the rector's wife, said the light has always been on.) (4) It's plain that no-one at Shamokin, or elsewhere, had any time for Schott. The Archbishop of the RC Diocese of Delaware said St Jude's Abbey was not a "legitimate order". "They advertise themselves as Catholic and non-denominational, they wear Franciscan-style robes and use Catholic trappings in their services." Schott admitted that his order still uses the Latin Mass - no wonder he was barely tolerated! (4) Better than TV!

A final note on the face on the cloth. It's natural, of course, to think of the face as the byproduct of light and shade on folds, but despite a concensus against moving the cloth, Knutti removes and replaces it over the ciborium at least twice a day, during morning and evening services. He admits he feared to move it too, to begin with. "Too many people were asking me what we had behind the veil, and I decided if it really was the work of our Lord, moving the veil wouldn't change it." (2,3) ...and it hasn't. Witnesses say the image "looks the same."
Shamokin, Penn, News-Item (1) 15 April 1977, (2) 23 April, (3) 28 April, (4) 5 May 1977; (5) Indonesia Times 23 April 1977; (6) Harrisburg, Penn, Sun-

day Patriot-News 5 March 1978. (Cr: source 5 to Ion Will, all other, with grateful thanks to Larry Arnold.)
Also: Houston Post 21 April 1977 (Cr: Kurt Lothmann.)

SPONTANEOUS PHOTOGRAPHIC IMAGES

The last time we mentioned images that spontaneously appear on film was back in FT18 - and we've collected a few since then - and others are being investigated. Here then is a selection of Fortean photos:

Mrs Lena Cheeseman, of Kings Cross, London, wrote to the magazine Weekend, saying that on the balcony of flats opposite hers she can see the ghostly figure of an old woman in a nightdress. Neighbours could see it too. Her son investigated but could find nothing to account for it. Weekend sent along their photographer, Clifford Kent, and he too saw the shimmering figure, and the photo below is the product of a minute's exposure of his camera. After taking the photo, he went and examined the door and balcony of the flat - it was empty and he too could find no explanation for the figure (which could only be seen from elsewhere.) Nor did he see any lights which might be causing reflections. Weekend 10 October 1973 (Cr: Cathy Purcell, Ivan Bunn.)

During New Year's Eve revelry, to usher in 1976, at the Plough Inn, East-bury, near Newbury, Berks, landlord Ken Thackway borrowed David Pounds' Pola-roid camera to snap the revellers. Over a week later, Ken and his wife Gladys noticed that the one taken of David himself and another person (*below right*) seemed to show a ghostly white face to the right of the picture above David's left elbow. Matters became even more interesting when another customer said they recognised the face in the photo as that of Violet Cotterill, the daugh-ter of a former owner of the pub, who died a bed-ridden cripple in 1945, and was buried in the churchyard opposite. The Thackways, who had only been in residence for almost a year, had sus-pected the pub was haunted - Mrs Thack-way said she had seen faces at windows, including the face said to be Violet Cotterill's in the pub's front door window. The newspaper suggested the face could have been formed from a camera flash bouncing off the gloss-painted wall...but the angles involved seem to me quite wrong, even if we knew whether a flash was used with the Pola-roid, which we don't. At the time the story appeared, I decided to approach the people involved through the news-paper, but got nowhere. If I remember rightly I was told the Thackways no longer had the photo and that they had been pestered so much that further en-quiries would be unwelcome. Perhaps someone else might like to pursue this, and keep us informed. Newbury Weekly News 15 Jan 1976.

The following letter appeared in Reveille 23 April 1976 (hmmm lots of 23s this issue too!) from Joseph Leath-erbarrow, of Morpeth, Northumberland: "A photographer friend was asked to take pictures of a woman's grave after her funeral. When he delivered the pictures the woman's daughter became very upset and accused him of 'some kind of joke". For there among the flowers and wreaths was the face of her mother.

Seen and photographed - the Kings Cross phantom (top left), Weekend.

David Pounds & ghostly face, (enlargement from Newbury W News).

The photographer had never met the mother, nor even known the family before being given the order. Nobody could explain the phantom face." (Cr: N Watson)

6½ months after the first visions at Shamokin, 2,000 people attended a healing service in St Anthony's RC church, Fitchburg, Massachusetts, presided over by Rev Ralph DiOrio - Sunday 30 October 1977. According to several eyewitnesses including a nun and a policeman, a woman took some Polaroid colour photos of the proceedings, and on one photo of DiOrio blessing a supplicant a faint image of a robed figure could be discerned behind the priest and above him to one side. The policeman, William Barrett, described the robe as white and the figure with blue eyes, a beard and arms extended. "In the right corner of the photograph was a faded image of Christ," said Barrett. "It was a real plain apparition, but faded compared to the side with Father DiOrio on it." The rest of the account goes on to describe DiOrio's brand of healing fireworks, full of fervour and speaking in tongues...and the healings apparently accomplished. DiOrio seems quite a showman. A young boy, who claimed his deafness had gone, was scooped up as he cried in relief, and taken by the priest toward the Boston TV station's cameras. DiOrio "told him to look at the cameras and raise his arms in praise to the Lord," which he did. So much for spontaneity! However that's all we know about the picture - and we'll definitely try to find out more. Worcester Telegram, Mass, 31 October 1977 (Cr: Loren Coleman.)

During a roaring fire which destroyed the United Methodist Church in the small Michigan community of Bear Lake, on 22 October 1977, a couple of strange events took place. As 78yr-old parishioner Laila Cooley watched the blaze from her nearby home, she saw, in the clouds of smoke the figure she is certain was Christ carrying a lamb - for 30 minutes she watched it fade and reappear. "It was very clear to me that the apparition was there, looking down on the people," Mrs Cooley said. "There is no question in my mind because it kept reappearing. If I had seen it once I would have thought it was just imagination. But it kept coming back again and again." The next morning at a meeting of the congregation, she told of her vision. All this is interesting enough, and guaranteed to keep a small community buzzing for months, but our present concern is the second curiosity

to come out of that fire, apparently an appearance of the opposition party. It transpires that Wayne R Wissner had taken several photos of the fire, and after developing them a week later he discovered a strange figure silhouetted against one of the blazing windows (see below). Probably in reaction to Mrs Cooley's vision, the folks at Bear Lake believe it was Old Nick himself. Wissner says: "My blood ran cold when I saw the strange figure. When I took the photograph, I saw nothing that could explain it. There was nothing leaning against the inside wall of the church because the floor had collapsed. It really does look like the Devil." The

photo was the second in a series of 3 taken at 1/25sec, one second apart, and the other two show no figure. It seems logical, I suppose, that if bearded and robed figures are generally interpreted as Christ, then a dark figure in flames would be seen as Satan. These types of events raise some major issues of great interest - by what processes do meaningful images manifest spontaneously on film; how do people perceive apparitions; how do we attach meanings to perceptions; and is it possible that these images and apparitions are associated with personalities living or dead? Story and photo from National Enquirer 7 March 1978.

These questions, of course, have been raised since the begining of spirit photography, and since the first apparition, and we still have no universally acceptable answers. The phenomenon cares not one jot for our dilemma and continues to manifest. Consider the drama over an identity card photo that Wendy Sternberg, of Buffalo State College, had taken in a photo-booth, back

in 1974. As you can see below, behind
her head to the right is the profile
of an old man or woman. As Wendy had
a flat screen immediately behind her,
and the booth was open to a line of
waiting students, there seems no possibility of anyone actually being in the
position suggested by the image. The

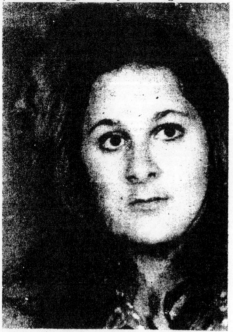

photo was investigated by the infamous
Committee for Investigation of Claims
for the Paranormal, led by Dr Paul
Kurtz. Kurtz's opinion (considered or
not) is that it is the profile of George
Washington from the quarter coin --
however Kurtz is at a loss to explain
how it happened: "We don't know..." but
suggest that "somehow" a coin was pressed against the film. If that's the
sort of explanations the Committee are
favoring, frankly, I'd prefer the more
aesthetically satisfying notion of
ghosts! Incidentally, when I first saw
the original caption to the photo I
misread the abbreviation for identity
card as implying this was a photo of
the girl's id...and therein lies another theory... From Midnight Globe 25
April 1978.

Finally, I have two miscellaneous
notes which have dark implications for
UFO photos, indeed photography gener-
ally, if there is any truth in them.
Firstly, according to John Reeves, of
Ashurst Wood, Sussex, the area was due

for a massive invasion of UFOs in Sept
1976. We can't tell whether it was or
not but John is convinced that he can
see great numbers of them in the skies
even though no one else can see them.
And, he says, he has many photos to
prove it. We are interested in his
method of photographing UFOs: "Just
point your camera at the pole star and
sometimes you get a clear picture with
UFOs in." (!) East Grinstead Observer
either 2 or 9 Sept 1976 (Cr: A Cromarty)
Similarly we have a brief note about
an unscheduled image that appeared on
film in an automatic camera at an unnamed rocket-motor testing station
somewhere in the UK Midlands. Between
the end of one test and the next the
camera should have been photographing
clear sky, and instead picked up an
unidentified object. It looked like a
highly-luminous object with a tail of
brilliant stars and was likened to a
"plucked ostrich neck". Experts said it
had nothing to do with the tests, and
examination of the film could not account for it. Too much vagueness about
this story as it stands - anyone know
any more? New Sunday Times, Malaysia,
10 July 1977.

HOLYGRAMS - AND OTHERS...
By the term 'Holygram' - cleverly
coined by our pal Ion Will - we mean
body images like the Turin Shroud. In
the last year the Shroud has received
much attention, and deserves a whole
article - but for a recent good exposition see the article by Ian Wilson in
the Sunday Times Magazine 26 March 1978,
previewing his imminent book on the
subject. For now, we'll give two cases
that recently came to our attention.
At 7.10pm on 1 Oct 1977, a busy Sat-
uday evening in Brakpan, South Africa,
a man was knocked down and critically
injured by a car. He was taken to the Far
East Rand Hospital, in Springs, where
he died at 8.30pm. He was later identified as Dirk Esterhuizen, aged 32. A
regrettable but not unusual occurrence
these days - the weirdness comes in its
wake. Esterhuizen had been laid on a
trolley bed which had a rubber sheet
between a linen sheet and the mattress.
When mortuary attendants came to remove his body they found a life-size
image of the dead man imprinted onto
the mattress. Hospital staff called to
witness the phenomenon said there was
no image on the linen sheet (which was
"a hotch-potch of bloodstains"), nor
on the rubber sheet (though one source
seems to suggest the image was on the

rubber mattress cover and not on the mattress). Apparently no amount of scrubbing will remove the image which include a representation of parts of clothing, a pen-top in the shirt pocket. And even weirder, the right arm and left leg are hazy, corresponding to fractures in the body. Dr J Botha, head of physics at Johannesburg General Hospital said that to his knowledge this image could not have been caused by any of the radioactive or Xray treatments used medically. The last we heard was that the case was under investigation by Prof JJF Taljaard, head of forensic medicine at the University of Witwatersrand. The Star, South Africa, 8 Oct 1977, Rand Daily Mail, SA, 13 Oct 1977, The Guardian 14 Oct 1977 (Cr: Chris Holtzhausen, Ian Thompson, Roger Sandell.)

A similar but less dramatic image is told of in the National Enquirer 26 Oct 1976. The image of a man's left hand as seen from the back appeared on a crushed velour bedspread owned by Mrs Irene Rogers, of Newport, Arkansas, on 1 Aug 1976. She says: "I was making the bed, and threw the spread back on - and there it was." Chemical tests stumped various experts who tried to duplicate the effect of the image. According to Dr John Beadles, Dept. Biological Sciences, Arkansas State University: "The fibers on the print are all lying down or twisted but none has been burned or scorched - which rules out the possibility that a plastic impression was used". Charles Beasley, manager of Sharon Rug Mills, manufacturers of the bedspread, was equally baffled. It was clearly not a freak product of the manufacturing process, he said after investigation. "I have no idea how this could have happen-

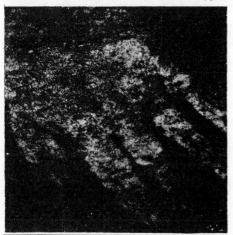

ed. It would take many tons of pressure - enough to crush a hand - to produce this effect." The image (see below *left*) shows wrinkles, knuckles, fingernails, and the shadow of a ring clearly visible - and the thumb appears to be slightly deformed. Mrs Rogers, herself, is convinced it's a sign from her late husband, Travis, who died of liver cirrhosis, the previous November. The Rogers had been married and divorced twice and Irene said: "He kept coaxing me to remarry him right up until he died. Travis had a lot of spirit. This might be his way of letting me know that he's thinking about me." A clincher, if you believe in such things, is the fact that Travis Rogers had a deformed thumb after a baseball injury. (Cr: G Abbott).

And finally, a lasting impression! Apologies for the pun...but here's an image, claimed by many to portray Christ, has appeared on the sole of a shoe, is attracting thousands of pilgrims to a Dominican convent near Quebec. The image was noticed by mystified churchmen who were unable to force a dead priest's left leg into his coffin - it says here - until the shoe was removed. (Died with his boots on eh?) Sunday People 9 July 1978.

SPONTANEOUS IMAGES IN NATURE

The following notes are a random assortment of curious images that have arisen in a natural context.

In Phenomena (p60) John Michell and I tell of a hen that laid eggs bearing designs, apparently on command from her owner who visualised the desired pattern in her mind. And in FT3p18 we told a similar story of a hen in Arkansas (hmmm Arkansas seems good for imagery) which laid an egg with a neatly printed **6** on one end. Well we've just found lurking at the bottom of the file a note from the Daily Express 23 March 1965, that a star hen on a farm at Rushall, Staffordshire, laid an egg with the letters 'WX' imprinted on it.

Another letter - this time in the News of the World 20 Nov 1977, from Lucy Wade: "My sister, a brilliant child artist, died young. Later I was sitting by a steamed-up window. As the steam cleared I was amazed to see a drawing of a face appear on the window. It was the same face my sister had once drawn in an art competition!"

The picture below received some publicity in the USA, but as it may be new to readers elsewhere we include it here. It seems that the most sacred of Sioux

rituals, the Horse Dance, representing
the coming together of the Sioux Nation,
whose 'circle' was broken by the shameful massacre at Wounded Knee, was dan-
ced at Waterloo, Nebraska, early June
1976. The next day a weather satellite
took this photo of clouds over the USA.

According to Omaha weatherman Benny
Gullach, who discovered this amazing
'Indian chief' image in the cloud-pat-
tern, the figure "appears to be look-
ing over toward Wounded Knee." Omaha
World Herald 18 June 1976 (Cr: Joe
Swatek.)

THREE-HANDED MADONNA

Every so often we hit some events
which give us an extra tingle, though
in all fairness we oughtn't to have
favourites, we are after all human (or
think we are!) Here's one... During a
Mass in the Greek Orthodox church in
the small town of Madaba, south of
Amman, Jordan, on the morning of Sunday
29 Jan 1978 a miracle was witnessed by
a large congregation. According to a
translated local report, the people saw
"A dark shadow and then a blue light
encompass the icon of the Virgin Mary,
and then a third hand appeared on the
icon behind the infant Jesus. The congregation immediately started praying
and praising God and the Virgin Mary
after witnessing this miraculous change."
We managed to locate a photo of the
transformed icon (top right) and see
there is no hand "behind" the Christ-
child figure - instead logic insists
the recent appendage to be one of those
on the left hand side, probably the
lower one.

There are a couple of interesting
additional points. The AP report adds
that in the congregation at the time
was Nasima Amatonios, a nun "reputed
to have performed miracles in Lebanon
and Syria in 1968". And as far as we
can tell, reconstructing from source
date, on the very same day, just over

the border into Israel, a calf was born
with three mouths (see the cattle sub-
heading in our section on 'Freaks and
Curiosities'). It seems as if that day
threeness was expressing itself, but
we haven't yet located a third triple
event for the same day! Assoc Press release 31 Jan 1978, London Evening Standard 1 Feb 1978, Aktuelt, Denmark, 31
Jan 1978 (Cr: Paul Screeton, Ion Will,
and Peter Juhl Svendsen of Forteana.)

THE CASE OF THE GLOWING CROSS

Back in my college days I irreveren-
tly proposed, for a design project, to
manufacture blow-moulded Madonnas and
other "grave furniture" on a modular
system that allowed design permutations
and which could be lit up from below at
night. It was turned down. Now, years
later, I'm brought face to face with
the genuine article - a grave monument
that shines out like an ad for After-
life! I've been sent a number of clippings but seem to have misfiled some
(blush!) and so I reconstruct from what
I have to hand.

The cross was originally erected to
mark the grave of William Thomas Thur-
ling Steenson, a 29yr-old railway guard
who died a hero, trying to stop a runaway railway carriage at Mullumbimby
station on 23 Sept 1907. The cemetary
at Lismore, New South Wales, Australia,
was closed in 1971, and many of the
monuments, including Steenson's, were
relocated further up the hillside. Each
night the cross glows brightly, and has
attracted regular crowds of the mystif-

ied, the terrified, gawkers and worshippers.

The cross is 2 meters high and made of apparently ordinary monumental granite. An industrial chemist investigated the suggestion that the cross had been coated with barium paint as a joke but analysis of the surface found nothing unusual. The nearest streetlights are nearly a kilometer away - and the cross glows even when the moon is hidden.

Locals, including Steenson's grandson, Neville, aged 55, believe the glowing has gone on nightly for the last 60yrs, even in its old position - but the story only became better known when a group of teenagers, straying into this deserted northern part of Lismore, became frightened by it and reported it to a local paper, in mid-Feb.

Sadly, no sooner had the story been broadcast widely, than vandals, in the night of 20 Feb, tipped the cross over and smashed chunks out of it, probably for souvenirs. Curiously, a prophetic event happened earlier that morning while it was still dark - the streetlights on a nearby bridge unaccountably failed. Daily Mirror,NSW, and Sydney Morning Herald, both 21 Feb 1978, Reveille 9 June 1978 (Cr: Richard King, Mac Lauria, Ion Will). For those interested in such things, Steenson's cross has the Masonic compass and square design engraved on the center!

RJMR

On the subject of Mystery Animals we
have several developments of the data
presented last issue (FT25pp33-36)...

THE BICKERTON BEAST

Last issue we gave a recent sighting
of a large dog-like MA in the Bickerton
Hills, Cheshire, from mid-Jan 1978. It
seems that we hadn't realised that this
MA had been seen before, both in that
area and in the pages of FT. See FT9
p20 for an account of the 'thing' that
was seen near the Delamere Forest in
1974.

THE 'SURREY' PUMA

Reader Chris Hall found a gap in our
Puma record (see FT25p47) and managed
to fill it with the following reports.
As far as possible we've reconstructed
probable sighting times - but our lives
would be made much easier if reporters
would put in details of time etc...

Sometime during the last couple of
days of June and the first two of July
1976, Sally Rose, mother of 3 and journalist, was returning to Hartley Wintney from attending a council meeting in
Bracknell in the evening. As she passed
Star Hill, on the A30, (an area of Roman roads, army camps, and a name evocative of the similarly army-inhabited,
UFO-haunted area near Warminster) the
animal crossed the road in front of her
car. She says: "I'd swear on oath that
I saw the puma or a very large cat-like
creature which wasn't like anything I'd
ever seen before...I was about 50yds
away when my lights picked up what I at
first thought was a large dog. It came
straight out of the bushes into the
road and I stopped. I immediately realised this was no dog, domestic cat or
fox - I knew it could only be the Surrey
Puma." Without turning its head the animal sauntered across and vanished into
the forest on the other side of the
road. Mrs Rose describes it as about
2ft 6in tall, 3ft long with a curving
tail about 2ft 6in long. It was a sandy
beige colour, with short smooth hair

and a smallish head, with noticeably
large paws. Mrs Rose told police but a
search found nothing. A spokesman from
Chessington Zoo was moved to comment:
"Let's just say it is a puma - it must
be getting very close to its maximum
lifespan, because these reports have
been coming in for about 12 years." We'd
guess 16yrs or more! Aldershot News 9
July 1976.

Close on the sighting by Mrs Rose, on
3 July 1976, Mrs Jane Skillicorn, a
Yateley schoolteacher, turned off the
A30 just before Hartley Wintney, about
10.15pm, and almost ran down a huge
"cat-like" fawn-coloured creature, on
the Eversley slip roadnear a sawmill.
She said: "I was terrified. I saw huge
green eyes in my headlights and slammed
on my brakes. It was definitely no dog
or deer. It was the puma." Police were
investigating her story too. Aldershot
News 9 July 1976. They were still investigating, and obviously finding nothing. Aldershot News 16 July 1976.

In a rather stupid piece, the same
paper from 30 July 1976, tried to jok-
ily explain the recent sightings, and
by implication those of the last decade,
as those of a large domestic ginger tom
owned by the Cruikshanks of Odiham.
It was discovered when police looked
into a call that a "black puma" was
seen in the grounds of Corridor House,
next door to the Cruickshanks...though
how any one can reconcile the large
black cat with a domestic ginger cat I
just don't know. Mrs Anne Barnes was
hanging out washing in the back garden
of Corridor House, High St, Odiham,
when she noticed a huge cat watching
her. It had frozen in its tracks, just
a few yards away from her - after a
couple of seconds it jumped a 10ft wall
and disappeared into dense woods. Mrs
Barnes decided the animal was not just
a large cat because it had "huge shoulders like a bear." Although the sighting isn't dated, a reference is made to
police still investigating the 2 A30

sightings above, so we'd guess it was sometime in mid-July 1976. Anyone with spare time could get dates and times from the daybooks at Odiham and Fleet police stations. <u>Aldershot News</u> 30 July 1976. (Cr: all above to Chris Hall.)

THE SCOTTISH 'LIONESS'

In giving the story last issue (<u>FT</u>25 p33f) of the livestock depredations and sightings of "a lion or puma" near Bettyhill, on the northernmost coast of Sutherland, we took the story up to 14 Dec 1977, having mislaid (blush!) some clippings sent to us by Jake Williams. They turned up eventually - so on with the story...

It seems police have records of sightings going back 2 years - but following the supposed wounding of the animal (told last issue) on two occasions they were mounting extensive armed searches on the moorlands and heaths near the village of Strathnaver, following the discovery of carcases on 12 Dec 1977.

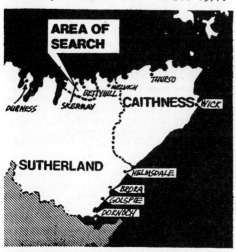

Thomas Todd, a crofter at Achneiskich, Bettyhill, found one of his sheep dead - its fleece had been removed and its flesh stripped. This was said to be the work of a predator. Mr Todd remembers earlier incidents: "The other morning I discovered paw prints about 3" in diameter in the snow; and I remember about 2 years ago finding a dead ewe which had been defending its lamb. Half its head had been ripped off and I realise now that it must have been this cat when it was younger." Of the present killing, Mr Todd said: "I have never seen anything like it. The skin was removed as cleanly as if it had been professionally skinned. The backbone and top of the skull were still there,

but the ribs had been chewed right into the vertebrae. There was very little sign of a struggle...whatever killed the sheep did so very quickly and efficiently." Scott Johnston, a vet called in by the police, said: "In my opinion the killing was the work of a member of the cat family. There is no conclusive proof, but the neatness of the kill, the spacing of the tooth marks and the crushing of the bones all point to a feline predator." Forteans following the gory saga of US cattle mutilations will note the curious detail of the clean "professional" skinning...and that for once we have convincing evidence of MAs linked to depredations.

That same day (12 Dec 1977) in the evening, Donald Mackenzie, of the Dunveaden Guest House, out hunting foxes with his son, shot and wounded a large animal they spotted swimming the River Naver, a mile from Bettyhill. He described the event: "My son Jim saw two red eyes in the river, about 9.30pm. We have permission to hunt foxes at night using a spotlight, and it was this that detected the eyes. The animal got out of the water and I realised what it was. It was about the size of an Alsatian, dark coloured and had a white chest. It ran across the fields and we chased it in the Landrover, but it was moving at incredible speed. I stopped and it stopped. I whistled and it started coming back towards us, so I aimed and fired. It spun round, fell down and got up again, then limped off into the darkness. I think I hit it in the rear end. It was a pity I didn't have my more powerful rifle with me." The Mackenzie's told Sgt Donald Bruce, of Bettyhill police, of their encounter, and having seen Mr Todd's sheep carcase - "I knew it was something different." - he organised the armed searches. He too recalled the time, 2 years earlier "when a couple of English tourists reported seeing a puma...They were very specific in their description and said it was a puma. For some reason their names were not taken, but now I wonder if they hold the key to all this. Maybe they let the animal loose because it was growing too big, and they didn't want to pay £300 for a licence to keep it."

Another man, Alistair McLean, a milkman from Skerray, said he saw the creature "a year ago" while fox-hunting with a crofter friend, Hugh MacKay, some of whose sheep had been killed. "It was about lunchtime and we were walking across the moorlands when this animal

got about 40yds in front of us and ran
off. I only got a glimpse, but it was
broad in the back, strongly built and
very fast. I thought it was a dull rusty
colour. I was convinced it was big game.
Since then it has been seen in Caithness
and other areas in Sutherland, and
locals have heard its screams in Skerray." Primary school pupil, Jaqueline
Carney, told of an animal she saw outside her home at Skerray a month ago.
"I was out playing at about 1pm when I
saw a large animal in the field below
the house. It ran across the park and
jumped over the wall. Its face was
round and cat-like and it had a long
tail. I was quite frightened. I ran in
to tell my mother but by then the beast
had vanished."

Curiously, the newspaper remarks on
the "odd coincidence" that almost exactly a year ago that week, schoolboys from
Skerray saw a strange animal molesting
sheep, 10 miles from Bettyhill, and one
of the boys was James, son of Mr Mackenzie above. In many of the Skerray depredations, the paper said, carcasses were
found skinned "with all flesh and many
bones removed." All these details from
The Press & Journal (Aberdeen) 15 Dec
1977 (Cr: Jake Williams.)

Then the beast seems to have laid
low - because the next we hear is that
on 30 Jan 1978, Mrs Helen Fitch saw
the beast in a field 100yds at Bishop
Kinkell, Conon Bridge. "Out of the corner of my eye, I caught a quick glance
of a large dog-like animal carrying a
black object in its mouth. I looked
again and saw it resembled a big cat -
similar to a small lioness or puma. I
have lived in Central Africa and seen
animals like that before. It was dark
tan but its tail and back were a darker
shade. It was very heavy in the shoulders and hindquarters and its tail curv-
ed upwards and curled at the tip. Its
stomach also sagged. I was convinced
it was a big cat. I reported it to the
police and they came along and took
casts of its prints."

Just over a mile from Mrs Fitch's
house, farmer John Henderson, of Lean-
aig Farm, reported large paw-prints
in snow in a field beside his garden.
The prints were 3-4" long and clearly
showed extended claws*(photo
shows Mr Henderson and prints.) From
Press & Journal (Aberdeen) 7 Feb 1978
(Cr: Jake Williams.)

* As a last minute thought, we realise
that cats walk with their claws retracted - a curious & puzzling detail!

At the time of the above report, no
depredations were noticed, but the next
day a carcase of a sheep was being examined by the health center in Wick,
but it was believed it was killed by a
large cat. The report, in the Press &
Journal is dated 8 Feb 1978, and curiously the previous day's sightings at
Conon Bridge are said to be "about 10
days ago." (Cr: Jake Williams.) Lastly
Jake confirms our supposition (FT25p34)
that there were two places called Farr
featuring in separate 'lion' sightings;
one near Bettyhill, and one 10 miles
south of Inverness.

Other 'lion' and 'puma' notes will
have to wait until we have more room.

RJMR

KORCHNOI'S COMPLAINT

As we type Viktor Korchnoi begins
to play Anatoli Karpov, in the Philip-
ines, for the title of world chess
champion - and our minds go back to the
defeat by Korchnoi of the Soviet Grand
Master and former world champion Boris
Spassky, in Belgrade, earlier this year.
On 27 Dec 1977, Korchnoi, himself a
Soviet Grand Master before his self-
exile, made the astonishing claim that
KGB agents were beaming microwaves "or
other mysterious rays" at him to disturb his concentration, thereby causing
him to lose 3 games in 10 days. He said
he realised what was going on when he
noticed Spassky leaving the stage after
each move - to get out of range, Korchnoi said. In the match he won, Korchnoi
said, Spassky made a mistake; significantly, while he was thinking on stage.
Even more mysterious statements were
made by British Grand Master Tony Miles
who saw the tournament, claiming that
Spassky was using hypnosis on Korchnoi,
who "felt his knees go numb" whenever
Spassky turned on the 'fluence. Petra
Leeuwerik, Korchnoi's secretary, added
that "Spassky himself may only have
been a medium - someone else in the audience could have been involved...But
Spassky looked as if he were drunk."
She confirmed that Spassky had studied
hypnosis since 1964 and had used it in
world championships before. Also quoted
was Dr Brian Fellows, of Portsmouth
Polytechnic. who reminded us that it was
well known that the Russians
          have had a long and serious
programme studying hypnosis at a distance, and even hypnosis by telepathy.
They all got together to beat Spassky's
or whoever's chess-whammy - and Korchnoi
went on to win the right to challenge
the Soviet wonderboy Karpov in what is
already shaping up to be an ideological
grudge match. Daily Mail 28 Dec 1977,
Guardian 13 Jan 1978, Sunday Times 26
Feb 1978 (Cr: Ion Will, Anon.)

US EMBASSY MOSCOW & MICROWAVES

The subject of mysterious beams also
arises in what is fast becoming one of
the great myths to come out of the Cold
War, the microwave bombardment of the
US Embassy in Moscow (I mean myth in the
fullest sense of the word, not its limited common usage implying a lie or 'not
true'). It transpires that the US State
Dept knew of the bombardment as far back
as the early 1960s, but it concealed the
problem, even from the embassy staff,
until 1975. The radiation level had been
fairly low (5microwatts/sq.cm - which
is about half the Soviet limit on exposure standards, and way below the US
standard of 10 milliwatts/sq.cm) - but
in 1975 the levels beamed at the embassy
briefly shot up to 18 microwatts. At
this time metal radiation screens were
put up at the windows, and the staff
alarmed at the danger and angry at the
dept's deception, demanded explanations.
The low-level bombardment continued
until the very mysterious fire - on 26
Aug 1977 - damaged the upper 'secure'
floors. In the weeks that followed intensity again increased, then dropped back
to a low level.

From 1975, when the danger became
known more openly rumours sprouted about
abnormal incidence of cancer and other
terrible afflictions among embassy staff
earned the Moscow office an "official
designation as an unhealthful post." (3)
In early June this year a Marine sergeant began a $1.75 million damages suit
against the US government on behalf of
his 5yr-old son, whom, he claims, was
born with severe defects caused by the
bombardment while he and his family were
posted to the embassy. (5) Conversely,
despite the appearances that 3 former
ambassadors died of cancer allegedly
contracted during their Moscow duty, ambassador Walter J Stoessel, the man who
ordered the metal radiation screens, has
publicly denied he had to move to the
West German embassy because the radiation aggravated his health. Is there any

health hazard? It's well known that exposure to microwaves can induce cataracts, ear and throat problems and even insomnia, (4) ...and it is known that the Soviet standards rest on the belief that continued low-level exposure can induce "behavioural changes, headaches, depressions, lowered sex drive and general non-specific debility." (8) Although there is no evidence at all yet of a cancer link, many experts acknowledge the added risk of blood disorders. Evidence that "1 in 29 adults" at the embassy had abnormally high counts of white blood cells (though without any apparent accompanying debility), came to light after the sudden radiation increases necessitated series of blood tests - but as these increases in lymphocytes continued after the screens were put up, others are not sure about blaming it on the radiation. The matter may be finally decided by a massive health study of all US personnel posted to the Moscow embassy over the last 25yrs - some 6000 persons - has been completed at Johns Hopkins School of Public Health, now in the final stages of statistical analysis (2, 3 & 7). Sources: 1) Times-Herald (Newport News, Va) 10 Nov 1976; 2) Daily Mail 5 Jan 1977; 3) Daily Press (Newport News, Va) 9 Nov 1977; 4) Houston Post (Tx) 27 March 1978; Observer 11 June 1978; 6) Sunday Times 9 July 1978; 7) Herald Tribune (NY) 14 July 1978; 8) Guardian 15 July 1978 (Cr: Ion Will, Gary Abbott, Kurt Lothmann, Paul Screeton.)

ELF POLLUTION

Something far more insidious than naughty gnomes or the Erisian Liberation front...there is a growing anti-microwave pollution lobby who see all kinds of physiological, psychological and even genetic hazards from low-frequency radiation. The main target in the USA are the high-tension power transmission cables whose numbers have increased dramatically, and largely until now unnoticed and unquestioned, in recent years. I refer the interested reader to a survey of the subject in Undercurrents 26 (Feb 1978) by Pat Coyne. Coyne says that British public apathy is matched only by the apparent unconcern of the Central Electricity Generating Board. Certainly this seemed the case when villagers from the Dorset village of Fishpond complained that ever since a special high-voltage power line was placed through the village, bees have become aggressive, in bad or misty weather birds mysteriously drop dead, TV sets blow up, and there is a persistent sizzling noise in their ears. Observer 15 Aug 1976). We'll give other reports some other time.

Before leaving the subject, I'd also like to refer to 2 articles in the Winter 1978 edition of Pursuit (see journal reviews for details). The first by John Ott, one of the top researchers on the topic, discusses the effects of ELF radiation from domestic fluorescent lighting on plants, animals and human eyes. Secondly Curt Sutherly and R Martin Wolf both suggest that modern life is filled with unseen but effective microwave radiations, from TVs, air-conditioning units and fridges, microwave ovens and fluorescent tubes etc...a problem even worse for those who live in mobile homes, aluminium boxes that reflect the ELF back and forth inside them. Can this fact play some part, they ask, in the significantly high proportion of UFO and Fortean events happening in or near mobile homes, or witnessed by those who live in such microwave traps?

WEATHER CONTROL, TESLA & RUSSIA

Andrew Michrowski, director of a group studying the application of Nikola Tesla's experiments to Canada's energy distribution problems, urged the Canadian Dept of Communications to analyse the mystery signals apparently beamed from Russia. Director of Operations, WW Scott, said that the signals had been severely curtailed before they could study them, but he could say that in the high-frequency range of 3-30 mHz, a signal came around the globe from the west about half an hour after a burst from the east; that they could have been harmonics of very low-frequency signals; and their brevity made the location of a low-frequency source very difficult. Dr Andrija Puharich, working with the Canadian group, said computation showed these signals were harmonics of the frequencies used by Tesla (6-60,000Hz), adding that one of the main components of the signals is in the 6-8Hz range and "happens to be the resonant frequency of the global sub-ionosphere, of radiowave travel-time through the earth" and very close to natural brain frequencies. The implications of long distance control of weather and human minds was not, I'm sure, fortuitous - especially in the light of the bombardment of the US embassy in Moscow. But the plot gets more frightening...

In Nov 1976, Associated Press, under the US freedom of information act, managed to see a partly-censored copy of a Defence Intelligence Agency report on Soviet microwave experiments. The report suggested that microwave bombardment might lead to disoriented behaviour, nerve disorders and heart attacks. The report also describes an effect called "microwave hearing" in which "sounds, even words, appearing to originate intracranially, can be induced by signal modulation at very low power densities." It warned that in a few years these effects might be controlled "to disrupt behaviour patterns of military or diplomatic personnel or as an interrogation tool." Speculations are offered that body chemistry, brain neurophysiology, and blood-brain chemistry could all be influenced from a distance." Alas poor Korchnoi...

That well known organ of urban paranoia, National Enquirer, saw good material in this to yell at the top of its journalistic and sensational voice that the Russians could now cause diseases, control minds and kill by microwaves from secret hiding places or at extreme long range. Their hysteria reached almost gothic proportions, painting a vivid picture of the strategic use of astral projection, teleportation, telepathy and clairvoyance, and the classical seance phenomenon of partly materialised hands. All these effects, they said, were described in another report from the DIA, declassified in May 1977.

Puharich speculated about the goal of weather control - much debated in recent years, along with earthquake induction, as a possible war weapon. Michrowski says his interest in all this dated from observations of astonishing luminous phenomena in the night sky over Ontario in March 1977 (We can't lay our hands on the files for this period at the moment) when, during a cold clear evening "the sky lit up with sheets of light traversing in a 360° pulsating pattern that lasted an hour." Michrowski is convinced this was no ordinary aurora but that it was a man-made phenomenon and part of Russia's continuing weather control experiments for agricultural and military purposes. Writing in the Guardian, Anthony Tucker calmly says the Russian harvests have not been all that good in recent years (because of drought etc) - and why over Ontario ? Ken Killich, a Canadian "science activist" whatever that is, says, with that beautifully simple reasoning that usually identifies a crank, it's all an error! They simply lost control and affected the whole world in a miscalculation that backfired on their own climate. Other papers went wild with this blaming the mysterious signals from Russia - we have many notes

on them in the file - for every freak of weather, plus the recent flue and even 'Legionnaire's Disease' (see our coverage of recent scourges, FT24pp17-20,33-37). This last accusation came just a few days before the CDC announced they had found the bacterium involved. Perhaps that too is part of a plot of lies! South China Morning Post 29 Nov 1976, & 5 Feb 1977, Corsicana Daily Sun (Tx) 8 Nov 1977, Guardian 19 Dec 1977, National Inquirer 15 Nov 1977 & 7 May 1978... also a 'Tommorow's World' documentary, BBC TV 15 Dec 1977, which alleged that a wave of mystery illnesses in the Canadian town of Timmins was attributed to the fact that the town lay directly on the path of an ELF signal beam traceable to the Soviet town of Kiev. (Cr: Ion Will, Gary Abbott, Tom Adams...and X's RBB nos 14-18 (1977).

LONG DELAYED SIGNAL?

Finally, a datum that would have had Fort's ears pricking up and a quick reaching for his tiny squares of paper on which he wrote his notes in code. It seems that the liner QE2, which took over the radio call sign of the old 'Queen Mary' - GBTT: Golf Bravo Tango Tango - suddenly received, out of the blue, the call sign from the old ship, followed by a routine position announcement, a call that must have been broadcast before the Queen Mary was pensioned off in 1967. Allan Holmes, First Radio Officer of the QE2, said: "It was uncanny...The radio procedure used was dropped years ago...it came from another age. I can't believe it was sent by a ghost...sometimes radio signals bounce off the moon and 'turn up' in Australia. This message could have bounced out into space more than 10 years ago and just zipped around until it found its way back to earth and we picked it up." Then if that's true, we are faced with the staggering coincidence that after 10 plus years the long delayed signal is picked up by a different ship using the original call code! Alas, no date for the incident is given, and if anyone can enlighten us, please do. Reveille 2 June 1978 (Cr: Dave Baldock.)   RJMR

WEBS

The following letter from Mrs Joan Davie, of Myrtle Cottage, Goodleigh, Devon, appeared in the North Devon Journal-Herald for 10 Nov 1977: "Something lovely seemed to have happened in the countryside the other morning. There had been a heavy dew which did not disappear. My friend and I took the dogs for a walk and on coming down the lane, looking into the sun, she said 'Look at that field, it is covered in cobwebs.' This large field was covered in a gossamer sheet - all over - and the other fields too. Gossamer hung from the trees and bushes, hedges and gates, and there were thousands of tiny black spiders in the air and falling on us. I would like to know if this was an aerial hatching-out in the sunshine plus what is called 'light airs' brought down by the condensation in the air which fell as the dew? There was no wind at the time. The whole thing was beautiful and wonderful to behold, especially when the dew hung on to the cobwebs in the early morning. I would very much like to hear an answer from some expert." (Cr: P Christie.)

So would we! Web falls were recorded by Fort, who noted that spiders are sometimes quite absent. In this case though we note the phenomenon of localisation - the women didn't notice the webs or spiders in the air until they were right by or in the field - aided no doubt by the absence of wind. And another thing - it's all very well to talk about aerial hatchings, but how did many thousands of the little buggers get up there in the first place?

Our second account took place just over a month before the above. On the morning of 11 Oct 1977, the residents of San Francisco's Bay area were astonished to see vast quantities of cloud-like lumps of white webs floating down from the sky. Some of the clumps were up to 20ft long, and made up of "super-er-thick" strings with "big white wads on it." Pilots at San Jose airport said they encountered it at 4,000ft - and one man in nearby Pleasant Hill, said his tennis ball got so covered in the stuff it went "Whoop!" when he hit it. Up to 100 miles away people were looking up to see wads coming down (I couldn't resist that) - webs were wrapped around lampposts, clinging to facades of buildings and trees, and covering cars. One entomologist, at UCBerkeley, ventured his explanation. It was called ballooning - baby spiders crawl to the tip of a leaf, twig or blade of grass and spin a length of web, and when the wind catches this, off they go into the blue yonder. The huge web-clouds, says Lennie Vincent, are made up of millions of smaller ones. One retired entomologist, Stanley Bailey, said that web-flying was not unusual in central California, but he was quite surprised to see it on this scale on the Pacific coast. But there are a couple of other questions we'd like to have raised: long-time residents of the area said they had never seen the phenomenon before, at all; neither the reports nor the witnesses make any mention of the spiders themselves, and surely many millions would have been involved, yet not one was reported seen on these Mary Celeste cloud-ships; where did they come from and why were they not seen until, in sizeable numbers, bulk and distribution, they were suddenly noticed coming down; where did the spiders go, and did anybody notice the population explosion which led to these numbers and if they existed and bred what happened to the even larger number of spiders this horde should have led to? The Atlanta Constitution, The Daily Oklahoman, Dallas Times-Herald all 12 Oct 1977 (Cr: Lou Farish, Tom Adams, John Gore.)

NUTS & BEANS

Bristol chess expert, Mr A Wilson Osborne and his wife, were returning from the church in Westbury Park, on Sunday 13 March 1977. They were heading

for their home to Northumbria Drive
from North View, and were outside the
White Tree garage, when a dark cloud
loomed over-head and it began to rain
nuts. Mr Wilson Osborne said: "At first
I thought it was a heavy hailstorm, but
no, they were hazlenuts. They were pep-
pering down on the road and bouncing
off the cars. They were coming from the
sky and coming from what I should estimate was a considerable height. I collected half a dozen or so to take home.
I tried one of the nuts later. (It) was
sweet, fresh and quite delicious." A
few minutes after they got home, a neighbour called. Mr WO continues: "Our
friend...said the most extraordinary
thing had happened to him - he too had
been showered with hazlenuts. It was a
very blustery day...I've heard of frogs
raining down from the sky - but I've
never heard of a storm of hazlenuts."
And neither have we, on reflection! Let
the dopes who seek refuge in the 'whirlwind' explanation for enigmatic falls
try to crack this nutty problem! From
Bristol Evening Post 14 March 1977 (Cr:
Ian Lawes.)
     Well we might not know of another
case of falling nuts, but there have
been falls of beans. In Phenomena (p15)
we quote from INFO Journal 8, the
story of the West African beans that
fell on a farm in NW Brazil - well
because Lou Farish sent us a copy of
the original clipping we are able to
be more specific. On possibly the 1st
of June 1971, according to the farmer,
Salvador Targino, the beans fell suddenly out of the sky. A State official,
who identified the beans as African,
speculated about a storm scooping them
up in Africa, carrying them for many
miles across the ocean, to dump them
in a small area in Brazil...but Targino says nothing about them falling
during a storm. He did boil some up,
however, and said they were too tough
to eat. Chicago Tribune 4 June 1971.
For bean-fall fans, we can add Raymond
Bayless gives an account, in Fate May
1964 (pp27-29) of two cases he personally investigated - one near Black-
stone, Virginia, on 2 Aug 1962; and
the other in San Fernando, California,
on 22 Jan 1964. This latter event is
mentioned by Ivan Sanderson in his
listing of falls (see Investigating the
Unexplained, Prentice-Hall, 1972) which
includes a fairly incomplete listing of
similar falls of wheat, barley, meal,
rice etc.

HAY & STRAW & A BIT MORE

Two old notes, untold, from July
1976...On the 22nd July 1976, for a few
minutes,it rained straw outside the Bar-
clay Arms, at Bosham, on the Hampshire
coast. Mrs Valerie Cresswell, a witness,
said: "It literally came down from a
cloud that was passing over. Luckily
one of the guests saw it as well because I thought I was going barmy. The
Met Office at Southampton could only
suggest "a sort of small-intensity tornado." It's true that some winds can
lift things, but most of our falls have
the characteristics,noticed by Fort,of
selectivity (ie nothing else came down
with the nuts, or the straw), and localisation. Note too that much testimony
stresses a cloud as being more noticeable than any "sort of" whirlwind. This
datum is from the Midhurst & Petworth
Observer, Hants, 30 July 1976 (Cr: John
Hitchens.)
     "Localised mini-whirlwinds" were also
blamed for hay-rains over Lincoln, coincidentally, on the same day as the
Bosham event (above), 22 July 1976. In
"late afternoon" straw from the sky
festooned buildings, roads and telegraph pole over a wide area of the city
stretching from the north to the south.
At Burton, Mrs Ruth Grace, of Beechwood,
said the straw was coming from the direction of Scampton and heading towards
Lincoln - we make that a heading of SSE,
following almost exactly the Burton-
Lincoln road beneath. In Lincoln, Peter
Twartz, of Lee Rd, said such quantities
came down it looked "as if somebody has
been going over in an aircraft and dropping bales of hay." A man in Yarborough
Crescent said: "The sky was full of
straw. People were walking around with
armfuls of it." As the phenomenon continued over the city, drifting southward,
a man in Hykham Road said there was so
much of it, it was blowing about "like
tumbleweed." At RAF Waddington, due
south of Lincoln, the sergeant's mess
was covered, and a spokesman said: "Our
traffic control had a report from a
light aircraft,west of Waddington, that
haystacks were being lifted to 3-4000ft,
but I imagine he meant large amounts of
straw." Despite an RAF met man's suggestion about "localised mini-whirl-
winds", it's clear this is pure supposition - and the light aircraft's
pilot, it seems, didn't actually see
haystacks being lifted, but supposed
this on encountering masses of hay at
his altitude. Scunthorpe Evening Telegraph 23 July 1976 (Cr: Nigel Watson.)

Five days later and about 20 miles due north of Lincoln, light showers of straw rained into the Thompson St area of Scunthorpe. At 1pm on 17 July 1976, a witness in Thompson St, and another in the Scunthorpe Borough Parks Dept depot in Station Rd, both saw "small amounts" of straw fall to the ground. This was discovered during a personal investigation by Nigel Watson that same day. Was it a separate fall or the tail end of the Lincoln shower? And if so how did it stay up there for 5 days?

Now we come to a datum that makes even a blasé Fortean sit up. At about 8.30pm on 8 Aug 1977, Poole, Dorset, experienced a shower of rain which stopped, then continued as hay. And that's not all - in with the hay were blades of grass, and clumps of grass with roots and soil still attatched. John Kay, holidaying at Rockley Sands caravan site with his family, insists: "I'm not crazy. It did happen. Grass fell on me! There had been a shower of rain...Then suddenly it began to rain grass. There was a large rain-cloud about 1000ft above us and it was coming from that." The London Weather Center, asked for a quote, said: "We don't understand." Daily Express 9 Aug 1977. Our day-log reveals to us that something strange was going on in West Country skies that and the following day: a strange high-pitched whirring sound filled the air over Bath, not many miles away, where it was heard again the next day, followed by flocks of frenzied birds wheeling over the city. We'll give full details the next time we run our 'Sounds' column.

SHELLS
We are very pleased to include the following account of what might have been a very localised fall of shells, experienced by our Coventry reader, David Tame:

"The year must have been around 1964-1965 - as I was then only a child. It must have occurred in the summer, because a brief heavy storm interrupted my outdoor play - but the ground was quite dry when I later went out again. It is certain that nobody else would have noticed the shells, for 3 reasons:

"1) They were only something like - taking my own smaller (relative) size into account - 0.15 inches in size on average...perhaps 0.2".

"2) It was only by virtue of the fact that we had a large white concreted area in our garden, causing them to show up, that I first noticed them. It was imp-

ossible to see any, even on close inspection, in the grass.

"3) A child lives close to the ground. Every pebble was a recognised and remembered obstacle for toy cars to avoid. Every blade of grass was known, with its history of cover for toy soldiers. There is no way an adult would now give the ground so close an inspection - and even if he did (see something) he'd think nothing of it. But I knew they had not been there before the storm. 'They' were half minute shells of some kind...the other half appearing to me to be an entirely different kind of biological formation, some kind of dead, dark, dry and hard aquatic creature. I mean that two kinds of things had fallen - unfortunately I can't remember details of their appearance. At first I thought that the storm must have knocked them all out of the grass, but on checking, I found them all up the garden path, out by the road, and in elevated positions such as on top of outdoor tables, lying perhaps an inch (?) apart. I did collect some, realizing this phenomenon to be something strange, and kept them carefully for a few years, but, yes, the inevitable story; much to my disgust one day I found they had been thrown out. Such was their small size that within a few days after the storm those on the ground were no longer to be found, I suppose, swept away by broom and weather."

IS THERE A CHEMIST IN THE HOUSE?
The small sample of mystery fibers that fell during a London storm, about 1964, have been examined under an electron microscope by Phil Ledger, and are not animal or vegetable matter. We need a chemical analysis - can anyone help? See FT25p13 for brief details of the fall - and write to me if you can help.

RJMR

Editorial Stuff/cont from p2...

OUT-OF-PRINT
We regret that once orders received have been met, we can no longer offer Hunt Emerson's FT poster. Backissues of FT are going out-of-print faster too! We printed 800 of FT24, and have none left - apologies to those who've missed out. We are increasing print-run to 1000, which includes stock & shop sales. We'll let you know if we reprint someday but until then you'll have to pay for a xerox-copy if you're desperate. Alas, copies of the second index (FT8-13, 1975) have also run out.

THE GREAT CAPER & ILLUMINATUS!

News comes that Ken Campbell's two great Fortean plays are on the move again.

The Great Caper - a synthesis of the major Fortean themes and theses - is touring England and will be at the following venues:

York Arts Center: 1-5 August.
Norwich Arts Center: 11 & 12 Aug.
ICA, The Mall, London: 15-26 Aug.
Everyman Theatre, Liverpool:
28 Aug - 3 Sept.
Bristol Arts Center: 6-8 Sept.
Humberside Theatre, Hull: 19-23 Sept.

Illuminatus! - the arse-numbing 9hr marathon compilation from the infamous trilogy by Shea & Wilson - will run for a season at the Empty Space Theatre in Seattle, Washington. It will be performed in 3 parts between 20 Sept and 31 Dec.

Those imposters masquerading as scientists, and who abuse every principle of scientific honesty under the banner of 'scientific inquiry' into such subjects as telepathy, astrology, psychokinesis, psychic surgery etc, and who have shown their true colours by their public avowal to stamp out such 'patent rubbish and superstition', fail to realise that their very negative attitudes predispose their efforts to apparent self-confirmation. They know these things are 'impossible'; therefore any results must be seen in terms of deceit, error or myth. No one is asking them to compromise their fanatically-held views, but in the name of science let us not be fooled by them! It is significant that things like the Committee for the Investigation of Claims for the Paranormal are happening now, at this stage of the obvious failure of scientific-materialism - it is equivalent to the age when blind faith in another world-view hatched the horrors of the Inquisition.

The 'investigators' of this stamp seem to imagine that gifted people are in some unspoken way obliged to perform before them, and when faced with obviously hostile people, irrational tests in strange and artificial conditions, and 'fact' that logic and analysis are the opposite of the intuitive and irrational paranormal effects (precisely the opposing functions of right and left brain hemispheres), it's no wonder that most testees fail. There is always the unspoken threat of being 'exposed' - or worse yet, 'explained-away' - in a scientific paper, rightly or wrongly, to bolster some cowboy's reputation for being 'rational', 'sceptical' and 'scientific'. I never blamed Geller one bit for refusing to jump through hoops for the New Scientist committee, and others. Like many witnesses to paranormal phenomena, too, these people are intimidated and then sickened at such displays of arrogance and bigotry. Many, like Doc, will say they couldn't care less about the disbelievers - they themselves Know!

So it is with particular pleasure that I learn that following last year's Parascience conference in London, that several sensitives and paranormal talents, including Matthew Manning (whom, we might add, has had nothing but praise from the scientists he's worked with), will form an informal 'union' to grade the quality of labs, scientists and their 'hospitality', and to take legal and 'industrial' action in cases of abuse. All power to them!

As we go to press, that mighty Indonesian volcano that shook the world in 1883, is rumbling again...and a dilly of a particle shower from a recent solar-flare is about to arrive soon (some poor Soviet astronauts up there had better be sure they packed their lead knickers!). If we can get it together in time, next issue should have a listing of all the weather and quake etc superlatives of the last 2 years.

We were intrigued by a story in the New Straits Times 6 June 1978, that a Californian evangelist, John Todd, has convinced members of the fundamentalist First Baptist Church, of Zionsville, near Indianapolis, that they must prepare themselves for a war against witches out to conquer the world. The members are stockpiling food and weapons and buying property at 'Christian retreats'. Todd, a 'born-again Christian' said he had been born and raised in witchcraft, but had been 'saved' 6 years ago, aged 22. Now he says he can reveal that he once participated in a high decision-making council of witches called the Illuminati. He said the Illuminati had been planning to create a major crisis in 1980 through disruptive strikes of food and transport systems. The base of the Illuminati in the US, he said, is the Council on Foreign Relations, and the financial backing comes from David Rockefeller and the Standard Oil Company. The farce be with us! (Cr: Jenny Cameron).

What then are we to make of the 261 page report published by the Pentagon, advising commanding officers and chaplains in the US armed forces on how to deal with the growing number of Satanists, witches and members of bizarre religious groups among the ranks? The advice to chaplins says the Satanists "believe in what the Christian church opposes" and that "it might be awkward to minister to them." When one dies, the report says, "the central grotto (Satanic HQ in San Fransisco) should be contacted." Among the other pagan and Black Magic cultists, is mention of the fast growing Native American Church, a cult founded by Indians which is allowed the legal use of peyote. Daily Telegraph 22 May '78.

Mark Hall sent us a clipping of a truly Fortean way to die! A 70yr-old Long Island woman, Eleanor Barry, was suffocated in her bedroom, on 18 Dec '77, when one of the many "towers" of books, old newspapers and press-clippings fell, knocking others, pinning her to the floor and muffling her cries. Minneapolis Star (Minn) 21 Dec 1977...

ƒortean ƒimes

diary of a mad planet... 6

75p:$1·50   5th anniversary!   FT27

UK ISSN 0308-5899

Fortean Times

A Contemporary Record
of Strange Phenomena

FORTEAN TIMES is a non profitmaking quarterly
miscellany of news, notes and references on current and
historical strange phenomena, related subjects and
philosophies. Formerly *The News*. Affiliated to the
International Fortean Organisation (INFO), and the
Society for the Investigation of the Unexplained (SITU),
and other Fortean journals in continuing the work of
Charles Fort (1874—1932). **SUBSCRIPTION** information
and details of other deals can be found on the back page.

Edited and published by Robert JM Rickard
Associate editor: Steve Moore
Contributing editors: David Fideler, Phil Ledger
Heading art by Hunt Emerson

**FORTEAN TIMES, c/o Dark They Were & Golden Eyed,
9—12 St Annes Court, London W1, England.**

Printed by Windhorse Press, at Sukhavati,
51 Roman Road, London E2.

FT27, autumn'78

FT and DAVID FIDELER

Thanks to the generosity of a member
of the '3-legged Toad Cabal', your editor, Steve Moore and Ion Will were
able to make a thoroughly enjoyable
trip to Washington DC, to this year's
FORTFEST. We had a great time, packed
with Fortean and synchronous incidents,
manic clipping of exotic papers, and
good conversation, meeting old friends
and making new ones. A high old time
was had by all in the FT hospitality
room. Our thanks go to all the FEST
organizers for their tireless efforts,
especially the perpetually worried Dick
Leshuck, and to Ray & Dottie Manners
for their generous transportations, and
to Al & Phyllis who put up with us for
a night after we missed a plane.

We were eager to meet Dave Fideler,
a young Fortean from Michigan, whose
energy and Fortean genius impressed us
all. Dave edits his own journal, the
excellent Anomaly Research Bulletin -
but the next issue will be his last
because he wishes to devote more time
to fieldwork, research and writing (I
know the feeling!) Seizing the opportunity we came to an agreement in which
FT will absorb the balance of his remaining subscribers, and Dave himself
joins us as FT's man in the New World.
We are honoured to be associated with
such a high-calibre Fortean and look
forward to many contributions from him.

US PRICE INCREASE

It was overdue, but the recent wob-
bly dollar makes our adjustment to the
US price more urgent. One way or another we have managed to keep our prices
stable for over 2yrs, at the same time
improving dramatically. Indeed some
US readers think we are underpriced
considering that much of our content
is unavailable anywhere else for any
price! Bearing in mind some plans for
our future expansion we have decided
that effective from next issue (ie the
first in 1979) our basic overseas rate
will be $8.00 per year, or $2.00 per
copy. This also absorbs the banking
surcharge on cashing foreign cheques,
so there will be no further need to add
10%. Airmail surcharge stays the same.
We are always looking for ways to improve our US mailings, so stay tuned!

MORE EDITORIAL STUFF

This last year has been an astonishing one for falling material, as regular
readers will know. This time we have
some accumulated ice-lumps and a small
assortment of weird substances.

ICE FALLS

Somme, France - at 10.30am on 11th
March, workers in fields at Becquerel,
near Abbeville, heard a loud explosion
followed by a whizzing sound, like an
artillery shell. Following the sound
they came to a fresh small crater containing a 25 kilo lump of transparent
ice with "greenish depths". The lump
stayed intact for about an hour, despite
the sun's heat - and eventually "experts"
arrived to take samples for tests. From
Liberation (Paris) 13 March 1978; Le Soir
(Belgium) 16 March 1978. Cr: Jean-Louis
Brodu, Henri Premont - trans: IAW & JB.

Cambrai, France - at about 4pm on
14th April, some kids training on a football field were startled by something
flashing through the air near them. It
fell from a clear sky in brilliant sunshine to embed itself in a nearby patch
of leeks. On investigation they found
a roughly spherical lump of ice, about
45cm diameter, weighing about 20 kilos,
that started to disintegrate almost
immediately. Cambrai is only about 60mls
from Abbeville, the site of the above
story almost a month previously. From
Nice Matin (France) 17 April 1978; and
Svenska Dagbladet (Sweden) 20 April 1978.
Cr: J-L Brodu, Ragnar Forshufvud (via
Malcolm Lowery of SIS).

Heverlee, Belgium - as far as I can
tell from the local lingo, a "Weer
ijsklomp" was from "hemel gevallen" on
or about 20th April, at Heverlee, near
Louvain, about 80mls NE of Cambrai (see
previous item). A fieldworker, Pierre
Hendriks, found two large lumps of ice
embedded 20cm into his topsoil. The largest lump weighing over 20 kilos, broke
into three (see photo). Belgian meteorological 'experts' offered the usual
explanations -- the only certainty is

that Northern France and Belgium were
bombarded with ice several times within
a short period! De Standaard (Belgium)
21 April 1978. Cr: Jos Verhulst.

Tennessee, USA - at about 3pm on 23rd
April - ie a few days after the Belgian
icefall above - a 51b block of green ice
fell from a clear sky near the small
community of Golddust, 60mls north of
Memphis, on the Mississippi. The police
said they were notified by someone who
had seen it fall, but they declined to
name the witness. A week can do wonders
for our data - especially when they are
mere 51b weaklings on a crash course,
for soon it was, in the eyes of some
papers, an impressive 251b hulk! The
local sheriff's dispatcher, Debbie Crowell, cooed: "It has a nice little odor

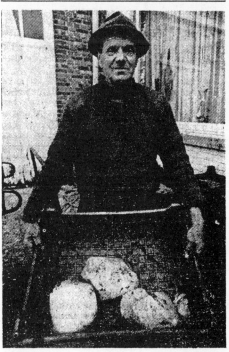

to it." But some people cannot see past a colour, and soon 'experts' are calling our hero nasty names.

Fred Farrar, a Memphis FAA spokesman, blamed the incident on leakage of toilet fluids in flight, indeed Mr Farrar seems to be fascinated by leaky toilets, referring to 14 such incidents in 1974 alone. He tells of one case, on 30 April 1974, when an engine dropped off a National Airlines 727 60mls east of El Paso. Later investigations showed that a valve used to empty a forward toilet had trickled fluid along the fusilage and into the air intake of the right rear engine. The ice built up and jammed the turbine, wrenching the engine from its mountings. "The human feces had hit the fan," sniggered Mr Farrar. Miss Crowell, and many others, remain unconvinced these tales of aerodynamic scatology account for this and other cases. Laramie Daily Boomerang (Wyoming), San Antonio Light (Texas), Indianapolis News (Indiana) 25 April 1978 (Cr: JL Mabie, TR Adams, DW Prater.) Washington Post 26 April 1978 (Cr: Paul Willis). Norwalk Hour (Conn) 28 April 1978 (Cr: JJ Patchen.) Herald Tribune 29 April 1978 (Cr: IAW).

Colorado, USA - on the morning of 3rd May, two ice chunks fell from the sky crashing through the roofs of two houses in the town of Arvada. Together the lumps weighed about 100lbs. Nothing more is known. Sherman Democrat (Tx) 5 May 1978 (Thomas R Adams.)

Henley-on-Klip, South Africa - sometime over the weekend 22-23 July a large chunk of ice plummeted into a garden in Shilingford Road. It was about 10cm thick and "as long as an arm", and certainly not a hailstone (according to CSIR scientists). More appeal to leaky toilets - must be a new fashion! Once again little more is known. Rand Daily Mail (South Africa) 28 July 1978 (Cr: CJ Holtzhausen)

Colorado, USA - on the afternoon of 23 July, a chunk of blue ice crashed through the roof of an apartment in the Windsor Gardens district of Denver, knocking over furniture before shattering on the floor a mere 10ft from the startled occupant. It measured about 1ft in diameter and weighed about 30lbs. Aviation officials said they had narrowed a culprit-list down to 3 planes, and expected to have found the guilty one within a week -- they think. We heard no more. Denver Post (CO) 25 July 1978 (Cr: Thomas Adams). Note this incident's rough temporal proximity to the Henley item above. (Cr. also: Loren Coleman.)

Meyterton, South Africa - a "few weeks" after the Henley-on-Klip incident above, a second ice-bomb fell in the nearby town of Meyterton, sometime towards the end of the third week in August - Mrs Hester Swart thought her geyser had exploded when the block hit the corrugated iron roof of her kitchen. Outside, she found shattered ice around most of the house and the remains of a 20cm thick piece which had dented the roof. For once an airline spokesman pooh-poohs the airplane theory - despite the fact that both incidents are below an air corridor to Jan Smuts airport - saying the air here is too warm for ice to form. He suggested instead that moist air trapped in a circulating current would form a block in layers until the updraught could no longer support its weight - and indeed, Mrs Allsworth, the Henley housewife who found her ice-bomb had broken some branches of a tree near her house, said that layers in the ice fragments could be seen through a magnifying glass.

But wait a minute! If the air is too warm to form ice on planes at high altitudes, how can they from in thermal updraughts in the same area? Pretoria News (South Africa) 25 August 1978 (Cr: Chris J Holtzhausen).

Illinois, USA - on the morning of 29 August, a school inspector and some others were nearly brained when they stepped onto the football field of the Stephen High School, Decatur - a chunk of ice "probably as large as a man's head or bigger" came down a narrow 30-40ft away. For once we have a datum in which a plane was noticed passing over - but it may not mean anything... Decatur Herald Review (Ill) 30 August 1978 (Cr: Loren Coleman.)

STRANGE WHITE DUST

A thin layer of an unknown white dust covering houses, cars, roads and yards startled the residents of Port Arthur, Beaumont, Texas, when they emerged from their houses on the morning of 16 May. In earlier days we could have heard exclamations of "Sahara sand" or "volcanic dust", but the fashion in explanations shifts with the times - in a pollution conscious world pollution is the immediate thought, looked for and found. The giant Gulf Oil cracking plant at Port Arthur said the stuff sounded like the white synthetic clay compound they use in their processing and which might have escaped through a faulty vent (at a cost of up to $200,000 to Gulf.) That sounded good enough for the investigating officer of the Texas Air Control Board, and Lo! it was pronounced synthetic white clay compound! Dallas Times Herald (Tx) 17 May 1978 (Cr: Thomas R Adams.)

BLOBS OF MOLTEN METAL

Shortly after midnight on the morning of 10 July, firemen were called to douse a small blaze at Third St and High School Avenue, Council Bluffs, Nebraska - and at the center of the fire they found a mass of splattered metal about 3ft in diameter and 3" thick at the center. It lay in a shallow impact crater. But this was not the first time such a strange incident had happened in Council Bluffs. On 5th July a similar splattered blob hit McGee Ave and Harrison St, and that too was so hot it could not be touched for 30 minutes -- and a third blob fell near Big Lake Park on 17 December 1977. In this latter case we are told that 'officials' branded it a hoax despite several reports of "a bright trail" in the sky that night. Adding to the puzzle, a USAF test of the December blob indicated that "it was neither meteor nor part of a space satellite". Results of any tests on the latest two incidents are not yet known, if indeed any at all were done in view of the 'official' opinion the events were hoaxed! Omaha World Herald (Neb) 11 July 1978 (Cr: Joe Swatek, Mark Hall.)

SLIME ATTACKS WASHINGTON

"It looked like a bad frost," said Jane Gillespie of the mysterious green slime that spotted her otherwise neat garden, in the Foggy Bottom area of Washington DC, causing her plants to wilt and blacken. The spots of goo seem to have fallen over 5 and 6 Sept and from high in the air, because the roof of a 12 storey building under construction was coated with the muck. Other residents reported their cats and dogs becoming nauseated "presumably after eating grass exposed to the substance" it was suggested, but initial tests by the Bureau of Occupational and Institutional Hygiene failed to identify the substance beyond: "It's green, soluble in water and alcohol...was very fluid when it came down...and turned more black as it thickened." Another resident, Mike Love, said his terrier's normally off-white hair turned to"blue or black"; for the period of several days it stopped eating.

Later news items said that tests eliminated the possibility of the slime being jet fuel or pesticide. A spokesman for the DC Dept of Environment said its principal components were nickel sulphate iron sulphate and manganese. It was "very highly acidic" and a "product of combustion" but "definitely did not come from an airplane." Its origin, however, remains a mystery. Washington Post 11 & 16 Sept 1978 (Cr: Al & Phyllis); Boston Globe, Arab News & Saudi Gazette (both Saudi Arabia) all 17 Sept 1978 (Cr: Loren Coleman, Ion Will); San Antonio Express (TX) 17 Sept 1978 (Cr: Thomas Adams.)

We don't know whether any significance can be attatched to the manifestation of slime so near the State Department, but we do note, at the limits of our chemical ignorance, a curious run of 'pollution accidents' or whatever, some of which also involved compounds of sulphur, in the wake of the slime-rain - we may as well give them here:

6 Sept - same day as as DC slimefall, the streets of New York were being sprayed with disinfectant during their Legionnaire's Disease crisis.

10 Sept - 17 cows dead at Rawmarsh, Yorkshire, as "lethel levels of fluorine" found on grass, origin a mystery.

13 Sept - 60 gallons of sulphuric acid spill on road near Canterbury,Kent.

14 Sept - 11 men hospitalized after a hydrochloric acid tank leaks, at Ashford, also in Kent.

18 Sept - 22 hospitalised as mystery 'chlorine' fumes sweep through building in Mayfair, London.

19 Sept - 3 die and 70 hospitalized as hydrogen sulphide gas fills a tannery in Genoa, Italy.

26 Sept - a drum of chlorine falls off lorry in Vancouver, Canada, creating gas cloud 3 miles long; 33 overcome, 100s evacuated.

And finally, prior to the DC slimefall over the first 2 weeks of August, a smelly green goo was bubbling up from holes in the inch-thick asphalt of a carpark in the Troy area of Detroit, Michigan. It throbs and slithers out in spurts leaving a slimy trail which dries to white powder as it flows down an incline. "Area chemists" say it could be hydrogen sulphide produced in the bed rock. Sources for this story: Washington Post 16 August 1978 (Cr: Al & Phyllis, John Michell); Lincoln Star (Neb) 19 Aug 1978 (Cr: Joe Swatek). Sources for the other incidents are on record here.
RJMR

diary of a mad planet '77

In FT18 we tried a summary of all
the major catastrophic events of 1976,
with some correlations to other synchronous events. That 'Diary of a Mad
Planet' was well received - and has
even spawned the notion of some kind of
chronology project, but more of that
anon. Such a project would be ideal for
our computer, of course - but that's
still in the future. Right now we have
no substitute for sitting down to a
monstrous heap of clipping and simply
working through extracting their essence, aided by our trusty but erratic
day-log.

Part of the impetus for this project
comes from our roving clipster Ion Will,
who has a keen eye for the superlative
event or comment, and each year seems
to bring more record-breaking phenomena - the "worst", "longest", "heaviest"
"coldest", "wettest", "hottest" etc.
The main purpose this time is to list
the main geophysical and meteorological
mayhem of 1977: 1978 in a few issues'
time.(Who knows, this may become a regular feature!) Regretfully many other
kinds of superlatives had to be left
out - the "worst" swarmings of insects,
the "worst" accidents, astronomical

events, appearances of monsters, out-of-
place animals and other parazoological
omens, and the mysterious aerial noises,
these will all be dealt with in coming
issues under their respective headings,
because we simply don't have the time
to put in on the basic correlation. The
end result - a mammoth listing that
could possibly fill an issue itself -
would be fairly boring in itself, and
we are considering Dave Fideler's idea
of publishing the whole correlation for
1977 as a special publication.

But for now, we give you the quakes
and storms of 1977. The events are very
briefly summarized on the day of event.
For explanation of the codes see after
the main listing. Most of the uncredited
sources were either clipped by FT'staff',
or sent in by a number of our regular
clipsters, among whom Ion Will, Mrs Valerie Martin, Gary Abbott, Thomas R Adams,
Paul Screeton and Nigel Watson contributed most to this section. To them and
to all of you who send in clippings, I
once again offer thanks on behalf of all
of us - not only are clippings the lifeblood of FT, they are important for the
record, and,as time goes by, invaluable.

2 - Indonesia: 2 mild Qs (1/4).
- Argentina: landslide kills 18 (2/3)
3 - Greece: mild Q (1/4).
4 - Argentina: strong Q (1/5).
- Missouri: Q, 3.6R (1/6).
6 - New Guinea: Q 6.9R (1/7,8).
8 - California: series of minor Qs up
to 4.6R (3/9; 4/9).
9 - N Pacific: new island from undersea
V activity S of Tokyo (1/10,11).
10 - Zaire: Nyarangongo V erupts (1/13).
11 - USA: major snowstorm sweeps US from
Canada, 20D (5/12).
12 - Italy, Switzerland, Austria: avalanches (1/13; 6/12).
14 - Spain: blizzards & severe cold
(7/15).
17 - New York: "coldest day in NYC's
recorded history," WCF-30F (5/18).
19 - Florida: snow "first in living memory (8/19; 9/20).
- Alaska: heatwave, T 20° above seasonal norm (9/20).
20 - Bahamas: snowfall "first in recorded history"; raging seas (10/20).
25 - USA: WHs bring cold to Deep South
(9/26).
- S England: WGs 60-91mph (9/26;11/26)
28 - USA: WSs "frigid blasts" drop Ts
from C Texas to Florida; N Illinois -80C; Minnesota -100C (2/30).
31 - Guadeloupe La Soufriere V erupts
with tremors (1/1 Feb).
Gen: USA: heavy snows make NY, Penn, NJ,
Ohio "disaster areas"; WCF-60F;
Buffalo, NY, has 155" snow "this
winter", average is 44" (9/31 Mar).
Mass unemployment as factories,
offices, schools close for lack of
heating. Ohio & Mississippi freeze
over. "Worst stretch of winter since
1872." As cold air blasts SE, Florida suffers "worst crop losses in
history." Massachusetts has "worst
winter fishing in 45yrs." (12/31).
"State of emergency" also declared
in Minn, Ind, Tennessee & Florida.
(12/7 Feb).
Gen: Japan: "Heaviest snows in north in
14yrs"; 31D; parts have "coldest
winter in 32yrs (9/4 Feb).
Gen: Italy: "worst winter for 10+ yrs"
(6/12).
Gen: Australia: "highest Ts in 13yrs"
up to 107F in NSW & Vic (13/31).

FEBRUARY 1977

3 - New York & Gt Lakes area: more severe blizzards; looters in Buffalo;
wolves in Minnesota (15/6; 14/1;
13/4; 9/4).
- W USA: severe drought; lack of snow

in Rockies & Sierra Nevada; California "abnormally low rainfall in
last 18 mths" (9/4; 12/31 Jan).
4 - N Japan: "unprecedented blizzard"
(9/5).
- French, Italian, Swiss Alps: snow
closes 13 passes (9/5).
5 - New York: Buffalo area declared
"major disaster area" (16/6).
10 - Alaska: "100 tremors a day", up to
3.7R, cont until 24th Feb (17/26).
11 - Madagascar: Cyclone Emilie, 30+D
1000s H (9/12,14).
13 - Yugoslavia: Q at Skopje (18/14).
19 - S Mozambique: "worst floods on record"; 25D, 10,000H (7/20).
- Aleutian Islands: Q 6.8R (1/21).
21 - Turkey: 4 "sharp" tremors (1/23).
25 - S England: rains, widespread flooding (9/26; 14/26).
Gen: USA: "Coldest winter since founding
of Republic 200yrs ago" says Nat.
Weather Service (9/17).
Gen: GB: "Britain's wettest winter for
100yrs" (29/9).

MARCH 1977

1 - Mindanao Islands: moderate Q (19/3)
4 - Romania: Q 7.5R hits Bucharest area,
felt all over Europe, est 2000D
(2/6; 13/5; 16/6). "Worst in Romania's history" (20/7).
5 - Kamchatka: "powerful" WT 110mph
(16/6).
6 - Aleutian Islands: V erupts (2/7).
7 - Yugoslavia: Q 4.5R (21/9).
Gen: California: 1-7 March raging
storms on coast, 37D (22/7).
8 - W Germany: Q 4R (23/8).
- Australia: "worst floods on record"
on NSW/Queensland border from WC
Otto, "disaster area" (9/9).
9 - Korea: Q 6.6R; felt locally, Indonesia (24/12), Malaysia (21/10),
Japan (21/10), Thailand (23/11).
14 - USA: "killer blizzard" hits Colo,
Kansas, Neb, Wyo & S Dakota; rain
& snow cause flashfloods in NY &
New England; 18D (2/15).
16 - California: "freak tornado funnel"
hits Orange Co (25/17,18).
18 - Philippines: Q6.8R hits Luzon (2/19)
21 - S Iran: Q7R (11/22).
22 - Colombia: Q (11/23).
25 - Lunar eclipse.
- Turkey: Q (26/).
- N & C China: "serious drought";
peasants urged to "fight the weather god"; no rain in 6mths (9/22,26)
30 - France: Ts plunge to -4F (9/31).

APRIL 1977

1 - <u>Bangladesh</u>: WT 100mph, 100sD
1000sH (9/5; 15/3).
2 - <u>Samoa</u>: Q7.5R (26/; 2/4).
3 - <u>India</u>: mild Q (27/4).
- <u>Japan</u>: 3 Qs of 7.7R (28/4).
5 - <u>Kenya</u>: mild Q (9/7).
6 - <u>Iran</u>: Q5.9R (26/).
8 - <u>GB</u>:   heavy snow & hail while the
south has warm sun (14/9).
- <u>Florida</u>: "driest spring on record"
(2/9).
- <u>Reunion Island</u>: V erupts "1st time
in 177yrs; 800 evac'd (9/14; 15/10)
11 - <u>Java</u>: Q5.8R (27/12).
12 - <u>N Haiti</u>: drought & famine kill 28
(9/13).
13 - <u>France</u>: grapes hit by "worst frosts
in 50yrs" (9/14).
16 - <u>Sicily</u>: series mild Qs (20/17).
- <u>W Kenya</u>: torrential rain, floods;
10D 3000H (29/17). Long drought ends.
18 - Annular eclipse of moon.
20 - <u>Soloman Islands</u>: Q series, main
one 6.8R (26/).
21 - <u>Soloman Islands</u>: Q8.1R (26/).
24 - <u>Bangladesh</u>: WC kills 13 (9/25).
- <u>New Zealand</u>: Q5.25R (10/25).

MAY 1977

5 - <u>Philippines</u>: Mayon V erupts (9/6).
7 - <u>Missouri</u>: 3 days of tornadoes &
floods make "disaster area" (2/8).
9 - <u>New England</u>: "freak snowstorm" &
WG 70mph create havoc in NY, NJ,
Mass, Conn & Vermont (9/10).
- <u>California</u>: heavy rain ends long
drought (9/10).
12 - <u>Burma</u>: Q5.7R (26/).
- <u>China</u>: Q6.6R near Peking; claimed
to be one of a cont. series of
aftershocks from the Tangshan Q
10 mths previously!!!(9/13,14).
13 - <u>Philippines</u>: Mayon V erupting,
8000 evacuated (5/15; 7/14).
- <u>Bangladesh</u>: WC 100mph + waves +
mild Qs (5/14).
- <u>Kenya</u>: "heaviest rains in 25 yrs",
100D 21000H; 40" rain in 5 wks
(average is 36"/yr)(5/14; 25/14).
16 - <u>Australia</u>: Q4.5R at Perth (27/17).
21 - <u>Philippines</u>: mild Q (30/22).
26 - <u>Turkey/Iran</u>: Q5.4R (26/).

JUNE 1977

1 - <u>Yugoslavia</u>: mild Q (27/3).
- <u>Cyprus</u>, <u>S Turkey</u>: Q6.5R (9/2; 27/3).
- <u>New Zealand</u>: White Island V erupts
(9/2).
- <u>Hongkong</u>: water rationing after
"worst drought in 128 yrs" (31/29).

2 - <u>Iceland</u>: Katla V shakes (9/3).
- <u>C Italy</u>: mild Q (9/3).
3 - <u>India/Burma</u>: severe floods,20000 D
(10/4).
4 - <u>Japan</u>: Totemic pandas in Tokyo Zoo
(gifts from China) perform rare
mating; at same time mild Q shakes
Tokyo (21/5).
5 - <u>Iran</u>: "powerful" Q in Kerman area
(9/6).
18 - <u>Oman</u>: WH kills 50 on Masirah Island
20,000H (15/19; 29/19).
19 - <u>S Carolina</u>: Q3R (32/20).
22 - <u>Tonga</u>: Q7.2R (6/22).
26 - <u>Greece</u>, <u>Turkey</u>: "highest Ts ever
recorded here" (152F) during "worst
heatwave in 50 yrs" (2/1 July).

JULY 1977

2 - <u>Pakistan</u>: "heaviest monsoon in 41
yrs", 220D 20,000H (33/2; 7/3).
5 - <u>Yugoslavia</u>: 2 mild Qs (34/7).
6 - <u>Abu Dhabi</u>: heatwave, 114F,11D (7/7)
10 - <u>Korea</u>: Seoul area "worst floods &
landslides in 5yrs", 200D (18/11).
- <u>SW France</u>: flooding "worst in 80
yrs", 30D (9/12; 7/10).
- <u>Pakistan</u>: more rain & floods, 12D
(35/17).
13 - <u>USA</u>: heatwave begins in earnest.
14 - <u>England</u>: Q at Stoke-on-Trent "worst
in 2 yrs" (13/15).
16 - <u>SwissAlps</u>: avalanche kills 7 (9/18).
17 - <u>Sicily</u>: Mt Etna erupts (36/18).
18 - <u>New York</u>: 100F "hottest in 11 yrs"
(2/20).
19 - <u>New York</u>: 102F "T highest in 47yrs"
7th consecutive day of Ts over
90F (2/20).
- <u>N Carolina</u>: "heatstorm", 15th consecutive day of Ts over 90F; no
rain for 2 mths; "1000s of fish die
of oxygen starvation" (2/20).
Gen: <u>USA</u>: heatwave in 48 States; 112F
in Arizona, 119F in Calif. (29/24).
20 - <u>Japan</u>: Mt Aso V erupts (2/20).
- <u>Pennsylvania</u>: 8" rain in 8hrs causes
12ft flashflood in Johnstown; apx
50D 1000sH (10/21; 13/22; 20/22).
Source (2/24,26) says 10" rain in
7hrs, like a "blob of precipitation".
21 - <u>New York</u>: 104F "highest T in NYC's
records" (29/24).
- <u>Vietnam</u>: WT Sara 82mph, heavy floods, havoc (34/31).
- <u>New Zealand</u>: Q7.2R (38/22).
- <u>Philippines</u>: Q6.6R (34/22; 27/23).
24 - <u>S Italy</u>: mild Q (9/25).
- <u>Japan</u>: heatwave; 95f; Japs flock
to beaches to engage in new sport,
63 drowned, 80 missing, total this
year of dead or missing on beaches
1600 (1635 in 1976!)(9/25).

25 - S Taiwan: WT Thelma kills 90, much
flooding, damage (37/26).
- California: drought; water rations
in 100 towns (2/24,26).
29 - Solomon Isles: Q7.3R (9/30).
30 - Alps: heatwave causing avalanches
8D (9/31).
31 - Canada: WS hits SW Ontario (27/2 Aug)
- N Taiwan: WT Vera 120mph (9/1 Aug).
- Japan: Mt Sakurajima V erupts
(39/1 Aug).

AUGUST 1977

1 - Antarctic: T on Australian Mawson
Base soar to 1.4C, first time in
24yrs above freezing point (20/13;
(27/12).
- Burma: drought during the 'rain
season', crops ruined (27/1).
- Indonesia: "major" Q, 105D.
- Korea: "worst heatwave in many yrs",
"millions" take to rivers & sea &
like the Japs some don't come back,
59 drowned (33/2).
2 - Antarctic: T at Mawson Base goes
up to an astonishing 6.7C (seasonal norm is -30C!)(20/13; 27/12).
6 - Sicily: Mt Etna erupts for 2nd
day (29/7).
- Japan: Mt Showa Shinzan V quakes
698 today (33/8).
8 - Japan: Mt Usu V erupts 3 times,
quaked 1056 times before eruption
covers 3600 acres with ash. Plane
flying overhead hit by rocks!
(34/8,10; 27/8,9; 40/9).
9 - India: Delhi area, floods kill 150,
200,000H (9/10).
- S Brazil: floods destroy animals
& crops, 6000H (9/10).
14 - Sicily: Mt Etna erupts (9/15).
16 - Nevada, N California: after the
drought, WH Doreen brings floods &
landslides, not on the fields but,
uh, out in the desert, "heaviest
where it was least wanted" (41/17).
17 - London area: "worst deluge for yrs"
floods & havoc (9/18; 20/18; 38/18).
19 - Indonesia: major Q beneath sea in
region of Sumba, Sumbawa & Bali;
8.3R (according to Swedish observatory) 8.9R (Vienna observatory);
"one of the greatest the world has
ever known" (13/20); huge waves
did most destruction; 116D (20/20;
38/20; 9/20; 42/20;34/20; 7/21).
- Philippines: WS floods 8000H (15/21)
- Japan: WS floods 2500H (15/21).
- South Africa: WS floods (15/21).
20 - Australia: Q7.5R Perth (43/26).
- Hongkong: Q7.7R (34/21).
21 - Australia: light Q at Adelaide
(9/22; 33/22).
- Japan:weak Q Tokyo (33/22).

- Illinois: WC kills 6 at Lake Mat-
oon (10/22).
22 - Sicily: Q4-5R (44/22; 23/23).
- Gambia: drought (21/24).
23 - Czechoslovakia: heavy rain, floods
(9/25).
25 - C Italy: 3 mild Qs (9/26).
26 - Indonesia: Q6.4R (21/27).
27 - Indonesia: Q7.1R (45/28).
- N Tanzania: drought (15/28).
- SE England: heavy rain, floods
(7/28; 46/1 Sept).
28 - Sardinia: Q5.2R "first Q ever
known here", "extraordinary and
exceptional" (21/30).
29 - Philippines: Q6R Luzon (23/31).
- Indonesia: Q at E Timor (47/30).
- C China: Q6.3R (23/30). Curiously
China denies the Q was in China &
places it at Luzon (9/31).
- S Spain: snowfall on Sierra Nevada
"1st time in 100yrs" (47/30).
31 - NW Colombia: Q4R (6/31; 45/1 Sept).

SEPTEMBER 1977

2 - Texas/Mexico: WH Anita 155mph (41/3)
3 - South Africa: Q (15/4).
4 - New Hebrides: Q6.5R (45/5).
- Aleutian Isles: swarm of Qs of 6+R,
"so many we didn't count them" said
the Tsunami Warning Center at Palmer, Alaska (21/6) So much for the
rigour of science!
9 - Indonesia: Q5.4R (48/12).
- Iceland: Myvatn V erupts (9/10).
10 - Japan: WT batters Okinoerabu Isle,
2000H (44/10).
13 - Chile: Q (9/14).
- Japan: 6 minor Qs (49/14).
- Hawaii: Kilauea V erupts "1st time
in 18 yrs" (50/15; 41/1 Oct).
14 - Missouri: heavy storm floods Kansas
City, "20ft wall of water", rain
15" in 36hrs; 23D 3000H considerable damage (10/14; 41/15,16; 38/15)
19 - N Philippines: WT Dinah rages for
4th day; 45D (9/20).
20 - Ibiza: 10" rain brings 15ft floods,
2D 1000s stranded (10/20; 38/21).
21 - Japan: Mt Usu V erupts (51/22).
23 - Albania: Q5.1R (9/24).
24 - Hongkong: "severe" WC (7/25).
28 - Hawaii: Kilauea V, 2nd day of
eruptions (41/30).
30 - Hawaii: Kilauea V, flow of lava
900ft wide, 8 miles long (41/10oct).

OCTOBER 1977

7 - Indonesia: Q6.5R on Sumbawa (26/).
8 - Soviet Azerbaijan: Lok-Batan V
erupts, rock, mud & flames (1/9).
- Lincolnshire: freak WC causes
havoc in Grantham (9/10).

9 - N Italy: violent WS rages for 4dys, floods, landslides isolate villages destroy crops & cattle, 13D (9/10).
10 - NE Italy: floods devastate Po valley (9/11).
   - Tonga: Q7.2R & tsunami (9/11; 5/11).
12 - Solar eclipse.
17 - Norfolk Isles: Q6.9R (26/).
   - Pennsylvania: 2 separate blizzards bring chaos, 12" snow (22/17).
23 - Mozambique: "one of worst ever hail-hailstorms" pelted Maputo for ½hr, some hail up to 1lb, 100s hurt (7/23; 9/24; 38/24).
24 - Sicily & S Italy: 4 Qs (9/25).
25 - S India: 7 days of monsoon rains kill 60 1000sH (9/26).
30 - Albania: Q (9/31).
   - Indonesia: Q5.5R (52/2 Nov).
   - Soviet Turkmenia: "exceptionally heavy snow" "worst in 50yrs"(1/1nov).
31 - S England: violent WS (10/31).

NOVEMBER 1977

2 - Greece: "torrential rains" flood Athens, 25+D (11/3).
4 - Aleutian Isles: Q6.6R (26/).
6 - Bulgaria: mild Q (9/7).
   - SW Virginia: severe floods (41/7,10)
9 - Iran: Q4.6R (26/).
   - N Midwest USA: "early" blizzard & WG 80mph cause havoc (41/10).
10 - London: "warmest Nov day since 1946" (9/11).
   - Australia: Sydney WG 80mph (9/11).
11 - Mexico: severe cold 7D (9/12).
   - S England: 36hrs of gales,floods, storms, rain, cold & snow (29/13; 9/12,14; 13/12; 10/12).
12 - England: WG continues 5D 9 missing 90mph (15/13).
   - India:"worst typhoon & tidal wave in more than a century", 12ft high it obliterated 8 villages in 30mins; Tamil Nadu state, 10,000D, 3000 missing, 200,000H (29/20; 9/22).
   - China: "thickest fog ever recorded" in Peking (15/13).
15 - Philippines: WT Kim 30,000H (9/16).
18 - E Tibet & SW China: Q6.7R (9/19; 26)
19 - S India: 100mph WC, 15" rain in 8hrs in Andra Pradesh state, "dozens of villages destroyed", est 20,000D & 2 million H (29/20; 9/22; 15/27).
20 - Nth England: hailstorm leaves 2" heaps on roads (9/21).
   - Somerset: hailstorm (9/21).
   - S Somalia: heavy flooding (9/22).
22 - Chile: Q7R (53/23).
23 - Argentina: Q7.4R (26/).
24 - Chile, Argentina, Uruguay, Brazil: Q7+R, 50D (9/25).
26 - China: Q near Peking (52/28).

   - C Italy: heavy snow, chaos (7/27).
27 - Philippines: mild Q (52/28).
28 - Argentina: major Q, 70D; "150 mild Qs since 24th Nov" (52/30).

DECEMBER 1977

1 - Sweden; "worst landslide in 50yrs" 6D (52/3).
2 - Iran: Q5.5R (52/3).
3 - Kamchatka: "strong" Qs (54/4).
5 - Argentina: Q (52/7).
8 - London area: flashfloods after heavy rain (10/8).
9 - Turkey: Q5.4R (42/10).
10 - Iran: Q5R (26).
13 - Texas: WC kills 1, many hurt, near Houston (9/14).
   - Mid Atlantic: Q6.5R (26).
   - N Pacific: Q6.6R (1/14; 55/14).
17 - N Greece: villages cut off by heavy rain & snow (9/19).
19 - Iran: Q5.8R in Kerman area, 800D 1000sH; during "bitter cold night" (26; 9/21; 20/21; 5/21). Q happened near midnight & most papers dated the event as 20 December.
21 - Japan Q6.9R near Bonin Isles (26).
24 - Britain: WG & floods; "worst in yrs" on Cornish coast (9/28;5/4 Jan).
27 - China: announces poor harvest after "one of the worst years for natural disasters since Revolution in 1949" (5/28)
28 - Red Sea: Q6.6R (26).
29 - Philippines: Q (5/30).
   - Yugoslavia: mild Q (39/30).
30 - Italy: strong Q (9/31).

--- o 0 o ---

Letter Code: C-centigrade; D-dead; E-east; F-farenheit; H-homeless; N-north; Q-quakes & tremors; R-Richter; S-south; T-temperature; V-volcano or volcanic activity; W-west; WC-cyclones or tornadoes; WCF-wind chill factor; WG-gales or strong winds; WH-hurricanes; WS-windstorm; WT-typhoon.

SOURCES -- the first number in the codes above (in brackets) gives the source; the second number gives the day of the month under which the citation is listed (unless otherwise indicated).
 1) South China Morning Post (Cr: IAW).
 2) Times-Union Jacksonville, Florida; (Cr: Gary L Abbott).
 3) Sunday People London.
 4) Blade Toledo, Ohio (Cr: Tom Adams).
 5) Guardian London.
 6) Reuters (Cr: K Rogers, P Screeton).
 7) Sunday Express London.
 8) Miami News Florida (Cr: Gary Abbott)
 9) Daily Telegraph London (Cr: V Martin)
10) Evening News London.
11) Evening Standard London.

12) Newsweek (Cr: IAW).
13) Daily Mail London.
14) Sun London.
15) Sunday Times London.
16) Sunday Telegraph London.
17) Houston Post Texas (Cr: K Lothmann).
18) Evening News Manchester (Cr: Peter Rogerson.)
19) China Post Taiwan (Cr: IAW).
20) Daily Mirror London.
21) Nation Bangkok (Cr: IAW).
22) Evening News Harrisburg, Pennsylvania (Cr: Larry E Arnold).
23) World Bangkok (Cr: IAW).
24) Indonesia Times Jakarta (Cr: IAW).
25) Los Angeles Times Cal (Cr: EC Krupp).
26) Earthquake Information Bulletin May 1978 (US Geol Survey, Virginia).
27) New Straits Times Malaysia (Cr: IAW)
28) Penang Star M'sia (Cr:IAW, J Klemes)
29) Observer London.
30) New Sunday Times Malaysia (Cr: IAW).
31) Straits Times Singapore (Cr: IAW).
32) Morning News Dallas, Tx (Cr: TAdams)
33) Star Malaysia (Cr: IAW).
34) National Echo M'sia (Cr: J Klemes).

35) Times-Herald Dallas, Tx (TR Adams).
36) New York Times NY (Cr: GL Abbott).
37) Evening Telegraph Scunthorpe, Linclonshire (Cr: Nigel Watson).
38) Daily Express London.
39) International Herald Tribune Paris.
40) Echo Sunderland, Co Durham (Cr: Paul Screeton).
41) Daily Press Newport News, Virginia (Cr: Gary L Abbott).
42) Times London.
43) Australasian Express London (C:IAW)
44) Mail Hartlepool, Co Durham (P Scrtn)
45) Post Bangkok (Cr: IAW).
46) Kentish Independant London.
47) Journal Newcastle, Nbland (P Scrton)
48) Guardian Rangoon, Burma (Cr: TAW).
49) Statesman Calcutta (Cr: IAW).
50) Amrita Bazar Patrika Calcutta (IAW)
51) Herald Melbourne, Australia (IAW).
52) Rising Nepal Katmandu (Cr: IAW).
53) Spectator Ontario.
54) Sunday Statesman Delhi (Cr: IAW).
55) Standard Hongkong (Cr: IAW).

- RJMR -

obituary

ROBERT CHARROUX

Erich von Däniken, in one of his books, expressed the hope that questions raised by Robert Charroux, Louis Pauwels and Jacques Bergier - as well as himself - would be answered in his lifetime. Charroux did not make this deadline. He died on 24 June 1978. He wrote 7 books, of which only a few have been published in Britain and America - special mention must be made of his One Hundred Thousand Years of Man's Unknown History (Berkley Medallion, NY, 1971).

It was Charroux's hypothesis "that before ours...there existed a very old civilization that had invented radio, TV, space rockets and helium bombs - until it was destroyed in a nuclear holocaust." (100 Years vol 1 p6) World history did not begin at Sumer, and science has conspired to keep from the public all finds that do not fit in with established theories, and Charroux made it his mission to disclose this falsification of history.

It will probably be of interest to readers of this magazine that he mentions Charles Fort as one of those who kept alive the search for the fantastic after Flammarion left off in 1862 (with his Inhabited Worlds.) Unfortunately, it cannot be said that Charroux's source

criticism equalled Fort's.

In Charroux's opinion, it was "ridiculous...to explain each and every miracle by referring to black magic or scientific hypotheses without foundation. The incredible development of science does, however, allow us to believe that in the foreseeable future we will witness a strong development also of the budding seeds of the occult sciences." (Vol 1 p64) This remark boomerangs on himself when he acts like a contactee claiming secret knowledge given him by extraterrestrials, or when he uses muddled occult sources as evidence, or references to the libraries in Vatican cellars and secret black books from the East in particular.

But I do not want to be unkind. Robert Charroux had the necessary courage - and deserves praise for that - to ask of orthodoxy a large number of inconvenient questions. We can then correct him where he·has been proven wrong - yes, we ought to - but at least he has given us a garden to cultivate, and we want to thank him for that.

KRISTIAN KRISTIANSEN.
(Reprinted, with kind permission, from Forteana 6 (1978). NB: citations above are from the Danish edition of 100 Yrs (Strubes Forlag, C'hagen, 1969))

Within a space of 5 months there have been at least 8 suicides by fire -- on 21 May, James Forrester died in Margate (D.Telegraph 22 May 1978); on 19 August, Terence Worton in Birmingham (S.People 20 Aug 1978 cr: R Skinner); on 9 Sept, an 'unemployed miner' in Ayr, Scotland (Detroit Free Press 10 Sept 1978 cr: Dave Fideler); 17 Sept, Pastor Rolf Günther in Falkenstein, E Germany (most papers); in last week of Sept, Naide Alves·Prestes, a Proutist, in Calcutta; 1 Oct, a man on an internal Japanese flight (D.Express 2 Oct 1978); on 2 Oct, Lynette Davis, another Ananda Marga Proutist, in Geneva (most papers); and on 4 Oct, Pamela Evans Cooper, near Windsor Castle (most papers) -- 6 of these within 2 months. And god only knows what's happened in Japan (apart from the one incident above) in the light (sorry!) of a note in the S.Express 19 March 1978, that in 1977 alone there were more than 100 suicides by setting fire to oneself in Japan. This is mainly to introduce our notes on cases where motive for suicide is either unknown or quite out of the question -- yes it's SHC time again, and we have quite a lot of data - too much for the space allocation here - so cases involving children, deaths in prison cells, poltergeist fires, or from 1977 and before 1975, will all have to wait a little. For now, please toast...

SOME SHC(?)s FROM 1976

Major John Lyons was woken by the smell of smoke about 7am on 20 August - it was coming from the basement of his home, 13 Cavendish Place, Bath. He called the fire brigade immediately, not realizing that his daughter was lying in the room dead or dying! When masked firemen broke into the smoke-filled room they found the "badly burned" body of Claire Lucille Lyons, aged 23. Detective Chief Inspector George Herbert said matches were found nearby. Then he added: "The fire is a mystery. There is what looks like charred cardboard and paper..." It was not known what Claire was doing in

the basement but it was thought she went down between 6-7am. Herbert speculated: "Somehow a fire started...which ignited Miss Lyons' nightdress." No conclusive or corroborating evidence could be found. Forensic people were examining the charred card, but we don't know what they found. Bath & West Evening Chronicle 20 August 1976 (Cr: John Michell.)

Kevin Copas came home from the pub about 10.15pm. His sister, Mrs Annie Kelly, 61, was still watching TV, so he went to bed. A few hours later he was woken by an explosion or "loud bang." He found his sister missing from her bedroom and went downstairs, shouldered his way into the lounge - the door was jammed - and saw his sister lying fully clothed on the floor of the smoke-filled room; then he made the fire call. The date of the incident is not known, but at the inquest it was said that Mrs Kelly smoked and drank sherry, and that an "almost empty bottle of sherry was found near the seat of the fire..." The Assistant Divisional Fire Officer, MV Jackson, said Mrs Kelly had extensive leg burns indicating the fire had started or burned on a low level. His theory was that she had fallen asleep watching TV after drinking sherry and that her cigarette had fallen on the carpet starting a fire there...but as in most cases we have to remind ourselves that this is supposition. Whether she was conscious or not, she had made little attempt to escape or deal with the flames - it's as though she just got out of the chair and fell over. She died, not of burns, but of inhaling carbon monoxide. Many might ask what we mean by including cases like this. In the first place there are many hundreds of cases like this in which the testimony includes varying amounts of pure conjecture (like: "She fell asleep while smoking "(plus or minus the "drinking" option.); or "...must have stumbled against the heater..." or "the pet must have tipped over the heater," etc). In the second place there seems reasonable doubt that the source and even some of the characteristics of the fire were wholly or partly conventional (Fg a fire confined to the chair area on a low level; are they sure a butt could fire the carpet, assuming she was smoking then anyway; etc). Lastly, if SHC exists (and we have no reason to think it shouldn't or doesn't) then its occurrence would create this kind of doubt and mystery. But as we say, like many cases the evidence is inconclusive - either way! Oh...and what the explosion was that woke Mr Copas, in his 52 Priory St, Corsham, bedroom, we are never told. Bath & West Evening Chronicle 22 October 1976 (Cr: John Michell.)

London Evening News 24 December 1976 - a brief note that Eileen McLinity, an 84-yr-old spinster, was found dead after a fire in her home at Hill St, Mayfair. Police supposed she was overcome by fumes and that the fire must have been started by matches...or cigarette. Either are to be found near any smoker. Curiously this small item is immediately followed by another even smaller. That a man was being questioned by police over a hammer attack on a 45-yr-old woman during a fire at Amhurst Rd, Dalston, on the other side of London. (Cr: Peter Hope-Evans.)

Mary Norris, 32, died in a fire at her home in Woodstock Ave, Isleworth. Although it was said to have wrecked her living room - this result may have equally been blamed on the smoke or the firemen's action - it was small enough to have been put out "in minutes." There are two interesting details, one suggesting fire-proneness, and the other a classic SHC symptom. Firstly it is said that earlier that summer a fire gutted one of her bedrooms. The second detail is that: "A fire brigade spokesman said he could not say what started the fire, or why Mrs Morris ((sic)) was unable to escape." (My underlining.) The incident happened on 29 December, and at the time of the report it was not known precisely how Mrs Norris died. Neighbours saw no smoke or flames. Slough Evening Mail 30 December 1976 (Cr: Peter Hope Evans.)

Note the clustering of these cases at the end of the year, if that means anything.

SOME SHC(?)s FROM 1978

On the 1st June the body of Andrea Deeley, 20, was found by firemen tackling the fire in the lounge of her home in Hunters Rd, Handsworth, Birmingham. She had died of carbon monoxide poisoning in the midst of a mystery - she was found still sitting on the settee which had

somehow caught alight. Leading Fireman Andrew Hodgkins, one of the firemen, gets to the heart of our interest: Andrea seems to have made no attempt to escape the flames or her predicament: "It looks a bit funny when a girl of 20 stays in an armchair ((sic)). You would have thought that she would have made some attempt to get out." And a fire dept spokesman said "...no suspicious circumstances..." Huh? We note another detail: in another room in the house Andrea's father lay bedridden. Birmingham Evening Post 2 June 1978 (Cr: Lynne Moffat.)

The next story we pick up from X's Res Bureaux Bulletin 39p2, cited from our own Manchester Evening News 3 August 1978 - for once no one sent any clippings on this interesting event! We quote X's synopsis: "On the night of August 2nd, neighbours heard a piercing scream from the flat ((in Harpurhey, Manchester)) of Charles Richards, which soon passed into the hall. Looking out of their doors they saw him blazing away with flames from 'head to toe'. He pounded on the door of a neighbour screaming: 'Betty save me.'...The door was blackened where he had hammered. Another neighbour ...tried to put out the flames with his hands, but by this time a second flaming body (Doris Howard) had entered the corridor from Richard's flat. 'I heard a commotion in the corridor and saw them like two torches. I picked up a rug and started beating the flames. Then I realized that I was doing no good and could feel my hands burning, so I ran to phone for help,' says Patrick Furey. Richards succumbed soon after; but Mrs Howard died the next day, without giving any clue as to how they caught fire." Police said an argument had been heard before the event and that the walls had a few smears of blood. A tin of lighter fuel was also found, and assuming you can answer the question of how they both came to be covered in lighter fuel from head to toe satisfactorily, there was still no sign of how they were ignited; nor, according to the "baffled" police, was there any "sign of fire in the dead man's flat." They also rule out actions of any third party or "suicide pact". A mystery, what? More mysterious to me is how come our Manchester Evening News readers - and I know there are a few - didn't see, or didn't bother to send us this one! Shows you how lucky we are for - and dependent upon - your vigilance and effort.

Early on the morning of 20 August Maud Primrose, 54, died in a fire in her apartment on Sullivan St, Biddeford, Maine. She was alone and the cause of the fire, or the lady's death, were not apparant. The note we have says the case is still under investigation. Bangor Daily News (Maine) 21 August 1978 (Cr: Loren Coleman.)

The body of Miriam Culine, 33, wife of a 70-yr-old travelling fairground boss, was found in a blazing car near rail tracks at West Cornforth, about 6mls south of Durham, at 5am on 22 August. At least the police think so - Mrs Culine had been missing since the 21st Aug, but beyond knowing the charred body was female, Detective Chief Superintendent Bill Connor admitted: "The body was so badly burned we may never be able to identify it. We are completely baffled..." Sun 23 August 1978.

HOT DOG - OR SAC?

It has been remarked by some researchers, Fort among them I think, that the deadly fire seems to strike only humans. We've reflected before on this and half imagined the element getting its own back for millenia of enslavement by man. However recently a case came to our attention which is not only suggestive but a good illustration of the conditioned reflexes of modern minds.

Doug and Jean Payne, of Queens Rd, Jarrow, Co Durham, own a 4-mth-old golden retriever called Hayes. On 6 Feb, Jean, 23 (aha!) was attracted by Hayes yelping "...so I went to the front window (and saw him) on the pathway with flames leaping up from his belly. A man was passing and he grabbed Hayes and rolled him in a puddle and on the grass. I was so upset I didn't even have time to thank the man or find out who he was." The

pup was rushed to a vet, treated and is said to be recovering.

Now, police, animal welfare officers and the newspaper reporter all assume this was the work of some fire-struck fiend who hates flaming animals. A reward was posted for any information about "the culprit". The report said the pup was "burned on its underside with matches...", then adding as if pencil poised it suddenly occurred to the man that no dog is going to simply stand there while man or loony repeatedly strikes several matches, "...or a lighter." It is always possible in this less than perfect and always surprising world that a loony could have squirted ubiquitous lighter fuel at the dog, then lit it and ran off. But I'm intrigued by a detail - neither Jean Payne or the rescuer seemed to have seen anyone bending over the animal or running off, and both were alerted almost immediately by the dog's cries. But what does it mean? Newcastle Journal 7 February 1978 (Cr Paul Screeton)

BAPTISM OF FIRE

A bizarre note from our Name Game file, of which more sometime soon. It seems that a young Italian girl, in Caserta, near Naples, was sitting near a fire, when a spark, or supposed spark, leapt from the hearth to set fire to her clothes. Within minutes she was "une veritable torche" and died later in hospital. The name of this unfortunate girl, somewhat predictable with hindsight, was Giovanna d'Arco, burned alive like her namesake! Point de Vue:Images du Monde 28 April 1978 (Cr: Henri Prémont. Trans: IAW, Janet Bord.)   RJMR

Grimbledon Down   **Bill Tidy**

Reproduced by kind permission of Bill Tidy and IPC Magazines, from New Scientist 10 August 1978. There were interesting words on SHC generally in the 'Pig Ignorant' column by Peter Laurie (New Scientist 23 (naturally) March 1978 (Cr: Mike Tuppen, Chris Hall.) Either we have closet Fortean inside NSci, or we're becoming a trifle respectable. That's shocking - I'd rather become a trifle!

DAMNATION!

Methods of defusing and dismissing Fortean phenomena

by Bob Skinner

DAMNATION

It sounds like an oath, and well it might be: the oath of an 'expert' when confronted with yet another piece of undeniable Scientific heresy. However, I use the word in the same sense as Fort used 'the damned', referring to data excluded by Dogmatic Science. Damnation is the process of condemnation by 'experts' of events or discoveries or observations that are unorthodox or anomalous to a currently accepted view of universal reality. In *The Book of the Damned*, Fort resurrected much of the data, letting it speak for itself.

When using the term 'Science', I do so loosely, to represent those ultra-conservative elements, generally in science, but sometimes in other fields; in both cases the so-called experts are often unconnected with the subject on which they seem to be commenting so authoritatively.

There appear to be three main factors which, in combination, affect the weight of evidence for any given report, and thus the form in which any damning reply will take!

i) The degree to which the event apparently contradicts known principles or beliefs (e.g. a heavy object levitating would require more severe damnation than would a heavy object falling from the sky, because it defies an acceptance of the universality of gravitation).

ii) The number, credibility or professional status of witnesses (e.g. accounts from police officers have to be dealt with differently to accounts from children)

iii) The presence or absence of physical evidence (e.g. filmed observations of Sasquatch have greater weight than do unsubstantiated sightings)

Damnation has three distinct elements, and Fort recognised these as Deny, Explain and Disregard. Using these slightly adapted as headings, I would like to discuss the range of processes available to the debunker [1], the weapons and ploys used, and the recurring motifs that appear.

DENIAL

This ploy may be used best only on events of little weight, although it is sometimes feebly brought to bear on more substantial reports. Usually it consists of trying to imply that an event did not happen, or if it did, certainly not as described by the witnesses. Weapons used in the attack are libel, ridicule and flattery, claims of coincidence and fiction, and the red herring and scapegoat decoys. These subdivisions are arbitrary, and one or more may be used together.

LIBEL

I think it is strange that there have not apparently been any legal actions taken against those who have so publically besmirched the characters of respectable citizens, just because they reported anomalies. Fort records some fine examples. A Rev. W. Read, reported to the *Monthly Notices* of the Royal Astronomical Society in 1851 that he had observed through his telescope, at 9.30 am, a host of self-luminous bodies passing at different speeds. The editor dared to suggest that the observation was possibly attributed to an abnormal state of the optic nerves of the observer. Did he really mean that he thought the vicar ought to get his eyes tested? He was rightly rebuffed by the good reverend in a subsequent issue. He had been a diligent observer, with instruments of a superior order for about 28 years, he said — besides two other members of his family had also seen the spectacle [2].

The mental stability of observers does not escape calumnous attack: A Professor Smith, commenting on a Dr. Hahn who had photographed and described fossils of microscopic invertebrates he had discovered in meteorites, called him 'a kind of half-insane man, whose imagination has run away with him'. Needless to say, the Professor had not examined the meteorites himself [3].

Insinuations of insobriety are more common: A Mr J.W. Robertson reported in a magazine his sighting in the Persian Gulf of two huge 'light wheels', from on board the SS Patna in 1880. He remarked on the size and the speed of rotation of the rays of the wheels. In a subsequent issue another correspondent says he thinks there must have been much 'splicing of the mainbrace' resulting in such a state that any ray of light would have taken on a rotary motion [4]. A reader of Fort will find many other instances of substantially identical light wheels being seen under the sea [5].

RIDICULE

The more ridiculous the report appears to be, or the sillier the witness can be made to seem, the better. A humorous, tongue in cheek, treatment of an occurrence when it is published in a newspaper or magazine, sows seeds of doubt in a reader's mind as to its reality. We tend to laugh at what is unknown; it is a release of the tension of fear, 'whistling in the dark'. Fort aptly described knowledge as ignorance surrounded by laughter [6]. However, to find something that is really meriting ridicule, one only has to read some 'expert' explanations of strange phenomena.

COINCIDENCE

Under this heading we come across the first of the three main motifs in explanation, 'it was on the ground in the first place'. It was commonly used about meteorites before their 'undamning' by science. As late as 1902, there were still doubters though, and a Member of the Selborne Society still argued that meteorites do not fall from the sky. He stated that they were lumps of iron — 'upon the ground in the first place' — that attracted lightning. The lightning was seen and misinterpreted as the fall of a luminous object [7]. The same motif is still used in the cases of reported showers of non-meteoric minerals and organisms. These are, they say, only noticed after the rainshower, and are thought to have fallen, by superstitious people. This argument cannot be used in the case of things or organisms not normally found on the ground that are reported to have fallen from the sky.

FLATTERY

If used skilfully, this one can be effective. The 'expert' appeals to the common sense of the reader, saying, for instance, that it is 'hardly necessary to suggest to the intelligent reader that thunderstorms are a myth' [8]. Anyone with at least a public (primary) school education should know better than to write that quartz had ever fallen from the sky, the 'expert' says [9]. The second well-worn motif, a development from the first, appeals to logic 'There is no . . . in the sky, therefore, no . . . can fall from the sky' — the spaces being filled with whatever is claimed to have done just that.

FICTION

This attack is rarely levelled. It is, however, safe to suggest that a report is a fabrication if it originates from a child, or some other individual who cannot defend himself adequately against such an allegation. It is also safe to use if the occurrence is reported to have happened, or is first revealed on, April 1st; or seen on the way home from a pub-crawl. Fraud has been alleged in cases of anomalous archaeological finds, such as Roman coins in American burial mounds [10]. Such a claim would have been correct in the case of the Piltdown Man find, but was never made, as the find supported a theory [11] many years passed before the hoax was revealed.

RED HERRING AND SCAPEGOAT

I have placed these two types of denial in the same section, as they both divert the reader's attention from the phenomenon.

Where an unimportant part of a story is exaggerated by the 'expert', or where an unconnected fact is brought in as an explanation, one can smell a 'red herring'. Such facts do not often explain even part of an observation. Damnation in some instances is by suggesting hypotheses that, in the light of the facts, are absurd. Clinkers were reported as having fallen in Kilburn in 1877, littering the street with an estimated two bushels in volume. A doubting investigator discovered that there was a fire station in the same street, and, apparently without vertification, suggested that the clinkers were raked from the steam fire engine [12].

The scapegoat explanation involves claiming that an occurrence happened as the result of a human agency. In most instances the person or persons are unnamed, or if they are, are unable to properly defend themselves. A child for example. This argument may not actually be used in the original published account of the phenomenon, but often appears as a footnote in a subsequent edition. A famous example is the supposed Worcester fishmonger, who was blamed for unloading his stale stock of winkles in the streets, and thus causing locals to superstitiously think they had fallen from the sky. The old on-the-ground-in-the-first-place motif does not explain how the molluscs came to be found on rooftops, unless we accept Fort's explanation of the impious, hardworking, but unnoticed fishmonger's assistants [13]. A report of a shower of blood and flesh over a tobacco field in Tennessee is eventually followed up by an explanation naming the scapegoats — in this instance negroes — who had pretended to see the shower and had scattered the decaying remains of a hog as a joke to test the credibility of their master. It seems highly unlikely that any negro worker, however much he might like the idea, would dare to actually do such a thing. It does not surprise me, however, that the poor workers could have been made to admit the crime [14].

EXPLAIN AWAY

If a reported phenomenon has more weight of evidence to support it, a more efficient method of damning, such as explaining away, is chosen. Often it does not deny the most salient features of a report, but the explanation offered does not fit all the details, or has some other characteristic showing it to be false. Occasionally a reasonable, logical explanation is offered, and until it can be shown to be false, it cannot but be tentatively accepted.

The only explanations that come under this classification are those that can be shown to be or are reasonably suspected of being, false. Most of the explanations cannot be categorised, but there are two major types. One is the third Motif of Damnation, 'Up from one part of the earth in a whirlwind, and down in another', and the other I have called 'Fell from plane/tree/building'. Referring to the strange atmospheric phenomena of 1883, Fort says that blue moons were as common as green suns. All this seemed adequately explained as the action of volcanic dust in the atmosphere from Krakatoa, which erupted in August 1883. Fort discloses two facts that throw doubt on this explanation. Firstly, the phenomena continued for seven years, except for a break in the middle of a few years — where was the volcanic dust then? Secondly, Fort triumphantly reveals that there were reports of the phenomena prior to the eruption of Krakatoa [15].

UP FROM ONE PART OF THE EARTH, IN A WHIRLWIND, DOWN IN ANOTHER

This is the third motif, a refinement of the other two. Included in this section are those explanations of falls of stones, slag and black rains as being results of volcanic action. The whirlwind theory seems credible, especially when it is explained how specialised falls could be the result of sorting by weight of objects picked up by a vortex of air. Rarely, however, are there other specialised falls at the same time such as could be expected if the theory is true. The actual whirlwinds are infrequently seen, and it is yet to be explained how objects can be deposited on small strips or areas of ground, rather than haphazardly [16]. The repetition of such falls at the same place, sometimes weeks later, is also unexplained.

FROM A PLANE/TREE/BUILDING

This title refers to the supposed source of a reported fall of objects, ice, animals etc. It is just a matter of deleting the inapplicable, or inventing your own source if necessary. Ice falls are invariably attributed to aircraft these days, despite the records of this phenomenon pre-20th Century, and research that attributes that cause to only about 7% of cases [17]. A fall of fish in Glamorganshire in 1859 is said to have been caused as a result of a practical joke. A Dr. Gray of the British Museum suggests that one person, scooping a bucket of water from a stream threw it over another, who thought that fish in it had fallen from the sky. The fish covered an area of 80 by 12 yards, and some were on rooftops [18]. Such an unadvised dismissal is typical of many that litter the land of the damned; absurd solutions, unadvised suggestions and emotional rationalisations. Fort records the case of a reported fall of frogs that was attributed to the amphibians having fallen from trees 'or other places overhead'. Did this include the sky? Presumably not [19]. Pieces of a brick-like substance which were reported to have fallen in a hailstorm at Padua in 1834 were attributed to the supposed destructive action of the hail on nearby buildings. Fort, however, records what he terms a concomitant; an accompanying phenomenon. Some of the hailstones had a light grey powder inside [20].

Fort describes the effect of explanations or orthodox assertions as 'hypnosis'. Provided the assertion is glib, suave, brief and conventional enough one seldom questions it and is soon forgotten.

DISREGARD

This is probably the most commonly used of all the weapons in the debunker's arsenal, especially in the form of censoring, of filtering of information prior to publication. This means that the majority of reports never see the light of day. A secondary element is the deliberate suppression or whitewash, where data, or results that do not conform, are deliberately destroyed or tampered with so as to make them suspect.

CENSORING/FILTERING

Few 'Fortean' reports reach the papers these days, compared with the numbers in previous centuries. I do not believe that this indicates a decline in the occurrence of the phenomena, but an increasing refusal by the press to handle such news. An exception is in the time of year referred to as the 'silly season'. This is usually in late summer, when parliament is in recess, and the papers for want of newsworthy material, often cover what are considered as trivial stories, generally in a tongue-in-cheek manner. Fort noticed the reluctance of scientific papers to cover unorthodox observations, and saw this as the restraining hand of the 'System', and the surrender by the magazines of their 'quasi-individuality' and independence — he dates the start of this process as the early 1860s. Some apparently held out as far as 1880, but few traces of their coverage of the strange reports are findable after 1890, except in the correspondence columns of *Nature*, and the *Monthly Weather Review*. The whole process was seen by him as a 'throttling', but as he says, many of the excommunicated creep in and to this day some of the strangled still breathe faintly [21]. The policy of regarding unconventional phenomena as unworthy of publication was also followed at the museums. Fort quotes at least two separate curators who admit that many strange substances have been sent to them with the assurance that they had fallen from the sky. Few, if any of the reports were ever published as the materials were of 'non-meteoric' origin [22]. Some of this 'filtering' must happen at source, that is, with the witness, since people are often afraid of being subjected to ridicule if they report what they have seen.

WHITEWASH

This is a charge against the scientific authorities that can rarely if ever be proved. It certainly seems that Kammerer, whose results tended to show the inheritance of acquired characteristics, was the victim of someone whose interference threw all of Kammerer's work into disrepute. By using a normally land breeding toad, and allowing it to breed in water, after only a few generations he managed to show that nuptual pads were developed. These horny surfaces on the forelegs of the amphibian aid in the actual mating process, allowing the male to firmly grip its mate. Specimens were shown to the astonishment of many leading biologists, who examined the pads microscopically. However, chemical analysis showed that the hands of the examined toad had been injected with black ink. Immediately Kammerer's results all became suspect including his work with the salamander and Ciona, a type of sea-squirt. Arthur Koestler, in his biography of Kammerer [23], shows that this tampering could have only been accomplished a week or so before the examination, and the toad had been seen by many biologists months before. His guilt seemed compounded by his suicide — which might have been for reasons other than this 'exposure' [24]. In the field of UFOs, governments have been suspected of tampering with evidence, confiscating photographs, and intimidating witnesses — but the borderline between this and 'Men-in-black' activity is not clear [25].

There are cases in which key witnesses to strange phenomena suddenly change their testimony, and this may be a result of pressure from the authorities, directly or indirectly, as in the case of the negroes in the tobacco field, cited earlier.

Having discussed the processes of damnation, it is now important to look at the reasons why Science so dogmatically excludes the possibility of the existence of extraordinary phenomena. I think there are two reasons — because they are not understandable on the basis of known Scientific beliefs, and are thus irrational; and because they may belong to a realm of existence that cannot be probed by science as it is at present.

The motive of maintaining the Scientific status quo was examined by Fort, who concluded that Science cannot maintain its approximation to consistency, stability and system without damning the irreconcilable and unassimilable [26]. This is like the logical viewpoint of a computer, which can only accept and reject on the basis of its programme. However, scientists should not be so blinkered as to be unable to see the need for an occasional change of programme. But Science changes slowly, in three stages according to Su Shu Huang. Firstly, a new means of experiment or observation is developed into a powerful tool, providing a fresh look at nature. Secondly, there is a proliferation of data not understandable in terms of known concepts and principles — this stage lasts the longest, and causes most frustration and bewilderment to scientists. Thirdly, sooner or later clarification comes in the form of a new concept explaining the baffling results naturally in a straightforward manner [27].

However, I do not believe that all phenomenal occurrences can be eventually explained satisfactorily by science. Because of its materialistic, nuts-and-bolts attitude, Science at present cannot accept or explain the spiritual, for example, and this leads to the damnation of phenomena that seem to be manifestations of that realm.

The study of any sort of mystery is bound to attract a fringe element, some with decidedly cranky ideas, and this inevitably makes Science loath to involve itself. However it would be good to see Science no longer damning, but investigating, accepting even the unexplainable, and recording such happenings until future enlightenment comes, if any. I hope that Science will one day no longer feel the need to fit inappropriate conventional explanations to unconventional phenomena.

Although I cannot support Science's dogmatic defence of the status quo, the alternative seemingly advocated by some, of a kind of anarchy with no physical laws, theories or reasonable explanations being even tentatively acceptable, is equally undesirable.

Bob Skinner — March 1978

Footnotes and References

1. 'Debunking' is a word that became popular to describe the USAF's dealings with UFO reports in the 1950s, originating presumably from the USAF side, as it means 'to clear of bunk or humbug, to show up (e.g. a theory) as False'. (Chambers 20th Century Dictionary)
2. The Book of the Damned by Charles Fort (Ace Star Books) p.206. (Books p218) [Eds note — since different Ace editions had different paginations, I've added, in brackets, the page from the 1941 & 1974 editions of the Complete Books of Charles Fort.]
3. Ibid, p. 84 (Books p.80)
4. Ibid, p. 252 (Books p.270f)
5. Ibid p. 252f (Books p.271ff)
6. Ibid, p. 30 (Books p.19)
7. Ibid, p. 32 (Books p.21)
8. Ibid, p. 108 (Books p.104)
9. Ibid, p. 118 (Books p.118)
10. Ibid p. 114, 115f (Books p.149f)
11. See also Phenomena by Michell and Rickard, p. 8f.
12. BOTD p.111 (Books p.111)
13. Phenomena p.8, 15 (Books p.548 ff)
14. BOTD p.49f (Books p.41)
15. Ibid p. 27f. (Books, p18)
16. See Ibid p. 90, 91 (Books p. 94f); 'Fish Falls and Whirlwinds', R. Schadewald, Fortean Times 22p 31f.
17. Phenomena p.17 Fortean Times 23 p. 17.
18. BOTD p.87f. (Books p.84)
19. Ibid p.85 (Books p.81).
20. Ibid, p.119 (Books, p.119)
21. Ibid p.224f.
22. Ibid p. 126f.
23. The Case of the Midwife Toad (Picador Books 1971.)
24. His death is a mysterious one, and the verdict of suicide may be suspect. Kammerer was found with a gun in his right hand, and the bullet hole in his left temple. See Ibid, p. 118f.
25. See Operation Trojan Horse by John Keel (Souvenir Press, 1971; Abacus, 1973)
26. BOTD p.27.
27. Quoted by Damon Knight in his biography Charles Fort (Gollancz, 1971) p.79.

NEW INDEX, AND OP ISSUES

Phil Ledger has prepared the index for 1976 (FT14-19), and this will be available from next issue. In the past we have sent a free index to all subcribers as a bonus - but because we could only print a small number we found that some subbers were going without while others received indexes for which they had no use. We want to try a better method this time. With this issue subscribers will receive a voucher, and if you wish to claim your free index please return the voucher ASAP before our next mailing (Feb 1979).

Some readers have asked whether we intend to reprint out-of-print issues. This is always possible and various ways are under consideration. Meanwhile, if you can't wait, we could make photocopies at cost to us plus a small cover-charge.

TRUSS FUND

...in which we thank the following for their generous and appreciated support: Sid Birchby; Richard Cotton; Jennie Cameron; Isobel Davis; Mrs W Furness; MS Kottmeyer; Dr EC Krupp; Anthony Smith; Mrs V Martin. Thanks!

TALES FROM THE YELLOW EMPORIUM

=ORIENTAL FORTEANA BY STEVE MOORE=

Our esteemed editor has allowed this improbable person a page or two per issue to present a selection of unsymmetrical notes on Fortean subjects relating to China. And so, without further ado...

'ELECTRIC PEOPLE' & CH'I ENERGY

Readers of John Michell and Robert Rickard's Phenomena will be well aquainted with the subject of 'electric people' (p36-7), where a conglomerate of inter-related phenomena may be found. One aspect I find particularly interesting (if I may be forgiven for a seeming lack of 'serious-ness') is that of those young ladies who, having developed 'electrical powers', put them on the stage. Not that this demonst-rativeness is particularly inter-esting in itself; but what was being demonstrated is. I summar-ise briefly: 'immovability', the ability to remain standing while four or five men attempt to push the demonstrator over; manipula-ting objects through 'invisible rays'; 'sticking palms', lifting people by merely placing the open palms on their backs; the admini-stration of electric shocks to bystanders, and so forth.

The interesting thing is that similar if not identical powers are attributed to the great T'ai Chi Chuan masters of China. Apoc-ryphal stories of 'super-powers' possessed by masters crop up rep-eatedly in the traditions and history of the martial arts of China, some perhaps exaggerated, some perhaps not. However, in the works of Robert W Smith, the noted American writer on the mar-tial arts, we find accounts at first, or at least only at second hand, either parallel to, or hau-ntingly suggestive of the powers of 'electric people'.

I choose the works of Smith simply because they come most easily to mind and hand, but sim-ilar stories can be found else-where. In an article, published in Fighting Arts magazine (Vol.2 No 6), paying tribute to the late master Cheng Man-ch'ing (d.1975) he quotes his wife's reaction to 'pushing hands' pra-ctice with Cheng: "It was so strange. When he touched me I felt an electricity-like surge go throughout my body but with-out the shock".

In 'Chinese Boxing: Masters and Methods' (Kodansha, Tokyo, 1974), Smith, concentrating less on the methods, as his usual wont, than on the men, has seve-ral tales of ch'i; many about or from the lips of the respected

master Cheng. "Ch'i" is difficult of definition in any sort of
everyday or scientific terms: it
is at once 'breath', spirit, non
-muscular energy, or 'inner power'. It is that energy which
flows along the acupuncture mer-
idians. It is also the energy
developed by practitioners of
the 'Internal schools' of the
martial arts, the most well-known
of which is T'ai Chi Chuan. But
if it is little understood it is,
according to Smith and other writers, frequently demonstrated.

In Chinese Boxing we find references to (and a photograph of)
Cheng 'rooting' himself to the
ground and resisting the efforts
of four men to push him over.
One master's 'rooting' is described as being so powerful that
his feet actually sank into the
ground. Another tale is from a
woman student of a master in
Shanghai: when she had attempted
to attack him, she found a force
propelling her backwards, and
then she started bouncing up and
down until her feet began to
hurt. 'Invisible rays'? Another
master, walking in the street
with a friend, was hit in the
back by a pedicab, which rebou-
nded 10 feet and tipped over.
The master, without a break in
the conversation, walked on as
if nothing had happened. Again,
Cheng invited another boxer to
strike his relaxed arm; he struck
once and withdrew, explaining
that his entire side had been
paralysed on contact with Cheng's
arm. And lastly, Cheng's teacher,
Yang Ch'eng-fu, controlled his
ch'i to such an extent that in
'pushing hands' he could magnet-
ise or attract his opponent's
arm so that it stuck to his own
as he moved.

As I said, the similarities
between the two sets of phenomena are remarkable; so is the
difference. For whereas the electrical phenomena of the west
usually arise spontaneously and
are later controlled, or are a
completely accidental nuisance,
the ch'i powers of the east are
produced by methodical training
and practice, usually in persons
who apparently have no spontaneous psychic or paranormal powers.

Whether ch'i energy is bio-ele-
ctric in nature is a question on
which I have no information to
hand, but the above tales do suggest this. I am unaware of any
attempts to scientifically test
this, or even if any attempt has
been made to register ch'i with
any sort of measuring instrument.
Perhaps martial arts practitioners who have reached sufficient
mastery to qualify as test-subj-
ects would consider it beneath
their dignity to have electrodes
attached to themselves while
demonstrating; similarly, many
might consider it an undignified
affair to have to demonstrate
ch'i to a skeptical group of
scientists in the first place.
Unless more information comes to
hand, we must let the matter
rest there.

But lest anyone should wonder
if those aspects of telekinesis
mentioned in the same chapter of
Phenomena have any counterparts
in the east, yes, they do. There
are mentions of projecting the
ch'i beyond the body to ring
bells and snuff out candles at a
distance. But it would take a
brave man or a fool to try to
sort out the fact from the fiction in those stories. Brave I am
definitely not...but I might give
it a try one of these days...
         *   *   *
And finally, does this sound
familiar?

"The world has no limit, and
therefore anywhere is the centre,
just as in drawing a circle, any
point on the line can be the starting point." - Ssu-Ma Piao (3rd
century A D).   SM

NEWS CLIPPINGS

If you see anything of interest to FT readers in your
reading, professional or scientific journals, or local newspapers, please clip it out, or make a note of it, add a
note of the source, date, and your name ... then send
it to us. It all helps and there are surprisingly few
duplications. Some readers have offered to scan their
regular reading matter, and if you would like to do the
same, please contact us for suggested periodicals not
being covered by others.

---

* NEWSLETTER *

...an informal postal exchange for
studies in paraphysics and the esoteric arts, founded 1944, Non-sectarian, non-demanding. For an introductory leaflet, send a stamp to NL,
40 Parrs Wood Rd. Didsbury,
Manchester M20 OND.

ᚱEVIEW ᚦUPPLEMENT

We welcome books and journals for review or ex-
.change on all topics of related interest. The details and
contents of journals are given in the next issue after
receipt, and the return favour in their pages would be
appreciated.

hardbacks

The Twelfth Planet by Zecharia Sitchin (G Allen & Unwin, 1977; £5.50;
pp384; index, illos, photos) -- At
first glance this well produced, and,
on the whole, pleasantly written, volume offers the promise of being a stimulating and serious attempt to reint-
erpret ancient Near Eastern religion
and human prehistory. Relying on Babylonian and Biblical mythology in the
main, and displaying some apparent erudition, Sitchin develops a model for
the origins of civilization that reminds
one at once of the catastrophist theories of Immanuel Velikovsky and Robert
Temple's claim of extraterrestrial intervention in the ancient Near East. The
primum mobile of Sitchin's cosmos is a
hypothetical 'twelfth planet', known to
the Babylonians as Marduk, which he
places on an enormous elliptical comet-
like orbit stretching from the asteroid
belt to the far reaches of the solar
system. Every 3,600 years, he claims,
Marduk returns to the vicinity of the
Earth, causing major catastrophes such
as the Universal Deluge, and as the home
of a race of superbeings called the
Nefilim, stimulating 'quantum jumps' in
the progress of human evolution and
civilization.

Sitchin begins with the famous Biblical verses concerning the "sons of
God" who mated with the "daughters of
men" before the time of Noah (Genesis
6:1-4). These verses are an old favourite of the extraterrestrial lobby, and

perhaps justly so. Sitchin points out
that the meaning of Nefilim, the product of this union, could be "those who
were cast down" rather than the conventional interpretation of "giants". Certainly some belief in "other beings" is
indicated, and here, if anywhere in the
Bible, could be a reference to extraterrestrials. The Twelfth Planet represents
some 30yrs of mulling over the identity
of the Nefilim, who captured Sitchin's
imagination in childhood. Anyone prepared to work his way through the anthropological literature making a comparative study of concepts similar to the
Biblical Nefilim would undoubtedly find
the task rewarding. Sitchin however
seeks a short-cut and simply assumes
that the Nefilim and the gods of the
ancient Near Eastern pantheons were
spacemen from the "Twelfth Planet" and
proceeds to "translate" a few Babylonian epics and Biblical passages into
histories of these ancient astronauts.

From the outset, Sitchin's approach
is marred by an extremely narrow outlook and frame of reference. He must be
one of the last people this century to
imagine that Mesopotamia was the center
of civilization, and that Mesopotamian
myths, by virtue of having been written
down earlier, are somehow the 'originals'
of those of other Near Eastern cultures
(including Greece and Egypt). He rest-
ricts himself almost entirely to a few
Babylonian epics (eg those of Gilgamesh,
Atrahasis and Enuma Elish) to develop
his grand rewriting of human history –
ignoring even Sumerian predecessors to
these tales. The effect of his "Twelfth
Planet" on the civilizations of America,
Europe, Africa and the rest of Asia is
not even considered, and outside of the
Near East and Greece, the mythologies
of the rest of the world are not even
acknowledged to exist. Sitchin's method
then is remarkable jejune - identify

the planets (up to 12) and 'spacegods' in the Epics and read the whole as history.

In making these "identifications" Sitchin displays a very limited understanding of Babylonian literature and civilization. He uses the Epic of Creation (Enuma Elish) as the foundation for his cosmogony, identifying the young god Marduk, who overthrows the older regime of gods and creates the Earth, as the unknown "Twelfth Planet". In order to do so he interprets the Babylonian theogony as a factual account of the birth of the other "eleven" planets. The Babylonian names for the planets are established beyond a shadow of a doubt - Ishtar was the deity of Venus, Nergal of Mars, and Marduk of Jupiter - and confirmed by hundreds of astronomical/astrological tables and treatises on clay tablets and papyri from the Hellenistic period. Sitchin merrily ignores all this and assigns unwarranted planetary identities to the gods mentioned in the theogony. For example, Apsu, attested as god of the primeval sweet waters becomes, of all things, the Sun! Ea, as it suits Sitchin, is sometimes the planet Neptune and sometimes a spaceman. And the identity of Ishtar as the planet Venus, a central feature of Mesopotamian religion, is nowhere mentioned in the book - instead Sitchin arbitrarily assigns to Venus another deity from Enuma Elish, and reserves Ishtar for a role as a female astronaut!

By ignoring the received and deduced knowledge of Babylonian religion Sitchin weaves an extended space fantasy around his own unjustifiable identifications. In doing so he reveals the sloppiness and shallowness of his thinking, rapidly becoming silly and credulous when he turns to the evidence of religious art. The curious and heavily symbolic glyptic art of Mesopotamian cylinder-seals is a dangerous playground for speculation, especially when the author - and presumably most of his readers - know nothing about it. In this and other areas of local representational art, Sitchin rapidly degenerates into the tedious "new euhemerism" (*) of the von Däniken school. Every strange costume is a spacesuit, every pointed artifact an imitation of a rocket, large stylized eyes must be goggles etc etc. (But can someone explain to me why supposed gog-

(* Euhemerus was a 4th C Greek philosopher who taught that mythology had a historical origin and that the gods were but the magnified and distorted memories of earlier great men - Ed.)

gles are so popular with the ET fanatics? Bikers, divers and welders, perhaps - but astronauts?) Sitchin has obviously put a lot of work into this book, but I cannot help feeling his labours have been completely wasted. His grand attempt to rewrite world history amounts to another weak exercise in the reductionism popularized by von Däniken, and one that is limited to a small part of the ancient world and flawed by innumerable errors of fact and interpretation. Sometimes it becomes merely pathetic - for example, in his discussion of the Babylonian myth of Etana (p153) carried to the skies on the back of an eagle, he comments: "We cannot help associating the ancient text with the message beamed to Earth in July 1960 by Neil Armstrong, commander of the Apollo 11 spacecraft: 'Houston! Tranquility Base here...The Eagle has landed!'... Eagle was the name of the lunar module." I'm sorry, but I'm not tempted by such silly insinuations! It is sad to see someone of Sitchin's intelligence wallowing in the same slavish worship of contemporary technology that forms the credo of von Däniken.

For anyone who expects a new direction in catastrophism or the study of extraterrestrial influences on the ancients, The Twelfth Planet will be a great disappointment. Sitchin seems to be totally unaware of - or not prepared to acknowledge - the work of Velikovsky and other catastrophists. Nor does it provide a single scrap of hard evidence for ET intervention: Twelfth Planet belongs to the same genre as Chariots of the Gods, not Robert Temple's Sirius Mystery. There are no references, and works are cited in the text by title only, no page numbers; most irritating of all, the bibliography contains an utterly useless list of the periodicals consulted by title only (not the issue numbers or even article titles) the inclusion of which can only be regarded as a pretentious attempt to appear scholarly.

Finally, Sitchin seems to have had trouble in following through his own theories. The dust-cover reads provocatively: "What happens when the Twelfth Planet returns to Earth's vicinity every 3,600 years?" Sitchin attributes the rise of Sumerian civilization, c. 3800BC, to an approach of Marduk, and one is presumably meant to believe that a return of the Nefilim can be expected around 3400AD. Fortunately, we don't have to wait that long to find out whether Marduk exists. It should have come round again c.200BC - but as far

as I know there were no cosmic catastrophes or influxes of spacemen around
that time, and if Sitchin is right, the
Hellinistic astronomers must have been
asleep when the planet appeared. Sitchin
forgets to explain to his readers what
happened to Marduk after 3800BC – but
after all, Twelfth Planet is an eminently forgettable book.

Peter James.

To Anger The Devil by Marc Alexander
(N Spearman, 1978; £4.25, pp203, notes, photos) — This astonishing
book plunges the reader straight into
a world that is, by ordinary standards,
fantastic, a world of spirit possession
and discarnate entities. This supernatural world exists today, and this is
a (selected) casebook of one of the
leading Church of England exorcists, Dr
Donald Ormand. The narrative unfurls
like a novel – and indeed Ormand here
benefits from being professionally
'written-up', compared to, say, the
equally interesting but more awkward
casebook of Dr Ormand's colleague Dom
Robert Petitpierre published 2 yrs ago.

The cases cover a wide range over
most of Dr Ormand's life, begining with
his ministrations to the circus. Later,
working as a journalist, Ormand investigated reports of Black Dog phantoms
seen on Kettleness Beach, reminding
Ormand synchronistically of the scene
in Bram Stoker's Dracula where the
Count is shipwrecked off this same
gloomy Yorkshire village and comes ashore in the form of a gigantic black
hound. As Ormand recollects this in
Kettleness graveyard, he and his companion come face-to-face with a genuine
Black Dog phantom radiating an aura of
evil. Ormand promptly splashed it with

a bottle of Holy Water. Later he is
involved in the exorcism of several
vampiric spirits, who generate violent
bloodlusts in their hosts, only to find
that the tougher of the cases involved
a man who once visited...Kettleness!
Such chains of coincidence are typical
of the evidence we are presented. Like
Dom Robert Petitpierre's book, and the
vast majority of books written from the
pulpit, as it were, the reader is not
given much chance to test the material,
but asked, indeed expected, to take it
all on faith. I'm broadminded enough,
and have read widely enough, to see
the material in other lights, and even
to me some of his cases seem too much
to swallow, and the fact that Ormand's
life, as presented here, reads like a
gripping and thrilling adventure film-
script, adds to the unreality.

But, says Dr Ormand, the powers of
evil are very real, or at least have
very real effects; possessed lions attack, haunted stretches of roads become
killer 'black spots', stolen idols
curse their owners with dispair, fear
and ruin, and a man is persecuted by
a vengeful phantom for some harm he
did in a previous life (or by an ances-
tor of the same name). But none of these
prove much of an obstacle for prayer
and the liberal application of Ormand's
favourite fluid. Nor is Dr Ormand a
piker, since he balks not at exorcisms
of truely heroic proportions – like
exorcizing the great Arctic icebarrier
and its seas (feared for driving sailors
to throw themselves overboard with 'Sea
Madness'), and even performing the same
for the Bermuda Triangle and Loch Ness
on the grounds that these areas have
become possessed. Dr Ormand discusses
the idea suggested to him by our own
FW Holiday and others that today's monsters may be forms of evil projected
from the past; their purpose, no doubt
anxiety and the spectre of insanity. It
all adds to a splendid medieval atmosphere in the book, since at the time
similar phenomena to those tackled by
the intrepid and fearless Ormand were
fanned into Europes shameful witchhunts,
scholars said the same about the enigma
of fossils – that God had placed them in
the ground to test the faith of men. In
this case though, our own pages have
recorded many sightings of that 'ancient
serpent' Nessie (remember, St Columba
stopped Nessie with the sign of the
Cross back in the 6th C) since Ormand's
visit in 1973 – so what hope for the
Bermuda Triangle? Ormand gives some interesting incidental information on
other water-monsters. He himself saw

one in 1967 in Loch Duich, Ross-shire, and again in the Troll fjord, Norway - he also refers to a monster in Lake Storsjon, Sweden (which he claims to have successfully banished), and one in Lake Vorota, Siberia (both these sites are discussed in Peter Costello's In Search of Lake Monsters).

But the gem of the book must be the long tale of the "displacer of souls" - a man who found he had the power to take over someone else's body, permanently, and body-hopped 4 times, ending truly repentent in the cancerous body of an old Syrian Arab. He asked Ormand to deprive him of his abused power, and before witnesses (sworn to secrecy) showed convincingly his ability to exchange souls...so convincing that one witness, a doctor, said: "The bottom was knocked out of my scientific world." One has some sympathy when faced with such pure Machen-esque (even Lovecraftian in places) tales with very little in the way of convincing evidence. One rightly hesitates to call Dr Ormand a pious fraud, since he comes across as a sound and intelligent person, and highly respected according to the numerous character witnesses, eminent doctors, psychiatrists and clergy, who insist that Ormand's word is not in doubt.

Strictly then, this is a book of anecdotes with little documentation, but nevertheless makes interesting, if chilling, reading, even if it leaves many questions unanswered. I for one would have liked to learn more about the mysterious Organization of Inquiry into Psychical Disorder (admission by election only, like a secret society) who form teams of psychiatrists, doctors & exorcists to study and cure cases outside normal medical and psychiatric experience. It is from this MI6 of the occult world that our psychic James Bond gets many of his 'assignments'.   RJMR

The Man who led Columbus to America by Paul H Chapman (Judson Press, Atlanta, Georgia, 1973; $6.00; pp202, index, bib, notes, apndxs, illos, photos) - The search for Lost America by Salvatore Michael Trento (Contemporary Books, Chicago, 1978; $9.95, pp284, index, bib, notes, apndxs, illos, photos) -- The man who led Columbus to America, Chapman convincingly argues, was St Brendan, the 6th C Irish navigator monk. Both as a mapmaker and as a sailor Columbus would have heard of, and become interested in, Brendan's voyages when he visited Galway, Brendan's deathplace. As a young

man it was Columbus's dream to sail west and he avidly collected all the descriptions of the Atlantic available to him, and thus, must also have been familiar with Brendan's Navigatio, one of the first ever 'best sellers' from the recently invented Gutenberg press. Chapman reconstructs each stage of St Brendan's expedition, showing how Brendan sailed "around the ocean" - ie up to the Faeroes, down to the Azores and across to Barbados, then up the coast of N America to Newfoundland using the Gulf stream all the way back home via Iceland. This route is almost the exact reverse of Tim Severin's recent attempt to reconstruct Brendan's voyage in a "leather banana". Severin, fearing such a flimsy craft was not up to mid-Atlantic weather travelled via Iceland and Greenland, against the Gulf stream; but Chapman has more faith in the arts of the old boatbuilders and believes that Brendan's boat did in fact make an open transAtlantic crossing using the N Equitorial current from the Azores. (Appendix B is a record of such a crossing in 1968.) At every stage, Chapman gives us all the navigational minutae, leaving the parallel "miraculous" narrative of the journey to be interpreted in charming drawings showing the encounters with an iceberg, a submarine volcano, and the first descriptions of various new islands, animals, fruits etc. With detailed appendices, maps, tables, and the relevant passages from the Navigatio, this book should become a standard reference on the subject.

In recent years the idea that Columbus was not the first to America has flourished, with lobbies forming for the Chinese, the Celts, Vikings, Phoenecians and Romans - and regarding St Brendan's Irish, Chapman quotes The Generall Historie of Virginia, written in 1626 by John Smith, governor of the first successful English colony, which in its first sentence celebrates them ("...they say a thousand years agoe they were in the north of America..."). Also remembered (and today, with great affection among the Americans) is the colonizing voyage of the Welsh prince Madoc ab Owain Gwynedd, some 600yrs after Brendan, and whom, Chapman ventures an opinion, may also have used Brendan's route-map. More recently a controversy has grown up around the work of Barry Fell, a Harvard professor, who claims to have found and deciphered inscriptions found on stones (mainly in New England and the Great Lakes area), ranging from the Punic of the Phoenecians, to Egyptian, Latin, Runes and a variant of the Ogham alphabet of the Celts (see Fell's book America BC, ie before Columbus). Sal Trento, a student of Fell's, has produced an encyclopedic study of those relics of early visitations designed to appeal to beginner and buff alike. It is extremely well done and will establish itself as a standard guide to the subject and to the thousands of standing stones, mark stones, inscribed stones, chambered mounds, tunnels and hilltop forts (many built in a recognizable style synonymous with European Celtic sites) that proliferate along the sea coast, the lake shores and banks of great rivers in America's eastern half.

There can be no doubt about Trento's thoroughness or enthusiasm for his subject as the great wealth of detail testifies - The Search for Lost America is rich in site photos and surveys, maps and drawings of inscriptions, tables, and an extensive listing of major stone sites; there is even a checklist for site observations and practical guidelines for would-be field explorers. Trento acknowledges the irony of the general lack of awareness by Americans of their own antiquities at a time when their interest is mounting in European origins. 'Lost America' becomes not just a euphemism for the ignored ruins in the local backwoods, but a comment on the crass indifference of the Establishment. Sal Trento hopes to kindle and encourage a new spirit of inquiry in American antiquities beyond the small band of his own enthusiastic helpers and the few others who care enough about the future to become interested in the past, not so much in academia, but among the new generation in their search for identity. This book should do it, and it is to be recommended to libraries, especially in schools, as a good starting point for the young and curious.

RJMR

The Stones of Atlantis by David Zink (WH Allen, 1978; £4.95, pp234, bib, apndxs, illos, maps, photos) - Secrets of Lost Atland by Robert Scrutton (N Spearman, 1978; £5.25, pp229, apndx, illos) -- Dr Zink's book is basically a personalized account of several expeditions to the Bimini Islands, led by himself, to search for the stones of Atlantis. The Bimini area was first suggested for the location of Atlantis by the trance 'readings' of Edgar Cayce - but the idea lay dormant until, in 1968, Dr J Manson Valentine, a Miami archeologist, and colleagues discovered portions of stone structure, artifacts, not natural form-

ations, since when others have been found including a section of "road" (a pavement of rectangular and polygonal stone slabs) all under the clear island waters on the seabed. In the course of 4 expeditions (1974 - 1977) Zink collected a motley crew of experts, interested amateurs and psychics, and armed with a battery of equipment and tests, set out to see for himself. Sites were mainly located by diving searches in areas indicated by his psychics, a technique that seems to have been successful in dicovering some important structures, and from the dating of samples, Zink is convinced he has found the remains of a fairly sophisticated seafaring megalithic culture - despite the admittedly contradictory dates of various samples (from 13,000 - 500 BC!) As one would expect from an English Literature professor, Zink writes an easy but rambling narrative. He speculates at every opportunity about the evidence, and often quite wildly drawing on the usual ancient histories and theories, with regular appeal to Velikovskyan catastrophism, sacred geometry, the 'new archeology' of dowsing and leys etc, paraphysics and 'higher energies', and the notion that in times past Earth was visited by the Pleions, from the Pleiades, beings "of radiance and light, emissaries of goodwill". It is hard to tell whether Zink's thinking is shallow in these speculations, or whether he was merely outlining possibly tangential matters for the general reader - either way he adds little to these subjects or our understanding of them. The main interest of the book is the accounts of the discovery and dating of their finds - and of some they failed to find (even with psychic help) like the mysterious and elusive stone pillar which its earlier discoverer claimed lit up the water around it with clouds of luminous radiation! Another interesting patch concerns a side expedition into the interior of Bimini to locate the fabled 'Fountain of Youth' of Ponce de Leon - and lo! Zink found it...or something like it...or thought he did.

The Secrets of Lost Atland is quite different and concerns another 'Atlantis' somewhere north of Britain, which colonized "the whole of the ancient world from the north Atlantic to South America from North Africa and India to the Balkans," founding the Athenian State and the Inca dynasty, which used Britain as a penal colony (nice irony there!) and which was destroyed in a Velikovskyan collision with a "runaway asteroid" around 2193 BC, and which might well have been itself a colony from the Atlantis of Plato. Phew! The presentation of the argument suffers from a major flaw: basically it is a continuation of Scrutton's previous book The Other Atlantis (Spearman, 1977) in which the key evidence was a translation of an ancient Frisian manuscript called the Oera Linda Book. This text is central to the continuing argument in this sequel and instead of providing a summary, or extracts, or indeed any helpful information at all, Scrutton merely and continuously refers the reader to the earlier book. This is useless for the new reader or those who don't have the earlier book, and actively obstructs the author's attempt to integrate the Frisian Atland (as he calls this Atlanean outpost) into the Western magical and mystical tradition (including leys, earth energies and occultism, sometimes with unfortunate references to suspect sources, like Madame Blavatsky's Stanzas of Dzyan). The result is a strange and compelling mixture of Velikovsky (Earth in Collision), James Churchward (the Mu series) Brinsley Le Poer Trench (The Sky People) John Michell (View over Atlantis) and Anthony Roberts (Atlantean Traditions in Ancient Britain). Again, minimal references and no index give little help to the reader. You must make your own mind up on this one!   RJMR

Hallucinations: Behaviour, Experience, Theory edited by RK Siegel & LJ West (J Wiley, NY, 1975; £16.90/ $29.40, pp322, index, bibs, illos, tables, plates) -- Throughout history the experience of hallucination has afforded philosophers the opportunity of expounding upon a whole range of subjects from ghosts and apparitions, to mental disease, human gullibility and the nature of reality itself, and yet despite the subject's interdisciplinary importance most of the works on hallucinations tend to be from specific viewpoints. The editors and contributors are obviously aware of the complexities of the subject and have collaborated to make a state-of-the-art assessment of the understanding gained from modern advances in psychiatry, psychology, neurology, pharmacology, biochemistry, anthropology, sociology, information theory etc. This substantial and well produced book is part of a biomedical series and as such is more concerned with the various mechanisms of hallucinations than their content or meaning - and predictably the main

points of discussion are visual hallucinations, and the use of drugs (both in society today and in archaic cultures). Hallucinations may arise in all the senses and in all combinations; and besides drugs they may be induced by disease, exhaustion, sensory deprivation, excitation and ecstasy, in some mental illnesses, and in some altered states of consciousness - but regretably these receive less attention.

The generally accepted definition of a hallucination is "a false perception in the absence of any corresponding external stimuli" - but although each paper seems to have its own redefinition of the word, they all seem to agree that the word "false" makes an unnecessary and confusing value judgement. A hallucination may produce as real effects (in terms of emotional, physical & metabolic response, for example) as any 'real' object - and indeed those who have experienced hallucinations in a positive spiritual or mystical context often describe the imagery as being in some undefined sense superior or "more real" than those of normal consciousness. Sarbin and Juhasz, in a paper on 'The Social Context of Hallucination', acknowledge the wide differences in usage of the term (eg between the clinical sense, the 16th C meaning of "ghosts and apparitions", and the modern derogatory popular usage implying character weakness or that the content is utterly inconsequential. Thus I find it very refreshing that the authors generally, regard hallucinations, not necessarily as the product of damage, disease or intoxication, but as "one of many forms of image thinking" and a state of consciousness with its own properties. Thus hallucinations, relieved of the stigma of abnormality, can be seen to function as part of the continua of consciousness of sane and everyday experience, for example dreams, daydreams, and even in the basic perceptual processes themselves. Afterall, our brains don't touch a brick, but reconstruct such a sensation from sense data and comparisons with related memories. Such considerations make another author, Ernest Hartmann, reverse the usual question "What makes us hallucinate at certain times?" and ask, more profitably, "Why don't we hallucinate all the time?" - then he proposes a mechanism of inhibition revolutionary in its simplicity. For anyone investigating Fortean phenomena with a psychological component a knowledge of hallucinations is essential, and whole sections of this volume are directly applicable, for example, to accounts of phantoms, religious apparitions, commanding voices, out-of-the-body experiences and so on. Each paper has a bibliography crammed with references to further material on hallucinations and related studies.

Ronald Siegel later wrote a long summary on 'Hallucinations' for Scientific American (237:4, Oct 1977, pp132-140) and this is well worth reading too (Cr: RM Wolf & SN Mayne).   RJMR

The Vanishing People by Katherine Briggs (BT Batsford, 1978; £5.95; pp218, index, bib, notes) -- The first lady of fairylore once again gives us a fascinating and informative distillation of her considerable scholarship and experience from a lifetime's wandering down the byways of folklore. After her recent Dictionary of Fairies (1976), Dr Briggs returns to the themes she studied in Fairies in Tradition and Literature (1967; RKP 1977): hosts and trooping fairies; fairy midwives and changelings; fairy wives and lovers; fairy homes and types; house-spirits and helpful fairies; fairy morality and gifts; fairy games; and beliefs about the origins of fairies.

One is struck by the similarities in many of the elements of fairy traditions to other phenomena in our studies; eg the abductions of mortals and the 'supernatural' lapse of time in Fairyland, first studied by Hartland in 1850, and which seems to have been translated without significant divergence into the modern psychomythology of abductions by UFO-entities. UFO studies, as well as the fields of religious visions, paranormal phenomena, spiritualist phenomena etc still have no agreeable method for dealing with anecdotal evidence - no effective way for comparative study of the subjective testimony of witnesses - and it is here that we might learn something from the folklorists. Disregarding (for the moment) whether fairies can be said to have a 'hard' objective existence, tales or accounts are evaluated by analysing them into their component themes and motifs, each allocated its own code. Dr Briggs usually includes in her books a list of these numerical codes, not only to identify, quickly, the recurring patterns of experience or detail, but also to serve brilliantly as a finely tuned index to story detail...thus, as a recurring motif, weird time distortion during an abduction is F377, or

---

'As phenomenalists, we accept everything; we believe nothing absolutely; we do not explain.'

Robert J. M. Rickard and John Michell

PHENOMENA

A Book of Wonders

fairies taking mortals up into the air is F329.3, etc. The coding structure was pioneered by Stith Thompson in 1966 and is now used internationally. Surely it is not impossible to adopt or devise a similar system to show up comparable motifs from other realms of experience (for example in terms of UFOlogy or religious experiences, F377 might apply respectively to a trip to 'another planet' or to heaven; and F329.3 (again respectively) might refer to rising in an anti-gravity beam or to levitation. So I mention this to show that fairy studies have many aspects from which we might profit - and if they help us make as fine a contribution to our own field as Dr Briggs does to hers it must be for the better.

'The Vanishing People' of the title are the fairies themselves, referring not only to their tricks upon the sight of mortals, but also to the fact that they are seen by far fewer people in this material age - but we are assured they are still there. Despite Dr Briggs attention to detail, general readers and those new to fairylore will not be put off. On the contrary, this book should delight all who have the slightest curiosity.   RJMR

Needles of Stone by Tom Graves (Turnstone, 1978; £4.95; pp213; figs, refs, ind) Having dealt with the practical techniques and applications of dowsing in his first book, Tom Graves moves on in his second to discuss its wider implications and correlations to a number of diverse fields, attempting to build up a coherent model of the 'Earth-energy' network and its relation to our psycho-physical environment. Writing in an easy, informal style, he provides a summary of recent dowsing research on terrestrial energy-paths and their connection with sacred sites, drawing on his own work and that of Underwood, Lethbridge, et al. From there, he becomes extremely eclectic, pulling together material on acupuncture, feng shui, energy fields, weather control, ghosts, spirits, demons and, to a lesser extent, Fortean phenomena; finally arriving at a vision of the 'living body of the Earth' criss-crossed by lines of energy analogous to acupuncture-meridians in the human body; and 'controlled' by megaliths and stone circles

analogous to acupuncture's needles.

The book has much to recommend it, but it has its faults too. It is well-illustrated, and well-referenced for the most part, although some of the material from 'other dowsers' seems little more than hearsay and speculation. The living-body model he constructs makes some sense as far as it goes, though Graves makes little attempt to extend it beyond the British Isles. There are points in the argument that need further investigation and clarification (as Graves admits) and such work would certainly be worthwhile. But there are places where I personally feel that he may only have drawn supportive evidence from sources which could just as easily have supplied a totally opposing point of view...

I think especially of feng shui, a quagmire of contradictions that positively invites fools to rush in (I speak as one with mud on my boots). Nonetheless, I feel the book has considerable value... though only time and further research will tell if its central thesis is valid.   SM

Strange Planet: vol E2 - compiled by William R Corliss (Sourcebook Project, Glen Arm, MD 21057, USA; $8.95, pp269, indexes, illos) -- The latest volume in Corliss' established and vital reference series is the second dealing with geological subjects. Its loose leaf/ring binder format and the cumulative numbering of cases allows the collation of material from several volumes under specific subheadings, as the series expands. This volume includes key source material (much of it from rare or unobtainable sources) on: fossil records of mass animal deaths, living toads in the hearts of rocks, sea-level changes, natural nuclear reactors, petrifying springs, myths of deluge, magnetic anomalies, spherical & cylindrical rocks, curious markings and impressions in rocks, tektites etc, ringing rocks, rambling rocks, 'inverted' strata, submarine canyons, craters and mounds, continental drift and topographical changes, etc. Once again it's worth saying that every library (from institutions to schools) ought to have a set of Sourcebooks.   RJMR

paperbacks

Sowers of Thunder by Anthony Roberts (Rider, 1978; £3.75, pp194, index, bib, apndxs, illos) — I've been looking forward to Tony's book for a long time, and its been worth it. Tony is a passionate advocate of Blake's vision of Albion and fascinated by the ideas of ancient races, sunken lands and mystical forces. This book examines the figure of the giant in myth, legend, and history, and is impressively researched, with chapters on gigantic hill-figures, the giant legends attatched to standing stones and ancient sites, and to the freakish giants of flesh and blood. But one can tell that it's the idea of giants that attracts Tony and there is considerable running discussion of the giant archetype as a power and energy motif in the unconscious   - and appropriately, the Albion giant in turn has evolved into a symbol of the revitalizing forces of the Earth mysteries. Tony's writing has never been clearer, and caught up in his own poetic insight, becomes a pleasure to read, and as informative and entertaining as Tony hopes it will be in his introduction. Although some of the subject matter overlaps with the exhibits of the von Däniken school, in that speculations are offered upon sunken Atlantis, the nature of the Elder Gods and their litter of artificial and natural monuments, Tony Roberts' appeals to the spirit where the former leave only vacuum. Tony also coins a new word, 'geomythics', describing the interaction between mystical topography, folklore, religion, anthropology and the physical landscape and its elements - more specifically it means the physical remnants, relics and records in our landscapes, antiquities and ancient sites of the existence in earlier times of the personifications of the raw powers of nature - and it is this dimension that makes it so much more than just a book about giants. Like all good symbols, the giant simultaneously reflects both an aspect of man and the greater external unknown he fears. Highly recommended as a good introductto all aspects of giantlore; with many illustrations; and appendices on Hoerbiger's occult giants of Ice and Fire, the giants of South America, Frank Buckland's encounter with a giant, and a useful list of the most significant and historically authentic giants. It deserves to be a giant success.   RJMR

The Testimony of the Shroud by Rodney Hoare (Quartet, 1978; £2.75 paper; pp128, index, bib, photos) - Shroud by Robert K Wilcox (Corgi, 1978; 85p, pp193, index, bib, photos) -- Both books cover the same ground - the known history of the Shroud of Turin, the representation of a body said to be Christ's, the analysis and experimentation, and tales of mystery and miracles. Both books have faults. The first is written from an uncompromising conviction the Shroud is the 'Fifth Gospel' - the second, more popularly sceptical, and contains slightly more interesting information.   RJMR

The Psychic Powers of Animals by Bill Schul (Coronet, 1978; 85p; pp176, index, bib) -- Having plundered pyramids and plants, its the animals' turn, but this collection of curiosa about our feathered, furred and scaley friends is competent, well written and often informative (though poorly referenced for those who wish to study seriously). Schul discusses many interesting aspects of animal navigation, ESP in animals, dogs and cats finding their masters across great distances, the intelligence of animals, special relationships between certain people and animals, animals that think and reason, and others who love being inside meditation pyramids, dolphins as super-beings, and of course the whole field of psychic qualities of animals, including whether they have souls etc. Well worth a read, but caveat emptor! RJMR

The Tumour in the Whale by Rodney Dale (Wyndham Universal, 1978; 75p, pp169, index, bib) -- Ken Campbell wrote a play based on 'Barroom Tales', those apocryphal stories that seem to crop up from all angles, in all countries, that happen to a friend of a friend etc. Dale has collected hundreds of such anecdotes, written them up in an entertaining style that relishes every irony and twist of grim humour, and illustrated them with Bill Tidy's brilliant, incisive and funny drawings. These modern folktales range from the ancient 'Jonah in the whale' types, to the stolen car with Granny's corpse on the roofrack; from mistaking a relative's ashes for packet soup in wartime, to microwave ovens cooking your kidneys; from bromide in the tea to the multiple

murder of Rasputin; myths, coincidences, fantastic and improbable events (many of them distinctly Fortean) and the echo of themes from fiction in reallife events. The only trouble is that Dale is so bent on getting laughs from the material (quite successfully too!) that he seems to scorn the idea that such events have ever happened in 'real' life. For example, entombed toads - he gives a few stories, but says "unfortunately" toads need, food and water to survive, and quotes William Buckland's famous (and in my view inconclusive) failure to confirm the toad's survival of entombment by experiment. And so the case is, like many others here, laughed out of court - rather uneasily, I feel. As we well know, who collect such material, there are impressive quantities of authentic accounts of living animals embedded in the hearts of solid rock. Dale is just as glib in dismissing SHC - but then he is citing Michael Harrison's error-filled book. On the plus side Dale has incorporated the apocryphal tales noticed by Katherine Briggs in her works on British folktales, and the efforts of the scholarly folklorists. However don't let my niggles put you off - this would make an excellent and amusing present for any Fortean, even if they don't go along with the maxim Dale quotes from Voltaire about the necessity of "being interesting rather than being exact..."   RJMR

The New Apocrypha by John Sladek (Panther, 1978; £1.50, pp376, index, bib, notes, illos) -- I didn't like this book when it came out in hardback in 1973, because of its expressed intention to debunk "myths and mythmakers". I'm more mellow now but I still think Sladek has a vindictive streak that fails him in his attempt to produce a sequel and update on Martin Gardner's excellent Fads & Fallacies in the Name of Science (Dover, 1957). Like Rodney Dale, Sladek writes well (he is an SF author) and wittily, and at the expense of his material, but unlike Dale he has comtempt for (not delight in) human gullibility. The book is the result of a prodigious feat of reading, surveying the twilight world of quackery, pseudo-science, food-fetishists, curious cults, von Däniken, UFOs, parapsychology, Lobsang Rampa and much more - however, despite his cleverness and erudition Sladek does not illuminate these beliefs much nor the obviously universal need for them. Interestingly, as in Gardner, Charles Fort is one of the few to emerge relatively unscathed (reluctant praise of sorts!) although his followers come in for some stick. **The New Apocrypha** deserves to be read by every Fortean as a critical study of human gullibility in areas of interest to us. Sladek also includes an extensive bibliography.   RJMR

Occultism Update edited by Leslie Shepard (Gale Research Co, Book Tower, Detroit, MI 48226, USA) — Last issue we reviewed Leslie Shepard's mammoth new **Encyclopedia of Occultism & Parapsychology**, sure to become mandatory for consultations on all aspects of psychic matters from personalities to subjects, terms and publications. **Occultism Update** is the first of four supplements to be issued, containing corrections, additions and new developments. After four issues the additional data will be incorporated into a new edition of the **Encyclopedia**. At ₤30.00 for the four issues, the **Update** seems rather expensive and is probably aimed at institutions and libraries, who should be encouraged at every opportunity to purchase the **Encyclopedia** - if this is unobtainable through normal book buying channels, apply directly to Gale at the above address. **Update 1** (1978) contains 51 pages of entries to supplement or expand the main listing, and 10 pages of cross-referenced index. Recommended (if you can afford it). **RR**

journals

We would be obliged if readers writing to addresses or answering adverts found in our pages would say they saw the information in *Fortean Times*. It helps us spread the word, and judge the effectiveness of these services.

Pursuit 43 (Summer 1978) - beamed power for starships; comments on TJ Constable's notions of UFOs as 'aerial lifeforms'; Clark and Davidson on cattle mutilations; underground cities; the physics of physics; phenomenological riddles; Schadewald on Fortean fakes; Eberhart on 'Witchcraft & Weather Modification' pt2; Larry Arnold on fiery phantoms of the sea; and more. Pursuit is published quarterly by SITU (Membership Services, RFD 5, Gales Ferry, CT 06335, USA) at ₤10.00/yr (or overseas ₤12.50 surface, or ₤15.00 air).

INFO Journal 29 (May/June 1978)- 19th C airship mystery; UFO notes; Fortean notes; the 'Force' of Star Wars; Monster Watch; Silbury Hill; Eberhart's 'Outline of Fortean Knowledge' & sug-

gested shelf arrangement for Fortean libraries. 30 (July/Aug) - conference on saquatch; Turin Shroud; Fortean notes. INFO: 7317 Baltimore Ave, College Park, MD 20740, USA. single copies ₤1.75/90p - published bimonthly at ₤10.00/£5.00/yr.

CHAOS: The Review of the Damned 1:1 - At last after much planning X's project to publish discussion of Fort's source material, and to reprint the original material itself, gets off the ground. The first issue deals with the torpidity of bats; ball lightning; the spontaneous burning of Countess Baudi (or Bandi?); Fort's letter to the NYT on 'Visitors from Other Worlds'written in 1924; observations on 'Vulcan'; the Colvocoresses'murder' in which there was no sign of a bullets passage thru' the clothes; falls of animals; the Alaskan city mirages and others; the various 'heights' of Mt Elias. X is to be congratulated on this restrained scholarly and invaluable contribution to Fortean studies, and I earnestly urge you all to subscribe to Chaos and ensure its survival - published 8 times a year: Canada ₤15.00; USA ₤ 3.50; UK £7.00; all others remit Canada rate: to Mr X, Box 1598, Kingston, Ontario K7L 5C8, Canada.
    X also publishes the very excellent Fortean newsletter **Res Bureaux Bulletin** available on exchange or contributions of information or clippings.

SIS Review, basically a forum for papers on Velikovskyan subjects - the Society for Interdisciplinary Studies also put out a members' newsletter called **Workshop** for news and active discussions and'informal' articles. SISR 3:1 (Summer 1978) is a summary of their recent successful conference in Glasgow, reprinting a few of the papers. One of particular interest to Forteans is Dr HA Meynell's 'Philosophy for Interdisciplinary Studies'. Membership for all interested in the serious study of catastrophist subjects is £8.00/₤16.00, or write for info to: Alan Hooker, 11 Broad Oak, Corseley Rd, Groombridge, Sussex.

Vestigia Newsletter - 2:1 (Spring 1978) experiments and results of 'spirit photography', plus discussion on ghost lights, Kirlian photos and polt cases (all under investigation by this vigorous outfit); 2:2 (Summer 1978) Vestigia's own statistical study of UFO patterns, more on 'lights'; 2:3 (Fall 1978) 'Spook light' update, plus aerial booms. Vestigia, one of the most active groups today, publish results of their investigations in VN - for more info write: Vestigia, RD 2 Brookwood Rd, Stanhope, NJ 07874, USA.

Stigmata - a newsletter on the investigation of the animal mutilation mystery - 4 (Summer 1978) contains a summary of reports and investigations so far this year. The whole of Project Stigma is being reorganized and revitalized, and after a hiatus will publish Stigmata in a new format from Jan 1979. Interested? Write: Project Stigma, Box 1094, Paris, TX 75460, USA.

Journal of Meteorology - indispensible to the Fortean interested in weather phenomena etc - 3:30 (July/Aug '78) worldwide disasters for April & May, seafreeze, waterspouts, cold & dry spells; 3:31 (Sept '78) worldwide disasters for June, drought & smog, ball lightning, severe frost and 'anticrepuscular' rays; 3:32 (Oct '78) worldwide disasters for July, the Newmarket tornado and others, the great Indian cyclone, floods & storms. For details write: JMet, Cockhill House, Trowbridge BA14 9BG.

EVP Newsletter devoted to experiments, discussion and news on the subject of 'electronic voice phenomena'. Editor Alan Cleaver will have an article on the subject in a forthcoming FT, but briefly EVP concerns the detection of coherent voices through various electronic methods; voices that are unaccountable since many have been positively identified as those of departed relatives! Others claim the voices emanate from the human unconscious or even contact with truly alien entities! The EVP Newsletter is

still fairly small and would benefit from your support - published monthly at £1.20/yr from Alan Cleaver: 72 Gladys Ave, North End, Portsmouth PO2 9BQ. EVPN is keeping abreast of developments in the subject - including the boggling prospect of establishing communication. Recommended!

The Ley Hunter 81 - a reader's issue packed with letters on a variety of issues, plus 'A Cotswold Ley' study, & report on the Moot '78; 82 - 'Old games & rituals'; Dr Derek Banks begins his discussion of theories of reality; and much much more . TLH is essential for coverage of the whole range of 'Earth Mysteries'. Bimonthly at £3.00 /yr (UK & Europe only), elsewhere £4.50 /$9.00 airmail. TLH: Box 152, London N10 1EP.

Institute of Geomantic Research, have a range of publications - the Journal of Geomancy 2:4 coldharbours, Bury St Edmunds zodiac, Wandlebury, the myth of Alfred Watkins' vision, Masonic France, Andover church alignments, plus index for vol 2. 3:1 moves to FT-type format, Winchester zodiac, Chephren's pyramid, telluric lines, John Michell on Watkins' vision, how wide is a ley? Glasgow 'druids'' temple, and more. JoG is £3.00/yr. IGR also publish occasional papers; no11 is Nigel Pennick on 'Ritual Magic in the Church of England', no12 is a reprint of an article by J Edkins the missionary on 'Feng Shui' (these papers 30p & 45p respectively). IGR are also experimenting with another general ancient mysteries mag, called Albion - I hope they aren't over stretching themselves? For more info write IGR, 142 Pheasant Rise, Bar Hill, Cambridge CB3 8SD.

The UFO Examiner - a new (to me) journal for 'private UFO investigations' - a UFO over an aircraft carrier in 1958, a Canadian UFO photo, the meteor of Jan 28, a Mt Pleasant UFO from 1920, sightings & news, did Carter see a UFO? report from France - for details see the ad on this page.

Flying Saucer Review 24:2 (Aug 1978) ufonauts plead for water in S Africa, 1951; encounter at Parkstone, Dorset; Puerto Rican encounters; sighting at Luke AF base; encounters at Risley, Cheshire, Spain, London; angel-hair case. FSR, West Malling, Maidstone, Kent.

*** We regret that many books, paperbacks and periodicals have to be held over to next issue - Ed ***

We have quite a collection of lightning deaths from the past few years, but
to trot them all out would be fairly boring.
The same goes for a long list of people
struck by lightning who got away with it.
Before moving on to a small selection
of some of the bizarre pranks of lightning from these lists, I'd just like to
note the 'filler' in the Daily Mail 15
February 1978, to the effect that retired park ranger, Roy C Sullivan, of
Virginia, had "just been struck by lightning for the seventh time in his life."
In fact the incident happened about 7
months earlier, in July 1977 - surely it
couldn't have taken that long to reach
British newspapers? Back in his fifth
hit (see INFO Journal 11) in 1973, the
force blew his boots off...and that same
year another bolt-struck unfortunate was
receiving offers to appear at Las Vegas
after lightning had welded the fly zip
on his trousers - see Daily Mail 20 June
1973. We'll have some recent cases, in
order...
Daily Mail 11 Sept 1975 - a bolt
vaporized electrical wiring on its way
to a fridge, killing a young housewife
in Knoxville, Iowa, even though she was
standing on a rubber-backed carpet. More
fortunately, the baby Vietnamese orphan
she was holding at the time miraculously
remained unharmed.
Sunday People 16 May 1976 - that on
15 May Freda Bell, of High Green Farm,
Middleton, Cumbria, had just tucked her
kids in bed and begun her ironing as a
storm began. "A flash of lightning ripped down the iron, bounced across to the
iron fireplace guard, then hit me," she
said. "I was hurled across the room and
found that the lightning had torn through
my overall, ripped off my trousers and
burned off my tights to below the knee
blistering my legs. (Cr: Nigel Watson.)
We noted at the time that Nature had only
recently printed an account of a ball
lightning attacking a woman in a kitchen

(see Nature 15 Apr 1976.) - but we'll
give this and other ball lightning cases
next time we run this heading.
Daily Mirror 22 March 1977 - Paula
Burgoyne, 20, walking on Dartmoor with
her brother Andrew, 13, received burns
on 40% of her body when lightning struck
a fancy buckle on one of her shoes. The
blast hurled both of them off their feet,
and Andrew was knocked unconscious when
his head hit a rock. When he came to he
couldn't walk, and so crawled to a car
park where the rest of their family were
waiting for them. They found Paula - "All
her clothing had been torn off and she
was burned black from head to foot." -
and rushed her to hospital, alive but
seriously ill.
Daily Mail and other papers for 12
April 1977 - John Prenderghast, 23, was
hurled backwards through the air when a
flash of lightning burned a hole through
one of his boots and three layers of
socks. His companion, Brian Peters, had
been sheltering from the wind, crouched
down, was also knocked over by the blast.
He dragged John to shelter, carried him
for five hours back to camp and alerted
a rescue team in the morning. (Cr: Peter
Rogerson.) They were on the peak of
Affric, Invernessshire, when John was
aghast and taken aback - on 11 April.
Daily Mail and other papers for 2 May
1977 - in a similar incident to the previous one, Angela Walls, 16, was blasted
unconscious by lightning that apparently
pierced a tin in her rucksack and burned
her clothes off her back. Strange, all
this burning of clothes off young ladies!
Some of her 24-strong party were also
thrown to the ground, but recovered their
wits enough to successfully revive the
girl with the kiss of life. This took
place on the 1st of May - a maiden sacrifice? - on Moal Siabod, Snowdonia. In
her own account, Angela mentions that
prior to the blast there was a "terrible
hailstorm..." (Cr: Peter Rogerson.)

Daily Mirror 1 July 1977 - that a Greek sentry on the Bulgarian border was killed when lightning struck his bayonet.

Daily Mail 20 July 1977 - that on 14 June, Kevin Scott, 18, was killed while crossing a playing field, in St Helens, Merseyside, when lightning struck the fashionable neck chain he was wearing. At the inquest a police constable said that 2 three inch deep holes were found near the body. In the **Daily Mirror** account (same date) the PC said: "They were probably caused by the heels of the boy's shoes pushing into the ground." !!! (Cr: Paul Screeton, Peter Rogerson.)

Sunday Express 28 August 1977 - Frank Gilbert, 44, had just prepared 200lbs of dynamite for blasting a section of a new road near Birmingham, Alabama...and, yes you guessed, lightning struck it! He said: "Normally I wouldn't go anywhere near explosives during a storm, but this one rolled in suddenly." The very first flash found Frank's dynamite. He was hurled 20ft into the air and was immediately buried by a huge heap of rubble and earth. In his sudden take-off Frank had the foresight to pull his hardhat down over his face, and when he was buried the air pocket kept him alive until he was rescued. (Cr: Peter Rogerson.)

Daily Telegraph 15 Sept 1977 - one for you, Larry! There were 8 people sitting around the coffin of a dead man, in San Foa, Northern Italy, in a wake that they'll remember for a looong time locally. Lightning blasted through the wall of the house and set fire to the body's hair and clothes as it lay in the open coffin, on 14 Sept. (Cr: V Martin.)

Lincoln Star (Nebraska) 20 & 26 May 1978 - two strange holes found in a field at Humphrey, NB, were said to be caused by lightning (see above to another case of a double lightning hole). In this case the holes measured 5" dia and 20ft deep, and 3" dia and 7ft deep, and lay in an oval-shaped impression with a white powder around the rim of each hole. Radiation equipment indicated there was metal at the bottom of the 7ft hole, but nothing could be found. UFO buffs, Civil Defense and US Army investigators all had a look, but the man whose explanation was deemed most plausible was John Say, a chemistry prof at Norfolk and a member of MUFON, who said the holes were most probably made by lightning, the white stuff being fused silica. But surely lightning penetrating the sandy ground (and none of the reports say specifically the ground was sandy) enough to fuse

silica grains into a mass, would leave the mass there for all to see? These fused masses can achieve wondrous lengths and shapes and look rather like a tree-root system made out of knobbly coral - an astonishing example can be seen in a photo in Vietmeister's **The Lightning Book** (MIT Press, I think; my copy is packed away somewhere!) - called 'fulgurites'. They shouldn't just vanish or vaporize - but the Humphrey holes were empty! (Cr: Joe Swatek).

Sunday Express 30 July 1978 - tells of an Austrian student, Georg Brachmayer, who was very fond of a "good luck" crucifix he wore around his neck. "Last week" as he drove cattle across a field at his parent's farm at Forolach, lightning hit the crucifix killing him. It also burned an imprint of the crucifix into his chest before melting it. Also **Post-Bulletin** (Rochester, Minn) 2 Sept (Cr: Mark Hall.)

We'll close with a tale which is almost apocryphal. Soon after the installation of COSMO, a brand new £5 million computer, in the Meteorological Office building at Bracknell, Berks, it was struck by lightning - or at least lightning blew its fuses (**The Sun** 16 June 1977). But then the weathermen should be used to the jolly japes of its more omnipotent (if cranky) namesake! A month after being zapped, COSMO forecast a very damp August (see Aug 17 in our 'Diary' this issue) - and sure enough fire trucks were called to the Met Office on Aug 17 to pump 4ft of water from their basement. Haven't they realized yet that something up there's hinting at greater mysteries! **Daily Mirror** 18 August 1977.

RJMR

We are pleased to present, in this column, a lengthy examination, by Paul Begg, of the infamous incident from the First World War in which cloud UFOs allegedly kidnapped a whole regiment. This mysterious disappearance of a large number of men, apparently well witnessed, has been told and retold by many esteemed UFO and Fortean writers, and so cannot be dismissed lightly.

That Paul was able to clear up the main misunderstandings in this tale shows the virtue of checking back to original or contemporary sources where possible. It is a shame that a small band of dedicated researchers, eager to probe the genuine mysteries that abound in the records and archives, have to first spend precious time in correcting the sloppy or non-existent research of the more popular authors who preceded them. There are so many errors and sheer fabrications in current circulation that such a suspicious and slow progress through the minefield of modern mysteries is unfortunately necessary, as, at any step, an unchecked fact or story may treacherously blow up in our own faces.

However, in this case, when the event is restored to verisimilitude, we are no nearer an answer, for in clearing up one mystery, Paul has uncovered other, more original, unanswered questions.

THE FIRST-FOURTH NORFOLK & THE KIDNAPPING CLOUD
by Paul Begg

The disappearance of the First-Fourth Norfolk 'Regiment', allegedly on 21 August 1915, during the Dardanelles Campaign, has been told many times, usually with reference to the following signed affidavit:

'The following is an account of a strange incident that happened on . . . [see note 1] . . . in the morning during the severest and final period of the fighting which took place on Hill 60, Suvla Bay, ANZAC.

The day broke clear, without a cloud in sight, as any beautiful Mediterranean day could be expected to be. The exception, however, was a number of perhaps six or eight 'loaf-of-bread' shaped clouds — all shaped exactly alike — which were hovering over Hill 60. It was noticed that, in spite of a four or five mile an hour breeze from the south, these clouds did not alter their position in any shape or form, nor did they drift away under the influence

of the breeze. They were hovering at an elevation of about 60 degrees as seen from our observation point 500 feet up. Also, stationary and resting on the ground right underneath this group of clouds was a similar cloud in shape, measuring about 800 feet in length, 220 feet in height and 200 feet in width. This cloud was absolutely dense, solid looking in structure, and positioned about 14 to 18 chains from the fighting in British-held territory. All this was observed by 22 men of No. 3 Section of No. 1 Field Company, New Zealand Engineers, including myself, from our trenches on Rhododendron Spur, approximately 2,500 yards south-west of the cloud on the ground. Our vantage point was overlooking Hill 60 by about 300 feet. As it turned out later, this singular cloud was straddling a dry creek bed or sunken road (Kaiajik Dere) and we had a perfect view of the cloud's sides and ends as it rested on the ground. Its colour was a light grey, as was the colour of the other clouds.

A British Regiment, the First-Fourth Norfolk, of several hundred men, was seen marching up this sunken road or creek towards Hill 60. However, when they arrived at this cloud, they marched straight into it, with no hesitation, but no-one ever came out to deploy and fight at Hill 60. About an hour later, after the last of the file had disappeared into it, this cloud very unobtrusively lifted off the ground and, like any cloud or fog would, rose slowly until it joined the other similar clouds which were mentioned in the beginning of this account. On viewing them again, they all looked alike 'as peas in a pod'. All this time, the clouds had been hovering in the same place, but as soon as the singular cloud had risen to their level, they all moved away northward, i.e., towards Thrace (Bulgaria). In a matter of three quarters of an hour they had all disappeared from view.

The Regiment mentioned is posted as missing or 'wiped out' and on Turkey surrendering in 1918, the first thing Britain demanded of Turkey was the return of this Regiment. Turkey replied that she had neither captured this Regiment, nor made contact with it, and did not know that it existed. A British Regiment in 1914-1918 consisted of any number between 800 and 4,000 men. Those who observed this incident vouch for the fact that Turkey never captured the regiment nor made contact with it.

We, the undersigned, although late in time, that is the 50th Jubilee of the ANZAC landing, declare that the above described incident is true in every word.

Signed by witnesses:
4/165 Sapper F. Reichardt, Matata, Bay
of Plenty.
13/416 Sapper R. Newnes, 157 King Street,
Cambridge.
J.L. Newman, 75 Freyburg Street, Octu-
moctai, Tauranga.' [1]

It is further claimed by Steiger and Whritenour, that a complete statement of the disappearance is recorded in an official history of the Gallipoli Campaign:

'They (the First-Fourth Norfolk Regiment) were swallowed up by an unseasonable fog. This fog reflected the sun's rays in such a manner that artillery observers were dazzled by its brilliance and were unable to fire in support. The two hundred and fifty men were never seen or heard of again'. [2]

The story was told on the occasion of the 50th Jubilee of the ANZAC landing, in fact at an old comrades at arms reunion on April 25, 1965 by Sapper Reichardt, who subsequently got two friends 'and fellow witnesses to sign the affidavit testifying to the truth of the story. This affidavit was printed first in the New Zealand journal *Spaceview* [1] , reprinted 6 months later in the American magazine *Flying Saucers* [3] , and thereafter reprinted in full or quoted by many noted UFO writers — Brad Steiger [2, 4], Jacques Vallée [5] , John Keel [6] , Ralph Blum [7] , Brinsley Le Poer Trench [8] , Charles Berlitz [9] — and others. (There is some suggestion that the tale has a pre-*Spaceview* origin, but I have been unable to trace it.) [10] .

Now for the big shock! To begin with, the First-Fourth Norfolk was not — repeat, *not* — a Regiment; it was a battalion within the Royal Norfolk Regiment. That it has been consistently called a Regiment is evidence that not one of the many writers who have told the tale have bothered to check the facts. Secondly, the 1/4th did not disappear at Gallipoli in August 1915 or at any time or place thereafter. Evidence of their existence during and after August can be found at the Imperial War Museum in London, where you can see a run of manuscripts, battalion orders and messages, even a ration indent for 545 men, all dated August 30 [11] . And in December 1915 the 1/4th were evacuated to Egypt to rebuild strength and numbers before being sent to another theatre of war.

However, whilst the 1/4th Norfolk did not vanish, it is an undisputed fact that the sister battalion, the First-Fifth Norfolk did — but not on the date or in the manner ascribed to the 1/4th. If Reichardt saw any Norfolk vanish, they could only have been from the 1/5th — so perhaps there could be some truth in his incredible tale. On, then, to mystery number two: The First-*Fifth* Norfolk.

Before progressing further it will be of value if we get the feel of and the background to this event [12] . The geography first: The Aegean is connected to the Sea of Marmara by the Dardanelles (the ancient Hellespont), a long narrow channel extending for about 40 miles along the Gallipoli Peninsula. Running for about a mile along the west coast of the Peninsula is Suvla Bay, beyond which is a large Salt Lake (dry in summer and reflecting the sun in a harsh glare), and beyond

that Suvla Plain.

From the end of April until October the sun burns down relentlessly; the flowers fade, the grass withers, and the earth is turned a scorched yellow-brown. The hard, sun-baked ground of Suvla Plain was dissected by dried water courses and broken here and there by a few stunted olive trees. In the distance a semi-circle of bleak hills stretch from north to south, giving Suvla Plain the appearance of a giant natural arena. To the north is Kiretch Tepe, to the east the twin heights of Kavak Tepe and Tekke Tepe, and to the south the Sari Bair range.

Sari Bair, Turkish for 'Yellow Ridge', has three summits, all about 1000 feet high and separated from one another by about ½-mile of undulating crest line. The northern peak is called Koya Chemen Tepe, the next is Besim Tepe (known to the British as Hill Q), and the third is Chunuk Bair. About ½-mile to the north of Chunuk Bair is Hill 60, the small hillock towards which Reichardt claims the Norfolk were marching when they vanished. A further 3 miles to the north is a cultivated area known as Kuchuk Anafarta Ova, the scene of the 1/5 Norfolk's disappearance.

The most practical route to the summit of Chunuk Bair is along a spur which the Allies called Rhododendron Spur after the red flowers which blazed along it during the early days of the campaign. It was on this spur that Reichardt claims to have been entrenched when he witnessed the disappearance.

Now let's turn our attention to the events leading up to the First-Fifth's disappearance.

When the Norfolk battalions (1/4th and 1/5th) arrived at Suvla on August 10 (as part of the 163rd Brigade of the 54th Division) the Allies were on the verge of defeat and would in fact evacuate the Peninsula before December. However, whilst it was not normal practice to plunge 'green' troops into battle without first giving them time in a quiet sector to grow accustomed to combat, Sir Ian Hamilton, Commander-in-Chief of the Meditteranean Expeditionary Force, believed that a major offensive by fresh troops would turn the tide of the campaign. He envisaged a bold, sweeping assault on Kavak Tepe and Tekke Tepe, the twin heights forming the central slice of the mountains dominating Suvla Plain, and proposed that on August 12, the 163rd Brigade should advance and clear the cultivated area Kuchuk Anafarta Ova of enemy snipers. During the night the rest of the Division would advance as far as the foothills of Kavak and Tekke Tepe, where they would wait until dawn on August 13, then attack the mountain heights.

At 4.45 pm on August 12, 1915, the Brigade began their advance. Sir Ian Hamilton later described what happened in a dispatch to Lord Kitchener, the Secretary of State for War:

'In the course of the fight . . . there happened a very mysterious thing . . . The First-Fifth Norfolks were on the right of the line, and found themselves for the moment less strongly opposed than the rest of the brigade. Against the yielding forces of the enemy, Colonel Sir H. Beauchamp, a bold, self-confident officer, eagerly pressed forward, followed by the best part of the battalion. The fighting grew hotter, and the ground became

more wooded and broken . . . But the Colonel, with 16 officers and 250 men, still kept pushing on, driving the enemy before him . . . Nothing more was seen or heard of any of them. They charged into the forest and were lost to sight or sound. Not one of them ever came back [13].'

267 men — vanished! Could these have been the men Reichardt saw kidnapped by a strange cloud?

This disappearance of 267 members of the 1/5th Norfolk (not even the battalion you will note) is a well documented event and there are a number of readily available accounts [12] including a substantially accurate version by Harold T. Wilkins [14], and it is well known that they did not totally vanish.

In 1919 a soldier of the occupation forces was touring the battlefield when he found a badge of the Royal Norfolk Regiment. Following inquiries it was learned that a Turkish farmer, returning to his property after the fighting, found the decomposing bodies of British soldiers strewn over his land, many within his farmhouse. He dumped the bodies in a nearby ravine, where they were later found.

Writing on September 23, 1919, the officer commanding the Graves Registration Unit in Gallipoli said: *'We have found the 5th Norfolk' [15]*.

He was slightly premature. Of the 180 bodies found, only 122 were 1/5th Norfolk, and only two could be positively identified, 240436 Cpl J.A. Barnaby and 1028 Pte W. Carter (not Cotter as stated in the *History of the Norfolk Regiment* and elsewhere [15, 16]. They are buried along with 114 unidentified Norfolk in Anzac Cemetary (6 bodies would appear to have been buried elsewhere) and their names recorded on the Helles Memorial [16].

Only 122 of 266 men were found, therefore more than half of those who vanished remain unaccounted for. Could *these* have been the men seen by Reichardt? Before answering that question we should perhaps turn our attention to the New Zealanders, upon whose credibility the whole story of the kidnapping cloud is based.

Who was Reichardt? Sapper 4/165A Frederick Reichardt was a sailor enlisted in the United Kingdom Section of the New Zealand Expeditionary Force on October 8, 1915, as a member of No. 3 Section, First Divisional Field Company, New Zealand Engineers, and he embarked for Gallipoli on April 12, 1915.

According to the *War Diary* of the First Divisional Field Company [17], Reichardt's Section was transferred to Rhododenron Spur, on August 13, Therefore, Reichardt was *not* on the Spur when the 1/5th attacked the day before. However, he could have been sent there during the afternoon of the 12th in order to begin work there at dawn on the 13th [18].

Part of the Royal Norfolk Regiment *did* vanish during that month but Reichardt named the wrong battalion (1/4th) and the wrong date (August 21). Is it possible that those Norfolk, disorientated and tired, totally new to Gallipoli and unfamiliar with the terrain, began marching towards Hill 60 and marched into a cloud. Reichardt was there, we were not. Are we justified in calling him a liar?

Mr I.C. MacGibbon, of the New Zealand Defence Liaison Office, has phrased the pertinent central issues, in his letter of 27 December 1974:

'No-one has been able to explain the disappearance of the 1/5th Norfolks, which certainly occurred. If Reichardt and his fellow Gallipoli veterans saw a 'bread-shaped cloud of light grey colour' lower itself into the path of the 1/5th Norfolks, why did they wait until 1965 before signing an affidavit to this effect? Would it not have been in order to have reported such an unusual occurrence to an officer at the time? or at least when the mystery could not be solved later? Possibly, however, they may have feared ridicule'. [18]

The strange 'kidnapping' cloud is not the only solution to the fate of the 1/5th Norfolk. We know that two, a Captain Coxon and Lieutenant C.S. Fawkes, were taken prisoner and spent the rest of the war in captivity in Asia Minor [11]. Other Norfolk men no doubt suffered a similar fate and Turkish prison camps being notorious for their appalling conditions, it is unlikely that many sick or wounded men would have survived. Moreover, conditions generally at Gallipoli were disgusting. An example is the often mentioned fact that bodies lay about in great numbers and burial was rudimentary at best. It was not uncommon to feel the squelching softness of a hastily buried body underfoot or see the face or hands of a former comrade protruding from the ground. In short, the loss of over 100 men is far from remarkable! And strangely, many of the missing were probably never missing at all. Sir Ian Hamilton says [13] that after darkness fell many of those involved in the advance returned to camp having lost contact with their comrades during the heat of battle.

Is Reichardt's story complete fabrication? I think not. One of the dates given by Reichardt, August 21, is of particular interest. So, too, is the entry in the unspecified official history of the Gallipoli Campaign, regarding the strange meteorological phenomenon, alluded to by Steiger and Whritenour [2].

None of the official reports consulted by the present writer contain the alleged entry, but the following extract can be found in *The Final Report* of the Dardanelles Commission [13]:

'By some freak of nature Suvla Bay and Plain were wrapped in a strange mist . . . We had reckoned on the enemy's gunners being blinded by the declining sun'.

The similarity between this account and the one in the 'official history' will not pass unnoticed and it is surely more than mere coincidence that it appears on the page opposite the account of the Norfolk's August 12th advance. The entry refers to a totally unexpected mist which was unseasonable but in all other ways perfectly normal, which descended during the afternoon of August 21, the day of the greatest offensive (in terms of numbers) ever fought at Gallipoli. That afternoon, shortly before dark, Sir John Milbanke, V.C., led the Sherwood Rangers into the swirling, grey mist. The Turks, situated above the mist, saw the advance and annihilated the Sherwood Rangers.

Is it too much to suppose that Frederick Reichardt, on the occasion of an old comrades reunion and looking back over 50 years, confused the disappearance of the 1/5th Norfolk with the unseasonable mist and the destruction of the Sherwood Rangers? Frankly, I believe that this is most likely what happened.

In the final analysis, however, we don't know what happened to the 1/5th, but people do vanish in wartime. The Commonwealth War Graves Commission's memorials around the world bear the names of 771,982 Commonwealth dead of the two world wars who have no known grave [16]. When faced with such staggering numbers is the fate of 145 missing in one of the worst theatres of war imaginable really all that mysterious?

Paul Begg — 1978.

References

1) 'A Day to Remember in August 1915', *Spaceview* No. 45 (Sept. 1965), Henderson, New Zealand. There is some confusion concerning the precise date of the alleged kidnapping. The article gives nothing more precise than 'August 1915' despite alluding to 'the above date'. Vallee (see note 5) substitutes for these words a dateline 'Gallipoli, August 28, 1915', and then confuses the issue by citing the August 21 date. No-one seems really certain. Also, most accounts that retell the story place the kidnapping 'at' Anzac. ANZAC is not a place but an acronym for Australia and New Zealand Army Corps.

2) Brad Steiger & Joan Whritenour; *Flying Saucers are Hostile* (Universal-Tandem, London, 1967), p57f.

3) *Flying Saucers* No. 46 (March 1966); Palmer Publications Inc., Amhurst, Wisconsin.

4) Brad Steiger; *Strangers from the Sky,* (Tandem, London, 1966).

5) Jaques Vallee; *Passport to Magonia* (Henry Regnery Co, Chicago, 1969); (Neville Spearman, London, 1970) pp98-100; (Tandem, London, 1975).

6) John Keel; *Our Haunted Planet* (Fawcett, Greenwich, Conn, 1971) p201; (Neville Spearman, London, 1971); (Futura, London, 1975).

7) Ralph & Judy Blum; *Beyond Earth,* (Bantam, NY, 1972) pp61-64; (Phillips Publishing Co, Springfield, Mass, 1974) (Corgi, London, 1974).

8) Brinsley Le Poer Trench; *Mysterious Visitors* (Pan, London, 1973); (JM Dent, Canada, 1973).

9) Charles Berlitz; *Without a Trace* (Doubleday, NY, 1977); (Souvenir Press, London, 1977) pp149-151.

10) [Editor's note — Both Mr DB Nash (see note 11) and myself feel that the whole myth may have inadvertently begun with Harold T Wilkins' book (see note 14). Written in 1958, Wilkins correctly summarises the fate of the 1/5th Norfolks but makes no mention of UFOs here. However, as his later books *do* deal with UFOs, Wilkins' Fortean scholarship brought his researches to the attention of the UFO world. Clearly this supposition is not proved, and the true origin of this classic 'UFO-kidnap' story has yet to be tracked down to its . . er . . liar!]

11) *The Vanishing Norfolks* (Information Sheet No 6; Imperial War Museum, revised November 1977). Also, correspondence between Mr DB Nash, Deputy Head of the Imperial War Museum's Department of Printed Books and the author, and Bob Rickard, Editor of *Fortean Times.*

12) Many sources were used for background information but the following were most useful on the Norfolks' case:
Brig. Gen. CF Aspinal-Oglander; *Official History of the War, Military Operations, Gallipoli* vol 2 (Heineman, London, 1932).
Tim Carew; *The Royal Norfolk Regiment: The 9th Regiment of Foot* (Hamish Hamilton, London, 1967).
Robert R James; *Gallipoli* (Batsford, London, 1965); (Pan, London, 1974).
The Times History of the War vol. 2 (The Times, London 1916).

13) *Final Report of the Dardanelles Commission,* Cmd 371 (HMSO, London, 1917).

14) Harold T Wilkins; *Strange Mysteries of Time and Space* (Ace, NY, 1958) p159.

15) *History of the Norfolk Regiment.*

16) Commonwealth War Graves Commission; letter (25 January 1974) to author.

17) *War Diary, 1st Field Company,* War History WA 61/1 (National Archives, Wellington, New Zealand).

18) New Zealand Ministry of Defence; letters (16 Dec 1974, 26 March 1975) to the author from Mr. I.C. MacGibbon to whom special thanks are offered.
Mr MacGibbon did attempt to locate Reichardt, but Reichardt did not attend later reunions. MacGibbon could not trace him, so presumed him to be dead.

[The Editor would like to acknowledge here the efforts of the few other researchers, known to him, who attempted to untangle this enigma — Roger Sandell, Nigel Watson, and Ron Dobbins, who pointed out (in a letter to *INFO*, 30 June 1973) that the case was also touted by Edwards, Warren and Otto Binder, the last of whom changed the location to *Luvla Bay, Australia* (!), and upped the numbers missing to a round 1000!]

MERMAIDS

'Recently', a Philipino fisherman claimed to have met a mermaid on a moonlit night, and she helped him "secure a bountiful catch." Jacinto Fetalvero, 41, said she was very beautiful, with "amiable bluish eyes, reddish cheeks and greenish scales on her tail." But alas little more is known - since letting that much slip, Jacinto has become the butt of jokes and media curiosity, and declines to say any more. Melbourne Sun

(Australia) 15 July 1978 (Cr: Has Thomas)
This recalled another recent 'mermaid'
note. According to the Pretoria News
(South Africa) 20 December 1977, a mermaid had taken up residence in a storm-
sewer in the Libala Stage III township,
Lusaka, in Zambia. It was first spotted
in the full drains - it was the rainy
season - by children playing nearby, and
soon a large crowd gathered. They told
the reporter that the creature appeared
to be "a European woman from the waist
up, while the rest of her body was shaped
like the back end of a fish, and covered
with scales." One girl said the mermaid
was "very pretty" with earrings and red
bangles on her arms. Then the story gets
confusing...another witness said he had
seen the mermaid "run out of a nearby
house toward the sewer. It dug a
deep hole in the ditch where it hid, but
surfaced later in the day much to the
bewilderment of onlookers." The report
ends with a description of local wags
trying to figure out how to run with
their legs tied together and fins glued
to their shoes! (Cr: Chris J Holtzhausen)
One has to wonder how a mermaid, whether
mystery animal or mythical, relates to
the imagination of a land-locked African
state. Anyway, this introduces two other
African oddities...

AMIN'S TALKING TORTOISE

A UPI release (24 Aug) said that
"thousands of Ugandans" believed that
there was a tortoise currently padding
around the countryside prophesying trouble
for Idi Amin. In fact the story worried
the Ugandan government so much that
officials, police, security chiefs and
loyal chiefs held several crisis meetings
and issued a statement which denounced
the entire population as "always drunk
with rumours." And 'Big Daddy' himself
held a press conference in which he
threatened to put anyone trading in such
rumours before a firing squad.
According to the Uganda government's
own report, the mysterious 'enfundu'(tortoise) waddled into a local village police station and demanded to be taken to
the town of Jinja, on the River Nile and
just outside Kampala. Once there it asked
for a private audience with the provincial governor and police commissioner,
having a message for their ears only.
Whether there was any possible truth to
the existence of such a magical oracle
or not, the two officials quite naturally
wanted to avoid a view of Amin's fridge
from the inside or having their vitals
garnish his grizzly meals - they hastily
denounced and denied the rumours. The

last we hear of the tortoise is that it
was "under arrest" in Kampala jail - but
the jailors, too, were quick to deny it!
This altogether weird story is typical
of Amin's influence on Uganda - he is
virtually a shaman-warrior to his people,
or at least to himself, having been
divinely elected in a vision, and through
a series of amazing escapes from attempted assassinations now firmly believes
his prophesied invulnerability.
One has to wonder too about the similarity with the Dogon myth of the beings
from Sirius - I imagine one small hard-
backed emmisary, rebuffed in his attempts
to get Amin to 'cool it', getting more
than he bargained for. Over the same period as the tortoise-rumour Amin himself
shot an enraged hippo that attacked his
boat as he sailed with his children. He
then ordered all government officials to
view the carcase, to be preserved at his
residence - thus demonstrating once again
his dominion over the powers of nature!
London Evening Standard 24 August 1978;
Daily Express, Daily Telegraph, Guardian
25 August 1978; St Louis Post-Dispatch
(MO) 27 August 1978 (Cr: Paul Sieveking,
Mark A Hall.)

THE DICTATOR & THE MERCENARY - a fable

Shortly after (28 days) the islands
(3 of the Comoro group, between Africa &
Madagascar) declared their independence
(of France) a man (Ali Soilih) declared
himself president with the help of a
mercenary (Frenchman Colonel Bob Denard)
and set about his idea of revolution,
destroying all machinery, raising a thug
army, bankrupting the economy, taking any
woman he wanted and generally becoming a
pain in his subjects' collective arse.
A mere 34 months was all they could take,
and on 13 May 1978 the same mercenary
again invaded the head island, Moroni
(yes, Moroni, you morons!), but this time
in the pay of those who thought the man
should go - quickly.
Fifteen days later the man was dead -
uh, "shot while trying to escape." Now
we come to the funny-business. A year
earlier, a witchdoctor told the man that
he could only be killed by a man with a
dog - so the man, superstitious to the
last, had every dog on the island killed.
Now it's a fact that when the mercenary
led his small force ashore in their
secret midnight assault he had with him
his mascot - an Alsation dog! The motif
here is instantly recognizable from the
legends of all cultures, from the prophecy of the half-shod Jason to Herod's
massacre of the innocents. Who says
myth is dead! Sunday Times 11 June 1978.
                                      RJMR

Fortean Funnies

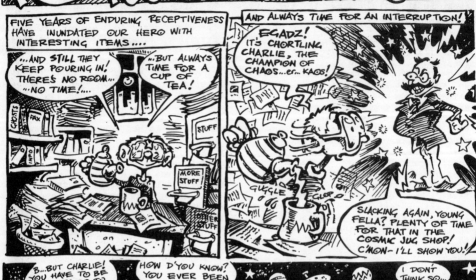

Predictions are ten-a-penny... or perhaps a little more expensive if they come from professional psychics and astrologers such as those consulted regularly by magazines like the National Enquirer at the beginning of each year. Looking back through our files, all we can say is that the famous have a remarkable talent for failure. So instead we draw our tales from humbler seers...

Plane-crashes: Perhaps the most remarkable story of the last couple of years is that of Lee Fried, an 18-year-old student at Duke University, N. Carolina. On 20th March 1977, he wrote some predictions on a card, put it in a wax sealed envelope, and had it locked in the office of university president Terry Sandford. On the 28th, with live TV coverage, the envelope was opened. Here's how Lee shaped up:

Boeing 747s crash, 583 dead. (March 27th, 2 Boeings crashed at Tenerife. Our clippings say Lee was wrong by 6 deaths...but the Guinness Book of Records gives the figure of 582),N. Carolina U. would lose the last basketball match of the season to Marquette, 68-58 (they lost 67-59), A TV hostess would wear a lavender outfit with cream blouse and silver earrings (she did), and the Supreme Court would hear 4 cases on capital punishment (right again). We only seem to have British sources for this (Daily Mail 1 Apr 77, S. Express 3 Apr 77, Weekly News 16 Apr 77. Cr: P Hope-Evans, P Roberts), short of details on how Lee arrived at his conclusions, but he claims he was just testing himself!

Another plane-crash prediction shows one of the famous getting it right for a change: 'psychic-astrologer' Jack Gillen predicted an aircrash at Evansville, Ind., on 12th December 1977. He made his prediction on a Florida radio station on 31 Oct, and repeated it on another radio show on 22 Nov. On 13th December (strange how these prognostics are frequently one out) a DC-3 crashed at Evansville, killing all 29 aboard. (National Enquirer, 14 Mar 78)

The New York City blackout: Time, 25 July 77 (Cr: Ion Will) has the following wondrous little tale: On the prior Tuesday, a small man with white hair and twinkling eyes turned up at the offices of the Seattle Post-Intelligencer, and offered to predict Thursday's headline. He gave his name only as Rogé (pron: Ro-jay), 52 yrs old, an ex-newsman come from Salinas, California,to attend a magicians' conference. He sealed his prediction in 5 envelopes. When Editor Stephen Green opened the envelopes on the Thursday morning, in Rogé's presence, he found written 'Massive Power Blackout hits New York City Area' which, of course, was exactly the same as his headline...

From out the mouth of babes: From the old to the young...when Cassy Holmes of Harborough Rd, Sheffield said relatives were about to arrive, her mother always put the kettle on...because little Cassy was always right. We say 'was' merely because our source is rather old (Weekly News 3 May 75, Cr N Watson) and have no news of her since. Cassy, at the time, was five years old, and had already been in the prediction business then for 3 years. Amongst her achievements: indicating that a picture would fall off the wall 2 minutes before it did; predicting the death of her grandfather's best friend, and the crash of a plane carrying Vietnamese orphans. Apart from prescience, Cassy knew quite a lot of science, too. She explained how blood carries oxygen to the brain with words her parents couldn't even pronounce! Like all good prophetesses, Cassy said nothing of how she did it, except she 'just knew it'.

Dreams: Shop-girl Mary Redding, 24, of Stirchley, Birmingham, dreamed she was going to win the football pools. I have several crumbling tomes of popular dream interpretation here, and seekers of useless wisdom might care to know that all of them agree that to dream of winning at gambling is a contrary dream indicating loss and lack of success. Not for Mary...5 days later, she picked up a cheque for £132,631 from Vernon's Pools. (D.Mirror, 17 July 75).

Another dreamer is Mrs Gwen Bridgland of Barrow-in-Furness, whose predictions were investigated by Dr John Beloff, a psychologist from Edinburgh University. On 2 Sept 1970, she dreamed of being on a crowded railway station platform, and seeing a man jump in front of a train with fatal results. In the dream, she said to her husband 'It's probably for the best anyway, Geoff, because the man was wanted for a sex murder'. On the 5th, she sent the dream to Beloff. On the 16th, a girl was sexually assaulted and murdered in Broxbourne, Herts. On the 19th, the man believed to have killed her died under a train. She also claims to have dreamed of being on a train which stopped, and men unloaded vast amounts of paper money; a few days later came the Great Train Robbery. This one appears to have occurred before she was working with Dr Beloff, however. Reveille 4 Oct 74. (Cr: N Watson)

The same source also tells of 28-yr-old American Shawn Robbins, who dreamed in February 74 that a large jet bound for London would crash in March or May, killing hundreds and leaving no survivors; and that a member of the US diplomatic service and his wife would die...though from the source it is uncertain whether these events were linked in the prediction. Nonetheless, 12 days later, on 3 Mar 74, a DC-10 on a Paris to London flight crashed in France, killing all 346 aboard; and including US Cultural Attaché Wayne Wilcox and his wife.

I noted above how some predictions are one out: to finish up, here's another with one detail wrong...thankfully for all concerned.

Mrs Frances Whaley, of Kay Gardens, Cockenzie, E.Lothian, Scotland, dreamed that her daughter Byrnice had toothache. In the dream, she phoned around and found a dentist in Musselburgh who could treat her. Arriving, she found the place was an old house with an ornate ceiling in the waiting room. Taking Byrnice to a toilet down a gloomy passage, she noticed black and white 'chessboard' lino on the floor, a bath with ornate feet. Still dreaming, Mrs Whaley returned to the waiting room while Byrnice went into the surgery. A friend came in and they chatted until the waiting room door opened and the dentist entered. He said 'I'm sorry, but your daughter has died under gas'. Mrs Whaley woke up sobbing.

And she forgot about it until 'months later', when Byrnice woke up with terrible toothache. She phoned around...the only dentist who could give her a quick appointment was in Musselburgh. It was of course, an old house: the waiting room had an ornate ceiling, the toilet black and white lino. And then, as a friend came in and they chatted, she realised her dream was coming true. Then the door opened, and the dentist said 'I'm sorry...I can't take out Byrnice's tooth. She's got a cold.' Mrs Whalen grabbed Byrnice and fled...though for the life of me I can't understand why she didn't do so sooner! And for those who like the loose ends tied up, Byrnice's tooth was taken out 2 days later...by another dentist. (Sunday Post, 1 June 75. Cr: N Watson)

SM.

To Wit! To Woo?

Some thoughts about Owlman

by Doc Shiels

In the Foreword to the catalogue of the 1942 Surrealist Exhibition in New York, Robert Allerton Parker pointed out the importance of the work of Charles Fort in relation to Surrealism. A sharp observation, methinks. Fortean reality *is* sur-reality, super-reality.

The Surrealist artists were and are magicians, shamans, tricksters, visionaries, adventurers, prophets, jokers, dreamers . . . they know a thing or two more, about the phenomenal pluriverse, than most ufologists, psychical investigators and monster hunters. Nature makes a habit of imitating art, and supernature often cocks an eye towards the super-real.

One of these fine days I will publish a lengthy text (already half-written) concerning the clues contained in Surrealist painting, films and literature, which relate, directly, to many aspects of Fortean phenomena. For now, let me concentrate on just one example . . . the Owlman.

Now I know the Owlman, as seen by young girls and Jungian psychologists, is a symbol of the negative animus; I know his first cousins pop up in the mythology and demonology of many cultures; and I know he flits through the pages of the comic-books and SF mags; but I also know that some of the most significant pointers towards an understanding of this weird winged thing are to be found in the statements and paintings of Max Ernst.

In 1906, at the age of fifteen, Ernst found his favourite pet, a cockatoo, dead and, at that very moment of this discovery, his father announced the birth of his baby sister. "The perturbation of the youth was so enormous that he fainted. A series of mystical crises, fits of hysteria, exaltations and depressions followed," wrote Ernst [1] . . . accompanied by a confusion between humans and birds. Following this interesting happening, young Max began his "excursions in the world of marvels, chimeras, phantoms, poets, monsters, birds, women, magi, trees, eroticism, stones" etc. You see? Already we are in Owlman territory.

In 1924, Max Ernst painted a picture entitled *Two Children are Menaced by a Nightingale*. Marcel Jean describes it as "the model of an hallucination". [2] It is a beautifully disquieting painting with an authentic atmosphere of strangeness about it. The nightingale threatens more than two, and by daylight.

"Men in ancient times," writes Marcel Jean, "believed that insects and serpents sprang spontaneously from the damp earth; Ernst gives a positive force to this old illusion: in his hands, pictorial material becomes alive and gives birth to new reptiles, mantises and birds of prey."

In 1941, Ernst traced the image of an Owlman in the sand of the shore of Lake Pontchartrain, New Orleans. He was, by now, living with the American artist, Dorothea Tanning. Her paintings began to be

"haunted by little girls in rags, seemingly turned into demons by their journey 'through the looking glass' " [2] Ernst continued to paint monstrous man-bird images, and young girls were never too far away.

In 1976, the Owlman of Mawnan frightened several young girls. In 1978, he returned to the area and frightened several more. June Melling's drawing of the Owlman (see illustration) is a splendid Surrealist image which could have flown out of a Max Ernst collage . . . a dream figure, a kachina, a magical phantom. It is funny-peculiar and funny-haha; decorative, too, like a man dressed in a primitive ritual costume, fright-masked and frond-winged on the top half, but with neat narrow trousers and black pointed shoes on the lower. He becomes slightly more monstrous in the sketch drawn by Barbara Perry. Here he is dressed in a one-piece outfit with feathered wing-sleeves. The winkle pickers have turned into cloven hooves or crab-claws. Sally Chapman's drawing dehumanizes him further, into an almost heraldic image, with angry glaring eyes and pointed teeth . . . menacing.

In June, 1978, 16 year old Miss Opie saw the Owlman and described him as 'a monster, like a devil, flying up through the trees'.[3] The Surrealist, Francis Picabia, once said, 'The Devil follows me day

(Top) Based on a sketch by June Melling - see note 5. (Above left) Drawn by Barbara Perry - see note 6. (Above right) Drawn by Sally Chapman - see note 6. (Previous page) Doc's daughter, Kate, photographed on Mawnan Beach in an attempt to summon the Owlman (FPL).

and night because he is afraid of being alone.' Well said, Francis! In August, 1978, his owliness returned to be observed by a trio of French girls.[4] This time he was white in colour, with big round eyes and a gaping mouth. The word 'gaping' put me in mind of hungry young birds . . . ah, there's a curious connection, folks! Do I mean sex-starved pubescent girls or downy chicks (here we go again) opening wide for a fat juicy worm (what did I tell you?).

In the wee small hours of the morning of August 8th, I dreamed a most curious dream. I found myself sitting on a high branch of a tree, looking down on a moonlit clearing in the woods near Mawnan church. There, spread-eagled on the ground, lay a naked girl. There was a churring sound and, suddenly, the pale figure of the Owlman came floating through the trees at the edge of the clearing, directly facing me. The churring song grew louder and I knew that it came from the gaping mouth-beak of the creature. Its eyes were large and red, its ten foot wings moved in slow motion and clapped together behind its head. It remind me, instantly, of a huge Lovecraftian whippoorwill as drawn by Lee Brown Coye in an illustration for *The Dunwich Horror*. Then . . . "No!" shouted a man's voice." . . . you are wrong, it is mine. I am the owl-mirror." I can't remember the exact words, but the accent was German and the shouter was Max Ernst. He sat on a branch of my tree, slightly above me. "Hello Max" I said, as if we'd been old friends for years.

The Owlman hovered three or four feet above the girl. She smiled and said "Hello" as if *they* had been old friends for years. "He thinks he's going to fuck her," said Max as the winged weird one floated above and between the girl's legs. "He can't," I thought, and said so . . . "he's no cock!" The girl laughed and the Owlman, curring fiercely, lifted his head and glared up at Max and me. It rose through the air, slowly, towards us, mouth gaping as if to swallow us and wings spread wide. "It's a cunt!" Max laughed . . . and that's exactly what it became—a gaping pink vagina between a pair of pale thighs. "That's a good trick," I thought. Then I fell out of the tree and woke up; so I don't know what happened to Max, but it must have been very interesting.

Interpretations? Well . . . I have a fair notion of my own libido, over which Freudian-minded readers will enjoy giggling. In recent weeks, one of my own teenage daughters has tried to bait the Owlman by waiting, sky-clad, in the woods (she was eventually discouraged from such experiments by a series of, possibly related, psychic backlashing 'accidents'). One evening in June we heard a strange churring song, like the trill of a nightjar. In the dream, Owlman first appeared to me as a large whippoorwill (an American name for the nightjar). This bird is also commonly known as the fern-owl or goat-sucker—names which evoke some significant imagery, like the fern-like wings of June Melling's Owlman. The name 'goat-sucker' conjures up thoughts of midnight witchery (and pink gaping mouths). Why was this innocent, insect-eating, little bird given such as emotive name? Has it, some time, been *seen* sucking goats? And were they she or *he*-goats? Max Ernst, or the dream Max Ernst, told me that I was 'wrong' to see the Owlman as a Lee Brown Coye whippoorwill. (Who's poor Will? Wilbur Whateley, perhaps?). He claimed the Owlman as his own, for he, Ernst, was the 'owl mirror' . . . reflective and reflexive, the magical

'looking glass' through which things can pass, the prankster, the Dadaist/Surrealist. Ernst's Owlman was not blessed with a feathery phallus. No cock, he. So Max, before this dreamer's very eyes, turned the winged gaper into a welcoming vulva. Why did I fall out of the tree? Maybe I was pushed, maybe I was taken aback, maybe I wasn't ready to become king. That owl-face-vagina image later reminded me of the Irish Sheelagh-na-Gig. . . those erotic carved figures, mouthless, with round staring eyes and exaggerated genitalia.

Whatever the owl-thing was or is, I fell out of the tree and thus avoided being wooed in the woods.

Doc Shiels—August 1978

NOTES

1) 'Some Data on the Youth of Max Ernst, as told by Himself'. In *Max Ernst: Beyond Painting* (Wittenborn Schultz, NY, 1948).

2) Marcel Jean, *The History of Surrealist Painting*, (Weidenfeld & Nicholson, London, 1960).

3) [Ed's note—Doc wrote to me, on 19 June 1978, to say that as a result of a small piece in the *Falmouth Packet* announcing Doc's intentions at that time to 'summon' up pixies, he had had several strange phone calls—the most relevant one was from a man calling himself 'Ken Opie' (more *Star Wars* links?) Opie being a fairly common name in the Falmouth/Truro part of Cornwall, Doc says. The man wouldn't leave his address or phone number, Doc continued, but "said he'd read the *Packet* piece and thought I might be interested in something his daughter had seen a couple of weeks ago (ie about 4 June) . . . "A monster, like a devil, flying up through the trees near old Mawnan Church"!!! He (and/or she) couldn't describe the monster except to say—and he repeated this—that it was "like a devil". I asked the age of his daughter, and he said "16", but wouldn't give me her name. I asked him what he was doing near the old church that morning, and he replied that "she wouldn't have been there on her own"!!! Then he rang off. It looks as if our Owlman is back!" Despite Doc's enthusiasm, he went on more cautiously, acknowledging that all the elements of this story could be found in the various published accounts of the earlier sightings (see notes 5 & 6), and from the news coverage of Doc's adventures. Curiously, although the *Packet* item was about a fairy or pixie summoning experiment, neither of Doc's anonymous callers mentioned the Little Folk!]

4) [Ed's note—Another letter from Doc, dated 6 August 1978, said that on Wednesday 2 August, Owlman was seen again near Mawnan church, this time by three young French girls. The landlady of the Penzance boarding house where the girls were staying told Doc that the girls had been frightened by something 'very big, like a great big furry bird," and that it was white with "a gaping mouth and big round eyes". It was "up in a tree, then went up higher and disappeared." That was all the landlady could tell, so Doc left word for the girls to ring him—but, as is the tantalizing way of weird phenomena, they never did. Several weeks later Doc wrote, appropriately: "Not a dicky bird (!) from the French girls yet." It's worth noting that during this period there were several UFO sightings of the lights-in-the-sky type—but we'll give the details some other time.]

5) Drawing reproduced from FT16p19, which also gives June Melling's story.

6) Drawing reproduced from FT17p17, which also gives the girls' stories.

UNIDENTIFIEDS

Sightings of monsters and unidentified animals continue at the usual pace, and we don't really have room for them all this issue - so, Nessie and some others will have to wait until next time, while we just mention a few very interesting and urgent items.

WATER MONSTERS

Perhaps it was inevitable? Less than 2 weeks after your editor, Ion Will, John Michell and Steve Moore made a phenomenal trip to Fortfest 78 in Washington DC, there were a series of sightings of a number of serpent-like monsters - likened to Nessie herself - in the Chesapeake Bay where the Potomac River (which flows through Washington) meets the sea. On the 25th July, Donald Kyker, an ex-CIA man, and his family, saw a creature in the lower reaches of the Potomac - it was between 25-30ft long and "about as round as a telegraph pole...or at least its head and neck was, seen before it dived. Kyker phoned the Smoots - No, I don't make them up! - who live a bit further downstream. Myrtle Smoot and hubby looked out and there it was - heading for the bay. Within an hour they saw three more - a large one about 36ft long, maybe longer, and the smaller ones between 5-10ft - this time heading upriver. Her husband, Mr Smoot (love that name!), shot one of the smaller ones in the neck, fired a few more times, and watched the critters dive. Another witness to this spectacle, CP Stemmer, the Smoot's neighbour, said that although they looked like "self-propelled logs", they were definitely alive, moving faster than the water and making wakes. On 27 June, another Smoot neighbour, Mary Lewis, swimming with two cousins in a pool by the Potomac, said they saw several things poking out of the water too large to be ducks, snorkel tubes...or porpoises (the latter answering some doubting official of the Potomac River Fisheries Commission.) Main details from St Louis Post-Dispatch (MO) 20 Aug 1978 (Cr: Mark Hall). Other accounts: London Evening Standard 18 Aug 1978; Daily Express, Sun both 19 August 1978 (Cr: Ion Will, Paul Burd.) Roanoke Times & World News (VA) 18 Aug 1978 (Cr: Gregory Bale.) Washington Post 26 Aug. (Cr: MA Hall).

A later report adds that Kyker thought it looked like "a big snake, about 100ft offshore...with a head the size of a cantaloupe." Since June about 30 people have seen the monster they have taken to calling 'Chessie', at the mouths of the Potomac, Rappahannock and Pautuxent rivers. The reaction from 'experts' runs from the usual allegations that people are seeing things - porpoises, otters, and "large rays"... director of the Calvert Marine Museum, Ralph Eshelman said: "I've seen 50 rays with their tails raised stirring up a boil in the water and it looks very strange." Interesting but is it relevant? - to the more helpful attitude of the Virginia Institute of Marine Science, where ichthyology dept head John Merriner said: "This is one hell of an animal to be in the bay. The trail is cold now, but we will try to track it anyway." There was also the usual appeal to ritual when reason failed - at Kimsale, Virginia, on the Yeocomico River, 200ft of plastic tubing crowned by a hobbyhorse head was formally shot at with a toy cannon. A week later, the Smoot's son, 11, saw the creature for the second time. Long live Chessie! St Louis Post-Dispatch (MO) 1 October 1978 (Cr: William Zeiser.)

Another new monster to come to our notice is the sighting of a water monster at the Grootvlei pumping station, near Vereeniging, South Africa, by four people - but that's all the report says. It is suggested that a Mr.B Byrne-Daly created the monster 14 years previously, when as editor of a local paper he pleaded for a road to the new Vaal Dam, and some kind of attraction out there like Nessie. "Within a week," he said,"the first wild-eyed believer came rushing in with the news that there was indeed a beast in the dam...And after him there was an absolute flood of people saying the monster had breathed at them. They had seen its huge red eyes glowing in the darkness like coals, from the safety of their treetop perches. It was remarkable...people camped out there for days, scanning the dam with telescopes." Amazing! Shades of the 'Angels of Mons'! No explanation is given as to why the monster should reappear (in any degree of solidity) after last vanishing in 1964 -- this present sighting was sometime in the week 17-23 April 1978. Maybe there is a monster there - stranger things have happened, as you know. Pretoria News (South Africa) 29 April 1978 (Cr: Chris J Holtzhausen.)

The third and newest monster surfaced in Lake Ikeda in the Satsuma peninsula of Japan's Kyushu island. One of the 20 witnesses, Yukata Kawaji, said he saw a huge monster with two humps swimming swiftly from north to south - after two minutes it sank from view. Straits Times (Singapore) 2 October 1978 (Cr: IAWill.)

AN AFRICAN 'BIGFOOT'

A French social scientist, Ms Jacqueline Roumeguere-Eberhardt, of the Centre National de la Recherche Scientifique, in Paris, has announced that she may have found the 'missing link' postulated by the Darwinians. She has researched among African tribes for 25yrs, the last 10 among the Masai of southern Kenya and their relations in the north. Over the years she heard many tales of strange forest beings but she took no notice until last November when a youth told her that he had been held captive for an hour by a creature that "seemed to be human but was very hairy on all his body and had a low forehead covered with hair." Then a group of warriors presented her with a bow, arrows and a bag, all of an unfamiliar design, which they said had been dropped by one of the creatures when they surprised him in the forest. Since then Ms Roumeguere has collected 31 accounts (she speaks fluent Masai) of sightings and encounters in 11 forests in Kenya, and has identified 4 distinct types of creature, which she calls 'Mr X'.

'X One' is a classic big foot, hairy and huge of stature. When one caught the young man, it examined him and his weapons carefully, broke arrows and put them back in their sheath. He has been seen carrying buffalo meat which suggests to Ms R-E that the animal might be social and intending to share with a group.

'X Two' is tall, thin and has a hairless beige-coloured body topped with curly black hair. They appear to live in caves, and 'children' have been seen.

'X Three' is "very old" (?). "Tall males have been seen felling a buffalo with an uprooted tree with its roots carved into spikes, and using a spear-like knife to cut out its internal organs which are then eaten on the spot."

'X Four' is a pygmy with a short fat body, hairy chest, back and thighs, and often carries a digging stick with which he unearths tubers.

X-One's seem to have great curiosity. A man taking a sheep to slaughter in the forest says he came face-to-face with one - the man ran off leaving the sheep. X-One "...only looked at it as though he had never seen one before. He did not beat it or kill it..." but examined its eyes and stomach. One woman was suddenly confronted by a "Mrs X-One" and to placate the creature the woman offered a calabash of milk. The creature did not seem to know what to do and gnawed at it spilling the milk. It seems that Ms R-E and the Masai are planning an expedition into the remote forests...so stay tuned for further details. The Australian 3 October; Guardian 4 October 1978 (Cr: Ion Will, Paul Sieveking, Douglas Watson.)

RJMR

letters-letters-letters-letters

HITLER IN LIVERPOOL

from K Harrocks, Cheshire:
In FT23p33, Robert A Wilson said that Hitler lived in Liverpool but this could not be confirmed. Well I remember seeing a series on Liverpool in the Liverpool Echo a couple of years back, and it showed, in a photograph, the street and house where he stayed with his sister. ((See also Tony Bond's letter, FT25p48. An item recently appeared in Sunday People 10 Sept 1978 (Cr: IAW) describing a diary kept by an Irish girl, one of whose relations married Adolf's brother Alois, settling in Liverpool. Adolf visited them in 1911 when he was 22, and yes he did have his moustache then. The diary was discovered by novelist Beryl Bainbridge, who has a novel based on it, Young Adolf,

coming out this November. She says the house was destroyed, ironically, during a German air raid. Curiously, the whole matter came to light in the _Times_ (10 Oct) in a note about William Hitler, the son of Alois and the Irish girl, Bridget Dowling. William Hitler emigrated to the US at the start of WWII, joined the USNavy and changed his name to settle down in obscurity.(Thanks to Sydney _Morning Herald_, Australia, 12 Oct – Ed)).

DARTMOOR PONY DEATHS

from Paul W Baines, Surrey:
Bob Skinner mentioned to me that you would be interested in hearing details of my investigation, 12 months ago, into the Dartmoor pony deaths in Cherry Brook valley near Postbridge. I understood from the locals – ie the residents of Powder Mill Cottages, near the scene of the deaths – that the carcasses had been discovered as far back as April '77. Pony deaths on the moor are considered to be a common event during winter, generally from a combination of malnutrition and cold. It was only when the pet-shop owner from Tavistock discovered them, in July '77, that public attention was drawn to the event.

I spoke to Mrs Joanna Vinson, veterinary surgeon and secretary of the Dartmoor Livestock Protection Association, who carried out the post-mortem examinations of the carcasses. She stated that the rate of decomposition was normal and that the carcasses had been ravaged by predators. She further suggested that the animals had fallen down the steep side of the valley where mutilation occurred by falling among the boulders that litter the valley. She concluded that something must have caused them to stampede over the steep side of the valley.

I visited the scene of the event early in August '77 and found nothing other than I expected. It seemed quite reasonable to assume that the animals, weakened by malnutrition in the winter months, could easily have fallen down the steep side, receiving severe injuries upon the many rocks . The reason for them taking fright and stampeding (if this is the case) remains obscure. Suggestions that they were chased by someone driving a landrover could be absurd...no four-wheeled vehicle could be driven in that terrain without having its bottom ripped out by concealed rocks. A skilled motorcyclist could, perhaps, have made it across that part of the moor. I do not feel inclined to jump to any conclusions about whether UFOs were involved in this case. ((We rounded up the pertinant reportage back in FT22p30 and FT23p3, and in the latter

citation we learn that the DLPA (whose secretary Paul cites above) suggested the ponies ate the poisonous bog asphodel The case still hasn't been accounted for convincingly – perhaps its too late and too cold now? – Ed))

THE FERAL EARL OF DERBY

from Paul Burd, Essex:
I've just finished the section in PHENOMENA on children brought up by animals, and I saw mention of an Earl of Derby being brought up by an eagle, and can add a little information. After reading in FT24p11 about eagles carrying off children, I was intrigued by the name of a pub in Brentwood, Essex – the 'Eagle and Child'. A notice inside told the story that an Earl of Derby (it doesn't say which) was out on his land (it does n't say where) when he saw an eagle carrying off a child. He gave chase and rescued the baby which was subsequently brought up as his son and heir.

For a touch of synchronicity, we drove down a lane called Eagle Way, about 2mls from the pub.

FATEFUL FAYETTE, & 'KANGAROO GIRL'

from AH Debnam, W Australia:
I was surprised at the omission, by Bill Grimstad (FT25p5–8), of the 'infamous' L Ron Hubbard, founder of Scientology, whose first name – whether adopted later or not I'm unaware – is Lafayette! He surely fits the theme. ((And Larry Arnold told us recently he was schooled at a Lafayette College. Hmmmm! – Ed))

I'm afraid you can scrap the Nullarbor (– no trees) Kangaroo Girl (FT25 p9) from your files. On excellent authority from a very close friend I'm assured this was a hoax. He was in the area for quite a while a month after the event (which was about May/June 1972). He met the people involved who informed him how the whole story had been rigged as a tourist attraction. They even went to the extent of showing him how they caught the 'roos alive and released them for the filming. The 'nymph' did _not_ live wild in the bush, nor, regretfully, did she run naked with the 'roos – though she did spend some time out there in a caravan. She, and the others involved in the hoax, left the area some months after the event.

HARRY PRICE AND ROSALIE

from Stan Farnsworth, Lakeside Hfx Co, Nova Scotia, Canada BOJ 1ZO.
For over eight years my associate in London, Mr Lester Macintyre, and I have

been researching the 1937 Harry Price/ Rosalie case ((see Ed's note below)) - on my part mostly by mail or on trips to London. Over the years many professional researchers, including members of the SPR, have tried to find the house in South London where the Rosalie seance was held, from the description of the house by Price, plus other clues, to decide once and for all whether the case was genuine or a fiction. In recent years the case was written up in magazines, pocketbooks and in David Cohen's Price and his spirit child Rosalie (1965); and last year the BBC made a filmed documentary on the case which has yet to be presented. Would any of your readers be int-

erested in helping us with this case? ((Interested parties please write to Stan at the above address. Price went to a private house in south London to investigate reports of a regular and full materialization of a medium's spirit guide, a girl of 11yrs. This girl, Rosalie, obligingly materialized and Price satisfied himself that she was warm, soft and breathing, and etherially beautiful. He wondered later whether he had indeed witnessed a "living or semi-living materialization", but the pressure of work prevented him returning to the house as he intended, and soon the case lapsed. The case still arouses passions, both for and against Price and his work - Ed))

FAIRY BATTLES

A few weeks ago the BBC screened their TV play on the Cottingley 'fairy photos' mystery - and I thought they treated the subject about as fairly as possible, giving a sympathetic treatment to all the angles pro and con. The whole thing was spoiled in advance by James Randi who gives a convincing portrayal of a man terrified of the least acknowledgement of the existence of mysteries. On behalf of the Committee for the Scientific Claims of the Paranormal (CSICP) Randi tried to get the BBC to preface the play with the announcement that the photos were decidedly faked by the two girls Elsie Wright and Frances Griffiths. To their credit the BBC refused. Randi bases his 'exposure' on the computer-aided analysis of the photos by William Spaulding and Robert Sheaffer, whose brief and hasty look at Doc Shiels' famous Nessie picture (see FT24p14) left much to be desired. Randi, however, is convinced that Spaulding and Sheaffer have found flat cardboard-like images and artifacts that look like string. Anyone familiar with the Cottingley photos will readily acknowledge that in many ways they are unconvincing in a way that immediately

arouses reasonable questions and suspicions...and yet after several professional examinations to date have failed to detect obvious signs of fakery. Indeed the most violent reaction against them has been of the kind: "Fairies don't exist - therefore the photos are fakes." Sheaffer has taken an across-the-board swipe at all those who have believed the photos genuine, or who have drawn attention to them (he would rather see them forgotten) in anything other than an attitude of disbelief - see his writings in Fate June 1978 pp 76-83, and Page Research Library Newsletter 20. See also Jerry Clark's response in Fate Nov 1978 pp68-71. While there is still room for doubt, about whether they are genuine photos of genuine fairies or projections of the girls' imaginations psychically imprinted onto film, or faked, and doubts too about Randi's exposé, I prefer to keep an open mind. True or false - and there is some truth in fiction and vice versa - the case against the photos has hardly been fairly presented. A brief report on Randi's crusade against the fairies is in New Scientist 10 August 1978.

HEAVEN COULDN'T WAIT!

On the 5th August Pope Paul VI was ill, so his doctors ordered a "complete rest". On the evening of the next day, 6 Aug, his condition worsened and he died at 9.40pm, taking his doctors' advice quite literally! Thus began an astonishing two and a bit months for Vatican-watchers and phenomenalists.

On that fateful 6 Aug the news spread rapidly throughout Italy and the world. As word reached the Druogno valley on Italy's NE border with Switzerland, we are told that "minutes later" torrential rain began that lasted 30 hours. The old folk said "The angels are weeping for the Pope." The damage was extensive, with the worst flooding in the Lugano area for 25 years. The "cloudburst" cut visibility down to 100yds, while hailstones the size of cherries smashed windows, destroyed crops and stripped leaves from trees. The waters accumulated so rapidly that one old couple on opening their front door were pushed back into the house as the torrent rose to shoulder height - cars were swept away, bridges shattered, communications knocked out, trees uprooted, and land was washed away. One report said the topography of the region has been permanently changed - at least 10 died and hundreds were made homeless. One old man said he had never experienced anything quite like this in all his 71yrs in the valley.

On 13 August, Cardinal Paul Yu Pin of Nanking, China, who resided in Taiwan since his expellation, died in a clinic in Rome.

17 August - the third tremor in 3 weeks rocks the northern suburbs of Rome - we don't know the dates of the first two tremors but they come within this portentious period.

After much public speculation Cardinal Albino Luciani was chosen to be the new Pope, on 26 August, and sadly, he died on 28 September, of a heart attack, as did Paul VI and Cardinal Yu Pin. Luciani chose the name John-Paul I in honour of his two predecessors and thereby became the first Pope since Simon Peter (technically Peter I) to have a double name. If you were pessimistic you might imagine that it was a bad start for any pope, to break a centuries-old tradition in a church with a strong belief in tradition for its own sake. There was more to come...John Paul decided that he wouldn't be crowned in full pomp, nor would he use the portable throne on which popes were traditionally carried on high in procession so their majesty could be seen by all. The result is that many Catholics, a bit baffled by the double name, could imagine he had not been fully installed, and many thousands, unable to see his diminutive eminence from behind the front rows of clergy, had to rely on newspaper and TV photos for their impressions. But I count the first uncomfortable omen to be the puff of smoke from the Sistine Chapel roof that signalled his election - it should have been 'white' for a positive decision and 'black' for negative - instead it came out grey, to the confusion of all observers.

For those following the omens, the week after JP's election was happier because the Holy Shroud went on display in Turin for the first time in 45 years, and on 19 Sept the powdered blood of St Januarius liquified on time.

On 5 September, the visiting second ranking member of the Russian Orthodox Church, Metropolitan Nikodim, collapsed and died during an audience with JP in the pope's private library - another heart attack!

On 16 Sept there was a total eclipse of the moon - but also on that day, and the two previous days (ie 14-16) there were reports of a brilliant yellow and green triangular shaped unidentified object in the skies of Sardinia, Sicily and Tuscany, which was also seen overhead in Rome on those days. Arab News, and Saudi Gazette both 17 Sept 1978 (Cr: Ion Will.)

John Paul was found dead in bed, the light still on, at about 5.30am on 29 Sept. He had apparently died, while reading Thomas a Kempis' Imitation of Christ, at about 11pm the night before - and unless I'm wrong, there's something ironic about the head of the Catholic Church dying without the last rites, one of the church's main rituals. Many thousands of people all over the world were shocked at his quite unexpected death. Evangelist Billy Graham said that in the series of deaths God had a message for the Church - but he didn't know what. Others suggested that this was God's way of saying the wrong pope had been elected. The cardinals on the other hand, who invoke God's guidance in their selection conclave, said they were absolutely certain that the Holy Spirit had neither reproved nor punished them. The lesson was one of death in the midst of life. Unhappily bad luck dogged even John Paul's funeral service as for the second successive day (3 Oct) Rome was "lashed with torrential rain"...and as if that were not enough

rumours were rapidly accumulating that
JPI might have been murdered by extre-
mists. There were also growing calls
for a post-mortem on JP (despite the
ban on papal p-ms by Paul VI himself)
from even ultra-conservative groups
within the Church. People began calling
TV phone-in shows with their beliefs
that the pope did not die a "natural
death". And matters were not helped
when the rebel archbishop Marcel Lefeb-
vre said publicly: "It is difficult to
believe the death was natural, considering all the creatures of the devil
which inhabit the Vatican." Now what
does he know? JP reigned only 33 days,
but his final audience, on 27 Sept,
was being claimed as the cause of a
change of heart in a leading member of
the racist/facist National Front party
in England. Although not a Catholic or
religious he was touched by the pope's
sincerity and has now resigned all NF
obligations.
    Now we have a new pope, John Paul II,
formerly Cardinal Karol Wojtyla, of
Krakov, Poland. Interestingly many com-
mentators missed this pope's portent.
Paul VI was in the habit of setting a
treasured alarm clock to wake him at
5am each day - it went off again unexpectedly at the moment of his death.
He had used the clock ever since, in
1923,he was a Vatican diplomat in Poland.
We have a few other numerological notes.
John Paul I was 23 when he was ordained,
and was the 263rd pontiff. The Shroud
was last shown in 1933...and although
there were 115 members of the Sacred
College of Cardinals when Paul VI died,
but due to inability to travel, or illness, only 111 could attend each conclave - in the last 150 years there
have been 11 conclaves averaging 11
days for election. Curiously the man
who ended up as John Paul I's successor
was one of those who missed JP's election through illness. The shortest ever
reign of a pope was that of Stephen II,
elected on 23 March 752 - an hour!
    Sources: Newsweek 31 July; Sunday
People 6 August 1978; Washington Post
7 & 17 August; New York Times 9 August;
Times 9 August; London Evening Standard
11 & 16 Aug, 29 Sept; Guardian 14 & 24
Aug; Dallas Times Herald 17 Aug; Daily
Telegraph 18 Aug, 30 Sept, 4 Oct; Sunday Times 27 Aug; London Evening News
5 Sept; The Australian 5 Oct; Daily
Mirror 17 October 1978. (Cr: Ion Will,
John Michell, Al & Phyllis, TR Adams.)

    According to a note in the Dallas
Times Herald 14 August 1978, Universal
TV and ABC have signed a deal to make
a 3hr version of Arthur C Clarke's
classic SF novel Childhood's End. If
you have never read the novel, do so -
it contains a good number of Fortean themes
and insights into UFOs & parapsychology.
(Cr: Thomas R Adams.)

    Another Illuminati plot? On 14 Sept
an attempt to deliver money to an ext-
ortionist who threatened to contaminate
Tucson, Arizona, with bubonic plague,
failed - the account doesn't say why or
whether the man was caught! Egyptian
Mail 16 Sept 1978 (Cr: Ion Will.)

FORTEAN TIMES

Fortean Times

28
75p:$2·00

visions
flying food
cranks
& more

strange phenomena

UK ISSN 0308-5899

Fortean Times

A Contemporary Record of Strange Phenomena

FORTEAN TIMES is a non profitmaking quarterly miscellany of news, notes and references on current and historical strange phenomena, related subjects and philosophies. Formerly *The News*. Affiliated to the *International Fortean Organisation* (INFO), and the *Society for the Investigation of the Unexplained* (SITU), and other Fortean journals in continuing the work of Charles Fort (1874–1932). **SUBSCRIPTION** information and other details can be found on the back page.

Edited and published by Robert JM Rickard
Associate Editors: Steve Moore, Paul Sieveking.
Contributing editors: David Fideler, Phil Ledger
Heading art by Hunt Emerson

FORTEAN TIMES, c/o Dark They Were & Golden Eyed, 9–12 St Annes Court, London W1, England.

FT 28 – WINTER 1979

EDITORIAL STUFF

The time has come for us to stop talking about our 'Great Leap Forward' and do it! This will be the last issue in the present format – to wait until the next new year would lose this opportunity; nor could it be taken up with this issue. From next issue (FT29) we will be a larger and more professional format, typeset throughout, better graphics, layout and legibility.

Our goal is to create an attractive and informative magazine, not only to lure more readers, advertizers, newsstand distribution, but to give reader and contributor alike the sense of appreciation we feel their respective efforts, and the material itself, deserves. We all want FT to continue, but not at the expence of the worrying, bodging, corner-cutting, penny-pinching inadequate budgets on which we have (against odds) survived our first five years. We believe that interest in Fortean affairs has never been higher and still rising, and that given the proper format the market could sustain our dream of a well-funded and sound journal in our subject. Stability can only come with a larger circulation and we believe we've proved we can do it. Help us, nurture us in the difficult initial stages, and we'll give you a damned fine Fortean journal – an FT you can be justifiably proud of.

Compromises will have to be made. A proportion of the contents will have to be aimed at introducing the general reader or newcomer to Fortean mysteries. But we don't intend to lose the flavour of the FT you know and love. If we make a profit, so much the better – it would be plowed back into improving the mag, paying writers, and even funding special research, projects or publications.

We are under no illusion about the difficulties, but we're game if you are! FT staff have put their own money up, but it's not enough – we need more capital, if you'd like to invest with a loan or donation. Otherwise, do all you can to bring in new subscribers. Your sub will be extended by 1 issue for each one you personally bring in. Write for our new expanded illustrated blurb – out soon. Lobby newsagents and distributors. Give gift subs. We're putting a lot into this behind the scenes – and we're sure you're with us. Excelsior!

OUR LADY OF BAYSIDE, NY

The BVM continues to visit New York, as she has done regularly for the last 8 years, making the visions of Veronica Leuken among the longest continuous visitation on record, whether recognized by the Church or not. We last heard of Mrs Leuken - an otherwise ordinary 50-ish housewife and mother - when her regular vigils on ground opposite the church of St Robert Bellarmine, in Bayside, Queens, had attracted such large followings, with pilgrims coming from all over the States, Canada, and abroad, that fights broke out between the devout and the irate, local citizens who protested about being besieged in their own homes - see FT15p3f. It seems the BVM couldn't fight City Hall, and conveniently intervened with a 'revelation' that the site of the vigils should be moved to Flushing Meadow Park, near a Vatican-shaped pavilion where Paul VI gave a blessing in 1965.

Veronica's experiences began while she was driving in 1968, when, as she prayed for Robert Kennedy - whose assassination had just been announced - a powerful scent of roses filled her car. Later she had visionary encounters with St Terese of Lisieux, who gave way in turn to the Mother of Christ herself in June 1970. At the mass vigils, Veronica is the only one priviledged to see and hear, and while a continuous Rosary is chanted (BVM's orders) Veronica articulates the messages for the benefit of a tape-recorder, interspersed by her own end of the celestial conversation and descriptions of the figures, movements, dress etc. Here is a typical scene described in recent literature from the group that has formed around her:

"Our Lady is coming down now from the right side of the sky. I didn't see her standing over, high by the trees. Now She's following, going across the sky to Jesus. She's going over to His right side. And over on the left side I can see Michael spreading his wings now. He's covering, like a protective shield, the whole sky over Our Lady's statue. He surrounds the whole grounds here with his being. There is no human way to explain the immense size of Michael...And also I can see now in the background behind Our Lady and Jesus many angels. I can see - not their faces; it's hard to describe the tremendous light - but the figures; they're clothed in white gowns."

The group, who call themselves the "Faithful and True Roman Catholics" hold their vigils on the eves of 28 major feasts in the Roman Catholic calendar, and depending upon the humour of the Almighty, Veronica may see, in addition to the regular appearances of St Michael, BVM and her Son, hosts of shining angels and glorified nuns, such luminaries as Sts Joseph and Bernadette and the Apostles, and perhaps vivid scenes of the coming catastrophic "Chastisement" of this sinful Earth.

In the past the BVM has encouraged pilgrims to bring and use their cameras but despite this approbation none of the many photos that have resulted are overwhelmingly convincing, except of course to the converted. One of my sources is a gently ironic article by Philip Nobile in the New Yorker for 11 December 1978. Nobile decided to attend a few of these vigils that Fall, and describes the crowds as mostly middle-aged women with a few men and children. "The majority appear to be simple Catholics, perhaps more devout than usual, from the lower middle class." Many have brought Polaroid cameras along, in the belief that a long exposure will give the BVM the opportunity to write messages using the trails of light from candles, car headlamps, street lights and the lights of planes coming into La Guardia airport. The photo below is typical of this kind of effect and is said to be the writing of Jacinta, one of the four children involved in the BVM visions at Fatima, Portugal, in 1916, who died in 1920. The BVM later revealed that a careful scrutiny of the picture from all angles would disclose the date of the "fiery Ball of Redemption" which will wipe out three quarters of the Earth's population. (Further details of the prophetic visions are transcribed in Grave and Urgent Warnings, etc by C Marystone - reviewed in our paperback section this issue).

Nobile said he was shown whole albums of similar photos, each of which held some special significance for the faithful. One lady had a set showing Veronica's 16yr-old son lying in his coffin after he was killed in a shooting accident. She told Nobile: "'See the top photo? It was taken with a flash. The boy is laid out in the coffin. But look at the other photo. It's dimmer because the flash didn't go off. But notice how the boy is floating above the empty coffin wrapped in a shroud.' I examined the set closely. 'The boy isn't floating in a shroud in the second picture, and the coffin isn't empty,' I said, trying not to hurt her feelings. 'This second shot was just taken at a different angle, farther back, so that more of the silk lining is shown falling down the side of the coffin.The boy is still lying in the coffin, only he appears higher compared to the angle of the first picture.' I placed the photos side by side to demonstrate the difference. She was speechless, as was the small gathering around us."

It is easy to talk of gullibility, but the problem is more complicated than that. All of us have certain levels of suggestibility - indeed it is the very cement that binds together the common concensus of reality - for without it we would have no agreement on the

A Polaroid picture taken by a Mr Eanzenberger at the Bayside shrine on 14 September 1971 - from Hartfield Courant (CT) 30 December 1978.

meaning of symbols, and thus means of communicating. For the role of suggestibility as one of the great shaping forces of society see that neglected work The Crowd (1897) by Gustave Le Bon. He showed that a crowd may be distinguished from a random group of people by their peculiar mental or psychical alignment - and the characteristics of this hypnoid state (ie like a hypnotically induced state) include a diminished individual consciousness with an increase in collective consciousness (ie a revertion to a more archaic level of consciousness); a loss of critical faculties and everyday values; and heightened suggestibility. The very act of being in a crowd becomes a trigger for this state in which the crowd as a whole can be swayed by the most preposterous notions - a fact orators and dictators have not been slow to take advantage of. We have no space to go into the subject but as I hope to show in a forthcoming book, a knowledge of these factors, among others, is essential to the proper analysis of Fortean and UFO phenomena, indeed all phenomena with intensely subjective experiental states. For now we only note that if Nobile's assessment was correct, then the vigil 'crowd' had created their own little bubble of belief about those photos, and his needle of rational analysis was enough to pop it - assuming of course that their speechlessness was due to the shock of waking up and not to anger at his impiety! This in no way denigrates the religious basis of their belief (which remains valid) nor their psychological need to believe (a subject we need to know a lot more about.) More examples of minority concensus belief below.

That said, there is no doubt people see things - it is only the physical and objective evidence that is ambiguous. This itself might be our single most important clue to the triggering of these kinds of experience. Again from Nobile, we learn that there is a strong tradition at these vigils of "heavenly doves" associated with the BVM apparitions at Bayside and Flushing Park, as there was at the visions at Zeitun, in Cairo (1968). (There are other similarities between Bayside and the visions at Fatima and Garabandal, Spain (1961) as several critics have observed.) On the evening of 2 October 1978, Nobile attended a vigil at the Park. "As I stood at the edge of the crowd examining a rosary that allegedly turned from tin to gold overnight, I heard a chorus of ahs. 'Look at the sky - see the doves,' said the man with the golden beads. I looked up and saw 5 luminous discs darting across the sky. They were like beams of light banked against the clouds, only no beams seemed to be coming from the ground. The discs disappeared simultaneously in a matter of seconds. 'They are spiritual doves,' a Puerto Rican in a white beret hastened to inform me. 'But sometimes they could be regular doves from a nearby pond ((!)) that are supernaturally inspired to fly by. It's a little treat that the Blessed Mother gives us.'" Spiritual doves, real doves, UFOs, telepathic hallucinations, meaningful coincidences - the versatility of belief is impressive - yet none of these explanations really, finally, explains anything. That's what's so damned fascinating! Incidentally, Nobile checked with La Guardia, but no UFOs had been reported - not that that particularly means anything.

The other aspect of the 'Bayside' visions of interest to us are their revelations. The prophecies, admonitions, messages and sermons in the BVM's locutions - Jesus himself doesn't speak but plants the words in Veronica's mind - have all the flavour of old-time fire and brimstone, aimed at all the corruptions of the modern world, especially that "cesspool of perversion" New York. But they also contain many themes of modern paranoia fascinating to contemporary folklorists, psychologists, ufologists, conspiritorialists and Forteans alike. For example, in September 1977, BVM warned that there was a genuine vampire on the loose in NY, who sustained humanoid form with the vital blood of others. Other messages spoke of hordes of hellish homosexuals sodomizing young boys; Satan as the 'Son of Sam'; an impostor Paul VI; John Paul I poisoned with curare. Top cardinals of the Curia (Villot, Benelli and Casaroli are vigorously named) are accused of worming their way to power in the Vatican with the aid of the Devil, and using an Italian actor (who had undergone plastic surgery at their request to look like Paul VI) in a plot to supplant Paul, who was kept prisoner in a secret cell. The BVM is credited with exposing their plan by causing a curious double exposure of a "miraculous photo" of Paul VI, taken during an audience in Rome. The group's advertisement in the Hartford Courant Connecticut, 30 December 1978 (Cr: Phil Ledger) adds that the BVM has identified the twin evils: that the rock music business is under the control of an international group of "Wicca" who consecrate each LP to Satan; and that the Illuminati are alive and well and own all media

in order to pervert youths through drugs and "school systems". Powerful stuff! But after the mass destruction of the misled (as Nobile refers to the Jonestown massacre) who's laughing any more? The "end days" might well be here!

DO YOU BELIEVE...?

In a major Gallup Poll in the USA, released on 25 May 1978, many Americans put their vote where their beliefs are. 57% said they believed UFOs were "real" (whatever that may mean), 3% up on the same question in 1973. Not much of an advance, but this is supposed to be an age of scientific rationalism (we are always being told), and skepticism went down by the same amount to 27%. For some discussion of these and allied statistics see Jerome Clark's column in UFO Report September 1978 (Cr: RF Landro)). However, belief in other aspects of the "supernatural" increased considerably, making belief in UFOs quite unremarkable. One in ten believed in witches; one in nine, ghosts, two thirds of whom claimed to have seen one. Two in five believed in the existence of devils and angels; while one in eight reckons the Loch Ness Monster and Bigfoot exist.

Like Fort before us, we note the use of the word 'believe'. Our position as Forteans is to "substitute acceptance for belief" - but of course some of us are also human. In the end it comes down to faith or belief for most people. Many scientists believe faith is the province of religion, but they're wrong. They couldn't proceed if they didn't have an equally fundamental belief that the 'laws' of science are consistent in all time and space. Faith is an absolute factor - with all the qualities of an extremity - leaving no room for doubt. You have it or you don't - and it comes and goes with devastating swiftness. Faith is the unconditional acceptance of dogma - and it is dogma in science or religion that draws the lines and decrees what is acceptable. Working covertly or openly it is also one of society's shaping forces, like suggestibility, and with the same qualities, including a hypnoid component of diminished critical faculties, intolerance of 'opposition', etc. Us doubters are all the time up against a paradox barrier: I may know what I mean, but that may not necessarily be the same thing you think I mean, or even the meaning you attach to the same words. How much simpler it is simply to relinquish the Babel of analytics and simply believe. Everyone knows what his symbol means to him and within limits is quite flexible in his belief. Belief, however is not the same as understanding - and I for one would like to understand the intricacies of an event in which apparently objective lights in the sky are seen by some as "doves", by others as UFOs, and by still others not seen at all.

Another example is the convergence of BVM visions with 'white lady' type apparitions. Within 2 months of moving into 14 Airth Drive, Mosspark, Glasgow, the Burns family were quickly rehoused (a few hundred yards away at 14 Arran Drive). In compiling a dossier of unusual lets or transfers by Glasgow's housing department, Councillor James Dunachie discovered the strange reason. It seems that no sooner had they moved in than they were persecuted by strange phenomena - noises, doors opening and closing, and apparitions. Their recorded complaint, according to the housing department, is that "a supernatural presence was affecting the family's health." Of central interest to us is that the neighbours recalled that the family, obviously shaken, said they had seen "visions of the Virgin Mary". And one member of the housing staff claimed the house "had a history of poltergeist activity" - although the latest tenants of the house have had no problems. Anyone familiar with the history of religious visions will know that visionaries are frequently the focus of poltergeist-type attacks, which in the religious context are seen as the work of the Devil. It is rare indeed to find a case that explicitly links BVM and poltergeist activity outside religious contexts, and even rarer to find ghosts being confused with BVM -- always assuming of course that the Burnses were not using their description carelessly (though even if they were, that would be interesting in itself).

As the papers picked up the story Mr Joseph Burns apparently had second thoughts - as though wishing to avoid involvement in a controversy of religion or local politics. He claimed that he was rehoused because of damp and the kitchen floor subsiding; and that all this fuss about visions was "rubbish". He also denied calling in a local priest for a service, but Monsignor Brendan Murphy, of the Cardonald parish of Our Lady of Lourdes - how appropriate! - remembers otherwise. He thinks his blessing worked successfully, since there has been no recurrence. We wish we knew more details about this interesting case, and hope an interested reader could look into it and send us a report. Glasgow Evening Times 14 December 1978, Glasgow Herald 15 December 1978 (Cr: R Watson).

Another area of apparitional experience in which the frames-of-reference of different witnesses condition their interpretations of that experience is in sightings of 'little people'. On FT7 p10, we told of a mother whose two children complained several times of being woken up from their sleep by a large-headed dwarf who wanted to play. Was this a case of fairy-contact, or the phenomenon of childrens' 'invisible playmates'? Or was it hypnagogic imagery - the hallucinations of faces or fragments of scenes etc, often very vivid, which intrude on the twilight state between waking and sleeping - yet another hypnoid state? Perhaps one child followed the other, competing for attention as children do, after being startled by a particularly vivid image? I'm not saying this is the answer, but it must rate a consideration. Reverie of some kind is a pretty constant factor in visionary and apparitional phenomena...For all we know the lady in Rowley Regis, whose mince pies were snatched by winged dwarfs (see the last story in our 'Flying Food' section) may simply have had a vivid daydream triggered by being momentarily dazzled during undemanding and routine kitchen work!

The Blade (Toledo, Ohio) 14 December 1976 (Cr: Dave Fideler) tells of a policeman who went to the aid of a man in obvious mental distress. The man claimed he was being persecuted by "invisible dwarfs" in his kitchen and cellar. The kindly cop did not arrest him, or turn away, but went into the house. He said: "I told the one dwarf in the kitchen to leave, and then went to the cellar to tell the others...They didn't put up much resistance and left." The man was so relieved he thanked the officer profusely, satisfied the little pests were gone. To judge such stories against a black-white conception of sanity-insanity is itself a form of madness. Hallucinations are as much a part of normal and even mystical life as they are of insanity. It is much more productive to to think not of sanity-insanity but of a whole range of different states of consciousness (see Hallucinations reviewed in last issue's hardbacks) in which hallucinations form an integral part of the normal (to that state) modes of perception. There are no easy answers. Consider people who hear voices. Socrates, the model of rational man, had his daemon which gave him useful information. However, some are ordered to kill their own children, blaspheme or commit weird crimes, while others, like George Fox,

go on to found the Quakers, or like Mohammed, write the <u>Koran</u>. Still others
hear the voice of their conscience, or
think the words come from UFO beings,
or the spirits of the dead! (We shall
have a section on 'Voices' in a future
issue.) Belief and context.

GUARDIAN ANGELS

Perhaps this story is another example
of the emergence of a small bubble of
self-contained reality. The concensus in
this case was the formation of a small
group of like-minded people, in St Paul,
Minnesota, to discuss occult and psychic
matters informally. In the <u>Midnight Globe</u>
8 August 1978, they claimed to have proof of the existence of guardian angels.
Jerry Gross, the group leader, told how
it happened. "During the discussions lights began to flicker, noises, knocks
and taps on the wall interrupted our conversation. We were just getting used to
these eerie events when we began to see
brief flashes of what appeared to be
ghostly apparitions. I began to wonder
if I could take a photograph of one of
these entities. One night at home alone,
I sat with my instant Polaroid camera. A
glow suddenly appeared in the dark room.
I grabbed the camera and started taking
pictures . The glow became brighter, then
at the top part of the glow, the brightest part, a face appeared. the face of a
distinguished bearded man. I managed to
take three photos, the first two showing
the glow expanding, the third ((opposite))
with the entity's face shown clearly."
The following night the group gathered
to try again - and the face of a young
woman developed on a print in front of
their eyes.
     So far nothing in this account diff-
ers from similar effects of psychic photographers, who, up to now, have claimed
these images represented either the spirits of the dead, or thoughtography (directly imprinting mental images onto un-
exposed film, etc). Later, Gross, who
claims psychic abilities, acted as medium in a seance. According to another
member of the group, "another voice"

Cross's guardian angel, Jeremiah - from
<u>Midnight Globe</u> 8 August 1978.

came out of Gross's mouth, identifying
itself as "Mora, a teacher from the Astral Plane." The voice then delivered a
series of lectures about the purpose of
life, preparation for death and life on
the astral plane - much of it conforming to, and confirming, their own beliefs, and just what they wanted to hear.
Mora also identified the face in the
photo (above) as that of Jeremiah, the
guardian angel of Gross. I could make
something of this, but I'll shut up for
once.
     In a sort of sequel to the above the
<u>Midnight Globe</u> 24 October 1978 gave the
floor to psychic Francie Steiger, with
the story of her own guardian angel called Kihief. Kihief first appeared to her
when she was 5yrs-old and her parents
had just moved into a new home. "I was
with my father in the master bedroom,
when I suddenly became aware of a being
descending right throught the ceiling.
He alighted so gently that I wasn't certain if he actually touched the floor.
He had a white robe draped over one shoulder. His hair was straw-coloured and
done in a pageboy cut. His eyes were light and wide-set. He had a large full
jaw. He was fair skinned and did not appear to have any facial hair." The being
spoke to her "in a falsetto voice", and
she turned to her father to say: "Dad,
look! There's an angel in the room." But,

she recalls, "He was caught in mid-motion in a state of suspended animation." He remained that way while Kihief and three other beings - "apparently females with darker skin, eyes and hair" - talked to her in sing-song tones. "He is not the winged creature kind of angel that we see in religious paintings, but an angel as I have come to understand them - higher intelligences from other dimensions." After this statement it should come as no surprise to many of you to learn that Francie is none other than the wife of Brad Steiger. Reader's of Steiger's own writings will recognize in these angels cousins of the UFO-entities, complete with time-distortion, selective perception, special mission to one who can see them truly, and lectures on the spiritual destiny of man, higher dimensions and the follies of modern materialism, etc. Some UFO writers have gone to the other extreme and linked UFO phenomena to the activities of demons (who, of course, were angels before the Fall).

THE VIEW FROM PARADISE

The following story sheds little light on the gloomy prospects of Iran today, but it has some interest for us.

It is said that on 13 December 1978, the Ayatollah Qomi, of the city of Marshad, burst into his mosque weeping with emotion, declaring that he had just had a visitation from the Imam Reza. Reza is one of the 12 Imams who succeeded the Prophet in the 7th century, and has become a 'patron saint' of the holy city of Marshad, being buried there after he was poisoned by Harun al-Raschid, the Caliph of The Thousand and One Nights.

The Ayatollah Qomi told his helpers that in the vision the Imam Reza denounced the Ayatollah Khomeini, exiled in Paris and recently triumphantly returned to Teheran - that he was the enemy of Islam and Iran and must be destroyed; and that the Shah must continue to rule. After the short period of shock it seems the people of Marshad, who not long before were chanting Khomeini's name, were quick to demonstrate and smash shop windows. Like all Islamic countries, where the traditions of prophecy and astrology are strong, it seems old men's dreams are still potent portenta for potentates in peril. The report in the Daily Mail 14 December 1978, added that when the news of the vision reached the holy city of Qom and Teheran itself, there were further riots. Since then we have not heard any more of possible splits between the Ayatollahs. The prospect of civil war is bad enough, but the increased fanaticism of a civil religious war is too awful to consider.   RJMR

The wags in Waukesha, Wisconsin, put up this sign to warn of unidentified leaping things - see p50 for details.

INDEX, INFO & CORLISS

We regret that the Index 1976 will have to be mailed out with the next issue, and not this one as planned, due to considerable pressure on our time. Fear not! All those who returned their vouchers will get their indexes - eventually!

We also regret that, effective immediately, we will not accept any orders or money for the INFO Journal or for the Corliss Sourcebooks. This is not intended to reflect upon them in any way - it is simply that the paperwork involved is becoming too demanding and our time very limited. We will continue to endorse both INFO and the Sourcebook Project and will carry their advertisements. Payments will have to be made direct, or through another agency. Meanwhile all orders received here up to 1st Feb 1979 will be processed; orders arriving after that will be returned to the sender. If our plans for development succeed then it may be possible to offer these and other reader services once again. We'll keep you informed.

KHOBALUS

by Robert Forrest

A friend of mine - a no nonsense, nuts-and-bolts materialist and Ph. D. chemist - scorns the idea that ghosts exist. Or Flying Saucers, for that matter. As to the possibility that people 'see' elementals in the region of ley-lines, well, you might as well tell him that the moon is made of Danish Blue. Yet he maintains a sincere belief in the Law of Universal Cussedness - that if a thing can *possibly* go wrong, it *will*. His slice of bread will always hit the floor buttered side down, and the queue at the Post Office in which he happens to be held up by a little old lady with some deviously insoluble problem, at the expense of all the other queues, which seem to empty at double the normal rate.

Whether the Universal Law of Cussedness is any more than a mode of perception is, of course, debatable. As are other curious 'laws' of Nature, or Laws of 'Perception', as the case may be.

One of these - and it is one that gives me great amusement - I call the Atomic Physicist's Dilemma. The game consists of juggling extremely obscure equations, introducing negative time, zero mass, and velocities greater than light, and thence predicting the existence of elementary particles which are more elementary than any hitherto known elementary particles. The Atomic Physicist then retires to his High Speed Betatron (or Gammatron or Zetratron, etc) or in the case of Quarks to the top of a hill, and, with disturbing frequency, and usually after a prolonged wait (like a Post Office queue, see above), discovers his predicted more-elementary-than-elementary particle. And what *particularly* amuses me about this Caucus Race is that many of its participants find ghosts a subject for mild amusement . . .

Now here's a thought. These particles of theirs - and I am willing to admit that, like dreams, in some curious way they 'exist', though not necessarily within our everyday frames of reference, since our ideas are governed by reference to a material world, and the last thing these particles are is surely to goodness material - these particles of theirs, suppose they are so flimsy that they appear only in response to the wishes of those equation-juggling physicists? I for one would like to see Uri Geller meet the Betatron . . .

But if obscure phenomena can somehow appear in response to the human will, then equally mysterious is what Arthur Koestler calls the 'Ink Fish Effect' - the tendency for certain obscure phenomena to evade investigation.

Koestler records evasive poltergeist activity [1], as indeed have many ghost hunters. F. W. Holiday records the evasiveness of the Loch Ness Monster (*Nessiteras Rhombopteryx*, as it is now known) as far as its apparent camera shyness goes [2]. And the refusal of various psychic faculties to operate under observation has long been known.

Why do not sub-atomic particles refuse occasionally to appear? Perhaps they do, but it is just that we never hear about them. After all, I cannot imagine that *Scientific American* would devote much space to the fact that I have never seen an elemental, not today, nor yesterday. (Though it must be admitted that the *New Scientist* did report at length on the non-conclusiveness of tests on Uri Geller, but I suspect that this had different motives).

Then there is the principle of Synchronicity - Jung's concept of meaningful coincidence. As Gustav Jahoda pointed out [3] it was fortunate that Jung chose the epithet 'chance grouping' as his term for 'fortuitous happening', as the term 'meaningless coincidence' rings somehow false. Every pattern is in some sense a 'meaning' when the mind comes to perceive it, and Mr Fortgibu's encounters with plum puddings [4] are surely to goodness as staggering as Jung's scarab-beetle case [5]. The following case (which I insert as it is now almost totally forgotten) does not conform to Jung's 'archetype activation' criterion for synchronistic activity, any more than Fort's 'multiple deaths' in *Wild Talents* do, and yet I cannot see for the life in me how such a case can be relegated to the realm of serendipity, whilst the scarab case becomes dignified with the title 'synchronicity'. It is from the old journal *Knowledge* (vol 1, p 270):

"The case actually occurred in France in 1794, and its details are sufficiently well known to obviate the necessity for their repetition here. Charged with robbery and murder, the innocent Lesurques was recognised, identified, and sworn to as the real culprit by various disinterested witnesses. Not withstanding strong exertions which were made to save his life, and, despite his previous high moral character and probity of conduct, Lesurques was sentenced to death and executed. Soon afterwards, the real culprit, a man who bore the closest possible likeness to Lesurques, was brought to justice. It was then seen that the similarity in features, stature, build and manner was so close as to have deceived the witnesses who gave evidence at the trial. On these grounds alone, and as a matter of common recognition and identification, the unfortunate resemblance of Lesurques to the real culprit had unwittingly led them into a 'Comedy of Errors' which resulted in a legal tragedy as its denouement. But more extraordinary to relate still is the incident well nigh unparallelled in the annals of coincidences, that Lesurques was marked by a scar on the forehead, and by another on the hand, whilst the real criminal likewise possessed similar markings."

If some 'principle' (law is such an inappropriate word here!) operates behind 'coincidence', then it is as meaningful as a child doodling on a piece of paper. Occasionally it may produce a scarab beetle at the right time, but it is just as likely to produce a grasshopper at the right time [6], or, for that matter, a plum pudding at the right time. Or, dare I say it, a sub-atomic particle at the right time.

But the law of Cussedness (a corollary of which is surely the Ink Fish Effect) and the principle of Synchronicity might only be whims of a higher 'law'. The word 'law' is again inappropriate. 'Factor' is better. I am talking now of another source of great amusement to me - the 'Absurdity Factor'. The Universe is playing with us. Or perhaps the game is two-sided. But no matter how hard we try to be 'grown up' in this universe, there is a streak of childishness in the game.

Jacques Vallee did a splendid job of collecting material relevant to this in *Passport to Magonia*. UFOs that make noises like sewing machines. Gnomes that dress Elizabethan style and poke about the roots of trees like traditionally industrious fairies. Boggle-eyed UFO pilots who come all the way from Ganymede to 'utilise the western hemisphere', eat pancakes, or request a bag of fertiliser.

FWH Myers recorded a similar 'meaningless' streak in encounters with ghosts [7], and Dennis Bardens has recorded a sublimely ludicrous case [8].

(I would here like to record my similar experience of 'encounters' with so-called ordinary people. But that is another matter.)

It makes one think that the 'meaningful' encounters - whether with ghosts, UFOs or the contents of coincidences - are only successful shams. That perhaps Jung's scarab only chanced (!) to be 'meaningful', in Jung's sense, because it was a part of a scheme that delighted in producing scarabs when scarabs were the, locally, 'in thing', just as grasshoppers were a locally in-thing somewhere else, or plum-puddings were a locally in-thing elsewhere again. The simple delight in producing patterns for patterns' sake - admittedly a meaningfulness of a sort, though hardly of the significance with which Jung seems to have been preoccupied. A delight in producing patterns because patterns are 'nice'. Because patterns are 'fun'. Kammerer's 'Serial Wonderland Universe' seems more appropriate than Jung's 'Synchronicity', with all of its part-time significance.

It almost appears as if the Universe is a living thing, and it likes to play with people occasionally. Who knows - perhaps the way it has made us hare round in ever-widening circles, on this mad-cap quest for order and significance that Man finds so compelling, is the Universe's biggest laugh ever.

The Greeks had a name for the god who delighted in perplexing people. They called him Khobalus. We in the twentieth century have a lot of fanciful terms for this or that effect - like synchronicity cussedness and neutrino. And yet I cannot see that we have progressed much beyond the ancient Greeks. We have a lot of fanciful words. The Greeks had one. Khobalus. How clever of them to fit all that into just one word . . .

In the spirit of Charles Fort, the author reserves the right to classify the above article alongside Darwin's *Origin of the Species*, Gardner's *Fads and Fallacies in the name of Science* and the complete works of Lewis Carroll. Q.E.D.

References:
1) Hardy, Harvie & Koestler: *The Challange of Chance* (Hutchinson, 1973)
2) FW Holiday: *The Dragon and the Disc* (Futura, 1974) p 184ff.
3) G Jahoda: *The Psychology of Superstition:* (Pelican, 1970) p 120ff.
4) Camille Flammarion: *The Unknown.* (Harper, 1900) p 194ff.
5) CG Jung: *Synchronicity* (Routledge & Kegan Paul, 1955) p 31.
6) as 1). p 185-6.
7) FWH Myers: *Human Personality and its Survival of Bodily Death* (Longmans, Green & Co; abridged ed, 1907) p 215-6.
8) Dennis Bardens: *Ghosts and Hauntings.* (Fontana, 1967) p 145.

[Editor's note – when we received this article from Bob I thought that his title was a clever pseudo-Greek for "cobblers" - I really should have known better! Bob sent the following clarification: "I had assumed that your interpretation of the name was an expression of opinion about the article, so I laughed along with you and left it at that. It never entered my head that the god Khobalus was so obscure that very few people would have heard of him, and that you might assume I had made the name up! He - or perhaps I should say 'they' - did exist, and I first came upon him/them in J Harland & TT Wilkinson's *Lancashire Folk Lore* (1882) p 16: 'The English Puck (the Lancashire Boggart), the Scotch Bogle, the French Goblin, the Gobelinus of the Middle Ages, and the German Kobold, are probably only varied names for the Grecian Khobalus, whose sole delight consisted in perplexing the human race, and evoking those harmless terrors that constantly hover round the minds of the timid.'"]

* * * * * * * * * * * * * * *

"I'll swear he knows we haven't got a camera"

Weekend 17-23 December 1975

From our 'Compulsions' file comes a sundry selection of snippers, slashers, snatchers and scratchers, who have pursued their strange work over the last few years.

SNATCHERS

A phantom spectacles snatcher was busy in Glasgow in 1975. On 21 July, teenager Alex Campbell was standing outside his home in Dalmally Street, Maryhill, when a man driving a yellow Avenger pulled up to ask directions. He wrenched Alex's glasses from his face and drove off. Five similar thefts had been reported in the city that year. Daily Mirror 22 July 1975. Three months later (?) another specialist began his work in the Thornton Heath area of South London. The Sunday Mirror 4 January 1976 said the police were "closing in" on this snatcher. In three months he had whipped glasses from eleven short-sighted women who couldn't give an in-focus description. But a witness, with good eye sight, who saw the latest incident involving a 15yr-old girl,was able to give some sort of description. By April, however, he (or another?) had claimed five more victims - all Asian women - and had taken to wearing a black plastic bag or cardboard box on his head. London Evening News 5 April 1976. He struck about 30 times in the Norbury, Croydon and Norwood areas in 1976 - by 1977 he started using violence, holding a knife to one woman's throat and thumping another from behind. A police spokesman said: "He must have a drawer full of spectacles at home. Heaven only knows what he does with them." Sunday Mirror 10 July 1977, Daily Mirror 4 August 1977.

16 January 1978 - a youth approached pedestrian Frank Dolman, in Chippenham, Somerset, and swiped his trilby. Further west, the phantom hat snatcher of Torbay, who has been busy for three years, struck at least 24 times by March. His targets were all women, with ages between 33 and 85. Sometimes he settled for scarves or turbans. Back in 1923 chauffeur Henry Hall of Harringay was done for stealing 164 ladies hats from the milliner who employed him. Easier work, but not so adventurous! Bath Chronicle 17 January 1978; Daily Mirror 22 March 1978; Daily Telegraph 30 November 1923.

8 September 1977 - a new hunt for the elusive scarf-snatcher of Paignton, Devon, who had struck at least 25 times in a year. Once he yanked a handful of hair from an elderly woman's head along with her scarf. Daily Mail 9 Sept 1977.

Shoes seem to be very popular! In the closing months of 1978 the high-heel hijacker of Seattle had been giving police a headache - was it mugging, sex-crime or assault? The victims were always young attractive women wearing heels at least 8cm high. In September he laid in wait in bushes - by November he was bolder, grabbing shoes just as they were raised off the pavements. Sales of flat shoes and sandals were booming. In 1913 a slipper-snatcher haunted New York. In 1924, London tramdriver John Pitman, 31, was caught in the act. Several incidents had preceeded. When asked why he did it he said: "I don't know. I am very sorry. I am married." Then, in 1929, shoes were snatched in Stockholm - only small dainty shoes. Reveille 15 September 1978. (Cr: Nigel Watson); Sydney Sunday Telegraph 19 November 1978 (Cr: Ion Will); Daily Express 23 April 1913, News of the World 25 May 1924, Star 20 November 1929 (Cr: G Ives).

Always odd shoes...as Fort said: "If Jack the Slipper-snatcher were in the secondhand business, he'd have manoeuvred girls into having both feet in the air."

SNIPPERS & SLASHERS

23 June 1977 - Graham Carter, a bespectacled school careers officer aged 23, was apprehended in Oxford Circus, London, after cutting a hole in Rosanna Reeves' dress. For six months he had prowled the Picadilly, Oxford Circus and Green Park underground stations, cutting out neat squares from expensive clothes and exposing the bottoms of at least 18 girls. He produced a diary logging these low-down deeds. One girl had walked almost the length of Oxford Street before anyone told her what had happened. But the case was far from closed - police received more complaints while their culprit was in custody. Said Carter's lawyer: "There is certainly one other person, if not more, doing this sort of thing." Daily Express, Daily Mirror, Sun 5 August 1977 & 2 September 1977; + unnamed US paper (Cr: AB & PR)

28 November 1978 - Stephen Jordan, 26, a motor mechanic from Woking, Surrey, with a marriage on the rocks, was in court admitting 9 snipping incidents at Earls Court station, London, between 6 September and 3 November 1978. But who was doing the snipping between the arrests of Carter and Jordan? Daily Telegraph, Daily Express, 29 November 1978.

Going back in time in our file we find a slasher of childs' boots in Portsmouth in 1901; a dress snipper who worked the upper decks of London busses in 1910; back in Portsmouth again in 1923 - and a dress-snipper in 1923 - and the cases of Stanley Scaife, Sheffield, 1932, who fastened to women's clothes pieces of copper wire attached to cotton wool soaked in sulphuric acid; and of Sidney Eastbury in Birmingham, busted in 1926 and 1935, who escalated his snipping into the world of art by throwing a mixture of chocolate and oil. Anon clipping 1901; News of the World 4 November 1910 & 1 February 1926; Daily News 7 November 1923; Reynolds' News 31 January 1932; Star 5 March 1935 (Cr: G Ives).

An interesting early case of an elusive 'Jack the Cushion-ripper' arose in 1921. Despite the vigilance of inspectors and plain clothes police he managed to slash 40 seats on the 'K' and 'S' bus lines. London Evening News 11 Mar 1921. (Cr: G Ives)

In February 1927, labourer James Leonard was "smartly punished" for slashing dresses in Halifax, Yorkshire, over a six month period. He had worked the theatre and bus queues, and was fingered, finally, when his peculiar nose was recognised. In 1938 an epidemic of slashing spread from Halifax to Bradford, then to Wigan, Brentford, Settle, Sale and Glasgow. Police believed that apart from the original slasher and his 13 victims, "an accumulation of incidents" had been attributed to a bogey man. At the height of the epidemic, boys in a Sheffield school took to slashing girls in the playground. News of the World 20 February 1927 Reynolds' News, 4 December 1938.

BITERS & JABBERS

From the Middletown, NY, Record for 23 April 1978 (Cr: AB & PR) we have a report of a man with a taste for fingernails. On 16 April a young man walks into an office, in Monticello, NY, admires the receptionist's long fingernails, takes her hand, bites off her thumbnail and walks out. Four days later he strikes again, asking a woman for the time. After admiring her nails he takes her hand and attempts to put it in his mouth. When she objects he tells her: "I just wanted to touch it to my teeth." Which brings us to the case of Rosana Vigil ((the Rosannas are for snatching, eh? Ed.)) in Denver, whose mouth was pried open by a man in the street who snatched her false teeth. Mrs Vigil, 60, told police: "He said, 'There ain't no gold here, so here's your teeth', and he gave 'em back." New York Post undated (Cr: AB & PR). Back in 1942, a bogus dentist plied his trade in Nottingham. His first victim was Mrs Mable Foulkes. He put her in a chair, opened her mouth and no sooner had he told her one of her molars needed attention than it was jerked out. "Isn't it a beauty?" he exclaimed before dashing away. Sunday Dispatch 21 June 1942 (Cr: G Ives).

More than a hundred women were cornered in Paris lifts in 1976 and jabbed in the breast with a fish-hook. No attacks in the winter, but by April 1977 the jabbing recommenced. <u>Daily Mirror</u> 6 April 1977.

21 September 1978 - Tokyo police arrested a 26yr-old draughtsman for scratching 12 young women on the face with a tiepin, on commuter trains. He said he was furious and exhausted from going to work on crowded trains, and it helped to dissipate his gloom. Police later said he was a manic-depressive who had been under treatment since his arrest last December

for assaulting two young boys. <u>Straits Times</u>, Singapore, 21 & 22 September 1978 (Cr: Ion Will). In 1924, a Greek named Setano was arrested in Paris for stabbing two young men with a tie-pin. The <u>Daily Mirror</u> for 18 March 1924 said: "He is thought to be the pest, till now undetected, who has been active in Paris for years."

Finally, ears...The Sydney <u>Daily Telegraph</u> 1 November 1978 (Cr: Ion Will) reported that Aboullah al Shirap, 52, a wealthy Arab stock-broker, had bitten off a girl's ear in a London flat. 'Ere, 'ere!

PS

QE2'S MYSTERY MESSAGE

In FT26p47 we mentioned the mystery radio signal received by the QE2 ocean liner. It was in an obsolete code and seemed to have been sent out by the old liner Queen Mary more than 11years before. Since then we have had further details which clarify earlier incomplete and in parts inaccurate information.

Alan Holmes, radio officer on the QE2, in the Atlantic bound for America, was on watch when he received a morse message: "GKS GBTT QSX AREA 1A". Recognizing that it was coded in a proceedure no longer in use, Holmes deciphered it as a routine position check from the old liner Queen Mary to the Portishead Radio, at Burnham, Somerset. There is a double curiosity here - not only the coincidence that the QE2 had inherited the GKS call sign from Queen Mary before the code was discontinued, but that the Queen Mary was pensioned off over 11yrs previously, sold to the City of Long Beach, California, as a floating conference center. When the news leaked out, Alan said in media interviews that he believed the signal was bounced back off something in space, perhaps 5 light years away.

On BBC TV, 11 August 1978, a spokesman for the Station manager smirked dismissively at the idea of a long delayed signal, saying (in roughly these words) that it was inconceivable that a message from his station could have left the Earth at just the right angle to hit a planet, or whatever, and then return to enter Earth's atmosphere to be received by the very ship that had inherited the old call sign. Pressed to explain he said: "I just don't believe it!" (Cr: John Michell). However, the Station manager himself, Donald Mulholland, said, in an interview with <u>Hello World</u>, the house magazine of the Post Office External Telecommunications Executive, that as far as he was concerned, "The most likely explanation is that someone was hoaxing Mr Holmes." What a thoroughly uninspired and unimaginative response from those whose daily business is radio transmission, and who must frequently come face to face with anomalous phenomena (as we shall shortly see!) In the same article Alan Holmes said he was fed up with justifying the event..."If I'd been alone on watch, I'd never have mentioned it...I was not alone in the radio shack at the time, and the message really did come in. I was listening out on a frequency used for radio telephone calls. I can't explain it." He had doubts about being the victim of a hoax. "(If it was a hoax) it's an elaborate hoax, rather difficult to lay on, and hardly worth the bother of laying on. The hoaxer would have had to know exactly what frequency we were listening out on, and when." Hello World Autumn 1978, p4 (Cr: Michael Goss).

Other possibilities have been mooted: transmission by UFO, or some freak of preservation that cannot be accounted for with present knowledge. We find an intriguing detail mentioned in the BBC report cited above - that shortly after the receipt of the message "a mysterious blackout silenced all messages to and from Atlantic shipping for a time." Since we don't know the actual date and time of the arrival of the message - the reports only say "earlier this year' - we cannot pinpoint any correlating phenomena or reports.

Curiously, in the same issue of Hello World (p11), is a description of another freak transmission, this time from the fishing vessel Kitty in the North Sea, which broadcast on the international distress frequency (2182kH). Normally this carries only a few hundred miles, but the message was picked up by Awarua Radio (callsign ZLB) some 10,000 miles away on the New Zealand coast. The report says Awarua then heard the German coast station Norddeich Radio dealing with the emergency, and Oban Radio dealing with a French ship off NW Scotland. Unfortunately no date is given.

ECHOES OF OLD BATTLES

The notion of picking up ancient undecayed transmission reminds me of Wellington's radio, in the Perishers strip in the Daily Mirror - no matter what station he tuned in he got the relief of Mafeking, and likewise his old phonograph would ignore your selection and belt out 'The Dardanelles'. Can EM waves sidestep in time? There have been cases like the QE2 story which appear to suggest that, and data on apparent temporal teleportations are of great interest to us. Just lately it's been message time-jump time...   ⟨she
In the Daily Express for mid-August 1978, appeared a letter from a Mrs Helen Griffith, who said that while crossing the English Channel in 1977⟨"heard" the sounds of a World War 2 sea battle. It may indeed have been since there is a strong tradition on the French coast that on the anniversary of the 19 August 1942 storming of Dieppe, the phantom

sounds of the battle can be heard in an eerie replay. The phenomenon was studied by the SPR in 1952 - and a useful summary appears in the Readers Digest Strange Stories: Amazing Facts (1975) p384f.

Anyway...we were unable to clip Mrs Griffith's letter, but we did catch another letter which referred to it. AJ Peterson, of Crayford, Kent, wrote that while his son was with the British Army in Borneo, 10 years ago, his patrol of the Green Howards picked up a radio message they couldn't decipher. "Back at base they handed the message to Intelligence who found it was in a long discarded code...a message sent during an action in the last war." Daily Express 22 August 1978 (Cr: Mrs L Chibbett). Makes you wonder just how many similar stories are lying around untold...and if there is the faintest echo of truth in these anomalous sounds then many branches of science will have to do some rethinking!

By far the biggest such story - it even made headlines - alleged that sounds from World War 2 sea battles are echoing around the North Atlantic. The US Navy has a network of super-sensitive hydrophones, called SOSUS - Sound Surveillance System - buried on the ocean floor, and linked to land stations scattered along the coasts where armies of listeners compare the incoming sounds with computerized libraries of submarine sounds and engine noises. According to a priviledged report in the US News and World Report (cited in the Telegraph as the primary source of the story) strange and unaccountable faint sounds have been picked up since SOSUS was installed in 1952. It was suggested these sounds, like distant explosions and cannon fire, were being perpetuated by freak conditions under the sea in much the same way as a coil immersed in liquid helium becomes 'superconductive', losing all resistence and allowing any current to flow virtually unobstructed for a very long time. One expert on undersea surveillance though the cause might be the known existence of deep channels which "act like huge natural telephone cables. Sound seems to be able to travel along them without deterioration in the signal. The sound goes back and forth, losing hardly any of its strength..." Strange currents and temperature conditions seem to create these 'deep sound channels', but there is a snag to this theory, as this expert admitted: "Not all sounds are 'stored' in this way for years. The sounds apparently have to have occurred at the right place...but how sounds get into this 'system' remains a mystery." It is well known that the sounds of undersea earthquakes and volcanic activity can carry extraordinary distances in the sea, and some critics have indeed explained these sounds this way. But the SOSUS experts could hardly have overlooked such an obvious explanation (if relevant) before coming out with this remarkable theory. They also admitted to being baffled by a "crying baby" sound, despite extensive analysis. They are definite that it is not caused by "a marine creature or some underwater natural phenomenon". The account in the Mirror spoke of a theory that the sound was "trapped" after a child drowned in a sinking boat - but where they heard this is conveniently unreferenced. Generally reaction from the Admiralty, and Britain's Institute of Oceanographic Sciences, is doubting - the main criticism being that sound travelling any distance through water would soon dissipate. Conditions would have to be anomalous indeed. Daily Telegraph 13 November 1978 (Cr: Anthony Roberts, Valerie Martin, Richard Cotton); Daily Mirror 3 January 1979; Weekend 10 January 1979.

VOICES FROM OTHER WORLDS

An alternative theory that occurred to us was prompted by the receipt of an article by Alan Cleaver on 'Electronic Voice Phenomena' (EVP) - to be printed next issue. EVP includes weird and often coherent fragments of human speech found on a tape recording, which were not apparent to the ear during recording. Perhaps, we wondered, the sophisticated microphones on the ocean floor manage to pick up sounds from other times when certain anomalous conditions coincide? This is a variation on the theory that specific places or stones can record violent events in their vicinity, to be 'decoded' by a human sensitive sometime in the future, who then sees a ghost or a vision. Perhaps not!

Our final item complicates or clarifies the mystery - according to how convinced you are about any of the cases. Eleven-year-old Tracy McCarthy was listening to a tape of home-recorded music. During a take of Donna Summer singing 'I Feel Love' the music suddenly gave way to "a crashing noise", followed by the chilling sound of screaming men. As men seemed to groan in pain and a boy whimpered, an eerie voice called out clearly: "Is there anybody down there?" Then a muffled voice mumbled some thing about dead bodies and the music returned. Tracy was shocked, and told her parents, who heard the disaster-scenario for themselves. Since then 'recording experts' are mentioned as having analysed

the tape in a fully equipped studio and confessing to being baffled - if it was faked they could not detect it. Tracy's mother Joyce said, at their home in Whiteheath, Birmingham: "We recorded the music some time ago and there was nothing like that on the tape. We have played it dozens of times before without hearing these dreadful noises. The ghostly voices suddenly appeared - the mystery has completely baffled us." Since the sounds were highly suggestive of a subterranean disaster, and there were several coal mines in the area in the last century, someone suggested it might be some ghostly recording of a mining accident. Sure enough one was found - the Black Bat mine, quite near the McCarthy home. It was closed in 1883, five years after several men and boys died in a roof fall! The report is slanted towards linking the two events - but this raises a lot of complicated questions. But how did the sounds get on the tape in the first place? EVP? Sunday People 8 October 1978.

IT'S CERTAINLY NOT GREEK...

While we're on the subject of mystery messages, here are a few linguistic spanners in the cosmic works...

A note in the Sunday Times 5 February 1978 (Cr: Ion Will), announced the launch of a 16yr project to compile a Sumerian dictionary, translating the world's oldest recorded language (it says here) from tablets at Pennsylvania University, Philadelphia. Apparently some of the ancient phrases are making the good professors hot under the collar...after weeks of analysis one still comes out as: "He put a hot fish in her navel." Just for the halibut, eh?

Not that it's much good trusting complex syntax etc. to computers, as is the trend today. One Finnish computer programmed to write poetry came up with the immortal words: "The green elephant makes love to jumping horses." Daily Mirror 5 July 1977.   RJMR

■■■■■■■■■■■■■■■■■■■■■■■■■■■■■■■■

TRUSS FUND...

Our sincere thanks are expressed to the following for their helpful donations: Lionel Beer; Ros Croson; RD Churchward; Alan Gardiner; Mrs PD Hall; Olive Oltcher; Richard Palcanis; Paul Pinn; John Peldyak; Bob Skinner; Mike & Linda Ward in memory of George F Haas; PJ Williams.

Over the last few years of collecting notes on all kinds of falling and flying objects, substances and animals, we have accumulated quite a few on aerial edibles. On FT15p17 we told of a string of sausages high among a tree's branches which seemed to have fallen from the sky...now head for cover as the phantom food flinger strikes again...

CHICKEN SURPRISE!

On several occasions a country school at Wokingham, Berks, was the target of UFOs - unidentified flying omelettes. Children would be sent scrambling for cover as eggs fell out of the sky to splat on the playground, and mothers, taking their kids to school, have seen eggs hitting cars, fencing, and even trickling from rooftops. Mrs Ann Norman, of Wokingham, said: "They must drop from high up because they make a terrific noise when they hit the ground." The mothers suppose they are being dropped from a light aircraft, and have named the phantom bantam the Rhode Island Red Baron - but a Civil Aviation Authority spokesperson, at Heston, Middlesex, didn't think too much of the idea. Plane noises have been heard sometimes when eggs have been seen falling, but no one can link the two definitely. These bombardments, which ceased suddenly, occurred in early December 1974. We note the school's name is Keep Hatch! If these events were an elaborate practical yolk no one could say what anyone would have gained by going to so much trouble. Sun 12 December 1974 (Cr: Anthony Smith).

Then a silence until 1977. It may be that our hoaxer (if that's what he, or it, is) went into retirement, and thirsting once more for the thrill of terrorizing mortals, began creeping around Abingdon, Oxfordshire, with an armful of six-packs. In mid-1977 he struck regularly on Tuesdays and Thursdays, usually restricting himself to West St Helen Street, over several months. James Heast of Glendale Electrical Services said they had been hit about 36 times in five months; and once a woman standing outside the estate agents next door was hit on the head. The estate agent's secretary said the phantom even worked nights, smashing eggs on parked cars. Shell-shocked shopkeepers, tiring of the hard rain, got up their own vigilante groups, but to no avail. The Abingdon police, though, claimed to have a suspect...but we never heard anymore about the affair. Perhaps some reader could look into it? London Evening News 9 September 1977.

Such cases are always interesting if only for their similarity to poltergeist-type incidents in which people are bombarded with stones or refuse, and to the so-called 'phantom sniper' cases of mystery bullets or wounding without any apparent penetration of the clothing or room etc. On its face value the evidence points towards some teleportive force. But none of this will convince the hardened sceptics, unlike the similar phenomena of falls and poltergeist outbreaks - but its that similarity which catches our interest, and we suspect that below the prankish appearances laid on by the Cosmic Trickster lies yet another clue to the mysterious forces of our existence. What can you make, for example, of the woman who found a perfect but cold fried egg beside her on her bus seat (Sunday People 9 July 1978)?...or of the unwrapped frozen chickens that appeared in the Centurion Inn, at Vicars Cross, near Chester? Landlord Les Brooke found first one in his bar, the next day two more still frozen, and the following weekend three laid out in a triangle in the pub car park. Whether or not the first appearances were the product of teleportation or absent-mindedness, we have some doubt about the continuing incidents, because the fowl fusilier has taken to making phonecalls. At first he just clucked into the phone; later he announced himself as the Chicken Man and said he'd leave more chicken surprises. After a few silent days he called again to say he'd been ill (chicken pox?) but had managed something. The Brookes opened their door and found a giant tin of peas. We suspect the demon distributor might be found among the Centurion regulars, elaborating an earlier mystery. Reveille 24 March 1978. For more of people who really dress the part, see our 'Strange Behaviour' section this issue.

DINNER'S ON THE HOUSE!

A particularly good case of aerobatic eatables was announced recently in the Sunday Express 3 December 1978 (Cr: Janet & Colin Bord, Richard Cotton), but we also have notes from the Guardian 11 November 1978 (Peter Rogerson) and the Niagara Falls Review 16 Dec 1978 (Cr: Dwight Whalen). A torrent of trajectorial treats, including black puddings, eggs, bacon, bread and tomatoes, have been hitting the doors of four old people's bungalows at Castleton, Derbyshire. Apparently the benevolent beanfeast bunger began his bombardment in late 1977 when a variety of fresh groceries, including legs of mutton,hit doors, windows, walls,and landed in the gardens. Like the chilled chicken chucker and the etherial egg ejector, the source of these cometary comestibles has eluded the grasp of the local police, despite the almost nightly watches mounted by the village bobby, Norman Young. The matter has even been raised at a local council meeting. Councillor Charles Lewis said: "It's annoying. The culprits are either raiding a deep freeze or have got a supply to be able to do it. Once a full 1lb black pudding was hurled. There have been entire loaves of bread, and a dozen large eggs at once." Mr Fred Robinson, 74, of Weaving Avenue, said: "Black puddings, bacon, tomatoes and eggs have all been thrown at my house. The attacks were irregular. Every other night...then nothing for weeks on end. But he hasn't struck since the police were brought in. We hope it stays that way." Mrs Ethel Bramley, said: "It's unreal, weird! If people want to give us food why not wrap it up and leave it on the doorstep?" Another added: "There's not much you can do with an egg once it has hit a door!" Police admitted that they had failed to trace the ghostly grocer - there have been no reports of thefts of quantities of food, especially black puddings, and no one has been seen buying large quantities...but we suspect that such searches may be a waste of time anyway if the stuff is coming down from, you know, up there!

The Daily Mirror for 8 November 1978

told of a rain of sloshy mashed potato over houses, cars and gardens in Kings Avenue, Kings Lynn, Norfolk. As with many reports of strange events, if there is a terrestrial, practical and halfway sensible cause, it is located pretty quickly - unlike the genuine mysteries which drag on until the press tire of publishing half-assed theories to explain-away the enigma - in this case a production fault at the nearby Dornay Foods factory resulted in granules of mashed potato being blasted out through an extractor fan. When William Bankes' car was hit by something from the sky on a motorway just 2 miles from his home in Ainsdale, Lancs, his inclination too was to explain it naturalistically. In a fleeting glimpse he thought it was a housebrick - there was no time to swerve so he braked hard and covered his face with his arms - then there was "a tremendous bang like an explosion. But despite the noise no damage was visible from the driving seat, so I got out to look at the front of the car. I was astounded to see, there in the road, the remains of a large frozen carrot, diced into tiny squares by the radiator grill, which with a headlamp surround was smashed. "I shudder to think what would have happened had it come through the windscreen, " said Mr Bankes, adding a guess that it must have been falling around 50mph. As he looked at the damage, he says he heard a flock of geese overhead, and speculated that one of them must have dropped the carrot since he knew of complaints of carrot fields being ruined by wild geese. These points were confirmed separately: the Wildfowl

THE UFO EXAMINER

The reality of the UFO phenomenon can no longer be doubted!!! Read about the following in the pages of the EXAMINER:

* CLOSE ENCOUNTERS WITH UFOs
* UFO LANDINGS
* OCCUPANT SIGHTINGS
* ABDUCTIONS
* UFO NEWS FROM AROUND THE WORLD

THE ONLY MAGAZINE WITH COMPLETE COVERAGE OF IOWA SIGHTINGS!!!

Only $6.00 for 4 quarterly issues ·
Send Check or Money Order to: PRIVATE UFO INVESTIGATIONS
Rt. No. 1, Hazleton, Iowa 50641 U.S.A.

Trust said flocks of pink-footed geese numbering up to 6,000 were known to be in the area; and the National Farmer's Union said there had been scores of reports of geese devouring carrot crops; then "physics experts" at Manchester University agreed that a carrot dropped by a goose at 100ft would hit the earth at about 50mph. I don't know how convenient all this strikes you as being, but I'm astonished! I know what an "expert" would say to me if I pestered him with questions about geese dropping carrots! Still...as far as everyone in the story is concerned, the case is solved and closed. But I wonder... Sunday Express 7 January 1979 (Cr: Janet & Colin Bord, Lionel Beer).

We also have a note, missed at the time by Fortean mags, that Stanley Morris, of Louisville, Kentucky, rushed into his backyard after hearing a noise like an explosion. He found it littered with bags of cookies - there were more on his garage roof and in neighboring gardens. They contained no writing or numbers or any means of identification, and, inevitably, were thought to have been dropped, or spilled, from a plane. I find that explosive noise interesting, since one often finds similar sounds associated with other kinds of falls. St Louis Post-Dispatch, Missouri, 10 November 1965.

TAKE ME TO YOUR LARDER!

Finally, I was intrigued by one of the current crop of UK UFO reports, which may be related to flying food phenomena as reasonably as carrots to flying geese or black puddings to invisible and unfindable marksmen. Mrs Jean Hingley, of Bluestone Walk, Rowley Regis, West Midlands, reported a close encounter to the local police. She said when she opened her back door..."there

was a blinding light" and three little green men with wings went past her into her lounge. "They had horrible waxy faces, like corpses." Jean offered them coffee - well, what would you have done? - but instead they asked for a simple glass of water. How often that detail recurs in close encounters, I leave to UFO researchers to calculate! Then, on their way out, they picked up a plate of Jean's mince pies, and said they'd be back sometime. Meanwhile keep your eyes peeled for a report of a fall of mince pies! Daily Mirror 6 January 1979 (Cr: Dave Baldock, Doc Shiels). RR

getting cross

Sometimes we can only shake our heads and wonder at the bizarre behaviour of religious devotees...still more so at the grotesque example of families and onlookers as they witness their loved ones immolating themselves.

Take, for example, the case of Eliana Maciel Barbosa, a 16-year-old Roman Catholic girl living in Rosario Do Sui, Brazil. For six months she had been tormented with nightmares and "evil visions". Medical tests proved negative so she concluded that her soul had been possessed by demons and evil forces. Finally, she had a dream in which a kindly old man "who looked like God" appeared to her, and told her how to drive out the demons. Yes, you guessed it: he told her to crucify herself. So on Friday 9 February 1978, she dragged a 44lb wooden cross, 9½ft tall, up the 450ft high Picucho Hill, in an arid, unpopulated part of the state of Rio Grande do Sul, was duly strapped to it, and hung there until the following Monday night.

We could understand this if it were simply the lone delusion of a hysterical girl, but this self-torture was carried out with the full knowledge and assistance of her family. Indeed, her father was arrested afterwards for slashing her wrists and feet with a razor; and that after the police had refused him permission to actually nail her to the cross. And as for the crowds...

The whole thing was like a circus, it seems: 20 chartered buses running in 5,000 people, many of them maimed and crippled, dabbing themselves in the girl's blood and praying for a miracle; to the accompaniment of crying beer and hot-dog vendors, preying on the faithful. Whether Eliana was actually cured, we know not...but by the time she descended from the cross, she was being proclaimed a saint throughout Brazil.

A personal Calvary . . . Eliana Barbosa and onlookers during her three-day self-crucifixion

Chicago Sun-Times, Washington Post, 14 February 1978, Sun, 15 Feb 1978, Guardian, Rand Daily Mail (SA) 16 Feb 1978, Sunday Times (SA), 19 March 1978. (Cr: Mark Hall, Chris Holtzhauzen, Ion Will)

If the crowd came hoping for a miracle in Brazil, in the Phillipines it seems they are more hardened to such scenes. We have an unfortunately unnamed UPI clipping of 1977(78?) (Cr: Kurt Lothmann) showing Juanito Piring, a former convict, being crucified, with nails this time, for the twelfth year running, "to make up for his sins". He got the crowds all right...but this time it was a jeering, unruly mob of 10,000.

The English, of course are much more practical about such things. Or would be if they were allowed to get away with it. Stuntman Eddie Shingler was intent on spending Easter 1976 nailed to a cross in Nottingham, and he was up to his tricks again in January 1978. But on both occasions police warned him that whoever drove the 7-inch nails through his hands and feet would be prosecuted for assault; so, after gaining some valuable publicity, the 61yr-old stuntman called off his attempts. But more practical? Well, not only did Eddie want to "prove the power of God";

he wanted to charge £3 to watch him being nailed up, and 50p to see him hanging on the cross! Daily Mirror, 13 Apr, 1976, Sunday People, 18 April 1976 (Cr: Nigel Watson), Sunday People, 15 Jan 78.

the 'muti' man

Not the phantom cattle-slayer of the American plains, though the name is suggestive: a "muti" man is a South African ritual murderer, and one of them was stalking Pretoria between 1974 and 1978. During that period, he attacked 12 girls aged between 7 and 10, all African except one who was "coloured", killing 9 of them. The victims had their throats cut, sometimes with the lid of a tin can, and pieces of skin cut from their bodies, usually from the thighs, though two had their tongues removed and flesh cut from their faces. The police were baffled and even called in local sangomas and witch-doctors to help, eventually bringing in "Mpapane", the most powerful sangoma in in the Transvaal, with his 10 assistants. But his powers failed too, and even when they gathered the parents of the dead children together and administered a special potion, they were unable to visualise the face of the killer. That was in September; but we're pleased to report that by November an arrest had been made. After another girl had been found with her throat cut, a man was held, and reported to have been carrying a human windpipe. And that, thankfully, is the last we've heard of him. Pretoria News, 9 January 1978, Sunday Express (SA) 10 September 1978, Rand Daily Mail 30 Nov 1978. (Cr: Chris Holtzhausen.)   SM

wizard pranks

A few more tales from the Dark Continent: In Togo, Adjata Koffi, 30, was arrested for beheading a man with a machete, and attempting to do the same to a woman, who received critical injuries. He was attempting to protect a new church from evil. Sun-Herald (Sydney) 15 October 1978 (Cr: Ion Will). This, of course, is an ancient ritual under a thin Christian veneer (extremely thin, in fact!) but we have purer tales of witchery...

A court case in Accra, Ghana: Mrs Sclina Laryea, 67, sued Nii Djan for defamation when he called her a witch. Seems that Djan's grandson, Alfred Odartey, is a schoolboy wizard, and he claims Mrs Laryea made him one. She put some drugs in his eyes, it seems, and he began to see fellow witches who at first sight appeared like white sheep. After that, he began "flying" nightly to "witchery banquets" near his school. And if he was left without money for his fare home, he simply flew. Though, if that was the case, we wonder why he used public transport in the first place. Neat trick, though! South China Morning Post 25 October 1977 (Cr: Guy Audebrand).

And finally, another goody from Accra: Togbui Siza Aziza, a Togolese jujuman, was placed in a coffin; the lid was nailed down; the coffin was lowered into an ordinary grave, piled with concrete slabs, a layer of mortar, then more concrete slabs. Aziza is a member of "Afrika Adzeu", a group which promotes African mysticism, and says he can spend 7 days undergound; but in this case he settled for 3 hours. His wife sat at the head of the grave with a bowl of herbal mixture, which could be seen to stir several times, while Aziza's voice could be heard   clearly from below ground. After two hours twenty minutes, as the crowd began panicking, he agreed to come out. The ground shook, and suddenly Aziza burst through the mortar, shoving concrete slabs aside. Not only that, but the lid of the coffin was still nailed down, a cloth and some "mystic equipment" were still inside. He also achieved

something else remarkable: emptying an entire football stadium while the match was still in play, when rumour got round that a dead man had risen from the grave. Aziza says he has had supernatural powers since childhood, vanishing when he was one year old and returning when he was seven, emerging from the village dumping pit. He claims to understand the language of animals, and to be able to cure a wide variety of diseases, usually after meditating underground. Pretoria News (S.A.) (Late 1974 (?)) Cr: Chris Holtzhausen)   SM

Covered with earth and mortar, Aziza climbs from the grave, watched by an incredulous crowd.

℞eview ⑂upplement

We welcome books and journals for review or exchange on all topics of related interest. The details and contents of journals are given in the next issue after receipt, and the return favour in their pages would be appreciated.

hardbacks

Mysteries by Colin Wilson (Hodder & Stoughton, 1978; £9.95, pp667, index, bib, notes) - The World Atlas of Mysteries by Francis Hitching (William Collins, 1978; £6.50, pp257, index, bib, maps, photos, illos) -- The recent flow of books relating to Fortean interests continues unabated. On the whole they tend to be both better written and better researched than the 'first generation' (the ancient-astronaut & Atlantis lives! type) which opened up the market. The new generation of books seem more willing to acknowledge the pioneering work of small magazines (most of those in our review section are represented, including FT) and the lone unknown researchers - eg: Wilson makes central to his thesis the sexual theory of evolution (unpublished) by Charlotte Bach, and the book on alchemy by Mary Ann South, both relatively unknown but very influential in their fields; while Hitching airs the little-known work of a French philologist on the alignment of towns with similar names, and the radical work of the scholarly 'Velikovsky groups' whose re-examination of the ancient history of the Middle East, for example, has been virtually ignored by the Establishment. If this is a trend it bodes well for the like of ourselves.

Wilson's long promised 'sequel' to The Occult proves to be as thick and encyclopedic as its predecessor, and follows much the same format. In his familiar rambling conversational style we are whisked headlong through dozens of summaries of books, theories,   potted biographies and anecdotes in search of a theory which will encompass the diversity of paranormal phenomena. I have always found Wilson eminently readable, and Mysteries is no exception - and I for one truly admire and appreciate the immense amount of work that must have gone into the condensation of so much information on this scale. But if Mysteries has the good points of The Occult it also has the latter's failings: over simplification, contentious interpretations of ambiguous material, and the tendency to weight the evidence in favour of his beloved 'Faculty X' theory. But I cannot blame him for this - it would be a dull book indeed without his driving opinion, which at least provides a perspective to the long and winding galleries of exhibits he has us tramp.

Unfortunately, the cover blurb carries the ambitious claim - that Wilson had set out "to write the Principia of psychic science, to explain all paranormal phenomena..." Leaving aside our own doubts that it is all explainable (or even part of it), or that explanations are necessary let alone desirable, he has set himself an impossible standard - whereas Isaac Newton was writing for the savants of his day, Wilson seems to be writing for an interested but relatively uninformed general reader (for whom, as one reviewer put it, "it is necessary to write of 'the poet Blake', 'the philosopher Bergson',"etc). Nor is Wilson any nearer his sought-after paradigm at the end of this book than he was at the close of The Occult - but again, no blame, since the journeying is fun even if the destination remains elusive - since the inherited premise (that Man has superhuman capabilities) is not materially improved upon along the way. This is ironic because at one point Wilson berates Charles Fort for having made "no attempt to present a coherent argument" (p200), and for failing to offer a new paradigm (p203). Familiarity with Fort's writing will show that his thesis is concisely formulated in chapters 1 and 3 of The Book of the Damned - and that Fort's notions of the 'Dominant' of an age foreshadows Thomas Kuhn's use of the word 'paradigm' in his model of 'scientific revolutions' by over 50 years. In Mysteries, what passes for a "comprehensive theory" is rather a collection of attempts to make sense of the variety of 'alternative' or 'fringe' explorations of paranormal phenomena - it is too wide a spread of the shotgun to discern a definite hit, and too fragmented to be consistent.

The book itself will not disappoint his fans. A long discussion of Tom Lethbridge's own wide-ranging works is followed by assessments of ancient-astronaut theories, Stonehenge, the 'Sirius Mystery', leys & feng-shui, ghosts, and ancient triumphs of navigation and surveying. There is a fascinating section on alchemy and its various schools and practitioners; a recurring theme of a "ladder of selves"; a review of scientific thought as the 'History of Human Stupidity'; and long sections on 'Faculty X'; archetypal psychology, hypnotism, revelations, dreams, 'life-fields'and other enigmatic forces, astral projection, precognition, sleep, sexual energy, evil, poltergeists, our need for stability, UFOs, monsters, states of consciousness, survival of death, and other subjects too numerous to mention.

The book is amiable and absorbing - however some of it evokes deja vu, being familiar from Wilson's previous writings. At nearly £10 it seems exorbitant, but otherwise well worth your while.

Where Wilson's book is one of eclectic speculation and synthesis, Francis Hitching's Atlas is more empirical and impartial. By testing the various solutions and theories associated with specific mysteries against each other, Hitching performs the valuable exercise of aiding the general reader to become more critical about the controversies and contradictory evidences involved, some due to scholarly differences of opinion, some to a division between the Establishment view and a new view, some to outright hoaxers, and some to a head-on collision of fact with outdated theory. Of course Hitching, like Wilson, has his preferences, but they don't get in the way: "Research on the Atlas showed time and again that after conscientiously examining the whole spectrum of possible solutions, it was the unorthodox that made best sense of the unexplained." (p7). What emerges is a refereshingly

critical guide to the 'alternatives' for "anyone uneasy about established views."

The biggest stumbling block for works of this kind is that so much of the subject matter lies in the past, remaining ambiguous even to the 'experts'. Even when you have something tangible - like the enigmatic 'writing' on stones found at Glozel, France - it is impossible to escape opinion, and therefore controversy - the French declared the site genuine, the British archeologists said it was a hoax and banned its discussion from the pages of Antiquity! With rifts like this in the Establishment, one is forced to question whether the 'official view' of history, animal and geological evolution, the nature of so-called primative cultures, etc has any right to exclude aspects it finds embarassing or for which it cannot account. Many of these sensitive areas, which bridge the Establishment and the unorthodox fringe, like the Glozel scandal, are fairly presented here, and the reader is left to make up his own mind, or not, as he wishes.

Also commendable is the way a great amount of information is presented visually, in maps (eg the early claims to America; long-distance migration; the European distribution of Holy relics, etc), charts (eg a comparison of the conventional and the Velikovskyan chronology for Biblical history; types of sea-serpents; leys & alignments; maze patterns; stonehenge, the Gt Pyramid and other sites; etc), and tables (eg a list of feral children; Plato's description of Atlantis; 10 ways the dinosaurs may have died out; 15 theories about the Mary Celeste; Velikovsky's astronomical predictions; etc). Major topics also include: evolution & Darwinism; catastrophist geology; aerial phenomena (inc. ice falls and UFOs); 'myths' of early history (eg the Deluge, who was Homer? and Noah's Ark); unknown energies; early civilizations and anomalous technology; some errors of von Daniken; appearances of monsters and disappearances of people; searches (eg the Holy Grail, King Solomon's Mines, and Shangri-la). As in other works of this scope (including Phenomena) errors are bound to creep in - the most serious being two conflicting dates for the Antikythera 'computer' (p 125); and the references in text and caption to Doc Shiels' Nessie photos when those shown were taken by 'Mary F' of the Cornish sea-serpent Morgawr (p 198).

Nevertheless, the Atlas provides a good basis for the newcomer to Fortean mysteries to thread his way through the maze of claim and counter-claim, hoax and whitewash, theory and fact. It is extensively illustrated and has an excellent reading list. (Coming out in USA in May, at ₤16.95).　　　　RJMR

Miracles and Pilgrims: Popular Belief in Medieval England, by Ronald Finucane (JM Dent, 1977; £6.95, pp 248, index, notes, photos) - Miracles by Geoffrey Ashe (RKP, 1978; £4.75, pp206, index) -- Finucane examines 9 medieval miracle cults (7 English, 2 French) that were established between 1066 and 1300, around the tombs of saints. Despite the considerable effort that has gone into researching the book and sifting through contemporary records of about 3000 miracle cures, the book never really comes alive. We are given tantalizing glimpses into the popular mind of the time but the opportunity to develop　　　　　insights into medieval man's belief in magical forces slips away. An example - in referring to the group of illnesses we'd today call mental aberrations, he mentions that an account might claim the victim slept out in a field, and "during sleep the victim was accosted by field or forest spirits which dwelt in the region." Such accounts, however, are very rare, but he knew of one, "...from Wulfstan's Collection, where three forest fairies interrupted a cleric's journey through a dark wood." That's it, apart from an obscure source reference that even a researcher would be put to some trouble to find.　Similar references to miracles and all kinds of strange phenomena abound, but Finucane (unfortunately for us) is more concerned with the memorabilia of shrine records, their administrations and the arbitrary investigations into the claims of cures by shrine officials, and the etiquette of the pilgrims (horrible scenes of cripples crawling around tombs, while others, presumably from a mixture of exhaustion, expectation and emotion, vomit over the tomb itself.) This dry approach has its lighter moments and the descriptions of "pious theft"　(the unscrupulousness of the monks in hoaxing relics, or stealing the relics of other shrines to improve their own business) verge on farce. He notes that as the original pure church spread out from Rome into a pagan and barbarian world, it had to make compromises (like incorporating pagan festivals, or taking over holy sites), and one wonders how far this contributed to the emergence of the importance of relics and miracles. On the other hand we know from the history of spontaneous radical movements and folk traditions that miracle healers and healing sites have always held important positions in the lives of early man, yet there is little light on it here. Just why medieval man was so ready to accept even the most preposterous 'miracles' without much desire for proof is only asked, not answered.

Geoffrey Ashe's book, on the other hand, says much about the numinous side of the miraculous, and suggests that the popularity of miracles might be linked with the emergence of the cult of the Virgin Mary. Tales of Mary's miracles, many of which seem quite outrageous to modern sensibilities, were very popular throughout medieval Europe both as an oral tradition and as a devotional device for sermonizing. They suit her elevated character too, since she alone stood directly between the Godhead and mortal sinners, and more than the saints had power to alter the course of divine judgement. Nor is Ashe blind to the BVM as the modern symbol of the eternal feminine. No book on miracles could avoid an attempt to define the term - but whereas Finucane seems content with the conventional understanding of "contrary to nature's course", Ashe goes back to its Latin root (mirus: wonderful) with a bold redefinition of a miracle as an exceptional and ordained source of wonder. In this way he is able to compare and discuss Christian miracles with those of other religions, notably Hinduism, Islam, Confucianism and Taoism - though these sections are lamentably brief. Ashe also argues that a belief in miracles is not a 'primitive' trait but based on an orderly conception of the cosmos which offsets the exceptions. Ashe proposes a novel theory for the Turin Shroud image, but anyone hoping for a juicy detailed discussion of stigmata, levitations, bilocations, miracles of multiplication, talking, weeping and moving statues, intervention in nature, etc, as I was, will be disappointed, for although these things are mentioned, it is in passing and briefly, like Finucane. After a quick account of the theological role of miracles, a whole chapter is devoted to those of the BVM, and another on the visitations at Lourdes (1858) and Fatima, Portugal (1917). (An astonishing omission is that Ashe barely mentions the numbers and influence of BVM visions in this century alone!) In slightly more detail than his references to miracles in other religions he gives a chapter to Tibet's folklore and lamas, but as a basis for the familiar theory of tulpas or materialized thought-forms, which the final two chapters elaborate into a model or paradigm for "magic". Thus in a few thousand words he adds as much to the subject as Colin Wilson does with his "quarter of a million words" in Mysteries (see above). Despite the impression that Miracles has been assembled from left-over chunks of Ashe's previous two books, The Virgin, and The Ancient Wisdom, it is well worth reading. RJMR

PSI and The Consciousness Explosion by Stuart Holroyd (Bodley Head, 1977; £4.95, pp235, index, bib) - Explor-

ations of Consciousness edited by Dennis Milner (Neville Spearman,1978; £5.50, pp439, indexes, bib, notes, photos, illos) -- Stuart Holroyd hacks his own path through Roszak country: the biofeedback business, 'executive ESP', hawkers of astral charms, bio rythmn computers and make-people-obey you-through-psychic-power courses etc. He is quite critical of the commerciality of the 'Aquarian Age'- what Robert Ornstein has called 'Tantrum Yoga' - the relinquishing of responsibility to a machine, a guru, a formula, a pill, while other psychic salesmen appeal to a gullible public's worst nature. Just take a look at the ads in Fate sometime (or any other psychic mag) and wonder where we are going. Genuine or not, the 'Aquarian movement' has certain themes which overlap with contemporary work in parapsychology. Holroyd identifies these as: 1) altered states of consciousness (ASCs); 2) a positive attitude toward the unconscious; 3) open to exotic cultural influences; 4) body and sensory awareness programmes; 5) the development of a field theory (dowsing, lifeforces, 'vibrations', planes of existence, psychotronic power etc). Detailing specific confirmatory experimental and anecdotal evidence he leads into a reassessment of what we know about telepathy, clairvoyance, precognition and psychokinesis. There are many omissions, but these are sufficient to show the 'state of the art', and to discuss their implications for science and Western culture. He comes to the conclusion that there has been a subtle but major paradigm shift, a far-reaching change in man's consciousness. But Holroyd is no naive dreamer who neglects difficult questions for glossy answers, and his deceptively modest book is essential and rewarding reading.

Dennis Milner's substantial book is a more specific proof of the same thesis - that the development and aquisition of psychic powers should be accompanied and consolidated by an equivalent evolution of consciousness. Milner is one of a group who met to explore their common interest in the "metaphysical understanding of nature". At one point they decided they all needed a direct experience of expanded states of consciousness, and embarked on a series of experiments based on the techniques described by GM Glaskin (Windows of the Mind, Wildwood House, 1976; also in paperback). One member performs a series of mental relaxing exercises designed to stimulate his powers of visualization. Soon he is in a deep reflective state, describing

his inner experiences in terms of scenes
or symbols, or voyages through vivid
landscapes. He is guided by another member who questions him, extracting descriptions for the taped record. Using
this simple procedure, the group developed a programme of exploration - each
symbol, description and experience then
subject to extensive analysis. What emerged was an astonishingly coherent and
very detailed cosmology, with insights
into nearly every branch of the physical,
biological and mental sciences. Under
Milner's skilful exposition, the unfolding of this knowledge seems natural, orderly and progressive in its drive toward
a creative synthesis of mystical, rational and imaginative thought, and done
without any significant reference to an
external source of information. If, as
they satisfactorily demonstrate, all
this knowledge is latent in each one of
us, it gives a whole new insight into
the history of human invention and culture. For its sense, discipline and encouraging vision, I have no hesitation
in recommending this book to anyone.
RJMR

The Cycles of Heaven by Guy Lyon
Playfair & Scott Hill (Souvenir Press, 1978; £4.95, pp368, index, refs,
photos, illos) -- This collaboration
with biophysicist Scott Hill takes Playfair in a somewhat different direction
to that of his earlier works on psychic
phenomena. And without denigrating those
books the change is to be applauded, for
he and Hill have produced a book which
may well become a standard reference in
the study of cycles and cosmic influences. It is a work of considerable scope,
deeply researched. The reference list
has almost 350 entries, a very large
proportion of which are scientific papers of very recent date, from a multitude of languages and apparently unconnected fields, including material from
Eastern Bloc countries, unknown or neglected in the West.
    The authors have done a remarkable
job in comprehending this data and assembling it into a coherent pattern, beginning with a study of the Earth and its
relationships to the sun and planets,
and the gravitational and electromagnetic influences upon us. And those influences are all pervasive, affecting virtually everything from earthquakes to
emotions. From there they move on to
discuss internal cycles (biorhythms,
biological clocks etc) and external cycles (sunspots, lunar phases, etc), Kirlian effects, bioplasma, man's 'energy-
body'...drawing a picture of man totally
indivisible from nature, immersed in a

web of cyclical and energetic influences. Science appears to have discovered
Fort's 'Continuous Universe'. An excellent reference book.   SM

Ancient Man: A Handbook of Puzzling
Artifacts, by William R Corliss (Sourcebook Project: Box 107, Glen Arm,
MD 21057, USA, 1978; $15.95, pp786,
indexes, illos) -- Some libraries
and potential purchasers of the invaluable sourcebooks tend to be put off by
their loose-leaf ring-binder format (intended to facilitate the accumulation
of material under each heading). For
this and marketing reasons Corliss has
brought out a jumbo selection from several different sourcebooks on the themes
of ancient man, his engineering, tools,
symbols and writing, plus relevant data
from the fields of geology, anthropology, biology and folklore. These notes
consist of quotes and illustrations from
original sources, some modern but mostly
rare or out-of-print. Thus invaluable
fundamental data is given under such
topics as: standing stones; graves and
mounds; ancient forts; walls and ditches;
stone circles, alignments and henges;
pyramids; unusual buildings; planning;
roads; canals & dams; mines & quarries;
stone artifacts; out-of-place artifacts;
high-technology artifacts; pictographs,
drawings, effigies, mosaics; symbols &
notation; fossil human footprints; fos-
silized technology; curious human skeletons; white tribes; linguistic oddities; plant evidence for early American
contacts; little people & giants; discoveries of America before Columbus,etc.
    An essential book for all libraries,
especially the Fortean's. (For more info on the sourcebooks, see the ad in
this section.)   RJMR

The Ghost of Flight 401 by John G Fuller (Souvenir, 1978; £4.50, pp319) --
In 1972, Flight 401 crashed in the Florida Everglades - the world's first Jumbo air disaster. Within months there
were reports of phantoms of the dead
crew being seen on the other planes of
the same airline - to the extent that
planes were being grounded because no
one would fly them. Rumours of these
psychic skyjacks reached Fuller, and another moneyspinning milestone of investigative journalism was born. A TV film
of the book (starring Ernest Borgnine)
has already been seen in the States, and
is soon to be screened by the BBC.
    Fuller, known for his books on the
Hills UFO abduction, and Arigo the Bra-
zilian psychic surgeon, is eminently
readable; even if the book does seem a

bit padded. There is a long and overly detailed account of the crash and subsequent events; then a section on the sightings and Fuller's own investigations; followed finally by Fuller's personal discovery of the wealth of material on the problem of life after death (he started out a self-confessed skeptic), culminating in the contact of a dead 401 crewmember via a ouija board. A worthy, if pricey, read.   RJMR

paperbacks

The World Before by Ruth Montgomery (Sphere 1978; 85p, pp222) - Grave and Urgent Warnings from Heaven by C Marystone (Box 41112, Minillas Station, Santurce, Puerto Rico 00940, USA, 1978; no price, pp418, notes) -- Evocative stuff by Ruth Montgomery, being a psychic history of the world from its creation up to the second coming of Christ, here declared for the next century. Naturally it concentrates on the more exciting material, like 5 gardens of Eden, Mu (Lemuria), 2 great cataclysms and an axial tilt shift of the planet. It seems a mixture of Velikovskyan cataclysms, Brinsley le Poer Trench's Sky People, Edgar Cayce and Lobsang Rampa...with St John's Revelations thrown in for good measure. Ms Montgomery's method is to meditate first thing each day with her finger resting on the typewriter keys, then, according to her, her Guides take over, drawing on material from the 'Akashic record'. Word clues like that, plus locating her Atlantis in the southeastern USA (like Henrietta Mertz in her excellent works) and many other details of her ancient world clearly suggest the possible origins of much of the material. She herself admits to reading The First Sex by Elizabeth G Davis prior to the essay on the division of the sexes by her Guides. So much seems cribbed from Edgar Cayce (the seer of Virginia Beach) that she complained of this to her own Guides. Quick as a flash they reply that: "all sources with access to the Akashic records will naturally report the same truths." Naturally! Be that as it may , some may take it at face value - secret conclaves meeting on Atlantis to plan the destruction of the dinosaurs; the creation of the earth by The Force (Ye gods?); a slave class of biological monsters; a giant crystal undersea off Bimini; the original sin was sex with animals; spirits teleporting to Mars; that the world's leaders are reincarnated Atlanteans etc etc. She ventures prophecy too; including a woman PM for Brit-

ain, and another shift in the earth's axis by the turn of the century. Her Guides are nothing if not quirky, favouring the death penalty, and stamping out roaches, which they say, have been interfering in mens' affairs far too long! Still, this kind of book has a long and respected tradition, from Enid Blyton (who worked the same way) through works of all shades of creative and mystical inspiration, to the Koran (dictated to Mohammed by an archangel).

Interestingly, one of Ms Montgomery's prophecies refers to the Second Coming of Christ being preceeded by the return to Earth of the Virgin Mary - however it is not clear if a bodily visitation or an apparition is meant. Mr Marystone's thick book is a very detailed compendium of "grave and urgent warnings" about the coming "Chastisement" of mankind - many of them compiled from recent visions of the BVM (including Fatima, Garabandal and extensively from the Bayside visions - see also our 'Visions' section this issue). Since my knowledge of Biblical prophecy is limited I cannot comment, but it does look thorough. Mr Marystone concurs that the end will be presaged by UFOs , Fortean phenomena (like rains of blood, etc), great quakes and weather chaos, and such astronomical portents as Velikovsky collected from records of earlier catastrophies. He originally intended a single work to extract all the known prophecies relating to the present era, both in the Bible and since - but there were so many the project has expanded to 3 volumes already, of which this is the first. It is impossible adequately to summarize or assess the scope of such a work in so short a review, but it is truly impressive, and one can only hope that it has a wider circulation (it seems to be a small private printing.) Although aimed at the "religious man", whose criteria are different from those of the skeptic, Mr Marystone is to be commended for including detailed notes, references and lengthy quotes of relevant data. He has also transcribed the divine locutions of the Bayside visions.   RJMR

Mind-Reach by Russell Targ & Harold Puthoff (Paladin, 1978; £1.50, pp 230, index, notes, photos) -- Sure to become an important sourcebook on their experiments with a range of 'sensitives' and types of phenomena or abilities. Subtitled "Positive proof that ESP exists", the book also counters the rather negative arguments of the critics of ESP research, and Targ & Puthoff prove, as much as anything can reasonably be proved, that man's perceptions are not limited to his sensory organs, nor the conventional understanding of space, time and energy. The experiments are bold (eg a clairvoyant journey to Jupiter), the writing lucid, and the subjects both human (Ingo Swann, Geller, Pat Price, Hella Hammid, Duane Elgin, Phyllis Cole and Marshall Pease) and interesting (out-of-the-body, remote viewing, precognition,, telepathy and psychokinesis). Particularly exciting are the long discussions of remote viewing and its implications, split-brain phenomena, and shifting paradigms, and above all   their clarification and correction of the attacks on their work with Geller (by Randi et al).   RR

Beyond and Back by Ralph Wilkerson (Corgi, 1978; 85p, pp237, notes) – Ralph Wilkerson is well-known in the USA – he blows his own trumpet loudly enough – as founder of the Melodyland Congregation, California, where he regularly preaches to crowds of thousands. At these meeting people are encouraged to stand up and tell their stories, and frequently some have told of dying and returning to life again after a trip to heaven. Wilkerson has collected many of these 'returned to life' anecdotes and added others from different sources in an unfortunately florid style which will put off all except the committed Christian. Each story gives him the opportunity to moralize and preach. Remarkable claims: Jesus went to church, God wipes out your memories in Heaven so you won't pine for any loved ones in Hell, dining and seeing the sights of the City are listed among the attractions of Heaven, and Heaven itself is called "the planet Heaven in the outer galaxy "! And describing waking up in Heaven after dying he says: "Imagine...feeling a touch and taking hold of a nail-scarred hand." Or the divine purpose behind the sterile precautions of the space programme is because God wants to keep germs and pollution out of Heaven. Meat for some...
RR

Alternative 3 by Leslie Watkins (Sphere, 1978; 95p, pp239) -- This book already has a cult following which implicitly believes that the prime forces of our existence are vast and secret conspiraces. This book plays on those fears – openly – and they love it! It was conceived as a TV documentary and networked by ITV at 9pm Monday 20 June 1977. It was intended for showing on April 1st, and said so in the credits,

but got delayed. It began in the usual way of documentaries - evocative scene setting - examining the strange disappearances of young scientists, tops in their fields. The fields of weather control, and all the sciences related to space colonization. The tack shifted to outline all the weather chaos of 1975/6 (remember?). Facts and figures were presented which suggested a huge conspiracy between the space programmes of USA and Russia. The climax was an interview with an American astronaut, allegedly invalided out because something he had seen on the Moon sent him loony for a while. This was nothing less than a fully operational base, built by the Americans and Russians before the first 'public' landing there. Allegedly decoded video records showed not only a Martian landing but some form of life moving under the dust. This space conspiracy was in fact a venture years more advanced than the feeble plodding explorations of space the public had been lead to believe were going on. In fact the Conspiracy had been faking the disappearances of leading young scientists and shipping them to the Moon and Mars to terraform the Red planet. It was brilliantly done - a mixture of fact and imagination, and based just enough on ambiguous real events to make it all plausible. It had me gripped, but I believed then (and now) that it was a superb fiction, with the employment of convincing po-faced actors as the scientists and astronauts etc. In the days that followed, it was Welles' 'Martian invasion' panic (1938) all over again - see the letter columns of the papers then for voices of panic, terror, dismay, anger and denial.
    Now comes the book of the documentary. It's all true! claim the authors. They say they were pressured into showing it on April 1st by the powers that be, out of fear of mighty reprisals. Panic was elevated to paranoia-conspiracy-cult proportions by the rumour that the entire first printing of Alternative 3 had been variously, bought-up, destroyed or mysteriously swiped from the Sphere warehouse. Well here it is, released again, and despite a world-dominating all-powerful conspiracy. Looking at it this closely one can see the sources - Fortean-type newsclippings on disappearances, UFOs, weather freaks etc, and some pretty half-baked UFO books. Nevertheless this is skillfully written (with several disguised bows to SF and Illuminatus!) Buy it - and leave the shop furtively! It just might be true!   RJMR

journals

Pursuit 44 (Fall 1978) - part 2 of
Larry Arnold's study of fiery phantom
ships; R Anjard on early colonization
of the Americas; report on a Bigfoot
conference; and an appraisal of Bigfoot
biology by R Walls; G Eberhart on the
early knowledge of Greenland; a suggestion for solving the Bermuda Triangle
erigma; a splendid note questioning the
basis of Freud's influence; a short account (with full page pictures) of the
Doc Shiels Nessie photos (by your Ed);
polluted rains; synchronicity experiments; thoughts on Canadian Bronze Age
fragments; plus some notes. Pursuit has
evolved into a fat, sleek and substantial journal - published quarterly by
SITU: (Membership Services: RFD 5, Gales
Ferry, CT 06335, USA) - $10/yr (overseas
$12.50; airmail $15.00).

ARB - special non-linear issue 23 -
David Fideler's parting shot before
taking up the cross of a more active
writer/researcher (and joining FT). This
special issue contains an article by
Loren Coleman on anomalous panthers and
pumas; Dave himself summarizing recent
kangaroo activity, and monkey escapes;
Martin Riccardo discusses vampires as
a living (!) tradition; plus other
notes on mystery animals and weird behaviour. Sure to become a collectors
item, despite its usual Fortean value,
because of the special 'mutant' envelope it comes in. $1.50 from Michigan
Anomaly Research: 303 East Fulton, Apt
2, Grand Rapids, MI 49503, USA.

Lantern 23 (Autumn 1978): East Anglian witchcraft; the legend of Black
Toby (ghost of a negro drummer hanged
for rape); UFO notes and gleanings from
backfiles of local papers; plus the sup-
plemental journal of the East Suffolk &
Norfolk Antiquarians (Spellthorn) - 24
(Winter 1978): the phantom house of
Bradfield St George; roadside & cross-
road burials; Spell thorn; and gleanings
from local newspapers. Lantern published quarterly by BSIG: 3 Dunwich Way,
Lowestoft, NR32 4RZ. UK sub £1/yr; over-
sea rates on application.

Journal of Meteorology (Nov 1978):
blizzards and snowfall freaks, sea damage in Dorset, weather disasters for
August 1978 (extracted from Lloyds List)
- (Dec 1978): correspondence on a fall
of 'star jelly' in Cambridge, weather
disasters fromSeptember '78, and records
of extreme conditions. Indispensible to
the Fortean interested in weather anomalies. JMet: Cockhill House, Trowbridge
BA14 9BG, Wiltshire. Write for details.
(The Dec issue has the index for vol 3).

Zetetic Scholar 1 (1978): As he explains in his editorial, Marcello Truzzi
helped to found the Committee for the
Scientific Investigation of Claims for
the Paranormal in order to establish a
proper dialogue - claimants for the
paranormal had publications arguing and
defending their cases, it was time, they
thought,for a forum for the defenders
of the orthodox position. They published a journal called The Zetetic which
attracted immediate criticism (from all
quarters) for its bigoted hostility towards all aspects of the unusual. Mr
Truzzi left to establish his own voice
because he did not feel it served the
true spirit of inquiry to takes sides
on an issue. The Zetetic Scholar , he
assures us,will not confuse skepticism
with dogmatic denial, and wishes only
to see that the proper rules of evidence
and procedure are maintained during the
debate itself, both for and against. We
sincerely wish him the best of luck,
and if the first two issues are anything
to judge by,he has succeeded admirably.
Even if you don't agree with ZS's form
of skepticism,   Truzzi's editorship
will enhance our studies in many ways,
not the least being his talent for compiling valuable and critical bibliographies. No 1 contains 5 bibliographies:
on the debate 'Pseudoscience or Science
Revolution'; books that 'debunk' the
claims for the paranormal; Uri Geller
and the scientists; 'Debunking Biorhythms'; and a random selection of books
on the Occult and Paranormal. Also included are articles on Carlos Castaneda,
'Skepticism, Science & the Paranormal',
'On the Extraordinary: an attempt at
Clarification'; and one on solar and
economic periodicities; plus book reviews. No 2 has a review of 'Anomaly
Literature'; Michael Persinger on UFO
experiences; and a philosophical examination of scientific procedure by WT
Rockwell. Bibliographies include: vampirism; scientific studies of astrology;
the Velikovsky debate; and more random
books on the Occult & Paranormal. Plus
interesting depth book reviews. ZS is
highly recommended to all committed
Forteans - $10.00/yr (3 issues) - ZS:
Dept of Sociology, Eastern Michigan
University, Ypsilanti, MI 48197, USA.

Nessletter - news and notes of any
interest relating to Loch Ness and mon-

ster hunting – edited by Rip Hepple, at £1.75 or $7.00/yr. Ness Information Service: R Hepple, Huntshieldford, St Johns Chapel, Bishop Auckland, Co Durham.

Specula – journal of the American Association of Meta-science and vehicle for the application of 'Many Worlds' physics theory to paranormal phenomena. No 3 (July-Sept 1978) has a paper on 'The Transmutation of Species'; and considerable discussion of psychotronic physics and warfare application, UFOs photography, and Bigfeet, and Tom Bearden's forthcoming book The Excalibur Briefing; plus reports on lectures and activities. $15.00/yr; overseas rates on application. Specula: AAMS, Box 1182, Huntsville, AL 35807, USA.

EVP Newsletter – devoted to discussion of 'Electronic Voice Phenomena' – No 9 included a plea for cooperation among researchers, letters and an EVP bibliography – No 10 had an analysis of Jurgenson's work & results by Prof Hans Bender; letters – No 11 continues Prof Bender's important article. Published monthly; £1.20 – overseas rates on application. EVPN: 12 Lime Tree Ave, Bilton, Rugby, Warks CV22 7QT. Editor Alan Cleaver will have an introductory article in the next issue of FT.

Forgotten Ages – new to us but now in its 6th issue – an intelligent and witty mag on the historical aspect of ancient mysteries. No 6 discusses a 'Fashion Show – 15,000 BC ; the 'Brotherhood of the Tat', the GT Pyramid and the mysterious Egyptian 'Hall of Records'; the 'Piasa Bird' and the Ica stones; and ancient use of lightning rods. $3.00/yr (12 issues); from JR Jochmans, Box 82863, Lincoln, NB 68501, USA. Much of it will tickle a Fortean's fancy.

Journal of Vampirism – quarterly of the Vampire Studies Society – poems, news, notes and book reviews on the subject; but serious scholars may prefer to sink their fangs into the bibliography and articles. $6.00/yr (sample $2); from VSS: Box 205, Oak Lawn, IL 60454, USA.

Stigmata – news, notes and reports of the continuing mutilation phenomena (mainly but not exclusively in USA) and field investigations – a thorough and important archive of data. The last issue will be published in July 1979 ($1) so order it, or inquire about back issues to Project Stigma, Box 1094, Paris, TX 75460, USA.

Catastrophist Geology – devoted to the study of "discontinuities in Earth history" – serious, scholarly and informative forum for this neglected subject and its implications – much of Fortean interest. Issue 2:2 (Dec 1977) (the latest one we have) contains: fossil cemetaries; criticism of the US Geological Survey's attitudes towards Fortean phenomena (eg quake lights, dowsing, etc); quake lights; neocatastrophism (ie discontinuities in geological and animal evolution); gravity & geomagnetic reversals; plus bibliographical and other notes. The price of $3.00 per year (2 issues) may be out of date. Write for details to Johan B Kloosterman: Caixa Postal 41.003, Santa Teresa, Rio de Janeiro, Brasil.

SIS Review 3:2 (Autumn 1978): a retrospect by the 'Old Man' himself, Velikovsky; isotope decay constancy; an alternative to the ejection of Venus; a critique of Velikovsky's new book Ramses II and his Time; Horemheb's place in Egyptian history; dating Merenptah; plus intelligent comments and book reviews. The SIS members' newsletter Workshop contains more informal material, including 'Angels & Catastrophism', and 'King Solomon's Mines?' The Review is quarterly -- write to the Secretary: 6 Jersey House, Cotton Lane, Manchester M20 9GL.

New Horizons – journal of this well respected Toronto-based psychical research Foundation – 2:4 (Sept 1978): Can humans detect weak magnetic fields?(No, or not very well, suggest two experiments): Mackenzie King & Survival; Two cases of Xenoglossia ('speaking in Tongues'); the problem of assessing UFO reports. For further details write, New Horizons Research Foundation: Box 427, Station F, Toronto, Ontario, Canada M4Y 2L8. Much interesting material.

Chaos 2 – Mr X's serial on Fortean source material: including original accounts of 'light wheels' under the sea ; strange meteorites,and meteoric stone showers of India, and a letter from Fort to the NY Times 1925 on the subject; an extensive listing of showers of blood by X; fire-prone Elizabeth Barnes of 1820; Carl Pabst with transcriptions of Fort's own notes, some a record of the writing of LO!; Charles Darwin's note of rains of dust on ships in mid-Atlantic; not a rain but a downpour of Black Ants; plus other shorter pieces. Essential to serious Forteans, and worthy of your support regardless. Canada $15.00 per year or C$2.00/US$2.00/£1.00 for single copies. Or write for details to X: Box 1598 Kingston, Ontario, Canada K7L 5C8.

MUFOB 11 (Summer 1978): Nigel Watson on the remarkable case of Paul Bennet (witness of UFOs, entities, angels etc); 'Are UFO witnesses public property?' asks Larry Tokarz; Paul Screeton finds curious details of a 1909 airship; plus book reviews, notes and part 16 of Peter Rogerson's catalogue of 'Type 1' UFO records. No 12 (Autumn 1978): re-examining UFO statistics; more on Paul Bennett, percipient extraordinaire; airships & panics by Roger Sandell; Peter Rogerson on UFO etiology, plus pt 17 of his catalogue. Quarterly £1.25/$3.00 (air) per year.

Journal of Geomancy 3:2: a Cambridge 7 church ley; Heinsch on the rediscovery of preChristian geomancy in Germany; proceedings report; Greek dragons; Ron Anjard on Kenyan stones; and more. 60p per issue or £3.00/yr, quarterly - from Institute of Geomancy: 142 Pheasant Rise, Bar Hill, Cambridge CB3 8SD.

NEARA Journal; a journal devoted to New England antiquities, and apart from regular features and discussions of new findings (stones, sites, artifacts etc), includes an open-ended series of early notes on American antiquities researched by the unsung hero of backfile safaris, Ron Dobbins. Quarterly: $10.00/yr. Write to NEARA Tresurer, Laura Linder: 12 Elizabeth Court, North Kingston, RI 02856, USA.

Minnesota Archeologist - many items relative to the ancient culture of the region, but particularly recommended is the long article by Mark A Hall on Bigfoot stories & sightings in South Dakota. Minnesota Archeological Society: Building 27, Fort Snelling, St Paul, MN 55111, USA.

Flying Saucer Review 24:3 (Nov 1978): UFOs that mimic; landings & encounters in Yugoslavia, British Columbia; Buck inghamshire, Tasmania, South America, Merseyside, Staffordshire, & Firth of Forth; plus account of woman's third encounter, a case of rabbit-snatching, a wave of Russian sightings, and the attitude of the Ministry of Defence. FSR Publications Ltd, West Malling, Maidstone, Kent.

The Visual UFO Book & Publication Catalogue - a well-illustrated listing of new, old and rare material on UFO & Fortean topics, including backissues of many mags reviewed in FT. Unfortunately no price is mentioned; but write to them, perhaps even send $6.00 for the Page Research Newsletter. UFO Information Network, Box 5012, Rome, Ohio 44085, USA.

Awareness 7:3 (Autumn 1978): VI Sanarov on European UFOs 1720-1721; Allen Greenfield on the 'Real Issues of UFOlogy; the Ark of the Covenant; 'Coincidence?, or a new approach' by Jenny Randles; JB Delair on 'Another UFO Kidnapping?'(the Australian pilot case); list of reports, etc. Consistently useful contents. For details, write Membership Secretary, Contact (UK): 28 Lodden Ave, Berinsfield, Oxfordshire. **The UFO Register** 8 (1977): a Danish airship of 1908; 1954 flap in Costa Rica; part 6 of Lucius Farish's 'Catalogue of Historical UFO Reports'; part 3 of a 'Provisional Catalogue of UFO Photographs' by Delair, Cox & Twine. Available to Contact members - see above address.

Earthlink - journal of Essex UFO Study Group - 2:4 (Autumn 1978) has items on the Australian vanishing pilot, a review of the USA cattle mutilations, and some weird new events at Warminster, use of hypnotism in investigating abductions; etc. Quarterly £2.50/ overseas £4.00 - singles 62p/£1.00. Write EUFOSG: 16 Raydons Rd, Dagenham, Essex RM9 5JR.

Wark - a review magazine for fantasy literature, films etc, comix and u/g mags, fanzines, semi-prozines etc, and letters. No 13 inaugurates a Fortean mag review column by Joseph Patchen. 3 issues for 90p/$2.00 - cash or POs only (Hmmm this is catching on!) Apply to Rosemary Pardoe: Flat 2, 38 Sandown Lane, Liverpool.

The Ley Hunter 83: John Barnatt on stone circles; Derbyshire mounds by TA Matthews; Don Robins on 'Scientists in leyland'; 'The Margate Grotto' by Valerie Martin; JH Fidler on multi-dimensional leys; mysteries in SW USA by Ron Anjard; plus leys, letters, reviews, & regular columns. Bimonthly: £3.00/ £3.60 Europe/$9.00 overseas airmail. TLH: Box 152, London N10 1EP.

Picwinnard - a journal of Wessex leys and folklore - No 5: Glastonbury, midsummer lore; Cornish language; ghosts; Wessex Forteana; and more. Bimonthly: £2.00. Write: Vince Russett, Hythe Bow, Cheddar, Somerset BS27 3EH.

---

* NEWSLETTER *
...an informal postal exchange for studies in paraphysics and the esoteric arts, founded 1944, Non-sectarian, non-demanding. For an introductory leaflet, send a stamp to NL, 40 Parrs Wood Rd. Didsbury, Manchester M20 0ND.

Conspiracy Digest - everything you've always feared about those big time conspiracies is paraded through the pages of CD, while readers and contributors throw rocks or praises, or dig up a few skeletons of their own. Good fun for paranoids. £6.00 per issue to Alpine Enterprises, Box 766, Dearborn, MI 48121; USA.

Alpha - as we go to press the first issue of a new professional newsstand magazine on the paranormal arrives. Edited by Roy Stemman, it will have a heavy paraphysics/parapsychology bias. This issue has items on psychic surgery; Geller and Prof John Taylor's retraction of his endorsement of Geller-effects; premonitions, automatic writing; and the Australian pilot who saw a UFO and vanished.; plus more. Bimonthly at 60p a time. Nicely produced and we wish them success. Alpha: 20 Regent St, Fleet, Hants GU13 9NR.

*** *** *** *** *** *** *** *** *** ***
We regret that a number of hardbacks, paperbacks, pamphlets and journals (many of them from overseas) have had to be held over for review next issue -- Ed.

other

THE WARP

Latest from the Science Fiction Theatre of Liverpool is The Warp, a cycle of ten plays about alternative cults and culture from 1958 to 1978, produced by that theatrical wizzard Ken Campbell (who brought us The Great Caper and Illuminatus!), in collaboration with poet and truth-seeker Neil Oram, who said: "I spoke, Ken typed, and we wrote 40 pages a day." The plays, performed one a night (2-13 Jan 1979; ICA Theatre, The Mall, London), and then all together as The Decathlon in three 18½ hour bouts of solid theatre, and 4 Demi-Decathlons (18-21 Jan), constitute a highly enjoyable circus of anecdotes, UFOs, conspiracy theories, sermons, melodrama, farce, music, and bawdiness which left me mellow and exhausted. Said the Financial Times (that other FT):"It makes the rest of our so-called experimental theatre look positively wan." And the Guardian:"Seldom in the history of theatre has so much been exposed by so many."

The play's opening came in the middle of multiple UFO sightings from New Zealand, Poland, Israel and Britain - and an encounter with 5 darkish skinned beings in pink suits who emerged from a landed UFO near Johannesburg. (Daily Telegraph 5 Jan 1979). ((And about the time of the close of the cycle of plays, Kerry Packer's cricket team comes onto the field, in Australia, in astonishing pink suits...Ed))

One theme of The Warp is that there are astral conspirators - Controllers - and their human agents,who prevent us from making life meaningful and "giving birth to ourselves" by thinking with our whole being. Hero Phil Masters is played with fantastic memory, skill and endurance by Russell Denton, who appears in virtually all 200 scenes. His part is eight times the length of Lear, and surely earns Denton a place in The Guinness Book of Records. Masters tends to see the universe in Manichean terms - a straight fight between Dark and Light forces. He explores Scientology (we learn a lot about auditing techniques), and the teachings of JG Bennett, Krishnamurti, Buckminster Fuller and Bhagwan Shree Rajneesh, all of whom appear in the plays (no, not in person!)

All kinds of visionary eccentrics and contactees appear (based, incidentally, on real people every one), like John Thrushman who tells us that Lafayette Ron Hubbard is a reincarnated captain of a flying saucer, who is gathering together his original crew to take off once more in a cosmic posse to smash the Controllers; the Yorkshire greengrocer (great performance by Jim Broadbent), who had visions of Ramana Maharshi and encountered lots of humanoids, and two men in a 40s black limosine; orator-tramp Billy McGuinness, who is God come to collect overdue royalties on the Bible (another great performance, from John Joyce); King David bearing messages from Orion and roaming the London streets in search of "blueprints"; a Yorkshire electrician who encountered children with enormous heads, a "flying mini" and was persued repeatedly by two beings with huge eyes in 18th century costumes or gaberdeen macs, who eventually allay his terror by telling him telepathically that he is one of them; a man who had been taken aboard a UFO and forced to make love to a beautiful woman covered in large freckles; and a host of telepaths, weirdos, saints and psychos. In fact, the wealth of splendid characters make up for the frequently clichéd dialogue - dozens of heads "explode into light", hundreds of things are "amazing" and so on. And the closing chapters smack rather of Peyton Place... but that's how it was, I guess...

I lost count of the numbers of cups of tea consumed: the thought makes my bladder ache. The company of actors, both professional and 'unknowns', were fantastic - particularly those mentioned earlier, and Bill Nighy, David Hatton, Maria Moustaka, Maggie Jordan and Mitch Davies, who can look completely Chinese or Turkish, and whose portrayal of the paranoid poet Marty Mission was arguably the most delightful of all.

The ten sets for The Warp, hurriedly got together in 3 days, work brilliantly. They were built around the walls of the theatre, with a pit covered in peat in the centre for the audience - a scaffolding structure overhead for the band. The action moved around from one set to another, with the audience scrambling off each one as it became illuminated. The audience was led a merry dance of real 'participatory theatre', and the overall impression is a fine bacchanalian whirl, well representing this Fortean round we inhabit. The band gave a fine performance with lots of songs, weird electronic noises, and overture and underture for each play. At one point, just as the hero heard a siren and thought Armageddon was imminent, the whole scaffolding somehow went live and some musicians got nasty shocks, narrowly escaping electric death. There is a curious prediction from one character about mass suicide rallies, written more than a month before the Jonestown People's Temple Cyanide Jamboree of 18 Nov 1978. The whole uproarious event came to a glorious climax 7 minutes before 10 on the first morning of the Year of the Goat - and outside, hundreds of people in 17th century armour were marching down the Mall. What a lovely world...
Paul Sieveking.

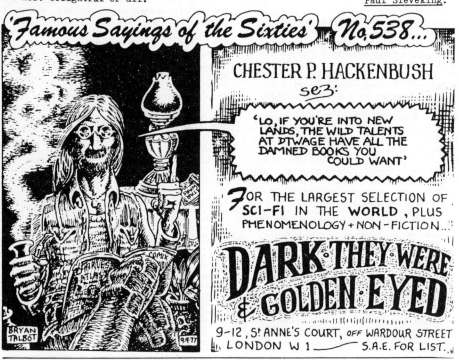

TALES FROM THE YELLOW EMPORIUM

=ORIENTAL FORTEANA BY STEVE MOORE=

PLUM BLOSSOM I NUMEROLOGY

Our subject matter this issue is rather technical and specialised and relates to a rather obscure mathematical aspect of the great Chinese classic, the *I Ching*. To those readers who are totally unfamiliar with the work, I can only offer an apology and refer them to some basic texts [1,2]; space is too limited for a comprehensive exposition. However, I will try to keep things as logical and simple as possible.

Plum Blossom I Numerology (hereafter referred to as PBI), is a numerical method of obtaining I Ching hexagrams without the use of coins or yarrow-stalks, and is attributed to the great 11th century mathematical genius, Shao Yung. 'Plum Blossom' means 'of multiple application' (as numerous as the plum blossoms); 'I' means 'changes' as in *I Ching*. The system was, as far as I know, first introduced to the west by Sherrill & Chu [3], and their book contains numerous examples of its extremely diverse application.

It is with the use of PBI in relation to date and time that we are most concerned, however. And perhaps we could best illustrate its use with an example . . .

TOTAL LUNAR ECLIPSE
– 16 SEPT 1978

The object of the exercise is to obtain an explanation for a portentous event, according to the time it took place. Purely at random, I decided to use the total eclipse of the moon as an example partly because it is an 'event' in itself, partly because of its possible relation to the succeeding Iranian earthquake, and also because, interestingly enough, it fell on the Chinese Moon Festival.

The eclipse took place on 16th September 1978. Lasting from 17-20 to 20-48 (GMT): totality from 18-24 to 19-44. Full moon was at 19-01, and this we can take as the median point.

Our first task is to convert to Chinese time.

1978 is attributed the Horary Branch number of 7 (See [3] for more details of this). 16th September is 15th day of the 8th month in the Lunar calendar. The Chinese day is divided into 12 'hours' of 2 hours each, starting at 23-00 on the 'previous' day. 19-00 hours falls 'on the cusp' of hours 10 and 11, so we shall look at both hours.

The eight trigrams of the I Ching are attributed numbers in this system, according to Fu Hsi's arrangement, thus:

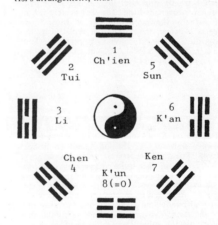

To obtain the upper trigram of our hexagram, we add the numbers for the year, month and day, and divide by 8:

$$7 + 8 + 15 = 30 \div 8 \text{ rem } 6.$$

For the lower trigram, we add the number for the hour to this, and again divide by 8:

$$30 + 10 = 40 \div 8 = 5 \text{ rem } 0.$$

These remainder numbers give us the trigrams from Fu Hsi's arrangement (0 = 8). To obtain the controlling line, we divide the final number (from the bottom) of the line. Thus our first hexagram looks like this:

By repeating the process, but using hour 11 instead of 10, we obtain:

In this system, the attributes of the trigrams and their positions are given at least equal emphasis the line and overall judgements, and it is the trigrams we shall use here. The lower trigram is considered to be 'inside', the upper 'outside'.

For hour 10, we have the trigram *K'un*, meaning both the earth and the dark yin principle, 'inside' the trigram *K'un*, meaning the moon . . . a perfect symbolic representation: the Earth is 'inside' the moon (ie, between moon and sun) and makes it dark. The overall hexagram is No 8 (Holding together), and when the controlling line changes, it becomes No 45 (Gathering Together).

A total lunar eclipse is a good example of the old established Chinese principle of enantiodromic reversal: when the darkness reaches its greatest extent, it turns into its opposite, and the light begins to reappear. Curiously, the 'turning point' of the eclipse (19-01) falls almost exactly on cusp of the hour (19-00). And in progressing to the next hour, the 8th trigram is replaced by its opposite, no 1. This is *Ch'ien*, meaning heaven, and the light yang principle. So at virtually the same moment as the eclipse begins to wane, the darkness is replaced by its opposite . . . the returning light principle. The hexagram is No 5 (Waiting), but when the controlling line is changed it becomes No 11

And here we see the strong light principle of *Ch'ien* 'inside' and pushing out the weak dark principle of *K'un* - movement in a hexagram is always upwards. As the judgement to 'Peace' says: "The small departs, the great approaches".

I find all this quite staggering: a perfect 'casebook' example. However I must also point out that this is worked out on 'standard' time (GMT) - observed from other parts of the world with different time zones the results would not be the same. Also having worked out similar auspices for the other three eclipses of 1978 - 2 solar, 1 lunar - the results are not nearly so impressive . . . in fact, apart from one or two interesting facets, they are not impressive at all. Call it a massive coincidence if you will . . . I content myself with having demonstrated how the system works.

DEVELOPMENT OF PBI CYCLES

So far go Sherrill and Chu, but they make

no attempt to apply this method to more than a single hour on a single day (not even taking two in tandem as we have done above). However, if we now work out the PBI omens for a whole day, we see an interesting cycle developing. For simplicity's sake, I take the Lunar New Year (1st day, 1st Month) of 1978 for my example. So the upper trigram is $7 + 1 + 1 = 9 \div 8 = 1$ rem 1. Now, taking each hour in turn, we arrive at 12 hexagrams, thus:

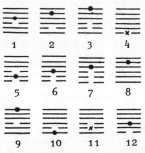

It will be noticed that the upper trigram remains constant throughout the day, while the lower trigram moves sequentially through the 8 trigrams, starting with that following the upper trigram in the sequence. The last 4 hexagrams repeat the first 4, but the controlling line, moving on a cycle of 6 rather than 8, has progressed 2 places. This is a standard pattern for all such daily cycles. We might say that the upper trigram controls the day, the lower trigram the hour.

If we now work out hexagrams for the first hour of the succeeding days ($7 + 1 + 2$, $7 + 1 +$ etc) we can see another cycle developing:

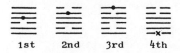

The upper trigram controlling the days also runs through the sequence in order, while the lower trigram for the first hour is that which will become the upper trigram on the following day. The starting position for the controlling line also moves on one step with each day.

And if we take the hexagram for the first hour of the first day of each month, we get:

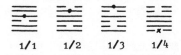

The same cycle developing once more. Thus we have cycles of hours, days and months, like interlocking rings, in cycles of 8, made more flexible by the controlling line which, moving on a cycle of six, modifies the overall meaning of each hexagram, still further. When we come to years, however, we come to a halt . . . for the Horary Branch numbers attributed to the years run in an arbitrary rather than linear sequence (eg:

1977 is 2, 1978 is 7).

Do these cycles have any significance beyond being merely pretty mathematical sequences caused by the addition of 1 every time? I frankly do not know. I have compiled and watched cycles for whole days and found them generally meaningless. On the other hand, when I have had occasion to take a PBI reading with regard to some event that might be conceived of as portentous, the result has frequently been relevant, to say the least, as in our lunar eclipse example above. It is as if the omens are 'logged in heaven', but must await some meaningful event in the sublunary world before they can themselves become meaningful.

However, if the reader will bear with me, I have one more example, in which a daily cycle can be used, both to demonstrate the flexibility of the system, and to provide another 'meaningful coincidence' . . .

THE DEATH OF
CHUKO LIANG

Chuko Liang (181-234 AD) was one of the most important characters of China's Three Kingdoms period, and his name will undoubtedly appear in this column again. Sage, statesman (Prime Minister of Shu), inventor (the multi-shot crossbow, wooden automata, etc), general (master of occult strategy based on the 8 trigrams) and supposed founder of one of Taoism's heretical magical sects, his reputation has expanded to legendary proportions.

Details of his death in the 8th month of 234 are sparse, however, and no historically verified date has been available to me. Ssu-ma Kuang [4], summarising official historical documents and usually so precise with dates, records laconically: "In this month Liang died, with the army."

We do have a date and some details from *The Romance of the Three Kingdoms* [5], Lo Kuan-Chung's historical popularisation of the 14th century. This is the 23rd day of the 8th (lunar) month, at night. This date may be more symbolically than historically accurate, for the 23rd of the 28 lunar asterisms is *Kwei* (The Ghost). Possibly this date is novelistic invention then, or possibly we have another meaningful coincidence.

Chuko Liang appears to have been chronically ill, and in his final years travelled around in a wheeled pushcart or primitive wheelchair. The *Romance* mentions coughing blood as one of the symptoms of the disease, so it sounds as if he suffered from tuberculosis of the lungs. Again according to the *Romance*, he spent his last day in a coma, waking at evening and, rather than resting, insisting on an inspection tour of his camps and military positions. This he made in a 'small carriage' (whether this is identical to the wheelchair is unclear), before the cold autumnal wind forced him to return to his tent. There, after making final arrangements and looking at the stars, he died.

The only problem is that *The Romance of the Three Kingdoms* is not considered in academic circles to be more than 70% factual. Lo Kuan-Chung drew on official histories, secondary written sources, popular cycles of legends, and, doubtless, his own novelistic invention. All of which makes Lo Kuan-Chung an unreliable authority doesn't it? Perhaps . . .

234 AD corresponds to year 51 in the sexagenary cycle, and so from Sherrill and Chu [3] we can work out that its yearly horary branch number is 3. And from there we can work out a PBI for the day. However, as Chuko Liang apparently spent the day in a coma, we need really only concern ourselves with the last two 'hours' of the day, from 7 pm to 11 pm. These give us this result:

Firstly, we see that the trigram controlling the day is Tui, which refers to illnesses of the chest [3]. For hour 11 we have hexagram 28 (Preponderance of the Great), imaged as an overloaded roofbeam or ridgepole. The lower trigram is *Sun* meaning wind, and one is tempted to see an attack of chest difficulties brought on by the wind. The hexagram as a whole also refers to illness of the lungs [6]. The judgement on the 3rd line reads: 'The ridgepole sags to the breaking point. Misfortune.' When the line changes, the resulting hexagram is 47 (Oppression, Exhaustion), which is also the first hexagram for hour 12.

Hexagram 47 as a whole also refers to illnesses of the lungs and chest [6]. The lower trigram is *K'un*, which apart from referring to the moon, also means water, an abyss, and danger. The controlling line is in the 4th place which, in the anthropomorphic structure of the hexagram refers to the trunk (the 1st line refers to the feet, the top line to the head, and so on). When the line changes, we have hexagram 29 (The Abysmal): doubled danger. And what does the controlling line say? "He comes very quietly, oppressed in a golden carriage. Humiliation, but the end is reached."

I leave the reader to make up his own mind. Personally, I'm on Lo Kuan-Chung's side . . .

* * * * * * * * * * * * * * * * * *

References.
1) Richard Wilhelm/C Baynes: *The I Ching* (RKP, London, 1951).
2) Hellmut Wilhelm: *Change* (RKP, London, 1961).
3) WA Sherrill & WK Chu: *An Anthology of I Ching* (RKP, London, 1978).
4) Achilles Fang (trans): *The Chronicle of the Three Kingdoms* (Harvard University Press, 1965): 2 vols, translated from Ssu-ma Kuang: *Tzu Chih T'ung Chien*).
5) CH Brewitt-Taylor (trans): *The Romance of the Three Kingdoms* (CE Tuttle, Vermont & Tokyo, 1959); translated from Lo Kuan-chung: *San Kuo Chih Yen-I*).
6). GG Melyan & WK Chu: *I Ching: The Hexagrams Revealed* (CE Tuttle, Vermont & Tokyo, 1977).

MAD MASQUERADES

We've always had a soft spot (in our heads?) for bizarre behaviour -mix that with fancy dress and you find antics that are both funny-ha-ha and funny-peculiar! And it's strange how most of it involves a strong anti-social bent. Just recently, in late December 1978, a handful (and I say that with fore-sight!) of French gangsters dressed up as Muppet characters, broke into a sanatorium at Nancy and relieved patients of their worldly cares to the tune of £16,000. As they fled in their stolen car, Kermit le Frog, Fozzie and pals were actually waved through traffic by bemused gendarmes on point duty, and enthusiastically cheered on by passers-by. Curious that; breaking into a sanatorium - it kind of restores one's sense of proportion. (News of the World 31 December 1978). In 1976, a man about to give evidence in Brighton County Court on a prosecution of squatting was dismissed for wearing a battery operated flashing red clown's nose (Sun 16 December 1976) - and in 1977 a modern-day bird-man was prosecuted for repeatedly buzzing a back garden, in Durban, South Africa, in which a blonde lady was sunbathing in the nude. As he shouted down: "I'd like to sleep with you!" the out-raged woman tried to hit him with a broom - but he was out of reach. I'm stretching, too, to include the hang-glider he was wearing as a fancy-dress, but the incident is not without relevant humour (Sun 23 March 1977). In Bergen, Norway, last February, unspecif-ied nuisance of another sort was caused by two characters dressed as Jesus and the Devil. After complaints from local citizens, the Devil was arrested and fined,

but being no less a man of princ-iple than his friend, refused to pay up on the grounds that he had been discriminated against, while 'Jesus' went free. As if that were not ironic enough, the report in the Sun (Sydney, Australia) 17 October 1978 (Cr: Ion Will) said the two had been on their way to a debate to protest about local priests practicing exorcism on a girl believed to be possessed by "a devil's ghost" (sic). It was also mentioned that the 'devil' who got nabbed was a member of the Norwegian Association of Heathens. Anyone know anything about this group?!

MONKEY SUITS

Then we have some monkey-busin-ess...When a gorilla escaped in a Tokyo zoo, terrified crowds were evacuated and a marksman called to fire a tranquilizing dart. When the animal had collapsed the zoo authorities found it was a man in an ape-skin, who later admitted he had been sent in secret to test the zoo security. Boy, is he glad they didn't use real bullets! (Reveille 19 March 1976. Cr: Nigel Watson). That puts me in mind of a similar but more recent incident - I blush to admit I've mislaid the clipping! In this case, as a pub-licity stunt, a man in a gorilla suit was to burst out of a speci-ally prepared cage to frighten the tourists...only one man - he might have been a Japanese, get-ting revenge on monkey-nuts no doubt - picked up an iron bar and bent it over the head of the sur-prised joker. If this sort of thing goes on in real life, I'm inclined to sympathize with the man who went on trial for murder in Lagos, Nigeria. He told the court that he shot his companion by mistake, thinking he was a

gorilla! (Daily Mirror 23 May 75).
When residents of Byron - a small
community near Flint. Michigan -
saw an 8ft hairy giant lurking
behind their apartment building
making growling noises, they were
sure it was Bigfoot and called the
police, who chased the creature
into woods where they lost it.
After much talk of armed hunting
parties in the woods, a rather
contrite prankster went to the
sheriff's office in Corunna and
confessed that he hired the suit
to play a trick on friends (Detroit News, Michigan, 2 September
1978. Cr: Mark Hall). More sinister is the report in the Houston
Chronicle, Texas, 19 July 1978
(Cr: Mark Hall), that two Bigfoot
costumes and three pairs of giant
feet were stolen from a hotel in
Hood River, Oregon, in use by Alan
Landsburg Productions, who were on
location with their drama-documen-
tary Monster Hunt (which, we understand from Bigfoot News Sept 78,
is to be released soon). For what
it's worth, we note that a year
before the theft of the Bigfoot-
kits in Oregon, a gang wearing
monkey masks began terrorizing
courting couples on the edge of
Epping Forest, Essex (Sun 6 July
1977).

DON'T FORGET THE BUNNY MAN!

Company director Michael Douglas
-Smith was driving home from from
a fancy dress party when a car
screeched to a halt beside his,
and he was dragged into it by 3
burly men. Mr Douglas-Smith was
dressed as a fairy at the time,
and whatever it was they wanted
they changed their minds, quickly
dumping him on the road and speeding off. Later the 3 men were
charged with assault at the Old
Bailey - one said: "There was a
bit of confusion". (Weekend, 29
June 1977). At times we all feel
like stragglers in some comic fancy dress ball and we don't know
the rules or the judges. I guess
the man in the duck suit in Seattle failed the test. He was advertising a local radio station but
was attacked by another player
wearing a driving cap, who pulled
off the duck's bill and beat him
with it. The socio-spacetime rul-
ing is clearer now - at that time
in Seattle it was peaks, not bea-
ks! (London Evening News 19 Sept

1977). On the other hand barman
John Collins could have been hos-
ting one of the judges, in his
Missoula, Montana, bar, without
knowing it. He ejected the man,
"dressed in an insect costume",
from the bar in the early hours
of the morning - however this bar-
fly objected to being shooed away,
returned and swatted Collins, then
buzzed off. When police arrived
all they could find were a pair of
wings flung into a corner! (The
Australian, early November 1978.
Cr: Ion Will).
Now for one of my favourite tab-
leaux...A bus travelling down a
dark stretch of road near Yately,
Hants, pulls in at a request stop.
Conductor Bill Perry nearly drops
his ticket machine as the door
opens to reveal the imposing figure of a 6ft man wearing a leopard's head mask and leopard-skin
gloves with long pointed claws.
Bill managed to ask him if he wanted to get on, but the Leopard Man
spoke not, and lifting his arm in
a gesture both imperious and menacing, merely pointed at Bill. The
bus was off down the road before
the doors had time to shut! (Daily
Mirror 30 October 1967. Cr: Anthony Smith). Finally, I come to a
note which says 'Don't forget the
Bunny Man' - see Fate (UK Edition)
August 1971, p36. He was first
seen by a young couple parked in
a wood in Fairfax County, Virginia
- they were rudely interrupted by
the astonishing sight of an obviously angry man in a bunny-suit
hacking at their windows with a
hatchet. It was believed the Bunny
Man was protesting about new housing developments in this Washington suburb, because he was discovered by a security guard, two
weeks later, chopping at a porch
post on one of the unfinished houses. "You are trespassing," he
announced to the startled guard.
"If you come any nearer I'll chop
off your head." Then he bounded
back into the woods. He was last
seen by 3 children in Seat Pleasant, Maryland, on their way home
from school, who told of seeing a
man on the street "with his bunny
suit on, with a hatchet."
...and believe me, there's lots
more stuff here on bizarre behaviour, but we'll dip into this dippy data again sometime soon. RJMR

We are very pleased to present the following extract from Peter Ratazzi's scholarly and fascinating guide to some of the less well known backwaters of Europe and their mysteries. *In Strangest Europe*, 1968, born of Mr Ratazzi's gentle but relentless curiosity and his notebooks, kept during more than 30 years of travelling byways, is full of Fortean titbits. A limited number of copies are still available, at £2.25 plus postage from Mitre Press, 52 Lincolns Inn Fields, London WC2.

HEALING WATERS FROM THE TOMB

by Peter Ratazzi

The River Tech, originating close to the Spanish frontier, tears brusquely through the Valley of Vallespir towards the Mediterranean and is bridged a few miles north of Le Perthus by the highway running from Narbonne to Barcelona. A secondary road from the intersection at Le Boulou accompanies its torrential waters for thirty miles back into the hinterland before ending in a cul-de-sac. Along the rocky, Colorado-like route lies Céret, the Mecca or Barbizon of Cubism, whose Provencal-Catalan air attracted Picasso, Max Jacob, Bracque, Manolo, Kisling and Juan Gris. The Museum of Modern Arts in the Carmelite convent contains some of their works. Next are the small towns of Amélie-les-Bains, a spa at the foot of a Vauban fortress, and Arles-sur-Tech, producing the first and finest apples of France.

Arles-sur-Tech grew around the abbey of Saint Mairie, founded by Charlemagne in A.D. 778 - the year of the merciless rearguard action near the clefts of Roncesvalles where, at the opposite end of the Pyrenees, the emperor lost Roland, Oliver, and other knights battling Basque partisans. Sheltered by the commanding summits of sacred Mount Canigou, magnetic peak of Roussillon lifting glaciers like frozen white flames skyward, Arles-sur-Tech is a pleasing place, enjoying the mildest climate, a folkloric centre set in a European Hindustan.

Local Holy Week celebrations are obviously related to those in Malaga and Seville. Processional altars aglow with candles and ornate floats sway slowly above the Stations of the Cross parade. Anonymous penitents move rythmically to the accompaniment of litanies and the mournful roll of muffled drums. Dressed in black robes and pointed hoods slitted for the eyes - costumes of the type worn by faceless escorts who walked alongside the barefoot chain-dragging miscreants to the scaffold - a column of repentant sinners crowds the plaza on Maundy Thursday. Backs are bent under the heavy *Croix des Opprobes,* some carry the sunburst of diamonds and the host of thorn-crowned waxen-faced figures with flowing locks and tears of pearl.

On other occasions the mood is gay. Midsummer Night Beacons are the signals of regional rejoicing. Mules are blessed. It is Muleteers Festival, alive with rousing Sardanas music and fraternal Catalan ring dancing. Miradors are festooned for the Cascavellada, and ancestral *festa mayor,* when revellers fight their friendly Battle of Flowers in fancy clothes, bear masks and espadrilles.

The present abbey and cloisters in graceful Provençal style date from the 11th - 13th centuries and shelter a splendid wooden altar-screen, gilded statues of the Persian princess Abdon and Sennen, and painted silver bust-reliquaries containing relics of these saints, who were martyred under the Christian-baiting Roman emperor Decius in A.D. 251. The entrance to the church is embellished by a Romanesque Christ in majesty and the first and the last letter of the Greek alphabet - the Alpha and Omega of the Apocalypse.

To the left of the central doorway and behind an iron railing stands a consecrated tomb. The discoloured, marble coffin - above which appears the wall effigy of Guillaume Gaucelme, Seigneur of Taillet (*d.* 1210), and with arms crossed over his chest - is attributed by archaeological experts to the fourth century. It bears Christ's monogram incircled by a wreath and may be read as IX (Iesous Christos) or XP, the Greek Chi-Rho symbol, the Chrismon, or the Labarum: the standard of Constantine. When surrounded with a ring or wreath the impression is that of a wheel. The *Signum Dei* of early Christianity stood for the founder of the religion as well as for universal peace - *Pax.* Two faded paintings of the Holy Monogram have been found on the garden tomb at Calvary-Golgotha. They incorporate the Alpha and Omega, and indicate that the sepulchre was identified in olden days as the Tomb of Jesus Christ, the First and the Last.

Although antiquarian sarcophagi (literally: 'flesheaters' supposed to consume the body within forty days) are not common in France, or anywhere else, there are still some on view. Several in Paris musea are Christian and show the Chi-Rho cipher. A few good ones may be seen in the southern parts of the country. The cathedrals at Auch (Gers) and Rodez (Aveyron) have perfect specimens from the fifth and sixth centuries. So has the crypt of St. Seurin, Bordeaux. Pagan and Christian sarcophagi discovered in and around Arles (Provence) are now in the archaeological museum of Marseilles. The local church of St. Victor has one said to enshrine the relics of Lazarus.

On the face of it, the heavy austere stone chest at Arles-sur-Tech seems in no way dissimilar to other sarcophagi of the same period. However, there is a difference that is unusual. It is associated with a riddle which has baffled generations of townspeople for the last thousand years. A riddle, by the way, not mentioned anywhere in the 1023 pages of the *Guide de la France Mysterieuse*. Apparently it hides some kind of spring bringing forth a pure, transparent and always fresh liquid of medicinal properties. Between 80 to 150 gallons of the tonic are siphoned by means of a small pump into bulbous phials every year. The little vessels holding the fluid are kept by young and old, and are also in demand outside Arles-sur-Tech, because the contents are believed to be efficacious in treatment of illness.

Mysterious healing water from the tomb!

A closed, free-standing tomb whose theoretical maximum capactiy has been estimated not to exceed 44 gallons!

Of course, there is a traditional tale. The relevant legend begins ten centuries ago when anthropoid apes infested the intensely folded ranges of the *montanyas regaladas*, and from where the ferocious mammals descended to the muletrails of the Vallespir and penetrated sporadically into Arles-sur-Tech. These gorilla-like simians – representations of which can be studied on an archivolt of the abbey – had a taste for tender felsh, particularly that of young children. Neither physical defence nor invocations could halt the scourge. From time to time infants continued to be snatched and eaten. As a last resort it was decided to send the abbot to ask the Pope for advice as to how it could be brought to an end.

One night, during his long journey to Rome, the people's emissary had a vivid dream in which the Persian martyrs, St. Abdon and St. Sennen, told him where to unearth their bodies so that their mortal remains, once transferred from the environs of the Eternal City to the Pyrenees, might protect and free the population from the persistent calamity. Having been granted

permission by the Holy See to disinter at the spot revealed to him, the pilgrim obtained relics from the neglected graves and placed them in a casket. In order not to draw attention of potential robbery the precious case was put into an ordinary barrel topped up with water and, in due course, shipped to Catalonia.

Disembarking with the timbered container on the coast of Roussillon, the faithful voyager engaged the services of a Spanish mule driver and they set out through the savage land in the general direction of the River Tech. When they came to a narrow track, in an area marked by vertiginous cliffs and obsolete iron mines, the mule refused to go on. To change his four-footed friend's mind, the Spaniard let out a string of invective which fairly horrified the good abbot. Before he had recovered from the shock, the stubborn animal had disappeared over a precipice. Now the muleteer, too, was speechless. Never, in those parts, could there have been a mishap so untimely and undeserved.

Utterly dismayed, the two men parted and wandered homeward on forlorn and separate paths. But after many hours the abbot heard a tintinnabulation in the far distance and when he arrived at last in his native town, stirred by joyous peals, he saw that the mule with the treasure had got there before him. *Pater, Ava, Gloria Patri*, the ecclesiastics and people of Arles-sur-Tech had understood the meaning of the event. It was a triumphant return and the happiest day of his life. Thanking God, the abbot poured the water from the barrel into the old sarcophagus and placed the casket in the chapel.

After a week or two the abominable simians began to leave the district. By the end of the season the dread menace lurking in the mountains was banished and the children were secure. Then something else was noticed. Persons in a poor state of health who had touched the water in the oblong receptacle felt stronger. Some patients drank a little of what they considered to be a miraculous cordial, and others added drops of the seemingly invigorating water to lotions. Invalids recovered. The cleansing, forti-

Painted, silver reliquaries (15th century) containing the relics of the Persian martyr-princes, St Abdon and St Sennen, in the Abbey at Arles-sur-Tech.

fying liquid gained popularity and, inexplicably, the tomb did not run dry.

A report set out in a municipal record takes over from the legend in 1794. That year the weighty lid of *la Sainte Tombe* had been upheaved by members of the Republican army of the Pyrénées-Orientales on their way to Spain. The sarcophagus had been emptied and filled with refuse. After cleaning the heavy box several women observed that linen cloths used as dusters became moist when in contact with its walls and bottom. The immense lid was put back in position, but within a month it was noted that ten inches of the aperient had gathered. In the presence of clergy, lawyers and councilmen the complete hard-limestone body was then examined at great length and the inexhaustible chest suspended in the air. No double bottom, no leads, pipes or holes were detected. The supporting bars were thoroughly inspected and proved to be non-porous. Throughout this testing, which lasted for a number of days, the coffin continued to secrete elixir.

Since those days the local position has been watched night and day during irregular but protracted intervals. More recent investigation has shown that the coffin's water level does not correspond in parallel fashion with atmospheric conditions. Furthermore, it has been established that the water tapped from the sarcophagus is of another compositon than the water filtered to the town, but precise chemical data do not seem to be readily obtainable in a place blessed with the rich golden light of the lazy southern life. A scientific analysis, especially if the amounts of trace elements such as arsenic, flourine and strontium, is required, is a complicated and quite costly undertaking for the individual outsider. Moreover, a laboratory would need at least l litre, which is far more than anybody can reasonably expect to collect. The minute ration actually dispensed to any genuine applicant might be sufficient, however, to determine the quantity of total solids, which would indicate if the water had been more or less distilled. It seems just possible that the tomb is in a damp corner and subjected to fairly large temperature changes which could cause condensation. If this were the case, since if is of marble, the water would contain small amounts of calcium bicarbonate and nothing else. In any event, humidity cannot possibly account for the large supply drawn off each year. It should also be borne in mind that the compact capacious sarcophagus is located in the luminous Pyrenees, the driest districts of France.

The region of Arles-sur-Tech is quite likely to have mineral springs - Ax-les-Thermes with much sulphur and flourine in its sixty warm streams rising from the ground not being too far away - but this is really nothing to do with the annual 80 to 150 gallons of 'miraculous.' Sceptics have suggested, of course, that churchmen might have replenished the drink off and on, but it is highly improbable that the abbots could or would mislead the inhabitants for a thousand years. The abbots and priors of Roussillon and Cerdagne have always occupied a special status. Pope Gregory XI was in his earlier years an abbot of Arles-sur-Tech. A single abbey, that of St. Michel de Cuxa (most of whose capitals were acquired by the Metropolitan Museum of Art in New York and adorn 'The Cloisters'), possessed thirty lordships as well as legal titles in 200 other places. Similar rights and responsibilities were exercised by the Abbeys of Corneilla de Conflent, Arles-sur-Tech and St. Martin du Canigou.

Of all the stories of miraculous healing waters - from sacred wells enclosed by chapels of granite to the hidden Fountains of Youth - this is the most remarkable. One thousand solid old Gold Francs, deposited decades ago by an intrigued notary of Arles-sur-Tech for the benefit of any person able to explain the phenomenon satisfactorily, still lie locked in the abbatial safe and await their claimant. "The fairest thing we can experience is the mysterious," opined a physicist and Nobel Prize winner. "It is the fundamental emotion which stands at the cradle of true science. He who knows it not, and can no longer wonder, no longer feel amazement, is as good as dead."

La petite Reine du Vallespir and the whole area from Font-Romeu to colourful Collioure of the sardine boats belonged for hundreds of years to Spain, until Louis XI, the first French nationalist, secured its cession from John II of Aragon. Since the transfer, in 1468, there exist the Two Catalonias, and French culture has merged agreeably with Spanish tradition. Fittingly, the popular, quotidian signal is "Aqui, Radio Andorra!"

For centuries July 30 has been a day of patronal feastrites at Arles-sur-Tech. The procession of the shrines of St. Abdon and St. Sennen then precedes the distribution of water from the sanctified sarcophagus, and this prayer: *Dieu tout puissant, qui avez lavé le monde dans les eaux du déluge et qui régénérez les ames dans les eaux du baptême, daignez, par la vertu que vous avez communiquée à cette eau dont notre foi nous inspire de faire usage, purifier notre ame de ses souillures et guérir notre corps des es infirmités. Nous vous le demandons au nom et par mérites de vos Saints martyrs Abdon et Sennon. - Ainsi soit-il.*

Occasionally letters with foreign stamps reach the abbey. They refer to cardiac, intestinal or rheumatic ailments, and correspondents request the curative agent. Tiny plastic bottles are mailed in reply. Some have arrived in England and America. Under the printed words *Nature de la Marchandise* on accompanying standard export forms the typewriting declares *Eau Miraculeuse*. One wonders what customs officers who deal with a variety of imports in this technological era have made of it before putting the rubber stamp of approval on to such packages.

On the site where Roman imperialists founded Arula on the Tech to the glory of Nature, *jeux de boules* in the *Boulodrome* by the Hotel de Ville now absorb the attention of citizens.

Agave, cork-oak and cactus; cherry, mimosa and peach-tree grow under the warm sky as in the years of early wondertokens when - with animated Perpignan, the Vermilion Coast and Balearic Isles - Arles-sur-Tech belonged to the quaint, short-lived Kingdom of Marjorca.

A Catalan priest siphons the healing water from the mysterious 4th century sarcophagus with Christ's monogram (just visible on the right side) at Arles-sur-Tech.

PETER RATAZZI 1968

JINXES

29 January 1978 - Alice Hicks of Youngstown, Ohio, died under mysterious circumstances. Her neighbours thought she was a "witch". Detective Mike Gilboy removed a six-inch doll wrapped in ribbon from her house - its head was turned backwards, there was a 2" needle in its chest and a thorn pierced its back. The day Detective Tony Cafaro put a piece of paper in Gilboy's desk, where the doll was kept, he slipped on some icy steps and broke his tail bone.. Detective Joseph Fajack, who rode to work with Gilboy, got sick for the first time in 12 years. Detective Clarence Greene caught pneumonia; Lieut. Don Malleske came down with flu for the first time in 20 years; and Patrolman Sam DuBose, who took home some of Mrs Hicks' voodoo books to read, had to have all his top teeth removed. Gilboy himself almost choked on a pepper seed stuck in his oesophagus a week after taking the doll. The next day he pulled a shoulder muscle...and a month later had a double hernia and torn groin muscles. In March he caught Russian flu. Then he was shoved into a swimming pool, breaking his neck and back. On 10 June Detective Steve Krispli moved the doll from Gilboy's desk to an evidence locker, and four days later was hospitalised with   severe chest pains. Lieut Sabatino finally burned the doll on 16 June. "My feeling was that this had gone on long enough," he said. National Enquirer, 15 August 1978.

In the summer of 1977 airline vice-president Ralph Loffert, of Buffalo, NY, his wife and four children visited the Hawaiian volcano Mauna Loa. While there they collected some stones from the volcano despite a warning from the natives that this would anger the volcano goddess, Madame Pele. Shortly after they returned home Mauna Loa erupted. Within a few months Todd, 10, developed appendicitis, had knee surgery and broke his wrist; Mark, 14, sprained an ankle and broke his arm; Dan, 11, caught an eye infection and took to wearing glasses; while Rebecca, 7, lost two front teeth in a fall. In July 1978, the Lofferts sent the stones to a friend in Hawaii who was asked to return them to the volcano. The disasters continued - Mark hurt his knee, Rebecca broke three more teeth, Dan fractured a hand bone, while Todd dislocated an elbow and fractured his wrist again. Mark then confessed he had secretly witheld 3 stones. They were returned to Pele and the trouble ceased. Grand Rapids Press (Cr: Davie Fideler) Columbus, Ohio, Dispatch (Cr: Loren Coleman) both 31 October 1978; Sunday Express 3 December 1978 (Cr: J & C Bord, Richard Cotton); Weekend 10-16 January 1979.

In June 1977, Terry Barlow's wife accidentally disturbed a robin's nest in their garden, killing two of the young. Since then Terry's father died, and his sons Mark, 17, and Simon, 12, ended up side by side in hospital after separate accidents. Someone was thrown through Terry's shop window in a street brawl, which also damaged his car. His aunt had a heart attack, and as he was attending to that thieves broke into two flats he owned and swiped the electricity meter money. The next day his wife's antique shop was burgled of £800 worth of goods. In April 1978 a lorry knocked down his garden wall. Terry, 44, a local councillor and heating engineer in Chesterfield, Derbyshire, said: "It's got to the stage where I'm wondering what will happen next." Sun

17 September 1977; <u>Daily Express</u>
10 April 1978. (Cr: Colin Mather).

TALES OF WOE!

In some cases no specific cause for a run of bad luck can be attributed. Perhaps someone (or something) up there (or wherever) is trying to get a message through to the hapless victims...

Roy Reep, 67, of Gastonia, California: - at 3 his brother accidentally shot him in the face; at 9 he cracked his skull; at 11 his father accidentally hit him on the head with an axe; at 13 an operation for sinus trouble revealed two teeth lodged in his nose. Later in life he fractured his pelvis and hips, and punctured his kidneys and bladder in a car accident. He was also shot in the chest by his alcoholic wife; burst a vein in his eye during a cataract operation leaving him blind in that eye; diagnosed a diabetic, and suffered a nerve injury to a hand. <u>Rand Daily Mail</u> (S.A.) 11 July 1977. (Cr: Chris J Holtzhausen).

Brian Chellender, 29, bricklayer of Bournemouth:- his latest reported exploit was bending down to pick up a pin for good luck, whereupon he was knocked unconscious by a falling brick. He reckons the trouble began when he was born on a Friday the thirteenth. As a boy he had a bad bicycle accident, was knocked out by a golf club and attacked by a man with an axe. He was stabbed at a fairground, pinned down by a 55-ton motorway earth-mover, trapped under a garage door, stunned by falling metal on a building site (he took his hat off in the heat to cool down), scarred for life by steam and rammed by a rowing boat off Bournemouth Pier. He is very well-known at the hospital. <u>Daily Mail</u> 24 Apr 1973; <u>Weekend</u> 13 June 1973.

Albert Goodwin, 53, of Peterborough: - he has broken both feet, fractured three fingers, dislocated his neck, fallen through a factory roof and been machine-gunned during the war. In December 1973 he was convalescing from an accident in his home, having just broken both wrists. Albert is a safety officer! <u>Daily Mirror</u>, 17 December 1973 (Cr: Bob Forrest).

Philip Ellis, 24, of St Albans: - He was knocked down by a Land Rover. While leaving hospital he was hit by a bus. A bridge he was crossing collapsed, dumping him on a passing car below. He has crashed in a glider, and in May 1978 he suffered a broken arm after being hit by an express train as he crossed a track. <u>News of the World</u>, 7 May 1978.

Nate Brown, 43, of Charleston, West Virginia: - Shot nine times; stabbed 15 times; knocked down by a car, a truck and a train. Carlisle, Cumbria, <u>Sunday Sun</u> 5 Dec 1976 (Cr: Peter Hope-Evans)

Sometimes the jinx falls more on those around the walking disaster area. Take Dr Max Benis, a specialist in allergies, who has been in the right place at the right time on at least 19 occasions to help people in distress. Wherever he goes people begin to drown, fall off high rocks right at his feet, choke on their food in the same restaurant, or touch live wires. Says the <u>Daily Mail</u> 6 December 77: "Not many of the victims seem particularly grateful to Dr Max."

Or consider Martha Matikia, a beautiful Bulgarian. A violent storm caused Martha to meet Randolph Eastman, and American touring near Sofia, in 1935, when he sought shelter in her house. They married within a week - two months later Eastman was struck dead by lightning, leaving Martha with £20,000. She bought her parents a new house and married Charles Martaux. While on holiday in Spain he was killed by lightning. In her sorrow she became ill and returned to Sofia where she was treated by a famous German doctor. On her recovery they went to Berlin, where they married. She left him when she found out he was a Nazi, but he pursued her. Near the French border his car was struck by lightning, killing him. <u>Weekend</u> 31 March 1976 (Cr: Anthony Smith). For other lightning freaks see last issue.

We have lots more on damned bad luck, but alas no room here. PS

NEWS CLIPPINGS
If you see anything of interest to FT readers in your reading, professional or scientific journals, or local newspapers, please clip it out, or make a note of it, add a note of the source, date, and your name . . . then send it to us. It all helps and there are surprisingly few duplications. Some readers have offered to scan their regular reading matter, and if you would like to do the same, please contact us for suggested periodicals not being covered by others.

STRANGE ENCOUNTERS IN YORKSHIRE

by Nigel Watson

A more than superficial look at the UFO literature reveals that UFO encounters are far stranger than mere lights in the sky and visiting spacemen.

A recent investigation by Graham and Mark Birdsall, area investigators for Contact International (U.K.), illustrates the kind of ufological scenario we are confronted with.

Their report deals with the sightings and experiences of the Ledger family, which took place in and around Clover Field, Leeds; this field being in the vicinity of Kirkstall Power Station, and located between Kirkstall road and Stanningley road, west Leeds.

The first sighting occurred at 2.0 a.m. one morning, in the first week of June, 1978, when Mr Barry Ledger (37) and his son, Reece (12) went rabbit hunting. They were walking towards Halfpenny Bridge, which leads to Clover Field, when they saw a stationary bright light ahead of them. The white light with a silver haze around it hovered about 2 feet above the ground. After they had seen it for a few seconds it shot away at a fantastic speed.

Three days later, Mr Ledger, his son, and daughter, Tracy (14), were out hunting at 2.30 a.m., in the same locality, when they saw at the far end of Halfpenny Bridge, a rugby-ball-shaped object. This appeared to be 20 feet in height and 30-40 feet in length, and was hovering only a couple of feet above the ground. They watched it at a distance of 100 feet for about 30 seconds until it 'simply disappeared.'

The next day Mr and Mrs Ledger were walking through the field when, at the same spot where he'd seen the object the previous night, they found a cluster of 5 or 6 holes in the muddy ground. In all they found 5 such clusters in the vicinity.

During the next week Mr Ledger, Reece and Tracy, visited the field again at night time. On this occasion they didn't see anything but instead they heard a whispering sound, so close to them that they were 'frightened to death' of this disembodied emanation.. Ten days after the original UFO sighting, father and son were yet again hunting for rabbits at 2.30 a.m. in Clover Field, when they saw a light in the corner of the field, which disappeared after 30 seconds.

By now Mrs Barbara Ledger was fearful for the safety of her family. So on their next rabbit hunting trip Mrs Ledger, Nellie their hunting dog and a friend, Eddie, attended the proceedings. On this visit they heard a loud screaming sound which seemed to emanate from the top of Kirkstall Power Station. Mr Ledger's hair stood on end, the children were terrified, and

Mrs Ledger claimed that: 'It sounded like something in pain, (it was) terrible, and I couldn't sleep that night, I'd never heard a sould like it in my life'.

The Ledgers were back in Clover Field, two nights later. First they heard the rustling of leaves, then their dog Nellie began to whine, which made Mrs Ledger turn round and look upwards. On doing this, she saw a monstrous shaped-object, which appeared to be 5 times bigger than their dog, swoop 1½ feet above her head. The 'bird' appeared to have no feathers, but instead had over-lapping scales, on the surface of it's wings and body. Mrs Ledger thought it looked mechanical and added that their dog jumped up at it as it flew over them.

The 'bird' or 'flying cross' landed on the ground ahead of them, close to the footpath. Their dog ran towards the object which began to wobble from side to side. It came towards the dog and then it suddenly vanished into, proverbial, thin air. Although the Ledger's could see nothing, their dog persisted in snapping and howling, as if something were still there. After this, the Ledgers had to have their dog destroyed by the RSPCA, because she began to go berserk at the sight of birds, and she would also attack cats and dogs.

A few days afterwards, Mr and Mrs Ledger were walking through the field when they found a heap of 5 dead, young starlings. The birds had no marks on them and rigor mortis had not set in, indicating that they had only been dead for a few hours. Looking around they discovered a total of 6 piles of dead birds, all separated by a distance of 12 feet from each other.

After an interval of 3 weeks, the bizarre happenings in Clover Field had ceased - but after this period, Mr Ledger, Tracy, Reece and Eddie, who were out rabbit hunting, were yet again confronted by the unknown.

This time Mr Ledger saw a strange light near his son, Reece. 'I haven't a clue where it came from', said Mr Ledger, 'it was suddenly there. I'd no idea how long it was there, for all I know it could have been an hour . . . it hurt my eyes I recall, yet I couldn't look down, we more or less came around to see the light had gone...

'It was then that I noticed I no longer had my rifle . . . I couldn't understand it at all, so we walked around searching for it, and I found it laid in the grass some 30 feet away from where I had been stood'.

Tracy and Eddie witnessed the light along with Mr Ledger, but surprisingly Reece, who was closest to the phenomenon, claimed that he saw nothing untoward.

As a result of this encounter, Mr Ledger

discovered that his wrist watch had gone hay-wire, and Eddie vowed that he would never return to the field.

On subsequent visits Mr Ledger has noticed that the wildlife in the area has diminished, but no more unusual events have been reported, by the Ledgers.

It would be simplistic and naive to take this report of these stange happenings at face value. From an objective point of view we might argue that the Ledgers' strange experiences can be explained in a perfectly rational manner. For instance, we could speculate that their UFO observations were nothing more than the lights of trespassing poachers - these and subsequent (mundane) triggers, inaugurating stange mis-persuasions in the minds of the Ledger family.

The rationalistic explanation is valid to a certain extent, but it does ignore the question of how such 'ufological fantasies' are triggered off, and to answer this we need to know more about the witnesses involved (still a neglected area of study despite the popularity of Keel's writings). Also many elements of the Ledgers' story - such as the dead birds, winged object, time lapse etc. - are prevalent in the Fortean literature, which indicates that such 'mispersuasions' are archetypal in nature. Indeed, within just the ufological context, we are confronted with a wealth of subjective and symbolic information which is worthy of more consideration than it has been given in the past. It is fortunate that more ufologists are beginning to realise this.

[We are pleased to announce that Nigel Watson has agreed to do a regular column of comments and notes on the Fortean aspects of recent UFO sightings, encounters and reports, beginning next issue - Ed]

FINDING THE FAMOUS

There have, of late, been a number of excavations, and subsequent controversies, concerning persons of ancient fame; perhaps the most notable being the alleged finding of the body of St John the Baptist at the St Makar Monastery, in the Natroun Valley, about 60 miles north-west of the Egyptian capital of Cairo. The details are extremely confused, and we have only reportage of reports in two Egyptian newspapers, Al Ahram and Al Akhbar, but I'll piece together the story as best I can.

According to the traditions of the Coptic Church, the body of St John, along with that of the prophet Elisha, was brought from Palestine to Alexandria in the 5th Century, and then secretly removed to the monastery in the 11th. This story seems to rest on oral tradition and two 15th Century manuscripts.

Earliest reports speak of two coffins being found in 1976, below a church within the monastery, which as a whole dates back to 360 AD. We first hear that only one of these had been opened, and had been found to contain the bones of Elisha, while the monks assured the reporter from Al Ahram that the second contained the remains of St John. This story soon changed alarmingly.

We are next told that a cave was found beneath the church, containing several undecomposed bodies, but this then changed again. The final version, as I understand it, is that the cave contained the bones of 14 people, and the skulls of 13: thus, 'obviously' the 14th man was St John. A wooden coffin was also found, which contained an undecomposed body, though no identification has been provided for him; except that he was not St John, for he had retained his head. Father Youhanna, the second most senior monk at the monastery, refused to say how the identifications had been made, but it is apparently customary for the monks to collectively fast and pray for long periods, until "heavenly secrets" are revealed to them.

All of which is very well, but the Roman Catholic Church also claims to possess the bones of St John, at Genoa, Italy. These were looted by one Gulielmo Embriaco from the city of Mira in Turkey, during the First Crusade, around 1100. The Genoese stole the bones, thinking them to be those of St Nicholas, but the citizens of Mira told him they were St John's. "So much the better!" he replied. Such is the way Ecclesiastical history is written, and I confess myself sceptical of anyone claiming to have received the body of St John, except six (or perhaps five) feet of his native soil. Story compiled from London Evening News, 13 Nov 1978, Daily Telegraph, Toronto Star, The Australian, 14 Nov 78, Guardian, 15 Nov 78, Bangkok Post, Toronto Globe & Mail, 20 Nov 78. (Cr: V Martin, V Thomas, D Whalen, I Will).

However, it should not be thought that I doubt the sincerity of the Coptic monks; but it seems to be a function of the human mind to make such assumptions as soon as any evidence, however fragmentary, appears in support of tradition. Schliemann, for all his brilliance as an archaeologist, was mistaken in thinking that he had found the remains of Agamemnon at Mycenae, and perhaps the same charge of assumption could be levelled at Manolis Andronikos, who claims to have found the tomb of Philip of Macedon (see FT 26). While Andronikos has undoubtedly found an important tomb of the right period, and has adduced some weighty evidence, his claim to have found Philip remains, at present, not proven.

Where religious considerations enter in, the situation is muddled still further. The alleged tomb of Christ at Srinagar, Kashmir, has received much coverage (Telegraph Sunday magazine, 4 June 78, Niagara Falls Review, 14 Oct 78 (Cr: D Whalen) and the book Jesus Died in Kashmir by Faber-Kaiser, reviewed in FT 26), but its contents can only remain a matter of conjecture while the Moslem Ahmadiyya sect refuse to allow the coffin to be opened. Their faith should, after all, be strong enough to be put to the test.

On the subject of the famous, I mention in passing that excavations continue at the tomb of Chin Shih Huang Ti (259-210 BC), the first unifier of China, at Lintung County, near Sian. Here, at least, there is some certainty that the right tomb has been connected to the right man, but I intend to give this much greater coverage in my oriental column next issue.

THE WAY WE LIVED THEN

An expedition of Egyptian and American archaeologists and geologists, led by Mr Farouk El Baz, returned from a two-week expedition to Egypt's Western Desert with a rather remarkable tale which has received surprisingly little coverage. That area of the desert they toiled through has not been explored in recent memory and, it seems, they will not know exactly where they were until they have referred to photographs taken by a sattelite which tracked their progress. But they started from Kharga Oasis, 520 km south of Cairo, headed south-west toward Bir Tarfawi and Bir Misaha Oasis, then west to Oweinat Mountain, covering 1600 km in all.

Somewhere along the way (the location is not given) they accidentally stumbled upon a "ghost city", a "cave-like" community dwelling, previously covered by the dunes and uncovered again by the wind. Within, they found hand-axes and spear-heads, petrified ostrich eggs, remains of a giraffe and cave-drawings indicating the area once had enough rain for grass to grow and cattle to graze. There were also traces of a 200 sq-km lake.

But perhaps the most remarkable part of this tale is the date El Baz attributes to the finds: 200,000 years ago. While this date, if true, will doubtless be eagerly siezed upon by those who advocate the possibility of lost super races in the dawn of time, I admit I have a mistrusting soul: to me, 200,000 seems a remarkably round number, and I'm willing to entertain the possibility that perhaps an extra '0' has been introduced into the reporting (though there is nothing to support this). But what niggles most, perhaps, is that nowhere in the clippings to hand is there any mention of how this date was ascertained, nor the names of any of the "prominent" scientists (except Mr El Baz). We must await further developments. Sunday Express, 22 Oct 78, Sydney Morning Herald, 23 Oct 78, Pretoria (S.A.) News, 30 Oct 78. (Cr: P Rogerson, C Holtzhausen, V Sumegi).

Whatever we may think of the above, it certainly makes England's oldest house a mere piker by comparison: an oval dwelling on a hilltop at Romsey, Hampshire, containing seeds radio-carbon dated to 6590 BC. Guardian, 8 Nov 78. (Cr: P Rogerson).

And some other antediluvian dwellings: In West Ukraine, Soviet archaeologists have found 4 oval huts, connected by a series of passages, made from mammoth bones and animal skins, 40,000 years ago. National Echo (Malaysia) 8 Dec 78. (Cr: I Will). Still in the Ukraine, a town of 700 acres, 1,500 buildings, some of them two-storeyed adobe constructions, built by the Tripolye culture, c. 3000 BC. Omaha World Herald, 17 Sept 72 (Cr: J Swatek). On the Mississippi River, evidence that the Indians lived in permanent houses and kept dogs, 9,000 years ago. D. Mail, 29 June 77. And at Rome, traces of a settlement existing 500 years before Romulus and Remus supposedly founded the city. London Evening Standard, 29 July 77.

And that touch of 'earlier than you think' leads us conveniently to our next section...

ANCIENT TECHNOLOGIES

We seem to have accumulated a quantity of material from communist countries, so, taking the Soviet Union first:

Central Kazakhstan: the 2,300 yr old skeleton of a young woman unearthed, and found to have had her amputated left foot replaced with bones taken from a sheep. She survived several years after the operation. World's first transplant? Observer, 24 Jan 71.

Bones excavated at Mezin, near Chernigov, in 1908, from a 20,000-yr-old Paleolithic dwelling, have been identified as percussion instruments. They are mammoth bones: two lower jaw-bones, a shoulder blade, a thigh bone, a fragment of pelvic bone and a fragment of skull, all painted with geometric patterns in red ochre, and struck with 'hammers' made of deer antlers and mammoth teeth. Stone-age rock? Novosti Bulletin, 24 Sept 74.

A Sarmatian burial mound of the first century AD, near Novocherkassk, in the Northern Caucasus, contained a copper mirror which appears to have been machine worked and incised with circles of "astonishing accuracy and finish".

It was in a case bearing similar designs, covered with a substance like glass. Soviet Weekly, 3 July 76 (Cr: RG Twine).

And from China: they struck oil first, it seems, 2,000 years ago, on the Yu River, in NW China. A contemporary historian (unnamed) spoke of a stream with fat on its water, which could be picked up; turned yellow, then black, and coalesced into ointment called 'stone paint'. When burnt it gave out bright flames. Sunday Times, 15 Dec 74.

The invention of papermaking, normally attributed to Tsai Lun (or, in the new phonetics, Cai Lun) in 105 AD, has been pushed back by excavation at the Ejin River in Kansu (Gansu) province. Two pieces of paper were found, the earliest being dated before 52 BC. Beijing Review (formerly 'Peking Review') 5 Jan 79.

A double-edged steel sword, excavated from a tomb of the late Spring and Autumn Period (approx 500 BC) at Changsha, Hunan Province, has pushed back the date of the first known steel-making in China by at least 200 years. Peking Review, 1 Sept 78.

And the ancient Tanzanians were no slouches when it came to steel making either, it seems. Reconstruction of smelting furnaces made by the Haya tribe, dating back 1,500 to 2,000 years and similar to those in use until the beginning of the 20th Century, has shown that they produced a temperature of 1,800 degrees C. This was at least 360 degrees hotter than anything known in Europe at the time, and the steel produced was thus of a considerably higher quality. The Star (S.A.) 27 Sept 78. (Cr: CJ Holtzhausen).

Excavations at Ban Chiang, Thailand, have turned up bronze artifacts dating back to 3,500 BC, 500 years earlier than any previous finds, which is something of a blow to the theory that bronze metallurgy began in the Middle East about 3,000 BC, and diffused from there. And also a blow to the notion that S E Asia was a backwater that only derived its culture from China. Evidence shows a flourishing permanent community, with excellent pottery, bronze work, and rice cultivation. Sunday Times, 17 Aug 75.

Archaeologists working at the Franchthi Cave, in the Argolis peninsula, Greece, have found evidence that seafaring began in the Mediterranean as early as 9,000 BC, 2,000 years earlier than previously known. Daily Telegraph, 27 Oct 78.

OTHER RECENT FINDS

A brief round-up:

The perfectly preserved bodies of six eskimoes, and their animal skin clothes, 500 years old, from a grave at Umanak, western Greenland. Melbourne Sun, 16 Sept 78. (Cr: H Thomas).

A Scythian gold statue from the first millenium BC, the first 3-D statue from the period, showing a wild boar thrusting its tusks into a hunter's leg. Site unknown. Sydney Sun, 15 Nov 78. (Cr: I Will).

A 45-feet long oaken boat, from Graveney, Kent, dated to 939 AD, the earliest boat so far discovered in England. London Evening News, 12 July 77.

A 13th century manuscript,

"Elucidation of the Astronomical Sphere", by Ubaidula Ash-Sheria, found in the archives of the Tajik town of Ura-Tyube. It contains theories about the formation of the universe, as well as astronomical data. Soviet Union No 335, Feb 78. (Cr: I Will).

Islamic glass, beads, pottery and traces of ships found while repairing a reservoir in Hong Kong, indicate foreign trade with south China in the 9th Century was much more extensive than previously thought. Denver Post, 18 Dec 77. (Cr: TR Adams).

A wooden bridge unearthed near Amphipolis, Greece, believed to have been built by the Spartan General Vrasidis, 424 BC. Sunday Express, 24 Dec 78. (Cr: C Hall)

A Roman temple, thought to be the largest in Britain, and four times as big as previous discoveries, at Northwood Farm, Hayling Island, Hants, believed to have been built on an earlier Celtic sacred site. The News (Portsmouth) 8 July 78. (Cr: N Maloret). SM

OUT OF PLACE

LARGE CATS

Our last note on the elusive "small lioness or puma" that has left sporadic tracks and mangled carcases in the Scottish Highlands, from Inverness up to the northern coast of Sutherland, was back in early February 1978 - see FT25 & 26. At 10am on 27 November 1978, a plasterer called George Gillanders, of Dornoch, spotted what he believed

was the 'puma' between the hotels at Aultnagar and Invershin, in Sutherland. He said: "It was quite near the road bounding away from me. It was black all over and just a bit bigger than a labrador, but it was definitely cat-like." Aberdeen Press-Journal 1 Dec 1978 (Cr: Jake Williams). Since then (ie about two days later) it was blamed for the killing of two sheep, and a third mis-

sing, from a flock high above Loch Shin, near Lairg, in central Sutherland. One of the sheep was partially eaten and had its ribs crushed, obviously by a powerful animal. This was the first such depredation since those of the previous winter (see FT25 & FT26). Glasgow Herald, and Daily Record, both 30 November 1978 (Cr: Jake Williams, J Lang.)

Signtings of the Scottish 'puma's' older southern cousin, the 'Surrey puma' seem to be getting fewer as the years go by. Let's hope that 1979 has more to offer than the few sightings last year (see FT25p33f) - for now we record a 'puma' scare in the are of Faversham, Kent - no dates are given but we guess the sightings occurred in the early days of January this year. A "large mysterious black animal" was seen by lecturer Peter Latham, near his house in

Boughton Street; and later his neighbour, Mrs Bernadette Kiely, found "unusually large paw marks" in the snow; and two local boys out ferreting said they saw a "big black creature" in the woods. Sunday Mirror 14 January 1979.

In the USA, mystery cats have been as mischievous as in previous years but also less frequently. On 23 Jan 1978, a woman in Loxahatchee, Florida, saw a lion outside her window - or thought she did! She called the nearby Lion Country Safari park to let them know. The lady who took the call at the park called a friend at a Loxahatchee grocery store - that friend called other friends who then did likewise and within a very short time the whole community was on alert. Three police patrol cars were sent to the area but they failed to pick up the scent. There were no lions missing at the park, and two residents who had lions as pets could account for theirs. When the tension dragged on for a bit people began to believe there was no lion, that the original caller must have been mistaken, or that it had left the area. An interesting little illustration of rumour...then the story fizzles out! Palm Beach Post, Florida, 24 January 1978 (Cr: Udo Schlegel).

A similarly inconclusive tale comes from the Millstone Road area of West Virginia. On 17 September 1978, Sam Tubaugh left his TV to go out of his front door, and in his yard, about 10ft away, he saw a large black animal which he first thought was a dog. He made a noise to scare it away and as it ran he realized it was a large cat-like animal. There was a light in the yard, and he thinks the animal was black, about 2ft tall "or more" and had a long tail. About the same time, or a little later, 2 local boys met it while they walked along the road - they too believe it was a large black cat with a long tail. The sightings caused the usual excitement; and the animal was blamed for the weird screeching noises some folks heard at night, and for the disappearance of neighbour Marcena Denny's chickens. The fuss was even compared to the 'Mothman' flap of nearby Point Pleasant (see the writings of John Keel) in the 1960s... and speaking of monsters, we note that Tubaugh was watching King Kong - he wonders if it was the panic-screams of crowds in the film that attracted the creature? As news spreads there are two developments. Firstly Mrs Denny sees a dog taking one of her remaining chickens and calls the County Dog Warden who manages to track and capture the canine culprit. The dog was undoubtedly wild, and black

and brown, but nevertheless in the minds of many people the mystery was solved! The other development was equally predictable and unsatisfactory to Forteans. Ray Knotts, a biologist with the McClintic Wildlife Station at Point Pleasant, visited Tubaugh to examine some traces - the tracks he dismissed as not cat-like, but various scratches and other marks could well have been made by a large cat...but no, he said: "There is no such thing as a panther in the United States...no wild mountain lions in West Virginia for over 75yrs.." but they do tend to range in colour from tawny yellow to chocolate brown. Since I don't want another rap across the knuckles from John Michell (see 'Letters' this issue) I point out this is the opinion of an 'expert' toeing the official line, and as such is traditionally in conflict with eye-witness testimony. For further discussion see Loren Coleman's account of black panther sightings in Ohio, in Fate November 1977. This story came from the Point Pleasant Register, West Virginia, 18,20 & 21 September 1978 (Cr: Tom Adams).

Curiously, less than a month later, the rare Eastern Cougar, long thought to be near extinction in Ontario state, was seen at least twice. In the second week of October, provincial police constable Art King saw one emerge from trees on the Bruce Peninsula while he was parked on a township road NE of Wiarton. He described it as about 30" high, around 200 lbs, and brownish-orange with a lighter coloured stomach. Like the Millstone Road incident above, there had been rumours of a creature haunting the area for at least a year. About a month later an animal, described simply as "a cougar", was seen by an award-winning outdoors writer (it says here) John Kerr, on the banks of the Saugeen River. Casts of the pawprints were obtained by Ontario's Ministry of Natural Resources, who now confirm the cougar's presence. Niagara Falls Review 17 October 1978; & the St Catherines Standard 17 November 1978 (Cr: Dwight Whalen).

Sightings of Thylacines - or the Tasmanian Wolf, as it is better known - are continuing in the coastal regions of southern Australia, but the situation is horribly mixed up by the persistence of the Australian press in confusing the Thylacine with the 'Tasmanian Tiger', a large marsupial cat widely believed to be extinct. And to make matters worse there have been sightings of large black panther-like cats in south western Australia (particularly New South Wales) and accompanying reports of savage sheep depredations. We'll cover these stories soon - in the meantime we're trying to locate an Australian naturalist (with Fortean inclinations) who could clarify and perhaps even tabulate the marsupial mysteries of the Land of Oz for us.

KANGAROOS & WALLABIES

A kangaroo was spotted in the fields of Bedfordshire, about mid-April 1978, by two ambulancemen on their way to a call. They reported it to the police, and the investigating officer caught up with it at Hockliffe, near Dunstable - but it got away by bounding over the fields. As usual, when the news reached the papers, the reporters ring around the local zoos, and as usual none of their animals are missing. Each time we get a report like this, I'm sorry to say, we are also given a lot of garbage which is supposed to pass for intelligent, informed and even witty comment from the zoo people - but, also usually, it is none of these things. The data I've just given you came from the London Evening Standard 20 April 1978 - and I'm sure that simply because the story was regarded as a light 'filler' they didn't bother which such heavy boring details like names or dates! We as Forteans and newspaper readers ought to do something positive, soon, about the declining standards of British newspaper reporting especially in the 'popular' papers - any ideas? But back to the zoos' comments - Whipsnade Zoo staff are cited as cynically stating such stories usually start "about pub closing time" when in this case the witnesses were public officials on duty during an afternoon! Also, the reporter was told that "no-one here" had heard of kangaroos running wild in Bedfordshire, and that it is more likely to be a wallaby. That last detail is correct: not only is the UK an ideal habitat for the wallaby, it is well known that there are at least 2 breeding colonies in England - besides, in my experience, escaped kangaroos are soon recaptured; wallabies it seems are more wily. Someone at the Woburn Abbey wild life park "denied any knowledge" of wallabies or kangaroos. They can't mean that they're entirely ignorant, and

A small footnote for marsupial kind. According to recent intelligence, kangaroos got their name when Cap'n Cook asked an Australian native about those strange animals he saw bounding through the undergrowth. The Abo replied "Kangaro..." Which, we are reliably informed, translates roughly as, "What the hell are you talking about?" Love it. -- Ed.

yet I find it hard to believe that they are unaware of the 2 feral colonies and the small number of escapes each! If this truly reflects the knowledge and opinion of these people it is pathetic! Here's something for them to consider... Sun 9 Nov 1977: a wallaby escapes from Cambridge University's animal research unit at Madingley (and that's not far from Bedfordshire!) - as far as I know it's still living in nearby woods (Cr: Paul Screeton). Sun 18 March 1978: a wallaby that escaped 2 years previously from a country park on the Isle of Wight was thought to be returning because she is lovesick, since a wallaby has been seen near the male wallabies. No one is quite sure if it is the same one or appearance of another (Cr: Nigel Pennick). Daily Mirror 10 August 1978: that a wallaby that escaped from Windsor Safari Park, Berks, on 30 July was recaptured on 9 August by 2 policemen at Forest Road, Winkfield. (Story also appeared in the Daily Telegraph.) And speaking of those wild wallaby colonies a note appeared in the Guardian 17 August 1978, that the directors of the Riber Castle Wild Life Park, near Matlock in Derbyshire, believe that one of the reasons the feral colony which has survived in the Peak District since 1939 have dwindled in numbers (apart from the devastating winter of 1962/3 which reduced their numbers to single figures) is their reduced hardiness through inbreeding. So they have selected a strong and virile young wallaby and released it near the known herd in the hope of revitalizing their genes. We would like to have seen more than one released, but we hope it works anyway.

Meanwhile, in the USA, kangaroos struck again in a repeat of the 1974 flap in Illinois and Indiana - see FT9p18f. These latest sightings began on 7 April 1978, this time in Wisconsin, in a suburban area west of Waukesha, and several undescribed incidents were enough to get the subject discussed on TV on the night of Saturday 8 April. Lance Nero, of Brookfield, was one of those who got a laugh from the airing - but as he had breakfast the next morning (9th April) he saw two animals that looked like kangaroos cross a road from a wooded area, hop across a field and another road. His wife also saw the animals - and later a Waukesha County Sheriff's Department officer took pictures of the tracks, which are said to be consistent with the notion of kangaroos. The next sight-was at 6.15pm on 12 April, by the Haeselich family as they sat down for dinner in their Mt Vernon Drive, Waukesha home.

Jill Haeselich said she only saw it out
of the corner of her eye but her husband
Peter and his mother had got a good look
at it about 50ft from their diningroom
picture window. Peter ran out of the
back door and saw it jumping off southwards over the hill. All of these reports mentioned that it was between 3-5ft
tall, the colour of a deer and very fast.
The next day (13 April) William J. Busch
was driving on Highway 83, just south of
Highway 18, at about 4.45pm,when a large
weird animal "which may have been a Kangaroo" flashed across the road 15ft in
front of him. He doesn't insist it was
a kangaroo, but it had short front legs,
very long back legs and looked about 3ft
tall - it seemed to be hunched forward
as it scampered across the road,but it
definitely was not a dog or a cat, he's
certain. On the 16th, at about 3am Mr &
Mrs Greg Napientek were driving on County Trunk A, just east of Waukesha,when
they saw an animal in their headlamps -
it reared on its hind legs and hopped
away. Greg said: "We got pretty close,
within about 30-35 yards." His wife
thought it might be a deer "...until it
stood up on its hind legs (and jumped
over a·ditch). I've seen deer before. I
know what a deer looks like...I know it
was a kangaroo." The Napienteks added
that they only learned of the other
sightings after they told friends of
their experience. Meanwhile the Sheriff's
Department was at a loss...the only zoo
in the area with kangaroos (Milwaukee
County Zoo) had none missing and no-one
was known to have one as a pet. Since
that date 'What made Waukesha famous...
has bided its time - it may be still
out there, but it's more than likely
the harsh winter has killed it by cold
or pneumonia, since kangaroos like. warm-
er climes than wallabies. We are intrigued by another detail (which seemed to
have evaded comment by local police and
naturalists), that the first sighting
distinctly mentioned a pair of kangaroos - is it too much to hope for little
bounders this spring? Sources: Waukesha
Freeman 13,14 & 17 April 1978 (Cr: Tom
Adams); Milwaukee Journal (Wis) 13 April
1978 (Cr: Mark Hall); San Antonio News
(Texas) 14 April 1978 (Cr: Tom Adams);
Ypsilanti Press (Mich) 17 April 1978
(Cr: Jerry Clark); Houston Post 21 April
1978, the source of the photo (Cr: Kurt
Lothmann): Daily Oklahoman (Oklahoma
City) 25 April 1978 (Cr: Tom Adams);
Daily Press (Newport News, Virginia)
25 April 1978 (Cr: Gary L Abbott). See
also the penultimate issues of Dave
Fideler's ARB for additional coverage.
                                    RJMR

letters-letters-letters-letters

THE VANISHING NORFOLKS

Patricia Villiers-Stuart, London:

I was reading with great gusto the
story of the disappearing regiment (FT
27pp35-38) because that area belongs to
my earliest memories. Alas I have only
negative evidence; although I knew personally some of the people involved it
was the first time I have ever heard
that the disappearance was attributed
to supernatural causes.

When I was a child we lived in Norfolk and my father, who fought in the
campaign, had friends in this regiment.
He was a captain in the Royal Fusiliers.
During the war my mother and I had our
portrait painted by Mark Milbanke, the
brother of the Sir John Milbanke mentioned in the story, and I remember meeting him several times later on. My father's family came from Ireland and had a
distinct liking for the supernatural,
and I feel very surprised never to have
heard this interpretation of the story
before.

I do know that my father felt the
whole campaign had been terribly bungled
and considered that both the Norfolks
and the ANZACs had a justifiable griev-
ance. I would certainly tend to agree
with Paul Begg's rather sober assessment
of the whole story. Congratulations on a
super edition of FT. Such a good collection of book reviews.

((You might like to know that the
'Vanishing regiment' and many other famous and infamous stories of disappearances have been given the benefit of
Paul Begg's "sober assessment" in a book
by him, Into Thin Air - to be published
this March by David & Charles - Ed.))

MYSTERY TRACKS

LR White Atkins, London:

Your footnote (FT26p44): "As a last
thought, we realise that cats walk with
their claws retracted - a curious and
puzzling detail!" (The evidence of claw
marks on the tracks) may not be so puzzling if we remember that the heavier

the "cat" or whatever, and the more slippery the snow it was walking on, the
more it might extend its claws!!

ATTACKS BY CONDORS

John Michell, Somerset:

I write to complain that false statements by supposed experts quoted without
correction in your mag have caused me to
look foolish in respectable company. At
lunch recently with Bruce Chatwin - author of In Patagonia, a book of interest
to Forteans for its descriptions of South American strange and not-so-extinct
creature lore, and of Bruce's quest for
a slice of Giant Sloth skin - I quoted,
from FT24p10, the information supplied
by a "condor specialist from the National Audubon Society, California" to the
effect that all the 40-45 remaining condors are in California and that it is
not in their nature to swoop on people.
Bruce contradicted this from a terrifying experience of his own, mentioned
briefly in his book (p140). The details
are interesting in the light of the recent 'Big Bird' attacks in Texas and Illinois (FT24).

"...Two condors dived on me. I saw
the red of their eyes as they swept past,
banking below the col and showing the
grey on their backs. They glided in an
arc to the head of the valley and rose
again, circling in an upthrust where
the wind pushed against the cliffs, till
they were two specks in a milky sky.
The specks increased in size. They
were coming back. They came back heading
into the wind, unswerving as raiders on
target, the ruff of black feathers ringing their black heads, the wings unflinching and the tails splayed downwards as
airbrakes and their talons lowered and
spread wide. They dived on me four times
and then we both lost interest."

This took place in Patagonia, disproving all the points stated by the Audubon "expert". Familiar features of the
'Big Bird' attacks and sightings, which
occur in the above account, are: huge
size, red eyes, grey colour, rigid wings
and rapid gliding. Compare the summary
of 'Mothman' cases in John Keel's Strange
Creatures form Time and Space: 10ft wing
span, glowing red eyes, most people described it as greyish, wings did not flap
in flight...incredible speeds.

Of course to suppose that condors travel secretly over thousands of miles to
swoop on mid-Americans is one of those
explanations which, as Fort would say,
needs to be explained itself. And there
are many cases which no condor theory
could ever be forced into fitting. But

there are many more condors about than
your Californian expert admitted, and
they do swoop down on people.
《 Thanks John...but I won't accept
responsibility for the pronouncements of
so-called experts. They're the experts -
we'll quote them. However I should have
qualified the quote by putting 'expert'
in quotes itself. I used his statement
because it was typical of some of the
ex-cathedra judgements on the 'Big Bird'
happenings made by careless 'experts' at
the time. The motto, regrettably,is:
Caveat emptor. Let the buyer beware! Ed》

FORTEAN TIMES

CONTRIBUTIONS of articles, artwork, notes and letters-
of-comment on related subjects are always welcome. YOU
CAN HELP by sending us a copy or clipping of any item
you think will interest FT readers—just add a note of the
DATE, the SOURCE and your NAME (for the credit). All
clippings go on file to be published in due course. Please
don't assume we must know about it already—there are
surprisingly few duplications. The editor regrets that it is
not always possible to reply to all correspondence.
Acknowledgements of money received will be sent only if
requested.

RIGHTS: All articles and artwork in FORTEAN TIMES are
the copyright of the authors and artists. The views of
contributors are not necessarily those of FT, and vice versa.
Uncredited material is byt he editors.

FORTEAN PICTURE LIBRARY (FPL)—We are laying the
foundations for a long-needed pictorial archive to satisfy
both research and commercial needs for the preservation
and supply of visual material on Fortean subjects.
Interested parties (users or those with materials) can
contact us via FT's editorial address.

Subscriptions: 1 year (4 issues) $ 8.00/£3.00
              2 years (8 issues) $14.00/£5.40
Airmail: add $ 3.50/£1.75 per year to sub rate.

Backissues:
Out of print: Nos. 1–12, 15, 16, 22, 24.
Otherwise $2.00/75p each subject to availability.
It is intended to reprint OP issues sometime, and this will
be announced in FT—but if you're impatient we'll
provide xerox copies at cost to us plus a small service
charge.

Indexes:
Subject to preparation and availability. From FT27
vouchers for a free annual index will be given for each year
of a new subscription or renewal, for use when the next
index becomes available. A few copies of 1973–4 (FT 1–7)
are left; but 1975 (FT 8–13) is out of print—see note
under backissues. Otherwise back copies of indexes may
be purchased at $1.00/50p.

PAYMENT
Cheques, postal orders, international postal money orders
or GIRO orders should be made out to FORTEAN TIMES,
and sent to:

FORTEAN TIMES (Dept S), c/o DTWAGE,
9–12 St Annes Court, London W1, UK.
US readers may find it more convenient to send subscription
money to:
FT: Box 1479, Grand Rapids, MI 49501, USA.
All other communications to London address

Fortean Times

The Journal of Strange Phenomena

UE No.29

PRICE: 75p $2.00

CHARLES FORT Prophet of the Unexplained.
NESSIE IN COLOUR 1977 Photos Examined.
PLUS Incorrupted Corpses, Vampires, Swarms, Psi powers
and other recent strange phenomena.

Summer reading from Thames and Hudson

The Ley Hunter's Companion
**Aligned Ancient Sites
A New Study with Field Guide and Maps**
Paul Devereux and Ian Thompson
Proving beyond question the reality of leys, this meticulously researched book details forty-one examples plotted with map and compass throughout England and the borders. Fully illustrated, it provides a guide to the country's most beautiful and mysterious places.
207 illustrations, 5 regional maps and 41 ley-maps £6.50 June 18

The Silbury Treasure
The Great Goddess Rediscovered
Michael Dames
Now available in paperback (together with Michael Dames's companion book, *The Avebury Cycle*), this controversial survey offers an intriguing and convincing explanation for Wiltshire's great enigmatic monuments. 'One of the most interesting contemporary attempts to reveal the true shape of prehistory' – *Rolling Stone*
109 illustrations £2.95 paperback

Phenomena
A Book of Wonders
John Michell and Robert J.M.Rickard
A brilliantly researched large-format paperback surveying, in words and pictures, over fifty curious and well-documented classes of strange phenomena that have defied the suppressions and explanations of the orthodox, including spontaneous human combustion, showers of frogs, teleportation, visions, stigmata, phantom beasts and cities in the sky.
209 illustrations £2.50 paperback

The Fantasy Book
The Ghostly, the Gothic, the Magical, the Unreal
Franz Rottensteiner
Franz Rottensteiner, author of *The Science Fiction Book,* surveys the world of fantasy as it appears in the literature of the West – from Transylvania to Middle-earth, from the clinical horrors of Poe to the nightmare bureaucracy of Kafka – anywhere where imagination reigns supreme.
203 illustrations, 40 in colour £2.95 paperback

The Earth Spirit
Its Ways, Shrines and Mysteries
John Michell
Proposing that the mysterious ritual monuments of antiquity were built in accordance with the ancient science of geomancy, John Michell discusses the earth's flow of vital spirit. Lavishly illustrated, it is one of the many large-format paperbacks in the *Art and Imagination* series. Others include: *Astrology, Celtic Mysteries, Creation Myths* and *The Tree of Life.*
113 illustrations, 22 in colour £1.95

Rose Windows
Painton Cowen
The rose windows of the churches of Western Europe are among the most spectacular and beautiful creations of the human mind. Painton Cowen shows that, serving as mandalas, they evolved to answer a perennial human need for a symbol of divine and cosmic unity.
141 illustrations, 59 in colour £2.95 Art and Imagination

Simulacra
Faces and Figures in Nature
John Michell
Simulacra – or shadowy likenesses to familiar objects on rocks, trees, clouds, insects – have fascinated artists and mystics from the earliest times. John Michell reviews the range of interpretations which have been applied to the extraordinary figurative sculptures and artwork of nature and illustrates them with his amazing collection of photographs.
180 illustrations £2.95 July 30

The Ancient Science of Geomancy
Man in Harmony with the Earth
Nigel Pennick
Geomancy concerns the subtle relationship between man and his natural surroundings. Nigel Pennick outlines the old knowledge of the ancient geomancers through folklore, legend, superstition, myth, ethnography, and esoteric doctrine.
128 illustrations £5.95

A Little History of Astro-archaeology
Stages in the Transformation of a Heresy
John Michell
Until recently ideas relating the design and location of megalithic sites to the movement of the stars, sun and moon were regarded as lunacy. Now they are seen as highly plausible. John Michell has charted the rise of these archaeological theories in a well illustrated paperback.
75 illustrations £1.50 paperback

Fortean Times

9-12 St. Anne's Court
London W1

The Journal of Strange Phenomena

Summer 1979.
ISSN 0308-5899.

Contents

Edited and Published by ROBERT JM RICKARD. Associate Editors: STEVE MOORE, PAUL SIEVEKING. Contributing Editors: DAVID
FIDELER, PHIL LEDGER. Art Director: RICHARD ADAMS. Section Heading Art: HUNT EMERSON.

FORTEAN TIMES is a quarterly journal of news, news, notes, reviews and references on current and historical strange phenomena, related sub-
jectsand philosophies. A friend to all groups and magazines continuing the work of Charles Fort in investigating, studying and discussing all
aspects of strange phenomena. RIGHTS: all articles and artwork in FORTEAN TIMES, unless otherwise stated. Uncredited material is by the
editors. The views of the contributors are not necessarily those of FT, and vice versa. SUBMISSION is invited of articles, artwork, cartoons
and news clippings on related subjects. The publisher can assume no responsibility for unsolicited material. CORRESPONDENCE: letters-of-
comment and personal experience are welcome. If replies are required please enclose a SAE. The editor regrets it is not always possible to
reply promptly. ADVERTISING AND DISTRIBUTION ENQUIRIES: contact the editor via the above address, or ring 01-552 54666.
SUBSCRIPTION INFORMATION: see page 56.

Editorial

Fortean Times was founded 5 years ago to collect and
circulate notes and studies of strange phenomena. It was
named after Charles Fort (1874 – 1932) an American
journalist who left us 4 of the wisest, wittiest, and most
informative books that ever questioned the belief that modern
man, especially in his persona as Scientist, is the omniscient
crown of creation (or apotheosis of evolution, if your prefer).

To judge from the proliferation of paperbacks dealing with
all aspects of the paranormal, the occult, ancient mysteries,
etc., interest in Fortean subjects is running higher than ever.
Yet media treatment of anomalous and non-ordinary events
and their witnesses is trivial at best, contemptuous of
genuine interest in accuracy and detail. FT aims to satisfy
that interest, presenting an open-minded overview of the
whole range of strange phenomena, with informed and informative articles and selections of recent Fortean events drawn
from our worldwide news-clipping commandoes. Anyone can
join in with a letter or clipping (remember to add your name
and the source for the credit), if not an article or cartoon.

FT is produced by an informal – some say unholy –
independent alliance of committed writers, researchers and
artists. Some of them are even devoted Forteans. FT is not
by or for a club, clique or movement, and is guided only by a
vision of an inclusive all-encompassing science. Each issue of
FT is a little miracle dependent on subscriptions, donations
and voluntary labour. With your help we'll be around long
enough to evolve into a fat, widely distributed, monthly news
magazine. Naturally we hope that can happen as soon as
possible. We want to publish FT to the highest standards of
creative and professional ability, giving our contributors the
fame and fortune they deserve. Profits will be ploughed back
into creative projects, field and archive investigation, special
commissions, and data processing. Already we have helped
found the Fortean Picture Library (FPL). If you like what
we're doing (even if you can't figure it out), support us.
Subscribe! Spread the word! Earn good karma by sending
gift subs to enemies, friends or libraries. If you like our peculiar mixture of scholarship, humour and iconoclasm, then
join us...regularly.

Finally, I'd like to thank all the friends of FT who have
supported us for 5 years, and who have given us the help and
encouragement to begin this new adventure. For you we
promise our very best – a Fortean magazine to be proud of.
Excelsior!

Bob Rickard.

Charles Fort and Fortean Times

Editor Robert Rickard explains the background, philosophy and modus operandi of FORTEAN TIMES, and outlines the influence of Charles Fort, iconoclast, trickster and philosopher, who laid the groundwork for much of today's interest in the paranormal, and who is still largely unknown.

Bertrand Russell once speculated that if Mankind had come into being yesterday, created with our planet, the Universe and artificial memories, we would have no way of proving it. To many of you *Fortean Times* will likewise seem to have sprung from nowhere, complete with on-going controversies, themes, corresponding readers and a 'past'. Unlike Russell's Man, and Adam, we have a real history behind us — or think we do. In fact this issue is number 29 of a series that stretches back to 1973, when we began life as a small newsletter called *The News*. Since then we have become better known as *Fortean Times*.

Fortean Times (abbreviated to FT) developed a network of friends extending all over the world, most of whom keep us supplied with newsclippings on all that is strange in their part of the world. We collated and edited them, writing them up under general headings in whatever combination the Universe, in its inscrutable humour, made topical. Each issue was a little miracle, put together as it was on a shoe-string budget, voluntary contributions of material and labour — a veritable labour of love. Most who knew us then believed we had the makings of a larger magazine of wider appeal . . . and so here we are.

We've had to make compromises of course, to ensure our viability and future, but we can reassure our old readers that we are still fuelled by our love for our chosen field. This change is not one of attitude — which will still be informal, informed, informative, slightly sceptical and amiably good humoured in the spirit of Charles Fort (on whom more later) — but a change in scale, enabling us to do all we used to do, but better.

A PROCESSION OF THE DAMNED

Humour was a weapon Charles Fort developed into a fine art as he mounted his single-handed "onslaught upon the accumulated lunacy of fifty centuries . . . and shot the scientific basis of modern wisdom full of holes," as Ben Hecht put it. Without humour this would have been a bitter and pointless crusade, but Fort's wit makes an elegant plea for an honest spirit of inquiry to make up our own minds. He didn't like being told what to think, and in turn urged each one of us to make up our own minds.

Fort was particularly concerned by a rigid conception of science, usually among scientists themselves, which excluded many instances of genuine events and phenomena because they were too fantastical or conflicted with the orthodox view of things. These sweepings from under the carpets of

science Fort called "The Damned", because in behaving like a dogmatic religion, science had effectively excommunicated them for serious consideration. They were hastily ignored, suppressed, discredited (often in shameful ways by respected scientists), or inadequately explained-away (which is a quite different thing from explaining a thing) [1]. Fort collected them and paraded them past the windows of the club of science.

What Fort had done was to spend the last 24 years of his life in the New York Public Library and the British Museum Reading Room sifting through journals and newspapers of all disciplines and countries, and the histories of the sciences, collecting notes on anything anomalous or mysterious. Most of these notes were published in his four books (see panel).

A brief selection of the diverse and arcane topics which interested him, and which still interest us, might include: the spontaneous flaming death; rains of frogs, blood, manna, ice chunks or stones from the skies; people like Kaspar Hauser who turn up from nowhere, and their mysteriously vanishing counterparts; wolf-boys and wild-men; stigmatic wounds; artifacts and human footprints found in geological strata laid down millenia before the 'evolution' of man; the evidence for 'Little People' and giants; the discoveries of America before Columbus; levitation and visions etc; 'living fossils' and the appearances of exotic animals outside their natural habitat, like the 'Surrey Puma'; sightings of the 'Tenth Planet'; coloured rains and snows; extraordinary mirage-like phenomena in the skies; strange lights; 'mass hysteria', panics and sudden deaths; bizarre coincidences; sea-serpents and other monsters; 'miracles'; and so on... [2]

Hence our eponym 'Fortean' applying to the study of strange phenomena.

Events in these and other categories are still going on today as the flow of clippings from all parts of the world testify. *Fortean Times* is continuing the work Fort began, collecting, recording and circulating contemporary reports and studies of Fortean phenomena. Join in the fun and send us a clipping of anything interesting you come across — but don't forget to add a note of the source, date and your own name (for the credit line). All clippings are gratefully received, and filed for use in our news and notes section.

SCIENCE'S FOOL [3]

After the publication of *The Book of the Damned* in 1919, American newspapers, whenever they printed some out-of-the-ordinary item, would say: "Here is another datum for

'I am a collector of notes upon subjects that have diversity, such as deviations from concentricity in the lunar crater Copernicus and a sudden appearance of purple Englishmen...But my liveliest interest is not so much in things, as in the relations of things. I have spent much time thinking about the alleged pseudo-relations that are called coincidences. What if some of them should not be coincidences?' Charles Fort *Wild Talents.*

that arch-enemy of science, Charles Fort." This was not quite true. Fort had no bone to pick with science — in fact he insisted on proper rules of evidence — it was only the slavish subservience to dogma in science, malpractise in institutionalized science and the arbitrary pronouncements of dilettante scientists who came in for his stick. Fort's whackings were never malicious, perhaps more in the detached spirit of the Zen master who beats a dozing meditator.

Fort argued that a major flaw in scientific philosophy lay in its exclusiveness. The scientific method lay in ever narrower attempts to define and divide things and to isolate them into units or categories. A scientific experiment, he wrote, is an attempt to define something by excluding the rest of the universe — a patent impossibility. The root problem was one of semantics and language — definitions, categories, measurements and meanings of words can only ever be *local* expressions, imperfect approximations to unknowable absolutes [4] . The language problem is further complicated by the inadequacy of our concepts of how to question the Universe or to interpret its answers, for as modern quantum mechanics has demonstrated, the 'answer' may be telling us more about the 'question' than the thing we were trying to query. Heisenberg wrote: "What we observe is not nature itself, but nature exposed to our method of questioning." [5] Or as the Duck said, in *Alice in Wonderland:* "When I find a thing it's usually a frog or a worm."

Scientists, often out of mental laziness, regard their 'laws' as absolute terms; whereas if they were rigorous they would agree with Karl Popper's conclusion that "every scientific statement must remain tentative forever. It may indeed be corroborated, but every corroboration is relative to other statements which, again, are tentative." [6] Whilst we are immersed in a world of ambiguous perceptions and hindered by the paradoxes of language we can only approximate to absolutes, which to our present form are ultimately unknowable. "If we could apply the word absolute to anything, say to a frog," Fort wrote to a friend, "that Frog would be God." [7]

I am not a believer in deliberate conspiracies to suppress knowledge, but I do accept that a great fear and loathing arises in the breast of the Establishment when it is confronted by the 'outlaw' — the Damned facts. The body of science behaves like any other organism that is threatened or invaded and closes ranks against the symbol of change and chaos [8] . Although the nature of science itself has changed since Fort's day, it is still practised by fallible humans, with their tendencies to fear change, to crave to be right or 'first' and their reluctance to risk their status, credibility and their job. It might be understandable but it doesn't make good science, and unfortunately such lowmindedness is fostered by an Establishment science subject more to the perfidious and arbitrary dictates of politics and economics than to the true spirit of free inquiry.

UNDERLYING ONENESS

What then is the alternative? Angrily, some scientists suggested the only alternatives would be to pointlessly check their 'constants' every day, or to abandon themselves to a Universe of chaos and insanity. This is the failure of the imagination of a rigid viewpoint. Chaos, being only the apparent indetectability of meaning or pattern, only shows up our inability to ask the right questions, and does not imply the Universe is a random meaningless existence. Fort was not a religious man but saw no harm in referring to the totality of things as 'God'. By the conventions of science alone this God would be an idiot " . . . drooling comets and gibbering earthquakes . . . " But Fort suggested a more inclusive approach, and out of his thousands of notes came a radical vision, bridging science and mysticism; that the Universe functioned, not like Newton's great machine, but like a single organism. He often likened it to a body — "The whole is God to its parts" — with its specialized cells, automatic reflexes, metabolic processes, growth and decay, reactions and drives, most of which would be incomprehensible to individual components, assuming they could think, and yet which function nevertheless in a coherent existence. An inclusive science would relate, not to hypothetical absolutes, but to the transience of phenomena.

Fort suggested a state of existence he called 'Continuity' in which all forms of phenomena and things were merely different expressions of the same fundamental organic existence, like islands in a sea, seemingly separate but connected in the bedrock of existence below the surface of appearances. All things are inter-related, indistinguishable at their merging points, "of an underlying oneness." [9] This radical view of phenomena came at a turning point in the history of physics, when Heisenberg was formulating his Uncertainty Principle, since when the pronouncements of physicists have often become interchangeable with those of mystics [4] . As we work out the implications of this, we are drawn towards new definitions of 'reality', new understandings of perception and meaning, and the patterns of simultaneous and cyclic phenomena [10] . Examples of coincidental phenomena include meteorites or aerial light displays during quakes; celestial periodicities in animal behaviour, plant growth or natural catastrophies; accident series, and sudden inexplicable waves of deaths or illnesses; events which mimic similar events in fiction; the phenomena of twins; the simultaneous filing of patents on the same thing by unconnected people; the relationship between appearances of monsters (like the Cornish sea-serpent 'Morgawr', the Sasquatch or Bigfoot) and UFOs, etcetera. Fort himself would have been amused to learn that at the same time he was writing about Continuity, the hapless Paul Kammerer was thinking about a related concept of meaningful coincidences he called 'Seriality' — and both prefigured the Jung-Pauli thesis of 'Synchronicity', which Jung described as an "acausal connecting principle" [11] .

'Every science is a mutilated octopus. If its tentacles were not clipped to stumps, it would feel its way into disturbing contacts.' Charles Fort *Lo!*

'Why don't they see, when sometimes magnificently there is something to see? The answer is the same as the answer to another question. Why, sometimes, do they see when there is nothing to see?' Charles Fort *Lo!*

TELEPORTATION AND UFOs

Sometime before 1920 Fort coined the word 'teleportation' to describe the instantaneous transport of people, animals and objects through space, solid matter and even time. In the course of his four books he developed the idea into a central hypothesis of the Continuous Universe — a primal shaping force of nature which survives now only weakly and sporadically as an atavism — a once powerful distributing mechanism which would show up in the appearances and disappearances of people, of alien animals roaming the countryside, of stones appearing and falling from a point in mid-air in a closed room, or of fishes snatched away from their ponds to fall from a far distant sky or to fertilize a new planet somewhere [12]. The notion that such a force could sometimes come under the control of humans, whether spontaneously, unconsciously or deliberately, was quickly taken up by John W Campbell, editor of the science-fiction magazine *Astounding*, who during the 1950s encouraged his stable of writers (many now famous names like Bester, Harness, Sturgeon, Heinlein, etc) to use Fort's material — and from there many of Fort's ideas, like teleportation and controlled psychokinesis (the manipulation of matter by mental effort only) passed into popular usage.

We also acknowledge Fort as one of the main influences and origins of today's interest in UFOs, life on other worlds and, indeed, other forms of life [13]. Long before the von Danikens of today he speculated about whether this earth had been visited in earlier times by voyagers from distant worlds in space — perhaps we were being developed as livestock, or were sitting tenants in some cosmic rent-war? He sincerely believed that one day space travel would be possible and visualized new wagon-trains of colonists trailing out into the vacuous prairie. Thirty years before Kenneth Arnold's classic sighting of "flying saucers" in 1947, Fort was collecting notes on strange lights seen floating, dancing or speeding through our skies — things that might be crafts from other worlds, unknown forms of natural phenomena (like ball-lightning), or even a strange luminous form of life. He discovered that such sightings often came in clusters or waves (called 'flaps'), as they did in 1896/7 and 1904/5 when "mystery airships" with powerful searchlights sped at speeds impossible for the time   through the skies of Britain and the United States [14]. Fort even anticipated the paraphysical and parapsychological dimensions of close encounter cases when he suspected of apparitional phenomena: "that many appearances upon this earth . . . were beings and objects that visited this earth, not from a spiritual existance, but from outer space." [15]

FASHIONS OF BELIEF

When *Book of the Damned* was published very few knew what to make of it since it presented a radical criticism of contemporary science, yet it was written in a difficult, unique and romantic prose-style. Fort himself joked that perhaps he was the forerunner of a new kind of literature in which the heroes and villains were droughts and comets, swarms and storms, volcanoes and plagues, and the backdrop for their adventures would be the sciences. His vision of a swirling tumultuous busy Universe contrasted with the formal ordered and sterile existance touted by orthodox science and inculcated in all of us at school . . . the world of the laboratory and the madhouse of life. Many readers will find Fort's writing difficult, but the insights are well worth the effort. He wrote with an eminently quotable wit, by turns poetic, violent and profound, but always with a sagacious humility, a gentle mocking at his own follies as well as those of so-called experts. He also has a sense of humour hard to match in any other philosopher of science. Considering his contributions to our understanding of the processes and phenomena of our erratic existence it is remarkable that he is still largely unknown, rarely acknowledged, and often misunderstood even by some who professed to love him [16].

If I seem to be eulogizing Fort there are good reasons, not the least that he opened up the interest in all of the subjects mentioned for myself and countless others. *Fortean Times* does not owe any special allegiance to Fort — this is as he would wish it — yet his work and his aims will serve as a model to our own efforts within these pages. He was above all a connoisseur of explanations. A favourite technique was to offer 'explanations' which were based on the same data but as absurd as the conventional explanations, sometimes more absurd and sometimes less. For example he would counter the 'whirlwind' theory of showers of fishes by emphasizing the anomalies of the data [17] and offering a vast, invisible "super-Sargasso sea" floating overhead from which things shake loose and fall. He never believed his own explanations and gently chides the reader if he takes them seriously. That seems pointless to some, but the humour is very instructive. Fort asks us to substitute acceptance for belief, if we are to get anywhere in our attempts to understand.

Explanations are subject to the whims of fashion — e.g., apparition phenomena, once the preserve of theologians and demonologists, is now the subject matter of psychic research. Fort wrote: "I conceive of nothing in religion, science or philosophy that is more than the proper thing to wear for a while . . ." The boundaries of science — even orthodox science — are changing all the time as the magic of yesterday becomes the technology of today. Voltaire scorned the notion of fossils; Lavoisier told the Academy of Sciences in 1769 that only peasants would believe stones could fall from the sky, because "there *are* no stones in the sky!", thus delaying the acceptance of meteorites until 1803; spaceflight was once considered "Utter bosh!" [18]. Today we see the big boys moving in on paraphysics and parapsychology; old herbals are plundered for new pharmaceuticals, and the practices of witchdoctors for new therapeutics; computer-time is lavished

'Science has done its utmost to prevent whatever Science has done.' Charles Fort
Wild Talents.

'When I come upon the unconventional repeating, in times and places far apart, I feel – even though I have no absolute standards to judge by – that I am outside the field of the ordinary liar.' Charles Fort *Wild Talents.*

on astrology, ley hunting and UFOs; and biofeedback machines bring diverse states of mind within ordinary reach. The task of *Fortean Times* will be to keep a track of and explore these shifting frontiers.

LAUGHTER AND IGNORANCE
As Forteans we don't wish to turn Fort into a cult-figure, but out of convenience and not a little respect use his name for our particular approach to the limitations of knowledge and the subject matter of strange phenomena, the non-ordinary, and discussions about the nature of phenomenal reality, plus a tip of the hat to all the other jovial proto-Forts in history [19]. Concerning a proposal put to him to form a 'Fortean society', Fort replied: "The great trouble is that the majority of persons who are attracted are the ones we do not want . . . persons who are revolting against Science, not in the least because they are affronted by the myth-stuff of the sciences, but because scientists oppose or do not encourage them." [20] When Tiffany Thayer went ahead and organised a *Fortean Society* in 1931, Fort thought it was a dangerous step and likely to turn his advocacy of free inquiry into a formal opposition to the scientific Establishment, thus becoming equally dogmatic itself. He refused to join it.

Independence of thought, open-minded inquiry, curiosity and balance-restoring sense of humour, then, are the basic qualities of a Fortean, and the attitudes to which *Fortean Times* will subscribe. Back in 1973 we were founded for the serious purpose of recording all the reported incidents of strange phenomena that are still going on. After Fort's death Thayer's *Fortean Society* continued the work of collecting and publishing notes and data on strange phenomena, but sporadically, petering out in the 1950s. In 1966 two Fortean societies were formed: the *International Fortean Organization* (INFO) by Ron and Paul Willis [21]; and the *Society for the Investigation of the Unexplained* (SITU) by the zoologist-author Ivan T Sanderson [22]. Both of these groups published journals for the discussion of Fortean phenomena, but their space for clippings on current phenomena was always limited. In 1973 we (or *The News* as we were known then) began to collect, record and circulate the reportage of contemporary phenomena, especially from Britain, which was being missed by the US journals. In 1976 we changed our name to *Fortean Times* and became probably the largest clearinghouse for Fortean clippings. We hope our contributors will continue to send in clippings since this is not only a prime source of information but essential to building up a proper archive of data.

Unlike most other commercial journals we are neither "just a magazine" nor in it solely for the sake of publishing. All of us associated with *Fortean Times* have a keen interest in Fortean subjects and studies and an involvement in free-lance research. We have certain aims in common and hope

the success of FT will allow us to achieve them and to serve you better. We have already established the *Fortean Picture Library* (FPL. Further information on request.) as the visual archive of our field. Further goals include a special publications programme of in-depth studies or rare and out-of-print reference material; a computer data-base of Fortean material; and a formal structure for funding research and field investigation. Further developments of FT reader services might include adding more pages to FT, publishing more frequently (e.g., bi-monthly), and a mail-order book service.

From our world wide network of readers and friends we receive a steady stream of news clippings, which are promptly sorted into rough general categories. Examples of these categories or Fortean topics are given elsewhere

Our practice until now has been to let the clippings accumulate until we have a sufficient quantity to make up an interesting selection, which is written-up for the FT data pages. If we are fortunate enough to publish more frequently we'll adopt the slightly different technique of using more categories in each issue but using only the most recent stories. Once the clipping has been used, it is filed in the main archive for posterity. This all sounds more orderly than it is in real (?) life, and in time we shall have to tackle properly the problems of data storage, retrieval and processing with the use of microfiche and micro-computer systems. Nor does any of this convey the general sense of hilarity and absurdity rampant at an FT clipping sort, and which we hope carries over into FT as gleeful wonder.

Our experience in Fortean publishing has shown us the problems of data gathering. In a so-called civilised community the ancient value of omens, portents, signs and wonders, curiosities and mysteries is neglected or derided. Once these phenomena were considered of central importance in man's relationship with the rest of the Universe – today they are often reduced to mere fillers by blase or busy editors. The nature of our data-gathering network prevents us from being bang-up-to-date, but we try, and will keep on trying. The data itself is of perennial interest and often it is more informative to keep a solitary clipping back until several similar cases accumulate – a technique we frequently employ to effect.

Nor do we ask you to be credulous. Our news and notes should be regarded more as clues than as the unquestionable truth. They are stimuli to your curiosity-buds – starting points for closer investigation – and should be tested by your own criteria before you accept them. Don't rely on the statements of so-called experts – there are no experts in the Unknown – not even ourselves! Fort said of himself, and we apply it to ourselves too, that our interpretations of the data are of little consequence ". . . but the data will be for anybody to form his opinions on . . . I shall find out for myself, and anyone who cares to find out with me." We extend the

'Horses erect in a blizzard of frogs, and the patter of worms on umberellas. The hum of ladybirds in England -the twang of a swarm of Americans at Templemore, Ireland. The appearance of Cagliostro – the appearance of Prof. Einstein's theories. A policeman dumps a wildman into a sack, and there is alarm upon all the continents of this earth because of a blaze in (the constellation of Orion)...All are related, because all are phenomena of one organic existence.' Charles Fort *Lo!*

invitation to you, but hang on . . . for as one reviewer of Fort wrote back in 1919, it'll be like riding the tail of a comet!

Bob Rickard

NOTES

1 For a guide to rationalizing and dismissive explanations see 'Damnation!', an article by Bob Skinner, in *Fortean Times* 27, pp15-18.

2 For a guide to the varieties and complexities of Fortean phenomena, and their historical continuity, see *Phenomena* by John Michell & RJM Rickard (Thames & Hudson, 1977; Pantheon, USA, 1978).

3 "The Fool does not lead a revolt against the Law; he lures us into a region of the spirit, where, as Lamb would put it, the writ does not run." Enid Elsford *The Fool: His social and literary history* (Faber, 1935).

4 The semantic problem is one of the main limitations on all inquiry, not just the scientific. Fritjof Capra (*The Tao of Physics*, Wildwood House, 1975) suggests that it is a consequence of the Cartesian Division (i.e., the separation of the world into religion and science, mind and matter, observer and observed, favoured by Descartes). This paradigm was not superseded until the advent of high-energy physics — its omen being a whopping paradox: that matter-energy manifested as a particle and a wave simultaneously, and that the very act of measuring a sub-atomic particle turns it into yet another equation . . . and physics merges with metaphysics.

5 Werner Heisenberg *Physics and Philosophy* (Allen & Unwin, 1963).

6 Fort delighted in discovering tautologies in scientific dogma. In a passage about a fall of red worms in Sweden in 1924, he wrote: If there is no change in the direction of a moving body, the direction of a moving body is not changed.' 'But,' continued he, 'if something can be changed, it is changed as much as it is changed.' So red worms fell from the sky in Sweden, because from the sky, in Sweden, red worms fell. How do geologists determine the age of rocks? By the fossils in them. And how do they determine the age of fossils? By the rocks they're in." *LOI*, chapter 1 (*Books* p547f).

7 Letter to Edmund Hamilton, 25 October 1926. Quoted in Knight (see panel) p173.

8 For the most authoritative study of the resistance of orthodoxy to the new in the history of science, see Thomas S Kuhn's *The Structure of Scientific Revolutions* (Chicaco University Press, 2nd edn, 1970).

9 In discussing Fort in his *Fads and Fallacies in the Name of Science*, Martin Gardner sums up Fort's "doctrine of the hyphen" (in which everything is in an intermediate state between extremes) thus: "Because everything is continuous with everything else, it is impossible to draw a line between truth and fiction. If science tries to accept red things and exclude yellow, then where will it put orange? Similarly, nothing is 'included' by science which does not contain error, nor is there anything 'damned' by science which does not contain some truth." (Dover Books, 1957, p48).

10 *Fortean Times* will be presenting articles on these and other topics in future issues.

11 A broad discussion of these hypotheses will be found in Arthur Koestler's *The Roots of Coincidence* (Hutchinson, 1972; Picador, 1974).

12 This force may now be vestigial. "The crash of falling islands — the humps of piling continents — and then the cosmic humour of it all . . . that the force that once heaped the peaks of the Rocky Mountains now slings pebbles at a couple of farmers near Trenton, NJ." *LOI* chapter 4 (*Books* p571).

13 Fort expressed a number of doubts about Darwinism, and offered several alternatives. One concerned his suggestion that people from other planets might be teleporting here (*LOI* chapter 4, *Books* p573f). In *Wild Talents* chapter 18, he elaborates: "I now have a theory that, of themselves, men never did evolve from lower animals; but that in early and plastic times, a human being from somewhere else appeared upon this earth, and that many kinds of animals took him for a model, and rudely and grotesquely imitated his appearance, so that today, though the gorillas . . . are only caricatures, some of the rest of us are somewhat passable imitations . . ." (*Books* p966).

14 Loren E Gross has written two scholarly and privately printed studies: *The UFO Wave of 1896* (1974); and *Charles Fort, The Fortean Society & UFOs* (1976) which detail sightings from 1895 to 1947 of "mystery airships" and aerial lights.

15 *New Lands* chapter 18 (*Books* p419f). Further and up-to-date discussion of the paranormal aspects of ufology can be found in John Keel's *UFOs: Operation Trojan Horse* (Abacus, 1973); Jacques Vallee's *Passport to Magonia* (Spearmen, 1970) and *UFOs: The Psychic Solution* (Panther, 1977); and *The Unidentified* (Warner, 1975), and *Creature of the Outer Edge* (Warner/NEL, 1978) both by Jerome Clark and Loren Coleman.

16 Tiffany Thayer, in his introduction to the 1941 edition of *The Complete Books*, and the late Ivan Sanderson in his own writings, at times seem quite unable to grasp the nature of Fort's detachment from the data and his method of arguing. Thayer even went so far as to urge readers to skip Fort's opening chapters in *Book of the Damned*, on the grounds that they are not as lively as the writing that follows them. These chapters contain the condensed essence of Fort's thesis, of which the entire remainder of this work is an illustrated elaboration.

17 Fort noted from many hundreds of authentic records of falling objects and materials that some kind of selection seemed to be involved — e.g., if seeds, or frogs fell they would all be of same species, age, rough size (with very few exceptions). If the contents of a pond (or whatever) had been sucked up by a whirlwind (the standard dismissive explanation) we should expect all kinds of debris, segregated by weight perhaps, to come down with the fall, but there is none. In the case of frogs Fort never found a single mention of tadpoles or old frogs – always adolescents. Many falls are confined to small areas or are repeated in the same place over intervals, or, in the case of a toadfall at Chalon-sur-Saone, France in 1922 (*Books* p546), lasting several days – characteristics which would rule out whirlwinds certainly. Finally it is worth mentioning the equally dubious explanation for chunks of ice falling from the sky: that they fall from planes. If a modern refutation ('The Ice-fall Problem' by JE McDonald, *Weatherwise*, 1960) is not convincing, consider the many authentic incidents from *before* the advent of powered flight!

18 For further discussion of what Arthur C Clarke called "the failure of imagination", see his *Profiles of the Future* (Pan, 1962).

19 The list of these proto-Forts would be long indeed. We'd inlcude a number of Indian, Chinese and Japanese Buddhist philosophers; some Taoists; the compilers of early natural histories; some travellers (like Giraldus Cambrensis); skeptical philosophers and neoPlatonists; some of the pioneering 'scientists' (like Kirscher, Cardan, Olaus Magnus, Lycosthenes); diaryists (like John Aubrey); collectors of curiosa (like Pu Sung-ling); etc.

20 Letter to Edmund Hamilton, 27 May 1926. Quoted in Knight (see panel) p172.

21 INFO: 7317 Baltimore Ave, College Park, MD 20740, USA. Write for details.

22 SITU: Membership Services, RFD 5, Gales Ferry, CT 06335, USA. Write for details.

Bibliography/Biography

Fortean Picture Library

CHARLES HOY FORT

THE BOOK OF THE DAMNED
1919, Boni & Liveright, NY.
1972, Ace (pb), NY.
1974, Abacus (pb), London.
1979, Sphere (pb), London.
NEW LANDS
1923, Boni & Liveright, NY.
1972, Ace (pb), NY.
1974, Sphere (pb), London.
LO!
1931, Claude Kendall, NY.
1931, V Gollancz, London.
1972, Ace (pb), NY.
WILD TALENTS
1932, Claude Kendall, NY.
1972, Ace (pb), NY.
THE BOOKS OF CHARLES FORT
1941, Holt Rinehart & Wilson, NY,
for the Fortean Society. Brief
index. Contains *Book of the
Damned, New Lands, LO!,* and
Wild Talents.

**THE COMPLETE BOOKS OF
CHARLES FORT**
1974, Dover Books, Ny. Basically a
reprint of the 1941 edition,

with the same index, and a new
introduction.

Recommended reading for introductory
discussions of Fort and Fortean
phenomena.
PHENOMENA by John Michell & RJM
Rickard (Thames & Hudson, pb,
1977; Pantheon, NY, pb, 1978).
**CHARLES FORT: PROPHET OF THE
UNEXPLAINED,** a biography by
Damon Knight (V Gollancz, London/
Doubleday, NY, 1970).
THE FLYING SAUCER VISION by
John Michell (Abacus, pb, 1974).
THE HAUNTED UNIVERSE by D
Scott Rogo (Signet, NY, pb, 1977).
**INVESTIGATING THE UNEX-
PLAINED** by Ivan T Sanderson
(Prentice Hall, NJ, 1972).
MYSTERIES OF TIME AND SPACE by
Brad Steiger (Prentice Hall, NJ,
1974; Sphere, London, pb, 1977).
**FADS AND FALLACIES IN THE
NAME OF SCIENCE** by Martin
Gardner (Dover Books, NY, pb,
1957).
THE UNIDENTIFIED by Jerome Clark

& Loren Coleman (Warner, NY, pb,
1975.
LIFETIDE by Lyall Watson (Hodder &
Stoughton, London, 1979).

CHARLES HOY FORT
Brief biography.

Biographical notes compiled from
Damon Knight's biography (see panel).
1874 — born at Albany, New York,
9th August.
1892 — Aged 18; left home to escape
tyrannical father; worked on a
NY paper.
1893 — Aged 19; made editor of a local
Queens paper; quit to hitch-hike
around the world, Southern
States, Scotland, Wales,
London, Capetown.
1896 — Aged 22; contracted malaria
leaving South Africa; back to
NY; nursed by Anna; married
her.
1897 — Aged 23; lived in Bronx; dire
poverty; journalism and small
jobs; broke chairs for firewood;
wrote 10 novels; collected
25,000 notes, but burned them
because "they were not what I
wanted."
1906 — Aged 32; virtually a hermit
between home and library;
began voracious reading of
scientific journals and papers
taking notes.
1915 — Aged 41; began writing *X* and
Y, and begins *BOTD.*
1919 — Aged 45; Dreiser gets Boni &
Liveright to publish *BOTD.*
1920 — Aged 46; in depression burns
40,000 notes; he and Anna
stay in London for 6 months,
then back to NY.
1921 — Aged 47; December, back in
London for 8 years; works at
British Museum; writes *New
Lands;* speaks at Speaker's
Corner for amusement; begins
again note collecting.
1929 — Aged 55; back in Bronx; working on *LO!*
1931 — Thayer and Sussman form the
Fortean Society which peters
out with Thayer's death in
1959.
1932 — Aged 58; after completing *Wild
Talents* Fort dies of unspecified
weakness in Royal Hospital,
NY, on 3 May; leaves 60,000
notes, now in NY Public
Library.

Among the more mystifying of mystical phenomena are the instances where the celebrated corpse refuses to decay normally, if at all.

Some of you might recoil from this subject feeling it typical of Medieval superstition and hardly creditable in the 20th century — but it happens, as we shall see. Although most of the known instances are from the hagiographies of the Catholic Church, cases of incorruption have been recorded from other countries and religious backgrounds. We have a note of a recent case involving the well-known yogi and teacher, Paramahansa Yogananda, who had settled in Los Angeles forming the Self Realization Fellowship. Part of his teaching was that an advanced yogi could put himself into a state of suspended animation in which all the vital functions were as undetectable as in death, or control his own aging process to live for centuries. However, he predicted his own death for 7 March 1952, and said that his body would show a sign that he was a true yogi. Though he seemed in perfect health he died of what appeared to be a heart attack on the appointed day, and according to his instructions his body remained on view in a glass-topped coffin for 20 days. It was not embalmed or treated in any way and was still undecayed at the time of burial and said to be exuding a mysterious fragrance (another detail familiar from many Catholic cases). Harry T Rowen, of the Forest Lawn Memorial Park, in Glendale, California, confirmed the "perfect preservation" of Yogananda's body in a notorized statement, adding that it was "so far as we know from mortuary annals, an unparalleled one." Grit 2 July 1972.

Typical of many cases is that of Nadja Mattei, who died in Rome, aged 2 yrs, in 1965. Her mother claims that for 12 years her daughter's voice would come to her in dreams asking to be fetched from her coffin. Early in 1977 the coffin was opened at last and they found the quite uncorrupted body of baby Nadja. *News of the World* 8 May 1977.

If any of you investigate the subject further — a good place to start is the excellent listing and bibliography of *The Incorruptibles* by Joan Carroll Cruz (Tan Books: Box 424, Rockford, IL 61105, USA; 1977) — you will find that a significant proportion of cases seem to involve discovery through dreams and visions. A disturbing case happened last year, which for once did not turn out as expected. Huge crowds gathered in a German cemetary on 26 February 1978, to witness the exhumation of Anneliese Michel after a nun had told the girl's parents that Anneliese had appeared to her 3 times in dreams saying: "Let my coffin be opened for all to see. They will find my body untouched by mortal decay, as you see me now, with the nail wounds of Christ on my hands and feet." The local authorities yielded to pressure from the parents and the Church to allow the exhumation, and many thousands stormed the cemetary near Klingenberg in the hope of witness-

ing a double miracle — incorruption and stigmatization of a corpse. *NOW* reporter George Edwards gives an account of the scene, as police tried to control the crowds, who were scaling walls and festooned on gravestones and monuments for better views. As the earth-covered coffin was taken into a mortuary to open a rumour swept wildly through the expectant crowd. Edwards heard a shout: "It's a miracle! She looks as if she's alive!"... but all present in the mortuary, including a Bavarian State prosecutor and the Mayor of Klingenberg, declared "Her body was in an advanced state of decomposition, just as would be expected after all the time she had spent in the grave." *Rand Daily Mail* (South Africa) 27 February 1978; *News of the World* 12 March 1978. The crowd dispersed disappointed and feeling "they had been cheated" — there is no mention of a nun being tarred and feathered...

Anneliese died in 1976, aged 23, after a protracted exorcism ordered by the Bishop of Wurzburg, after her family, fiance and local priests believed she became possessed by at least six demons, one claiming to be Hitler. In a saga that shocked Germany the fiasco at the cemetary was followed by the trial of the exorcists themselves for criminal neglect, since they had starved the girl — she weighed less than five stone at her death — as part of their treatment. Doctors alleged the girl need not have died if both parents and priests had been more caring and less fanatical and the inquiry that was to

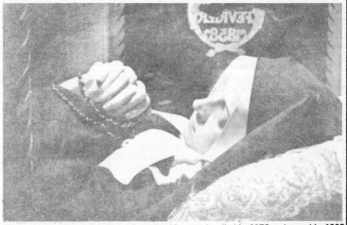

The incorrupt body of St Bernadette Soubirous, who died in 1879, exhumed in 1909 and 1919 (from Cruz).

follow arose out of a doctor refusing to sign the death certificate. We will return to this fascinating case in a future section on recent possession cases.

In Espartinas, near Seville, Spain, a family grave was opened in mid-1977, to inter the body of a local man. The cemetary keeper was shocked to find that the body of the man's son was still intact after 40 years. Jose Garcia Moreno had died of meningitis in 1937, aged 11, and his brothers deny that he was embalmed. The whole village, who all saw for themselves that night the preserved body in its rotting grave-clothes, believe the boy must have been a saint, and have begun agitating for his case to be sent to Rome for the long process of canonization. *Reveille* 30 September 1977.

It is' traditional to think of such phenomena in the context of religion, and often, to the Church's chagrin, apart from any consideration of piety which is usually awarded in retrospect as in the case of the boy Moreno (above). In *The Brothers Karamazov* Dostoievsky has a scene of grim humour in which the corpse of a holy ascetic shows unmistakable signs of mortal dissolution, much to the disgust of other characters who take it as a sign the recluse was a hypocrite. The Church's attitude is simple and stern — 'miraculous' phenomena are not automatically indicative of God's favour since (in their terms) they can be imitated by the Devil. The Church prefers to canonize on the basis of a holy and heroic life, keeping 'miracles' as secondary evidence. In this view, strictly, any 'miraculous' phenomena not associated with piety and humility are labelled 'diabolical', which damns at a swipe all similar occurrences outside the religious context.

We recently learned of a case with minimal religious colouring, from *New Thrill* (Malaysia) 6 December 1978. Unfortunately *New Thrill* is not one of the world's most reliable sources and any reader who knows of good references to this story is invited to tell us. A beautiful Hungarian countess, Zofia Bosniakova, died in 1644, aged 35, having been married twice and bearing one son. Her first husband died within a year of her marriage at 17; and the brawling promiscuous ways of her second husband — Franco Wesselenyi, a swordsman, diplomat and governor of Hungary — caused her to withdraw into

a lonely, simple and pious life in Strecno Castle, northern Slovakia. During renovations at the castle in 1689 (45 years after her death) her coffin was opened to reveal her flawless beauty. Our source says that 'The Lady of Strecno', as she is known to villagers who believe she is a saint (though not canonized), lies in state today, in a church at Teplic in Czechoslovakia, dressed in a robe she herself embroidered, and still looking beautiful.

As a postscript we might as well record here a case mentioned in *Grit* 2

July 1972, which is unrecorded by Cruz, or by Father Herbert Thurston (*The Physical Phenomena of Mysticism,* 1952). In the church of Our Lady of Merov, in Madrid, Spain, lies the fresh-looking body of Sister Mariana Novarro Romero who died in 1625. She is dressed in a nun's habit, and her smiling face and exposed hands and feet show no sign of decay after nearly three and half centuries.

Credit: Chris J Holtzhausen, Peter Hope-Evans, Colin Mather, Joe Swatek, Ion Will. RJMR.

Uri Geller's metal bending feats have been well publicised and the debate about his honesty drags on, with many of the so-called rational 'explanations' as wild and far-fetched as the supposed talents. Looking through our files we see these talents are widespread — some out of control, some volitional...

ELECTRIC PEOPLE

Back in 1928, Wilfred Batt, 18, a farmer's son from near Ashford in Kent, was plagued by weird warpings and whirlings shortly after a wireless set was installed in his home. Iron bars which he held suddenly bent almost double. One bar was attracted so violently to the earth that it pulled him flat on the ground. Going up to bed, he saw a candlestick jumping downstairs to meet him and then follow him about. A silver tray leapt at him; a dining room gong began to sound loudly. His wrist watch stopped. All kinds of things would become excited by his presence: lumps of coal and wood, furniture, ornaments, matress springs, would all jump about his vicinity. Once a heavy crowbar, which the boy could scarcely lift, shot from his hands and drove through the galvanised iron roof of the coal shed. *Weekly Dispatch* 5 Feb 1928.

In the late 1950s, a girl called Andrea Kolintz (possibly a pseudonym), from upstate New York, found she had a very disturbing influence on her environment, had accidents, objects would fly about and doors open and slam. In an interview, in Illinois about 1976, she said:

"I don't eat in restaurants any more because of the embarrassments. I've suffered with cutlery bending all around me, and waitresses having accidents and dropping things. I've had mattresses burst in hotel rooms for no apparent reason, and bottles inexplicably start falling from shelves in shops. Our neighbours were startled once by an unexpected fall of monster hailstones ...after I'd returned home tense from a tiff with a boy." Once upon a time people were burnt as witches for this sort of thing; today they tend to be seen as heroic throwbacks or else forerunners of coming evolutionary developments. Author Stephen King claims he based his best-seller *Carrie* on this girl. She links the onset of her powers to head injuries received during World War II. "They began during the months I spent recovering in hospital. I was very angry and upset and as I walked towards a cupboard, a pitcher suddenly moved towards the edge of a shelf and smashed to pieces." *Reveille* 25 Feb 1977.

"As Kant observed, it is just as inconceivable that I should move my arm as that I should be able to move the moon in its orbit." (So says Charles

Julie Knowles, of Trowbridge, Wilts, concentrates on moving a mobile of plastic straws enclosed in a bell jar—it turned 60 degrees. *National Enquirer* 26 Oct 1976. Professor John Hasted with some results of experiments with junior mind-benders . . . curled metal sealed in a glass sphere; a folded metal strip (left); and 4 metal rods (in glass case). *National Enquirer* 15 Feb 1977.

McCreery in his *Psychical Phenomena and the Physical World*, 1973). It is only the familiarity of limb-moving that obscures its mystery. The cases of telekinesis and poltergeist activity given above are roughly analagous, let us say, to involuntary muscular action, eg Parkinson's disease or Dr Strangelove's arm. We also find, however, volitional telekinesis.

THE TELEKINETIC KIDS

Following Geller's first British broadcast on 23 November 1973 (see FT2p5) people all over the country began to discover their own paranormal powers. Mark Shelley, 7, of Ipswich, found he could bend cutlery by rubbing it and thinking hard. A journalist who witnessed his power in action said it took about 20 minutes. The next evening, on TV, five children were claiming similar abilities, including Russell Jennings and Alison Lloyd, both aged 11. Joseph Greenless, of North Somercotes, tried with his 11 yr-old son Kevin to bend cutlery without success. After lunch however, he was astonished to discover that the bars of a budgie cage had bent out of shape. *Daily Mail, Daily Mirror* 28 Nov 1973; *Sun* 30 Nov 1973; Scunthorpe *Evening Telegraph* 27 Nov 1973.

A couple of spoon-benders were reported from South Africa in 1974: Sheri Ableman,.10, and David Friedman, 15, both from Johannesburg. When David met Geller, Geller said he was the 11th junior metal-bender he had come across, the other 10 being in England "under close research", some only 5 yrs-old. Apparently they were mostly children of divorced parents. By May 1975 magician David Berglass in England was offering £5000 for conclusive evidence of metal-bending by inexplicable means. Among those taking part in the nationwide competitions were Philip Jesney, 12; Terry Pickering, 8; John McNeill, 13; Mark Henry, 11; and Malcolm Holland. Said Keith Newton, 10: "I don't really think about anything or feel different when I'm doing it. It just happens." So far as we know no-one collected off Berglass. Johannesburg *Star* 10 Aug 1974; *Rand Daily Mail* May or June 1974; *Daily Express* 4 Nov 1974; *Reveille* 7 March 1975; *Daily Express* 22 & 23 May 1975.

Six girls tested by Dr Brian Pamplin at Bath University in September 1975 were spied upon by scientists through special mirrors and were caught cheating. "Instead of benders I found twisters," said Pamplin. Angry parents subsequently claimed that the conditions were wrong — the place was too hot and brightly lit — and the girls weren't given much time, and felt they were obliged to produce results. Susan Clark, 12, cheated because she felt pressured. Her mother said she had been bending things paraphysically for two years. Julie Knowles, 14, didn't cheat, but nevertheless failed the University test. Previously she had bent knives, forks and scissors — even the buckles of her shoes disintegrated when she absentmindedly fiddled with them. By the end of the year Julie was being studied by Prof John Hasted, of Birkbeck College, London University, who had helped develop radar in WWII. She managed to rotate, by 85 degrees, an object floating on water under a glass dome (see photo), and bend a metal bar without touching it. She was also able to predict accurately the major 1976 Chinese earthquake (see FT18p18) and the Moroccan invasion of the Spanish Sahara. One day she met herself in the street. "I heard a noise like footsteps in a corridor. I turned around and I could see myself. It was all misty round my feet." She was living near UFO-infested Warminster and said she had seen UFO occupants several times in her mind. "I've heard them talk once but it didn't make sense," she said. *Sunday Mirror* 14 Sept 1975; *Bath & West Evening Chronicle* 3 Oct 1975 & 3 Feb 1978; *Reveille* 5 Nov 1976; *National Enquirer* 26 Oct 1976.

Professor Hasted also did experiments with four schoolboys between 1975-1977. Nicholas W, 18, was able to bend three door keys suspended on wires 13 feet away in an adjacent room. "After a few seconds, Nicholas told me: 'I think they're bent now.' To my utter amazement two of the keys had snapped and the third was still bending." The experiment was repeated successfully too. The boy also twisted two pieces of metal around each other in a spiral and stood them on end... from another room; and bent pieces of brittle metal 180 degrees in his pocket without touching them. Andrew M, 12, was able to twist paperclips into a column sealed inside a glass globe in another room. Willie G, 14, could make straws swivel while they floated on water inside a glass jar. And Graham P, 15, snapped a zinc bar simply by stroking it. Graham's mother described strange events that often happen to him, recalling classic poltergeist phenomena: "On two occasions I have found him squatting on top of a door, lodged between the door and the ceiling. He tells me it just suddenly happens...he finds himself floating through the air. When Graham is ill objects fly through the air towards his head. He has no control over it at all." *National Enquirer* 15 Feb 1977.

Researchers like Genady Sergeyev with his work on Ninel Kulagina in USSR, and Prof John Taylor of London have tried to show that telekinesis and metal-bending are mediated by low frequency electromagnetic radiation coming from the human body. Indeed Kulagina was shown to emit biomagnetic pulsations in rhythm with her brain pulse when moving objects from afar — see *Psychic Discoveries behind the Iron Curtain* by Ostrander and Schroeder (Abacus, 1973, 1977), and *Superminds* (Palladin, 1976) by Prof Taylor, in which is also detailed his experimental work with child metal-benders. (It should be noted that Prof. Taylor has once more reverted to scepticism, his change of mind being fully documented in *Alpha* 1, March 1979). Prof. Hasted thinks differently, favouring the "many worlds" school of quantum theory. In this school's view there are an infinite number of "worlds" which do not normally interact because they are naturally orthogonal, ie at right angles to each other. Hasted hypothesises a convoluted "active surface" or interface between two "worlds", which travels through space and may posses rotational properties affecting metal-bending. (See his article 'Physical aspects of Paranormal Metal-bending' in *Jour.SPR* 449: 779; Philip Creighton's article 'Bent Spoons, or Bent Reality' in *Flying Saucer Review* (known as FSR); 24:1; and Tom Bearden's article 'Species Metapsychology, UFOs and Cattle Mutilations' in FT26p14-20, for further discussion.)

Dr Richard Muttuck, senior physicist of the Orsted Physics Institute in Copenhagen, tested Lena Duns, 17, every two months between June 1974 and June 1975, during which time, he says: "Her powers never failed. She was successful in moving and bending objects 100% of the time." Under strictly controlled conditions she bent thick nails by stroking them; bent a nail sealed in a glass tube; boosted the temperature of a thermometer by 9 degrees Fahrenheit while holding the end opposite to the bulb; sent a compass needle swinging through a 30 degree arc without touching it; and advanced the hands on a wristwatch 3 hours just by holding it. *National Enquirer* 28 Oct 1975.

The spectacle of secret hordes of kids with powers over ordinary objects might invoke fantasies of wish-fulfilment. Will they hold the world to ransom ? Will they use their powers for gain, or be used in turn in a new form of psychic warfare? The children themselves seem to relish the attention their abilities gain them more than their possible applications. Mark Shelley (see above) seemed to speak for many when he said: "It seems a waste of time doing this (spoonbending). I'd rather play football for Ipswich." The more adult benders imply the only limits to their powers are the limits of imagination. Alejandro Baez, 37, a civil engineer from Mexico City, can put himself into trances during which he has moved chess-pieces 20 feet away in another room, and made chalk, suspended over a blackboard, swing leaving a half inch mark. These experiments were witnessed by Dr Carlos Trevino, head of the Mexican Society of Parapsychology, another doctor, a psychologist and a Jesuit priest. Said Baez: "Under self-hypnosis I can step out of my body and I'm free to voyage where I wish." *Reveille* 18 July 1975.

RUSSIAN MOVES

Quite a bit has been written about Ninel Kulagina, 54, alias Nelya Mikailova (qv. Ostrander & Schroeder). She has been studied by many eminent Soviet scientists. We have reports of further wonders by her. In one experiment a beating frog's heart was placed in a glass jar about 2½ feet away while she concentrated on it, willing it to beat faster or slower — cardiograms confirmed the heart response. Five minutes into the experiment she willed it to stop beating — and a second heart was stopped in 23 minutes. Genady Sergeyev of Leningrad University said: "Ninel drew energy somehow from all around her — electrical instruments proved it. On several occasions the force rushing into her body left burn marks as long as 4 inches on her arms and hands. I was with her once when her clothing caught fire from this energy flow — it literally flamed up." Once she burned the arm of a Finnish scientist, Dr Jarl Fahler, just by touching him, even though a thermometer next to his flesh registered no change. The red burn marks lasted several hours, but had completely gone the next day. She also transmitted heat to the arm of Dr Keil, a psychology professor from the University of Tasmania. This time a thin sheet of lead shielded her hand, apparently preventing a burn developing. Several times in experiments — during which she has moved, from a distance, objects weighing over half a pound, and been filmed moving others — Kulagina has herself lost several pounds and fallen unconscious. In 1975 she had a heart attack, and the strain of her wild talents was implicated. *Daily Mirror* 18 March 1968; *Sunday People* 14 March 1976; *National Enquirer* 24 Aug 1976.

At the end of 1975 we had a report on the psychokinetic powers of a hospital research technician, Felicia Parise, 37, from New York, studied by Charles Honorton, director of parapsychology research at the famous Brooklyn Maimonides Medical Center. Felicia caused a bottle to move in a 4 inch curve and back again. Observed by Dr Graham Watkins at Duke University, she rotated a compass needle 15 degrees West and held it there for 25 minutes, during which time it was totally unresponsive to a magnet brought near it. Watkins compared her to Kulagina — in fact Ms Parise said her powers developed just a few months after seeing a film of the Russian woman in action. "I lost about 15 pounds in the first weeks of doing this," she said. "I perspire freely; sometimes my nose and eyes run and I tremble. It takes a tremendous physical effort — such an effort that I can hardly speak afterward." A movie was made in her apartment of her mentally moving a water-filled plastic vial, several corks, pieces of tinfoil and a compass needle, all under a glass bell jar. Her ESP and telepathic abilities were also found to be remarkably developed. *National Enquirer* 30 Dec 1975.

Alla Vinograd, 42, tested by Dr Victor Adamenko at the National Institute of Normal Physiology in Moscow, could move objects weighing up to half a pound and make a light bulb, lying on a table, flash on and off. And Boris Ermolayer, 36, during experiments at Moscow University under Prof Venyamin Pushkin, was able to levitate a pingpong ball, a matchbox, several pencils and plates. Plates were the easiest, he said. *Sunday People* 14 & 21 March 1976.

FRENCH LEVITATOR
Tests in France at the begin of 1976 brought another object levitator into the limelight, Jean-Pierre Girard, 33. Physics professor William Wolkowski, of Paris University, Swedish physicist Georg Wikman, of Goteborg University,

and Dr Raymond Viltage, senior lecturer in chemistry at the University of Orsay, outside Paris, all witnessed Girard move 15 fountain pens placed on a concrete floor 3 feet away from him — and than levitate four of them, causing them to hover 5 inches off the ground for 30 seconds. "The tests were done under laboratory conditions," said Wolkowski. "I'd set up a metal meter to test for hidden magnets, and an electroscope to detect any electrical or electromagnetic disturbances." Further feats included mentally bending a fat steel screw 20 degrees in a sealed container held by Wikman; changing the colour of heat-sensitive crystals by gazing at them; and causing a thick coin in a reporter's hand to curl.

More tests were conducted by M Charles Crussard, research director of the metal firm Pechiney Ugine Kuhlmann. Girard was apparently able to produce martensite-like transformations in metals by paranormal means. (Martensite is a component in a hardened steel produced in a normal way by a complex heat treatment.)

In November 1977, Girard attended the first International Congress on Paranormal Phenomena, in Mexico City, where he moved various objects from a distance, and bent a solid bar of titanium alloy. The performance was videotaped. However, he failed a 2 hour test in a Paris lab on 19 January,

directed by physicist Yves Farge, and organised by the French TV channel TFI. He complained that he was hampered by the short duration of the test. Various researchers have pointed out the significance of the disposition — hostile or supportive — of those present during this kind of performance. Failure might well be due to an unfriendly atmosphere. *National Enquirer* 17 Feb 1976 & 3 June 1978; *Observer* 11 July 1976.

In the *New Scientist* 16 Feb 1978 (p431) Crussard's experiments are discussed, and Girard is cited as admitting "he sometimes cheats to avoid disappointing the public, but insists that he nevertheless has genuine psi power." Interestingly Crussard asserts that arch-demystifier James Randi has psychic power too but refuses to acknowledge the fact, although using it to inhibit Girard's during a test!

BENDERS GALORE
Professor Hans Bender, the investigator of Annemarie Schneider, in 1976 kept a watchful eye on Sylvio Meyer, 34, from Berne, Switzerland. In an experiment at Freiburg University's Institute of Psychology, Meyer stroked a plastic spoon which promptly bent. Said Bender: "We were just about to put the spoon bent by Meyer on the table to *continued on p20*

"His stigmata's playing him up again, Doctor."

Strange and Wonderful News

For the greater part of its history mankind universally believed in the correspondences between astronomical events and unusual natural phenomena, bizarre occurrences and the mysterious rhythms of growth and decay. Peoples of all nations and times believed that such phenomena stimulated or preceded changes or critical events in the affairs of men, for better or for worse: a magical cosmology that reflects the workings of the unconscious and which is inborn in each of us, and has only been denied by the recent dominance of scientific materialism. The ephemera of earlier centuries are gold mines of records of strange phenomena for the modern Fortean, and illustrate the historical continuity of phenomena which still happen today. It is only the fashions in explanations which have changed. Leslie Shepard has contributed learned introductions to many books, written a few himself, and edited the massive ENCYCLOPEDIA OF OCCULTISM AND PARAPSYCHOLOGY, published last year by Gale of Detroit. He has a particular interest in early Broadsheets and street literature, and offers this guide for the Fortean.

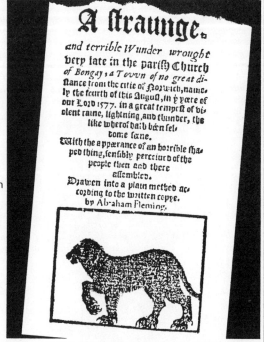

Broadside ballads were the printed sheets of verses sold by hawkers and pedlars for four centuries since the dawn of printing. Chapbooks were cheap pamphlets of news, songs, jokes, riddles and stories. While books and newspapers proper were the literature of the well-to-do classes, the street literature of balladsheets and pamphlets catered for poorer people. They were a printed folklore, in which traditional tales of battles, heroes and folk myths merged with love songs, religious rivalries, bawdy ballads and topical events. They were also the protest literature of their day. Essentially, they were the forerunners of the popular cheap newspaper and today's mass media of paperback books, radio and television.

Because of the class divisions of earlier society, balladsheets and chapbooks were much neglected as sociological and historical materials until the scholarly study of folk music was stimulated by Bishop Percy and his *Reliques of Ancient English Poetry* in 1765.

Balladsheets and chapbooks are of particular interest as popular journalism in recording stories of prodigies and portents, the 'strange and wonderful news' of comets, earthquakes, monstrous births, weird aerial phenomena and other unusual events that were the front-page news, so to speak of their time. Most but not all of the broadsides were in verse, while the chapbooks were mainly prose. In practice, it is difficult to make absolute distinctions between chapbooks and other pamphlets except perhaps in bulk and price. Larger pamphlets were known as 'small books'.

There was much interaction between high and low literature, and often strange news of the day was printed equally in street ballads, news pamphlets and the more substantial small books. Sophisticated writers copied popular tales and beliefs into their books and plays. Shakespeare refers frequently to street ballads, although it was fashionable to disparage these as a kind of unreliable yellow press.

From the sixteenth century onwards, public fascination with marvellous events was reflected by ballads and pamphlets about monsters, human and animal. The word 'monster' comes from a Latin root meaning 'to warn' and suggests an awful event to be interpreted as an omen. The birth of monsters was regarded as a sign of God's wrath with a wicked world, and the penny broadsides as well as the pamphlets made monsters the excuse for moralizing about the sins of the day. In the year 1562 alone, there were five monsters reported — two children and three monstrous pigs, while in 1566 a ballad described twins joined together at the stomach and another monster born with ruffs around its neck. In 1568 there were popular verses on a monstrous child born at Maidstone, Kent, with a mouth slit on the right side like a leopard's ('terrible to behold'), the left arm joined to the breast, with stumps on the hand, the left leg growing upwards towards the head, and the right leg bending to the left leg, with the foot growing into the left buttock, and also with a strange rose-shaped hole in the middle of the back. The verses were captioned 'A warnyng to England':

> This monstrous shape to thee, England,
> Playn shewes they monstrous vice,
> If thou ech part wylt understand,
> And take thereby advice.

Symbolic morals were drawn from each abnormality, rather in the style of the hieroglyphs in prophetic almanacks.

In the popular superstitious atmosphere of the sixteenth and seventeenth centuries, all unusual events were considered omens, and a comet or an earthquake ranked equally with a monstrous pig or fish as a signal of divine reproof. Because of this, many broadside and pamphlet stories of marvels are somewhat exaggerated. Some reports of monstrous fish may have referred to nothing more remarkable than sharks, whales or cuttlefish. However, one fish story suggests a mermaid: *The most true and strange report of A monstrous fishe that appeared in forme of a woman from the wast upward Seene in the Sea* (1604). Stories like this prompted Shakespeare's sly humour in *The Winter's Tale,* when the pedlar Autolycus offers his balladsheets: "Here's another ballad. Of a fish that appeared upon the coast on Wednesday the four score of April, forty thousand fathom above water, and sung this ballad against the hard hearts of maids; it was thought she was a woman, and was turned into a cold fish, for she would not exchange flesh with one that loved her. The ballad is very pitiful and as true."

Because people believed in marvels, the ballad writers and pamphleteers sometimes invented them. Nobody, for example, seriously credits the story in 1614 of the 'strange and monstrous serpent (or dragon) Lately discovered... in Sussex, two Miles from Horsam' who slaughtered 'both Men and Cattell by his strong and violent Poyson.' Another dragon story (in 1609) is titled: *The worldes warning of an Alarum from sinne by the vision of 2 Dragons seene fightinge in the ayre neere Gaunte.* Another aerial vision was: *Strange fearful & true newes, which hapend at Carlstadt, in the kingdome of Crotia* in 1606, when 'The sunne did shine like Bloude nine dayes together and... two Armies were seene in the Ayre, the one encountring the other... also a Woman was delivered of three prodigious sonnes, which Prophisied many strange and fearefull thinges, which should shortly come to passe'. In 1580, *A Blazyng Starre or burnyng Beacon, seen the 10. of October laste (and yet continewyng)* was interpreted as 'Gods province, to call all sinners to earnest & speedie repentance.' Typically Fortean is the 1597

story in both pamphlet and ballad of the rain of blood and brimstone which deluged the city of 'Strale Sonet'. Less credible is the 1620 ballad of *The Lamenting Lady* who mocked a woman who had borne twins (it was a folk belief that this indicated two lovers). The unfortunate lady was punished by herself giving birth to no less than three hundred and sixty-five children, one for each day of the year, at a single delivery!

One persistent theme in ballads and chapbooks was the Pig-faced Lady, immensely rich, who needed a husband. This fable lingered in popular belief for nearly three centuries from 1639 to 1815, and seems to have originated in folklore.

The moralizing of prodigies and natural disasters was turned to account as political propaganda at periods when religion and politics were inextricably entangled. One of the most famous examples of such propaganda is the three volume collection of tracts *Mirabilis Annus* (1661-2), which lists fifty-four signs in the heavens, twenty-three on earth, ten on water and twenty-seven judgements on individuals. These were regarded as divine signs against the iniquities of the Crown and the Anglican Church. An earlier work in the same style was Henry Jessey's *The Lords Loud Call to England* (1660) which catalogues 'judgements or handiworks of God, by earthquake, lightning, whirlwind, great multitude of toads and flies, and also the strikings of divers persons with sudden death'. Such material is fascinating to the student of Forteana.

Even late eighteenth century chapbooks and broadsides recorded strange stories, such as the 'most surprizing savage girl who was caught wild in the woods of Champagne, a

(Left) Record of the famous 1577 'Black Dog' incident at Bungay, Suffolk. *(Below)* An Italian with parasitic twin, born in Genoa in 1617 (from Rollins' *Pack of Autolycus*).

province in France' (1795) or the poltergeist which moved furniture and other objects in *An authentic, candid, and circumstantial narrative of the astonishing transactions at Stockwell... on... the 6th and 7th January, 1772.* A popular subject in the early part of the nineteenth century was the astonishing story of Kaspar Hauser, the mysterious foundling of Nuremberg, reported alike in pamphlets, newspapers and books. Even though chapbooks and small books were often penny-a-line rehashes, they are still valuable to the researcher for the light they shed on popular beliefs of the time. It was an early European chapbook which gave author Bram Stoker circumstantial material on the real-life Dracula.

But there are special difficulties in separating fact and fiction. Most of the nineteenth century chapbooks of the prophecies of Old Mother Shipton are uncritical rewrites of earlier stories, and Mother Shipton herself appears to have been entirely mythical. To make matters worse, the nineteenth century authority on street literature Charles Hindley perpetrated a hoax in adding to Mother Shipton's mythical prophecies some modern ones of his own, in which the world was supposed to end in 1881. These verses created a minor panic at the appointed time, and in spite of Hindley's subsequent confession, the verses are still often quoted as authentically those of Mother Shipton, notwithstanding her own nonentity!

Like the oral tradition of folklore from which the printed tradition of broadsides and chapbooks grew, it is difficult to disentangle the mythic view of life in which real and imaginary events were reported uncritically and interpreted in the light of the religion or philosophy of their time. It was not until the more pragmatic outlook of the nineteenth century, with a developing rationalism, that fact and fiction began to be more clearly discerned. But while the educated classes were beginning to enjoy more accurate standards of reporting in newspapers, these were still too expensive for the working and lower middle classes, who relied upon the sensationalist and catchpenny news in verse, retailed on the penny ballad-sheets. Indeed, the folklore tradition of singing the news did not finally die out until the end of the nineteenth century. Of persistent fascination were the Dying Speeches and Confessions of criminals, at a time when public executions were still a popular holiday spectacle. These were a survival of the sixteenth and seventeenth century last farewells of political and religious prisoners before execution, but many of the nineteenth century sheets were written long before the actual event!

Somebody once said: 'History is what actually happened folklore is what people thought happened.' The student of history as well as the lover of the bizarre and strange, and the researcher into Fortean phenomena of past ages, will all find broadside ballads and pamphlets of great interest and fascination, especially if studied in conjunction with the sophisticated literature of their times. The folklore element of myth-making and even deliberate fabrication must be given special attention, since the recurring belief in certain phenomena is closely related to the framework of religion and philosophy of any given period. Folklore is also timeless, and certain types of phenomena are persistently reported through many centuries and ironically find validation in actual occurrences from time to time, as nature follows art.

Even in modern materialistic times, fantasy plays as large a part in our everyday lives as fact, and the plea of escapism

Woodcut of a 'monstrous birth' in 1654, of a child, a serpent, and "a lapping toad", (from Rollins' *Pack of Autolycus*).

hardly does justice to the paradox. Where ancient civilizations nourished the imagination by other-worldly stories of gods and goddesses and the nostalgia of ballad heroes, a modern world has a special place for the ritualized mock battles of football and baseball, and the endless fictions of novels and television screens. And after all, we already spend nearly half our lives in the world of dreams.

Fact is important in its correct context, but fiction is not simply phoney fact. I believe that myth is the poetry of the human psyche, and facts are sometimes less meaningful than allegories, dreams and intuitions. Modern history has shown how materialistic societies without creative dreams and ideals degenerate into a morbid fantasy of vandalism, violence and senseless destruction.

Selected Bibliography

Ashton, John. *A Century of Ballads illustrative of the Life, Manners and Habits of the English Nation during the Seventeenth Century,* 1887; Detroit, 1968

Ashton, John. *Chap-Books of the Eighteenth Century,* 1882; New York, 1967

(A) *Collection of Seventy-Nine Black Letter Ballads and Broadsides... between the Years 1559 and 1597,* 1867; Detroit, 1968

Hindley, Charles. *Curiosities of Street Literature: comprising 'Cocks', or 'Catchpennies', a large and curious assortment of Street-Drolleries, Squibs, Histories, Comic Tales in Prose and Verse,* 1871; The Broadsheet King (John Foreman), 1966, 2 vols

Rollins, Hyder E. *An Analytical Index to the Ballad Entries, 1557-1709 in the Registers of the Company of Stationers,* London, North Carolina, 1924; Tradition Press, Hatboro, 1967

Rollins, Hyder E. *A Pepysian Garland. Black Letter Broadside Ballads of the Years 1596-1639. Chiefly from the Collection of Samuel Pepys.* Cambridge University Press, 1922.

Rollins, Hyder E. *The Pack of Autolycus or Strange and Terrible News . . . as Told in Broadside Ballads of the Years 1624-93,* Cambridge, Mass., 1927

Shepard, Leslie. *The Broadside Ballad; a Study in Origins and Meaning,* 1962; EP Publishers/Legacy, Hatboro, 1978

Shepard, Leslie. *John Pitts, Ballad Printer of Seven Dials, London, 1765-1844, with a short account of his predecessors in the Ballad and Chapbook Trade,* London/Detroit, 1970

Shepard, Leslie. *The History of Street Literature; the story of broadside ballads, chapbooks, proclamations, news-sheets, election bills, tracts, pamphlets, cocks, catchpennies and other ephemera,* London/Detroit, 1973

Thomas, Keith. *Religion and the Decline of Magic,* London/New York, 1971 (contains important material on the relationship between broadsides, chapbooks and religious beliefs)

Thompson, C. J. S. *The Mystery and Lore of Monsters,* 1930; New York, 1968   *Leslie Shepard March 1979*

TALES FROM THE YELLOW EMPORIUM

=ORIENTAL FORTEANA BY STEVE MOORE=

THE FIRST EMPEROR'S ARMY

In May 1974, members of the Hsiyang Village People's Commune, in Lintung County, were digging a well. Four metres down, they discovered a life-size terracotta warrior's head, and hands and body soon followed. Their report to the county authorities was passed on, and the State Cultural Relics Administration sent archaeological workers to the site. And as the summer went on, the First Emperor's terracotta army was exposed to the daylight for the first time in almost 2,200 years[1].

The site, 30 kilometres east of present day Sian, in Shensi Province, is part of a complex of remains centred round the ancient capital city of Hsienyang. And the man responsible for building this 'underground place' lies two kilometres to the west, in a vast mausoleum known as 'The Mound of Li' (standing just north of Mount Li, with which it is often confused). He was Chin Shih Huang Ti, China's first unifier.

There had been 'Emperors' before, but the Shang (1766-1121 BC) and Chou (1121-256 BC) dynasties could hardly claim overlordship of the entire country. Indeed, Chou rule was completely bankrupt by 480 BC, China being divided up into a number of petty states. During the two and a half centuries that followed, half a dozen of the major states fought amongst themselves for control. Finally, the state of Chin conquered all its rivals, bringing the 'Warring States' period to an end and establishing the Chin dynasty (221-206 BC).

Cheng Chao was born in 259 BC, son of King Chuang-hsiang of Chin, whom he succeeded at the age of 13. Twenty-five years later, he had conquered the entire country, and taken the title *Chin Shih Huang Ti,* 'First Emperor of Chin'. Revelling in Imperial grandeur, he was a builder on a monolithic scale, being responsible for roads, canals, the Great Wall, no less than 270 palaces and a mausoleum that took 38 years to complete, surrounded by underground palaces. And in one of these he put his army.

Excavations are by no means complete; in fact they have barely begun, and proceed with the slowness one would expect from a team of six archaeologists assisted by spare-time peasant and commune workers. But it is estimated that there are 6,000 life-sized figures buried there, and about 100 chariots (perhaps the magic number 108?) The complete vault is 210 metres from east to west, 60 metres north to south, and from 4 to 5 metres deep. When last we heard, a strip at the eastern end had been excavated; an area of 1,100 sq. metres out of the total 12,600, in which 591 figures and 24 horses had been found; and three test-pits, one at the western end, the other two in the centre.

The army faces east, away from the tomb. On all sides, rows of soldiers three deep face outwards, surrounding six columns of chariots and three of soldiers. The vault was originally roofed over, and five entrance ramps have been found, leading down into the eastern end of the vault (or perhaps they are *exit* ramps?).

Each soldier stands between 1.75 and 1.82 metres high, and is constructed in four basic parts: body, hands and head. And each warrior is individually fashioned, with varying posture and costume and differing facial features. Some are intent, others arrogant, smiling or courageous; as if an entire (living) legion had posed for their own individual statues. There are archers, spearmen, swordsmen, and they were all armed with real weapons, many of which have been found with them. Spearheads, arrow-heads, cross-bow mechanisms and many truly beautiful bronze swords have been found. The swords especially have retained their lustre and sharpness over 2,200 years, and spectro-analysis throws some interesting light on the state of ancient Chinese metallurgy. Apart from the basic copper and tin, the swords contain 13 other elements: nickel, magnesium, aluminium, zinc, iron, silicon, manganese, thallium, molybdenum, vanadium, cobalt, chromium and niobium. Other finds have included objects of gold, jade and bone, iron farm tools, linen, silk and leather; 10,000 relics in all.

And the chariots were real, too, though their wooden frames have stood up less well to the ravages of time and fire. According to the historian Ssu-ma Chien (2a&b) when the Chin dynasty fell to Hsiang Yu in 206 BC, he burned Chin Shih Huang's palaces, both above and below ground,

STEVE MOORE

The statues show a wide variety of individual expressions and differing facial characteristics.

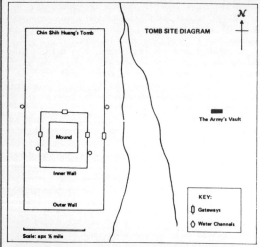

TOMB SITE DIAGRAM

Chin Shih Huang's Tomb

N

The Army's Vault

Mound

Inner Wall

Outer Wall

KEY:

Gateways

Water Channels

Scale: apx ½ mile

Chin Shih Huang was obsessed with numerical symbolism, and especially with the number 6. No large-scale accurate maps of his tomb have been available to us, but the simplified map we have does suggest some interesting numerical ratios.

The outer wall of the tomb is 108 units by 48. The inner wall is 33 un. north to south, placed 50 un. from the north (outer) wall and 25 from the south; it is 30 un. from east to west, and placed 9 un from the side walls.

The burial mound is 18 un. square, placed 6 un. from the north (inner) wall and 9 from the south. It is 6 un. from both (inner) side walls.

The tomb complex is aligned to the cardinal points, and the Army's vault lies 66 un. east of the outer wall. Our calculations suggest that each unit measures 66 (Chinese) feet, but this is not confirmed.

and there is evidence of this fire in the charred remains of the chariots, columns and roof-boards. Each chariot was drawn by four horses, also modelled in terracotta, and standing 1.23 metres high. These too are extremely life-like, especially in their facial features. Each chariot contained three or four men, and was accompanied behind by 12 foot soldiers.

In the earlier Shang and Chou dynasties, it had been the practice to bury chariots, together with living horses, chariot-eers and slaves, to serve the Emperor in the next world, though by the Warring States period this barbarous practice had been stamped out, giving way to small pottery figurines instead. The first Emperor's legion probably served the same purpose, though this is the first time life-size figures have been found; and the sheer quantity is astounding. At the present rate of excavation, it will probably be years before the entire legion has been unearthed, but there is talk of restoring the vault to its original roofed glory.

TALES OF THE TOMB

What I find truly astonishing is that only two kilometres away lies the actual mausoleum of Chin Shih Huang, its position known (it never having been 'lost') and yet completely unexcavated. I can imagine few western archaeol-

ogists being able to keep their spades and trowels out of a potential treasure-house such as this for long, let alone confine themselves to minor, if notable, sites related to it. And yet there it remains, with a fair possibility of being intact from the day it was sealed. Both Topping(1) and Cottrell(3a) state that Hsiang Yu broke into the tomb when he burned the palaces, but there is no mention of this in Ssu-ma Chien in either his biography of Chin Shih Huang (2a) or of Hsiang Yu (2b); merely that the latter burnt all the palaces, and the fire burned for 3 months. There do not seem to be any other recorded desecrations.

Building of the tomb commenced as soon as Cheng Chao assumed the throne of Chin at the age of 13, and was not concluded until a year after his death in 210 BC. Ssu-ma Chien (2c) has this to say of it:

"As soon as the First Emperor became king of Chin, excavations and building had been started at Mount Li, while after he won the empire more than seven hundred thousand conscripts from all parts of the country worked there. They dug through three subterranean streams and poured molten copper over the outer coffin, (an alternative translation by De Groot (4a) suggests that the entire crypt was made of copper, as protection against the three streams) and the tomb was filled with models of palaces, pavillions and offices, as well as fine vessels, precious stones and rarities. Artisans were ordered to fix up cross-bows so that any thief breaking in would be shot. All the country's streams, the Yellow River and the Yangtse were reproduced in quicksilver and by some mechanical means made to flow into a miniature ocean. The heavenly constellations were shown above and the regions of the earth below. The candles were made of whale oil to ensure their burning for the longest possible time."

Ssu-ma Chien has been vindicated as a historian so often of late, as in the evidence of the burning of the underground vault mentioned above, that we suspect much of his description may be accurate. Many wonders may be found within; and also, unfortunately, the bones of the artisans who designed the tomb's defences, immolated with their secrets, and also of the First Emperor's childless wives, murdered on the orders of his son.

The tomb was built as a square three-layered shape, like a 3-step pyramid, more than 300 metres per side (i.e. bigger than the great pyramid), oriented to the four cardinal points. It apparently consisted of brick or stone-lined chambers, with earth heaped over the top, and stood some 50 metres high. The tomb stood at the centre of an 'inner city' or 'spirit city', containing sacred stone tablets, inscribed soul towers and temples, and this in turn lay within an 'outer city', about 1000 metres east to west, 2,200 metres north to south and surrounded by a wall 7 metres broad at the base, with watchtowers at the corner. These walls and outbuildings have virtually disappeared. Only the tumulus remains above ground.

There is speculation that there may be corresponding underground vaults to the north, south and west of the tomb, perhaps containing life-size figures of officials, ministers and court ladies, though we have no reports of any exploratory digs that might be going on to find them. We do have a brief mention that figures of female court attendants were unearthed 'some time ago', but absolutely no details of their form or location. Perhaps these supposed other vaults will also have to wait for accidental discovery.

A certain amount of folklore has built up around the tomb, too. Writing before the discovery of the vault, Cottrell (3b) mentions that the mound was supposed to have been connected with Mount Li by subterranean passages; and that the mound is only the 'Great Gate', leading to the actual grave, which is within the mountain. There the Emperor's wooden boat-shaped sarcophagus floats on a quicksilver sea, always moving just out of reach if you try to get hold of it. And another story in the same source relates that buried within the mound are Chin Shih Huang's "Ascend the Cloud Boots", which enabled him to ascend to heaven, his "Drive the Mountains Whip", and his "Measure the Fields Rod" which when waved in the air caused the defeat of his enemies.

And we have another interesting tale, drawn from the *Miscellanies about the Western Metropolis* (4b), a work variously attributed to Ko Hung (circa 290-370 AD) or Liu Hsin (1st C BC). It is said that two statues of *ki-lin* (the Chinese 'unicorn', though hardly akin to the western beast) which had once stood on the grave at Mount Li, were removed to a position near the Palace of the Five Tsoh Trees. They were 13 feet tall. The left foreleg of the animal on the eastern side was broken off, and the fracture secreted a red, blood-like substance. The elders said the substance possessed supernatural power, and the populace took it as a tonic.

Before leaving Chin Shih Huang, we might also record that excavation work is being carried out at the ancient capital city of Hsienyang itself, which lies 15 kilometres north-west of Sian. Excavation began in 1960, and was resumed in 1974, and has mainly concentrated on the Hsienyang Palace, the hereditary home of the Chin kings from the time of the city's foundation in 350 BC. The palace grounds cover 6 km east to west and 2 km north to south, and are centred in the northern part of the Yaotien commune. Some 1,000 relics have been discovered, though the finds are by no means as impressive as at Hsiyang, being mainly of architectural significance. Many decorated bricks and tiles have been found, as well as some severely damaged murals. Pottery, bronze hinges and knockers, iron nails and jade ornaments have been found, as well as silk fabrics, some of which were carbonised (presumably by fire). The palace had at least two storeys, and may have stood 17 metres high. See (5) for more details.

GRAVE UNDERTAKINGS

While dealing with the wondrous interiors of famous graves, I may as well give an airing to one of my favourite tales. It concerns the tomb of Chuko Liang (181-234 AD), the sage, strategist and inventor mentioned last issue. The story is undoubtedly apocryphal, if not entirely mythical; but worth telling nonetheless. It is said that the Emperor Hung Wu, the first sovereign of the Ming dynasty (reigned 1368-1398 AD), and his councillor Liu Po Wen, found themselves in the neighbourhood of the tomb, which lies in the Ting Chun mountain, and determined to visit it. As was the custom of the time, both were wearing iron armour; yet they managed to force an entrance and found themselves in an ante-chamber. There they saw an inscription to the effect that the grave's occupant would bind the hands of any visitors, and indeed, in squeezing through the narrow entrance to the grave, they had had to wedge themselves so as to be incapable of using their arms. From the ante-chamber, they broke down another door, and found themselves in a second chamber. This contained several figures made entirely of loadstone, which attracted the armour of the intruding 'guests'. Terrified at the unknown force which was dragging them forwards (though the loadstone was known to the Chinese from the time of Chin Shih Huang onwards), they cast off their armour and fled. Though not before noticing another inscription, which Dennys (6) renders thus:

"I'll strip off the skin
Of who ventures in
To open this my grave."

As may be gathered, the Emperor and Liu did not stay to survey the tomb in detail, and it was closed once more. The tradition of the visit is still allegedly recounted by neighbourhood story-tellers, though whether it had any basis in fact, we know not.

The story may well be nothing more than folklore, typical of the sort of tale that springs up about the tombs of famous men, especially those reputed to have had some skills in the magic arts. A similar tale is told of the grave of Confucius (6th Century BC) though he was hardly a magician, and comes from the same source (6). Confucius's disciple, Tze-kung, is said to have covered his master's coffin with loadstone. And here our tales wind about full circle, for it was the First Emperor, Chin Shih Huang, who came visiting. The First Emperor was not fond of Confucian scholars; he had 460 of them buried alive at one point in his illustrious career; and thus his approach to the tomb was somewhat less than reverent. He ordered his soldiers to open the tomb, but the loadstone attracted their pickaxes and armour, making the work impossible. Thus the tomb of Confucius was never violated. As to whether there is any truth in this story either, I can only say that I have.. *grave misgivings!*

SOURCES:

1. Material on the excavations at Hsiyang is drawn from the following:
   Peking Review. Vol. 18, No 30 (25 July 1975) p21.
   Chinese Literature. 1975, No 10 (October). p109-110.
   Chinese Literature. 1975, No 11 (November). p102-107.
   China Pictorial. 1975, No 11 (November). p22-25.
   China Reconstructs. Vol 25, No 2. (February 1976) p38-42.
   National Geographic. Vol 153, No 4. (April 1978) p440-459. ("China's Incredible Find", by Audrey Topping).
   New Archaeological Finds in China, Vol 2. (Foreign Languages Press, Peking, 1978) p59-64. ("An Art Treasure-Trove of Chin", by Tu pao-jen & Han Han).
2. *Records of the Historian,* translated by Yang Hsien-Yi and Gladys Yang (From the 'Shih Chi' of Ssu Ma Chien) Commercial Press Ltd, Hong Kong, 1974. a) p195. b) p221. c) p186.
3. *The Tiger of Ch'in,* by Leonard Cottrell (1962). Pan Books, London, 1964. a) p195. b) p173-5 (quoting largely from *The Great Wall of China,* by W E Geil, John Murray, London, 1909).
4. *The Religious System of China* by J J M De Groot. (Leiden, 1892-1910) Reprint: Literature House Ltd., Taiwan, 1964. Book 1, Vol. 2. a) p399-401. b) p823.
5. *China Reconstructs.* Vol. 28, No. 2. (February 1979) p64-66.
6. *The Folklore of China,* by Nicholas B Dennys. (London, 1876). Reprint: Oriental Press, Amsterdam, 1968. p135-136.

Steve Moore is associate editor of Fortean Times.

continued from p13

photograph it when he said, 'Wait! It's going to break.' And before our eyes it snapped in half!" Meyer also placed a Swiss franc on his forefinger. In less than a minute it flopped over his finger like a Dali clock, bent almost double. *National Enquirer* 4 Jan 1977.

Commenting on Meyer's feat, Russell Targ of the Stanford Research Institute said: "I don't know of anyone else, including Uri Geller, who has demonstrated a psychic influence on plastic." But even in our few examples some plastic items are mentioned. Not long after, we had note of another plastic bender. Orlando Bragante, 17, was tested by Dr Aldo Martelli at Bologna University. By concentration he straightened paperclips in his hand, bent keys from a distance, as well as steel and plastic bars, and a fork in a sealed container. *National Enq* 27 June 1978.

A couple of children who could bend things just by picking them up... Emma Waters, 11, of Forest Row, Sussex, put the usual kinks in cutlery, as did Gloria, the 2 yr-old daughter of famous psychic Peter Hurkos. However Gloria also bent several dentist's high-carbon drills merely by touching them. Said the Los Angeles dentist, Dr Peter Doerken: "Afterwards, I tried to bend one of them back, but because the steel is so hard it broke." Hurkos claims she has inherited psychic powers from himself, just as he had done from his mother. We remember elsewhere reading that his psychic abilities developed after he fell from a ladder onto his head. Perhaps there is something here worth investigating since the legendary Eusapia Palladino and the proto-Carrie, Andrea Kolintz (see above), also linked the emergence of their powers to head injuries. *National Enquirer* 16 March 1976; *News of the World* 9 Jan 1977.

At Drexel University, in Philadelphia, Karen Getsla, 32, gave physicists food for thought by bending a 9 foot laser beam. "We monitored every possible occurrence around Karen — temperature both inside and outside the laser, air flow, humidity, vibration, sound and barametric pressure," said biophysics researcher David Faust. Karen stood on a wooden platform about a foot from the laser, put her hands against the walls of the cubicle,

which surrounded her, and rocked back and forth. She was able to repeat the laser-bending effect several times in each 5 minute experiment. *National Enquirer* 7 Feb 1978.

Elaine Fortson, 44, managed to exert a quarter-pound pressure on a metal beam without touching it, when tested by Dr Will Franklin at Kent State University, Ohio. She also set a pendulum in motion by a glance, while another next to it remained stationary, and sent self-generated electricity down wires to repeatedly flip a switch. Her other talents included reading a doctor's case histories through sealed brown envelopes by placing her hands on them; and psychically locating a crashed plane on a hillside in North Carolina. *National Enquirer* 21 March 1978.

Michael Morse, 9, of Anaheim, California, was tested by Dr Jerry Cunningham, of Pepperdine University, Los Angeles. 25 broken watches were spread out on a table in front of him. He passed his hand over them said he thought he could "fix" about 7 or 8. In the event he mended 6 just by holding them. In another test he successfully identified the suit of the odd

card out in a line of playing cards lying face down in 12 out of 20 tests. The chances of doing this by guesswork, we are told, are less than 1 in 2000. *National Enquirer* 29 March 1977.

Finally a couple of enigmatic aspects of these powers — if that's what they are. On 3 November 1978, Mrs Elizabeth Sandys-Pemberton 78, was in hospital in Hampshire, while Uri Geller was making a broadcast from the top of the Blackpool Tower. While eating her lunch, a fork fell across a newsphoto of Geller's eyes, and bent 90 degrees. Portsmouth *News* 9 Nov 1978. Then, to deepen the mystery, let me mention what happened on the Day of Innocents 1978, when stage magician Jose Diaz appeared on Spanish TV posing as 'Professor Mendoza' with paranormal powers. Thousands called TV and newspapers, nevertheless, with claims that the 'Professor' had indeed mended their clocks and bent their spoons. *Daily Mail* 30 Dec 1978.

Credit: Alan Cleaver, Chris Holtzhausen, Peter Hope-Evans, George Ives, John Michell, Tony Roberts, Peter Rogerson, JDM Start, Nigel Watson, Ion Will. PS

SWARMS and MIGRATIONS

The last few years have seen proliferations of many kinds of insects and animals beyond the usual seasonal fluctuations in their populations. Our last listing of swarms was back in 1977 (FT20p21-23), so it's about time we had another.

ANTS

Britain's hospitals have been facing a growing nuisance — plagues of tiny yellow-brown Pharaoh ants. Teams from afflicted hospitals throughout Britain attended crash courses in combatting these and other pests (eg the cockroach) at Wexham Park Hospital, Slough, Bucks — according to the *Daily Mirror* 24 October 1978. Then — the irony of it — just months later, Wexham Park has to close a large surgical ward after it was overrun by ants. *London Evening Standard* 7 January 1979. But that was nothing compared to previous invasions. An entire 17-storey block of

council flats, at World's End, Chelsea, became infested for a short while in 1976 (London *Evening Standard* 25 November 1976), a situation which was repeated in another council block, this time at Erith in Kent, causing the residents to petition Bexley Council for action. *Kentish Independant* 21 September 1978. Earlier that same summer, Kent suffered a bigger plague of ants, affecting the town of Deal and blamed on the dry weather (!). London *Evening News* 14 June 1978. Huge swarms of flying ants caused chaos on the seafront at Southsea, Portsmouth, Hants, in September 1978. Four old age pensioners were driven off a golf course; one lady's pink cardigan became a living black garment; and cars pulled over as ants covered their windows. Portsmouth *News* 23 Sept 1978.

Strange how things come and go... The *Sunday People* 6 March 1977 announced a programme to breed ants after a "massive heath blaze" killed millions — an estimated three-quarters of their population — at Hartland Moor, near Wareham, Dorset. It seems they were being studied by the nearby Institute of Terrestrial Ecology at the time and their work was also destroyed in the fire, otherwise the disaster would not have been detected. Then in November a huge colony of red ants — estimated at about 300 million, and believed to be the world's largest "of its kind" — was found in Switzerland. *Daily Mirror* 4 November 1977.

In 1976 a warning was issued by American entomologists that the dreaded fire ant could multiply throughout the southern States. Already there had been tales of lingering deaths and ruined crops (see FT20p22) as this native of South America, which has periodically scourged the South for the last 25 years, took advantage of the warm weather and the dwindling use of Mirex, a pesticide potent to fireants but no longer manufactured after it was suspected of causing cancers in laboratory animals. Georgia is estimated to be two-thirds overrun, and parts of Mississippi have as many as 200 of the 2ft ant mounds per acre. This danger was brought to our attention again recently by the announcement that fire ants now infest 230 million acres in nine States, and have split into two varieties, a black kind in Texas and the south and a red kind in the east. In South America the ants are kept in line by other ants who attack and kill their egg-laying queens, but in the absence of natural predators and suitable chemicals their spread to the western States is estimated at 50-100 miles a decade. They are called fire ants because of their powerful toxic venom — in most cases it causes an itchy welt at the bite, but has been known to cause shock, infections and gangrene. In 1976, one-year-old Mary Harper, of Taylorsville, Mississippi, crawled into a bed of fire ants and was stung 70 times. These ants hang on with large jaws, jabbing repeatedly with their stingers. Within minutes she was gasping for breath as her top lip

ballooned to block off her nostrils. She would have died there and then had her father not been a doctor and quick witted. Even now, Mary has to have monthly injections of a fire ant desensitizer, and probably for the rest of her life. Less lucky was an asthmatic in Holden Beach, Florida, who died during an ant attack earlier this year. The latest death occurred at the end of January when a salesman in Vidalia, Georgia, felt a painful bite in his foot — within an hour later he had died of a cardio-pulmonary arrest. *Newsweek* 26 April 1976; *Toronto Sun* 16 February 1979.

FLIES, APHIDES AND LADYBIRDS

In the summer of 1976 the east and south coasts of England experienced an astonishing invasion from the Continent, only these tourists were ladybirds, thriving on a hot summer that followed a mild winter (see FT20p21). One naturalist writing in the 'Day by Day' column of the Scunthorpe *Evening Telegraph* 25 January 1977, noted that usually the bugs vanished as the weather got cooler, but this year there had been so many that: "Right up to the recent frosts, one came upon batches of them, or saw them scattered on the pavements in most unexpected places...I had not realized they were a hibernating species, but there is no other way of accounting for the rows of little red bodies in the overlap of wooden fences, chinks in walls, under loose bark, etc."

After the veritable orgy of eating these huge swarms embarked upon there couldn't have been an aphid or greenfly left in England, and yet come July 1977, we hear of huge aphid infestations covering "hundreds of thousands of acres" of crops in southern and eastern England, particularly threatening the corn crop. One source said that aerial spraying organizations were using every available pilot and hour of daylight to nip the plague in the bug, as it were, and relying on the tiny red army of ladybirds to eat the stragglers. I kept my scissors at the ready but not a single note of ladybird abundance that summer did we see... *Daily Telegraph* 16 July 1977; *Sunday Times* 17 July 1977. In August came the answer to their prayers — not the ladybirds which were by now acknowledged to be unexpectedly low in numbers, but huge swarms of hoverflies. Although migratory, these swarms were said to have been "blown across the Channel from

Holland" as though by Providence. Sunbathing girls screamed when masses settled on them, open-air concerts were abandoned. Between Broadstairs and Bournemouth, and on the East Anglian coast, dead flies were heaped "for miles" At first these harmless small wasp-like flies were declared a pest, but a month later they were heroes as their larvae made inroads on the aphids. *Daily Express* 19 August 1977; *Sunday Telegraph* 19 Sept 1977. And last summer the ladybirds were on hunger-strike again, it seems, as swarms of greenfly sent holiday-makers scrambling off beaches at Skegness, Lincs. *Sunday Mirror* 30 July 1978.

A correspondent to the London *Evening News* 3 July 1978, asked where all the flies had gone that summer. Where indeed? — it seemed as if the country had been abandoned. But we do have notes of swarms of other kinds of flies than houseflies and bluebottles. Unidentified flies, in swirling clouds numbering thousands, drove people from the beach and seafront at Whitstable in Kent, about midday on 16 May. A spokesman for the Natural History Museum in London suggested a low-tide and humid conditions encouraged the swarm, but our correspondent Valerie Martin notes that day had a cold east wind despite being sunny. *Whitstable Times* 19 May 1978. In August, residents of the Tullibardine area of Auchterarder, Perthshire, complained about a plague of flies. They blamed a nearby potato dump, described by a Tay River Purification Board spokesman as "a quagmire". But James Fordyce, the potato merchant who owns the dump, is protesting too — he says the flies are not potato flies and are coming in from the Fife coast. *The Scotsman* 14 August 1978. In September, tens of thousands of tiny ant-like flies descended on the Belgian town of Chatelet, near Charleroi, covering trees, cars and buildings. Charleroi *Le Rappel* 11 Sept 1978; *Le Soir* 14 Sept 1978. And in Florida a relatively new pest — the citrus black fly — was threatening crops for the third year, and being fought with stingless wasps imported from Mexico. *Time* 28 August 1978.

SPIDERS, MILLIPEDES AND SNAILS

1978 got off to a good start for spiders. A plague of deadly funnel-web spiders affected hundreds of homes in Sydney.

Reports say they were maddened by both their "mating season" and the heat-wave. One woman was bitten to death, and two others seriously ill in hospital. *Daily Express* 12 January 1978; *Sunday Express* 5 February 1978. In Arizona a plague of black widow spiders gave birth to a new sport — nighttime gettogethers at which neighbours drunk beer and chased spiders with sticks and flashlights. This abundance is described as "unusual". *Time* 28 August 1978. Black widows popped up in England too, though only four of them, and mercifully dead. They were found in a crate of spare parts for Lynx helicopters which had been undergoing tropical trials in California. The box was opened after routine "de-bugging" by mechanics at a Ministry of Defense base at Boscombe Down Airfield, Wiltshire. Then came unconfirmed rumours that more spiders and hundreds of eggs were found in a hangar on the same base. A spokesman assured us all that the cold would have killed them all anyway. One report said that the last time black widows reached England from America was in 1970, when a young man working at the USAF base at Lakenheath, Suffolk, was bitten as he pulled on his trousers. Then a middle-aged woman, living near the base, was bitten while sitting on the toilet. Apparently nesting under toilet seats is favoured by the nasty little devils. Ugh! *The Sun, Daily Express, Daily Mirror, Daily Mail* all 20 Sept 1978.

Millions of millipedes invaded Floyds Knobs, Indiana. The residents of this small community couldn't keep them out, even with kerosene, turps or oil filled moats around their houses, and they have become reconciled to the sound of crunching underfoot. One, Thomas Picket, said: "They move *en masse*... millions of them. One night my neighbour's truck just spun on the roadway because he couldn't get any traction on them." Pickett himself puts a coat of paint on his bed legs so they don't crawl all over him. The inch long insects, which don't bite or sting, first appeared in June 1978, brought out, according to one expert, by a hot dry summer following a mild winter. He suggests they are looking for moisture and decaying vegetable matter. Worthington, Minnesota *Globe* 28 August 1978.

In September 1977 there was a massive invasion of NE India by African snails. The people of Dimapur, about 74kms from Kohima, in Nagaland, were waging a continuous war to save their crops. The snails were said to number "lakhs" (hundreds of thousands). Calcutta *Sunday* 2 October 1977. Snail wars were also reported from California, although this one pitted snail against snail. In 1977 Halix aspersa, a large brown snail, was gobbling up gardens and vegetation along freeways and roads and generally the bane of gardners everywhere. It is known that it was originally introduced to the area by those who love to eat snails, but as usual in such introductions, the absence of natural predators stimulated a population explosion. Ted Fisher, a biologist at the University of California at Riverside, was commissioned by the California Transportation Department to develop a biological control, and had the idea of pitching cannibals against the vegetarians. The cannibals — Rumina decollata, a smaller faster breeding snail that thinks other snails are good enough to eat — were already adapted to the Californian environment, although no one is quite sure how or when they got there, like the Helix, from Europe. Fisher bred thousands and turned them loose. He says it'll be three years before the plans effectiveness can be assessed. *International Herald Tribune* 11 July 1978.

WORMS AND SHRIMPS

In 1976, the migratory armyworm ate nearly $20 million worth of corn, peanuts, soybeans and other crops and pasture, in Georgia, USA. The damage was nearly matched in 1977, in Georgia and Virginia, when the drought added to the voracious worms' hunger, causing them to eat anything in their path. Jacksonville, Florida, *Times-Union* 1 April 1977; Newport New, Virginia, *Daily Press* 19 Sept 1977. By 1978 the army worm was reported in Pennysylvania and Maryland (estimated 75% crop loss) attacking the corn along with the corn-ear worm and the European corn borer. In California lygus bug infested cotton was sprayed with an insecticide which also killed off the bollworm's predators — so farmers are dreading a bollworm resurgence. *Time* 28 August 1978.

Masses of migrating worms brought trains to a slippery halt on a steep railway in Japan, as they covered the tracks. *Daily Mirror* 5 Oct 1976. Similarly, millions of worms disrupted train services in Bulgaria. *Daily Mirror* 16 May 1970. It is unusual to hear of mass migrations of earthworms, but a note recently came to our attention. A correspondent had written to the *Gainsborough News* 6 June 1975, that a friend had witnessed the event in daylight in Gainsborough, Lincs, during a spell of wet weather. "One day recently while walking along the pathway of The Avenue, she saw... in front of her... a moving, heaving mass of earthworms, a wide track from out of the dyke bottom, up over the pathway slabs, on over the road to the grass verge on the other side of the road. Just a live trek moving ever forward to some unknown destination, regardless of any hazard or obstacle. The traffic on the road was just crushing through them, leaving writhing, wriggling or flattened worms — not a pretty picture". Another migration, this time a vertical one. Millions of small-finned greenish worms 2-4 inches long, which usually live in lagoon mud, surfaced in Venice's Grand Canal on 17 May 1977. *Daily Telegraph* 18 May 1977.

Worms and creatures in your tap water...it seems to happen more often that you'd think. When Tubifex worms were found in the supply of an anonymous hospital, the cause was quickly located — the loft space contained dead birds, feathers and droppings, and undoubtedly the birds that used the place contaminated the water tank which had no lid. London *Evening Standard* 11 July 1977. More puzzling were the harmless shrimps found in tap water at Corby, Northamptonshire. Local officials said they'd flush them out, but we suspect there was little they could do but flush themselves. *Daily Express* 25 Oct 1977; *Sunday People* 30 Oct 1977. A year later, authorities in Essex dealt with worms in the pipes by adding Permethrin, allegedly harmless to humans. We wait and see... *Daily Telegraph* 2 Oct 1978. For 2 days (1 & 2 Sept) unidentified fuzzy half-inch red worms slithered from water taps in the Lafayette Parish community, near Broussard, Lousiana. Water engineers put a standard dose of chlorine into the supply, and then a second dose when it became apparent the first was not enough. Eggs or larvae had somehow penetrated their filter screens, and although the problem was

The curious regimented swarming of the Processionary Bombyx, as they march out of their nest.

cleared quickly, local residents still shudder when they turn on taps. *Daily Mail* 5 Sept 1978; *Grand Rapids Press* (Michigan) 6 Sept 1978.

The townsfolk of Elphin, Co. Roscommon, in Ireland, were flabberghasted when they protested to water engineer Joe Corcoran about the bodies in their water. Terrt Leyden, a member of the Dail, the Republic's parliament, said: "Elphin has the most wretched water in Ireland. It's not fit to be put in whiskey." Cornered Corcoran tried elfin humour. "It's one of our tests," he bluffed. "If the creatures are alive then the water is safe to drink." This did not amuse Elphin councillor Seamus Scott. He roared: "How would you like to look in a glass of water and see things swimming in it and then drink it?" Joe declined his offer. Later in a council meeting, Scott brandished the English reportage of the incident. "Even an English newspaper thinks it is a farce," he said. The council was given a report on a major new water supply scheme for the area, but I imagine the news raised more fears than it was intended to quell — the source for the scheme was named Polecat Springs! *Reveille* 9 & 23

June 1978.

The most recent case to hand of shrimps thriving in tap water comes from Northamptonshire, where a months-long cleansing operation of underground mains has begun after families complained about their squirming liquid. *Sunday People* 29 April 1979.

Our final shrimp note is of Wellingborough, Northants, where the water supply was discoloured for 4 weeks over August and September 1978, as engineers tried to flush out tribes of thriving shrimps. They said that the shrimps were harmless and the water still fit to drink — but would you? *Daily Telegraph* 25 Aug 1978.

CATERPILLARS AND GRUBS

Spring, in London, heralds the itchy season as millions of Brown-tailed moth larvae hatch, and their irritating hairs fall on skin or clothes on washing lines. This menace has been noticeable in the last 20 years, some say several centuries, and has got increasingly worse since the mild winters of '75 and '76 followed by hot dry summers encouraged their breeding. Although they can

be found throughout southern England no one seems to know why they favour the north bank of the Thames, from Canvey Island to Tower Hamlets, nor how they got there since they are not natives. We mentioned the 1976 invasion in FT20p22...but the only note we have for 1977 is simply a warning from health authorities to be prepared. London *Evening News* 23 June 1977. If they hadn't appeared by June it's likely the nuisance was minimal that year. Another mild winter brought fears of a large plague in the spring of 1978, and many boroughs were asking for the authority to compel home owners to search for and destroy the cocoons in their gardens, and some sent leaflets to homes in their area. The Natural History Museum stepped in with an idea they said proved popular and effective "in the 1700s": - a bounty on every bucketful. *Kentish Independent* 9 Feb, 6 July 1978; *Kentish Times* 9 Feb 1978; *Daily Mirror* 8 Feb 1978; *Daily Mail* 10 Feb 1978; London *Evening Standard* 26 May 1978; *Weekend* 13 Sept 1978.

As expected the confused Spring this year delayed the arrival of this irritating pest, but also many nests had been destroyed, so their numbers were noticeably down in the Borough of Newham. However, Canning Town and a few other isolated pockets were as overrun as Barking was in 1978. As we work on the paste-up of this issue we learn that a plague of Brown-tailed moth caterpillars was wreaking havoc in the West Sussex Town of Chichester. *Barking & Dagenham Post* 14 June 1979; *Daily Telegraph* 21 June 1979.

But London's problems are tiny compared to the devastation by caterpillars in parts of Canada and the northern United States. The two main culprits are the spruce budworm and the forest tent caterpillar, which apparently swarm on a regular cycle, but according to a statement from the Center for Short-lived Phenomena, Cambridge, Mass, for the first time since 1955 the two cycles have coincided. Between them a vast swath of oak, maple, spruce, fir and balsam trees around the Great Lakes have been effected. In Maine alone an estimated 8000 square miles of spruce and balsam have been lost, and in Indiana 55 square miles of deciduous trees were completely defoliated. Minnesota, Michigan, Ontario and New Brunswick were also badly hit...or bit. And as if that wasn't enough, a 20 square mile area around Columbus Georgia was infested with another kind of caterpillar. Harrisburg, Pennsylvania *Evening News* 27 July 1977; *Newsweek* 15 August 1977; *Sunday Express* 18 Sept 1977. The same scourges remerged in 1978, afflicting the same areas only worse than before. In Maine cars were skidding on carpets of squished caterpillars. The forest tent caterpillar stripped an estimated 30 million acres in Ontario, where it is believed about 100,000 billion hatched within a few days of new buds opening — and in Vermont the devastation was the worst in 25 years among the maples and other hardwoods. However, Vermont was saved by a mysterious disease which killed off many millions of the caterpillars. An estimated 150 million acres of spruce and fir have been infested and largely defoliated by spruce budworm in Maine and southern Canada. *Observer* 25 June 1978; *Time* 28 August 1978.

The same late summer saw a relative, the eastern tent caterpillar, devastating orchards in Georgia and other south-eastern States, right up to the Rocky Mountains. This scourge which hits wild cherry trees, peach, plum and apple trees, is said by the Georgia Dept of Agriculture to be the worst in 10 years. Not surprisingly we find the menace has a cycle of 10 years. *Extra!* (USA) Oct 1978.

In Majorca millions of unnamed caterpillars munched their way through the island's pine woods for the fifth consecutive year, despite tons of insecticides, isolation breaks created by felling thousands of trees, and the latest ploy, the issue of a million shotgun cartridges to blast the football-sized nests. The locals are worried — legend has it that 500 years ago a Moorish prophet predicted the island would flourish only as long as the pine groves. *Sunday Express*. The pine forests of Sutherland and Western Caithness are also under attack from furry hordes of Pine Beauty caterpillars. They are indigenuous to Britain having a taste for the Lodgepole pine, and also known on the Continent (as the Owl moth) where it favours the Scots pine. In 1977 they stripped around half a million trees in north Scotland, despite insecticide spraying. In 1978 a stronger insecticide was used — but apparently to little effect. Already this year the Forestry Commission has warned that they may pose a worse threat to these Isles than the Dutch elm scourge. *Daily Telegraph* 19 May & 19 June 1978, & 9 Feb 1979.

When a green army of caterpillars marched down a tree into her garden, a housewife in Bournemouth, Dorset, went understandably berserk. She managed to phone the council, and when workmen arrived they found her singlehandedly fending off the onslaught by rushing round madly, flatting all she could see with a hammer. Messy! *Sun* 4 July 1978.

In June 1978 we also learned of a plague of caterpillars of the Umber moth, uncommon in Lancashire but nevertheless swarming in millions in the Alum Scar Wood, on the Woodfold Estate at Pleasington, near Blackburn. Oddly the swarming is confined to the wood, defoliating all kinds of trees. At Lumb Bank Farm, which borders on the wood, they tell of the eeriness of walking down the lane with fine threads hanging from the trees in place of leaves. Gordon Moulden, of the farm said: "It's just like a horror movie. There are threads hanging all over, and you walk into them. You can hear the caterpillars eating and moving about — it sounds like it's starting to rain." *Guardian* 17 June 1978.

We have considerably more material on swarms of lice, fleas, ticks, maggots, beetles and bugs of all kinds, jellyfish and other marine nuisances, but we'll have to unload these some other time.

Credit: Gary Abbott, Larry Arnold, Jeremy Beadle, Lionel Beer, Paul Burd, David Fideler, Mark Hall, RTA Hill, Peter Hope-Evans, Nick Maloret, Valerie Martin, Paul Pinn, Henri Premont, Ken Rogers, Peter Rogerson, Paul Screeton, Leslie Shepard, Anthony Smith, Has Thomas, Nigel Watson, Dwight Whalen, Ion Will, Jake Williams. RJMR.

occult crimes

Occasionally in our gleanings we come across intriguing hints of occult criminology, as though paranormal abilities were being used secretly, sometimes for gain, but more often for the utter confusion of us mortals.

THE PHANTOM WALLBANGER

The area around Danby Street, Peckham, in south east London, was the cause of some excitement between July and September 1977; excitement and devastation, for someone, or something, was attacking garden walls with some relish. By the end of September, 25 walls had been damaged or destroyed, and there were said to be 'dozens of unrecorded incidents.' Despite continuing watches by police and residents, no one seems to have been arrested... nor was the wallbanger even seen in the act.

The damage varied: sometimes an entire wall would be knocked down, at other times there would be damage to pillars and canopies, at other times merely the top-section would be knocked off the wall. Sometimes householders would hear two or three loud thumps, and then rush out to find their wall shattered; at other times, there would simply be the sound of the collapsing brickwork. And no one ever saw him do it.

At first, police and residents logically assumed that *someone*, armed with a sledgehammer or pickaxe, was responsible, and thus the press coined names like 'Harvey Wallbanger' and the 'Phantom Wall Smasher.' An identity was even invented for him... an out-of-work bricklayer who was making work for himself. Children were discounted, for though some of the smaller walls could have been been pushed over, others required great strength to destroy. And if such was the wallbanger's design, he could have reaped a large profit; damage ran from a minimum £20 per incident to several hundred pounds.

And they should have been able to see him, or at least to have seen him running off. The first victim had finished tidying his garden in the evening, merely nipped into the house to get the milkbottles to put out, and returned to find no wall. Other attacks seem to have taken place mainly at night (though never on a Tuesday night) and residents have been at their windows in seconds. And two separate residents told police that they had been keeping watch, then turned away from the window for no more than a few seconds, only to turn back to see dust settling round broken bricks. Even so, there was no one to be seen. By the time of our last clipping, there was talk of a 'ghost wrecker'; perhaps an acknowledgement that the Phantom Wallbanger might be less or more than human, after all. *Daily Mirror, The Sun* 24 August 1977; *The Job* (Metropolitan Police newspaper) 30 September 1977.

...AND HIS THIEVING FRIENDS

We sometimes like to speculate that the universe takes a dislike to a certain spot or building, and unleashes 'mysterious forces' to eradicate the construction. Or perhaps there are human thieves of such audacity and know-how that they can achieve the absurd. In Shickshinny, Pennsylvania, police were hunting for a gang who allegedly stole a 150 foot long dry stone wall from the property of John Levyak. *Sunday Express* 12 September 1976. And in France, police were also searching for a gang of thieves, after Pierre Lestienne and his family drove to their prefabricated seaside cottage at Dunderque, only to find it... gone! London *Evening News* 8 June 1977. And if these seem ordinary enough, ponder this: members of a British Railways cricket team turned up for their first match of the season at their ground at Hartlebury, near Kidderminster. Alas, the pavilion had disappeared! And just *how* do you steal an eight-room building without anyone noticing? *Reveille* 9 June 1978.

And there was a fair amount of pondering by police in Hillsdale, Michigan, on 14 July 1977. Someone stole 700 railroad ties from a storage area in nearby Hanover Township. The ties were worth $7,000, and weighed a hefty 122,000 lbs. And on the very same day, the DCA Food Industries wholesale distribution centre reported that their 30-foot wide cement loading dock had been moved five inches off its foundation by some unknown means. And that would certainly have been no pushover! *Jacksonville* Journal. (Florida) 15 July 1977.

THINGS THAT GROW RICH IN THE NIGHT...

Or perhaps there are occult gangsters, going about their invisible business and introducing a little chaos into our lives? Some may be giant, making free with our loading docks... and others diminutive, making free with our money...

Police in Buntingford, Hertfordshire, were looking for a very thin man, after a break-in at Wydiall Hall, home of city stockbroker Michael Boyd-Carpenter. A *very* thin man, for it was assumed that *someone* had crawled through a tiny catdoor, and then let in a gang of thieves. They got away with a valuable haul of silver. But... a *cat-door?* London *Evening News* 12 July 1974.

Or perhaps they have no substance at all... At Athens, our tale has a dignified beginning. Under the watchful eye of police, bank men and airport officials, $ 200,000 in cash was placed in crates, duly sealed, and loaded aboard a plane bound for New York. The creates made it in fine shape... but the money didn't. When the crates were opened at New York, not one single cent was found. *Sunday People* 4 September 1977.

59-year old Charlie, his wife Jaqueline, and their 17-year old son David, lived on the premises at the butchers, in St Marychurch, Torquay, Devon. But there was 'something evil' there which ruined both the business and a marriage of 32 years. Money kept disappearing. One morning they opened the safe to find the cashbox empty of £5 notes, though the locks on the safe and outer doors were untouched. And he was audacious, this spectral speculator. Even when the family slept with the money under their pillows, or held in their hands, still it would go missing. The family had the house blessed by the Reverend Michael Malsom, but still the cash disappeared. In final desperation, Mr Harding moved out, hoping to take the evil influence with him. No luck. At last, Mrs Harding and her son seem to have left the ghostly gangster behind when they too moved out, and were hoping to rejoin Mr Harding. But we can only wonder what happened to the next occupants... *Daily Mail* 14 May 1977.

TAKING DELIVERY

Sometimes the themes of our stories overlap and run into each other. From Malaysia we have a tale of a phantom midwife who turned her hand to kidnapping... and this only a week after the scare about the 'Bloodthirsty midwife' (recorded in our section on Vampires) had surfaced. We have met the kidnapping *Orang Bunian* (invisible forest elves) before in these pages (see FT 23 p 6). But now we have a new and curious tale, worth telling at some length...

It concerns Ramlah Binti Mat, a 48-year old woman living at Kampung Perlis, about three miles from Balik Pulau, Malaysia. She already had a son, Asmawi, aged 6, and, when she became pregnant again, claims to have carried her second child for 13 months. In June 1977 she went to the Ayer Puteh clinic, about seven miles away, for x-rays and specialist examination. A nurse, Zainab binti Ahmad, confirmed she was pregnant—

continued on p37

Nessie: The Shiels 1977 Photos

In May 1977 Doc Shiels was lucky (!) enough to see and photograph Nessie. The story has been told in notes scattered through various issues of FT, and recently your editor summarised the saga for two USA Fortean magazines, PURSUIT and SPECULA. Our new format provides a good opportunity to show Doc's photo. properly in colour for the first time in any Fortean magazine (see back cover). It also gives us the occasion to present the results of three photographic examinations by experienced investigators who have studied the colour slide original, and to establish what is known about the photos.

Enlargement of ANS-1

Enlargement of ANS-2

A BRIEF ACCOUNT OF THE PHOTOS

Anthony 'Doc' Shiels is a professional wizard. Late in May 1977 he left his home in Cornwall, with the street-theatre group *Tom Fool's Theatre of Tomfoolery* (which comprises most of his talented family) for a working holiday at Lock Ness. About 8 am on the morning of 21 May, Doc, his wife Christine, and four others, watched three 'humps' break the surface of Borlum Bay, from the carpark of the Inchnacardoch Lodge hotel. They believe they saw three creatures rather than one many-humped one.

Later that afternoon, Doc and Christine sat in the grounds of Urquhart Castle — they had other sightings that day and

kept a camera by them, primed. Suddenly up popped a head and neck about 100 yards away. Christine wasn't looking and Doc had time only to grab the camera and shoot two frames before the creature slid smoothly down out of sight. Describing the sightings and the photos, he said later: "...the part of the neck showing above the waterline must have been around 4 or 5 feet. Don't take any notice of what appear to be eyes... I could see no eyes as such in the original. The light patch above the mouth (if mouth it is, and I think it is) is merely a reflection of a kind of ridge...Skin texture, smooth and glossy. The animal was visible for no more than 4-6 seconds. It held itself very upright, very still, except for a turning of the head and a straightening of the neck... It had powerful neck muscles. There is ... possible evidence of a parasitic growth at the back of the neck, on the dorsal ridge, as a pale yellow-green patch is visible near the water. Also in both pictures, a round pale object floats on the water close to the neck." Doc told us he thought it might be an empty McEwan's beer can.

The two medium-long shots of the head and neck were designated ANS-1 and ANS-2. The originals were taken on high-speed Ektachrome transparency film, in a Zenith EM 35mm SLR camera, at between f11 and f16 at 1/500th of a second, through a Chinon 135mm telephoto lens. They were developed professionally, back in Cornwall.

Copies of ANS-1, slightly enlarged, were made by a photo journalist, Frank Durham, and sent by Doc to many interested parties, including Jerome Clark, associate editor of *Fate* magazine and one of the field's leading Fortean and UFO investigators. The original was lent to Tim Dinsdale, the explorer and author whose own association with Loch Ness goes back many years, and who, in turn, showed it to many experts, including Sir Peter Scott, and Dr Vernon Harrison (until 1976 president of the Royal Photographic Society). All have expressed their conviction the transparency was genuine and showed a large unknown aquatic animal. ANS-2 was lent to another photojournalist, David Benchley, who made a glass copy-neg enlargement, before Doc packed the original off to his friend and colleague, the US magician Max Maven. Disaster struck! The envelope arrived empty. ANS-2 had vanished; and Benchley's glass neg broke! Fortunately Benchley had taken off a few trial prints, and the best of them, which we present here, contrasty though it is, is now the only remaining evidence of ANS-2.

These two photos are the clearest still pictures of Nessie to date — one in colour — and as such constitute serious evidence for the existence of some kind of creature in Loch Ness. As such they deserve to be taken seriously and thoroughly examined both to corroborate their authenticity and for whatever additional information they might contain.

CONTROVERSY

Through the offices of Jerry Clark, one of the enlarged copy slides of ANS-1 made its way to William Spaulding of the UFO photoanalysis group Ground Saucer Watch (GSW). GSW attempted an analysis using computer-aided methods which they admitted were hastily assembled (from several other kinds of analysis programmes) and previously untested on 'monster' photos. Their basis for comparison was a "quickly acquired" selection of Nessie photos "digitized...for any patterns". Although their report was never fully published anywhere, a summary of their findings was given in FT24. Briefly, they found an "alarming" feature: the creature seemed to be transparent and waves could be seen "penetrating" the edges of the image. Its bright patches were said to be "unnatural" and the image was smaller than the apparent size and must have been further away than "100 yards" judging by wave size etc. They also commented on the lack of water displacement.

It was quite clear that GSW thought the picture was a hoax, although they don't say how. Rickard and Dinsdale (FT24), and Bord (see below) have expressed their own reservations about the GSW analysis. In the first place the copy slide which GSW saw, one of a small number sent to

interested Forteans, was never offered as primary or first-hand evidence and never intended for analysis. In the second place, many of the results of the GSW analysis (image-flatness, loss of colour, increase of contrast, and the size anomaly) could be accounted for by the fact that GSW were looking at an enlarged copy transparency and not the original. Had they seen ANS-2 also, they would have noticed a strong displacement of water as the creature appears to turn slightly and straighten its neck before diving. Dinsdale also wonders if the apparent transparency of the creature as found by GSW might not be an 'artifact' of the electronic image enhancing methods used — a remark all the more interesting in the light of Colin Bord's examination (see below) of the remaining duplicates of the GSW slide in which this 'edge transparency' could not be found.

It is regrettable that GSW did not examin the original. Their own findings are far from conclusive (bearing in mind, also, the hastiness and tentativeness of their programme) and must remain conjectural until they are confirmed or not by any further examinations. Doc has never objected to the detailed examination of the ANS-1 original by experts — to the contrary, he has always encouraged it for whatever new information it would add to the subject. It would be a foolish faker indeed who hastened his own exposure in this way.

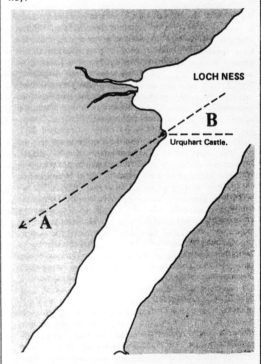

A map of the Urquhart Castle area of Loch Ness showing:
(A) a line pointing to the position of the sun ("up-sun") at 4 pm on 21 May 1977;
(B) the sweep of view within which the monster appeared, from the grounds of Castle Urquhart.

Recently other doubts have been raised: could the dense black patch in or on the water where the creature's neck enters the water be a shadow, or artificially produced by painting or as a composite picture? Another nagging question is why there should be a strong difference in contrast between the two pictures? The former questions are reasonably settled by the observations of Bord, Dinsdale and Harrison from their studies under high magnification. There is detail in that dark patch and it has the characteristics of a reflection, which in turn confirms the relative positions of the sun and photographer at that time and place. The question may have been stimulated by the black and white reproductions in FT22 and *Pursuit* Fall 1978, which simply do not do the colour original its due justice. Several stages of black and white rephotographing and photographic printing, and the mechanical process of screening or reducing to dots to make the printing plate, and the vagaries of printing itself tend to increase the contrast of any continuous toned photograph at each stage, effectively pushing the subtler tones towards white or black. The result is that the dense graduations of the darker grey in the reflection inevitably 'block in'. Although colour printing is subject to the same handicap, we hope that the laser colour-separation process used to make the plate on the back page will give a more helpful picture.

The difference in the contrast between the two photos is the result of different copying methods, as explained. ANS-1 is copied directly off the colour slide original. ANS-2 is probably the only remaining print (and not a good one) off a glass negative. The relation of this glass negative to the original print is not known precisely, but it is likely to be only once or twice removed from the colour original of ANS-2, both now lost to us. This glass slide was obviously intended for press reproduction and the contrast heightened deliberately in order to print the sort of image newspaper editors prefer (ie with less background, etc).

The mysterious dangers of the modern postal system are the only obstacle to further analysis — they've already claimed the original of ANS-2! Were it safe to do so we'd be only too happy to lend the original of ANS-1 to any sceptic for his own battery of tests and analyses. FT and FPL will attempt to procure a 'second opinion' here in the UK. In the meantime we offer the colour portrait of Nessie on the back page, printed as carefully as possible from a copy transparency prepared by Colin Bord to match the original for tone, colour and detail. We also take this opportunity to present the opinions of three expert examinations of the original of ANS-1, which go a long way to answering some of the questions raised.

COLIN BORD COMMENTS

As a co-founder of the Fortean Picture Library (in cooperation with Robert Rickard and my wife Janet) I am able to examine at leisure one of the two original frames of High Speed Ektachrome which Doc Shiels made at Loch Ness on 21 May 1977 and of which black and white reproductions have subsequently been published in FT22 and *Pursuit*, Fall 1978. I have been a professional commercial photographer for 25 years and have spent considerable time in studying the nature of light and its interactions with the physical world, as well as the problems involved with the

reproduction of this interaction by photographic means and the subsequent reproduction of photographic images on the printed page by photo-mechanical means.

WHAT DO WE HAVE? First let me state what I know does exist. FPL has in its safe keeping the original 35mm transparency of the first of the two colour transparencies (ANS-1) that were shot by Doc Shiels on 21 May 1977. The film used was High Speed Ektachrome and the camera and the exposure details have been published in FT22 and *Pursuit*, Fall 1978. The subject is under-exposed by about ½ stop and has fully saturated colours. The image definition is good (i.e. it is a sharp picture). The image of the object within the 24X36mm frame (standard 35mm size picture) is approximately 2mm from top to underline (please note this is a measurement of the size of the **image, not** an estimate of the size of the object photographed). So you can see it is quite a tiny image in the centre of a large expanse of water. I have spent appreciable time studying this transparency through a high-powered magnifier. I have also projected it on a screen to get a picture approximately 3 feet high. This represents a magnification of approximately 40 times, giving an image of the object over 3 inches in depth. All who have seen this have been impressed, though sceptics are not necessarily won over immediately.

The general appearance indicates that a warm toned low-angle light is coming over the photographer's right shoulder and illuminating the object, and this agrees with the details of location and time which the photographer gave us. The areas of light and shade suggest that this object is three-dimensional and approximately circular in cross section.

The object naturally reflects from the surface of the water, the reflection being broken by wavelets which conform to the surrounding water pattern. Within the object's reflection can be seen small patches of the same blue as the surrounding water, where the surface of a wavelet has reflected the sky, indicating that this is a completely natural reflection, and that the water is reflecting it and surrounds in a completely natural way. The pale tawny band does reflect in the water as would be expected and the image is naturally broken up by the wavelets, though the reflection does not have the same brightness as the original above it. The difference in brightness between this highlight and the rest of the reflection is very slight, and on the 8X6" black and white prints which I have carefully made via a black and white copy negative, the tonal variation is just discernible. A magazine reproduction made from such a black and white print would most likely lose this tonal variation unless it were made to the highest standards on a glossy paper. The loss of these tones in the shadows would cause the reflection to appear completely black. In fact, a study of the original transparency reveals that the highlight on the "teeth" appears to be no brighter than the brightest part of the pale tawny band on the front of the object. If it looks brighter in a magazine reproduction, that is due to the vagaries of the printing process.

CRITICISMS CONSIDERED. Now let us consider the objections:
1. Some critics reveal their confusion about the difference between shadows and reflections. This is not uncommon with people who are unfamiliar with both optics and photography. For a variety of reasons shadows can rarely be seen on the surface of water, especially at a distance. As the

transparency clearly shows that the sun is behind the photographer, criticisms based on the belief that the object is in silhouette (i.e. photographed with the sun shining into the lens) are quite irrelevant.

2. Some critics are apparently disturbed by the solid blackness of the reflection in the second picture (ANS-2). The difference between the two black and white reproductions is due to the fact that they were made from copy negatives made at different times by different people. The black and white copy negative used to produce the print of ANS-1 was carefully made by me working from the original colour transparency and I tried to retain maximum detail and tonal separation. The history of the print of ANS-2 is somewhat more involved. It seems that the second transparency was lost by the postal services en route to the USA. All that remained in England was a glass copy negative, very contrasty and lacking in detail. By the time the PFL had been formed and I was involved in the matter this glass negative had been accidently broken and all that remained of ANS-2 was a glossy black and white print of poor quality. I have made the best copy negative of this print I can, but when the mid-grey tones of a photograph have been lost by contrasty copying it is of course impossible to replace them.. When printing my copy negative of ANS-2 I have tried to match it to the tones of ANS-1. There is a little tonal variation within the 'neck' area of ANS-2 and the reflection does show some paler patches where the wavelets are breaking the image, but the tonal differences are so subtle that they will almost inevitably be lost when reproduced on a printed page. This happened when the pictures were reproduced in FT22 and although I have not yet seen the relevant issue of Pursuit I expect that it has happened here too.. Incidentally there are what appear to be a retoucher's brush marking the copy print of ANS-2, at the point where the neck enters the water. It looks as though some lighter areas near the underline have been 'toned down'. As this ANS-2 copy negative was made by a press photographer the retouching was probably done on the glass copy negative. The contrasty 'soot and white-wash' quality of this copy negative is typical of the type of negatives that newspaper blockmakers prefer to work from, as it gives a brighter reproduction on a poor quality newsprint than would a negative with a softer tonal range.

3. Forteans and Ufologists should not be dazzled by the phrase 'computer analysis'. A computer is simply a sophisticated electronic tool, and the usefulness of any tool depends on the skill and experience of the craftsman handling it. In the past GSW have revealed a very basic lack of knowledge of photographic technique and terminology, and most of the points of criticism made about the ANS-1 picture (and published in FT24) are ones which might be expected from the examination of a duplicate transparency. But they have no relevance to the original picture shot by Doc Shiels. As to their allegation that they can see wave ripples through the 'neck', I only wish this were true. I have examined the original at 40X magnification, but no wave ripples can be seen. I wish I could see some because this could support a theory advanced in the forthcoming book Alien Animals (written by Janet and myself, and to be published later this year). I have also examined an enlarged duplicate transparency similar to the one given to GSW, but can find no wave ripples in the 'neck' of this

either.

CONCLUSION. If these pictures are faked, I cannot detect how it was done. Such fakes certainly could not be called "crude". If they were produced by double-exposure or superimposition, they would need the services of a skilled laboratory staff and have to be the work of a skilled and well-equipped photographer. Having met the man, I do not think that either his photographic equipment (a fairly simple SLR) or his knowledge of photo techniques are up to it. The alternative is that he took a boat out into the loch with a buoyant life-size model abroad, popped it into the water, went ashore, photographed it twice in such a way that it changed shapes between shots, and went out again to retrieve it. All this on a fine afternoon in May at a famous tourist attraction. I find it simpler to believe in the existence of water monsters.

COLIN BORD
26 March 1979

TIM DINSDALE COMMENTS

I met Doc almost by chance about three years back when down in Cornwall investigating the Morgawr sea-serpent reports — and found him to be a quietly spoken, educated and amusing fellow, in contrast to the image he seems to create of himself of a somewhat wild eyed and outspoken eccentric. Later we corresponded at length about his undoubted encounter with Morgawr and the photos he and his co-witness obtained. Having had such a vast amount of correspondence with 'witnesses' at Loch Ness and Loch Morar over the years one gets quite good at assessing the veracity of their accounts by the manner in which they are presented. Certainly in Doc's case I got the feeling I was corresponding with a man of refreshing wit and honesty — with a real interest of both the paranormal, and the enigmatic but solidly real phenomena from Ness and Morar (vide 400 yard 'V' wakes for instance).

2. Subsequently, when he obtained the two colour stills at Loch Ness of a 'head and long neck-like' object in late May 1977 — my interest was aroused and I was intrigued by the events which followed resulting in the loss of the second original slide when posted to the USA, and the reactions caused by the first. It all seemed to be par for the course. Dramatic new photography obtained at Ness invariably produces a fierce backwash of opinion, claims and counterclaims, explanations and denigrations and a polarisation of views.

Later Doc sent me the original No 1 colour slide, and asked me to take care of it for him. I examined it microscopically, and found in it detail of profound interest to me as a photographer, pragmatist, and serious monster researcher, and fieldworker (I have spent some 430 days and nights living on and observing the surface of these lochs from boats and some ten years of shore based long-lens expeditionary work).

3. The next step was for me to ask Anthony Nicol Shiels if he would write an affidavit as to the circumstances of the photography — which he did on 14th November 1977, duly sworn out and witnessed under the provision of the Statutory Declarations Act 1835. [Copy on file with FT-Ed.]

4. Armed with this document I made private approaches to Royal Photographic Society of which I have long been member — enquiring whether it might be possible for one

of their scientists to examine the original colour transparency of the No 1 colour picture on High Speed Extrachrome. Within a short period a recent president of the RPS — Dr Vernon G.W. Harrison, a most distinguished photographic expert, examined the original, and wrote me a letter about the study he had made of it, which did not reveal anything to suggest that the picture had been faked. On the contrary, there was some very subtle detail in it which he had discovered when examining the image microscopically. He could not, however, commit himself as to what the image represented. It is necessary to read this letter in toto. [See below-Ed]

5. In December of 1977, I circulated a private and confidential set of notes about the Shiels pictures to those who I felt might be interested, and subsequently in early 1978 a private meeting was held in London, at which his photography, and the short super-8 colour movie sequence of a 'head and neck' obtained from shore at Loch Ness by Peter and Gwen Smith in August 1977, was shown and discussed. This resulted in the better sequence being submitted to the RAF for study — it being felt that with movie film there was a better chance of gaining definitive comment — and also because Dr Harrison's letter had already been written about the Shiels picture.

That is where the matter rests at present.

SOME PERSONAL OBSERVATIONS: Of the various objections, doubts and fears expressed over the Shiels pictures — which in truth are understandable, and in a way desirable, if we are to retain the use of our critical faculties — several can be explained away quite logically — and others reconsidered in the light of circumstances; for instance... the excessive illumination of the 'head and neck-like object' seen in the No 1 picture is in fact characteristic of objects seen on water in bright sunlight, where they are directly illuminated, and also indirectly receive a double dose of light reflecting off the water surface at a low angle. This produces an astonishing 'cine light' illumination effect, recognizable by those few people who observe such objects, over water, and under these conditions...furthermore, the excessively 'blue' water surface is again a combination of photographic circumstances — the sensitivity of H.S. Extachrome to UV light, the excess of UV light in bright sunlight over water, and reflecting off it produces an imbalance of 'blue' in the photograph...the reflections on the water have nothing to do with "shadows" cast by a sun behind the object— 180 degrees out of position as described by the photographer, who said it was behind him. Reflections are not shadows, for heavens sake, etc. etc.

An enlarged study of a big-as-possible print made from the No 1 picture reveals some astonishing and intricate detail which seems both natural, in one sense (the subtle curves of what appear to be neck muscles, for example) — and unexpected in another (the appearance of what could be eye and nostril features on the head).

All things considered, and this includes the possible alternatives such as models, painting, divers with glove puppets etc., the two Shiels pictures interest me enormously, and of course if they are real pictures, even a child can see they are the best still pictures ever obtained of what must surely be the head and neck of a large unknown animal.

At the same time, as still pictures they are proof of nothing but pictures...that is until further similar stills or movie photography are obtained by independent witnesses, showing similar objects.

Finally, in terms of the ever important human analysis, I place great faith in direct speech — the sort of down to earth comments people make when they are coming under fire. Under these circumstances, people tend to say exactly what they feel — and mean it.

TIM DINSDALE
27 March 1979

DR HARRISON'S LETTER TO DINSDALE

I have examined the photographic transparency stated to have been taken by Mr. A.N. Shiels on Saturday 21 May 1977 from the shore of Loch Ness in the vicinity of Castle Urquhart. This examination has been made through a binocular microscope at all magnifications up to X100. I find the transparency to be quite normal and there is not evidence of double exposure, superimposition of images or handwork with bleach or dye.

The object depicted is certainly not a branch of a tree, a trick of the light or an effect of uneven processing. Under magnification a small reptilian head is seen looking towards a point on the right of the photographer. The lighting comes from behind, and somewhat to the right of the photographer; and the foreshortening of the water shows that the object was photographed from a considerable distance through a long focus lens. The creature has a wide mouth, partly open, and light is reflected strongly from the lower lip, which is presumably wet. There is an indication of two eyes and a stubby nose. The head is attached to a long neck whose girth increases as it approaches the water. The neck is smooth and reflects the light strongly, and it appears to be paler in colour on its lower side. The course of the neck can be traced for some inches below the surface of the water until it is lost to view because of the turbidity of the water. The image of the submerged part is distorted by the surface wavelets of the water, and I find these distortions to be entirely naturalistic. There is even a wavelet that has been reflected back from the left side of the neck and caught the light of the sun.

It is not possible to say from a single still transparency exactly what the photograph represents. The obvious explanation is that the photograph depicts a living creature strongly resembling a Plesiosaurus. However, it could be a hoax. For example, a diver might have made a model of the head and neck and be holding it above the water while he himself was submerged. A third possibility is that the photograph is not of an outdoor scene at all, but is a reduction of an imaginative painting executed by a competent artist. To produce a sufficiently deceptive painting would require skill and a detailed knowledge of the effects of light reflected from, and transmitted through, rippled water; and it is just these effects which I find so impressive in the photograph.

While I feel that the alternative explanations I have suggested are not very plausible, they can only be excluded by a study of any independent evidence that may be available.

VGW HARRISON
3 December 1977

LAST WORDS

Quite apart from the relative merits or demerits of the photos themselves, there are two other factors that mitigate the acceptance of Doc's testimony and photos:

Firstly, Doc has never concealed the fact that he is a well-known Cornish eccentric, showman and magician (both on stage and in belief). He has written books on stage illusions for other magicians. Doc believes that he 'invoked' Nessie just as he 'invoked' Morgawr, the Cornish sea-serpent, by the use of ancient magic and psychic power, with the aid of a world-wide group of psychics who were conducting this specific experiment, and the help of a group of witches, including his daughters, who enacted their summoning ceremonies both in secret and in a well-publicised "sky-clad" swim off Mawnan Beach in the Helford Estuary (see FT16, and Doc's article in FT27). In his letters to us over many years Doc has shown himself to be widely read, extremely intelligent, refreshingly honest about every aspect and stage of his endeavours and experiments, and deeply interested in the relationship between Fortean phenomena, surrealism and magical belief. He will readily acknowledge that much of what he does is a song and dance, but points out that not only does humour have a purifying, protecting and sanity-stabilising effect, but there are strong correspondences between things and forces and the images of them. In his writings he shows a sound grasp of Fortean philosophy, and knows that his eccentricities will influence the credibility of his evidence. Nevertheless, he has pleaded for the impartial examination of that evidence.

Secondly, Doc seems to have defied the laws of probability according to those who value such things. There are people who spend much time and money, visiting Loch Ness or wherever every year in the hope of seeing something and each year leaving disappointed. But prior to the May 1977 photographing of Nessie, Doc had seen Morgawr (Cornish for 'sea giant') twice in the Helford Estuary. The second time, he was accompanied by David Clarke, editor of *Cornish Life;* they both took photographs, but Clarke's camera jammed giving a triple exposure (see FTs 19-23).

If this was a run of luck, Doc has not benefited from it much. In fact he firmly believes that this series of incidents has somehow "backfired" and made his family the focus of accidents and misfortune. So much so that Doc has asked us to announce his 'retirement'. In a letter dated early April, he writes: "Within the next few weeks I'm getting out of the psychic game. My witch-daughters are retiring from the monster-raising business too. As a final fling, Kate and I will have a last crack at Owlman (see FT27 — Ed.) and Morgawr... so we can say our farewells to them. I want to get on with other things, like painting and writing...we're all fed up with the 'backlash effect' of too much psychic gameplaying. Its caused some misery in the last few years. We — Kate and I — would like you to announce that we're no longer playing witch and wizard after May 1st. I may give up busking too, for a while. BUT...please don't think I'm turning respectable! Perish the thought...I know that some of our supporters would prefer me to be less 'odd', but as I've said before, that would be dishonest."

I feel sure we haven't heard the last of Doc, or his photographs.

BOB RICKARD

Spellcraft
A Manual of Verbal Magic
ROBIN SKELTON

Robin Skelton, the distinguished poet and man of letters has written a readable and informative account of the making of spells. Spells are, of course, a staple ingredient of magical processes and can be used for good ends and bad. Robin Skelton firmly supports their use in white magic and as a weapon in the sexual armoury. The book concludes with a chapter on how to make them for one's own purposes. 0 7100 8887 6   *Illustrated* £3.95

The New Waite's Compendium of Natal Astrology
With Ephemeris for 1880-1980 and Universal House Tables
COLIN EVANS
Revised and brought up to date by Brian E. F. Gardener
'There is a mass of information in this book of great interest to astrologers. A notable work.' – *Light*
0 7100 0183 5 *Illustrated* **now in paperback** £2.50

The Mantram Handbook
EKNATH EASWARAN

A mantram, the repetition of of spiritual formula requires no special setting, time or equipment, and it can be used effectively by people of any age or way of life. Here Eknath Easwaran explains how the mantram can bring about evenness of mind and increased concentration, physical relaxation and freedom from undesirable habits.
0 7100 8974 0   *paperback* £2.50

The Tao of Health and Longevity
DA LIU

By contrast with the West the Chinese have an ancient Taoist tradition which regards healthy longevity as not just a problem for the elderly but for the young as well. Here Da Liu explains this approach and shows how Taoist health and longevity practices when performed correctly can affect all aspects of life, spiritual as well as physical.
0 7100 0079 0   *paperback* £2.95

Routledge & Kegan Paul
39 Store Street, London WC1

RKP

Now, if we're sitting comfortably, I'd like to welcome you one and all to the utter depths of filth, degradation and depravity, for this column — those of nervous disposition and/or a tendency to lose control of their bodily functions are advised to beat it smartish — is devoted to a vile and pernicious canker: rock music, with special and peculiar reference to science-fictional, or even (if we're lucky) Fortean content and things that go bump in your tweeters. May I therefore, then, extend cordial and slime-pickled thanks to your courageous editor for allowing something so low on the evolutionary scale as (shriek!) a rock critic access to these pages; may he remain free of ulcers or coronary thrombosis on my account...

Of course, I always thought rock'n'roll (as we australopithicenae are prone to refer to it) was about wholesome, lighthearted activities like sex and drugs and cruising freeways in decomposing Studebakers and love and a spot of how's-your-father in the backseat and, well, sex and probably more sex as well, but even my parents suspected different; they knew it was all a germ-warfare pinko plot to enslave the pointed little minds of Western youth. How right they were. Myself I haven't voted since I discovered the stuff and am now sufficiently steeped in this dangerous substance to actively shun the attentions of Young Conservatives and church outings to *No Sex Please, We're British.*

But, y'know, this all came as a total revelation to me, and I am therefore much indebted to the demented Mrs Leuken[1] and her jovial 'Faithful and True Roman Catholics' for certain information on the matter contained in one of her public service diatribes; "Your children are bringing demons into your homes... called 'rock', 'hard rock' — they were produced in the temple of Satan (sic)... You do not understand, my children, but many of your... recording companies are under the control of Wicca, the international organisation of witches and warlocks. Do not laugh! It is true!" O c'mon, dear Mrs Leuken, not one infinitely weeny titter? No, don't mock, because — leaving aside the fact that may have occurred to the more perceptive among you, that Mrs L. can't point to so much as one gold chalice inscribed with festive qabbalistic symbols, presented by said companies for enslavement of one million souls — there's a terrifying inference here and it boils down (Heh, heh, bubble, bubble...) to this: if your old lady has a scar on her left wrist, under her left (blush) breast or is given to leaping out the window clad in nowt but foul-reeking ointment, she's not only a witch but (shriek!) a *record executive.* Do not laugh! It is true! And since my present in-house ladyfriend is quite partial to a spot of Todd Rundgren or Dwight Twilley on occasion, I can only

conclude that I should henceforth ensure that my coffee doesn't bubble or squeak before imbibing.

Not that Mrs Leuken is alone in her cute, acute observations, oh no. Not only do I seem to recall the same feeble-cranial tirades emanating over the years from a rancid rag called, inspirationally enough, *The Plain Truth,* but I have in my possession (if it hasn't spontaneously combusted, that is) an amusing little document headed *The Illuminati*[2] (obviously a punk band) by one Dr Charles C Younts, BR.ED., B.TH., DD., Pastor to the Calvary Baptist Tabernacle, Professor to the Toledo Bible College and meal ticket to his analyst, in which we learn that John Todd[3] is behind all this. And who's behind *is* John Todd, anyway?

Well, it appears that Todd, Ohio's entry in this year's Aleister Crowley Lookalike Contest, is "Manager of Zodiac Prods., the largest Rock Concert Booking Agency in the world", even, and "Zodiac Productions features (sic) the Beatles who took their name from Scarab of Egypt". I don't suppose it'll do much good to cough politely and shuffle-footedly proffer the information that not only don't Zodiac Productions **exist**, but the Beatles haven't made any records (hellish or otherwise) together for ten years, and those they've produced apart aren't worth an incubus's fart, now, would it? What label are Scarab of Egypt on, anyway?

Let's dig deeper into the goo. It also appears that Three Dog Night are in a coven in Arizona (probably 'cause nobody else would have them) and Santana are in a coven in South America, which is peculiar, because Devadip Carlos Santana — he of the antiseptic white suit and consecrated guitar — is prone to cut albums of such luminous, God-glorifying, devotional intensity that no critic worth his earring will touch one with a ten-foot, incense-flavoured taper. And hot on the heels of this little bauble, as if to clinch the whole soggy deal, we are regaled with the intelligence that Crosby of Crosby, Stills, Nash, Freud and Jung, is "almost dead from a $200 a day heroin habit". Startling news, since said Crosby is currently bouncing with ruddy health, weighs in at about fifteen stone and closely resembles the Beach Ball from the 'Dark Star' movie with a walrus moustache. Furthermore, it does occur to your brainwiped scribe that Neil Young, of that illustrious combo, was so horrified and shaken by the twin deaths of his friends Danny Whitten and Bruce Berry from hitting the needle that he toured (with Crazy Horse) with a show that totally alienated his audience, in which he sang harrowing, sickly little songs like 'Tired Eyes', 'The Needle and the Damage Done', and 'Tonight's the Night' in a shaky, lost voice while a single lightbulb burned over the stage, the whole purpose of which was to scare potential hard-drug users witless. The resulting semi-live album, *Tonight's the Night* lost him about eight zillion sales units as a consequence, and he's shown no signs as yet of having been programmed or otherwise zapped by Mr Todd. Like someone once said; everything you know is wrong. Including that.

Wait, there's more. It seems that nobody can make a record without first proving their Occult connections, the mandatory mutilated left wrist, see? Now, in order to check out this rivetting snippet, I chanced to peer rudely at the left wrist of the last recording musician I chanced across — in point of fact it was Ashley Hutchings of the Excellent Albion Band, whose records I commend to you, and he's made simply scads of the little buggers, believe me — and by this serious study (I really *did* look, y'know) ascertained this either to be a palpable untruth or Ashley is a genius with body makeup. But, of course, I'm in the music biz myself and you shouldn't believe me; rock journalists are world-renowned for making things disappear instantaneously in a puff of ozone, particularly drink, food, drugs, women and advance pressings of records.

And then Dr Younts hits paydirt: "The rock group Kiss were ordered to form. Kiss means *King in Satanic Service*". Furthermore, we learn, their music comes from demons and is bespoke to enslave the susceptible and three of them are fairies, too. Well, I dunno about the last bit but I'm damn sure that their sex organs in no way resemble yours. Or even mine, perhaps. But there's a bit of twisted-ass truth in here somewhere.

Kiss, in point of fact, are a loathsome aggregation who do sell millions of elpees (as we pseuds call them) in the US by the simple expedient of dressing up in cretinous, studded-leather, lizard jumpsuits, cavorting from one lunatic pose to another and playing music (?) of such assinine ineptitude that only a teenager or a person with tin ears would get off on it. As if that didn't threaten my security enough, they also peddle a nasty concept called the 'Kiss Army', borrow the lightning-flash SS symbol of Third Reich fame (one of the great hits of the forties) and seem to get photographed drooling over the shoulder of everyone from Jimmy Carter to Johnny Cash. Oh yes, they're never seen without their greasepaint either.

Personally, I think they're the goods, the real McCoy. Kiss don't possess the intellect of an enchanted, inebriated toad (three-legged or otherwise) yet they probably could, right now, mobilise a zomboid, rabid mob large enough to overrun the White House, the Pentagon, Wembley Stadium or any other major centre of occult practices. Dr Younts doesn't need the Illuminati; one look at the word 'Kiss' and I said twelve Hail Marys and jumped out the windown.

Next time I'll probably (if I'm allowed to live after this) be revealing how the state of Tennessee is full of musician descendants of the lost Sumerian tribe of Banjo. Perhaps.

Oh, a last quote from Dr Younts: "Christian Rock is also satanic". Mr Rock , are you gonna take that lying down? Call your lawyer. Now!

NOTES
1) For Veronica Leuken's visions of the Virgin Mary at Bayside and Flushing, NY, see 'Visions' last issue — FT28p3-5.
2) A duplicated pamphlet published by the Society of Jesus Christ, Box 6919, Toledo, Ohio 43613, USA. (FT received a copy through the good offices of Dave Fideler's Michigan Anomaly Research outfit, who was sent it by Sig Humanski, an FT reader and teacher in Toledo. Sig was presented it by one of his students who in turn received it from his father. True!—Ed.)
3) See the piece on John Todd's bizarre involvement in FT26p52.

Steve Burgess is an editor of Dark Star magazine.

Roger STEADman 78

The **Full** and **True** Text of a *Notorious, Remarkable* and *Visionary Speech* made by John, Viscount Amberley, Earl RUSSELL, on the 18th., of July 1978 at 9.8p.m. in the **HOUSE OF LORDS.**

"The Police should turn into the Salvation Army... Mr. Brezhnev and Mr. Carter are really the same person... Naked bathing ought to be universal.. Three quarters of the National Income should go to girls being given houses of their own at the age of twelve to have as many husbands as they liked, the men to live in communal huts... The Royal Family is pampered, decadent and snobbish.. The official rating of the human race in the Northern Hemisphere is TOAD! What are you? spiritless papal bumboys? Forward the Creative Spirit!.."

and much much more! Now available at 60 pence including post & packing from OPEN HEAD PRESS, 2, Blenheim Crescent, London, W.11.

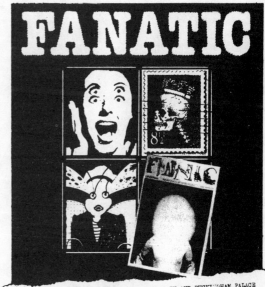

FANATIC

WHICH MAG DARES FLYPOST THE LAW COURTS, CENOTAPH AND BUCKINGHAM PALACE TO PROMOTE ITS VISIONARY WARES? **THE FANATIC!** Issue number Five out now: with Robert Crumb on This Here Modern America, Abbie Hoffman fucking Communism up the Bum (from somewhere on the Run), David Solomon (author of first acid anthology) writes on the New Ordure, or the Shape of Shit to Come, extracted from Shit Power! (to be completed when the powers that shouldn't be release him from Bristol Jail), John Michell finally demystifies Hitler & reveals him as a failed comic with some hitherto unknown and choicely selected sparks from the Fuehrer, the Love Life of Elizabeth II, Hermaphrodite Spread Shots, the full text of the Secret Gemstone File, Unusual Tortures, Nameless Wildness and much much more that's either unmentionable or unspeakable. 60 heavy pages plus colour "A stunning new bloom in the radical press desert.." £1.25 (incl) from OPEN HEAD PRESS, 2, BLENHEIM CRESCENT, LONDON, W.II. INN.

BILL SANDERSON

Devil Names and Fortean Places

Many Fortean researchers have noted the high correlation between names of places and the strange events that happen in their vicinities. Often it is the Devil who gets the blame for the weird, and here leading Am-American researcher Loren Coleman, author of numerous Fortean articles and co-author of THE UN-IDENTIFIED, 1975, and CREATURES OF THE OUTER EDGE, 1978, enlarges on the theme.

When Western Europeans landed in the New World, and started spreading across what was later to become America, they discovered what the Amerindians already knew; there were some strange places in this new land. Certain locations were "strange" because the early explorers and settlers would see, hear, smell or feel strange things — e.g., weird globs of light, eerie screechings, sickening sweet odours, cold drafts of air as well as UFOs, mystery animals and other "inexplicables." [See David Fideler's companion article for a Fortean's idea of just what these "certain locations", these "gateways" are all about, beginning next issue — Ed.] The interface between these newcomers and the decidedly unexplainable phenomena produced place-names which attempted to reflect the notion that the locales were special, different and indeed, strange. The names can take many forms, but I have long noticed an American historical acknowledgement of Forteana-ridden places by way of the use of the word "devil" in the naming of these localities. A few examples will illustrate this point:

A) Some of the more frequent sightings of California's phantom black panthers occur in the Diablo (Spanish for "devil") Valley, east of San Francisco. The Las Trampas Regional Park booklet notes the black cat is referred to as "The Black Mountain Lion of Devil's Hole", because it is frequently seen on the slopes of Mt. Diablo, and in the Devil's Hole area of the park. Mystery lights also turn up in the Mt. Diablo — Diablo Valley area frequently. [1]

In 1873, a live frog was found in a slab of limestone in a mine on Mt. Diablo, and in 1806, Spanish General Vallejo encountered a man-like apparition (which had exotic plumage and made "diving movements") while battling the Bolgones Indians. [2] Monte de Diablo is a very strange place.

B) The territory known as Devil's Kitchen in southern Illinois was avoided by the region's Amerindians because of their awareness of its sinister nature. Southern Illinois, in general, is a frequent host of mystery animals and UFOs [3,4] as well as the site of pre-Columbian stone walls which form a rough alignment between the Ohio and Mississippi rivers. [5]

Near Grand Tower, also in southern Illinois, is a small rocky hill known as the Devil's Bake Oven. South of that prominence is a longer hill known as the Devil's Backbone. Speaking of the Devils Bake Oven, folklorist John W. Allen observes: "On those nights when the hill was flooded with gentle moonlight, visitors would report that they had seen a weird and mistlike creature . . . floating silently across their pathway to disappear among the rocks or in the dense bushes on the hillside. This disappearance was often followed by moans, wails and shrieks such as only a ghost can make". [6]

C) Devil's Lake of Wisconsin has its share of geological oddities such as glacier scratches on unusual rock formations and petrified sand waves of an ancient sea [7], but it is the Amerindian mounds which are especially interesting. Three major effigy mounds are located in Devil's Lake State Park. "One in the shape of a bear and another which resembles a lynx are at the north end of the lake. A bird-shaped mound is at the south end". [8] Did the mound-builders wish to acknowledge real animals or phantom creature forms which haunted the shores of Devil's Lake?

From nearby Baraboo (a mere three miles north of Devil's Lake on Wisconsin 123!), at least a decade ago, there were stories circulating of giant ghost elephants. Or were they mastodons? [9] And finally, August Derleth, author and follower of H.P. Lovecraft, liked this area of south-central Wisconsin because he felt it contains "Cthulhu power zones". [10]

D) One of my favorite examples of the reflection of Fortean phenomena via a "devil name" comes from one corner of the inland town of Chester, New Hampshire, on Rattlesnake Hill. A cavern there of "great notoriety in all the country round" bears the name of Devil's Den. According to local legends, the path leading to the cave "was always kept open, in summer and in winter, by the passing to and fro of evil spirits who frequented the place, though themselves invisible to the eyes of mortal men." [11]

The poet J.G. Whittier put the Devil's Den traditions into verse, and the following two stanzas from that poem give deep insight into bedevilled places, in general:

"Tis said that this cave is an evil place —
The chosen haunt of the fallen race —
That the midnight traveller oft hath seen
A red flame tremble its jaws between,
And lighten and quiver the boughs among,
Like the fiery play of a serpent's tongue;
That sounds of fear from its chambers swell —
The ghostly gibber, — the fiendish yell;
That bodiless hands at its entrance wave, —
And hence they have named it The Demon's Cave.

Yet is there something to fancy dear
In this silent cave and its lingering fear, —
Something which tells of another age,

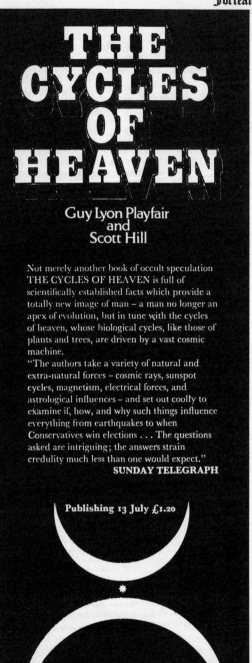

THE CYCLES OF HEAVEN

Guy Lyon Playfair
and
Scott Hill

Not merely another book of occult speculation THE CYCLES OF HEAVEN is full of scientifically established facts which provide a totally new image of man – a man no longer an apex of evolution, but in tune with the cycles of heaven, whose biological cycles, like those of plants and trees, are driven by a vast cosmic machine.

"The authors take a variety of natural and extra-natural forces – cosmic rays, sunspot cycles, magnetism, electrical forces, and astrological influences – and set out coolly to examine if, how, and why such things influence everything from earthquakes to when Conservatives win elections . . . The questions asked are intriguing; the answers strain credulity much less than one would expect."

SUNDAY TELEGRAPH

Publishing 13 July £1.20

Pan Books

Of the wizard's wand, and the Sybil's page,
Of the fairy ring and the haunted glen,
And the restless phantoms of murdered men:
The grandame's tale, and the nurse's song —
The dreams of childhood remembered long;
And I love even now to list the tale
Of the Demon's Cave, and its haunted vale. [12]

Simply stated, the strange events of the past are often remembered in the geographical names of the area. Place-names can be a Fortean's clue to the "haunted vale". I know of over one hundred and twenty-five places with "devil names" in the United States, and I am finding more correlations with this list and Forteana every day. I suspect many more etymological connections exist. My list of "devil names" is just the tip of the pitchfork.

Indeed, the United Kingdom abounds with fertile devil sites for the curious researcher. Evan Hadingham in *Circles and Standing Stones* writes: "There are countless names and stories connecting ancient sites with giants and devils, such as the Devil's Arrows alignments at Boroughbridge, Yorkshire, or the name Devil's Quoits associated with Stanton Drew." [13]

Geographical "devil names" worldwide may indicate, as they seem to in America, locales high in Fortean energy and strangeness. These places deserve some extra attention, for from the stray sod to the fairy ring, and the haunted glen to the Devil's Den, there lies many a riddle to unfold.

Loren Coleman

BIBLIOGRAPHY

1. Coleman, Loren
   1978   "California Odyssey: Observations on the Western Para-panther," *Anomaly Research Bulletin* 23, Special Non-Linear Issue.
2. Brandon, Jim
   1978   *Weird America* E.P. Dutton, New York (pp. 42-43).
3. Coleman, Loren
   1971   "Mystery Animals in Illinois," *FATE*, March.
4. Clark, Jerome and Loren Coleman
   1978   *Creatures of the Outer Edge*, Warner, NY, NEL, London.
5. Coleman, Loren F.
   1970   "Pre-Columbian Stone Structures in Southern Illinois", *NEARA Newsletter*, Milford, New Hampshire. (Also, in William R. Corliss' *Ancient Man: A Handbook of Puzzling Artifacts*, Glen Arm, Md., 1978.)
6. Allen, John W.
   1963   *Legends and Lore of Southern Illinois*, Southern Illinois University Press, Carbondale, Illinois.
7. Wisconsin Writer's Project
   1941   *Wisconsin*, Duell, Sloan and Pearce, New York.
8. Folsom, Franklin
   1971   *America's Ancient Treasures*, Rand McNally and Company, New York.
9. Auburn, James
   1970   Personal Communication.
10. Brandon, Jim
    1978   Op. cit., (p. 245).
11. Drake, Samuel Adams
    1971   (reprint) *A Book of New England Legends and Folk Lore*, Charles E. Tuttle and Co., Rutland, Vermont. (Originally published 1884).
12. Whittier, J.G.
    1971   (reprint) In Drake ibid.
13. Hadingham, Evan
    1976   *Circles and Standing Stones*, Anchor Press/ Doubleday, Garden City, New York.

continued from p25

nant. "In fact the whole kampung knew," she added. But the doctor told Ramlah that she would have to be operated on, and she became scared and kept away from him.

So far so good. On 17 February 1978, she went into labour, at her home. Her husband, Hamzah bin Abbas, was at home too, but there is no mention of him witnessing what followed... indeed, he is hardly mentioned at all, neither confirming or denying his wife's story, which runs as follows:

"After having the pain for more than an hour I became dizzy and just then I saw a woman dressed in white. The woman circled around me three times and took something out of a basket and choked by throat (sic; we do not know if the 'something' was choked by the throat, or whether it was Ramlah's throat that was choked. But on with the story...) Then I felt relieved and saw only the navel and feet of my baby. I felt cold kisses on my cheek and saw the woman taking away the baby. I pleaded with her not to do so but she left the house and disappeared".

The ghostly woman, also said to be wearing a yellow shawl, was not seen by anyone else, though Cik (Mrs) Salasiah, a padi planter, came to the house and saw Ramlah in labour. But she did not see the baby being delivered, or any blood. However, she thought she heard someone leaving the house when Ramlah felt no more pain. On the following night, the baby was apparently brought back for Ramlah to breastfeed, but then presumably taken away again. And there, too, our story runs out, alas... *New Straits Times* (Malaysia) 19 February, 1978.

Credit: Garry Abbott, J P Kain, D Tame, Ion Will. SM

Recent issues of FT have seen torrents of data on falls of ice-chunks slime, spiders' webs, nuts, clods of grass, stones and money... and there seems no end to these events. They still happen. We hadn't heard the good old 'Sahara sand' explanation for quite a while, so this time we'll have a few sand falls.

MUD IN YOUR EYE

In mid-February a "yellow snow" fell on part of Vienna — about a week later reports from Poland and Yugoslavia, facing their worst winter in years, also reported a blanket of yellow snow. In Poland, it was said, examination disclosed that a layer of sand had fallen on the snow discolouring it. Vienna's meteorological institute claimed a solution: this gaudy grit had been sucked up by whirlwinds in the Sahara, swept across Europe "by a fast upward airstream" to come down with the snow in Northern Europe. Satisfying as this theory may be to tiny meteorological minds, one has to boggle at the notion of such quantities of sand i) keeping together in the air; and ii) not decorating the intervening countries on the way! *Sunday Express* 18 Feb 1979; *Daily Telegraph* 24 Feb 1979; *Guardian* 26 Feb 1979.

In 1976 the Swedish National Science Council set up a Sahara dust study group, with international scientists. A Swedish geographer, Prof Anders Rapp, said the precise processes of dust formation and transport are "poorly understood", but notes significantly that the famous dust storms are not made up of sand — sand tends to be blown *along* the desert, not upwards — but topsoil is disappearing at an alarming rate. Writing in the *Sunday Times* 4 Sept 1977, John Worrall said that there was "little evidence of Sahara or Sahel dust moving southwards; the main movement is westwards across or into the Atlantic,

"though he does acknowledge that there have been identifications (or alleged identifications) of Sahara sand from Israel to Scandinavia, as well as the Cape Verde Islands, Bermuda, Bahamas and the West Indies. As regards the westward erosion, atmospheric sampling by aircraft suggest the movement of a staggering 40-60 million tons of dust a year across or into the Atlantic.

Westward. 1977 seemed a year for wet sandstorms. 3 March — red dust found on top of fresh snow in the Minneapolis-St Paul area of Minnesota. The local US Weather Bureau, who haven't yet heard of the Sahara getout, blamed a dust-storm over a drought area in the south-west. *Independent* (Marshall, Minn) 4 March 1977. I don't know if there was a dust-storm then in the south-west US, but coincidentally (whatever that means) a few days later, over the weekend 5-6 March, a "red rain" fell over parts of West Scotland. The Scottish weathermen are à la mode — Sahara blamed. *Daily Telegraph* 8 March 1977; Wolverhampton *Express & Star* 8 March 1977. End of March — a "fine yellow dust" settling on Japan. I suppose if you keep going west from the Sahara, you'd reach any part of the East! This time we're back among the backward: droughts in north-east China are blamed. *Daily Telegraph* 30 March 1977. 20 June (I think) — a rain of dust, said to be Sahara sand, fell on Nuremberg, West Germany, for 2 hours. *Reveille* 24 June 1977. 13 August — during the night yellow dust coats the trees, houses and cars of Springwell Estate, Sunderland, Co Durham. A novelty...local officials are at a loss to explain! Sunderland *Echo* 18 Aug 1977. Late Dec — during fierce wind and rain damage bad enough to have a state of emergency declared in one Californian county, northern parts of the state were treated to a celestial facepack as rain reportedly fell through a dust cloud created by 100mph winds. *Daily Telegraph* 23 Dec 1977.

I can be as discriminating as our selective whirlwinds. I separate out 2 accounts of yellow rains from the jaundiced jactitations of 1977, because not Sahara sand is blamed, but a veritable blizzard of bee dung. Over the last 3 weeks of June 1977, yellow spots kept appearing on cars, patios, roofs etc of Des Moines, Washington. It was bee-dung said the Puget Sound Air Pollution Control Agency. It was moth-dung said professor of zoology, John Edwards, University of Washington. Interestingly, mention is made of an airborne malaise that began in the Seattle area in April 1954 — an oily ash that ate holes into windscreens — spreading to California, Oregon, Ohio and Illinois. *Constitution* (Atlanta, Georgia) 30 June 1977; *New Castle News* (Pennsylvania) 6 July 1977. Mysterious yellow rains repeatedly fell on the Cameron Highlands of Malaysia, drying to a powder. The exudations of insects was mooted, but others pointed out that the falls were reported over a huge area. Regretfully no other details available. *New Straits Times* (Malaysia) 7 July 1977 (or 7.7.77, for number freaks).

We have a few other unrecorded dust falls. On the 1st July 1968, a fine powder the texture of womens' face-powder fell on many parts of southern England and Wales. Dust coloured white, yellow and orange-red were reported, and rains of yellow and pink. At Cardiff there was both a layer of red dust and red hailstones up to 7cm diameter, about tennis-ball size if you've no ruler handy. Exceptionally high temperatures over Spain were blamed for keeping Sahara sand aloft after storms in North Africa — pretty hypothetical as usual. *Leicester Mercury* 1 July 1968. Ron Dobbins sends us a datum not in Fort's *Books* — that on 13 & 14 Feb 1870 showers of fine reddish sand fell in parts of Italy with the rain. Nothing changes much — Sahara sand blamed. *Eclectic Magazine* June 1870, 74: 766.

On 29 January 1979, residents of Hoboken, Belgium, awoke to find a carpet of black snow. Police said they had no explanation, and a local anti-pollution group made the most of the opportunity to 'investigate' the Overpelt lead works in the town. If the factory was the culprit why hadn't it happened there before? *Melbourne Sun* (Australia) 30 Jan 1979.

From the Guillotiere district of Lyon, Belgium, we learn that sometime early in February 1979 (unfortunately no date is given), locals found spots and stains covering stationary cars and the fruit and vegetables of the market-gardens at Place Jean-Mace. A light shower of blue water had left indelible marks everywhere. The reporter in *La Lanterne* (Belguim) 12 Feb 1979, theorizes about particles of paint in suspen-

sion in the atmosphere, brought down by the rain. If so, how the particles were accounted for is omitted.
An interesting detail : just prior to the blue rain, residents noticed strong gas-like smells of unknown origin lingering all over the area.

More recently a strange orange rain fell on the Crimean city of Yalta, leaving a layer of thick rust-coloured dust when it dried. Soviet newspapers quoted their scientists blaming it on airborne dust from Turkey. This proves nothing except the sameness of scientists everywhere. *International Herald Tribune* 24 April 1979.

FISHING LINES AND SEEDS
Automotive plant worker, John Wright, saw something snagged on a bush behind his Greensburg, Ohio, home — it was a fishing line. He pulled it off the bush but it seemed to have no end, trailing off into the sky. With the help of neighbours he pulled in about 1000 feet of line, filling 8 reels, with no sign of a kite or whatever to account for its continuing presence in the sky. It broke and floated away, with people following it until it was lost sight of in the sky. Perhaps it was Charlie, sitting on the edge of his Super Sargasso Sea, toying with us. After all he did write: "I think we're fished for." Story from *Post-Dispatch* (St Louis, Missouri) 24 Sept 1978.

Pensioner Rowland Moody, of South Mill Rd., Southampton, claims that in different days various kinds of seeds came down with the snow into his garden — maize, dried peas, mustard and cress and broad beans. He called in the police in case he was the victim of a, uh, vegetable plot. He believes the first rain of mustard and cress seeds was genuine, and that as news got out local wags began playing tricks on him. Mystery unsolved. A Sunday night 'consumer' show on BBC TV, had a few laffs at this story's expense — but I suppose I'm more amazed that something Fortean got airtime. A new sensation — we're becoming respectable! *Daily Mirror* 19 Feb 1979.

When we spoke to Mr Rowland, who remembers the 1968 sand-fall, he readily gave us more details. The falls began on 12 Feb, occurring intermittently over the next few days. He was in his conservatory potting seeds, and outside it was snowing from the East with strong gusts of wind. He heard the

seeds hit the house, cascading onto the roof, falling into his garden and the neighbouring gardens each side. The first fall was of cress seeds. They were cylindrical and coated in a jelly which glued them to fingers, shoes and other surfaces. Mr Rowland insisted he was not exaggerating when he said "millions" came down — he estimated about 500 in any 6 inch square. With the recent thaw and rain the little devils are sprouting everywhere (doormat, cracks in paving, flowerbeds, etc); now an inch high and tasting like normal cress. The second fall was of mustard seeds, tiny spheres with a distinctive smell, also in great quantities. Although he regrets not going upstairs to see these falls, he says that the neighbour's boy, 13, saw one fall, teeming down from a small black cloud! The maize, beans and peas seemed different to the observed falls, in that these seeds were *dried* and just appeared on the ground. Mr Rowland suspects a prank by local boys, since the mysterious appearances stopped as soon as the police were notified. Mr Rowland called the press, hoping to get some university or government scientists to investigate, and he's disappointed nothing came of that. Several weathermen he spoke to acknowledge the phenomena of falling materials and animals, but would not mention it publicly. The usual explanation for such falls is — a whirlwind. But where would such quantities of different seeds lie around waiting to be snatched into the sky? Mr Rowland couldn't tell if any vegetation and debris came down with the seeds — at least none was noticeable. He still has some seeds — if any of our readers could properly identify them, please contact us as soon as possible. Here's a good opportunity for a thorough study.

Finally, a conjectural fall. On the back doorstep of a house in Lyndhurst Avenue, Grimsby, a medallion dated 1923-24 was found after recent snow had melted. It had not been there before the snow. Praps it teleported? Scunthorpe *Evening Telegraph* 24 Feb 1979.

Credit: Frank Adey, Janet Bord; Ron Dobbins, Mark A Hall, Valerie Martin, Paul Pinn, Paul Screeton, Thoth, Henri Premont, Has Thomas. RG Twine, Nigel Watson, Ion Will, Will Zeiser.
RJMR

Of all the phenomena with which we deal, perhaps the most common is that of poltergeists and ghosts, from simple apparitions to furniture hurling furies, overlapping with nearly every other category of phenomena. Here we present a few poltergeists who play with fire.

ETHEREAL ARSONISTS

Returning to our own shores, we have a tale of the Blagdon Inn, Paignton, Devon, and the ghost of John Henry, who lived in the pub a hundred years ago, and committed suicide. At least, he's the one who's blamed for strange noises in the night and smashing bottles. Unfortunately, 'John Henry' rather lost his temper after a New Year party in 1978; Landlord Ian Emslie had hired a local comic to raise a laugh at the party. The comic's theme was funny phantoms... and perhaps it's coincidence, and perhaps John Henry was annoyed... but the pub burned down that evening, soon after the guests had left. Emslie blamed the ghost, and I suppose a man who's just sustained £30,000 worth of damage to his pub has the right to blame whoever he chooses! *Daily Mirror* 4 January 1978.

And another tale of revenge: John Ingham, 43, his wife Dylys, 40, and their daughter Lorraine, 18, had lived quite peacably in their 400-year old cottage for some time. Then Mr Ingham, a construction company manager, decided to renovate the cottage, which stands in the Isle of Sheppey, Kent. Beneath the floorboards he discovered a rough wooden effigy, about a foot tall; a man with his hands by his side, and seemingly wearing some sort of monk's habit. Mr Ingham "knew it was evil", wouldn't let anyone else touch it, and burned it immediately. Perhaps that was a mistake...

Shortly afterwards, Mrs Ingham began to have forebodings. The sideboard would shake, the windows rattle, and their Christmas tree was thrown over as they watched. They never saw the ghost, but Mrs Ingham would hear a child giggling and calling her name. She tried talking to the voice, and it told her

its initials were M.S. and that he had curly ginger hair. But when asked to leave, he merely giggled. Events centred on the study, where the effigy was found. Daughter Lorraine refused to stay in the house on her own after hearing the voice one night. When her parents returned home she was hysterical, not daring to go into the study in case 'it' grabbed her.

Mr Ingham became a changed man too. He and his wife began to have violent rows for the first time in 23 years of marriage, and eventually he walked out and stayed with a friend for two months. And while he was away, a fire started: as his wife was sleeping under heavy sedation upstairs, a blaze began in the study, apparently at the spot where the effigy had been found. A passing coalman saw the fire and rescued Mrs Ingham, but police and firemen could find no logical cause for the fire. After that, Mr Ingham 'came to his senses' and returned home, since when the disturbances have subsided somewhat.

Checking in the Kent County Council archives, they found that a family called Sole lived in the same street 200 years previously, and that they had a 10-year old son who drowned; but they could not find his initial. Nonetheless, they decided he was probably the one responsible, and a spiritualist that visited the house confirmed their view. A convenient conclusion, but we can only wonder what connection there might have been between an apparently ritualistic effigy and a 10-year old boy who didn't even live in the same house...*News of the World* 15 January 1978.

And still the fiery furies rampage through the world. They seem to have a liking for throwing stones, too, and that is how our next tale begins. Ex-boxer

Lazarus "Tucks" Pochaka and his then-pregnant wife, Annacleto, lived in the Orlando East area of Soweto, South Africa. On 10th May 1978, a stone was hurled through the bedroom window, and Mrs Pochaka was slapped and throttled by the 'creature'. In the next few days, curtains began to catch fire, and the furniture was wrecked and burned too. Mr Pochaka's shoes and socks began to cavort through the air, and a shoe hit him on the thigh. On Sunday the 15th, a church service was held in the house, in an attempt to discourage the poltergeist. Nonetheless, on the Monday there was the usual pitiful sight: burned and wrecked furniture dumped in the yard, most of the windows broken, and Mrs Pochaka scared to go into the house.

However, on Tuesday an unnamed official from the West Rand Administration Board turned up and "explained" everything: it was all an electrical fault, he said... nothing but a short-circuit. The Pochakas didn't believe him. They organised another prayer-meeting for the same night, during which a bag of salt was hurled from the kitchen into the dining room, which is where the group were praying. Perhaps the ghost was trying to exorcise the exorcists, but unfortunately we have no more details of how this confrontation worked out. *Rand Daily Mail* (South Africa) 16 & 17 May 1978.

And lastly, the ghost of a fire itself. The story comes from the little village of Bepton, near Midhurst, Sussex, and was recorded from the witness, an elderly villager, in the 1930s. Sherwood's pond, near the Shamrock Inn, used to be a favourite skating rink when it froze over in the old, cold winters, and great bonfires were built to illuminate it for midnight skating. One night, when the villager was walking near the Shamrock Inn, he saw a burst of flame leap across the road, apparently without source. The fire left smoke spreading over the road and into the nearby trees, before that too dissipated in the darkness, leaving all as it was before. The villager was convinced that he had seen some sort of ghost light, and at this late date, we can find no grounds for disagreeing with him. *Midhurst & Petworth Observer* 5 May 1978.

Credit: J Hitchens, Chris Holtzhausen, Colin Mather, Paul Screeton, Nigel Watson. SM.

Bram Stoker could hardly have realised the effect he would have on generations to come when he epitomised the archetypal vampire in Count Dracula - for 80 years later his sanguine nobleman still stalks through the popular consciousness with a mighty stride, as witness the recent theatrical versions of DRACULA, and the forthcoming spate of films.

VAMPIRE TALES

Every year, scores of people visit a churchyard in Whitby, Yorkshire, searching for the nonexistent grave of the fictitious vampire — such is the hold of Dracula on the imagination. *Daily Express* 17 April 1978.

But perhaps they are looking in the wrong place, for a very solid slab of granite turned up at Peckham, South London, bearing the words "Count Dracula, 17.12.1847". Workmen found it buried deep in the earth while carrying out renovations to a house in Peckham Hill Street; but a couple of days after the story appeared in the press a former resident, David Perrin, came forward to say that he had buried the stone as a joke, 13 years previously, when he was 15 years old. Mystery solved, but there are some curious aspects too. Site agent James Davis remarked that he had been to the house at night to watch for vandals, and found the place extremely spooky; also that his Doberman Pinscher would not go into the garden. Perhaps next-door neighbour, James Francis, summed it up best, though: "It's eerie. If they find any dead'uns in there, I'm moving out. Let alone undead'uns". London *Evening News*, 15 & 17 August 1978.

And then there are mysterious tales of Dracula's bones; or rather those of Vlad "The Impaler" Tepes, Dracula's historical forerunner. Somewhere along the line they disappeared; or perhaps they were never found. His body was believed to have been buried beneath the floor of Snagov Chapel, on Snagov Island, in a lake near Bucharest, Rumania. But excavation revealed only ox-bones in the alleged grave though the dig, in 1931, did uncover some

human bones near the chapel door, in company with jewelry and pieces of silk bearing the Tepes emblem. These bones were taken to the Bucharest Museum, from which they have since "mysteriously" disappeared. *National Examiner* 30 August 1976.

Perhaps Don Blyth has them. He runs a Weird Museum in Hollywood, and one

According to Don Blyth, owner of the Weird Museum of Hollywood, these are the remains of Dracula. Blyth points to the fang-like teeth and the caved-in chest (where a stake might have been driven) as his proof! *National Insider* 17 Nov 1974.

of the main attractions is "Dracula's" corpse. He claims the body disappeared near the end of World War 2, and turned up some years later in a shop in Meza, Arizona. They woudn't say now they got it, but Blyth paid $3,045 for it, and has statements "from various experts" as to its authenticity. Vlad Tepes, as far as we know, had a fairly normal physiognomy...but as you might expect Blyth's "Dracula's corpse" has two large, hooked fangs protruding from the upper jaw. Blyth insists the teeth are genuine: a natural outgrowth from the bone, rather than a clever insertion job. And if that is the case, we'll at least admit he has some very peculiar remains in his possession. But as to whether two missing rib indicate that the body once had a stake thrust into its heart, well... Too good to be true? Up to you...! *National Insider* 17 November 1974.

And talking of 'lost and found' in an obvious publicity stunt, Los Angeles producers of the play *Dracula* decided to fly in a box of earth from Rumania, to line the Count's coffin with. But when the box arrived at the airport, the dirt had disappeared. Or so said the producers. *Detroit Free Press* 29 October 1978.

All of which demonstrates in, uh, a jugular vein the evocativeness of the vampire count. But what ghouls we mortals be; there are some who take the subject more seriously...all *too* seriously, alas...

BLOOD SUPPERS

These, then, are the vampires, blood-drinkers and plasma-thieves of the 1970s; a less-than-supernatural lot of obsessives for whom "the blood is the life"...usually life-imprisonment...

Farm labourer Alan Dyche, 20, of Abergele, Denbighshire was somewhat less than discreet when he became interested in black magic. He told people he was a vampire, and took friends along when he was making blood sacrifices to the devil. He killed 6 sheep, 2 lambs, 4 rabbits and a cat, and drank their blood. The law replied in similar style: 5 charges of killing animals, one of burglary, one of theft of rabbits. Dyche got off with three years probation. *Daily Mirror* 26 November 1971.

Our 'vampires' are loose in all parts of the world these days: from New England researchers Ed Warren and his wife Lorraine claimed to have encountered two local blood-drinkers, both again connected with witchcraft and magic. The first, named simply as "Lilith" (a suggestive name in itself, for in Hebrew myth Lilith was the progenitor of the sexually-vampiric incubae and succubae) told of her encounter with a young man in a cemetery. He tried to kiss her, but she buried her teeth in his neck and held him down with an "unnatural surge of strength" until she had tasted blood. That was the first of many attacks, though she never thought of herself as vampire in the traditional sense, merely "a very evil person who liked the taste of blood. I just liked being evil." However, when one of the coven that she had joined suggested using her own father as a blood sacrifice, she decided to call a halt. The second vampire, Carl Johnson of Rhode Island, developed a "thirst for blood" one night. He crept into the bedroom of his sleeping sister, delicately pricked her leg and sucked her blood. He later started a Satanic coven and claimed that when he sucked his victim's blood he could feel himself getting physically stronger. Both vampires are alleged to have been cured by the Warrens, though how this cure was carried out we are not told. *Sunday People,* 9 June 1974.

From the above, it should already be obvious that there is a strong sexual motivation in our 'vampires'; from here on, it only gets worse...

We mention Zdzislaw Marchwicki merely for the sake of completion, as he was christened 'the vampire of Silesia' by the press. He was arrested in 1974, charged with terrorising the area around Katowice, Poland, between 1964 and 1970. Lying in wait for lone women, he would knock them out with a bludgeon, rape them and kill them with a home-made steel-whip. After a lengthy trial, the 48-year old Pole was found guilty of 15 murders and 6 attempted murders, and sentenced to death. Krzysztof Plewa, 27, also named a 'vampire', was at work in the same area at the same time. He would strangle his victims with a noose, then rape them while they were semi-conscious. He was convicted of 17 attacks, and sentenced to 25 years. *Chronicle* (San Francisco) 30 March 1974; *Evening News* (Reading) 19 September 1974, *Daily Express* 24 July 1975.

Returning to our blood-drinkers, we have 41-year old deaf mute Kuno

Hofmann of Nuremberg, W. Germany. He admitted removing the bodies of at least 30 women from their freshly-dug graves at 15 cemeteries in Germany to drink their blood. Hofmann was accused of shooting a sleeping couple in a car, in May 1972, and drinking the blood from their head-wounds; also of a number of mortuary break-ins, and the attempted murder of a mortuary attendant whom he shot when disturbed while looking for bodies. He told the police: "I drank the blood of the women because I wanted to feel it in my body. I need a litre of women's blood every day. I've got used to it now." Brought to trial in August 1974, he refused to answer questions put to him in deaf-and-dumb language, merely staring blankly ahead and occasionally pointing to the public gallery. He had, it seems, spent 19 of the previous 24 years in prisons and mental institutions. *Daily Mirror, Toronto Sun, Omaha World—Herald* (Nebraska) all 6 August 1974.

From Germany again, Hamburg this time, a fine example of a Dracula obsession taken to the limit. The neighbours lived in fear of 24-year old Walter Locke: they heard eerie sounds at night and had to address him as Grand Master or Count Dracula; he ate raw meat, slept during the day and roamed the streets at night. Of course, burly 30-year old electrician Helmut Max knew nothing of this when the tall young man dressed in black came up to him in the street and knocked him unconscious with a karate chop. Helmut woke up in a coffin lined with white silk, in a small candlelit room. Locke, who had a "stabbing, hypnotic look" announced himself as Dracula, and that he lusted for human blood. He then hit Helmut in the face with great force, and collected the blood that flowed in a white enamel bowl. Then he drank it. With seemingly unnatural strength, Locke lifted his victim out of the coffin, and the latter fell at his feet, begging for mercy and swearing to be his slave for life. When Helmut had kissed his feet, Locke accepted his submission, and together they ran through the deserted streets to a cemetary half a mile away. There, while Locke performed 'obscene rites' before an ivy-covered vault, his victim escaped and ran to fetch the police. When he had finally persuaded them to believe him, he led them back to the room where they found Locke

asleep in his coffin. Despite all this, doctors did not believe Locke was mad, and he was charged with kidnapping and causing grievous bodily harm. *News of the World* 27 October 1974.

Behaving like an officer and a... gentleman? Ian Officer, 41, had a somewhat obsessive dislike of prostitutes, especially when he was drunk. His fantasy was to murder one, steal her money and drink her blood. And one night in August 1974, he set off for St Anne's Court, Soho (mere yards from our current mailing address!), armed with a sword-stick, knives, whips, a bayonet and a razor, intent on making his dream come true. The girl of his choice managed to stay out of range of his swordstick, while screaming for help, so Officer could only steal £9.60 and flee to the street. Now the tale degenerates into farce, for two policemen had been brought running by the screams, and Officer duly ran into the officers. He lunged at one, who sidestepped and was nearly knocked down by a passing car; as it was he was struck on the arm. The other policeman grabbed a cripple's crutch and beat Officer into submission. He got life-imprisonment, later being transferred to Broadmoor mental hospital. *Daily Express, Daily Mail,* 18 April 1975, *Daily Mirror, Daily Mail* 21 February 1976.

From Indonesia, an astonishing tale; though our astonishment is as much at Indonesian justice as anything else. 25-year old Bahya Lenpeng, living in a village in South Sumatra, had six husbands in two years...and killed five of them. On their wedding night, no less, she would give each new husband a sedative, prick his artery and drink his blood while he slept. After a month of this, the husband, suspecting nothing, would die of anaemia. With husband number six, however, she erred; for he was the local police constable, and he only pretended to drink the drugged tea. When it was her turn for some liquid refreshment, he promptly slapped the cuffs on her and dragged her by the hair to jail. And the verdict? A suspended sentence for manslaughter (!) — and a welcome home from her new husband. *Sunday People* 22 June 1975.

Little Tracey Robson, 9, was walking through a field, Collin's Meadow, with two friends, not far from her home in Canonsbrooke, Harlow, Essex. Suddenly a man wearing a stocking mask leaped from the bushes and began to chase them. The two friends managed to run away, but Tracey tripped and the man, wearing grey checked trousers and a red pullover, was upon her. He bit her viciously on the cheek, but did nothing else to her; then jumped up and ran off with blood on his lips. As far as we know, he was never found. *Sunday People*, *Sunday Mirror* 5 October 1975; *Daily Express* 6 October 1975.

Another unpleasant tale: Michael Ireland, 23, knew he was a dangerous man; he was obsessed with the full moon, subject to blackouts, and already had a history of violence, having beaten up his girl-friend, amongst others. He had made attempts to see a psychiatrist, but the hospital cancelled the appointments 3 times. And then it was too late. Susie Giles, 10, laughed at him while he was drunk. He dragged her into a garage, subjected her to violent sexual assault, bit her and tried to suck her blood, hit her 11 times with a brick and then set fire to her body. Next day he met his 54-year old ex-scout master, dragged him into a sewage works, threw him into a silo and pelted him with stones, bricks and lumps of concrete. He was finally cornered on the roof of his girl-friend's flat, where he held out for two hours before jumping. He appeared in court on crutches, pleading guilty to manslaughter on the grounds of diminished responsibility, and causing grievous bodily harm to Mr Bath. *Daily Mirror*, *Daily Mail*, *Daily Express*, 27 May 1976.

With relief, we come to a tale without violence; terror, yes, but no bloodshed. In Lauderhill, Florida, a man 6ft 4ins tall with long hair was terrorising school children, at Castle Hill and Paul Turner Elementary schools, Lauderhill Middle School and an (unnamed) high school. He wore a cape and fangs, and ran up to the kids spreading his arms wide; they, in turn, ran home crying. Reports said local officials' "blood was boiling"! *Dallas Morning News*, 20 May 1977.

And in Lubbock, New Mexico, 5 pints of blood were taken to the bus station as an emergency shipment to a hospital in Hobbs. When a man turned up and said he had come to collect it, the clerks handed it to him. Oops... wrong fella! Following a tip-off from an apartment manager, the blood was found in a vacant apartment, untouched, still packed in its freezer container. As to the reason for it all, we can only wonder... *Dallas Times Herald*, 1 November 1977.

Back to the sadists: Robert Smith, 50, continually beat up and degraded his common-law wife Barbara, 46, over a 10-month period, including carving his initials in her back with a razor-blade and drinking her blood. At times Smith, of Wimbledon, South London, would growl like a dog. He got an 18-month suspended sentence. *Sun*, 1 February 1978.

And in Chesterfield, a man of about 20 pinned a girl, also aged 20, against a wall in Calow Lane, Hasland, and bit her neck before running off. *Nottingham Evening Post*, 8 February 1978.

A scare story from Malaysia: Reports that a midwife at a government clinic in Batu Pahat had been sucking blood and eating placenta were striking terror among expectant mothers. The rumour began in January 1978, and went on for at least a month. We suspect the story may have been no more than scaremongering, but women were threatening to boycott the clinic, and pressing the Ministry of Health for investigation. *New Straits Times* 12 February 1978. See this issue's 'Occult Crimes' section for another tale of malevolent Malaysian midwifery.

From Bangladesh, a racket where the suckers are the criminals, not the victims: a well-organised gang extracting blood from sleeping victims to sell to the needy in the port city of Chittagong. One girl, Rahela Khatun, 18, said she woke up to see a stranger standing over her holding a syringe. Before she could cry out, he overpowered her and put her to sleep with chloroform. London *Evening Standard* 3 July 1975.

And back to Germany for our latest report on blood/lust: an unnamed student, 22 years old, was arrested in Frankfurt after a 15-year-old girl went to the police, and charged with causing dangerous bodily injuries, seducing minors and possessing illegal drugs. He is alleged to have seduced a number of girls aged between 12 and 15 with the aid of drugs, and to have then drawn off blood for drinking. A search of his flat revealed large syringes, bottles with traces of human blood, marijuana, cola, leaves, arsenic and four large butchers' knives...the last of which, thankfully, he doesn't seem to have got round to using. When last we heard, he was being held pending further inquiries. *Daily Express*, *Daily Mirror*, *Shropshire Star*, *Pretoria* (S.A.) *News*, 3 January 1979; *Ceylon Daily News*, 4 January 1979.

(See also the letter, this issue, from Michael Hoffman, mentioning hypodermic vampires—Ed)

STAKE-OUTS

And then there's the other side of the coin...where there are some who believe themselves to be vampires, so there are others who see themselves as vampire-hunters. In this so-called enlightened age, there are still those who take the legends literally: that there are corpses that rise from the grave at night, and which must be staked down again to prevent them working evil. We have a couple of recent reports to hand...

St George's Church, Camberwell, London, was the target of raiders in early September 1977, who smashed their way through a wall to gain access to the burial vaults. 12 of the 128 lead-lined coffins in the vault were smashed open, and bones and well-preserved, embalmed corpses from the Victorian era were strewn over the floor. Two corpses were beheaded, another had a wooden stake driven into its chest. Whoever was responsible seems to have gone about things with the fury and organisation of a commando-raid: concrete blocks were smashed aside, coffins ripped open with what looked like "some kind of giant tin-opener". *Sunday People* 4 September 1977.

Perhaps more misguided than obsessed, two boys aged 10 and 13 broke into a grave in a churchyard at Wyke, Bradford, only a month later. They prised off the lid of the coffin, containing a woman buried a year earlier, and poked the shrouded corpse with a stick. Magistrates, handing down conditional discharges, attributed the desecration to too many Dracula films. *Daily Telegraph*, 5 October 1977.

Finally, as we go to press, we learn of the conviction, in Palo Alto, California, of Richard Chase, 28, for the first-degree murder of six people. He confessed to drinking the blood of at least one of his victims. London *Evening Standard* 9 May 1979.

Credit: Gary L Abbott, Tom R. Adams, Janet & Colin Bord, Loren Coleman, Gene Duplantier, Lucius Farish, Dave Fideler, Chris J Holtzhausen, Anthony Smith, Joe Swatek, Nigel Watson, Ion Will. SM.

U.F.O Commentary by Nigel Watson

UPSIDE DOWN, DOWN UNDER

One of the more bizarre stories in the annals of ufology began on the evening of Saturday, 21st October, 1978.

Frederick Valentich, a 20-year-old Australian with 150 hours of flying experience, took off in a Cessna 182 aircraft from Moorabbin Airport, on a routine flight to King Island. During this flight he reported to the Melbourne Flight Information service that he could see a long shaped, un-identified aircraft, which was 1000 ft. above his own altitude of 4,500 ft. Minutes later the young pilot radioed that his engine was rough idling and beginning to cough, but he still stated that his intention was to continue towards King Island.

Then at 7.12 p.m. Frederick said in a calm voice; 'that strange aircraft is hovering on top of me again. It...is hovering and it's not an aircraft'. Those were the pilots last words which were followed by a strange metallic sound — like two drink cans being banged together — and then all communication was lost. Most of this material has been reported extensively in the media and so it is not worthwhile to spend time and space in rehashing the full story of the unsuccessful RAAF search for Valentich and his aircraft.

The media immediately jumped to the conclusion that Frederick had been abducted by a UFO, and this idea was reinforced by reports that on the same day, numerous UFO sightings were made in the Melbourne locality. The Victorian UFO Research Society and the Blue Mountains UFO Investigation Bureau, were kept particularly busy investigating these claims.(1,2,3.)

When Frederick hadn't been found — despite an extensive search — the Australian Department of Transport decided that they ought at least to offer some sane explanation for his disappearance — officialdom doesn't like mysteries. So a spokesman advanced the Australian 'up and under' theory, explaining that Frederick; 'wasn't very experienced and could easily have accidentally turned the plane upside down and seen his own lights reflected in the sea'.

Brad Forrest of the Sydney Sun(4) retraced Frederick's flight path and proved to his own satisfaction that the missing pilot had indeed become a victim of disorientation and had thus crashed into the drink — ignoring the fact that he had disappeared in perfect flying conditions and was an instrument-rated pilot with 15 hours experience of night flying(5,6) — the media doesn't like mysteries it can't solve.

A strange twist to the story occurred on Thursday, 26th October, when 16-year-old Miss Rhonda Rushton — Frederick's girl friend for the previous 6 months — turned up at the Bay Pines Motel at Apollo Beach. Miss Rushton asked Mrs Joyce Ford, the motel owner, if she could see Frederick. Later Mrs Ford told reporters: 'When I said there was nobody by that name stopping here she seemed to cry. 'She said she had arranged to meet him at 7 o'clock. She just stood there for several minutes as if she couldn't believe me and didn't want to leave'.(7) This story led hordes of

journalists, reporters and photographers to Apollo Bay.

A couple of Frederick's friends also surfaced in Apollo Bay, and they were not too pleased to find that the media suspected a hoax. One of the friends told a reporter: 'If I find out who started this rumour I'll shoot the bastard down like a dog'.(8) These friends felt that Frederick had crashed into the nearby Otway Ranges, and they planned to search for him. Frederick's father, Guido Valentich, an Italian who had migrated to Australia in 1955, said: 'It is outrageous to suggest he is hiding somewhere. I believe he was sucked up into the air by a UFO and then forced back to earth somewhere — perhaps in Central Australia'.(6)

With speculation rife, and with no clue as to his where-abouts, the story was abandoned by the media in Late November, 1978. Like the legendary story of Captain Mantell's tragic encounter with a UFO — which he saw "...directly ahead of me and still moving at about half my speed. The thing looks metallic and of tremendous size,"(9) before he and his aircraft disintegrated over the land of hope and glory — the Valentich case is left to the hacks of ufology to disinter. In the Mantell case a UFO was seen by other witnesses, and the main dispute was whether Mantell had been fooled by a secret Skyhook balloon, or whether he had been zapped by the electro-magnetic field of an extraterrestrial flying saucer.

The Valentich case presents several discrepancies which indicate that Frederick wasn't just an innocent victim of saucer napping or disorientation. These discrepancies can be listed as follows:

a) Frederick only filed a one-way flight plan to King Island, although he had indicated his intention of returning the same evening.(10)

b) He made no arrangements for the landing lights at King Island to be switched on.

c) Police found no one who had arranged to sell crayfish to Frederick — the stated intention for his flight.

d) The aircraft's long range fuel tank was filled to its 303

Airman missing at sea

PILOT SAW A U.F.O.

MELBOURNE: A young pilot flying over Bass Strait near Cape Otway disappeared last Saturday night minutes after reporting a UFO.

In the six minutes before his radio cut out with a metallic noise, the pilot, Frederick Valentich, 20, was able to describe the UFO and its behaviour to Melbourne Flight Service.

What the pilot said

7.06 pm — Valentich:

litre (80 US gallon) capacity.

e) Cape Otway lighthouse keepers and Bass Straight fishermen did not report seeing any light aircraft in the vicinity.[11]

f) Despite ideal radar conditions, at no time was the aircraft plotted on radar.[1,12]

g) There were rumours that Melbourne police received reports of a light aircraft making a mysterious landing not far from Cape Otway, at the same time as Frederick's disappearance.[1]

h) Although Bass Straight — and later Cape Otway and King Island — were searched for signs of wreckage, nothing was found.

i) He had 300 dollars cash on his person.

j) He, arranged to meet Miss Rushton on the same evening at 7.30 p.m. — a date he couldn't have possibly kept.

k) Frederick's father claimed that, 8 or 10 months before his disappearance: 'My son told me he had seen a large, brilliantly-lit object in the western sky which was flying at a tremendous speed from south to north'.[13] His father also stated that Frederick firmly believed in the existence of UFOs. Yet no mention was made of a UFO during his last radio communication.

l) On the tape recording of the last conversation with the young pilot, there is no hint of panic in his voice.

People have tried to explain Frederick's disappearance by suggesting that he was: smuggling drugs, hoaxing everyone, flying upside down, executing a bizarre form of suicide, or was abducted by a UFO. My own theory is that he was on a suicidal acid trip, and whilst enjoying the effects of flying upside down, he was banged between two UFOs (thus creating the reported sound of two beer cans clanging together), as a consequence of this he was atomised into the twilight zone. Any better theories?

DESTINY OR DESIGN?
On the evening of the 9th July, 1968, Gene Ruegg was fiddling with his 5,000 dollar radio-telegraphy equipment, in the bedroom of his home in Memphis, Tennessee. All was normal until he heard the pilot of an aircraft, coded Delta four-zero, who reported over the crackling static: 'I am being attacked by unidentified objects, I think I...'

The transmission died, and then the pilot's voice returned again, saying: 'They're closing in on me. I am unable to steer a course. 'Something is happening to the plane... I am being taken along by this thing. I require assistance. I require assistance...' Gene then heard, 'a strange, searing noise like scraping metal and the pilot shouted something I couldn't identify. Control tried without success to establish contact, but they couldn't, he said. According to Gene, a USAF spokesman confirmed that a Phantom jet had, in July 1968, gone missing in mysterious circumstances from the Southlands, Tennessee, air base.

The US Air Defence Command has possession of Gene's tape recording of the last dramatic minutes of Delta four-zero's communication, but it is 'still being studied and assessed'.[14] Could Frederick Valentich have based his disappearance on this, the Mantell case, and other reports from flying saucer lore?

CAN YOU PICTURE IT?
Aircraft being abducted by UFOs has been a theme

employed by the cinema since 1950s. One of the best and earliest films to portray this ufological scenario was Joseph Newman's *This Island Earth* (1955). The plot of this classic SF film develops when the naughty but desperate Metalunans suck a light aircraft up into their gigantic flying saucer...

In *Star Trek*'s first season (1966-1967) D.C. Fontana's story, 'Tomorrow is Yesterday', sends the USS Enterprise back into the skies of the 1960s. A USAF jet pilot who is flying in the vicinity photographs the Enterprise which he mistakes for a UFO — silly fellow — and from there the plot cleverly revolves around the abduction of the pilot and the manipulation of time. Even Spielberg in *CE3K* used the factual disappearance of Flight 19 as the foundation for his monumental cinematic faction. (An excellent exposition of the Flight 19 saga has been written by Mr X[15].)

The imaginative fuel supplied by these celluloid marvels only reinforces the view that ufology is a brew of 'faction' (fact and fiction) — the degree to which each influences the other is one hell of a maze.

BODYWORK
At the first Iberian conference on the subject of UFOs, held in Oporto in October, 1978, a startling revelation was announced by MJ Fernandes at the start of the conference, and repeated at the close of the conference by R

'UFO' PILOT: DID HE FLY INTO THE SEA?

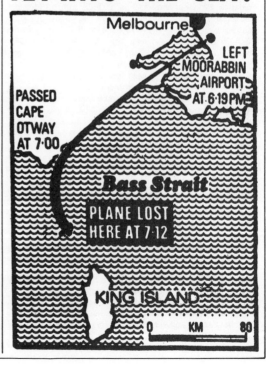

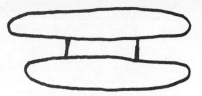

Mark, 14, of Geelong, drew this sketch of the object he saw in the sky during a tennis match on October 21 . . . "It had a color like a sort of metallic silk."

A Geelong woman's sketch of the objects she saw at Cape Otway on October 21 . . . "What puzzled us was that the two objects were flying with such precision."

Sketches of objects seen in Melbourne skies the same day Valentich disappeared. Melbourne *Herald* 25 Nov 1978.

Berenguel.(16,17) Their story was that on the 2nd November, 1959, two UFOs were seen in broad daylight over Southern Portugal. From them fell a cloud of cottony filaments, which rained down on the region for a period of 4 hours.

A Portuguese professor collected one of these cottony filaments, in a test tube. He discovered that it was a 'living organism about 4mm long, equipped with tentacles ending in a 3-pronged fork, and which took up defensive postures'. The living being had a cross-section of 1mm and owned 10 tentacles.

Eventually after 2 years the organism broke up — probably under pressure from sceptics. Soviet scientists were also alleged to have obtained similar specimens, recently.

At the 9th annual MUFON convention, held in Dayton, Ohio, in July 1978, Leonard Stringfield repeated some hot gossip. This consisted of the story about 30 alien bodies — they must be breeding! Previous reports only mention 12 bodies — Wright-Patterson have on ice.(18,19,20). Leonard's sources for these stories come from former government employees. However, in reply, John Williams, the director of Richland College Planetarium, said that: 'I'm inclined to think that's a misinterpretation of possibly true events, including early American rocket experiments that sent monkeys into near space. Perhaps there could have been an accident with one of these and the recovered wreckage of the craft and body could have been misinterpreted as extraterrestrial craft and beings'.(21)

Williams also commented that   military intelligence often circulate bizarre stories in order to detect any security leaks. Through the Freedom of Information Act, the Ground Saucer Watch (GSW) group intend continuing to file lawsuits, this time against the National Security Agency. GSW director, William Spaulding, spent $15,000 on suing the CIA who had to cough up 340 documents. If GSW have

hopes of finding any alien bodies, I'd advise them to look at Patrick Moore; the only alien body the USA has is a sometime peanut farmer.

In 1977 a couple of police officers were sent to upper Manhattan, at 6.30am, after reports that a disorderly crowd were gathered around an alien spaceship. The policemen found a dozen people surrounding a cone shaped object which was emitting flashing lights and a gurgling sound. Nearby they found a small, dead, humanoid body (another peanut farmer?). The officers took the capsule and body to the 34th Precinct, where they discovered that the body was a GI Joe doll covered in clay, the capsule was a mass of wires and two tape recorders.(22)

Could it have been an elaborate hoax by the aliens? If they were to disguise themselves as dolls, or monkeys, or minute organisms, or Steven Spielberg, or Jimmy Carter — who knows what havoc they could provoke?

NOTES
1) *The Australian* 23 & 24 Oct 1978.
2) *The Australian* 31 Oct 1978.
3) *The Herald* (Melbourne) 25 Nov 1978.
4) *The Sun* (Sydney) 7 Nov 1978.
5) *The Sun* (Sydney) 23 Oct 1978.
6) *Sunday Telegraph* (Sydney) 29 Oct 1978.
7) *The Weekend Australian* 28-29 Oct 1978
8) *The Age* (Melbourne) 28 Oct 1978.
9) *The Truth about Flying Saucers* by Aime Michel (Criterion, 1956) p.39.
10) *The Australian* 25 Oct 1978.
11) *Daily Telegraph* (Sydney) 16 Nov 1978.
12) *Daily Telegraph* (Sydney) 27 Oct 1978.
13) Article by Arch Maclean — unidentified newsclipping.
14) *Sunday Echo* (Malaysia) 17 July 1977.
15) *INFO Journal* vol 3, no 4, Feb 1974.
16) *Le Progres* (Lyons, France) 7 Oct 1978. Trans: Phil Ledger.
17) *The Herald* (Sydney) 10 Oct 1978.
18) *Daily Freeman* (Kingston, NY) 30 July 1978.
19) *Morning News* (Dallas, Texas) 21 Jan 1979.
20) *Fortean Times* (June 1975) 20p14—15.
21) *Morning News* (Dallas, Texas) 21 Jan 1979.
22) *Paris News* (Texas) 18 May 1977.

Credit: Thomas R Adams, Greg Axford, Rev AH Debnam, Lucius Farish and the UFO Newsclipping Service No 113, Les Herring, Phil Ledger, Ion Will.

Nigel Watson is a leading researcher for UFO Investigator's Network (UFOIN), and a frequent contributor to UFO periodicals.

It's bad enough having the place over-run with Londoners every weekend!

Hardbacks

LIFETIDE *by Lyall Watson (Hodder & Stoughton 1979; $ 5.95hb, pp376, index, bib.)*

I was taken to task for my opinion of Watson's last book, *Gifts of Unknown Things* , because I suggested it was a different kind of book from Watson's well known first two books, in that there was a definite trend in his writing, from the scientifically based biologist of *Supernature* to the mystic of *Gifts* who alternated between wide eyed awe at the wonders of nature and dispair over the banalities of technological man. I said, in a review in an earlier FT, that Watson seemed to be undergoing a personal re-evaluation and that should he successfully integrate the scientist and the mystic his fourth book should be well worth the wait. I am pleased to say it is !

The subtitle – 'a biology of the unconscious' – indicates well in advance that his scientific knowledge is to be placed at the disposal of a creative, speculative and intuitive interpretation of the age-old fundamental dichotomy of mind/body, or the internal and external worlds. Using fascinating examples drawn from recent work in nearly every field of biological and psychological science, Watson has bravely attempted a new synthesis - and I believe he has succeeded ! His exposition gives us exciting insights into man's relationship with the world of external phenomena on the one hand, and the perplexing world of the paranormal on the other, and his clear restatements of problems and phenomena allow the development of fresh approaches.

In essence, Watson takes his primary clues from the way in which paranormal phenomena seem to bridge the internal and external worlds, and his belief that the 'nonsensical' and paradoxical aspects of these strange effects, meaningless to the materialist scientist, does indeed have meaning and relevance. It comes down to the business of learning to see again but in a different light, as the magicians, the shamans, the mystics of all ages have repeatedly said. Biologically, Watson argues, man is a composite creature; his physiology is a subdivided whole representing simultaneously different stages of physiological evolution, each with its own brain or neurological structure, and its own needs, consciousness and conflicts, dreams and memories.

This in turn confirms that there are many layers to the mind, though it might be better to state that not in terms of a hierarchy, but as a dynamic fluctuating gestalt of different but contiguous states of consciousness. Watson's most interesting sections deal with Jan Ehrenwald's notion that pregnancy is the "cradle of ESP", and that the foetus is conscious, although due to his limited sensory inputs, this functioning is on what we might call an archaic level and similar to Jung's hypothesis of the 'collective unconscious'. In this primary state we can postulate the origins of most psychic phenomena (including their puzzling 'childish' qualities) and the mechanisms of reality-shaping. Naturally, this leads Watson to consider the theories of archetypal forces and symbols, and the new hypothesis of alternate-realities (as discussed by Joseph Chilton Pearce *et al*), and of paranormal beings and objects (eg UFOs, apparitions, monsters, etc.) as projections from the unconscious mind that materialised or became apparently real. There is also the suggestion here that such effects, along with psi phenomena, ESP, etc

may be part of the normal abilities and repertoire of the human mind before they 'disappear' , either eliminated by the process of 'growing-up' (i.e. conforming to the adult concensus of reality in which these phenomena are less real), or that they are swamped by the 'roof-brain chatter' (as Castaneda put it) of everyday consciousness. Jung apparently suspected this since he thought it "probable that we continually dream, but consciousness makes while waking such a noise that we do not hear it." Watson goes on to link the paradoxical state of 'active sleep' (in which dreams are lucid and not linked to the rapid eye-movements of normal dream-sleep) in which foetuses are known to spend most of their time, to the archaic hypnoid states of trance typically associated with paranormal phenomena. Buy the book and read on.

Along the way we get other clues, like the paranormal phenomena associated with children or the emotionally childlike. The book opens and closes with Watson's encounter with the well-publicised case of the Italian girl who could turn tennis-balls inside out mentally, and how she lost the ability, or her interest in the ability, when the onset of adolescence made her more physically aware of herself and others. Also along the way we pause for many fascinating nature lessons, and as a guide Watson is clear and apposite. Recommended for its concise restatement of the problems presented by paranormal phenomena, and indeed of our very existence, and for the valuable detailed bibliography of 600 items. *RJMR.*

THE LEGEND AND BIZARRE CRIMES OF SPRING HEELED JACK *by Peter Haining (Frederick Muller 1977; $4.75 hb,180 pp, illos; index)*

Spring Heeled Jack has been an enigmatic figure in popular British tradition for nearly 150 years, but if Peter Haining is to be believed, the mystery is now solved. He puts forward a convincing case, which briefly is that the idea of Spring Heeled Jack originated with the Marquis of Waterford, a practical joker who dressed up in a flowing cloak and mask and, with steel claws on his fingers and springs in the heels of his boots, during 1837-8 terrorised London by leaping out at unsuspecting young women, breathing fire into their faces, ripping their clothes off, and then escaping. Any reports later than 1838 can be attributed to other people emulating Spring Heeled Jack, Haining tells us. He makes out a good case; nevertheless some doubt remains. Apart from the danger of lynching if Jack were ever caught (which may indeed merely have added spice to the eccentric behaviour, if it were he), the discriptions given by people who saw Jack are of interest: eyes like balls of fire, the ability to vomit blue and white flame, pointed ears, claws instead of fingers , clothes which included a helmet and oil-skin like garments. The British ghostly black dog, reported over many centuries including our own, very often has glowing red eyes, and sometimes it belches fire. Alien visitors to our 20th century world sometimes have claws, and often have pointed ears. They also are on occasion dressed in helmet and bright, shiny garments.

Haining considers the 'alien visitor' theory in his last chapter, 'Was Jack a man from Outer Space ?', using to present the theory a 1961 article from *Flying Saucer Review* which in the light of what we have learned about UFOs in the intervening 17 years is somewhat naive and does not help the theory. If we forget about ' a man from outer space' and consider Jack instead as yet another denizen of that other world whose location we are yet uncertain of, this possibility is still feasible, despite Haining's conviction that Jack was several terrestrial jokers. For as well as Jack's revealing appearance, some later encounters are not so easily dismissed as Haining makes out, for example, sightings of Jack at Caistor, Lincolnshire in 1877 (including at New Barracks), at Aldershot's North Camp in 1877, and Colchester barracks some time during the 19th century (why the interest in army premises ? Surely the most likely place

MITCH DAVIES

for such an intruder to get shot ?), and the relatively recent, and apparently his last , appearance in Everton, Liverpool, in 1904 when Jack was seen on several occasions, finally putting on a display in broad daylight which included leaping from roof to roof before he mysteriously vanished. The Aldershot appearance is especially intriguing, because two soldiers shot at Jack with rifles, and (I quote Haining) ' the bullet seemed to pass right through the being' and ' their bullets seemed to have not the slightest effect' (both page 90). The uselessness of guns in fending off alien beings has also been reported in encounters with Sasquatches, black dogs, and UFO occupants. Haining does not deal with this aspect (which apparently undermines this 'terrestrial jokers' theory), but presumably if questioned on it would say that the men were too frightened to aim properly. In fact on the first occasion the figure was immediately in front of the soldier who fired, and it would seem to have been difficult for him to miss. Or was Jack wearing bullet-proof garments ? But wouldn't such garments weigh him down ?

Despite the fact that the solution to the mystery is not as clear-cut as Haining would like to think, this is a useful book to have for it is the first to document Jack's career. However, an author with more knowledge of ghostlore, Forteana and ufology would have handled the puzzling aspects of this still enigmatic figure with more understanding than Haining

does. The book is illustrated with period engravings, but unfortunately many are rather murky in reproduction.
Janet Bord

A DICTIONARY OF OMENS AND SUPERSTITIONS *compiled by Philippa Waring (Souvenir Press 1978, $4.95 hb, pp264.)*

Dr Johnson felt he must touch every wooden post along a certain road whenever he frequented it. He couldn't explain it, and had no intention of desisting for fear of calamity or bad luck. Contrary to the beliefs of materialists, superstitions have very real functions, and their practicality is ensured long after their purpose has been forgotten or sunk out of view of the narrow conscious mind. For all those who wish to propitiate fate here are countless time-honoured ways. Other entries deal with special requests, prophecy, psychic self-defense, symbols, animal and nature lore, old wives' tales and folk medicine, etc. Surprising how many of the entries deal with modern superstitions (e.g. US airmen crossing the belts in unoccupied seats. Or in the north of England a belief persists that consumption can be cured by swallowing a baby frog!) *RJMR.*

THE FRIAR OF SAN GIOVANNI *by John McCaffery (Darton, Longman & Todd 1978; $3.95 hb, pp143, glossary, photos.)*

Pio Forgione, better known as Padre Pio, died in 1968. He had displayed in his body the wounds of Christ' s crucification for 50 years, the longest of any recorded stigmatic. Loved and adored in his lifetime as a saint, his *cultus* has more than once drawn warnings from the Vatican asking his admirers to desist. The Church has a policy of not canonising a living person, and certainly not on the evidence of miracles alone, tales of which proliferated around this shy monk. The telling criteria of sainthood, in the Church's opinion , are the 'heroic virtues' of piety, humility, obedience and faith - and on these counts one may say of Padre Pio that his canonisation is only a matter of time.

There are many accounts of his life, stigmatization and alleged miracles, but most are written for the faithful (or credulous, according to your point of view), and lack the very details that interest researchers and Forteans. Some are simply hard to obtain. A very few contain good accounts of the medical examination of Pio's stigmata and their periodic bleedings. In fact of their existence and the pain they caused him continuously there can be no doubt. Over the years millions attended his masses and confessed to him, and one of the most consistent of the 'miracles' claimed for him was his power to (telephatically ?) see into the hearts of men. But he was also said to have healed the sick, been in two places at once, walked in the rain without getting wet, and appeared in visions to people.

I had high hopes for this book - but it turns out to be a collection of personal reminiscences of the 'living saint', both first and second hand, of the author who lives as a journalist and a businessman in Italy. McCaffery admits that he writes from memory and that some circumstantial details may not be completely accurate, but this will not bother the faithful as they plough through the many short chapters recounting healing miracles, clairvoyance, and the wit and wisdom generally of Padre Pio. But I was hoping to learn more about the stigmatization, about the background and make-up of the saint-elect, his early illnesses and strange experiences. Instead this is a different book, one which concentrates on the last years of this simple and good-humoured holy man, and the lives of those in close contact with him, and indeed the lives he touched by his existence. *RJMR.*

VOICES FROM THE GODS by David Christie-Murray (Routledge & Kegan Paul 1978; $6.95 hb, pp280, index,bib, notes, plates.)

'Speaking in tongues' is an ancient phenomenon, and although the main thrust of this book is in the role 'glossolalia' has played in the Christian West, Christie-Murray is obviously aware of its universality,e.g. in shamanism or spiritualism, and before beginning a chronologically structured analysis of the various Pentecostal and 'heretical' movements that have kept the practice alive and shouting, devotes chapter 1 to a brief survey of 'possession' among other cultures. The Christians, of course, distinguish possession by spirits from possession by the Holy Spirit; for them the utterances spoken in the latter state are the virtual outpourings of divine communication.

Christie-Murray divides the subject into two: glossolalia (paranormal speaking in tongues) and xenolalia (paranormal speaking of foreign languages allegedly unknown to the speaker in normal state), and after the historical survey discusses the psychological and anthropological aspects of tongue-speaking. The number of Christian sects which were founded upon glossolalia are more than one would at first think, ranging from groups within the Russian Orthodox Church, to the Camisards of the 17th C, to Mormons and Quakers and Shakers. It is strongly linked to religious revivals and was prominent in the great Welsh revival of 1905, during which Fort noted the appearances of UFOs, mystery animals, spontaneous combustions and other phenomena. Then begining with the first Pentecost feast after the Crucifixion (Whitsun), and the 'revivalist' meeting of the early Christians as they spread through Asia Minor, our author charts the 'family tree' of glossolalia through the charismatic sects to their many descendants today, and which show the 'love-bombing' techniques of disarming and converting newcomers practised (or malpractised) by the Children of God and other modern sects is nothing new at all. The early Church used the techniques of tongue-speaking meetings to establish their mission and unity. The Apostle Paul frequently spoke in tongues as both prayer and worship, but later seemed aware that the chaos and 'babel' of these meetings could mislead outsiders into blurring the two kinds of possession. Eventually, Church worship settled down to more ritual forms since the great majority cannot readily or practically reach such heights of inspiration – and thus gradually glossolalia was pushed to the fringes of Church practice, until it was particularly associated with heretical and fanatical sects.

In truth, as Christie-Murray discusses in the later parts of the books, both glossolalia and xenolalia become more complicated the more you look into them. With the rise of the Spiritualist movement there emerged many authentic examples of both phenomena; but shorn of their Christian context, the strange languages were here said to belong to the non-human world of spirits, or even to one's own past lives in other times and places. At the same time, the foundations of psycho-

logy were being laid and in systematising mental phenomena the pioneer psychologists recognised two groups of relevant phenomena. First, the psychopathologies of mental illness in which a consistent symptom is the hearing of loud and often abusive voices,whether internally (e.g. 'Someone is putting voices into my head.') or as external projections (e.g. hearing accusive voices from radios, or superimposed on the voices of other people.) The second group involved the paradoxical phenomena of Mesmerism, hypnotism, somnambulism etc and the way in which they occurred or could be induced in quite ordinary healthy people, helped establish the hypotheses of the subconscious and unconscious. Now, from the burgeoning of psychic research we have to add another possibility...ESP or psi, and the new 'electronic voices' on tapes etc.

It is quite impossible to do justice to the thought and scope of this book here. Christie-Murray, himself a Friend, admits that despite the mass of evidence, no one theory seems to be capable of definitive proof. The phenomenon exists, and in a wide variety of forms, each with its supportive theory. He agrees that more experiment is needed... or more faith. Recommended. *RJMR.*

MIRACLE by Des Hickey & Gus Smith (Hodder & Stoughton 1978; $4.50 hb, pp172, brief bib.)

You may remember the splash in the papers in 1976, when among others, Pope Paul canonised a Scottish martyr, Blessed John Ogilvie, and it came to light that one of the main and convincing pieces of evidence considered by the Consistory of Cardinals was the miraculous cure of docker John Fagan, of Glasgow. In 1965 he had a major resection of the stomach and colon after the discovery of a massive carcinoma. The recovery was temporary, and by 1969 the mass had grown again, and he was sent home to die. He was given the Last Rites by a local priest who gave him a medal of Blessed John Ogilvie, and advised the family to pray to the martyr for his intercession. A few days later medical examinations confirmed the disappearance of the abdominal mass and Fagan's steady recovery.

The authors reconstruct Fagan's case from the records and testimony of those involved, and against this background give an account of the life and martyrdom of John Ogilvie (d. 1615), and stages of transforming his beatification into a full canonisation. RJMR.

INTO THIN AIR: People who Disappear. by Paul Begg (David & Charles 1979; $5.95 hb, pp184, index, notes, plates.)

To satisfy the public's, or the publisher's, demand for a constant stream of 'true mystery' stories, too many writers have been content to copy out stories from earlier books and articles without any attempt to check their authenticity. The 'Forteana Corrigenda' column in FT has begun the daunting task of investigating some of the old chestnuts that appear from time to time in monster, mystery and UFO books, and which often disappear into thin air when closely examined. Paul Begg carries on the work, and in this work the thin air consumes more legends than people. Among the distortions, inaccuracies and downright lies which he exposes are the myths of David Lang (from material in FT18) [see also Janet Bord's letter in this issue --Ed], and the alleged kidnapping of the Norfolk Regiment by UFOs

[see Paul Begg's article in FT27 --Ed], and the *Mary Celeste* mystery. Also demystified is much of the data used by lazy, gullible or unscrupulous writers to support theories about the 'Devil's Sea' (off Japan) and the 'Bermuda Triangle', scenes of disappearing ship and plane incidents whose actual circumstances are generally far less strange than their legends.

Paul Begg has sought out the original sources of 'disappearing people' stories, and his book is useful, sensible and clearly written. The only pity is that he does not follow up on Fortean ideas on disappearances. There is no mention of UFO -- or fairy-linked abductions, nor does he refer to the testimonies of people who have vanished in strange circumstances and returned with even stranger stories. It is odd that a writer on this subject, who apparently knows his Fort, has nothing to say on teleportation, or on people who have mysteriously appeared somewhere after presumably vanishing from somewhere else. Verdict: a good book as far as it goes -- shame it does not go further. *John Michell*

PATHWAYS TO THE GODS by *Tony Morrison (Michael Russell 1978; $5.95 hb, pp208, index, bib, plates).*

Morrison produced a documentary for BBC TV on the enigmas of South American civilizations (shown in November 1977), which dwelt in part on the work of Maria Reiche in mapping and exploring the famous ground lines and figures on the arid stoney plains of Nasca in Peru, and of Dr Gerald S Hawkins in surveying and analysing the data on the lines for significant patterns and signs of astronomical alignment. In the course of the filming Morrison explored further afield and stumbled upon the discovery of a straight line mystery directly analogous to the European ley-line enigma. In a recent *Ley Hunter* (TLH84) editor Paul Devereux and John Michell discussing this book claimed they could find no real distinction between the newly discovered alignments in the Andes and the examples of Leys rediscovered in England and Wales by Alfred Watkins. Primarily both linked hills, villages and shrines, both were deliberately straight, and both seemed to have

---

UNDERCURRENTS

June-July 1979　　　　　　No 34

Crabapple Revisited—Pam Dawling
Commune sehse and sensibility

Romance and Reality—Ann Pettit
Self-sufficiency as she is lived

The Co-op Lesson: Learning the Hard Way—Iago Mephistopheles
An interview with a would-be socialist entrepreneur

Hanging Separately—Jenny Thornley
Two co-ops that failed

Green Danube—George Wood
An alternative to the Vienna UNCSTD conference

Doing without the State—Ghulam Kibria
How the feudal socialists squashed AT in Pakistan

A Collective of Shopkeepers—George English
A year in the life of Earthcare Retail Co-op

Pricking the Nuclear Balloon—Sheryl Crown
What feminists can bring to the anti-atom struggle

Atom Scandal—Eddie O'Rio
Monkey business among Brazil's nukes

Looking Forward to 1984—Geoff Wright
An interview with Ian Lloyd MP

Whale Talk—Bill Hall
Make jaw, not war, on our cetacean cousins

Engineering on the Dole—Martin Ince
A bleak look at the future of Britain's industry

plus News, Reviews, Events, etc. 48 pages for only 50p from 12 South St, Uley, Dursley, Glos GL11 5SS.

been used as paths.

Morrison sets the background by outlining the work of Reiche and including Dr Hawkins' Nasca study; then follows a very readable and well-illustrated account of the 'pathways in the Andes' (or *ceques*), and other mysterious ruins, like forts and reservoirs. The accuracy of these lines over great distances argues for a purpose to their construction, but Morrison admits that "Why?" has to be left unanswered for now. Fascinating problem well explored, and essential reading for all interested in ancestral mysteries.*RJMR*.

Paperbacks

ROBERT FLUDD by Joscelyn Godwin (Thames & Hudson 1979; £2.95 pb, pp96,bib. engs.)

Forteans today, no less than the orthodox scientists, are to some extent bound to the 'Dominant' as Fort called it, the pervading paradigm that the Universe has to be separated into mind and matter, subjective and objective (etc.) before sense can be made of it. Forteans have felt this as a drive to make their work more 'scientific' -- but the comparison ends there. Forteans can be distinguished from mere scientists by their subscription to an inclusive cosmology, a sense of Continuity (again as Fort put it), against the divide and subdivide *reduction* of science. This Continuity is partly a rationalisation of the mystical and logical sense of unity of all things that all things interpenetrate and influence each other to a greater or lesser degree. In our strivings we Forteans would do well to look to the past, for there are men, like Robert Fludd, who in seeking to understand the sheer variety of phenomena, tried to develop systems which integrated God and Man and the world of phenomenal appearances.

Fludd was born in Shropshire, and studied and taught at Oxford before travelling around Europe's centers of learning in the 17th century. He was truly a Renaissance man (though a little late); a philosopher, musician, doctor, astrologer etc. True, he laboured under the 'Old Dominant' (Descartes had not yet arrived on the scene to tip the Church off its pedestal, replacing it with material science) which probably influenced him to study the Cabala and other systems of occult

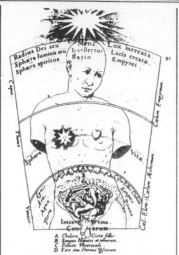

knowledge -- but he knew archbishops and scientists (Harvey, Keppler,Inigo Jones etc.) and he was proud his writings were acceptable to Calvinists, Anglicans and Catholics alike. The main influences in his philosophy seem to be Paracelsus, Pythagoras and the early Rosicrucians. He conceived of a major 3 volume encyclopedia of knowledge, and completed most of the sections. This book is an introduction to those works, profusely illustrated with engravings from the originals, and which attempts to show that there is much in common between Fludd and the philosophical synthesis (between occult science and natural science) going on today. The book can be read with great profit by Forteans, and the illustrations, showing Fludd's accomplishment as an anatomist, astronomer, mathematician, engineer, natural historian, theologian, cosmologist and systematiser are full of the most evocative symbols. Miss Godwin is to be congratulated , and her book (in T&H's 'Art and Imagination' series) is to be recommended. *RJMR*..

EVOLUTION by Colin Patterson (RKP & British Museum [Natural History] 1978; £5.95 hb, £2.95 pb, pp 197, index, bib, diags, drgs, photos, glossary.)

A brilliantly informative and concise book that manages to summarise the official dogma of Darwinian evolution, and by treating it historically Patterson includes the challenges to Darwinism from recent developments in genetic science, tissue-typing etc, and the

emergence of 'neo-Darwinism'. In full awareness of Prof Popper's criticism that Darwinian evolution is not a scientific theory but a "metaphysical research programme" (by which he means the theory is more akin to a metaphysical proposition than a scientific one, but accepting it allows the development of a research programme) Patterson discusses the basic notions including species, heredity, genetics, mutations, natural selection theory, origin of species theory, the origin of life, evolution and man; and an interesting section on classification and typology which shows the radically different effects of different typing methods used between say a geneticist and an anthropologist, and even between biologists of Darwin's day and today, very much proving the inescapable influence of your particular point of view. Apart from the book's obvious value as both a reference and a primer for all interested in evolution theory, Forteans could also find some interest and advantage in the chapter which discusses theories of science, and tests neo-Darwinism according to their criteria. Lamarck's notion of 'acquired characteristics' is discussed sympathetically, but it has to be admitted that it has not opened itself to the wealth of evidence, discovery and experiment that Darwinism has, and although it survived to become a political tool in Russia under Lysenko, the essential confirmations are still lacking. True Forteans can find many instances which defy Darwinistic theories of natural selection etc, but these too still lack their systematising model. It is well argued here that neo-Darwinism, with its faults, "is still the best we have". The whole tone of the book is genial, informed and clear, a nice touch being to end with a photo gallery of leading figures in the debate for and against. Recommended. *RJMR*

THE OTHER ATLANTIS by *Robert Scrutton (Sphere 1979; £1.25 pb, pp 251, glossary, plates.)*

In 1871 a Frisian antiquarian told the world of a manuscript that had been in his family for generations, since 804AD in fact. The writing was in an ancient Frisian dialect and told of Atland, a culture and land mass around the north and east of the British Isles, which was contemporary with the more famous Atlantis, and which some believe was the model of the Hyperborean tradition. It survived the Atlantean cataciysm by thousands of years to perish itself in a Velikovsky-type catastrophe — an asteroid collision forming the north polar crater and tilting the spin axis to the present, is suggested here — in 2193 BC. The legacy of Atland was astonishing. It is here suggested that Frisian heroes and kings (etc) were the real life models of the Norse Odin, the Cretan Minos, the Roman Neptune, Minerva, and Temple of Vesta; that English Common Law was founded on Atland's law, and that our numerals are not based on the Arabic but Ancient Frisian, and that the Greeks derived their writing from Frisia, via Phoenicia; that Ulysses is mentioned by name as trying to wrest a 'magic lamp' from a Frisian priestess Kalip (Calypso); that the Indian epic, the *Mahabharata* was written by Frisian colonists who settles in the Punjab; that Britain was Atland's 'Botany Bay' etc.

If this is true then this book will have a far-reaching effect on nearly every aspect of official and occult western history. Why haven't we heard of it before? Well, it is said to be a typical tale of human disbelief, apathy, stupidity and fear. Shortly after its translation, it seems, articles in London newspapers attracted it considerable attention, but so sensational were its contents and implications in academic circles that the establishment historians assured the world it was a hoax. Their word in those days was law, the furore died down, and the manuscript, called the *Oera Linda Book*, fell again into obscurity. Robert Scrutton here re-discovers and re-interprets the *Oera Linda Book* — apparently based on the long out-of-print English translation by William R Sandbach, of 1876 — and presents whole extracts followed by his commentary relating the text to "modern scientific knowledge, archaeology and traditional mythology and occult doctrine".

On many levels the book deserves to be widely read and discussed and this edition should facilitate that. Recently Neville Spearman published the sequel to this book (*Secrets of Lost Atland* in hardback, reviewed in FT28) which deals with the mystical and material sciences of the Atland legacy, and we understand this too will be eventually released as a Sphere paperback. I understand some scholarly and detailed refutations exist, but in German and unavailable to us. The Velikovskyans have serious reservations about the *Oera Linda Book*. Read with caution. *RJMR*.

THE MEDIUMSHIP OF THE TAPERECORDER *by DJ Ellis (Published by the author from: Fernwood Nightingales, Welt Chiltington, Pulborough, West Sussex RH20 2QT, 1978; £1.50/$5.00 pb, index, bib, glossary, diags, tabls.)*

David Ellis was the Perrot-Warrick Student of Trinity College, Cambridge, for 1970-72, and the terms of his brief involved study of 'voice extras' on tape recordings as possible evidence for the continuance of human existence after bodily death. These voices are heard on the playbacks of tapes recorded by a variety of methods from open microphone monitoring room noise or running water to microphones linked to radios tuned to random or white noise frequencies, or by replacing the microphones with a diode. Apart from a degree of press interest in the EVP (electronic voice phenomenon) in 1971, following the English publication of *Breakthrough*, Dr Konstantin Raudive's account of his experiments based on the pioneer work of Friedrich

Jürgenson, interest in and experimentation on the EVP was left to a small band of researchers (see *EVP News* in our journal reviews). In this case, though, Ellis was able to make use of the Perrott-Warrick award for original psychic research to conduct a long term study of the EVP. The book is a collation of his progress reports over the period, and although his ultimate conclusion is negative as far as the EVP is concerned — "it does not seem to be anything paranormal" — Ellis does admit that it may be triggering the psychic abilities of the experimenter, and investigations on different briefs may be more rewarding. The book constitutes an important record of experiments (usually unsuccessful), interviews, conferences, book critiques, discussions and analyses of recordings. *RJMR.*

Journals

FT will have a policy of helping the research field as far as we can, not forgetting that we too were a small magazine once and grateful for any mention we could get. In the new FT we will continue to list other magazines on an exchange basis. The only general rules for inclusion here, are 1) that your magazine must have some relevance to our studies, and 2) you establish an exchange with us. Each issue we list the mags we have received on exchange since the previous issue, and give their basic details. No mag, no mention -- Ed.

PURSUIT 11:4 (Fall 1978) -- report on a conference on Sasquatch and similar humanoid monsters; antiquarian records of climatic changes in Greenland by George Eberhart; Larry Arnold with more on phantom ships and strange fires; our editor's account of the Shiels Nessie photos; Ron Anjard on the colonization of the Americas in 2000 BC; Britton Wilkie on Bronze Age enigmas, and more. *Pursuit* is the quarterly journal of the SITU, the Society for the Investigation of the Unexplained. $10.00/yr (Overseas $12.50). Apply to:SITU Membership Services, RFD 5, Gales Ferry, CT 06335, USA.

INFO JOURNAL 31 (Sept-Oct 1978)-- the physical characteristics of Bigfoot; interviews with Big Bird witnesses (complete with incoherent,uh, inter-

jections); plus fewer notes of clippings than usual. *INFO JOURNAL* is the organ of the International Foretean Organization. $10.00/yr. Write for details: INFO. 7317 Baltimore Ave., College Park, MD 20740, USA.

SIS REVIEW 3:3 (Winter 1978/9)-- 'A chronology for the Middle Kingdom and Israel's Egyptian bondage' by Dr JJ Bimson; Dr Velikovsky identifying the Biblical 'Kima and Kesil' as the planets Saturn and Mars, respectively; Dr I Wolf on Shakespeare's use of myths and omens in *Hamlet*, its parallels with the legend of Orestes and some legends in the *Popol Vuh* of the Quiche Mayas, and that these parallels may indicate an archetypal drama of a celestial catastrophe; plus letters & notes. *SIS REVIEW* is the journal of the Society for Interdisciplinary Studies which explores the work of Velikovsky and catastrophic geology. For details, write: RM Amelan, Secretary SIS, 6 Jersey House, Cotton Lane, Manchester 20.

JOURNAL OF METEOROLOGY 4:35 (Jan 1979) -- remarkable mirages at Hastings and the Humber estuary; a tornado at Hitchin; unusual cloud; Shetland's greatest storm; positively charged lightning; and 'World-wide weather disasters' lists for October and November 1978. Plus weather summaries and other articles. 4:36 (February 1979) --some hard European winters; floods, blizzards and tornadoes; the Thames 'frost fair' 1814; a mini ice-age? origin of giant ice-meteors; 'World-wide weather disasters' for December 1978; other weather summaries and articles. Indispensible to the Fortean interested in weather anomalies and records. Monthly. £9.50/yr (Overseas $22.00 surface, $28.00 airmail). *JOURNAL OF METEOROLOGY*, Cockhill House, Trowbridge Wilts BA14 9BG.

NESSLETTER 31 (Dec 1978) -- summary of the JARIC examination of Nessie on 22 Aug 1977, plus statements from some of the witnesses; plus notes on the Potomac and Canadian monsters. *NESSLETTER* is published by the Ness Information Service as a clearinghouse for monster sightings and related information. Monthly: £1.75/$7.00/yr. Editor, Rip Hepple; Huntshieldford, St Johns Chapel, Bishop Aukland, Co Durham.

EVP NEWS 12 (Feb 1979) -- German interview with Jürgenson; news and letters on EVP; article by professor Hans Bender. A newsletter for researchers and all interested in the 'electronic voice phenomenon' (EVP). Editor Alan Cleaver has written us an introduction to the weird voices that appear on tapes for a forthcoming issue of FT. *EVP NEWS* is monthly: £1.50/yr (Overseas airmail £4.50/yr), from Alan Cleaver, 12 Lime Tree Ave., Old Bilton, Rugby, Warks CV22 7QT.

VESTIGIA NEWSLETTER 2:4 (Winter 1978) -- articles on 'Plasmas' and the nature of mystery lights ('spook lights'), and notes on related subjects. Vestigia is an active Fortean fieldgroup in New Jersey, who are investigating local reports of Bigfoot, UFOs, mystery lights, and lake monsters. Write for details. Vestigia, RD 2 Brookwood Rd, Stanhope, NJ 07874,USA.

RES BUREAUX BULLETIN - regular summary of Fortean clippings and related matters from Canada. Available for exchange, clippings or other support. Edited by Mr X., Box 1598, Kingston, Ontario K7L5C8, Canada. Mr X (legal name) also edits the periodical **CHAOS** dealing specifically with Fort, his writings and notes, his cases, and his sources of materials, with the purpose of keeping in circulation this valuable and hard-to-obtain material. This project is threatened through lack of support. Send C$2.00/US$2.00/ £1.00 for single copies. Third issue just out — to be reviewed next issue.

FORGOTTEN AGES 12 (Winter 1979) -- mainly two articles: the search for Atlantis pt 3, and the 'Clones of Enki', not a SF novel but a Sumerian inscription apparently describing the production of biological duplicates by the manipulation and artificial impregnation of genetic material into host mothers. *FORGOTTEN AGES* is published monthly by J R Jochmans, being informed and expansive comment on the various alternatives to orthodox history. $3.00/yr. JR Jochmans, Box 82863,Lincoln, NB 68501, USA.

NEUROLOG 4 -- special *What is reality?* issue -- produced by The Network in association with the 'Corps of Reality Engineers', with articles on Fortean phenomena and societies; alternate geography; magick, healing, animal mutilations; MIB comics; paranoia; health and diet; UFO; and several on 'reality'. A real bonus is that each copy contains a piece of 'The Fabric of the Universe' This splendid effort forms a good introduction to Fortean and alternate reality topics, and we recommend it to everybody as a good place to start; and there is a large and useful annotated bibliography thrown in. Available from The Network, Box 317, Berkley, CA 94701, USA.

THE LEY HUNTER 84 -- John Michell and Paul Devereux on Morrison's book on the straight lines of Peru; R Rickard on 'The Straight and Crooked'; Tony Roberts on giants; Sid Birchby on the 'Hummadruz'; Dr Derek Banks proposing an 'Experiment on Reality'; Hopi traditions and the vibrating plateau of Colorado; and the other features on ancient stones and alignments; letters and reviews. Now that it is typeset throughout TLH looks and reads a fine magazine. THE magazine of 'earth mysteries' published bimonthly: £3.00/yr (£3.60 Europe; Overseas airmail $9.00). TLH, Box 152, London N10 1EP.

AWARENESS 7:4 (Winter 1978) -- Jim Lorenzen with 'New Light on the Thomas Mantel case'; Martin Straw on possible connections between 'Seers,

saints and sunspots'; and Vera Perry on North American Airforce radar sightings of UFOs (or are the UFOs looking at the radar?); news, notes, letters etc. Published by the Contact(UK). Write to their PRO, P Flatman, 17 Quarhill Close, Over Norton, Oxfordshire.

MUFOB 13 -- articles: on close encounters that begin with 'Strange Awakenings' and which, argues Keith Basterfield, have parallels with hypnagogic images; Jenny Randles gives more examples of 'sleep' associated UFO phenomena; Peter Rogerson attempts a 'Revisionist History of Ufology'; and editor John Rimmer goes straight for the throat as he cuts to pieces the apalling standards of British press reportage of UFOs; and another instalment of Rogerson's painstaking catalogue of important close encounter cases. *MUFOB* is Britain's leading journal of UFO theory, published quarterly: £1.75/yr (overseas airmail $4.00). MUFOB: 11 Berkeley Road, New Malden, Surrey KT3 4AW.

NORTHERN UFO NEWS -- the monthly newsletter of the Northern UFO Network, detailing investigations and reports of regional sightings. Published 8 times a year; editor Jenny Randles,23

Sunningdale Drive, Irlam,Salford M30 6NJ. The other four times a year it changes name to *NORTHERN UFOLOGY* and attempts more analyses and articles than reports. Jenny Randles seems tireless in her active pursuit of cases to investigate and write up!

BUFORA JOURNAL 8:1 (Jan-Feb 1979) -- notes, news, investigations, sighting lists of recent cases. Published for members by the British UFO Association. Write: BUFORA Membership Secretary, Mrs A Harcourt,'Berways', Stocking Pelham, Buntingford, Herts.

SKYWATCH -- news, notes, some articles, local sightings and investigations, published by the Manchester Aerial Phenomena Investigation. Write to editor David Rees, 92 Hillcrest Rd, Offerton, Stockport, Cheshire SK2 5SE.

We have quite a few foreign journals on exchange and these will be included next time. Meanwhile all those responding to ads and notices in these pages might mention where they saw the information. It helps us judge the effectiveness of these services --Ed.

Letters

THE HUMMADRUZ

In 1975, the late Fortean pioneer Chibbett (see obituary in FT25) lent me some press-cuttings and letters about people who claimed to have heard unexplained humming noises. His attention had been aroused in 1954, and thereafter he noted some dozen cases and wrote to many of the people concerned. In fact, his file showed that there had been *hundreds* of cases. In 1954, the science correspondent of the *Daily Telegraph,* having examined 40 reports, agreed that there was a noise, but could not find a common pattern.

Consider also the writer Edward Hyams, whose wife had been plagued for 5 years by a low-pitched hum on the edge of audibility. A doctor and ear-and nerve-specialists found nothing wrong with her except lack of sleep, and prescribed drugs. The noise still woke her. The GPO took out the phone and slackened the stay-wires on the poles. The hum went on. Hyams campaigned for an official enquiry and received 400 letters. In 1961, a question was raised in Parliament: reply: 'No evidence'.

Harold's file provides the evidence, but even he could not suggest an answer. There the matter might have rested, but by chance I remembered reading about something called The Hummadruz whilst searching old press files some years previously. In 1878 there had been letters in a Manchester paper about a mysterious noise called 'The Hummadruz' (hum+drone+buzz, no doubt) which had brought to light some 14 cases dating back to 1727, and recorded by such people as Goethe, Oliver Wendell Holmes and the naturalist Gilbert White.

Obviously, the noise is more than a Sunday-press gimmick, and one can also see in the light of 3 centuries of records that each generation has tried to explain it in terms of its own technology, despite earlier accounts when such technology did not exist. In 1974 it was radar; in 1879, telephony. About 1828, the whirl of machines in Manchester's factories. In 1769, on the Hampshire Downs, Gilbert White likened the noise to the humming of bees, although none were seen.

Cases have continued to be reported since 1975, with equally-suspect explanations. It is said, for example, that the hearers may be sensitive to a continuous signal allegedly put out by the Ministry of Defence, perhaps as a hot-line to Polaris submarines; and as "evidence" a certain make of commercial pipe-locator is said to make canny use of it. All one can really say is that the Hummadruz has been reported for centuries, whatever it may be.

We need more data, and I have recently started an informal Working Party for this purpose. Already, the results are encouraging, and anyone else who would like to take part is invited to write to me, *enclosing return postage.* Reports from those who have heard the noise are especially welcome, but much useful work could be done by searching records. May I say that the purpose of a working party is to *work,* and that its members must be ready to do so. Requests for information from casual enquirers are not wanted.
SL Birchby
40 Parrs Wood Ave, Didsbury, Manchester M20 0ND

PEOPLE'S TEMPLE MASSACRE: VOUDOO MOON RISING?

Jonestown aka 'Village of the Dead' was headed up by a bi-sexual cross-roads christian (bible seasoned by a somewhat older religion which also venerates the "sign of the cross") and son of a masonic ku klux klansman. In black street parlance "jones" means an obsession or addiction as in "Jim Jones had a 'jones' for demerol" (a synthetic opiate).

Jim Jones and aides laid out the bodies of some of the victims/martyrs in a HALF MOON shape. Shortly afterward, Harvey Milk, a homosexual official in San Francisco, was gunned down along with the city's mayor. (Source for half-moon reference: *NY Times* 12 Dec 78).

San Francisco or "Frisco" was plagued throughout the summer and autumn of 1978 by the murders of gay people some of whom were discovered in the HALF MOON Bay area (source: *The Advocate,* 29 Nov 78 pp.7-8) including murder victim and gay Arthur Tomlin Goodman III.

Jim Jones had his headquarters in Frisco. In the slang of the first part of this century "Frisco" was a term used

GREAT·MOMENTS·IN·SCIENCE

'I was present one day [11 March 1878] at a meeting of the Academy of Sciences. It was a day to be remembered, for its proceedings were absurd. Du Moncel introduced Edison's phonograph to the learned assembly. When the presentation had been made, the proper person began quietly to recite the formula as he registered it upon his roll. Then a middle aged academician, whose mind was stored — nay saturated — with traditions drawn from his culture in the classics, rose, and, nobly indignant at the audacity of the inventor, rushed towards the man who represented Edison, and seized him by the collar, crying: "Wretch! we are not to be made dupes of by a ventriloquist!"'.

Camille Flammarion *The Unknown* (Harper, 1902, p3).

Other absurd moments spring to mind - but why should we have all the fun? Readers are invited to submit their own favourite candidates to be illustrated in this spot by Hunt Emerson.

HUNT EMERSON

---

to describe fellatio. Mammy Pleasant, the voudoo madame whose bordellos doubled as voudoo temples had her final temple — Beltane — at a ranch in the VALLEY OF THE MOON area of California. Her other temples had all been in "Frisco".

Endnotes: MARTIN is a voudoo patron saint on a par with John. *MARTIN* is a new movie by Geo. *(NIGHT OF THE LIVING DEAD)* Romero about a vampire who uses only hypodermic needles and razors for extracting blood. Jim Jones, according to the *NY Times* for 12 Dec 78, murdered at least 70 people by injection with a cyanide laden hypodermic syringe(s). In a recent issue of *Occult Review* Colin Camber states that death by vampire bite has the same symptoms as death at the hands of an Obeah (voudoo) Man. When Geo. Romero revised the vampire bite in modern terms, was his muse picking up some *une sorte de musique de fond* from

Jim Jones' modern version of Obeah Power?

The Hazards of Opinion: Observe caution when driving thru paranoia about blacks who do magic. American jazz, Jamaican Rastafarians, Jimi Hendrix, marijuana, are all part of a potent transformative wave which has its macabre aspects, just as the European Gothic era had its danse *macabres*. The figure of Christ is as heavy with sorcery symbolism as any of the native earth sorceries of which Voudoo is a part. If Druidic ritual sacrifice is right why is Voudoo wrong? Of course with plutonium around things will get nasty.

PS: Masonic Lodges Stateside are often named NITRAM or MARTIN backwards. Jones had his People's Temple in the Albert Pike Memorial Bldg in good ol' Frisco in 1971.

Michael Hoffman
Geneva, NY.

DAVID LANG REVIVED?

An item in FT18 (pp.6-7) told how research has shown that David Lang never existed, and the story that he vanished in 1880 in Gallatin, Tennessee, in full view of his wife and children was a purely fictional entry in a lying contest. Jay Robert Nash tells this same story in *Among the Missing* (Simon and Schuster, 1978, pp.327-30), but there the unfortunate 'disappearee' is one Orion Williamson, the place Selma, Alabama, and the date July 1854. At the end, Nash comments as follows:

'This story is now famous, not only for the weird "facts" that it relates, but because it has been altered from its very real site. Over the years, a thorough investigation on the part of the author and his staff revealed, Williamson's name and place of residence have been changed for various reasons by several writers. This began when a wandering salesman named McHatten from

Classified Ads

Cincinnati was trapped by a snowstorm in 1889 in Gallatin, Tennessee. With nothing to do except drink, McHatten sat in the Sindle House Hotel and rewrote the Williamson story in an attempt to make a bit of extra change by selling it as an original report. He changed Orion Williamson's name to David Lang, the site of his disappearance from Selma, Alabama, to Gallatin, Tennessee, and the date of the occurrence from July 1854 to September 1880. McHatten's story, except for the basic facts of Williamson's disappearance, was a gross fabrication that has been almost universally accepted and rewritten and published in a score of reputable journals and books, not the least of which is the recent *People's Almanac*. No such person as David Lang ever existed in Gallatin, nor did any family named Lang during this period. Orion Williamson was no figment of the imagination but a real, live resident of Selma, Alabama — until, of course, he slipped into eternal mystery.'

Janet Bord
Montgomery, Powys.

Fortean Times

Subscription

Taking out a subscription helps us in many little ways. Newsstand sales are excellent as far as they go, but there is no substitute for the stability of a growing and regular subscriber list. Subscribing also ensures you receive your *FT* immediately and without anxiety, and makes you eligible for any of the bonuses we'll cook up to your advantage from time to time. You are also entitled to a free copy of our annual index whenever we publish one.

SUBSCRIPTION RATES
(includes UK & overseas surface postage)
1 year (4 issues) £3.00/$8.00
AIRMAIL surcharge: add £1.75/$3.00 per year.

GIFT SUBSCRIPTIONS: A subscription to *FT* makes a novel, thoughtful and stimulating gift for birthdays, Christmas, etc, which lasts a whole year. For every gift sub you give, or for each new sub you bring in, we will extend your own sub by an extra issue. Send us the details and payment and we'll dispatch the current issue with a gift/compliment slip. Or send us details of someone who might like to know of *FT* and we'll send them a leaflet. Copies of our leaflet are available on request, free.

PAYMENT: cheques, postal orders, international money orders and Giros in Sterling or US Dollars, made payable to *FORTEAN TIMES.* Write details clearly, and send order with payment to the address below. Receipts will be issued only on request.

FORTEAN TIMES (Dept S)
c/o DTWAGE, 9-12 St Annes Court, London W1, UK

Next Issue

Michael Hoffman on the strange case of the Son of Sam murders...Was Berkowitz himself a convenient and willing victim in a larger, more sinister conspiracy? **David Fideler** begins his 3 part study of the UFO and Fortean phenomena of the state of Michigan. **John Michell** previews his forthcoming book on the mysterious realm of spontaneous images in nature. A photo-feature on a blind heretical Spanish Archbishop, who also bears the stigmata. **Plus** more Fortean notes.

Loch Ness Monster snapped unawares by Doc Shiels, May 1977. *See p26.*

© FP

Fortean Times

ISSUE No. 30   The Journal of Strange Phenomena   PRICE: 95p $2·50

SIMULACRA:John Michell on Nature's Art;
+ Son of Sam; 1859 Fish Fall; Stigmatic Heretic

Fortean Times

The Journal of Strange Phenomena

Contents

Cover painting by Una Woodruff, whose thoroughly recommended book *Inventorum Natura* is reviewed among our paperback reviews this issue

Published by Fortean Times Ltd: 9-12 St Annes Court, London W1. Editor: ROBERT JM RICKARD. Associate Editors: STEVE MOORE, PAUL SIEVEKING. Contributing Editors: DAVID FIDELER, PHIL LEDGER. Art Director: RICHARD ADAMS. Comix Editor and section heading artwork: HUNT EMERSON. Photosetting by Wordsmith Graphics, 19A West End, Street, Somerset. Printed by Bija Press, Beeches Green, Stroud, Glos.

FORTEAN TIMES is a quarterly journal of news, notes, reviews and references on current and historical strange phenomena, related subjects and philosophies. A friend to all groups and magazines continuing the work of Charles Fort in investigating, studying and discussing all aspects of strange phenomena. RIGHTS: all articles and artwork in FT are the copyright of the authors unless otherwise stated. Uncredited material is by the editors. The views of the contributors are not necessarily those of FT, and vice versa. SUBMISSION is invited of articles, artwork, cartoons, and news clippings on related subjects. The publishers can assume no responsibility for unsolicited material, but all reasonable care will be taken while in FT's possession. If material is to be returned, please enclose SAE. CORRESPONDENCE: letters-of-comment and personal experience are welcome. If replies are required please enclose SAE. The editor regrets it is not always possible to reply promptly. ADVERTISING and DISTRIBUTION ENQUIRIES: contact the editor at the above address, or ring 01 552 5466. SUBSCRIPTION INFORMATION: see inside back cover.

Editorial

Your appreciation is our reward. However we have had to reassess our goals recently and bring them into line with the small resources available to us — some of the more obvious and tangible reforms are apologised for and explained in an accompanying letter to our subscribers.

Even before last issue's experiment in newsstand appearance, many readers thought FT was professionally run and funded. We are flattered, but this is not so. We are entirely dependent upon the voluntary, unpaid and sparetime efforts of a few loonies, and funded mainly. by your subscriptions, some shop sales and valued donations.

Over the last couple of issues our subscriber list has nearly doubled — but then so has our printing, production and postage bill , and the balance is as shakey as ever it was. Seedling ventures like FT are very much affected by the successive waves of price rises, union actions, shortages and deteriorating services, each threatening to swamp our little boat. As of writing more postal rate increases are looming, and other rises are on the way.

Our only refuge lies in gaining more subscribers. As an incentive we will continue to peg our sub rates for as long as possible, but effective from this issue we have to put up our cover price. This makes the present sub rate an even better bargain, saving almost 30% over the cover value. Helping us get more subscribers will help you in the long run by keeping the sub rates down and fending off the spectre of a drabber, thinner FT. For each new sub you bring in we'll extend your own sub by an extra issue. There's no limit, but you have to claim this giving the name of your catch. Copies of FT blurbs are available free, in any quantity, for the asking.

Finally, I'd like to thank all of those — too numerous to mention — who have helped and advised us over the last six months. Thanks also to our patient contributors and artists who donate their material when they could be earning bucks elsewhere. Thanks especially to Una Woodruff for her truly astonishing cover painting this issue, to illustrate John Michell's article. It really is encouraging that we can attract such talent. And last but not least, thanks to all our readers, without whom this would all be empty vanity.

Bob Rickard.

Spontaneous Images and Acheropites

'Conditioned by rationalistic beliefs, our view of the world is duller and more confined than nature intended,' writes John Michell in his recent book **Simulacra** (Thames & Hudson, 1979), an eloquent denial of the 'single vision' that William Blake proclaimed the error of small and narrow minds and of scientific materialism. Faces and figures can be seen by anyone, in or on any form or surface, at any time. To 'the manifold vision innate in all of us' they are not without beauty or meaning or transcendent logic. **John Michell** here outlines his thesis of the interplay between nature and imagination, with illustrations from **Simulacra.**

One type of strange happening which intrigued Fort was the appearance of forms or images, produced by nature, which people interpret as spontaneous ikons, portraits or symbols of topical significance. These 'simulacra' or deceptive likenesses served well to illustrate his view of the world as anorganic entity of which we ourselves are part and which our human desires and imagination are largely responsible for shaping.

In *Lo!* Fort described a number of contemporary instances of the spontaneous image effect, including, typically, the reports in the *Bath Weekly Chronicle* during 1926 of the appearance on a stone pillar of the Abbey Church at Bath of certain damp stains which strongly resembled the figures of a soldier with pack in full marching order. In the course of several weeks it kept changing shape but the likeness remained. On the same pillar were exhibited the tattered colours of the heroic Somerset Regiment, and the opinion of 'local theosophists' was that the damp-stain image was shaped by the concentrated imaginings of the thousands who had been to view these moving relics. The literal-minded clergyman in charge of the Abbey thought differently. He disclaimed the miracle, denounced it indeed, and rebuked everyone who saw the image as anything other than the chance, meaningless effect of natural causes.

The tendency of the human eye to see its own image reflected in the appearances of nature and to detect faces and figures in the interplay of light and shade or any variegated pattern is well known. It has been much used by mystics for purposes of divination and by imaginative artists. Many of the designs by prehistoric and aboriginal cave painters, and also the mythic events they served to illustrate, seem to have been suggested by natural cracks or marks on the rock face. Leonardo

advised his pupils: 'Stop sometimes and look into the stains of walls, or the ashes of a fire, or clouds, or mud, or like things, in which, if you consider them well, you will find really marvellous ideas.' Alexander Cozens in the 19th century followed a well-established tradition among painters when he daubed ink on to crumpled paper, thus obtaining the background of rocks and scenery for his landscape drawings. It is a tradition that has its roots in deepest antiquity. The ancient science of geomancy, by which were divined the proper sites for temples and for all other human additions to the landscape, was based on the idea that apparent likenesses and symbolic shapes in rock formations give clues to the hidden nature of the countryside and to the fortunes of its inhabitants. The modern prophet, Antonin Artaud, recaptured this type of vision when, as described in his *Journey to the Land of the Tarahumara*, he saw repeatedly in the shapes of the Mexican mountains the same ancient, alchemical symbols — which he then recognised in the designs and artifacts of the local people. Nature, he realised, had stamped a whole district and all its inhabitants with its own characteristic set of images. It came to his mind that a forgotten science, Universal Esotericism, which was still preserved in the secret rites of the Tarahumara, had once read and made use of these natural symbols. 'When one knows this' he wrote, 'and when one suddenly finds oneself in a country that is literally haunted by these signs, and when one recognises in them the gestures and rites of a race, and when the men, women and children of this race wear them embroidered on their clothing, one feels uneasy, as if one had arrived at the source of a mystery.'

The Bath clergyman who objected to the pious interpretation of the damp stain on the wall of his

Abbey would doubtless have agreed that Artaud deserved the treatment he received from the mad-doctors for insisting on the importance of his vision in the Tarahumara mountains — incarceration and electric shock 'therapy'. Authorities, both religious and psychiatric, are inclined to draw firm lines between the world as it is and as we perceive it, and to ignore the indissoluble relationship between these two sources of reality. This relationship arises from the fact that our human ways of seeing things have been developed as part of the same processes of nature that have created everything we see. Our vision is a part of nature and thus, according to Fort's view of an organic universe, related to every other part. As we are programmed from birth to respond to certain forms and symbols, so is nature correspondingly programmed to manifest repeatedly these same images.

Consider the face pattern, which is the first thing a baby sees, which it has been found to respond to instinctively. This pattern continues to haunt our imagination throughout life. It is the most popular subject with painters, and it recurs again and again in the designs of nature.

In *Simulacra* are illustrated some of the many face patterns in the markings of creatures and natural objects. Apart from the skull on the back of the ominous Death's head hawk moth, there are well-defined face patterns on the wings and thorax of many kinds of insects, notably on the closed wings of the various types of Underwing and on the half-opened wings of the Eyed hawk moth. Several spiders, even tiny ones, are similarly marked. The most obvious example is the round, sun-god face on the abdominal plate of the trap-door spider. It uses this plate to block up the entrance of its hole, and the face pattern has been thought to act on the other creatures as a symbol of warning. On the back of the *Dorippe* crab, found off the coast of Japan, is the distinct image of a samurai mask, while another crab, inhabiting English waters, bears the markings of an irrascible Englishman! Most extraordinary of all is the chrysalis of a small, north American butterfly, *Feniseca tarquinius,* only about a quarter of an inch long, which is marked with a human face clearly resembling the features of a local Indian. Two other similar types of chrysalis are found elsewhere. In each case the pattern of a face marked upon them is characteristic of the locality.

Explainers of the Darwinian natural selection school have made all kinds of attempts to account for these face patterns throughout nature, some laughable indeed. For instance, Julian Huxley 'explains' the samurai face on the Japanese crab as being the result over the years of the more human-looking ones having been thrown back into the sea rather than eaten, even though he admits that the Japanese do not eat the crab anyway. And this of course fails to account for the English face on the inedible English crab.

We are left with this observation: we are inclined to see patterns of faces and nature is similarly inclined to produce them.

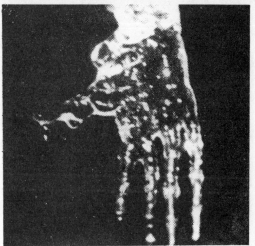

The strangest of all the wonderful, naturalistic effects which are created by combinations of the elements are those which in some way are timely, as if intended as omens or as comments on human affairs. This icicle hand appeared at the kitchen window of Carol Alspaugh one morning in the winter of 1979. 'I wondered if someone was trying to tell me something,' she said afterwards to her local paper, the Press *of Grand Rapids, Michigan. 9 Feb 1979, because on that day she was due to take her sister to hospital, for a hand operation. When they arrived, the surgeon said he could not operate on account of a new injury to the sister's arm. It had been wounded the previous day -- by a falling icicle.*

Consider now acheropites. They are defined in Brewer's *A Dictionary of Miracles* as 'likenesses not made by the hands of men'. The Shroud of Turin, which appears inexplicably to be a negative photograph of a nobly bearded figure from the time of Jesus, is an acheropite. Closely related are 'veronicas' which are cloths marked with a face which is supposed to have been imprinted by the sweat of Jesus when a woman, Seraphia, wiped his face as he was walking to Calvary. The notion that the cloth was twice folded explains the existence of three veronicas, one in St. Peter's, Rome, one in Milan and the third at Jahen, Spain. A case of a similar effect is recorded in Sir Henry Halford's *An Account of the Opening of the Coffin of Charles I* 1813. He says that when a piece of cerecloth was unwrapped from the face of the royal martyr, it was found to bear the imprint of his features.

Modern Church authorities look askance at acheropites, fearing outbreaks of cultism. Not even the Turin Shroud is above suspicion, for the late John Paul Mark I at the start of his papacy was dissuaded from his intention of making a pilgrimage to it on the grounds that he would thereby encourage pagan superstition. Yet, whether as a spin-off from the growing Shroud cult or for some other or no particular reason, there has

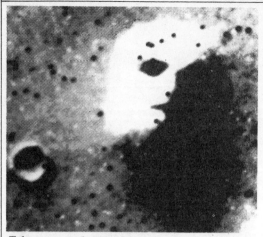 

Telescopes and microscopes have extended the range of face images visible in nature. The one on the left, from a photograph of the surface of Mars taken by Viking 1 Orbiter on 25 July 1976, is about a mile wide. The other, figured in the National Enquirer *12 July 1975, as a 'happy virus', is a microscopic cell, photographed in the laboratory of the Children's Hospital, Philadelphia.*

recently been an absolute spate of spontaneous holy countenance images. Many have been faithfully recorded in *Fortean Times* (see *FT* 7, 16 and 26). The hierarchies of the older churches have generally been quick to denounce them. For instance, in early April 1976 the Bishop of Nimes ordered the village church of Suave to be closed after crowds flocked to see the image of a face which somehow appeared on the wall of the nave. He said they 'came to see a spurious miracle rather than to worship.' Another case of official dampers applied to an acheropite and its cult occurred in 1978 when the Archbishop of Santa Fe denounced a fried tortilla, a kind of local bread, on which the New Mexico woman who had cooked it discerned the familiar bearded countenance. She enshrined it in a reliquary and persuaded the local priest to bless it. Unlike normal tortillas it did not decay after a few days. Once more the crowds flocked despite the Archbishop's attempts to restrain them *(International Herald Tribune* 25 July 1978 from *LA Times).* More excitement, flockings and official disapproval followed the recognition by a woman in a village near Voronezh in Russia of a 'miraculous' damp stain on the ceiling of her house as a portrait of her grandson who had recently died. 'Excursionists have taken her house by storm', said a Communist Youth newspaper, quoted in the *Guardian,* 19 September 1978. 'They beg, they plead, they demand, they threaten, they try to break in by force.' The paper called on the local anti-superstition zealots to take action against the damp stain and its cult.

What about the 5,000 students and their teachers at the Voronezh Institute of Scientific Atheism, it asked. 'They well know that neither the damp spot nor the rumours about it are going to disappear just like that.'

Sometimes, however, particularly in newer churches and those remote from the seats of authority, the local priest can not resist taking spontaneous divine portraits, when they occur in their churches, at literally face value. For instance, at Shamokin, in the case described at length in *FT* 26, when crowds of pilgrims swamped his Holy Trinity Episcopal Church following his discovery on an altarcloth of an apparent Shroud-like countenance, the Rev. Frank Knutti welcomed them with the services of spiritual healing. *FT* 18 reported that similar images in churches in New Mexico and Denver, Colorado were graciously received by the priest and minister concerned. In the latter case, the Rev. H. D. Wilson of the Episcopal Church, Denver commented on a 'face of Christ' that appeared on a windowpane of the church school, 'We feel it is a sign that what we're doing in the church is right.' Despite what their superiors may say, these simple churchmen have most authoritative precedents for not looking their spontaneous ikon gift-horses too closely in the mouth. After all, the world's most fanatically revered religious object, the Kaaba stone at Mecca, is an acheropite — a heaven-made image of God that fell from the sky.

The world is full of acheropites, formed fleetingly in clouds, in growing or rotting timber and, more lastingly in rock formations. In every group of rocks the eye can see images, but there are certain spots about the world where they are particularly clear and numerous. Anyone interested in such things should visit the Brimham Rocks, on a high plateau above Pateley Bridge in Yorkshire, where a remarkable collection of rock-figures, carved by the wind and grit, are grouped together like prototypes for an alternative creation. Another such spot is the Forest of Fontainebleau in France where nature has wrought masterpieces of natural statuary, including three distinct elephant-rocks and herds of other creatures. Robert Charroux in *Le Livre du passe mysterieux* refers to such places as *points d'amour* or life-generation centres, giving as an example the

Nature's tendency to stamp likenesses of human features on insects' wings, crabs' shells, the backs of spiders etc. has never been explained by the evolutionists, whose ingenious but contradictory attempts to do so bring to mind Fort's dictum: "There never was an explanation which did not have itself have to be explained." The matter becomes more interesting when, as in the case illustrated here, the 'face' seems to resemble the local human type. Right is a chrysalis, magnified from its natural ¼ inch size, belonging to the small blue North American butterfly, Fenesica tarquinius. Two other such chrysalids are known elsewhere in the world, in Asia and Africa. In each case the 'face' markings they bear reflect the features of the indigenous locals, and Fenesica tarquinius gives an accurate portrait of a noble Red Indian. Evolutionists claim obscurely that the similar chrysalids from Asia and Africa are mimicing local types of monkey rather than men, but the theory fails to account for this example from North America where there are no native monkeys.

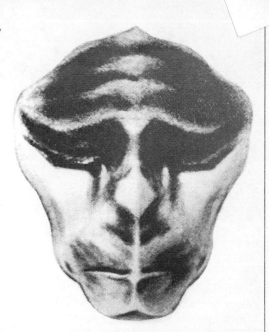

Good photographers have an eye for 'simulacra' or figurative effects of nature. This beautifully modelled ice bird, created by freezing rain on a twig of a tree, was photographed at Uzwil in Switzerland. International Herald Tribune 25 Jan 1979.

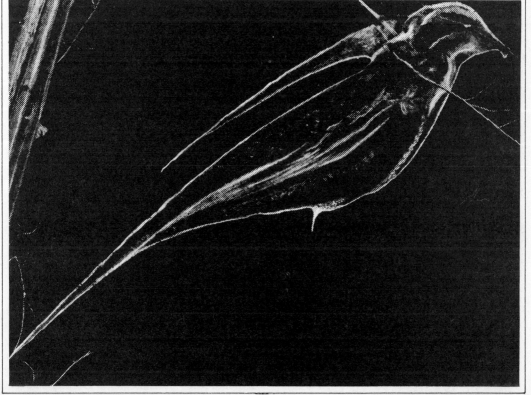

In rock formations all over the world people see images which seem to resemble the characteristic human features or animal types of the district. These images are sometimes taken as representations of local heroes or episodes in mythology. One of the most striking is the natural rock portrait of a mitred figure near Chermoog in Armenia which the Armenian Church recognizes as an acheropite of St. Vartan, a 5th-century bishop, who was killed nearby ina battle against the invading Persians. The revelation of his image in his native rocks is said to have taken place on the day after the battle and to have brought great comfort to the Armenian survivors.

Marcahuasi plateau in Peru where Daniel Ruzo in 1952 discovered a vast gallery of natural human and animal sculptures, visible only at certain seasons under particular conditions of sunlight, which he thought to be the work of a mighty, lost civilization. The same idea occurred to Artaud when he called the Tarahumara country 'one of those sensitive spots on the earth where life has shown her first effects.' This belief in a mystical connection between the generation of life-forms and places where these forms are indicated by folds in the earth is as ancient as nomadic times, when fertility rites for the increase of various creatures were held at spots where those creatures were seen represented in the rocks and landscape.

The eye that detects simulacra in all nature's patterns is the primeval eye, the use of which is still enjoyed by children, tribesmen, mystics, madmen and dreamers. Shakespeare describes how it was regained by the banished Duke in *As You Like It*, holding outlaw court under the greenwood tree, who found 'tongues in trees, books in running brooks, sermons in stones, and good in everything.'A wonderful account of its modern use is given by Strindberg in *Inferno*, of how he descended into the loneliness of a room in Paris, began alchemical experiments, and found himself led by promptings from the signs and images around him to invoke a series of amazing coincidences through which he gained the information needed for his research.

This brings us to the really interesting part of the simulacra phenomenon; the appearance or recognition of spontaneous images in circumstances that make them seem significant as guides, portents or commentaries on topical events. A legendary example, illustrated here, is the rock-acheropite of St Vartan, the 5th-century Armenian hero, which was revealed to his disconsolate followers after his death in battle against the Persians near Chermoog in his native land, where it is still to be seen. Natural rock-heads, recognised as portraits of local characters, are not uncommon, but accounts of such timely representations in this medium are rare. A recent case was the discovery, soon after the assassination of President Kennedy, of his familiar profile in lava rocks on the island of Maui, Hawaii. Fort gave several examples of images not made by men appearing in times and places which gave people grounds for viewing them as portentous. These include the mysterious marks that appeared on windows in Germany in 1872, which were seen as images of French cavalry soldiers waving banners. It happened just after the Franco-Prussian war when feelings were still inflamed. The authorities ordered the windows to be smashed! Another Fortean classic is the item he culled from the *English Mechanic* 12 June 1908, about a fall of large hailstones at Remiremont in France. Stamped on the hailstones were shapes recognised by witnesses as very exact representations of the Virgin of the

Hermits, the object of a local cult. A week before the event the town council had banned the Virgin's annual procession, but this, said the town's priest, was 'a vertical procession that no one could forbid.' (For details of some other Fortean characteristics of this happening see *Phenomena* p59)

The spontaneous image effect embraces a wide range of phenomena, among them stigmata — the symbolic markings which appear on certain people's skin in apparent imitation of the marks of crucifixion on Good Friday or some other significant season — and images projected on to sealed film or some other surface by proved 'thoughtographists' like Ted Serios or Eusapia Palladino (see *Phenomena* 'Projected thought-forms'). The invention of photography last century, closely followed by the first offerings of 'spirit photographs' and the like, has yielded a vast new crop of mysterious images. A number of contemporary examples of photographs, showing faces or figures which were not present when the photograph was taken, and which the photographer recognized as having some personal meaning, were shown and described in *FT* 10, (others in *FT* 26), where it was suggested that, like the 'thoughtographs' of Serios, these images were involuntary products of the photographer's or someone else's mind. Perhaps photography in general is less impersonal than is generally considered. After all, what is it that distinguishes a good photographer from a bad one when both have steady hands and the same equipment?

The strong evidence that the appearance of photographs may be influenced by human thoughts or desires reopens the old question of the extent to which these same thoughts and desires may influence appearances in the world at large. This question is central to Fortean studies, as it has also become central in the modern study of physics. Whatever conclusions we come to, experience warns that they should be lightly held; for in this world, where theories drawn from observation of phenomena begin to affect the phenomena themselves, nothing ever can be cut and dried. Forteans are likely to sympathise with the *idea*, though not with the *certainty* of the Bath theosophists that the damp-stain image on the Abbey wall was shaped by the pious thoughts of visitors. And the same goes for the idea [the certainty] of the sceptical vicar that it was shaped by blind chance. How could either party finally judge between these or other possible theories? Explanations in general being arbitrary and conditioned, we have the choice of patronizing whichever we want, whichever seem most delightful and beneficial. Exercising that choice, the ancients invoked the gods and powers of the earth at places where nature displayed a god's symbols or image. And, following that increasingly recognized effect of experiments tending to justify a theory, perhaps these invocations were successful.

John Michell

OUT OF PLACE

There seem to be more mystery animals roaming the British landscape than ever before. As we go to press more sightings of our phantom feline friends are coming in, to be given next issue.

'Surrey Puma' Lives...

Stories of large cats — lions, pumas, cheetahs, leopards, lynxes etc — living wild in the British countryside have been regularly reported since the early 1960s. These exotic aliens are seen strolling in fields and surprised in lanes; they are heard yowling at night; they scare domestic animals and leave tracks. They are hunted by big game hunters, police and experts from London Zoo — but nothing conclusive is found. The experts retreat to London convinced of what they knew all along — that the countryfolk had been 'seeing and hearing things' again and letting their imagination get the better of them. We could suppose that these animals have a phantom existence conjectured from the effects they leave behind them. These effects themselves are phantoms, usually recollections of an encounter, or thoroughly ambiguous or inconclusive physical evidence. The lesson is obvious: this poor state of affairs is usually the result of the involvement of an 'expert', whose function in the scheme of things is to extricate himself with his world-view intact and unmodified in a way which leaves the affair even more confusing than before. But on with our story...

Before sightings this year our last note of the 'Surrey puma' — which is confined neither to Surrey nor to puma — was from October 1977 (see FT25 p33). All 1978 it laid low, or was unobserved or unreported. It was seen again early in January this year, this time in Kent. In woods at Boughton Street, near Faversham, two boys out ferreting saw a 'big black animal'. A lecturer, Peter Latham, spotted it near his house, and a neighbour, Mrs Bernadette Kiely, found 'unusually large' paw prints in the snow nearby. *Sunday Mirror* 14 Jan 1979.

The next sightings in the Faversham area came a few weeks later, but our net of clipsters caught the tiny note in London *Evening News* 31 Jan 1979, that a police hunt for a large cat, thought to be a 'puma', was going on at Waldershare Park, stately home of the Earl of Guildford. Waldershare Park is about 4-5 miles from Dover and perhaps 17 miles from Boughton. No details of the sightings that stimulated the hunt are given, but we note the use of the term 'puma'. Pumas are large sandy coloured cats, whereas a large black cat would have to be a pigmented leopard or jaguar, or a panther. Popular insistence on the term 'puma' for all these sightings provides an easy target for the scorn of big city 'experts'.

Nevertheless, a black 'puma' continued to be seen in the Faversham area. Chris Flood, who has a farm at Uplees, Faversham, was among a number of people who reported their sightings to Faversham police. Flood, who thinks it could be a panther, says: 'At first people round here thought it was just a large domestic cat but it is far too big for that,' Prints were found on Flood's farm, and police confessed themselves mystified. There were no reports of escapes from zoos or circuses. Not taking any chances they issued a public warning to beware of a 'dangerous large black cat'. *D.Star* 21 Feb; London *Evening News* 24 Feb 1979.

Chief Inspector Carey told papers 'Some very sensible people have made reports of seeing it so we can't dismiss it as nonsense.' Their own searches revealed nothing, except the mysterious paw prints. Like a good Chief Inspector, Carey sent casts of the prints to Howletts Zoo, Canterbury, but despite the accompanying suggestion that the prints might be panther or puma, the keepers there said they could not be sure what kind of animal made them. Like good keepers they decided to let someone else make fools of themselves identifying them. The Last Resort for perplexing zoological questions: London Zoo. After all, justifies Chief Inspector Carey: 'They have the best brains in Britain on this kind of thing.' London *Evening News* 5 March 1979. London Zoo did not diappoint us for once — like good puzzled zoologists they passed the buck to a higher authority. Back came the word from the Natural History Museum: 'Dog.' This was good enough for Chief Inspector Carey, who, like a good policeman, shelved his own earlier reservations ('It could be a big dog but everyone who has seen it says it does not look like one.') in favour of *ex cathedra* judgement. He said: 'At last the residents of Faversham can stop worrying... Two of the county's top experts say the print is not made by anything from the cat family and is almost certainly a dog. Now the mystery is over.' We bet it isn't. London *Evening News* 14 March; Kent *Adscene* 15 March 1979.

We have often reflected on the quiet, comfortable and untroubled life we would be able to lead if we weren't curious. To be able to change convictions as easily and quickly as Chief Inspector Carey would get us out of many an awkward position. But we have some reservations about these paw-casts: two zoos (full of living animals) were unable, or reluctant, to pronounce upon them — then, in steps the Natural History Museum, which normally side-steps controversy. The Museum is a weird place — a visiting extraterrestrial could be forgiven if he came away with the idea it was a shrine to glassy-eyed extinction, where an invisible priesthood have set out to kill, stuff or pickle at least one of every different living thing, displaying the victims of their unguessable rituals in a celebration of the abhorrence of life and movement. It's said that the only way to tell a member of staff from a specimen is to wave a wage packet in front of the creature — and even that's been known to fail. But what excuses have they got? Only that they follow in the impeccable tradition, subscribed to by institutions, authorities and experts all over the world, of knowing better than locals and witnesses what the latter have seen and heard. Such superior knowledge at a distance would make a case for clairvoyance if it weren't wrong much of the time.

What guarantee have we that the paw marks were made by the sighted large black cat. If they were indeed made by a local large dog — any large dog — what more convenient way to squash a mystery?

So...having been cynically dismissive about an expert opinion have we anything to put in its place? Only the original and firsthand reports of witnesses

that a large black panther-like creature, distinctly feline, visited the Boughton area in January and February. Valerie Martin, one of our correspondents in Kent, spoke to a woman who lived in Boughton. 'I asked her about the animal,' wrote Valerie. 'She had not seen it but knew several people, including children, who had. The animal was seen in the main village street during the recent snowy weather in the third week of February. Two sheep were also found dead and mutilated. The villagers were most annoyed at the 'expert' opinion of it being a dog. They say it was definitely feline in appearance, and not a golden retriever, labrador or fox, nor as had also been suggested, a large domestic tom.' Valerie observes that the countryside is full of lonely wooded places which could shelter predators. She also recalled that a few miles south-east of Canterbury is John Aspinall's zoo park. 'He keeps tigers, lions, cheetahs and black panthers but I've not heard of any recent escape. Remembering the terrible fuss many years ago when one of his panthers did escape and was shot, I do not think another such occurrence would pass unnoticed.' This generates another hypothesis, that we have the ghost of a shot panther haunting the area, and like ghosts everywhere appears sometimes solid and sometimes immaterial, but always neither one thing nor any other.

A Sussex Panther?

As so often happens in our subjects the 'mystery' closes down its operation in one locale and sets up shop elsewhere. Alan Gardiner, another of our vigilant readers, has been keeping his Fortean eye on the 'puma', or large black cat, that turned up in his Sussex backyard at mid-year. Alan was alerted when, in the course of the conversation with a colleague at work, Colin Carter, Carter confessed that he had seen a 'puma' 3-4 weeks previously. He knew nothing of the history of the 'Surrey puma', and had not mentioned his encounter to anyone except to his mother a week later. She asked if it was like a puma, and that's when the oddity of the event sank in. The following details are from a statement made to Alan Gardiner on 31 Aug 1979.

Colin Carter was walking along the South Downs, in the Belle Tout area, east of Eastbourne, at about 9pm on either Saturday 30th June or Sunday 1st July. A large black animal crossed the path about 10 yards in front of him. Before it was lost in the undergrowth he got the impression of a cat-like creature 'the size of a small pony'.

The creature, or one like it was next seen on 10th September. The story is pieced together from the Brighton *Evening Argus* 14 Sept 1979, and yet another statement obtained by Alan Gardiner, this time from witnesses John and Frances Clarke. That Monday was warm and overcast and found John and Frances at midday strolling through picturesque Tilgate Forest, near Crawley. Suddenly ahead of them they saw the large cat-like creature, about 75-100 yards away. It was motionless, gazing at them, as though it too had been surprised in its walk. After an eternal 10-15 seconds, during which they could see the animal clearly, John whistled. The creature turned swiftly and retraced its steps with long bounds, then turned aside into the undergrowth. Frances said: 'I don't mind admitting I felt quite panicky. I picked up a stick and carried it until we got to the car.'

The Young Turk who shocked the Curators at the Natural History Museum by actually studying Live Specimens!

The Clarkes estimate its height at 2 to 2′6″, with a small head, pointed ears and a long tail. Its colouring was 'either black or very dark brown.' Like most people, the Clarkes knew very little about the 'Surrey puma', but when they told their story in their pub that night, they were told other stories in turn. Crawley Council, who administer the Tilgate Forest, said that their woodland workers had seen no sign of the beast.

I guess it's still out there!

Scottish Cats

In previous issues we have kept a beady eye on the 'Surrey puma's' friends north of the border, in Ayrshire, Sutherland and Inverness-shire. Two of these have been reactivated.

Either the Inverness 'lioness' (see FT25 p34) moved south and east over the Cairngorms, or we have another outbreak of phantom feline, this time in Angus. On the edge of the bleak Forest of Alyth, between Alyth and Glen Isla, is the small village of Kilry, in wild Macbeth-country. Witnesses told police that a 'large black cat-like creature' was seen twice, at 8am and 1pm, in a snow covered field opposite the village store. It was described as 'bigger than any domestic cat or dog', and about 2ft high. No date is given but we'd guess at 8th or 9th February. Scottish *Sunday Post* 11 Feb 1979.

In late August the 'puma' returned to its Ayrshire haunt. After being seen several times in the Holmston district of Ayr itself, SPCA Inspector Robert Dunbar saw it for himself. He said: 'It has all the characteristics of the puma family. Without doubt it is the largest cat I have come across...his body length is about four feet.' Witnesses agree this puma-like animal is big and black. Then, about 1st August, Sharon Sloan, 18, and her neighbours saw it several times in the back gardens of Glencairn Road. Pictures of a large cat were shown to the director of Calderpark Zoo. Scottish zoo-keepers it seems are just as conservative as their

English cousins — he said it was an ordinary domestic cat. To be fair there is no real indication of scale in the picture, and any cat looks smaller when hunched in a defensive posture. Inspector Dunbar was undaunted — he planned a safari. But before he got very far a girl on a pony was frightened into a 'near-hysterical' state by a large black animal that fitted the description of the creature. Casts of paw-prints spanning four inches across were taken, and they appeared to match those taken from the Dundonald area of the same county during a 'puma' hunt there last year. We have no further details on either series of sightings. This may be because Inspector Dunbar did a fatal thing. He said: 'I'm keeping my fingers crossed that more sightings will be made.' As far as we know none have been reported. *Glasgow Herald* 6 & 8 Aug; *Weekly News* 11 Aug 1979.

Bear-faced Monkey Business

Sometime in July this year — none of our sources say precisely when — a change came over the woods on Brassknocker Hill at Claverton Down, about 5 miles south of Bath, Somerset. Ron and Betty Harper, who live at Sun Cottage on the hill, reported that something had stripped the bark off a 40yr-old oak tree beside the cottage — and whatever it was had badly frightened their goat. Dubbed the 'Beast of Bath' by the papers, the mystery animal became an object of great curiosity, and so did the tree. Local gardener, John Harris, 70, thought it might be the work of squirrels, but when he saw for himself he changed his mind. 'Squirrels usually walk across the tops of branches and strip off the top bark. This damage looks as though it has been done by an animal hanging under the branches. The bark has been ripped off all the branches from about 20ft up to the top.' Another account, perhaps carelessly, says the lower 20ft. Another old-timer who lives on the hill, Frank Green, 81, said that since the incident all the birds had gone and the wood was

strangely silent. He said: 'It must be some kind of creature which can cling upside down and lean over. I suppose it could be a bat, but it would need to be a terrific one to strip bark like that. I think it's some sort of monkey.' Ron Harper thinks it 'has got to be a rodent' after a Bath Parks official made a nervous joke about him having a 'squirrel 10 times bigger than normal'. Harper adds: 'The teeth marks were 10-20 times the size of a squirrel's.' One paper quotes him supposing it could be an escaped monkey or raccoon.

Harper's neighbour, Mrs Jean Blunt, said her cat went missing the night the Harper's goat was frightened. She woke that night to hear a terrible scream. Later, Mary Silk, a nurse, said she and a colleague at nearby Winsley Hospital also heard the noise, at 4am. Mrs Blunt later found her cat with a 7 inch gash across its belly. The accounts imply the scream was made by the 'Beast', but it could have been the cat when attacked.

By the 1st August we learn that about 50 trees had been found stripped, though none of them to the extent of Harper's oak. They were mostly oaks, and a few beech — the 'Beast' seems partial to the softer sweet pith between the bark and the trunk. 'Experts' say this is the behaviour of some monkeys but none have been reported missing recently. We have news for them — in February 1977, 3 baboons escaped from Longleat Wildlife Park, not 10 miles south of Claverton Down, and as far as we know were never caught. *D.Mirror* 1 March 1977.

People began seeing things which may or may not have been the 'Beast of Bath', who may or may not have been a giant bat, giant squirrel, racoon or monkey or baboon. Albert Miner, sitting in the garden of his Bradford Road cottage at Claverton, saw a 'strange animal come through the gap in my garden wall. I followed it to the garden gate but did not get a look at its face. It crossed the road and went into the wood opposite.' It was dusk but he made out that it was about 2ft high, about twice the size of a cat, stood upright, and was bushy and grey in colour. On the 9th August a 3-man team claimed to have almost caught the creature and are fully convinced it is a *fully grown chimpanzee*. Search leader Alan Heaslop, of Combe Down, said he and his men had been in the wood several hours when they heard and then saw 'this black creature swing from tree to tree above our heads.' It dropped to the ground about 20ft away, and seemed tame, or at least curious. The men approached and Alan dived. 'I caught it by the leg, but it let out a high-pitched screech and jerked free.' Once again it was poor light but they describe the chimpanzee as 'about 3ft tall with a flat face and patches of grey and white on its chest.'

A feature story in the *Guardian* later gave the experience of Christopher Morris, returning from a fishing trip with a friend. 'We were driving through Monkton Combe at about 12.30am, and it stood in the middle of the road, right in our headlights. It was 3-4ft high and scrambled through a hedge. To me it looked like a baboon. My friend thought it looked like a chimpanzee. It had bright white rings around the eyes, rather like spectacles. We hadn't been drinking.' Baboon, chimpanzee – a world of difference – yet our two eye-witnesses cannot agree. But wait a minute: white rings around the eyes? Mrs P Lawless, of Bath, also spotted that one and wrote to the *Guardian* pointing out that quite a few zoos have Spectacled Bears with precisely that distinctive feature, and could not our 'Beast' be an escaped one? Now bears — splendid! But police and zoo officials kept reassuring us that there were no known escapes — experts in these things usually end up blaming a hypothetical owner of some exotic animal who lets it loose or from whom it escapes, but they can never say where, when and from whom. I'm tempted to be as 'scientific' as any expert and refuse to believe in such imaginary and inept zoophiles on the same grounds as the well-tried logic that resists 'Surrey pumas', yeties and Nessies.

That was the last we heard about anything. Like all our mysteries, the 'Beast' was never identified positively and press interest, or sightings, or its very existence ceased as mysteriously as it had begun, leaving only a confused record of a haunted wood which was for a short time visited by a were-thing seen, heard and touched in the form of a baboon, a chimpanzee and a Spectacled Bear. Story assembled from: *S.Express* 29 July; Bath *Evening Chronicle* 30 July, 1, 7 & 10 Aug; *Guardian* 23 & 25 Aug 1979.

Encore for Exotic Escapes

Speaking of monkeys:

Residents of Exton, Leicestershire, are claiming that a band of monkeys are raiding their dustbins and greenhouses during the night. Mrs Nancy Nicholls, of Exton, in what used to be Rutland, said she saw one climb into her greenhouse and begin eating her tomatoes. Up to five at one time have been seen. Peter Taylor, a pub-keeper at Barkby, said it could be his capuchin monkey, which escaped sometime previously. But Mrs Nicholls doesn't think so: capuchins are tiny, she says, and the monkey she saw was as big as a spaniel. Into the debate steps the inevitable zoo spokesperson, in this case Molly Badham, billed as a 'Twycross Zoo expert'. Mrs Badham, expert on Twycross Zoo, pronounces that a band of five monkeys is highly unlikely — it is probably only one. (You

figure it out.) Naturally, puzzled as to its /their origin, she blames our old friend and zoological bogeyman, the phantom pet-keeper. Curiously, we have on hand Mr Taylor; but he doesn't count because he lost the wrong kind of monkey, the fate of which has passed beyond human ken. The last note we have is of a band of monkeys 'believed to have escaped from a travelling circus' seen swinging through trees at Stamford, Lincolnshire. A quick glance at the map showed that Stamford was only a few miles from Exton, over the border. *Leicester Mercury* 7 & 8 Sept; *D.Express* 10 Sept; *D.Mirror* 12 Sept 1979.

But what about bears? Well we've noted sightings of bear in Yorkshire in these pages (FT9p15f). In the week beginning 11th June there was a bear scare in the forest at Thetford, Norfolk. From the descriptions given by motorists travelling along the A1066 at Snare Hill, it was supposed to be a small Himalayan or Malaysian bear, eascaped — you guessed it — from a travelling circus. I wish I had £1 for every travelling circus that's sneaking along our byways distributing exotic aliens. Sussex *Bury Free Press*, Sunderland *Echo* and national press for 15 June 1979.

[Credit: Tom Adams, Janet & Colin Bord, Mollie Cairncross, PL Catlin, Richard Cotton, Peter Christie, Alan Gardiner, Chris Hall, Peter James, J Lang, Valerie Martin, John Michell, Colin Mather, Nick Maloret, Paul Pinn, Mike Rickard, Roland Watson, Sam] **RJMR.**

It's funny! Now we're actually face to face, I'm not the least bit frightened.

Behind many a grim datum we've detected the sure hand and black humour of the cosmic prangster. For your edification we present a selection *In memoriam.*

Thankamma Mathai (20) wore an artificial bun at her wedding in Trivandrum, near New Delhi. She collapsed and died as she walked down the aisle. A doctor found a snake bite on the nape of her neck. It was supposed that a small snake had coiled up in her bun overnight. Recent research at Melbourne University has shown that every year after mating, the entire male population of the marsupial Stuart shrew keels over and dies. Immediately after his marriage in Council Bluffs, Iowa, Greg Cundiff (23), stricken by nerves and heat, hit his head on the altar steps and never regained consciousness. *S. Express* 10 July 1977: Madras *S. Standard* 8 April 1979; *D. Mail* 26 June 1979.

•

Paul Gleffe (12) of Milwaukee, taught himself to lose consciousness to amuse friends. He died after collapsing and striking his head on the school playground. London *Eve. Standard* 29 May 1979.

•

A man was knocked down by a car in New York, got up uninjured, but lay down in front of a car again when a bystander told him to pretend he was hurt and collect insurance money. The car rolled forward and crushed him to death. Mark Harrison was killed as he worked in a field by bouncing wreckage from a plane that crashed nearby. The same fate befell his father a few years before. Malaysia *New Sunday Times* 10 July 1977.

Fish knifes man. A South Korean fisherman, preparing his catch landed in New Zealand, thought the tuna he was about to gut was dead. It flicked its tail sending the knife he was holding into the luckless man's chest. *Shropshire Star* 4 June 1979.

•

Nitaro Ito, 41, a Japanese restaurant owner from Osaka planned a bizarre campaign to be elected to Japan's House of Representatives. He asked friends to beat him up, and then stabbed himself in the thigh, hoping to draw sympathy from voters and the publicity of running his campaign from his hospital bed. Unfortunately for him he had stabbed too deeply and died from loss of blood in the 20 yard walk from his car to his house. *AP* 20 Sept; Vancouver *Sunday News* 23 Sept 1979. Curiously, about the same time, Paul Williams, 24, a police recruit in North London, carried out a similar but non-fatal attack upon himself, hitting his head with a brick and stabbing himself with a penknife. His wounds were impressive enough to attract an award after hospitalization. He was caught out when other false alarms were traced to his own extension in the police station. He said he had expected police work to be more exciting. *Sun* 26 Sept 1979.

•

A man was accidentally killed in Thonburi, Thailand, in a fight with his friend over which came first, the chicken or the egg. He said it was the egg. *S. Times* 15 Jan 1978.

A boy of 2 was killed in Florida when a wind-propelled beach umbrella pierced his heart. A French woman of 30 met an identical end on a beach at Roquebrune-sur-Argens on the French Riviera the following summer. *D. Mirror* 29 Aug 1978; *Int. Herald Tribune* 24 July 1979.

•

Jean-Marie Escoubes (54) was killed while inspecting a double wheel on his truck at Pau in France. Both tyres burst simultaneously in the heat and hurled him 30 yards. This happened sometime in the week up to the 9th July 1978. An AP press release of 30 June 1979 (San Francisco) told of the sudden end of a San Jose quarry worker, Virgil Romero (48). The 7 foot tyre he was blowing up — blew up with a roar heard miles away. *S. Express* 9 July 1978; *NY Times* 1 July 1979.

•

A stone flung up by a mower in a Surrey field entered a car window and almost decapitated a 19-year-old nurse taking a driving lesson. A year later, a Tel-Aviv woman was killed when a fizzy drink bottle exploded in her hand. A sliver of glass severed the main artery in her neck. *D. Telegraph & D. Mirror* 15 July 1978; *Guardian* 27 June 1979.

•

A woman in Boise, Idaho, had a cornea graft died from rabies transmitted by the donor, 7 weeks after the operation in Atlanta, Georgia. *Rising Nepal* 18 March 1979; *Guardian* ? March 1979.

•

12 men in a village near Rawalpindi died in succession as they went down a well which contained gas leaking from a kerosene-powered water pump. And 7 died of suffocation near Ahmedabad after a man fell into a cow dung pit and 6 others jumped in to rescue him. Delhi *Statesman* 12 April 1979; *Guardian* 30 July 1979.

A youth of 22 died after inserting a knife in his chest at a dargah in Jamnagar, India, believing it would do him no harm. He had seen people inserting a needle or a thin piece of iron into their lungs or other parts of the body with no ill effects. *Times of India* 29 May 1979.

•

Student David Reynolds described in an essay how he was shot dead at a Hartford motel where he worked as a night clerk. A few nights later he was shot by a mystery intruder. He had even got the time of death right. *Weekly News* 23 June 1979.

•

53 Hindus returning from a religious dip in the Ganges were killed and 12 injured when their bus plunged into a river, 65 miles from Allahabad. Unsympathetic magic? *Leicester Mercury* 9 Feb 1978.

•

Villagers cut off the heads of a religious leader and his wife in the Philippines after challenging them to prove there was a life after death. *Reveille* 11 May 1979.

•

A man who went fishing on the banks of the Amazon's Rio Negro was attacked by infuriated bees after he struck their nests while trying to free his line from a tree. To escape, he leapt into the river, where he was devoured by piranha fish. *D. Telegraph* 12 Aug 1977.

•

During the British fireman's strike, one of the army's Green Goddesses rescued an old lady's cat from a tree. After tea and biscuits, the army left and ran over the cat in their fire engine. *Sun* 14 Jan 1978.

•

[Credit: Janet & Colin Bord, Chris Hall, D MacAdams, Peter Rogerson, Paul Screeton, Has Thomas, D Whalen, Ion Will, Joe Zarzynski.] **PRAdeGS.**

Algernon Blackwood wrote: 'It is impossible to know whether or not plants are conscious; but it is consistent with the doctrine of continuity that in all living things there is something psychic...we must believe that in plants there exists a faint copy of what we know as consciousness ourselves.' *The Man Whom The Trees Loved.* We don't consider plants much... but they were here on this planet before we were a twinkle in a mud critter's eyes, and for all we know we may have been used...

Plants — Down to Earth and Skyward Ho!

'It's like something from Outer Space' is a frequent, post-triffid reaction to fearsome and futuristic flora, and Mrs Halliday and her dog suspected that it might be so. So did Mr Bill Halliday, who found some seeds while walking on the Fells (!) which he planted in his garden in the hamlet of Quaking Houses, Co. Durham. There grew a 'strange menacing' 6ft high plant, eventually and authoritatively identified by experts as a *'Dispsacus sylvestris*, one of the Teasel family'. Helpful, but no-one could explain why at night it emitted an 'eerie white glow'. (*S. Express* 25 June & 2 July 1978).

Equally exotic were farmer Joe Carr's crop of luminous potatoes, Pentland Firth variety, from his field at Pica, Cumbria. 'It's as if they had been scattered with glitter dust', said his wife Sadie, 'but they make super

chips'. Local wags dutifully dubbed the starry-eyed spuds Identified Frying Objects. *D. Express* 29 Jan 79). Russian botanists reported from Tunguska that the area before the 'event' of 1908 produced only stunted wirey trees, but has 'recently become a mighty coniferous forest and the natural rate of genetic change in the flora of the region has increased twelvefold'. Unusual silicate dust particles, thought to be the remains of whatever it was that exploded on arrival, have been found trapped in nearby layers of moss. *S. Times* 4 April 1976.

We glimpse the growth of a far-flug fertiliser and seed delivery service — an Interstellar Interflora — our planet's plant life occasionally requested to relay a genetic chain-letter to the outer galaxies. And since human migration has always been used by plants to accelerate their colonisation of *this* world, we are not surprised to find them active in space exploration and busy developing new forms designed for long journeys to new lands.

'Brilliant, much brighter than usual' gladioli were a big hit at Moscow's Botanical Gardens — grown from bulbs that had spent several months in orbit in Soyuz 20. 'The space trip seems to have worked wonders' said the bemused botanists. Well you see, they flowered *23* days earlier than is considered normal. (*S. Express* 4 April 1979.) Then, in May 1979, the cosmonauts on board Salyut 6 harvested and ate their first crop of orbital onions, with a witches' salad of fennel, parsley and garlic to follow. We trust that the undeservedly little-known cult of onion-worshippers in France (*Herald Tribune* 14 May 1979) were consoled by the news that a Soviet computer-programmer got six years hard labour for speculating in closely-related tulips from a State tulip farm only ten days after a tulip was sent aloft by supply rocket to grace Salyut's sacrificial supper table. (*D. Telegraph* 15 & 26 May 1979.) [About a week after these words were penned, we learned that the Salyut cosmonauts had returned to earth. The news that 'doctors had to relieve them of a large bouquet of gladioli handed to them after landing because of the strain on their weakened muscles' (*D. Telegraph, Guardian* 21 Aug) provoked disruptive hilarity at the weekly FT editorial meeting. Later, another datum of galactic gardening turned up. According to *Soviet Weekly* 4 Aug 1979, tulips grown in space will send out shoots up to 20 inches long but the buds refuse to open. The current crew of Salyut will administer remedial doses of earth-gravity in a centrifuge. — Eds.]

'For all I know' mused Charles Fort in *Lo!* (chap. 4) 'some trees may have occult powers'. So, should, in continuing karmic compensation, a new wave of Tulipmania engulf the USSR, you heard it here first. Plants have had time to develop any amount of wild talents, including leading Cleve Backster up the garden path.

Heroic Sago
Training for survival under extreme conditions has been going on for some time: further reports that Mother Nature looks after her own come from Fukien Province, East China, where a 1000 year old lichee tree still bears fruit every year in the courtyard of the Sung temple in Putien county (*New Straits Times* 21 Feb 1978; *China Pictorial* June 1979); from Mendoza, Argentina, where 2000-yr-old seeds of the Quinca (a variety of pigweed) were successfully germinated and throve (*Washington Post* 12 Jan 1977); and from Saga, Japan, where a 4000-yr-old acorn discovered during excavations grew into a 5ft oak in a museum garden (*Shropshire Star* 21 Sept; *Melbourne Herald* 22 Sept 1978). In the last two cases the life-support system was a simple sealed jar.

Harry Potter is a keen gardener, so a wooden clothes peg he used to mark a row of seeds in his greenhouse at Bebside, Northumberland, sympathetically took root and grew 4 sturdy shoots. 'Millions-to-one fluke of nature' hoped an expert – but what about the 'mystery plant shoots up to a foot long' growing out of David Cowan's new kitchen-

door frame at W. Bridgeford, Notts., or the runner-bean poles fueled by elephant manure at Dudley Zoo, Worcs., which grew into a row of poplars with 40ft trunks? *D.Express* 10 Jan 1978; *D. Mirror* 13 May 1976; *Weekend* 5 Dec 1973.

A cornucopia of fabulous fruits, voluminous veg and magnificent mushrooms suggests that low-gravity planets are desirable destinations for floral frontier scouts. Consider the 17 pound mutant mushroom in Villafranca, Majorca, which had a 'cluster of heads, some a foot wide, all sprouting from a central stalk' (*S.Express* 17 Sept 1978); and another, 6½ ft in diameter weighing 19 pounds from the Shoumen region of NE Bulgaria (*Times* 24 Oct; *Le Soir*, Belgium, 25 Oct 1978); and the profusion of 4 pounders which dotted the lawns and boulevard verges of the town of Osh, Kirgizia, Soviet Central Asia (*S. Express* 20 May 1979). 'Tear Mushroom eats 80 houses in Sapporo, Japan, Jan 23' indicates the next field of research — the marauding *Merulius Lachrymans*, which oozes tears of wood-rotting liquid enzyme, has found ideal conditions in houses insulated to beat heating-oil price-rises (*Ceylon Observer* 25 Jan 1979). Scotland produced a 42 pound world record swede (*D. Telegraph* 21 Feb 1979) and the 'biggest ever' tapioca, weighing 28 katies

(look it up!) was uprooted during the Malaysian army exercises at Kuala Kelawang (*New Straits Times* 27 Nov 1978). We have further data on giant cabbages and brussel sprouts, potatoes, tomatoes, pineapples and even gooseberries. The current champion, a 297½ pound pumpkin, grew in, uh, *Petal*uma, California (*Nevada State Journal* 19 Oct 1978), but who remembers its 140 pound precursor found in a garden in Vaucluse, France, which was flown to London's Savoy Hotel to feed 400 US tourists at Thanksgiving? It preferred suicide to fraternisation and exploded in the kitchen! *Weekend* 5 Dec 1973.

Plant research lost a precocious pioneer when an 'ugly sort of rubber plant gone wrong' was thrown into a family dustbin. It lived next to Mrs. Josephine Cooke's TV set in Stockton-on-Tees, and learned to move slowly from side to side to grow away from the light and, when watered, to utter moans. It is not known whether this attempt at intra-species communication was directed at Mrs Cooke or the one-eyed electric lodger, but nature is prodigal. We await further developments. *S.Express* 24 June 1979.

[Credit: Chris Hall, Mark A Hall, Dave Hill, Janet & Colin Bord, Valerie Martin, Richard King, Henri Premont, Anthony Smith, Sam, Paul Screeton, Has Thomas] **IAW & PRAdeGS.**

Our last review of sexy spectres was in FT22, since when the randy wraiths have been busy with more ectoplasmic erotica and horny horror.

Asking For It.....
For the most part, the recipients of these astral affections are female, and all seem to be post-pubescent, which contrasts with

many of the 'usual' poltergeist cases centering around adolescents. We suspect that sexual frustration and wish-fulfilment may play a large part in some of the following tales, but as our reports don't deal in detailed personal life-histories, we have to reserve judgement. But we note that if wish-fulfilment *is* the root cause, it seems mostly to be sufficiently unconscious for the ghostly groper's attentions to be unwelcome, if not horrifying. On the other hand, some folks just seem set on letting themselves in for trouble....

In a series of articles on the perils of the ouija board by Paul Pickering (*Reveille* 24 March 1978), we have mention of a certain Mrs June of Marske-by-Sea, near Redcar, Yorkshire. Mrs June, obviously a mature woman with a 10-year old son, became obsessed with the ouija, which in turn led to automatic writing, the communicating entity being 'a long-dead spirit called Leonardo'. Dead he may have been, but he still knew how to write a good love-letter, and he even claimed to want a child by Mrs June. A few weeks after the automatic writing began, Mrs June saw a floating shadow in the bedroom; then she felt the bed-clothes move. Leonardo had arrived...and was, it seems, furious to discover she was taking the contraceptive pill. (Eventually she did have another child, physically by her husband, though she is convinced it was conceived because of the ouija board.) This doesn't seem to have dampened lusty Leonardo's enthusiasm though. Mrs June is quoted; 'I would feel his presence, even his strength of feeling when he wanted to make love. He was a competent lover and must have been on earth. But human love is more satisfying. With spiritual love, there is no warmth of flesh'. What eventually became of Leonardo is not, unfortunately, recorded...

And Getting It....

Cynic that I am, I confess there is something about the dating of our next story which makes me suspicious. A mere two days after Mrs June's expression of disappointment in Leonardo was published, we find Jenny Price, 20, of Shenley Lane, Wedley Castle, Birmingham, claiming complete satisfaction with her own ghostly gallant. *News of the World* 26 March 1978; *Kansas City Times* 13 April 1978. It seems that Jenny's mother, Olive, 50, wrote to the NoW to reveal her daughter's spectral sex-life, which perhaps qualifies Olive for a place in our 'Strange Behaviour' section. But on with the story...The family had known that the house had a ghost for years, but had never told Jenny about it. The first amorous approach was to the elder daughter, Lorraine, but it merely touched her shoulder. Then, three years prior to the report, Jenny was sitting up in bed one night when she felt invisible hands round her neck. With great strength, the hands pushed her down on the bed. Frightened, she tried to scream, couldn't, and thought the ghost would strangle her, but then realised the ghost had other intentions. After that she was scared to go to bed in case the attack was repeated, and a week later, it was. She soon realised that the ghost meant her no harm, however, and began looking forward to his visits, which began to take place as often as three times a week...

By the time three years had passed, the biggest problem appears to have been how to get Jenny out of bed, she being too intent on staying there waiting for her invisible lover to show up. It begins with a kiss on the shoulder, then hands come under the covers and caress her before he gets into bed beside her. 'I just let him do what he wants,' she says, 'and he does it beautifully ...he can certainly love.' But always silently, it seems.

Olive Price wanted to get in on the act too, so she swapped beds with her daughter for three weeks (what her husband Trevor thought about this is not recorded). But the randy wraith didn't show up. Prefers blondes, apparently. Still, you'll be pleased to hear that Olive doesn't think anything immoral's going on. She asked to see the vicar, and he said ghosts probably don't bother with morals. So that makes it okay. Doesn't it?

By George!

Or, more precisely, 'Why George?' Why does the name George turn up so often in our tales of amorous ghosts? If it were merely a case of an affectionate label, 'George the Ghost', all would be clear. But it's not so simple. A quick skim through our two previous selections reveals a George Lane, and a George Dexter, whose dead brother was supposed to be going a-haunting. And now we have more:

George Meyer had a friendly ghost at his converted stable home at Iver, Bucks, which introduced itself to his wife by slapping her bottom...this seems a fairly regular prank amongst our high-spirited spirits. But this ghost restricted himself to butt-smacking, making noises in the night, moving jewellery and switching off lights. *Daily Mirror* 18 May 1970.

Diane Moloney started work at Liverpool's Adelphi Hotel and was given a room on the fifth floor. The first night, she woke at 5 a.m. to find a man standing by her bed. Diane, 24, was not particularly reassured to be told it was 'only' George the Ghost...*Reveille* 10 June 1977.

While at the Black Horse pub at Windsor, Berks, another George the Ghost can't keep his hands off the bar-maids...he pinches their bottoms. *Daily Mirror* 5 Sept 1977.

At least two, and perhaps more, ghosts were haunting the Betts' household in Clacton, Essex, especially when Steve Betts, 24, was on night-shift. His wife, Ross, 22, seems to have been the centre of attention, but our clippings are a little contradictory. The *Daily Star* 15 Feb 1979, claims one ghost whispering sweet nothings in her ear, another materialised in her bed at 3 am, and yet another tagged along when she went for a bath one day. The *News of the World* 18 Feb 79, tells it a little less salaciously, and with only one major ghost, which had been plaguing the house for two years before an exorcism ejected it. Taking a bath one day, Ross heard footsteps moving from one bedroom toward the bathroom door. Wrapping a towel round herself, she opened the door... and nothing there. In bed one night with her 4-year old son Craig, she found the bed moving up and down at 2 am, followed by a loud banging in the ceiling; plaster fell on the dressing table. And on another occasion she saw a large black cat in the lounge, which her husband couldn't see. But here's the clincher: they would put young Craig to bed, and then hear him talking to a girl...the girl's replies could also be heard...and her name? You guessed it...Georgina!

Pun-worshippers may like to contemplate the fact that the name George derives from the Greek word for 'Husbandman'...

More Pub Polts

Landlady Sheila Jones of the Whitchurch Inn, near Tavistock, Devon, thought one of the customers was getting a bit amorous when she felt a 'warm hug'. But as no one was to be seen when she turned round, the furtive fondle was attributed to the resident ghost. It had also moved bottles and ornaments, and on another occasion upset a flower vase while the family was out. The two gallons of water in the vase simply disappeared. *Reveille* 9 Feb 1979.

Goosing the landlady in the bathroom seems a popular prank among our phantom fingerers.

Barbara Barnes, 31, was getting into the bath at the Albion Hotel, Bolton, Lancs, when she felt a hand caressing her bottom. At first she thought it was her husband, but on looking round... no one there and the door still closed. Still uncertain, she dressed and went downstairs, only to find her husband hadn't moved out of the bar. So 'Fred' the ghost got the blame. Fred has also dried up the beer in the pumps, turned off gas-taps in the cellar, and one night, caused beer to flow unceasingly from one of the taps. *Sunday Mirror* 29 July 1979.

And, as we learn from the house magazine of brewers John Courage Ltd (*The Golden Cockerel* July 1979), the Liverpool Arms in Kingston-upon-Thames, Surrey, has another bathroom invader. Licensees Leila and Fred Mudd took over the pub about 3 years ago, and became aware of the ghost shortly afterwards. And while Leila's mother has heard heavy breathing, it is Leila herself who attracts most attention...perhaps not surprising as she is former Miss Great Britain. On one such occasion she felt someone was standing in the doorway, and a shadow passed across the room as if someone was blocking out the light. But so far, the ghost seems content to play the Peeping Tom...or perhaps that should be the Peeping George...

But at the Old Vic pub, Winchester Street, Basingstoke, landlord Bob Williams is something of an exception to the rule. He shares his bed with a female ghost. He isn't too happy about it either. But Bob, 24, is not the object of her affections. He simply hears her heavy breathing and sighing, but he sees (and, apparently, feels) nothing. 'It's as though there is a woman lying next to me making love,' he says. 'She sounds a very passionate sort of woman.' Bob hides his head under the bed-clothes until

the panting stops... *Sunday People* 4 February 1979.

And in Naples, Italy, police were called in to hunt a sexy spectre that was trying to seduce women hotel guests. Perhaps the other guests need protection from the victims too...the latest one, newly-wed Annalisa Fusco, screamed so loud when she felt cold hands in bed that she woke up all 300 of the other guests! *Sun* 13 March 1978.

Back To The Bedroom

We have a couple more fairly straightforward stories to recount before we get on to the exotica...

The Hardie family of Stockton, Tees-side, had heard strange noises in the loft for a long time, but things started happening after the council did some modernisation work on the house. Daughter Margaret, 19, was lying awake in bed one night when she heard a thumping on the landing. The bedroom door opened, the bed shook. The bedclothes were slowly lifted, and then she felt a hand slide down the outside of her nightdress from her shoulders to her legs, where it rested. Paralysed with fear, she next saw a bald-headed man in a Victorian cape, who kept his face hidden from her. 'Come to the bathroom, Margaret,' he said, four or five times. Margaret still couldn't move, but eventually let out a scream. Her mother found her wringing with perspiration. After that, Margaret slept downstairs, but the ghost followed her, making regular visits (presumably of a similar nature). Her mother, Bessie, 57, sister Valerie, 20, and brother Bob, 24, have all seen the ghost also. The family were hoping to have the house exorcised. *Sunday People* 13 August 1978; *South Africa Sunday Times* 6 August 1978.

Divorcee Flo Dyke has been living in her 40-year old council house in Laburnam Road, Cannock, Staffs, for 30 years; but now she's had enough. Though

Flo has seen the ghost, he seems generally to leave her alone; it's her daughters he's after. The ghost is said to be in his 30's with greased black hair, and wearing a baggy, wide-lapelled suit over a vest. He first appeared to eldest daughter Yvonne 26 years ago, when she was 17, staring at her while she slept in the front bedroom, and he also took a look at middle daughter Annette in bed when she reached the age of 17. Three exorcisms seemed finally to have removed him, until...

Until youngest daughter Denise reached 17, too. Our early reports (*Sun, Daily Mirror, Daily Express, Daily Star,* all 11 June 79) play the story for laughs and sex, intimating that the saucy spectre had on several occasions popped out of the wardrobe and into bed with Denise, grabbing her arms and legs, holding her pinned to the bed, tickling her legs and so on. But later word (*Daily Star* 20 August 79) indicates that Denise woke one night to see the figure standing over her bed; tried to scream, couldn't; tried to move, pinned down; screamed again, succeeded, and woke Flo who swore at the shadowy figure. He laughed and dissolved away. Since when neither Flo nor Denise have slept at the house, and they've applied for a new house.

There is a tale that a Polish soldier was billetted in the street just after World War 2, fell in love with his host's 17-year old daughter, and hanged himself in the nearby woods on Cannock Chase when his suit was rejected. Now he is thought to have returned in search of his forbidden 17-year old bride. Only trouble is, it's the wrong house!

And another ex-serviceman: an unnamed couple living on the site of the old Croydon Airport, near London, are haunted by a young pilot who appears in flying helmet, oxygen mask and leather jacket. At first he simply appeared, standing there for up to five minutes. But the man of the house is a collector of military memorabilia, and a dummy in the hall, wearing an SS uniform, was hurled 10 feet one night. Later, he appeared to the wife in the bedroom, while she was ironing. Then another couple came to stay, and while the man was in the bathroom, the bedclothes were whisked off his wife. Finally, the couple had the house exorcised: yet while the exorcism was in progress, the wife felt the amorous airman plucking the straps of her bra. Wizard twang, what! The exorcism has apparently failed; phenomena continue. *Daily Star* 21 August 1979.

Some Nasty Ones

Certain of our bedroom invaders seem more intent on violence than passion, though we note that most of the first encounters with sexy spirits feature some kind of attack, frequently strangulation.

Madge Hislop and her family decided to move out of the old house in Oldmeldrum, Aberdeenshire, after only 9 months residence. They'd heard footsteps, strange violin music, and seen faces at the window. The last straw came when Madge was sleeping alone: the room went cold, the smell of roses pervaded the air. A voice called 'Marjory' three times and a pair of hands enclosed her throat. Madge screamed, the hands fell away... and when she put the light on, there were red marks round her neck. Exit the Hislop family, hurriedly. *Sunday Post* 7 May 1978

In *Midnight Globe* 15 August 1978 we have author Frank DeFelitta claiming that his new book *The Entity* had to be written as a novel because he couldn't publicly name those involved, but it was all true and the horrible tale he had to tell wasn't a publicity stunt to sell more copies, no sir! Be that as it may, we retell the tale briefly. In 1975 DeFelitta heard from UCLA parapsychologists Barry Taff and Kerry Gaynor of a woman who was being taken sexually by a force they could not pin down. The attacks took place nightly, with beatings, bites and marks appearing all over her body. DeFelitta recalls watching the woman one night: she screamed as the thing approached her, then a gaseous green light took on the form of an arm, shoulder and neck. The woman described the entity as a man about 7 feet tall, Chinese-featured, savage, but in a way loving. DeFelitta apparently spent several months with her, though no explanation was forthcoming...nor is there any mention of any attempts at preventative measures. The drama is, it seems, still being played out without resolution.

And then there's always a spectral spoilsport lurking around somewhere too: Steve Mikloz and his bride Debbie moved into their new flat in Rounds, Northants, on their wedding night, got into bed, put out the light...and Debbie, 17, realised they were not alone. Seconds later, so did Steve. Something grabbed him by the throat and dragged him out of bed, gasping for breath. After that bit of invisible interference, the couple got dressed and left, and haven't been back to the flat since. A spokesman for the landlord said quite plainly that the flat wasn't haunted: 'The disturbance must have come from the flat next door.' Rowdy neighbours, huh? *South Africa Sunday Times* 5 November 1978.

[Credit: Steve Hicks, Chris J Holtzhausen, Nick Maloret, Colin Mather, John Michell, Paul Screeton, Anthony Smith, Roger Waddington, D K Watson, Nigel Watson, Sam] **SM**.

Coincidence abounds in the world of twins and their double lives often run uncannily parallel.

Twin Speed Speech.

'Genebene manita.'
'Nomemee.'
'Eebedeebeda. Dis din qui naba.'
'Neveda. Ca Baedabada.'

This is a snatch of a tape recording of Poto and Cabenga, or Grace and Virginia Kennedy, as their parents call them. The identical twins were born in South Georgia in October 1970 of a German mother and an English speaking father. Their father remembers that the day after they were born, Grace suddenly raised her head and stared at him. She was having a 'convulsive seizure'. Virginia did the same thing the next day. These seizures continued periodically for six months, in spite of treatment. At 17 months, they began to improvise (or receive?) their very dense and rapid ideoglossia ('own language'), their only concession to English being 'mommy' and 'daddy'. At 2 they moved to California, but there were very few other children in the neighbourhood for them to meet. For five years they spoke nothing but their own language, although they clearly understood their parents' English and the German of their grandmother who looked after them when the parents were out. (Mrs Kunert herself spoke no English)

Then the speech therapists at the Children's Hospital in San Diego, California, began to study and tape them, and coax some English out of them — which they speak with a curious high-speed delivery. In May 1979. Dr Hagen (head of the Speech Pathology Department) said: 'Right now the big problem is to reduce their speech rate to a level understandable to normal ears.'

Some of the keen therapists have even tried to talk to Poto and Cabenga in their new language. 'They look at us as if we're crazy and laugh' said Anne Koenecke. 'Snap aduk, Cabenga, chase die-dipana' said Poto masterfully. (Poto and Cabenga at once began to play with a doll's house.)

They will celebrate their 9th birthday in October 1979, and they will be speaking English. As we see so often, a wonderful wild talent has been taught into woeful submission. Perhaps they are boat people from an alternative universe or early kundalini graduates (remember those 'convulsions'?) Perhaps they got sent to the wrong space-time by the Universal Reincarnation Company...But I digress. *D.Mirror* 19 Sept, *Nat. Enquirer* 15 Nov, *Daily Oklahoman* 23 July 1977; *D.Mail* 14 Sept 1978; *Observer* magazine 20 May, *Herald Tribune* 13 Aug 1979.

Double Lives

Prof. Thomas Bouchard of Minnesota University said that only 73 cases of monozygotic (identical) twins who have been raised apart have been recorded. At least three have come to light this year. In fact the air has been positively crackling with synchronicity for the devious or delightful duos.

Jacqueline and Sheila Lewis were adopted at birth by different families, and neither knew the other existed. 27 years later, they were admitted to Southmead Hospital, Bristol, on the same day with the same hereditary skin disorder, and put in the same room. They soon discovered they were identical twins and Sheila's husband had died on the same day, two years earlier, that Jackie had divorced her husband. *D.Mail* 2 July, *D.Telegraph* 3 July, *Nat. Enquirer* 31 Aug 1976.

Sometime in August 1939 in Piqua, Ohio, identical boy twins were adopted by two families who were told that the other baby had died. The Springers lived in Dayton, the Lewises in Lima 80 miles away. 6 years later, while completing adoption papers, Mrs Lewis learned by accident that the other twin was alive. When she said that she had called the child James Edward, the court official said: 'You can't do that. They named the other little boy James.' James Springer grew up thinking his twin was dead, while James Lewis didn't know where his twin was, and hesitated for many years before tracing him through the red tape jungle of adoption courts. In February 1979, at the age of 39, they met. In their lives apart the two James married and divorced Lindas and remarried Bettys; and had taken holidays on the same beach in St. Petersburg, Florida. Both were into carpentry and mechanical drawing, both had had police training and occasional 'law enforcement' work. One is now a security guard, the other a records clerk. They called their eldest son James Alan and James Allen. When they met, their families noted similar speech patterns, mannerisms and posture. But Lewis had short hair combed back and Springer long hair combed forward...

On July 27 1939, a few days before the birth of the Ohio twins, an unmarried Finnish student, Helena Jacobsson, gave birth to twin girls in Hammersmith Hospital in London. They were christened Dagmar Margaret (Daphne, the elder by twelve minutes) and Gerda Barbara. Both were adopted, Barbara growing up in London and Daphne in Luton. In May or (?) June 1979, at the age of 39, they met. Barbara Herbert and her family live in Dover, while Daphne Goodship and her family live in Wakefield. Both their adoptive mothers died when they were children: both had worked in local government offices; both miscarried their first babies, then each had two boys followed by a girl — though Daphne had two more children later; and both had met their husbands at Town Hall dances when they were 16. They both like carving, tho' Barbara uses wood and Daphne soap; and they were wearing identical white petticoats at their reunion. This time the difference was one of weight: Daphne had been dieting. *Boston Globe 20 Feb, South Middlesex News* 22 Feb, *D.Mirror* 24 Feb, South Africa *Sunday Times* 4 March, *Midnight Globe* 27 March, *Sunday People* 10 June 1979.

In July 1979 twins Ruth Johnson of Lowell, Mass. and Allison Mitchell Erb of Mount Vernon, Maine, met for the first time since they were adopted 26 years ago in New Hampshire. Each is a hairdresser, with a daughter called Kristen and one other child each. The previous June they had both watched a TV discussion on the right of adopted persons to discover their origins, and both started to search for the other. *The Spectator* (Canada) 24 July, *Herald Tribune* and *Daily Mail* 25 July 1979.

Mrs Martha Burke (49) of California, suffered terrible burning pains in her chest and stomach as her non-identical twin was burned to death in the Canary Island plane crash in 1977 which claimed 582 lives. A year later she was sueing the airlines for lack of sympathy, but maybe she is lucky to be alive. Mrs Joyce Crominski wrote to the Melbourne *Truth* about her identical twin sisters Helen and Peg. At 11.15 one evening, Helen (19), awoke white-faced and screaming, with a terrible chest pain. Her parents sent for an ambulance and she died on the way to hospital, as did Peg, who had been in a car accident at exactly the same time as Helen awoke. The steering wheel had penetrated her chest. Lisa and Mark (3 months) died within minutes of each other in Dublin. The twins were in different cots, and the cause of death was unknown. Ida Torrey and Freda Palmer — twins born in Geronimo, Texas, in 1905 — died on the same day 350 miles apart. *D. Telegraph* 10 April, *National Enquirer* 6 June, *D. Express* 7 Feb 1978; *Psychic News* 11 Aug 1979.

Two By Two

We note that sometimes the universe goes in for clumpings of bifurcation. In 1978 there were nine sets of twins among the 285 pupils in the village school of Herrick in central Illinois, a village of only 600 souls. And there were five twin births within a few hundred yards of each other in Rose Hill, Loughborough, near Derby in England. Paul Slade wrote to the *Guardian* (30 July 79) that no less than 80 per cent of all the hen's eggs his family had eaten in the previous three weeks were double yolked. A 10-year-old gave birth to healthy girl twins in Indianapolis University Hospital in June 1979; and the next month Leslie Wallace (25) of Sydney gave birth to identical quadruplets — possibly the first recorded. *D. Telegraph* 2 June 1978; *D. Mail* 2 June, London *Eve. Standard* 27 June, London *Eve. News* 8 Aug 1979.

Twins Jacky and Geraldine Herz had had babies within days of each other on 12 occasions.

Other twins have managed this feat once anyway, often with greater synchronisation. Renee and Bernee married on the same day and gave birth within hours of each other in Las Vegas. Gill and Susan Partridge carried it off in August 1979. Twins Paul and Fritz married twins ten years ago in Silesia. Two years later they became fathers within two hours of each other. And both sued for divorce on the same day. *The Star* (USA) 24 Aug 1976; *Houston Chronicle* 5 April, London *Eve. News* 9 Aug, *News of the World* 7 Jan 1979.

Conversely Mrs Crocifissa Micchia had a baby girl at home in Marianapoli, Sicily, but continued to have pains. Next day she was taken to San Cataldo, 20 miles away where another girl was born. Four days separated the birth of twin boys to Mrs Walker in Tottenham in 1940. 'Four days apart' twins were also born to the wife of a Walthamstow baker in 1936. The greatest recorded interval between twin births is, supposedly, 136 days in a case reported from Strasbourg in 1846. *Herald Tribune* 17 July 1979; *News Chronicle* 9 May 1940. A case of twins 12 days apart is reported in a reader's letter in *D. Mirror* 24 Sept 1979. An Egyptian woman, Mrs Aziza Amin, 31, had twin boys in different countries. The first was delivered on the way to Cairo airport. It died, but Mrs Amin felt well enough the next day to travel to Athens, where she again went into labour. This time the baby, only 2lb, survived. *D. Telegraph* 22 Sept 1979.

Mrs Nebis Ramos, of Chicago, has double trouble — beating odds said to be 55 million to one, she has given birth to four consecutive sets of twins. Identical twin boys arrived in 1970, identical twin girls in 1975, and fraternal twins in 1977, the girl surviving the boy who died suddenly of the infant death syndrome. The latest pair, again identical twin boys, were born on the 3rd of August, and one has developed a breathing problem. Mrs Ramos is finding life hectic. She told a reporter: "I can't talk to you now. I've four loads of washing to do, dinner to fix for

Grace & Virginia Kennedy, alias 'Poto' & 'Cabenga', aged 8.

everybody, then get back to the hospital for the twins' breast-feeding." Mrs Ramos is separated from her husband, and on public assistance. Both we can believe! *Toronto Sun* 8 Aug 1979.

In 1978 there were reports of a German woman who had twins, one white and one black. Since we reported this case in FT26, p.11, some other cases have come to light. One was in the USA in 1810; another sometime between 1914 and 1924 in Liverpool; and in September 1939 a black woman in Hokerton, North Carolina, had twins, a white son and a black girl. In this case the father of both seems to have been 'coal-black Herbert Strong'. Blood tests have also shown that twins had different fathers, though both were white. Cases from Vlborg in Denmark and in Stockholm in 1934; and from Berlin in 1939. *Sunday Referee* 7 Oct 1934 and 5 March 1939; *D. Mirror* 9 Dec 1940; *Newsweek* 25 Sept 1978; *Moneysworth* USA Dec 1978; *Times* 4 Sept 1978.

For other tales of genetic complication involving twins in some form, see our 'Freaks' section.

Twinchronicity

Our files are bulging with case histories of twin telepathy, twin-chronicities and extra-sensory empathy pains. The extraordinary examples of wound and pain transference seem to point beyond mere astrological identity to a shared Destiny... a single entity by fate or intention manifesting in two physical bodies.

Take, for starters, the bunch of letters sent to the *News of the World* (7 May 1978). A woman found she had trouble moving her arms and legs. She also had a large red mark on her arm. Her twin sister had been in an accident, and was given an injection in the same place as the red mark. A girl won first prize in a raffle with the number 38; two weeks later her twin sister won again with the same number. A woman went to get ear-rings for her twin sister's birthday, only to find that they had been bought for her the previous day by her twin. Jayne Wilkinson, 5, fell and

broke her nose; and her twin sister Claire had a nose-bleed. Their father and his twin brother both suffered the same leg injury playing football on the same day in different places. Mrs Sheargold went to hospital with a leg injury and her twin brother was kept awake by the pain. Later he cracked a rib, and *she* felt *his* pains. And so on.

Another case of wound empathy concerns the 5-year-old Spanish twins Silvia and Marta Landa who were being studied by the Parapsychology Society of Spain. When Silvia burnt herself on a hot iron, Marta felt the pain 12 miles away. Both developed a burn scar on their right hands. Shannon and Sharon Egner (7) both lost front teeth on the same day. Then Sharon broke an arm, and Shannon did the same a few days later. Helen Fry (13) was out shopping with her grandmother when she began to stagger about quite dazed and had to be taken home where she fell asleep on the settee. Her identical twin Lorraine was in hospital for a minor operation, but both twins had experienced the anaesthetic. On

two occasions when Yvonne Green had a baby, her twin brother Christopher Gool had labour pains 300 miles away. Another time Christopher hurt his arm in a brawl (he is a policeman), Yvonne fell over and had to go to hospital to have her arm injuries treated. *National Enquirer* 18 Oct, *Reveille* 18 Nov 1977; *Rand Daily Mail* 29 Dec 1976; *Weekend* 9 May, *People* 25 March 1979.

Finally, what are we to make of the story related in *Fate* (Sept 79)? Sheila Doxtader gave birth to a girl in an Eaton Rapids, Michigan hospital. Within the hour another Sheila Doxtader gave birth to another girl in the same hospital. So far as the two Sheila Doxtaders know, they are not related. A subtle joke by the cosmic puppet-master, or a typo in the genetic code? A near-miss twin-birth or 'just one of those things'?

[Credit: Gary Abbott, Tom R Adams, Richard Cotton, Peter Hope Evans, Chris J Holtzhausen, Bob Forrest, Jackie Klemes, Valerie Martin, Nick Maloret, Colin Mather, Mark A Hall, Peter Roberts, Paul Screeton, A W Szachnowski, Thoth, Dwight Whalen, Ion Will, John Rimmer.] **PRAdeGS**

The black and white twins from Germany, Heiku and Bernd, aged 8. Daily Mirror *29 May 1978.*

FREAKS

This year has seen an extraordinary number of Siamese twins and extra-uterine pregnancies.

Siamese Gods

Once at an FT clipping sort, our utterances departed from the usual banter and cries of delighted astonishment. The topic was the future of the yet-to-be-born Fortean Institute (or whatever). One visionary, jokingly (I hope), suggested that we might have a department of genetic engineering to manufacture and supply living gods to pantheistic cultures — many-headed, multi-armed, blue-skinned types to India, for example. Well, like so many of our speculations, there will be no need for our Mail-Order god programme because genuine prodigies are being born all the time.

On 17 Feb 1979, the first Siamese twins to be born in England in 10 years were delivered by caesarian section at the West Kent Hospital, Maidstone. The boys were joined above the waist and so shared most of their vital organs. They died 10 days later, of 'natural causes', within 90 minutes of each other. No separation had been attempted, and it is not known if this operation — almost certainly fatal to one of them — had been planned, since the distressed parents requested all details to be kept private. *D. Express* 21 Feb 1979; London *Evening Standard* 22 Feb 1979; *Kent Messenger* 2 March; *D. Telegraph* 28 Feb 1979.

Within a few days of the Kent twins, two girls were born on 20 Feb, at Albert Einstein Medical Center, Philadelphia. They were joined from above the breast-bone to below the navel, sharing an unusual six-chambered heart and a liver. In the first week of March they were separated at St Christopher's Hospital for Children, also in Philly, in a 6 hour operation involving 17 doctors. One of the twins had to be 'sacrificed', the other was in a stable condition for a while but later died too. Parents requested anonymity. *Grand Rapids Press* 5 March; London *Eve. Standard* 17 May 1979.

Twin girls, joined from chest to navel like the Kent girls, were born on 3rd May to Mrs Eleni Alifteras, 20, during a 'difficult' caesarian section in the Greek town of Larissa. Later they were transferred to Salonica, and then to Evangelismos Hospital, Athens, where, two and a half months later, Dr George Tolis and his team separated them in a half hour operation. The weaker twin died so that her survivor could have the heart and liver they shared. The last we heard her condition was hopeful. We can only hope the outcome was good news and therefore not worth reporting in the papers. *D. Telegraph* 5 May; *Guardian* 27 and 28 July 1979.

Siamese twins, or uniovular asymmetrical twins, are said to be one in a million or more, yet the law and disorder of chance sent us two together in February, and now another not long after the Greek twins. On 6 June twin girls were born to an Indian woman, Veeran Rani, at the JP Hospital, New Delhi (see photo). Although characterized by the *Daily Telegraph* (of all papers) as a 'two-headed baby', it is clear that these girls are two joined beings, having distinct nervous systems, heads and lungs. Unlike our earlier twins, the Rani girls share a third hand, with eight fingers, on their common shoulder. At the time of the reports no extensive examination had been made to determine what organs were shared — only one heart had been located. Doctors were not underestimating their chances of separating the twins, and if their worst fears are confirmed — that the girls indeed share a heart and other organs — then the operation, as in previous cases, will mean certain death for the weakest and slender chances for the survivor. While doctors were deliberating

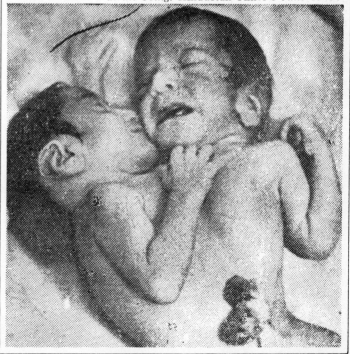

The Rani twins: a divine being. Hindustan Times *8 June 1979.*

the curious effects of a double nervous system — one laughs while the other cries, one lies awake while the other sleeps, etc —the babies have drawn huge crowds who are in no doubt about the status of the babies; I should say 'baby' since the crowds, like the *Telegraph*, believe them to be a single being. In their eyes the baby is a goddess since only a *bhagwan ka roop* (divine being) can laugh and cry at the same time. Our last news was that the babies' condition had deteriorated. *Hindustan Times* 8 June; *Rising Nepal* 9 June; *D. Telegraph* 9 June; *Times of India* 10 June; Delhi *Statesman* 11 June 1979.

Finally, on 30th May, another pair of Siamese twins were in the news. They were Lisa and Elisa Hansen who had been joined at the head since their birth 19 months previously (Oct 1977). They were separated in a Salt Lake City hospital in an operation lasting 16 continuous hours. They made a reasonable recovery and were soon allowed home. But because of the seriousness of the operation and their vulnerability, doctors were watching them closely. Our last note reports that in late July Elisa was admitted to the Utah University Medical Center for surgery to 'adjust incisions in her head'. *Hindustan Times* 8 June; *D. Mail* 19 July; London *Evening Standard* 30 May and 20 June; *Herald Tribune* 30 and 31 July; *S. Express* 3 June.

[Credit: David Fideler, Ian Lawes, Peter Rogerson, Sam, Has Thomas, Ion Will].

Their Brother's Keeper

Following on from the topic of Siamese twins, and twins in general (see our 'Twins' section) are a few notes we could call 'twins which might have been'.

At the King George Hospital, at Visakhapatnam in south India, a foetus was removed from the abdomen of an 11-year-old boy. Dr Viswanatha Rao, who performed the 3 hour operation early Sept 1977, said the foetus appeared to have developed to the fourth month stage. Dr Rao believes that it was one of a pair of twins, which died and was then incorporated into the body of the living twin. Texas *Eagle* 14 Sept 1977.

Recently, a Viennese mother of four was found to be two people, giving rise to another case of biological complication. During a routine blood-test before transfusion to one of her children, it was found that her child's genes did not match her own. Half the child's genes were identified as inherited from her father, said Dr Wolfgang Schnedi, but the other did not match those of a woman who gave her birth. The enigma was only resolved when the woman recalled her own mother saying that she thought she was carrying twins, then she gave birth to only her. Dr Schnedi examined the woman and discovered that she was carrying her own twin, partially developed in her own womb. Then something even more unusual happened — genetic material from this partial twin somehow passed on to her

children instead of her own genes. *Titbits* 8 Sept 1979; *Nature* 277 p211; *New Scientist* 18 Jan 1979. *[Credit: Tom R Adams.]*

Wombless Wonders

It is not uncommon in these days of widespread sterilization by severing of the fallopian tubes to hear of the occasional case of a woman discovering herself pregnant after such operations. Usually a fertilized egg has luckily made it before the scalpel, but sometimes we hear of the spontaneous healing of the tubes; such a case happened recently, see *Sunday People* 17 June 1979. But the following cases are characterized by foetal development *outside* a womb, some in cases where there was no womb at all. In reviewing these cases we note the regularity with which doctors, unaware of the other cases, claim theirs to be unique or the 'first of its kind'. In some cases they may be right — either way the situation is extremely unusual. Doctors attending the Chapel Hill birth (see below) said only 50 extra-uterine births had been recorded in medical literature. Eggs slipping out of the other end of the fallopian tube are estimated to occur once in 10,000 pregnancies, and those lucky enough to find somewhere to take root usually die within the first three months. Whatever the odds, it is a fact that we now record six extra-uterine births which have all taken place within *4 months* of each other.

The first was tiny Martin Trott, born on 31 March to Alison Trott, 23, at Musgrove Park Hospital, Taunton, Somerset. Alison had a hysterectomy after the birth of her first two children. The gynaecologist who performed the operation to remove her womb 11 months previously, and who delivered Martin by Caesarian, revealed that Alison had had an abnormal womb, but managed to carry to full term two normal children before the operation. He added, 'Only half the uterus had developed, the other side simply wasn't there... In this case the baby developed in the 'horn' which would have been the other side of the uterus had it ever

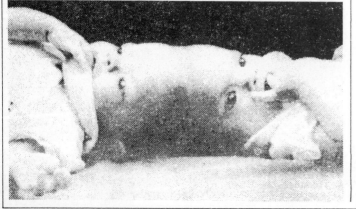

Lisa and Elisa Hansen before their separation. D.Star *1 June 79*

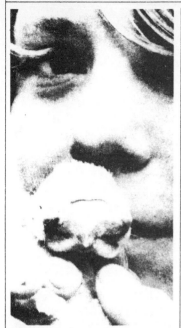

On - uh! - 23 July 1979, a stray cat in Montreal gave birth to the furry freak pictured below. National Enquirer 2 Oct 1979. Coincidentally, another two-faced feline, called Tom & Jerry, was born around the same time in Indianapolis (above) Niagara Falls Review 7 Aug 1979. Both had normal siblings, and both died later.

developed. Not only did the baby implant itself there, it grew to full term. This case, where the foetus had secured itself and stimulated a formerly non-existent uterus to support it, is, as far as I or the staff can ascertain, unique.' *Western Morning News* & Melbourne *The Age* both 17 April; *Philadelphia Inquirer* 5 April; *Guardian* 17 April 1979.

Next we have a note that sometime on the weekend 5-6 May an extra-uterine baby was delivered by caesarian section to a woman in Southeast Medical Center, Dothian, Alabama. The baby, said to be in good condition, had developed for 8 months in the abdominal cavity, but it was not said where. *Niagara Falls Review* 9 May 1979.

Margaret Martin had a hysterectomy after the birth of her third daughter. Eight months later she gave birth to a healthy girl, delivered surgically and one month prematurely at the National Women's Hospital, Auckland, New Zealand, on 15 May. Her doctors said that she must have become pregnant about two days before the operation last September, the fertilized egg remaining in the fallopian tube when the uterus was removed. In this case the egg fastened itself to the woman's

bowel and other organs in her abdomen and drew enough nourishment from them to develop normally. Doctors induced the birth because the baby's growth rate had slowed and was apparently beginning to starve. Mr Martin described his wife as 'naturally plump', and despite complaining of morning sickness and cravings her own doctor had refused to believe she was pregnant until about two months before the birth. Dallas, Texas *Morning News*, & Harrisburg, Penn *Evening News* both 17 May 1979.

The case of Janet Sickles is slightly different. After two normal births previously her third child was said to be developing normally. In fact a fertilized egg had somehow escaped the fallopian tube and attached itself to the exterior of her ovary. On 25 April, three months prematurely, Mrs Sickles haemorrhaged causing a dangerously low blood pressure. She was rushed to Montrose Memorial Hospital, Colorado, where, to save her life, Dr Hamilton Lokey, said he expected to lose the baby and perform a hysterectomy. As soon as the incision was made doctors were astonished to find the baby, safe in its embryonic sac, in her

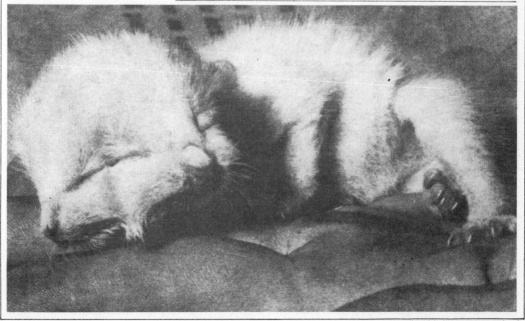

abdominal cavity. Despite being unusual and premature, the gratefully named Miracle Stacy Sickles, and her mother are doing well. Dallas, Texas *Morning News* 17 May 1979. NB: This and the previous case were both reported on 17th May, and a few days after the Alabama case!

The arrival of David Lee Patterson on 18th July, at North Carolina Memorial Hospital, Chapel Hill, North Carolina, was very similar. His parents had been trying for a baby for 13 years, however it was not until shortly before his ETA that it was discovered that the baby had developed outside Shirley Patterson's womb. The fertilized egg had escaped from the fallopian tube and attached itself to blood vessels near the pelvis. Shirley had been admitted because of pre-natal complications when tests confirmed the doctors' suspicions. Dr Linn Hatley, chief gynaecologist, decided on a caesarean. 'When we opened the abdomen, the first thing we saw was the placenta. Then I found the baby's feet, and the baby started kicking and screaming'. Harrisburg, Penn *Evening News* 19 July; *Indian Express,* & *D. Telegraph* 20 July 1979.

Our sixth case is short on detail because the parents request anonymity. A baby girl, called LaKesha, was delivered by caesarean on 31 July, at Mercy Hospital, Benton Harbor, Michigan, after developing normally in her mother's abdominal cavity. *Niagara Falls Review* 11 Aug 1979.

Finally a case of an abdominal foetus that went wrong. On 23rd May — a date that plugs the gap in our sequence of extra-uterine pregnancies above — an 83 year-old woman underwent an operation to remove the calcified remains of a foetus from her abdominal wall. She had been vomiting and complaining of abdominal pains before seeking medical help. An adopted son, translating for the Spanish-speaking woman, said that she had married but never had children, and although she had been in hospital before had never been x-rayed. The attending doctor believed the woman must

have become pregnant when 12-13 years old and carried the foetus for about 70 years. He believed that it may have been an abnormal tubal pregnancy that the body tried to abort, pushing it into the abdominal cavity and walling it off with tissue. In the light of the above cases, it could also have begun life — or death — as a fertilized egg escaping the fallopian tube to develop for a

little while in the abdominal cavity. Either way the foetus had become calcified. A curious side-effect was that the woman had not menstruated in all those years — her body believed she was still pregnant, said a doctor. Houston, Texas *Post* 2 June 1979.

[Credit: Tom R Adams, Larry Arnold, Jenny Cameron, Chris Hall, Kurt Lothmann, Valerie Martin, Peter Roberts, Sam, Has Thomas, Dwight Whalen] RJMR.

Synaesthesia, the apparent displacement of perception of one sense into the language of another, may be related to Psi, according to world wide reports.

Russia

Russian work in this field has been covered in some detail in Ostrander & Schroeder's *Psychic Discoveries Behind the Iron Curtain,* (Abacus 1977) and Gris & Dick's *The New Soviet Psychic Discoveries* (Souvenir Press 1979), so we will be brief...

We have an old and unreferenced clipping concerning Vera Petrova, an 11-year-old girl from Ulianovsk, who could read with her fingers, distinguish colours, and sense shapes and outlines through thick layers of wood, plastic, metal etc. She had normal sight, but the 'sixth sense' only worked when she was blindfolded. She could read a magazine article placed under three large books, and 'see' a picture placed under a carpet. She managed to convince Prof. D Fedotov of the Institute of Research Psychiatry, Moscow, who quotes three explanatory theories: that skin-sight is 'connected with infra-red radiation of human hands'; that some people have built-in rudimentary photo-receivers; that it's connected with telepathy. L. Teplov, of the *Literary Gazette,* disagreed though, claiming it was all fakery, and that claimants of the

power were always mentally unbalanced or children, and therefore irresponsible individuals. Younger readers may not care for this implication...

Some time later, 22-year-old Rosa Kuleshova appeared on the scene, also with perfect sight, and able to distinguish colours with her fingers. Poor old Teplov seems to have been overruled, for it now seems that a programme is underway to teach the blind to develop the same abilities, and the Russians are claimimg some success...though the hows and whys are apparently still unexplained. *Reveille* 1 July 1977 & 20 March 1979.

China

Some kids are content with wiggling their ears; 12-year-old Tang Yu of Sichuan Province goes one better. He can see through his ears. Tang is the youngest of three sons of a rice-farmer in Dazu County, and discovered his powers in 1978. He can read Chinese characters even when the paper they are written on is folded up, distinguish between pen and brush writing, reproduce pictures 'seen' through his ear, and when tested, reproduced the letters A, B & C, though he is not familiar with the western alphabet, and did not know how to pronounce the letters. Tang describes the process thus: he holds the piece of paper up to his ear, then feels 'an electric current in his brain' and a picture of the word appears to him, in the correct colour. Tang can also obtain good results with his fingers and feet, which leads us to wonder if the sensing process might actually be located in the fingers holding the paper, rather than the ear. Tang was investigated with apparent thoroughness at his home, and produced the goods...but (same old story) when he was taken to the big city (Chengdu) and hounded by investigators and a curious public, his powers began to fade...which eventually led to the *People's Daily* (Renmin Ribao) denouncing the whole business as superstition.

But not before a couple of other wonder-kids had shown up: a brother and sister in Anwhei Province, 100 miles south of Shanghai, claiming the same powers (no further details); and an 8-year-old girl in Peking who heard of Tang Yu's feats and said she could do it too. And it seems she could... *Times of India* 26 May 1979; *National Enquirer* 12 June 1979; *Reveille* 13 July 1979.

Japan

If nothing else, Tang Yu's appearance on the scene should have scotched the notion that eyeless sight is a talent peculiar to females, which was current when Sayuri Tanaka, aged 10 in 1976, was causing an uproar in Tokyo. Her 'third eye' is positioned on the left side of her nose and has 20-20 vision. Amongst other things she can, while thoroughly blindfolded: ride a bicycle along a straight line, read a book, catch a ball, identify playing cards, play basket-ball (and score), and draw a pencil line through a maze drawn on paper. But whereas our other cases imply either telepathy or the necessity of touch, Sayuri's watchful nostril seems to behave exactly like an eye...blindfold her and hold a hand in front of her nose and she can't see a thing!

Sunday Times 25 Jan 1976; *Daily Mail* 5 June 1976; *Weekend* 17-23 Jan 1979.

And Elsewhere

We have mentions of investigations in Poland and Albania, but no details. Meanwhile...
USA: Patricia Stanley of Michigan can accurately distinguish colours when blindfold. *Reveille* 1 July 1977.
France: Jean Flauret, 14, has been blind since birth, but can see well enough through his hands to ride a bicycle through his home town of Orleans, deal with speed and direction of traffic, distinguish shapes of trees and colours of houses. *Weekend* 17-23 Jan 1979
Egypt: In 1942, an unnamed boy in Alexandria was injured in an air raid, losing his sense of smell (later restored by surgery) and becoming totally deaf. He later discovered he could 'hear' by placing his hand on the radio, or on the throat of the person talking to him. And though this

might be seen 'merely' as hyper-sensitivity to vibration, every word is apparently clear and distinct. *Weekend:* 5-11 Dec 1973.
And lastly...James Jordan, nationality unknown, a botanical artist blind since childhood, produced a book of full-colour flower paintings, distinguishing colours by the 'heat' they generate...red is hot, blue cool, green cold. While researchers at Rome's Institute of Mental Research suspect the pineal gland of responsibility, theorising that it translates impressions received by the subconscious into images that can be understood by the brain. *Weekend:* 17-23 Jan 1979. It's as good an explanation as any other, we suppose...but it doesn't explain *how* the signals are received through the skin in the first place. But then the other explanations don't do that *either...*

[Credit: Jane Brecha, Peter Roberts, Peter Rogerson, Anthony Smith, Martin Straw, Sam] **SM.**

Bolts of lightning seemed more vivid and active this summer, there being several dramatic deaths and coincidental events. Next issue; Ball-lightning.

Thunderbolt Terror

Every year has its quota of lightning deaths, and the tragedy that gripped the public imagination this year was undoubtedly the thunderstorm that suddenly and severely descended on Skegness, Lincs, at 3.30pm on 29th July.

Six-year-old Louise Hough, and her sister Lianne (4), three other children and a group of three married couples were on the beach at Skegness, near the Derbyshire Miners' Holiday Center. One of the women took the children down to the water's edge, and as they were all

balancing along the top of a wooden breakwater, there was a shattering thunderclap knocking them all into the water. Young Louise in the lead seemed to have been hit directly by a vertical bolt of lightning, her father, Eric Hough, said later. Eric ran towards them in horror. Then a second flash, very near him, left him with a severely numbed leg. He crawled towards Lianne and began resuscitation until other rescuers took over. In all 11 people were rushed to hospital — most were simply shocked; some had burns. Louise was dead and Lianne barely alive. Lianne recovered and was later released.

Donald Mitchell, assistant manager of the Derbyshire Miners' Holiday Center, said: 'It had been marvellous weather — bright and sunny all day. Then suddenly, about 3.30, the clouds gathered and really torrential rain poured down. I've never seen rain like it — not even in the monsoons in the Far East. Along with the rain there was endless forked lightning, which went on for about an hour. We could see it bounce off the sea. One bolt hit our games room. The lights went out, and plugs and switches were burnt off the walls.' Story in most national dailies for 30 July; additional material in London *Evening News* 30 July, and Scunthorpe *Evening Telegraph* 31 July 1979.

Before we begin a round-up of lightning strikes and deaths, we must mention a couple of vague but interesting reports. Firstly, the year seemed to kick off with a weird omen of lightning. According to the *Daily Express* 18 Jan 1979, a farmer in South Africa, who had been praying for weeks for rain, had his prayers answered in a way he hadn't bargained for. Along with the rain came a bolt of lightning which struck and killed his wife! The other cases came from *Weekly News* 9 June 1979, and refer to unspecified storms earlier that month:

At Leigh, in Lancashire, a mother and 4-yr-old daughter were hurled backwards across their living room as a bolt hit the house. As the TV was thrown into the air, said Mrs Hazel Radcliffe: 'it's sides and top blew off, shelves and curtains came away from the walls, and all the light switches were wrenched from the walls.' And at a farm near Chester, Steven Wilson, 16, was walking across a field. The next thing he knew was waking up in hospital. His father found him staggering around the field in a very dazed condition. His mother said: 'His shirt, underpants and socks all melted, and his trousers were ripped to shreds. His wellington boots acted as insulators and saved him from certain death before they were blown off his feet.'

Lightning Strikes

April

8 — L hits 11 soccer players at Caerleon, Gwent, 4 hurt, 1 seriously. *J.Met* 4:39pl50.

17 — L rips through row of houses triggering explosion in Shogi village, near Simla, India. 14 killed, 7 hurt, 4 seriously. *D. Telegraph 18 April 1979.*

19 — L hits tanker *Seatiger* near Port Neches, Texas. 1 dead, 30 hurt. *Lloyds List.*

25 — L hits lady golf pro, Leatherhead, Surrey. Unhurt. *D.Telegraph.*

28 — L hits Anglia TV weatherforecaster David Brookes, on golf-course at Cambridge. *S.Express* 29 April 1979.

May

17 — L blows roof off house in Scunthorpe, Lincs. 'Big blue flash' from phone receiver startles youth in phone-box nearby. Scunthorpe *Evening Telegraph* 18 May 1979.

23 — L hits house at Sacriston, Co Durham, cracking walls. Woman stoking grate at time blown backwards across soot-filled room. Newcastle-upon-Tyne *Journal* 24 May 1979.

24 — L hits an angler's rod killing him at Vimerby, south Sweden. *D.Telegraph* 25 May 1979.

31 — L kills 17 cattle on ranch near Piedmont, South Dakota (see 12 Aug).

June

3 — L kills one at Niigata, Japan. *Int. Herald Tribune.*

7 — L hits house at Sparkbrook, Birmingham; fuses blown, TV damaged etc. Lady hurt. Birmingham *Evening Mail.*

? — About this time the two cases described above occured; one at Leigh, Lancs, and the other at Chester.

16 — L hits house in Scandia, Michigan. Man on porch hurt. *Grand Rapids Press* 18 June 1979.

20 — L hits the National Guard's Camp Grayling, Michigan. 45 hurt, 3 seriously.*Grand Rapids Press* 22 June 1979. L hits 2 girls picking strawberries at South Haven, Maine. 1 killed, the other hurt. *Grand Rapids Press* 1 July 1979.

29 — L starts bush and forest fires in Arizona, over several days.*Lloyds List.*

July

29 — L strikes at least 3 times on beach at Skegness, Lincs. 1 killed, 10 hurt, 2 seriously. See our first story above for details.

31 — L hits 2 British climbers on Denti del Sassolungo, in Italian Alps. 1 dead, the injured dangled for 2 days before rescue. London *Evening Standard* 2 Aug 1979.

August

4 — L kills 4 West German climbers on Denti di Terrarosso, also in the Italian Alps (see July 31). *S Telegraph* 5 Aug 1979.

6 — L hits climber on Mt Yarigatake, central Honshu, Japan. 2 killed, 4 hurt. *Int. Herald Tribune*, & *D.Telegraph* 7 Aug 1979.

12 — L kills cattle on ranch near Piedmont, South Dakota, just 3½ miles from identical incident on 31 May (see above). *Omaha World Herald* 15 Aug 1979.

20 — L hits Leon Swiech, mowing a lawn in Houston, Texas. Recovering. Lightning pulled the 'Swiech' and witnesses said he 'lit up like a bulb.' *D.Mail* 22 Aug 1979.

September

2 — L kills soccer player and knocks over 50 spectators at Enschede, Holland. *D. Telegraph* 3 Sept 1979. Same day as L kills 7 horses and 1 rider at Düsseldorf, West Germany. *D.Mail* 3 Sept 1979.

[Credit: David Fideler, B Hain, Valerie Martin, Paul Screeton, Joe Swatek, R Watson, IA Will, Nigel Watson. Undated items from J.Meteorology 4:40 & 4:41] Sam] **RJMR.**

As we receive and sort your clippings we often become aware of running themes and trends.

Skylab Funnies

The remains of Skylab finally fell to earth on the night of 12 July. After a man-made meteorite display of bright red and orange sparks accompanied by a thunderous sonic wave, it pitched into the great desert beyond Kalgoorlie, in Western Australia. Like good Forteans we kept a beady eye on the media during the run-up period of trajectorial trepidity, and gleaned much. Suffice it to say that people everywhere were seeing things plummeting out of the sky. Loren Coleman has assembled the data and will present an article in FT shortly. One particular event, the fall of a blob of green plastic on Mississauga, Canada, on June 16, attracted a lot of attention, including that of our colleagues, Dwight Whalen (whose home town it is) and the intrepid Mr X. We hope to include a report on the fall next issue.

Suddenly falling things were all the mode. We clipped quite a heap of falling planes, people falling or leaping from buildings — even a stuntman whose bid to leap a line of cars ended in a fatal rain of machine and rider. But perhaps the real fun began as Skylab passed into living legend. Early on, when fears that the junk would re-enter over the USA, there were several attempts to shift its orbit by thought power — one by an enterprising mentalist, and the other by a radio appeal for a million people to concentrate for 7½ minutes on 25th May. Then President Reddy of India denounced the space-lab publicly as a demon from which only God could save the people.

It seems the people of India entered into the spirit of the event. Surjit Singh, an accountant with the Punjab State Electricity Board, named his son, born on 11 July, Skylab Singh. An Indian woman ran away with her lover after her horoscope predicted that a chunk of debris would kill her husband. An old Indian, who set aside a lot of money for his sons at his death, was fooled into handing it over, when his boys convinced him the village was going to be destroyed. And one farmer pioneered a lucrative business selling 'genuine' pieces of Skylab to his credulous neighbours, until one, a bit sharper than the rest, found he'd bought part of an old stove.

In Brazil another baby was named after the space-lab — Marcos Skylab Galisa — and his unmarried mother was encouraged to write to NASA for financial support. Another unexpected claim — this time for damages — came from a South African restaurant owner who reckons the US Government are responsible for his extensive period of 'mental anguish'. Less lucky was Simeon Galvez, 58, who died in Manila of a heart attack. He awoke from a nightmare, crying: 'Skylab! Skylab!', and then collapsed. And just in case we didn't get the message it was underlined just over a week after Skylab fell, most appropriately, at the Miss Universe contest at Perth, Australia, when before the assembled stars the stage collapsed precipitating another unscheduled descent of heavenly bodies. On a large display behind the girls was one of Skylab's blackened oxygen tanks, rescued from the Western Australian desert, and doubtless piqued at being upstaged! Aberdeen *Evening Express* 17 May 1979; *Guardian* 9 July 1979.

But the best joke of all must be the news that on the very same day that Skylab fragmented into hundreds of smouldering pieces prior to pelting Australia, the meteorite shield 'inexplicably' fell off the model of Skylab displayed in Washington's National Air and Space Museum — the same piece that fell off during the launch of Skylab itself in 1973! Finally, as we are about to go to press, we learn that some UOD (unidentified orbital debris) has re-entered over Australia's Western Desert, on 7th Sept. Residents of Albany reported 'soaring lights' coming down very near the resting place of much of Skylab. The Western Australian Observatory said 2 Cosmos satellites were due to re-enter, and this might be Cosmos 900. Don't they know? It could be that Skylab will continue to reign over the world for some time to come. And why not? It's as probable as anything else in this wacky saga. Aberdeen *Evening Express* 17 May 1979; *Guardian* 9 July 1979; Omaha, Nebraska, *World Herald* 12 July 1979; *Washington Post* 13 July; *London Evening News* 10 July 1979; London *Evening Standard* 11 and 20 July 1979; *Daily Telegraph* 12 and 21 July 1979; *Australasian Express* (London) 13 July 1979; *Observer* 8 July 1979; *International Herald Tribune* 9 July & 8 Sept 1979; *Toronto Sun* (Canada) 15 July 1979; *The Spectator* (Canada) 13 July 1979.

[Credit: A&P, David Fideler, Joe Swatek, Dwight Whalen, Ion Will, Jake Williams, Heathcote Williams, Sam].

A Modern Myth in the Making

When General Zia Ul-Haq of Pakistan hanged his former prime minister, Zulfikar Ali Bhutto, he must have hoped Bhutto's influence would die with him. In actuality the popular feeling for Bhutto has increased, and Zia must be thoroughly dismayed that Bhutto has become not just a martyr but a saint who, rumour has it, has performed several 'miracles' after his death.

The Delhi *Statesman* 19 April 1979, just two weeks after Bhutto was hanged in Rawalpindi, proclaimed the execution ended a bizarre series of coincidences. It began in 1929 when one Bhagat Singh shot and killed a British police officer in Lahore. (He had been aiming at the Superintendent of Police!) A tribunal passed sentence of death on him despite a split verdict. The man who hanged Bhagat Singh was the father of the man who hanged

Bhutto, Tara Massih. The witnessing magistrate at Bhagat Singh's death was Nawab Mohammed Ahmed Khan, later killed in an ambush laid for his son Ahmed Raza Kasuri in 1974. The ambush took place at the spot where Bhagat Singh was hanged, the jail having been demolished in the meantime to make way for a new road. The ambush also led to Bhutto's death, since it was alleged that he had ordered it. The tribunal that passed the death sentence on Bhutto did so on a split verdict. That, you'd think was that — but since the *Stateman*'s item we've learned that Tara Massih has been rushed to hospital dying from tuberculosis. *Daily Telegraph* 11 July 1979; *Guardian* 17 July 1979.

Even more curious are the stories of Bhutto's post-mortem miracles, which cannot be backed up with any documentation or authority but which have that enduring character of the best folk stories. The first miracle was said to have occured at the end of the traditional 40 day mourning period as thousands gathered to watch the ceremonies outside the walled graveyard at Naudero, in Sind, where Bhutto had been secretly(?) buried. It seems a pickpocket had made a good haul of watches and wallets and was on the point of escaping when he was mysteriously and suddenly struck blind. In panic he confessed all and the religious leaders proceeded to return the purloined property. As the last wallet and watch found their rightful owners, the man's sight was 'miraculously' restored. The second miracle was that a rose, taken from Bhutto's grave to a sick woman in Bhutto's Larkana constituency who was cured after eating the petals. This rumour has led to the widespread practice of pilgrims bringing flowers to the grave and taking others. The third miracle was said to have occurred as Bhutto's wife, the Begum Nusrat, and his daughter, Benazir, a former president of the Oxford Union, met with the executive of Pakistan's People's Party in Larkana. A phone call alerted them to a strange phenomenon to be seen on the moon. All present rushed into the garden, and stared in astonishment at the profile of Bhutto, clearly seen among the lunar features. *Guardian* 7 July 1979.

[Credit: Ion Will.]

Food for Thought

It began simply in April when a large quantity of 'brilliant yellow wax-like substance' was found washed up on Sennen beach, near Penwith, Cornwall. Analysis by the South West Water Authority said it was quite safe — it seemed to be the sort of fat used in the manufacture of margarine! Where it came from, they couldn't say. *Western Morning News* 23 April 1979. Within days an even stranger mystery was being unearthed at Milton, in Staffordshire. Two neighbours in Leek Road dug up, between them, three packets of sausages. No one knows how they got there. *Sun* 21 May 1979. After years of collecting such ephemera our practised eye notes the layers of acausal punning. What does Leek Road have to do with the Santa Anna freeway outside Los Angeles? Probably as much as a truck full of carrots has to do with a truck full of salad oil. Nevertheless two such trucks colided in that place creating what the Highway Patrol described as 'the biggest carrot salad ever'. London *Evening News* 28 June 1979. Similarly the *Daily Telegraph* 25 July 1979 reports that a lorry load of dressed chickens collided with another carrying barbecue sauce on New York's George Washington Bridge. The chickens obviously dressed for dinner, ended up fried in the flames — bet that smelled good! The London *Evening News* of the same day adds that also in the collision were trucks containing coffee and preserved fruit. It is given to a few of us to know how we'll meet our end — but we know of one poor soul who ended in meat! Driving his car under a Kansas City motorway bridge, he was hit by several tons of frozen beef of a lorry above. *Weekly News* 14 July 1979. And for afters? To go with the coffee and fruit, how about ice cream? Yep! 20 tons of the stuff blocked Cannock Rd, Wolverhampton, after its transporter jack-knifed on 7 August. *Daily Star* 8 August 1979. A late comer to the meals-on-wheels feast were the 18 tons of baked beans, which warmed up when their lorry caught fire on the M6 near Rugby, Warwicks. *D. Express* 28 Sept 1979.

[Credit: Chris Hall, Peter Roberts, Ion Will, Sam].

Nessie Notes

The 1979 'silly season' opened on schedule with announcement, in the media at least, of the annual expeditions to Loch Ness. Among these were the teams of Dr Rines, Tim Dinsdale and Adrian Shine, plus the usual quota of TV film crews and tourists. Expectations were raised by the news that the stars of this year's Academy of Applied Science Circus were to be a pair of dolphins. The dolphins, Susie and Sammy, were trained at a Florida aquarium to carry cylinders on their backs containing strobe lights, camera, sonar and battery. Both cameras and sonar have been improved by Rines' team-members Harold Edgerton and Charles Wyckoff over previous experiments and minaturized to fit the special harnesses. The use of dolphins' mobility and curiosity, and their ability to be trained, has a highly questionable history, the most infamous exploits of which were the underwater intelligence and mine-placement experiments of the US Navy in Vietnam. The news of their use in the freshwater Loch brought a storm of protest, and the Scottish SPCA said they would 'watch the project closely' since dolphins are salt-water creatures. The Rines team countered: the dolphins would be kept in special tanks and would only be allowed into the Loch for short periods before being recalled. *Glasgow Herald* 2 April 1979; *New Scientist* 21 June 1979. The excitement was shortlived, for all were sorry to hear that Susie died in late June, the day after the pair were flown from Florida to Boston prior to their departure for Prestwick in Scotland. Susie had travelled much in her 14 years (10 of them in captivity) and although the move was not being blamed the

(Top) The famous portrait of Nessie taken in April 1934, by London surgeon RK Wilson. Compare it with this enlargement (center) from Admiral R Kadirgamar's film of an elephant swimming off the coast of Sri Lanka. (N Scientist 2 Aug 1979), and one of Frank Searle's questionable Nessie photos from 1972 (Bottom). The gents who proposed the idea (see story, Right) that Nessie sightings are simply of swimming elephants, have failed to observe its venerable antecedent as a Pictish symbol, spotted by one of our vigilant readers, Mike Crowley (see 'Letters' section).

cause of her death remains a mystery even after the autopsy. Glasgow *Evening Times* 4 July 1979; *New Scientist* 5 July 1979. It was rumoured that Rines was moved enough to abandon the idea but according to the *Daily Telegraph* 1 August the Boston Academy team are looking around for a pair of English dolphins to train up for another trial next spring, or perhaps even later this year.

Curiously, just as we were warming to the idea of the dolphins escaping and adapting to a feral life in the Loch, news came of further bizarre neighbours for Nessie. Lawrence McGill, 31, who owns a small waterfront hotel at Dores, on the north-eastern corner of the Loch, revealed that he was taking delivery of two King penguins from the Falkland Islands. The birds, at a monstrous £1,000 each, should adapt very well to the Loch, and their weaving manner of swimming should cause splendid havoc. Scottish *Sunday Express* 15 July 1979. As for 'out-of-place' animals in the Loch our prize for the most novel hypothesis of the year must go to Drs Dennis Power and Donald Johnson, who beat Prof Waldemar Lehn (University of Manitoba) into a cocked hat. Lehn (*Science* v205p183) explains Nessie sightings as temperature inversion mirages of protruding sticks or rocks; while Power and Johnson (*New Scientist* 2 Aug 1979) more ingeniously compare the famous Nessie photos to the behaviour of swimming elephants [see illustrations]. This theory, undoubtedly meant to raise a smile, has already had its supporters and sceptics (*New Scientist* 16 & 23 August 1979) but as Fort observed truth and fiction are continuous and often inextricable.

Finally; clairvoyant Kim Tracy, of Chatham, Kent, predicts that Nessie will surface in a big way in September. She also claims to have had a 'vision' of 'tunnels and caves deep under Urquhart Castle' when she visited the place, and that Nessie has about 20 companions down there. As far as we know, nothing surfaced in September. (Unidentified newsclipping) 27 April 1979. If you miss that show, make a date to be at the Loch in May of 1981, when, according to the *New Civil Engineer,* a new bridge over the River Ness will be completed. If that means nothing to you then we refer you to the prophecies of the Brahan Seer, otherwise known as Coinneach Odhar, who lived on the Isle of Lewis in the 17th century, and whose prophecies have a reputation for considerable accuracy. Our source says that in this case (though we find no trace of it in the little data we have on the Seer) the prophecy runs that 'when the Ness River is overbuilt nine times, the river shall be emptied, and a powerful sea monster will appear.' Needless to say, the new construction will be the ninth bridge. *Spotlight* 12 1979.

[Credit: Larry Arnold, Clive Akass, David Fideler, Nick Maloret, Mark Hall, Martin Straw, Paul Screeton, Peter James, Roland Watson, Ion Will, Joe Zarzynski.]

Weasels Ripped my Tyres

The *Guardian* for 1 August told of reports from Switzerland of a new menace: weasels gnawing through car tyres and even cutting electric cables. Dr Donald Jefferies, of the Nature Conservancy Council in Huntingdon was asked to comment — and he did. It is possible, he speculated, 'that the smell of hot rubber is like the smell you get from the female in the mating condition.' Then he added: 'To a weasel, at least.' A spokesman for a leading tyre company (there's a pun there somewhere!) doubted the story. He thinks it escalated from an old tyre-dealers joke about badly chewed-up tyres — but do the Swiss joke about such things? That would have been the end of it if Katherine East, of Dorking, hadn't written to the *Guardian* (9 Aug) that her cat will eat the rubber off her Wellington boots with great relish. Only the right boots, she notes.

Now that we smelled a trend, a quick sortie through our new clippings disclosed the fate of a police car in Sunnyvale, California, whose driver had

called for a rescue squad. The car was found in the middle of an intersection, driver stranded inside, with two large bull terriers chewing and actually puncturing its tyres. *Niagara Falls Review* 12 July 1979.

Finally, Helen Mills and her young daughter were driving around Windsor Safari Park, Berkshire, when they had to stop behind some other vehicles. To her horror a large tiger pounced on her car and savaged a rear tyre before running off to attack a minibus. It was half an hour before wardens could tow her away and replace the rear wheel. *Daily Mail* 14 August 1979.

[Credit: Dwight Whalen, Ion Will.]

Hot Cross Fun

A bizarre running theme in recent weeks is attacks on churches and clergymen. On 8 July parishioners in Pattada, Sardinia, gasped as priest Don Guiseppe Mura collapsed after sipping Communion wine from a chalice. Police believe it was a murder attempt because Mura had mediated between the Mafia and relatives of a kidnapped West German. In the event Mura survived and is keeping quiet. *Guardian* 9 July 1979; *Weekend* 22 August 1979. A British born Jesuit, Fr Bernard D'Ark, was stabbed in the back while taking photos during a riot in Georgetown, capital of Guyana. Still smarting from the 'Peoples Temple' massacre, the riot was part of a continuing protest about the regime of Prime Minister Forbes Burnham, who had allowed the Jim Jones colony to flourish there. This demonstration was about the activities of yet another bizarre cult, the controvertial 'House of Israel' founded by 'Rabbi Washington', alias the fugitive US convict David Hill. Witnesses said Father D'Ark's attacker was a high-ranking member of the 'House of Israel'. *Guardian* 16 July 1979. Did Fr D'Ark have notions of being a martyr?

A bishop was beaten and shaved by an angry mob on the Greek island of Cephalonia, and narrowly saved from lynching by

police. Islanders say the bishop and 140 priests agreed to cut up the embalmed body of St Gerasimos and peddle the parts to other churches and pilgrims 'to make money'. *Daily Star* 16 June 1979.

Earlier this summer a Protestant missionary went down well with his flock, in the remote Cotabato area south of Manila, Philippines. They ate him! *Observer, & Sunday Telegraph* 15 July 1979. And in New York, 36yr-old Woodrow Webb decapitated deacon Robert Williams outside a church. Webb believed he was the devil. *Guardian* 11 Sept 1979. About the same time Webb came to trial, a bizarre case was being tried at Chipping Norton court. Father Anthony Colella, 48, of St Phillip Priory, Begbroke, near Oxford, had cycled into the country to pray and collect flowers, only to be knocked off a bike by Edward Addison, 45, head game-keeper of Lord Rotherwick's Cornberry Park estate, Oxfordshire. Colella was wearing a large yellow hat, knicker-type shorts, T-shirt and dark glasses when he was assaulted by Addison, who accused him of being 'a bloody weirdo.' It seems that a lady walking along a country road with her two children became frightened by Colella's appearance and demeanour, and complained to Addison. Colella denied peering at the woman and insisted he was saying his prayers. He protested: I was wearing pants down to my knees...Anyone who knows me will confirm that I am no pervert.' *Guardian* 12 Sept 1979.

In this time there were at least two cases of suspected arson in churches — *Guardian* 18 July & 27 Aug 1979 — and several robberies. On May 5th two teenagers attempted to steal the Holy Shroud from Turin Cathedral. They were caught by the elaborate alarm systems before they could locate the casket containing the relic. It was said to be the fifth attempt in seven years. *Daily Telegraph* 8 May 1979. Next, another gem from our bizarre crimes file. When the congregation saw the mantle on a statue of the Madonna moving, on a shelf behind the altar in the Italian parish church of Pietralcina, the stupified crowd thought they were witnessing a miracle. The crowd surged forward shouting: 'Miracolo, miracolo!' Women fainted. But it was only a thief stealing the jewels sewn onto the BVM's mantle. In the chaos he got away with about £12,000 worth. *Daily Telegraph* 9 August 1979.

Finally, after surviving a visit to Ireland, and the reformists in America, Pope John Paul was nearly brained by a huge iron cross during an outdoor service at Pompeii, Italy. As a gust of wind felled the cross in his direction he stepped back just in time. It was re-erected, but fell again, harmlessly. *D. Mirror* 22 Oct 1979.

[Credit: Paul Screeton, Valerie Thomas, Peter Christie, R Watson, Ion Will., Sam].

Stop Press. As we go to press we learn of more attacks on church folk. A Dominican nun was found clubbed to death not far from the Driefontein Mission Hospital, Rhodesia, where she worked. There was no sign of assault, and guerillas were not blamed. London *Evening Standard* 6 Nov 1979. On 7th November Luciano Esposito, 26, forced his way into the Vatican, brandishing a knife and insisting: 'I have to see the Pope. I want to kill him.' The honest assassin was disarmed by a Swiss Guard's deft handling of an antique halberd and a colleague using judo. *Herald Tribune* 8 Nov 1979. Anagram king, John Michell, tells us our would-be Papa-popper's name rearranges as: 'Oi! I can oust Poles.' The farce is with us! Nor has the armed seige of the Great Mosque in Mecca, an unparalleled sacriledge of Islam's holiest spot, gone unnoticed in FT's offices. It began perhaps on 18th Nov, just a handful of days after the Miss World contest in London, the annual signal to the UK press to lay in its own special seige-by-spotlight of the contest organisers...Mecca Ltd.

RJMR.

CAUSE AND EFFECT?

We have noted that after we bring out an issue, events occur in the outside world related to that issue's contents. If an issue is long in preparation, as this one was, these real-time events pop up with monotonous inevitability shortly after we've finished off a section of notes...hence the occasional stop press.

Loren Coleman told us of a rash of 'mystery illnesses' in New England shortly after receiving our plague issue, FT24; and again that after Doc Shiels' 'Owlman' article in FT27 many owls turned up in New England rarely or never before seen there. In FT28 we described compulsions to snatch and jab, and eccentric crimes performed in fancy dress. Well, we soon noted more spankers and a gent who swiped false legs, a flasher with a false nose, an entire fire station contingent debagged while they slept, attempted rape by a man dressed as a bottle, and bank robbers in Sicily dressed as Zorros.

It's been suggested we run a 'We told you so' department as a catch-all for this eerie echo effect. We'll see what happens after we mail this one out.

There — that's another awkward space filled.

TELLY KINEX
by JH Szostek.

Clemente Dominguez: Pope, Heretic, Stigmatic

Traditionally the stigmata are bodily representations of the wounds of Christ's Passion – in hands and feet, in the breast and circling the head. The Catholic Church distinguishes between divine stigmata, borne in humility, piety and often secretly, and diabolical stigmata, which prick their bearers on to sins of pride, ostentation and impiety. **Bob Rickard**, who has an interest in the Fortean aspects of religious and mystical phenomena, recently learned of the following case: an intriguing mixture of stigmata, heresy and visions in dubious circumstances.

The purple-robed archbishop is led toward the high altar. It is 9 in the evening and the service usually lasts 9 or even 12 hours. Most of the rituals are made up from those forgotten or abandoned in the modernisation of the Catholic Church, and in the various liturgical reforms. But this isn't just another of those local rebellions against the Vatican decrees, clinging to the old Latin (Tridentine) Mass in opposition to the instructions from the Holy Father that such Masses should be said in the local lingo. Archbishop Fernando of Palmar de Troya, Spain and both Americas — alias Pope Gregory XVIII — alias Clemente Dominguez Gomez — has it from the Virgin Mary (BVM) herself that he is on the ultimate and holiest of crusades.

The setting for this drama is appropriately bizarre. Clemente has built his own 'Vatican' — an exhibition-hall-like building made of scaffolding and sheets of green corrugated plastic that resembles more a Fellini film set than a cathedral in daily use. It sits in a deserted Martian landscape at the foot of Christ-the-King hill at the back of the small town of Palmar de Troya, near Seville, in Spain's Andalusia province. The green cathedral is surrounded by a 6 metre high wall, built on the instructions of the BVM — a tangible symbol of the strange battles fought around this very hill for the sole privilege of establishing a shrine to Mary and thereby founding a new and inevitably lucrative pilgrimage center.

It all began back in 1968. Two 15yr-old girls — Maria-Luisa Vila, and Maria Marin — became the focus of a series of visions in which messages were received from the BVM. It is said that in Andalusia there are a dozen BVM apparitions a year to young girls, and indeed they would have been forgotten among all the others were it not that they took place on Christ-the-King-hill, which looms over the vineyards of the aged Baroness of Castillo Chirel. The 93yr-old Baroness took a great interest in these local visions — not only was she an extensive landowner and red-wine producer, but was area treasurer of an extreme right-wing politico-religious group, advocating a return to 'Traditional Communion'. To the horror of her family she made out a will leaving 17 million pesetas (about £100,000 at the time) for the development of a shrine on the hill. She died before she could see the weird circus she set in motion.

When the news spread at least six of the 'top' visionaries in Andalusia turned up, to contest their claim. No one seems to have thought it odd in the light of the strong traditional female visionaries that all the contenders for the Baroness's millions were male. According to one source, these included a 12yr-old boy (Pepito) and 4 priests (Fathers Luna, Porfirio and Felix, and Brother Nectario). The sixth was Clemente, then 22 and a clerk in a Seville insurance firm — wait for it — the Archangel Raphael Insurance Co!

We learn that since he was a lad Clemente had pious aspirations. He attempted the priesthood, but was refused ordination, it is said, by the archbishop of Seville, Cardinal Bueno y Monreal, because of Clemente's indiscreet relationship with the flamenco dancer Carmelo, and Manuel Alonso, a fellow accountant at Archangel Raphael Insurance — the three were notorious throughout Seville as 'The Three Brotherly Lovers'.

The battle of the visionaries lasted about 2 years. The 40,000 pilgrims from round-about saw six pious seers swept away on the tide of extraordinary divine grace on the local Holy Mountain. Other eyes saw only the spectacle of six pious frauds, each trying to outdo the others with more and more bizarre and amazing close encounters with Christ, saints and angels, but always the BVM, to the awe of a fascinated and credulous crowd. There were grumblings in Rome.

By late 1970, Clemente was king of the hill. Literally. Having been rejected by the orthodox Church, he now had the resources to set up on his own — under the aegis of the BVM, of course. He began issuing bulletins of the orders and admonitions of the BVM, given to him personally during his regular trances. One such, given on 24 Feb 1971, warns of a group of Satanists in the Vatican, operating the coming destruction of the orthodox Church, and unless things improve, the coming destruction of this world. The basic content is little different from those conversations with apparitions of religious entities at Fatima, Garabandal, Bayside, San Damiano, Landeira and many others. Each of them have become centers of vigorous resistance against the reforms attempted by the Vatican, advocating a return to more dogmatic, traditional forms of worship, penitance and ritual. Clemente was soon joined by his old friends, Carmelo the flamenco dancer, and Manuel Alonso. Alonso became their business manager and guardian of their new wealth. About this time Clemente displayed publicly a divine stamp of approval — see photo(4). During a vision on 2nd April 1971, at 6am, he says, Christ himself branded his forehead by touching it with a crucifix that was dripping blood! From this time on Clemente was predisposed to the occasional stigmatic wound.

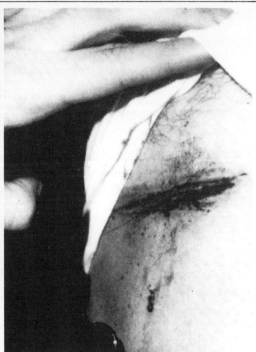

During regular expiation Masses, Clemente passes into ecstasy and manifests variously the 'Crown of Thorns' (above left) and the 'ferita' or chest wound (above right & far right).

So it went for several years, until the winter of 1974/75, and an event which lifts our narrative out of the ordinary. The 'Three Brotherly Lovers' flew to Rome for an audience with the elderly Vietnamese archbishop Petrus Ngo-dinh-Thuc brother of the assassinated dictator Ngo-dinh-Diem. Whether or not the 'Three' knew the archbishop was a big fan of BVM visions, and played on it, is not known. The fact is that the Spaniards told the Vietnamese that Mary had appeared and had requested to speak to the archbishop at Palmar de Troya. Archbishop Thuc did not stop to ponder why the Queen of Heaven and of countless miraculous apparitions could not have appeared to him in Rome, but when he heard this (as he said in a later letter) 'I backed my bags at once.'

Once in Spain the venerable archbishop seems to have been on the receiving end of the sort of treatment he'd find very hard to resist — the personal attention of the BVM. Once, during one of Clemente's nocturnal vigils. Thuc was ordered to hold out his arms to receive the Infant Jesus. In others he was told it was Mary's vehement wish that he should ordain Clemente and his key followers as priests, and then immediately after as bishops. This was done on 11 Jan 1975, according to the ancient and proscribed rite. So it was that Clemente became bishop Fernando, Manuel became bishop Isidoro, and Carmelo the flamenco dancer became bishop Elias. What a moment of triumph this must have been to the 'Brothers' — now they had the full and legal authority of a bishop.

One of Clemente's first acts seems to be one of foolish bravado. The triumph had gone to his head. In full bishop's uniform, with some embellishments of his own, he swaggered into the office of the archbishop of Seville, Bueno y Monreal, for a show-down. Within minutes Cardinal Bueno informed a shocked Vatican of what had happened — and three days later the Papal Nuncio to Madrid, Monsignor Luigi Dadaglio, had read a full *excommunatio specialissima* on Christ-the-King hill. But it was too late. There was no doubt about the legality of the ordination, and the laying on of hands, in a direct transmission of power and authority, from bishop to bishop, back to the very founders of the Church. Thuc was unceremoniously bundled off to virtual house arrest in Rome, where he is said to be abjectly 'sorry'.

The threat to the Catholic Church of this event is enormous. Its whole authority rests on the exclusive and unquestionable authority of its bishops; ordination being a magical rite of the highest order. Only a properly ordained priest, with authorization to ordain others, can do so. Throughout the history of the Catholic Church there have been heretical sects founded by breakaway priests who have (legally) ordained their own successors. There are a number of traditional Catholic movements who have done this within the orthodox body of the Church. Then there are the 'Wandering Bishops' who are not attached to any particular see, diocese, monastery

or whatever, but who travel where they will, ordaining who they want. But as far as I know, this is the first time a layman has tricked an ordination. And Clemente is no ordinary layman - he has the truth as given to him in his visions, that his alone is now the true Church, and the Vatican now a mere 'cave of robbers'. That is why archbishop Thuc had come to Palmar de Troya.

What is going on at Clemente's green plastic cathedral must seem like a black farce and a nightmare to the Vatican. It is said that the only qualification for being made a priest or bishop are that you attend the programme of services at the cathedral   showing some kind of willing. Without a glimmer of humour, one commentator baldly states that your chances of ordination are better if you are a handsome young boy. Since 1975 it is estimated about 300 bishops have been ordained – no-one keeps count – 70 of whom stay on at the cathedral. Since he doesn't recognize the authority of Rome, it's clear that Clemente doesn't care whether this clerical inflation embarasses the Vatican. Besides, the BVM told him he would be the next Pope after the death of Paul VI. (It is not known how Clemente reacted to the death of Paul on 6 August 1978, or to the election of the two John-Pauls, but I'm sure he relished the attendant confusion – see FT27 p 51). After his excommunication in 1975 he made himself and his two cronies, archbishops. Recently we heard he'd declared himself Pope Gregory XVIII. P'raps he made Carmelo and Manuel Alonso popes too?

These trances are becoming more dramatic. Recently he issued a document stating that we are in the 'Last Times'. It also deplores the moderation of post-Franco Spain. In fact while he was about it he made Franco a martyred saint for his fight against communists. He has also canonized some 60 anti-communist activists, plus a weird collection of medieval nuns who mutilated themselves to death for the glory of something or other. At the same time he uttered dire anathemas against 'Muhammedans, Masons, King Henry VIII of England and the diabolical Second Spanish Republic.' Although he has a lot of support from various reactionary elements in the Catholic Church, our Clemente hasn't made too many friends. On a recent visit to Colombia, he was booted out by the Cardinals for 'disrespect' to church officials.

The ritual performance goes on all night every night, crammed full of different kinds of Masses and services, Laurentian litanies, Pope hymns, Hearts of Jesus, Rosaries and Sacraments, Cross-carryings and ecstasies. The entire drama, garnished with the occasional miracle healing, is said to be an expiation ceremony, to avert the coming cataclysm. The bishops also made no secret that they were praying for the Pope (then Paul VI); since the BVM had revealed to Clemente that a secret group of Satanist Cardinals had imprisoned the Pope, drugging his Mass wine every day — thus Paul VI could be forgiven the 'error' of excommunicating Clemente and his followers because he was not himself. The rigor of the regular

expiation marathon is matched by   high morale among the young bishops. By Mary's order they are to do nothing but eat and sleep all day — work is out, steak and wine is in ('I need strong bishops!'). Cigarettes are kosher — Clemente is a chain-smoker — but regarding the housekeeping, Mary reserves the woman's privilege of changing her mind. One day beards are ordered, the next day prohibited, then demanded again. Chocolates, puddings, cheeses etc are forbidden one day and prescribed the next. Room changes every 3 days in the church's houses, says the Mother of God, to prevent 'attachments'. Despite this, millions of pilgrims come by coach, and donate. One Swiss lady has sent them a total of £5000. Many of the pilgrims themselves have visions and stay. Although Clemente himself controls not one penny, financial control is in the able hands of his crony, archbishop Isidoro, who has four bank accounts in his name, as well as the deeds to the Plastic Cathedral, 6 houses in Seville and half of Palmar de Troya. Ironically, Isidoro, alias Manuel Alonso, is the only one of the founding Brothers who has not been vouchsafed visions by the BVM!

But apart from these antics we are interested in Clemente because of his stigmata. The accompanying pictures — obviously taken at a time when beards were in celestial favour — show both the heart wound (or ferita) and the 'Crown of Thorns', of Christ's Passion. But while we can piece together the above story from our sources we know very little about the stigmata themselves. The 'Crown' must have appeared or disappeared (we have no idea of the order of the photos) very quickly, since it is not visible in other photos, obviously of the same set.

The stigmatic phenomena occur during the trances of the expiation programme, in which the conversations with the BVM alone may take up to 3 hours. They appear to be   recent phenomena, and one wonders whether they are related in any way to the car crash (on 29 March 1976) in which Clemente was blinded? However doubtful the cross on the forehead may appear, these classical stigmatic wounds look quite genuine. Their public display in this manner alone would be enough for the Vatican to denounce them as of diabolical origin. We cannot avoid a Fortean observation: if the events are quite genuine then there is a strong element of farce in them, on the other hand if the entire Shamanistic circus has been the product of hoax and fraud, then there are aspects of it which are convincing imitations of genuine phenomena.

Bob Rickard.

Sources

Anyone who has tried to research facts relating to the charismatic and visionary phenomena of religious movements will appreciate that they are in short supply and usually hidden within masses of dogmatic and subjective material. For instance, I would love to have learned more about the 'secret box' kept by Clemente in which he is said to keep 'an embodiment of the Holy Ghost' in the form of a pinned butterfly; but that's all we're told. So it goes.

Our primary source was an article in *Stern* No 24 (June 1978), 'Der Pabst von Sevilla' ('The Pope of Seville') by Conrad Zander, translated for us by Ion Will. Our photographs, mainly by Klaus Meyer-Anderson, are from this article.

Other sources were: *High Times* April 1979 (Cr: Michael Hoffman); and *Je Vous Salue Marie* tome 1 (July 1971).

PHENOMENOMIX

TALES OF MISUNDERSTANDING .... by HUNT EMERSON

THE CHAP WITH THE *WORRIED LOOK* IS INTERESTED IN WHY'S AND WHEREFORES!

...AND WE END OUR NEWS WITH REPORTS OF A GIRL IN ITALY WHO TURNS TENNIS BALLS INSIDE OUT WITH HER MIND....

HE EXPERIENCES A *FLASH* OF *INSIGHT!*

OF COURSE!! IF SHE IMAGINES WHAT THE INSIDE OF A TENNIS BALL WOULD LOOK LIKE IF IT WERE ON THE OUTSIDE!...

...WHY, I COULD DO IT MESELF!

TIME PASSES....

MEANWHILE, IN TENNIS BALL FACTORIES ALL OVER THE WORLD....

THAT'S T'FORTIETH CRATE THIS WEEK.. ...RUINED!!

EE, OUR ALBERT! HAST THOU SEEN OWT LIKE IT?

BOWNSERS BEST TENNIS BALLS

NAY, NOT IN A LIFETIME OF TENNIS BALL MANUFACTURY, YOUNG SPROG!

MORE RUBBER! BUY MORE RUBBER!!

WE'LL BE RUINED!

...AND, IN THE FAR EAST, VAST TRACTS OF RUBBER PLANTATION ARE CLEARED TO MEET INCREASED DEMAND!!

BOING

THEY SAY THAT *NATURE* ABHORS A VACUUM! WELL, SHE SURE DON'T THINK MUCH OF THIS SUDDEN *LACK* OF RUBBER IN MALAYA (WHICH, AS WE ALL KNOW, IS FAMOUS FOR THE STUFF).

DO SUMP'N ABOUT IT, AN' PRON TO!

...AN' YOU! GIT THAT GODDAM THERMOS FLASK OUTA HERE! Y'KNOW TH' RULES!

OK MA!

?GULPE S-SORRY, MA!

WHAT IF WE PUT THE RUBBER SOMEWHERE THEY'RE NOT GOIN' TO IMMEDIATELLY CHOP IT DOWN?!

GOOD THINKING, ROBIN!

UNCLE CHAO'S COZMIK FIXERY

STUF FIXED CHEAP

AND SO, IN THE *HOCK SIEW KONG* TEMPLE AT *TELOK,* A WOODEN STATUE OF A WELL-KNOWN LOCAL DEITY GROWS A STRANGE BEARD....

etc

John Ellis

The Great Fish Fall of 1859

Of all the phenomena Charles Fort pursued and described, showers of frogs and fishes, perhaps, most typify the Fortean event. They are tangible enough to be subjected to the scrutiny of a scientific viewpoint, and yet the details defy explanation according to the current theories leaving an anomaly that raises more questions than can be fairly answered. **Robert Schadewald**, an American science writer with a more than passing interest in Fortean enigmas, investigated one of Fort's classic fish falls, one of the very few in Britain, to determine the extent of the evidence.

Mention fish rains, and most Forteans automatically think of John Lewis and the 1859 incident at Mountain Ash, Glamorgan Wales. That's because the Mountain Ash fall is included in almost every article written about the falls (including three by me). Usually, the writers have merely borrowed from Fort, or even borrowed from other writers who borrowed from Fort.

Most modern accounts of the incident are thus based on the testimony of John Lewis, 'a sawyer in Messrs. Nixon and Co's yard,' who reportedly told the following story:

'On Wednesday, February 9, I was getting out a piece of timber for the purpose of setting it for the saw, when I was startled by something falling all over me — down my neck, on my head, and on my back. On putting my hand down my neck I was surprised to find they were little fish. By this time I saw the whole ground covered with them. I took off my hat, the brim of which was full of them. They were jumping all about. They covered the ground in a long strip of about 80 yards by 12, as we measured afterwards. That shed, (pointing to a very large workshop) was covered with them, and the shoots were quite full of them. My mates and I might have gathered bucketsful of them, scraping with our hands. We did gather a great many, about a bucketful, and threw them into the rain-pool, where some of them now are. There were two showers, with an interval of ten minutes, and each shower lasted about two minutes, or thereabouts. The time was 11am. The morning up-train to Aberdare was just then passing. It was not blowing very hard, but uncommon wet; just about the same wind as there is today (blowing rather stiff), and it came from this quarter (pointing to the S. of W.). They came down in the rain in 'a body like'. [1]

Before examining the story in detail, it's useful to know something about Mountain Ash.

Mountain Ash is a village on the Cynon River, in the valley of Aberdare. It is in the parish of Aberdare, about 4 miles southeast of Aberdare proper, 30 miles northwest of Cardiff, and 37 miles northeast of Swansea. The region is mountainous, and averages several inches of rain per month.

In 1859, Aberdare parish was painfully dragging itself into the 19th century; its population more than doubled between 1841 and 1851, and again between 1851 and 1861. The Industrial Revolution was going strong, and there was a tremendous demand for coal. The local mines yielded a very high grade, and it was used in the local iron works, and also shipped out in quantity, mostly by rail, partly via the Aberdare Canal. John Nixon, John Lewis's employer, was a major pioneer in the Welsh steam coal trade, and the 'Nixon's Navigation Steam Coal' from his yard was world famous.

I have been unable to find the population for Mountain Ash for that era, but it must have been small, a few thousand at most, since the 1861 population of the entire parish of Aberdare was 32,299. Mountain Ash had a railway station, Post Office, St. Margaret's Church (seating 500) and a newspaper, *Y Gwladgarwr*, published every Friday. Sadly, there seems to be no file of the latter extant.

The earliest surviving reports of the Mountain Ash fish rain appear in the Monmouthshire *Merlin* and the Merthyr *Telegraph* for Saturday, February 19th, 1859. The reports are slightly contradictory, and appear unrelated.

According to the former, 'Much excitement has been occasioned in the valley of Aberdare, by the fact of a complete shower of fish falling at Mount Ash, on Friday last. The roofs of some houses were covered with them, and several were living, and are still preserved in like and apparent health in glass bottles. They were from an inch to three inches in length, and fell during a heavy shower of rain and storm of wind.'

'Friday last' apparently means the 11th, or the writer would have said 'yesterday.'

The Merthyr *Telegraph*, apparently published at Merthyr Tydfil, 5 miles north of Mountain Ash, reported as follows: EXTRA-ORDINARY SHOWER OF FISHES—We are informed on credible authority, that a most singular shower of fishes occurred a few days ago in the neighbourhood of Nixon's Yard, Aberaman, and in the immediate district. The shower appears to have fallen in an easterly direction, and to have extended over a large tract of country, as some of the fishes have been found at Troedyrhiw. The shower was so large that besoms were called into requisition in order to clear them away from doorways, &c. We have seen one of the fishes, which appears, from this one, to be of the whiting kind, and about the size of a small minnow. Many gentlemen in Aberdare have also possessed themselves of some, and a few have been sent to Merthyr Tydfil, so that all doubters may examine.'

Aberaman is halfway between Mountain Ash and Aberdare, but I can't find Troedyrhiw on a map.

Chronologically, the next account was written by Aaron Peters, Curate of St. Peter's, Carmarthen (about 40 miles to the West). His letter, dated February 25th, was published in the London *Times*, March 2nd, 1859, and said in part:'On Friday, the 11th of February, there fell at Mountain Ash, Glamorganshire, about 9 o'clock a.m., in and about the premises of Mr Nixon, a heavy shower of rain and small fish. The largest size measured about four inches in length. It is supposed that two different species of fish descended; on this point however the public generally disagree. At the time it was blowing a very stiff gale from the south. Several of the fish are preserved in fresh water, five of which I have this day seen. They seem to thrive well. The tail and fins are of a bright white colour. Some persons attempting to preserve a few in salt and water, the effect is stated to have been almost instantaneous death. It was not observed at the time that any fish fell in any other part of the neighbourhood, save in the particular spot mentioned.' [2,*]

Reverend Peters then quotes the note from the Monmouthshire *Merlin* verbatim.

On Saturday, February 26th, accounts appeared in two papers, the Merthyr *Telegraph* again, and the Cardiff and Merthyr *Guardian*.

The former mentions the incident in passing, again placing it at Aberaman. It notes that 'those who could possess themselves of one of the wonderful fishes, have done so; while the less fortunate have contented themselves with repairing the shop windows, where some of the mysterious creatures have been swimming about, in blissful ignorance of their late ethereal tour.'

The account in the Cardiff and Merthyr *Guardian* (published at Cardiff?) is long and mostly independent of the others given above. It begins, 'The curiosity of the inhabitants of Merthyr and Aberdare has been greatly excited during the past week by the fall of a shower of fish into Mr. Nixon's yard, at Mountain Ash, Aberdare. Some few are also said to have been picked up at Troedyrhiw...'

The *Guardian* writer notes that in places the fish had to be swept out of the footpaths, and says that it is firmly established that 'this took place on Wednesday, the 16th inst...that the fish, thousands in number, were many of them alive, and remain so; that they are about an inch in length, of the minnow kind, or, strictly speaking, having more of the characteristics of roach or dace; and that they live in fresh water. They are dusky green on the back, and a silvery white on the belly; the dorsal fin commences rather behind the middle of the back; the head is larger, and the eyes more prominent than those of the minnow; and the tail is more deeply forked.'

The account notes further that 'they fell upon the tops of a shed, and some adjoining houses; a man who was passing by at the time had his hat covered with them...' The writer then goes into a pretentious (and not very well informed) discussion of the mechanism of whirlwinds, and concludes that the fish were picked up and dropped by a waterspout, which was unseen because it was on the other side of a mountain. He winds up with, 'But whatever may be thought of the suggested explanation, the fact is certain; we may have seen the fish, and accept the testimony that they fell in a shower.'

The account from which the testimony of John Lewis was quoted earlier was not written until March 8th. The author was John Griffith, vicar of Aberdare. The vicar called John Lewis 'the principal witness,' and notes that he took down Lewis's testimony on the spot where the incident happened. He recorded the testimony, so he says, 'for the purpose of being laid before Professor Owen, to whom, alas, I shall send tomorrow, at the request of a friend of his, eighteen or twenty of the little fish. Three of them are large and very stout, measuring about four inches. The rest are small. There were some — but they are since dead — fully five inches long. They are very lively.' [1,*]

Griffith's letter was reprinted in *Zoologist* 1859-6493*. Apparently the fish reached Owen, for in *Zoologist* 1859-6541*, the editor notes that the fish are to be seen in the Zoological Gardens, Regents Park. He says that one is a minnow, and the rest are

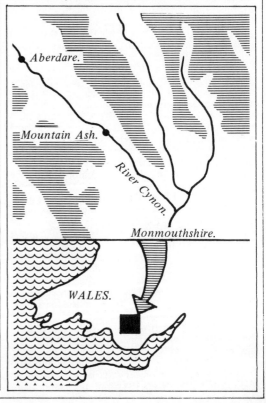

smooth-tailed stickleback *(Gasterosteus leiurus).*

On the same page is a letter dated April 2nd, from JE Gray of the British Museum. Dr Gray has seen some of the fish, and says that they are 'very young minnows,' and are 'very unlike those taken up by whirlwinds in tropical countries.' He thinks John Lewis was hoaxed by someone who thew a pailful of water and fish on him.

In *Zoologist* 1859-6564*, there is a letter dated May 18th from Robert Drane, Cardiff, disputing the hoax conclusion. Drane says, in part, 'from information obtained from many sources and very careful and minute inquiry, I am quite convinced that a great number of fish did actually descend with rain over a considerable tract of the country. The specimens I obtained from three individuals, resident some distance from each other, were of two species, the common minnow and the three-spined stickleback; the former most abundant and mostly small, though some had attained their full size.'

The incident is mentioned in the Welsh journal *Seren Gomer* 1859-142 as follows: 'A SHOWER OF FISH—Friday, 11th February, a heavy shower containing many hundreds of small fish fell in and around Mr. Nixon's yard, Mountain Ash, near Aberdar. It seems that most if not all of the fish were sprats.' [3]

The Rev W. S. Symonds read a paper about the Mountain Ash fish fall before the British Association for the Advancement of Science. A summary of the paper was printed in *Reports BAAS* 1859-158* as follows: 'The evidence of the fall of fish on this occasion was very conclusive. A specimen of the fish was exhibited, and was found to be the *Gasterosteus leiŗus*, Cuv.' William Samuel Symonds is best known for his writings on the geology of Wales, and his original paper would be an invaluable source. Unfortunately, it, along with most of the other early papers of the BAAS, has perished. [4]

From the above confusing and sometimes contradictory mass of data about the Aberdare Valley fish fall, three conclusions emerge immediately. First, there can be no doubt that it actually happened. Second, everybody and his brother grabbed some of the fish and put them in water, as living souvenirs of the bizarre incident. Third, the incident passed immediately into folklore.

The folklore aspect is important, because it helps to explain some of the confusion over details. Consider how a modern newspaper, with a staff of professional reporters, can botch a story it actually investigates. In 1859, the small Welsh newspapers were weeklies, put together by tiny staffs from rumours, letters, unpaid contributions, and material lifted from other newspapers. There were no reporters usually, and the editor wrote his stories from whatever sources he could get. Small wonder then that the details, partly gathered from pedlars in pubs, got a bit garbled.

Now, more than a hundred years after the fact, it is impossible to be certain when the Aberdare Valley fish rain occurred, unless additional and better sources can be uncovered. The earliest dated sources point to Friday, the 11th. The longest, seemingly best researched account, says Wednesday, the 16th. The man who was clobbered with the fish was reported (a month later) to have said Wednesday, the 9th. A clear majority of sources point to the 11th, but historical truth cannot be determined by vote. [5] In my opinion, it happened on Wednesday, February 9th, as reported by John Griffith.

John Griffith was vicar of Aberdare, only 4 miles from Mountain Ash. Though his letter to the London *Times* was dated March 8th, there's reason to believe he interviewed John Lewis long before then. For one thing, he was obviously very interested in the incident, and one would assume that he talked to Lewis as soon as possible. Indeed, he took the trouble to interview Lewis on the spot where it happened, and some of the fish were still swimming in a rain-pool at the time. Griffith may have written an earlier, similar account that was published in Wales. Note the account in the Cardiff and Merthyr *Guardian* of February 26th seems (impossibly) to draw on Griffith's letter of March 8th. Though Griffith alone gives the date as Wednesday, February 9th, I believe he's correct.

Suppose I'm right, and the fish fall actually happened on the morning of the 9th. Suppose some excited citizen of Mountain Ash gathered what information he could and wrote a breathless letter (probably in Welsh) to *Y Gwladgarwr*, beginning, 'A remarkable thing happened this morning...' If the letter was printed verbatim in the next issue of *Y Gwladgarwr*, Published Friday, the 11th, other papers lifting the story might mistakenly assume that the incident happened on the 11th. Then the writer for the Cardiff and Merthyr *Guardian* discovered that it actually happened on a Wednesday, but guessed the 16th, a week too late. All this is, of course, speculation, and I wouldn't bet much on it.

The time of the incident is given by two sources, Aaron Peters (9.00am) and Griffith (11.00am). Again I trust Griffith.

It was raining (water) and windy when the fish fell. The Monmouthshire *Merlin* account says 'a very heavy shower of rain and storm of wind.' Aaron Peters mentioned the rain and 'It was not blowing very hard, but uncommon wet; just about the same wind as there is today.' Griffith says the wind the day of the interview was 'blowing rather stiff' and that Lewis pointed to the south of west to indicate the direction of the wind. Interestingly, the writer for the Cardiff and Merthyr *Guardian*, who tries to make a case for a whirlwind, makes no mention of the wind conditions at the time! None of the accounts mention storm damage, or the kind of violent winds that typically accompany tornadoes (and I presume, waterspouts).

Regarding the location and extent of the fall, the title of W.S. Symmonds' BAAS paper was 'Account of the Fish-rain at Aberdare in Glamorganshire.' This and the accounts in the Monmouthshire *Merlin*, the Merthyr *Telegraph*, the Cardiff and Merthyr *Guardian*, and the

Zoologist letter by Robert Drane all suggest that the fall covered a wide area in Aberdare Valley. Apparently, there was a tremendous concentration of fish at Nixon's yard, and some people weren't aware that the fall was much more extensive. There is some confusion over whether Nixon's yard was at Mountain Ash or Aberaman. John Nixon ran a huge coal business, and perhaps he had several yards in the area. Whatever the cause of the confusion, I trust Griffith, who says he interviewed John Lewis 'on the spot' at Mountain Ash.

As to the fish, they were successfully kept alive everywhere in fresh water. There were more than one kind, and the various accounts mention sprats,

whiting, minnows, three-spined stickleback, and smooth tailed stickleback. The first two are questionable, but the presence of the last three species seems well established.

Both the Cynon River and the Aberdare Canal run through the Aberdare Valley. I will leave it to the reader to judge whether or not a whirlwind lifted fish from one or both of these sources (or from any other source), dumped a few thousand of them on Nixon's yard and John Lewis, and scattered the remainder over the surrounding countryside.

Robert Schadewald

Notes:
* Denotes a source used by Fort
1) Griffith, John. Letter dated March 8, 1859, in London *Times* of March 10, 1859. Reprinted in *Zoologist* 1859-6493 and (I believe) *Annual Register* 1859-14.
2) Also reprinted in Cardiff *Times*, March 5, 1859.
3) Translation courtesy of Cleo Vaighe of the National Library of Wales, Aberystwyth.
4) Letter of 25 January 1977 from Miss Joan H. Dring, Senior Administrative Assistant for BAAS.
5) That makes about as much sense as taking the average, and declaring that the incident happened on Frisat, the 11.6th.

AUTHOR'S NOTE
I would like to extend my thanks to G.A.C. Dart of the Central Library, Cardiff; G. Davies of the Central Library, Aberdare; Miss J.H. Dring of the B.A.A.S.; Mrs Patricia Moore of the Glamorgan Archive Service; and Cleo Vaighe, of the National Library of Wales, Aberystwyth, whose research efforts in my behalf made this article possible. It takes a special kind of person to take time out from what must be more important business and rummage through musty archives seeking information for a stranger a quarter the way round the world.

FACTS YOU MIGHT FORGET! *by Pokkettz.*

U·F·O Commentary by Nigel Watson

Jaws Encounter

A young messenger for a Panamanian doctor made an amazing discovery when he stumbled across the skeleton of an extraterrestrial child on a stretch of beach at San Carlos, Panama.

The skeleton consisted of a bony shell instead of a rib cage, and the vertebral channel appeared so large that the being must have had a large heavy, intelligent brain encased in a huge skull.

Naturally the president of the Center for Panamanian Extraterrestrial Investigations (CIPE) — Dr Francisco Ramon de Aguilar — was very excited about this discovery and paid 1,000 dollars for the precious skeleton.

Dr Aguilar said that his skeleton was proof that: 'they exist, are here among us and carry out a task of selective education among humans, the results of which we will soon see.'

A similar skeleton was found on Erendira beach in 1972, and another one — though in a poor state of preservation — was found in February 1978 in Manta, Equador. [1]

Are there star wars over South America? Is some incredible battle going on which we know little of, except for the discovery of odd bones and rotting skeletons? Mr Spock would have delighted himself in trying to answer this galactic riddle. Spock never materialised to solve this problem, but a doctor and a Jesuit Priest, Ignacio Astorqui, felt that he had the answer.

On a beach in Nicaragua a similar skeleton was found, and Astorqui, an expert in zoology and ichthyology, examined the specimen.

His verdict was that it was the head of a dead shark. He said: 'The disagreeable smell like rotten fish was suspicious in an extraterrestrial, unless he should come from a planet of fish-men. Neither is it very convincing that an 'evolved being should have a rigid skeleton and thus not be too functional.' [2]

A Star Is Born

Frances Steiger — wife of Brad Steiger the well known author on the subject of UFOs and related topics — started it all by dreaming about two men who said to her: 'Now is the time. Now is the time.' The profoundly philosophical nature of this statement is quite astounding, evidently 'now is the time' verifies the validity of the telephone speaking clock system, and what better way than in a dream?

Frances, however, decided that her dream meant that she could reveal that herself and thousands of other people are Star People.

Star People have more sensitivity to sound, light, electricity and electro-magnetic fields. They are subject to: chronic sinus trouble, subnormal blood pressure, lack of any long periods of sleep, lower body temperature and an unusual blood group usually flows through their veins. The Star Person is complete when they discover that they have an extra vertebra and psychic ability.

Bonnie Davis, a Star Person, claims that: 'The Golden Age is coming. When it arrives there will be no sickness, poverty or illness.

'People will live long, happy lives free of trouble and worry.'

Another Star Person, Faye

Thompsen, states: 'I feel that the reason Star People are on Earth is to prepare earthlings.

'We are making it easier for you to accept us. The Golden Age will be here before the year 2000.'

When asked for an opinion the Earl of Clancarty made the astute remark that: 'People may not know that they are descendants of aliens until they get some message.' [3]

I keep getting visions (no comments, please) of a bug-eyed monster scratching out millions of letters, saying: 'Dear sir/madam, You are an alien. The side-effects are nearly harmless and in return you will live to see the arrival of The Golden Age. Just send 2000 dollars to the above address and await further instructions. Yours etc....'

Mind Games

'My place is not of this solar system called a star galaxy,' says Lydia Stalnaker who after several hypnotic sessions believes that she has been implanted with the personality of an alien being called Antron.

In defence of her weird story Lydia says that: 'This may seem like science fiction to many people, but to me it is now becoming a way of life. I have come to know some of these (alien) people and feel that they are friends. Sometimes I begin to miss them, just as I miss earth friends whom I have not seen for some time. I want to call them and talk to them just to be sure everything is all right with them.' [4]

Lydia's awareness of Antron began in 1974. One evening during that year she was driving near Jacksonville when she thought she saw a plane crashing, until the aerial object stopped behind some huge pine trees. Lydia blacked out as soon as she got out of her car to investigate, and when she regained consciousness she found herself driving her car again.

The day after her sighting she had a short violent attack of illness which terminated abruptly. Then: 'I suddenly became psychic. I started knowing who was on the phone. And I was seemingly able to tell people what to do — mentally,' she said.

Another side-effect of the encounter were terrible nightmares about an operating theatre which led her to seek the aid of Dr James Harder. He carried out a series of hypnotic regressions on Lydia and during these he discovered that she had a UFO encounter when she was 9 years old.

During one of these sessions Lydia related to Dr Evelyn Brunson that during her 1974 encounter 'she and another woman were on separate tables head to head with a mechanical device that covered part of their heads. They were spun around and around. This supposedly merged them together and made it possible for Antron to be with Lydia,' said Dr Brunson who carried out 26 hypnotic regression sessions with 36-year-old Lydia.

Antron is a female alien who resides in a glass tube onboard a spacecraft in the vicinity of Earth. There are other aliens on the spacecraft who communicate telepathically between themselves. Antron is thousands of years old and she comes from a green planet which has 2 suns and is situated in another galaxy.

Antron has a powerful personality and it took Lydia several years to accept and feel comfortable with the thought that another living being was within

herself. She said: 'I go off to a far corner of my mind when Antron wants to do something. She just takes control.' [5]

Unfortunately the aliens don't have a very welcome message for humanity, since: 'They tell of the time ('Now is the time' — N.W.) soon to come, when earth changes will occur,' says Lydia.

Antron (via Lydia) explains that: 'Man was here originally, in the beginning, as we are. He was built to live forever, but he failed and now we have come to take the people that have chosen of their own free will to live correctly. They will be re-colonized to live as in the original beginning. We are sent to do this job.' [4]

Presumably if we are not to have a Golden Age on Earth the chosen people — with the aid of the aliens — will fly off to some extraterrestrial utopia.

Indeed an alien named Jay (via a Scotsman called Andrew) claims that a total of 100 million people have been secretly blasted into space. They leave on a flying saucer which is launched on the 8th of each month at 3.35am from the Florida Everglades.

Apparently these people are sent as zombie workers to the Moon or Mars. Although Rex Dutta, a director of the Viewpoint Aquarius magazine, believes that there are colonies on the Moon and Mars (being a convert to the ideas expounded in

the 'Alternative Three' science fiction story), he was able to rumble Jay's story.

Jay's downfall was due to the fact that he claimed that the flying saucer which shuttled between Florida and an anonymous lunar colony used the same VHF frequency as the Northampton and County police headquarters — and even Rex Dutta was unable to swallow that! (Even though his appetite for believing such stories is almost inexhaustible.) [6]

Body Games

59-year-old Eugenio Siracusa, a retired Customs officer, was a Star Person who went on trips to Venus and Mars for his holidays and had regular communication sessions with the aliens.

He set up a Cosmic Brotherhood which was financed by two Americans — Kelly Meadowcroft and his wife Leslie.

Siracusa 'called us to Sicily,' said Kelly, and 'we bought him a villa where he could install the brotherhood and erect the glass pyramid which he used to 'communicate' with the UFO pilots.'

Whilst the Meadowcrofts stayed under the spell of Siracusa's stories at the Brotherhood's HQ on Mount Etna, Kelly was sent on long trips to meet space visitors or leave boxes for them to pick up.

All these expeditions were futile but Kelly said: 'I believe him about my missions. Everytime I'd get back and tell him I hadn't met anyone he would say it was only a test.'

Siracusa's intentions were not entirely honourable and whilst Kelly was on his stupid travels, he intended having a close encounter with Kelly's wife.

Leslie said that when Siracusa tried to make love to her 'he said a son would be born from our union. The son would be known as the prophet Elias and he told me he was acting on orders from a cosmic being named Adoneides.'

When Kelly found out about this state of affairs, Siracusa was arrested with charges of adultery, embezzlement and tax evasion to his credit. [7] Will he be another

A. KRAUZE

Zombie worker for the Moon colony work-camp?

Not Yet

Mark Block and his three female helpers declared to the people of San Diego County that the enigmatic space people were planning to drop in for a visit.

On the appointed date — 21st June, 1979 — at the appointed location — an unfinished stretch of the interstate 15 freeway 20 miles north of San Diego — 1,000 people gathered to see the event of the century.

The UFO party began at 6pm in anticipation of the landing at 11.49pm. With the prospect of seeing city-sized space ships and bendy-toy aliens, a tense excitement must have descended on the expectant crowd as the minutes slowly approached the most momentous time in the history of mankind.

For reasons unknown to humanity the landing was abandoned, and when it was clear that nothing was going to occur, Block disappeared from sight as quickly as a Venusian scout craft. [8]

Not Yet, Again

Prediction is a tricky business as Jo Ann Dunaway will no doubt agree when we consider that she prophesied that 'spacemen from a highly evolved planet will land in the United States in 1977. The landings will occur near West Palm Beach and in the Connecticut-Rhode Island area. The spacemen will be short with reddish curly hair. They will speak every language and dialect —and they come to help.' [9]

When 1977 emerged without any significant UFO landings, another psychic, Mrs Shawn Robbins, boldly claimed: 'The world will have its first contact with a UFO in 1978.'

She said that the contact would occur during a screening of the film, 'Close Encounters of the Third Kind' and that the audience would receive a message which 'will contain three important parts. First, it will be the first positive confirmation that they're here from outer space. Second, that their presence on earth is in the

interest of peace. Third, that there will be mass landings in the U.S., Middle East and Russia.'

Miss Kebrina Kinkade, a Los Angeles psychic, pronounced: 'I predict that we will have actual communication in 1978 from planets like Pluto and Saturn.' [10]

Is there anybody who would like to predict that 1980 will be the 'Year of the UFO?'?

The Pinocchio Complex

There seems to be a widespread need for mankind to believe that we are being visited by aliens. This need drives people to buy shark skulls; it makes them gather on unfinished freeways; it sends them on wild goose chases while their partner is being seduced; it makes them believe in colonies on the Moon and Mars; it makes them believe that there will be mass landings; most fundamental of all they believe that they can communicate with the aliens and in extreme cases many believe they are one of the Space People.

By combining the most compelling aspects of religion and science the UFO myth becomes a powerful symbol of the technological saviour who will deliver us to utopia and beyond.

More importantly we must ask whether we are responding to valid external stimuli or whether there is some need within ourselves which makes us want to believe that there are external stimuli. Or to put it more simply: are we the manipulated or the manipulators?

Notes

1) *Cronica* (Buenos Aires) 3 April 1979. Trans: Jane Thomas*.
2) *Cronica* (Buenos Aires) 20 April 1979. Trans: Jane Thomas*.
3) *Reveille* 3 Aug 1979, 'Was your Dad really a UFO man? by Midrim Jones.
4) *Florida Times-Union* 4 Feb 1977, 'Hypnotic Sessions reveal 'Experiences' by Ralph Goff.
5) *National Enquirer* 12 June 1979, 'Alien from Space shares Woman's Body and Mind' by Bob Pratt.
6) *Guardian* 7 March 1979, 'Outer Space Believers stand firm' by Michael Parkin.
7) *Reveille* 5 Jan 1979.
8) *The Hour* (Norwalk, Connecticut) 25 June 1979.
9) *Florida Times-Union* 4 Feb 1977, 'Psychics and UFOs' by Ralph Goff.
10) *National Enquirer* 31 Jan 1978, 'Psychics predict Space Beings will communicate with World this year' by Bud Gordon.

*[Credit: *Lucius Farish's* UFO News-clipping Service No 119, Gary Abbott, Joseph Patchen.]*

Nigel Watson is a regular contributor to Fortean Times

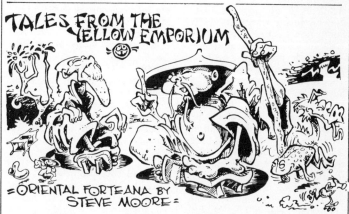

TALES FROM THE YELLOW EMPORIUM

= ORIENTAL FORTEANA BY STEVE MOORE =

The Hairy Boy of China

They called him Zhenhuan, meaning 'shock the universe', and the kid has indeed created something of a stir. Western journalists have handled his story in the usual degrading fashion, calling him 'monkey-boy', 'wolf-

boy', freak, mutant...but to the Chinese he is simply *mao hai*, a hairy child.

Yu Zhenhuan was born 30 Sept 1977 in Shaotzugo People's Commune, Zhouyan Country, Liaoning Province, NE China. His parents, Yu Wenguang, 27,

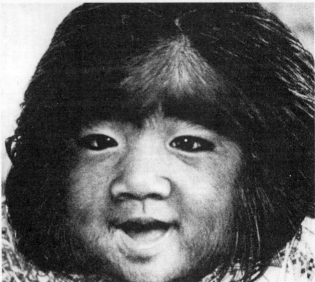

and Song Baoqin, 25, were horrified to find Zhenhuan covered in jet-black hair at birth: his eyebrows merged with the hair on his forehead, and his entire body except for his lips, palms, soles and the tip of his nose was hirsute...the kid even had hairy ears!

There was, it seems, some dispute about whether Zhenhuan should be allowed to live, but he survived long enough to come to the attention of the Chinese Academy of Sciences, and after that his future was assured. His family now has a new house and a state subsidy to look after him, and at 8 months, Zhenhuan starred in his first movie...a documentary film shot at Shenyang, the provincial capital.

Zhenhuan's hair has now turned from black to brown, and varies in length: 7cms around the shoulder, 4.5cms on his back, 2.5cms on his abdomen. Apart from that, he's very much a normal child; all his senses are in good working order, X-rays and intelligence tests show nothing abnormal. He has a slightly enlarged heart, and at 4-5 months was taller than an average child. His head and ears are large, and he cut his teeth late, at about one year. He laughs much, cries little and, apart from a little trouble with a boil and eczema, is perfectly healthy. The hair parts at the side of his body and

thickens toward the mid-lines of the back and abdomen, forming whorls at various places.

Zhenhuan has a sister two years older than himself who is perfectly normal. Apart from his maternal grandfather and uncle, who have slightly hairy calves and thick beards, none of his immediate relatives show similar traits.

The average Chinese is perhaps the least hairy individual on the planet, which makes the *mao hai* phenomenon all the more unusual. All human foetuses are covered with fine down after 5 to 6 months development, but this hair is usually shed before birth. The cause of the 'mao hai' atavism apparently remains mysterious, but it has been determined that the trait is inheritable. And the hirsute individual keeps his pelt throughout his lifetime...

More of the Same

Despite the pedagogic pronouncements of the *National Enquirer*, Yu Zhenhuan is not unique: 19 other cases have been found in China, and more elsewhere. We shall catalogue briefly those we have details of:

1. Yu Zhenhuan; Liaoning. Described above. [1-4].

2. An old woman of the same village as Yu Zhenhuan heard, when she was young, old folk

(Top Left) The hairy girl Zhu Xiulian, 11 days older than the more famous hairy boy, Yu Zhenhuan (Top Right and Below). Photos from: Ta Kung Pao 10 May 1979, and China Pictorial 1979:5.

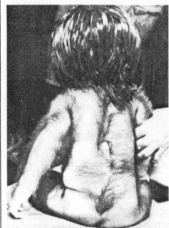

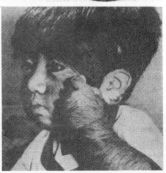

saying that a woman not far from there had given birth to a similar black haired infant. The mother's father-in-law killed it with a blow of a pick-handle. [1]

3. Shandong Province, 40 years ago. [2]

4. Li Pao-Shu: born in the late 1940s near Peking, with a handsome black-and-white mane. Treated as a freak and exhibited in a travelling show [2].

5. Qi Rong, born 1969, Shachou Country, Jiangsu Province. At ten years of age, he measured 1.25 meters tall. [2,3].

6. Name unknown: boy, born 1968, Hsincheng County, Hebei [2].

7. Zhang Xing: born 1950, Hebei province. He has a sound physique and is 1.76 meters tall. Fond of singing and playing the flute, and a model worker. [3].

8. Jiangsu province: a hair-covered child born to a woman with the same condition. However, the mother shed much of her hair after her marriage, and though still not smooth-skinned, her condition has improved 'dramatically'. [2,3].

9. A family in Liaoning Province having hairy persons covering three generations. [3].

10. Zhu Xiulian. Born 10 September 1977 in Guangdong Province. Active and intelligent. Covered in black hair. Her nose is wider, the ditch between nose and lip deeper, her lips are thicker and her ears are bigger than normal. Body and IQ normal. Parents Zhu Shaowen and Li Muqong are members of a people's commune. [5].

11. Other *mao hai* cases reported from the following Chinese provinces: Shanxi, Qinghai, Henan, Sichuan, Anhui and Zhejiang, but no details. [3].

12. Russia, 19th Century. A father and son in a peasant family. [1,2].

13. Burma. An entire family of hirsute individuals. Date unknown [1].

14. India. A case where the condition occurred in three successive generations. No further details. [2].

Further examples may be found in Charles Darwin's *The Descent of Man and Selection in Relation to Sex* (1871).

Sources

Major sources on Yu Zhenhuan
1. *China Reconstructs* Vol 28, No 3. March 1979, p60-61.
2. Ceylon *Weekend* 31 Dec. 1979: reprinting on article from *Asiaweek*.
3. *China Pictorial* 1979, No 5 (May 1979) p42-3.

Minor references:
4. *Rising Nepal & Guardian* 23 Oct 78; *News of the World* 29 Oct 78; *Daily Star* 17 Feb 79; *Daily Telegraph* 24 Feb 79; *National Enquirer* 24 April 79; Belgium *Het Volk* 25 Oct 1978.
And for Zhu Xiulian:
5. Hong Kong *Ta Kung Pao* Weekly (English) edition No 672. (10-16 May 79) p12

[Credit: Jane Brecha, Blomme Ronny, Anthony Smith, Ion Will.]

I Ching Studies, Anyone?

Would any of our readers with a serious interest in the I Ching and related subjects be interested in participating in an informal postal exchange of information (in circular letter form)? Material would tend towards the esoteric and technical, e.g., structural and mathematical aspects, numerology, horoscopy, military usage, bibliographical work, etc. The idea would be to set up a loose working group, so participants would be expected to contribute as well as receive material. Dependent on sufficient response, the project would get underway in early 1980. Write for details to Steve Moore, c/o *Fortean Times* (SAE would be appreciated).

Steve Moore.

For almost a half decade I have lived in the Boston area, and thus I sometimes forget how driving from the urbanized East Coast of the United States into the Midwest is a culturally shocking event. The megapolis of the Washington - New York - Boston complex often stymies life and the natural world, as well as the imagination of man. Despite some articles of recent years about the encroachment of wildlife into North American cities, these fingers of urban nature are generally nothing more or less than the occasional raccoon, opossum or deer. Only when you get away from the overcrowded, concrete jungle do you find the kind of space, the corridors of vegetation which allow the creatures of the netherland to roam freely. New England is beautiful and wild, but the temperate climate and open territory of the Heartland has reserved a special place in its

soul for the kind of unknown animals I love to pursue. Be they ape-like, feline-formed, or thunderbird-shaped, the beasts of the Midwest make a Fortean's drive through Ohio, Indiana and Illinois an exciting trek. Having recently returned from just such a journey, here are some stops along the way.

Phantom Panthers

Westerville, Ohio, is a town a mere mile from Interstate 270, the vast ring of highway which keeps the sprawl of Columbus so neatly contained. 270, like the others of its kind in America that separate wildlife from man, suburbs from the city, does serve as a barrier. But Westerville is not a suburban community of square little houses and clipped lawns; rather Westerville is a gathering of cornfields, of country roads where speed limits are difficult to enforce, of homes and farmhouses here and there,

Plastercasts of the mystery 'panther' tracks found at Lake Estates Home Park, Westerville, Michigan, on 10 June 1979, near the Marks' home. (Copyright: Loren Coleman.)

and of course, trailer courts.

Most cities in the States move their corporate limits into an area, and among the new sidewalks, stop signs, and sewage systems they bring with them, they also introduce zoning laws which quickly eliminate trailer courts. Mobile home parks are forced, therefore, to move beyond the new city limits. Residents of trailers are becoming the new pioneers of our civilization. They relocate on the edges of the country, with often only a thin sheet of metal between them and the unknown. Very often, as quite a few researchers have discovered, many occupants of trailer courts find their confrontations with the unexplained more frequent than they desire. My travels led me, once again, to quite a number of trailers and their owners.

Following up on a lead supplied by David Fideler of Michigan, I stopped by the Lake Estates Home Park in Westerville, Ohio, to check on the recent accounts of a panther seen thereabouts in June 1979.

Elusive, phantom panthers are

nothing new to central Ohio. Back in 1947, Stanley Belt saw one near Kirkwood. The reports have come in periodical waves since then. Black panthers have been seen in virtual flaps in 1955, 1962, and 1973, in the Urbana-Springfield region of the state, and the Bluffton area was the site of the 1977 activity. Ron Schaffner's investigations of 1978 revealed sightings near Minerva. Not too surprisingly, the phenomena continue to date.

Starting late in May, 1979, Delaware County Sheriff Bill Lavery began getting calls from residents who claimed to have spotted a large cat-like animal, a 'cougar'. In the village of Delaware, a big feline had killed some sheep, and in nearby Sunbury, some people had actually spied the cat. As with the Bluffton, Ohio, panther reports I investigated in 1977, [See *Creatures of the Outer Edge* (Warner 1978) pp209-217; or 'Phantom Panther on the Prowl', *Fate* November 1977 pp62-67.], the pattern of livestock kills,

sightings, and foot-print finds was repeated in Delaware County, Ohio, in 1979.

In the midst of all of this 'cougar' activity, the animal made a visit to the Lake Estates trailer court. Charles and Helen Marks, co-managers of the court for three years after having moved from Toledo, did not think they were going to get involved in 'cougar tracking', when suddenly on June 10, 1979, they found huge footprints at their doorstep.

This is the way Charles Marks described the course of events to me: 'Someone had called the police, and said that the night before, they were fishin' out here (at the little lake next to the trailer court). 'See we got a lot of good fish in this lake here. It's stocked. He was out fishin' and he'd seen these prints. Then he called the Delaware Sheriff, and they came down Sunday morning. The guy showed them the prints; he'd staked them all out. Then we hightailed it out here to see what was going on.' Helen Marks added: 'We didn't know if it was a dead body or something. But it was these prints, some with claws, some without.

Charles Marks had some plaster of paris from the time he had repaired a broken leg of a pet, and Marks tried his hand at making some casts. His wife, in the role of 'operations director', told Charles to make a cast of the more exciting clawed tracks, and thus these were the ones shown to the police. The authorities quickly labelled them as 'dog prints' — an event familiar to anyone interested in mysterious feline accounts.

The Marks found over 200 prints in the small muddy and grassy field across from their trailer, and next to the little lake. They are convinced they had discovered 'cougar' prints, for they also came upon a patch of vegetation with clear signs of where the animal had lain. Helen Marks recalled: 'And you could even see the tufts of grass sticking up between the place the head had rested, and the five foot long depression where the body was.'

Later on that eventful Sunday, the discovery of the prints unbeknownst to them, three boys were out playing in their 'fort' behind the trailer court. Quite suddenly, they encountered a large, tan panther in a tree. Donnie Grady, 12, said the cat jumped from the tree, landed on all fours, and fled. Ricky Smith, 10, obviously taking the meeting very personally, told of how the thing 'looked at me and jumped from the tree'. Travis, Ricky's eight year old brother, said 'when it growled, I saw those BIG front teeth'. The boys, residents of the trailer court, later saw the 'cougar' on a nearby roadway, and then learned of the Marks' discovery of the prints.

More reported encounters with the panther took place during that next week in June. A woman on nearby Fancher Road was taking out some trash when she met the big cat, and promptly fainted. Other sightings filled the newspapers for a few days, but like many elusive creatures of the borderland Midwest, this one too faded from the view and the minds of the residents of central Ohio.

The percipients of such incidents, however, do not so quickly forget the events which touched their lives. This came clearly into focus in Illinois.

Big Birds

In 1977, Lawndale, Illinois, was visited by two big birds, one of which carried a ten year old boy a few feet before his frightened mother's screams seemed to make the bird drop the boy. [see *Creatures of the Outer Edge* pp225-227; and FT 24 pp10-12.] My brother, Jerry Coleman of Decatur, Illinois, had been able to interview Marlon, Ruth, and Jake Lowe on two occasions in 1977, within hours of the incident. During my 1979 trip I planned to reinterview the Lowes and inquire into the occurrences since the time of their encounter two years previous.

Their trailer (!) had not changed any since the photographs Jerry had taken in 1977, and the prophetic black birds on the shutters were still there to greet us.

Ruth Lowe was cautious, to say the least. This was a woman who had obviously been hurt, but I was soon to hear the surprising depths of this sorrow. And harassment.

After Marlon Lowe was lifted into the air, and the media carried the story, individuals started leaving dead birds on the Lowe's front porch. Right after the first press mention, Ruth Lowe found a 'big, beautiful eagle' spread out at the foot of their door. The next day, a circle of six birds was placed there. The authorities seemed unable or unwilling to help the Lowes.

The dimension of the human tragedy was great for this family. Turning to my brother, Ruth Lowe asked: 'You know how red Marlon's hair was? He had the reddiest hair you'd ever want to see on a kid.'

Lowering her tone, she continued, 'Well, he wears a hat all the time now. For a year the kid won't go out after dark. I started coming home early before he got off the bus to clean off the front porch. I had hawks, owls, you name it, I had 'em on the

front porch here. And I started coming early from work *just* to clean off that front porch. Now that's when I started getting hysterical when I found all the birds, the little notes, and got all the telephone calls. But about a month after it happened, I was washing his head, and I mean to tell you, the only red hair he had on his head was just the top layer. It was just as gray as could be.'

After the initial shock, and her mistake of telling Marlon sent him into hysterics, Ruth Lowe cut his hair short and debated whether to put a color rinse on it. Slowly the locks of gray seemed to disappear. She reflected: 'It grew out. It's not a red. It's not a blonde. It's a gray.'

And the reason for the change was not shadowy to Marlon's mother: 'It was the shock of it. And we are still putting up with a lot. The poor kid gets in one or two scraps a week.'

Subdued, Ruth Lowe observed: 'They call him 'Bird Boy'. He's quite a fighter now.'

In juxtaposition to the human consequences of the 1977 encounter, there are the numerous confirmations of those scary days. 'I'll always remember how that huge thing was bending its white ringed neck, and seemed to be trying to peck at Marlon, as it was flying away,' Ruth Lowe commented, in a new detail which did not come out two years ago. Although she said the massive size of the bird reminded her of an ostrich, the bird itself looked like a condor. She had spent some long hours in the local library, poring through bird books, trying to come up with a clue to what she had seen. She was certain it was not a turkey vulture, as an area constable would have her believe.

'I was standing at the door, and all I saw was Marlon's feet dangling in the air. There just aren't any birds around here that could lift him up like that,' Ruth Lowe told us.

And there were the other sightings which have continued quietly up to the present in the Lawndale area. In nearby Lincoln, one of the big birds was flying down the middle of the main street, when the cab company's dispatcher yelled over the radio: 'There goes that son-of-a-bitch now.' But his report was silenced.

A December 1977 account of the killing of one of the birds was likewise kept under wraps for fear of ridicule. Apparently a woman was on her way to work in Beason when she saw something like a 'man standing in the road with something over its arms'. (A description which conjures up the images of Mothman.) The woman collapsed, was hospitalised, and recovered some time later. A group of men, hearing of this report from the local grapevine, went out to the spot, killed a large bird, and burnt it. Whether it was one of the big birds will never be known, but this kind of story demonstrates the level of emotion these creatures can activate in such generally calm

Midwestern towns as Lawndale.

Ruth Lowe's sister-in-law was even involved in a frightening big bird run-in at Belleville, Illinois. A large bird landed on top of one of the mobile homes (!) in the trailer park where she lives. The thing flapped its wings once, took off over the trailers, and left many residents gasping in disbelief at its 18 foot wingspan. Needless to say, this creature was the talk of the trailer court for some weeks.

The local reports and the memories have given the Lowe Family many haunted moments, for as Ruth Lowe knows and quietly told me...'They're still around here!'

Loren Coleman is a psychiatric counsellor and co-author of two books (The Unidentified *1975, and* Creatures of the Outer Edge *1978) and numerous Fortean articles.*

some cerebral activity since the Klaatu saga is wondrous strange and may prove an interesting diversion from the usual, everyday rains of frogs and spontaneously-combusting aardvarks and all the other exploding, floating, falling, and flitting bric-a-brac with which this journal is usually concerned.

Anyway, Klaatu released this album in the sort of cover that hadn't generally been seen since people started using their kaftans to wash the car, all sunflowers, field-mice, 'cozmik' vision and mushrooms (for those who spend late summer wandering around football fields with downcast eyes) and were immediately taken for a new outbreak of 'Beatles', a strange disease that ranged throughout the western world in the sixties. Apparently some American deejay — shorthand for 'banal, mealy-mouthed, patronising creep' got hold of both a copy and the whisper and trumpeted it all over the polluted airwaves of the USA with such mad, vigorous glee that 'Klaatu' sold millions of units and the NME — that's *New Musical Excess* or 'The Enemy' to you — was forced to spend a disproportionate amount of space pricking the bubble (sòrry I can't refer to the issue in question for you, the cats have long since used it to transact their private business). In fact, the record did indeed resemble a reformed Beetle wingding: most thought it inferior to the real thing, but this critic for one — not given to viewing the Moptops' career through a rose-tinted glass onion — thought it distinctly better than the real thing although it was transparently obvious to even those recently fitted with tin ears that Klaatu were not the real McCoy, let alone the real McCartney. After all the Beatles might just have been able to bash out the Yellow-Sub-Period upheavals of the 'Sub Rosa Speedway' but they sure as hell never did anything like 'Anus of Uranus' which resembles, say, 'Hey Jude' the way Donna Summer resembles Bruckner.

If I were to just casually drop the name Klaatu into the very first sentence of this column, chances are the more erudite amongst you might find yourself host to a vision of Michael Rennie bringing fast relief for tummy upsets from the planet of the same name. Was it in *The Day The Earth Stood Still?* Or was it just something you ate?

No matter, to us blouson-clad and sneaker-shod inmates of the Music Biz asylum, Klaatu is a group of faceless (as opposed to merely chinless) wonders from Canada, land of caribou-steaks and quick-frozen mounties — who always get their man and I wonder where that leaves the women, but I digress (I *always*

digress). And Klaatu, who burst upon the market-place with all the force of an imploding kipper and an eponymous album, have subsequently come in for the sort of scorn usually reserved for Cliff Richard's latest fab waxing or every other Dylan elpee (*Slow Brain Coming* at the time of writing). Which is a bit of a shame, 'cause they're ALIENS, y'see.

Well, so says John Squire Esquire in his breathless communique to the *Paranormal & Psychic Australian* — sure hate to meet one of *those* — of September 1978, a claim which at first sight perhaps strikes one as a load of old cobblers but warrants

And up there in the tundra three crazy-like-foxes musicians threw another husky on the fire and laughed all night (and since the nights, I'm given to understand, can be several months long, this is not a feat to be attempted without expert supervision).

Ultimately Klaatu remain in the semi-consciousness of most rock lovers (I'm quite fond of boulders too – I'm sorry) for having penned an elegaic and rather lovely piece called 'Calling Occupants of Interplanetary Craft' – subtitle 'The Recognised Anthem of World Contact Day' — last seen on a clear night in the northern quadrant of the charts after a disgraceful mangling by the nauseous Carpenters. But they did go on to make more records (bad luck) – the first one of these, *Hope*, beaming down into the stores sometime in '77. The cover was a thing of astonishing beauty to behold; the record it contained – supposedly the second part of a related trilogy – was drivel. Coming on like Queen at their most chintzy and lacy-knickered, words fail me to convey the depths of musical degradation that this record plumbed. As we critics portentously are wont to proclaim, it sucked dogs on ice. Whatever that means.

Enter John Squire with a likely excess of THC in his bloodstream. It seems our antipodean charlie scrutinized the merry, festive hieroglyphics with which *Hope* is festooned and decided that they were 'symbolic messages that only the most intelligent human being would be able to decipher' and spent over three months playing with them, eventually coming up with over 36 pages of 'almost unbelievable data' that prove beyond doubt's shadow that Klaatu are not of this Earth but are instead genuine, card-carrying BEMs (Bug Eyed Musicians of course). One could interject at this point that if a mere earthling can successfully unravel these Geigeresque ciphers it may be entirely possible that another human being might have constructed them in the first place, but will let it pass; Mr Squire has no use for such sophistry.

'My next step', he continues, 'was to deeply study the 36 pages, from this I was able to get visions of what the front and back cover of Klaatu's third album may look like. I also began to receive psychic visions in the form of dreams, detailed graphic pictures...somehow I knew this was the cover of Klaatu's third album'. In point of fact our addled Aussie enclosed photos of his own designs but the *P & PA* didn't see fit to publish them, so we're unable to have a cheap chuckle at Mr Squire's expense. And if you're wondering how I can be so condescending about these things, sight unseen, it's simply because, when the third album – *Sir Army Suit* – appeared, the cover contained NOTHING CRYPTIC WHATSOEVER. Har Har.

In all fairness we should let Mr Squire have the last word before they cart him away: 'So far there exists no other person apart from the Klaatu members who have been able to discover the amount of of data I have uncovered on this amazing mystery group'. Is that crystal clear or is that piece of mangled syntax actually as meaningless as it first appears?

Actually, the real reason why I can be so disgracefully patronising about the whole soggy business is that I know who Klaatu are. I said I KNOW WHO KLAATU ARE (wake up). At least I have grounds for suspicions that Sherlock Holmes would not have sneezed at (unless he'd been at the nose-candy again, of course).

You see, once upon a time there was another Canadian band called – with singular inspiration – The Stampeders, and they made so many records that (to borrow Mike Nesmith's joke) they should have been awarded a gold record for releasing a million different ones. Now, these albums vary from the reasonably acceptable to the downright execrable and, since any number of them have been inadvertently released over the years by some luckless division of the semi-comatose EMI group, it was on the cards that I would eventually end up with one or two of the buggers at my disposal. It has come to my attention that, for example, on the '73 effort (and I'm sure it was) *From the Fire* there is a track called, er, 'Chariots of the Gods'. By the time '74 had rolled round, however, there was something called *New Day* mouldering in the racks and *that* contained a dippy ditty called 'Brothers of the Universe' which is (synchronistically?) the exact converse of 'Calling Occupants' by Klaatu and, stripped of the cod-Beatles schtick of the latter, remarkably similar in style and content: 'Hello earthman, listen to me, I'm a captain of a UFO, blah blah.'

Now this is where the fancy mental footwork comes in, because, in 1976, The Stampeders, having strewn copies of their dozen-or-so totally unwanted albums all over the Western Hemisphere and giving in the process every indication of continuing to do so for eons to come, abruptly disappeared without apparent trace, probably because EMI would have gone bust years earlier had they continued with this arcane practice. A rethink perhaps? A smart gimmick to break the years of futile slog-and-riff, maybe? I think so. By the way, Klaatu record for Capitol. Capitol is an EMI label. Nuff said, Klaatu are Rich Dodson, Kim Berly and Ronnie King. I hope.

Next issue: is Elvis Costello really a malignant alien parasite? Are the Easter Island statues really discarded promotional freebies for some ancient record company? Is Bob Harris really an android with an exhausted power-pack? And of course, are Grateful Dead?

Now where did I leave that police box? Happy Phenomena everybody.

Steve Burgess is an editor of Dark Star magazine.

The Sun of Sam

The psychopath who signed himself 'Son of Sam' presided over a reign of terror in New York between the summers of 1976 and 1977. Even Mafia boss Carmine Galente was moved to order his 5,000 'soldiers' to 'get Sam'. By the time he was arrested – ironically by officers investigating a parking offence by David Berkowitz – he had killed six young people and wounded others. Mysteriographer, **Michael Hoffman** (author of **Masonic Assassination** – see our Booklet Reviews), speculate on the occult aspects of the case.

David Berkowitz was not the Son of Sam. He was a scapegoat-loser jammed full of Central Intelligence Agency LSD in Korea where he served as a son of Uncle Sam and listened between the lines to *Purple Haze* by Jimi Hendrix.

At King's County Hospital he told psychiatrists he was part of a 'network' of zombies ruled by spirits who could have 'sex with the dead' and by monsters 'too real to be called delusions'. At Marcy Psychiatric Center he told Maury Terry, a reporter for the Gannett-Westchester newspapers, that others would go to jail if he revealed all he knew. Two eyewitnesses to separate murders attributed to Berkowitz described the assailant as tall and thin with long straight hair. The accused is of average height, obese and has short, kinky hair.

Berkowitz was supposed to be friendless and yet employees of a dog kennel in the area insist that he looked over German Shepherds, with a companion, two days prior to his arrest. The companion was described as tall and thin with straight long hair.[1]

Official NYC police spokespersons continue to maintain that Berkowitz was a 'lone nut' without ties to any other individuals.

On June 5, 1977, Jimmy Breslin, a columnist for the *NY Daily News*, received an expertly handlettered missive mocking the first victim of the Son of Sam — Donna Lauria — and predicting more killings on the anniversary of her demise (Sirius Rising, June 29, 1977). In June the official casualty toll was three women and one man dead and 4 others wounded.

New Yorkers were in a panic. With the publication of the letter which was so brazen in its hostility toward human life and so controlled in its rage, the Dreaming Mind of 9 million people entered a psychological pressure-cooker courtesy of the *Mystere du Zombeisme*.

Handwriting analysts say Berkowitz did not pen it. Others cognizant of his mediocre intellect and limited education believe he could not have composed its hauntingly sinister prose:

Dear Mr. Jimmy Breslin,
Hello from the gutters of NYC which are filled with dog manure, vomit, stale wine and blood. Hello from the sewers of NYC which swallow up these delicacies when they are washed away by the sweeper
trucks. Hello from the cracks in the side walks of NYC and from the ants that dwell in these cracks and feed on the dried blood of the dead that has seeped into these cracks.

J.B., I'm just dropping you a line to let you know that I appreciate your interest in those recent and horrendous .44 killings. I also want to tell you that I read your column daily and I find it quite informative.

Tell me Jim, what will you have for July 29th? You can forget about me if you like because I don't care for publicity. However you must not forget Donna Lauria and you cannot let the people forget her either. She was a very, very sweet girl but Sam's a thirsty lad and he won't let me stop killing until he gets his fill of blood.

On July 13, 1977, at the height of the deathwatch, NYC went totally dark due to a power failure. At zero-day plus 2 (July 31st) on the burned-over dog-daze asphalt, the same .44 handgun trademarked 'Bulldog', which already claimed 10 victims, blew away Stacy Moscowitz and blinded her friend, Robert Violante.

The fatally prophetic letter had been signed: 'Son of Sam, The Wicked King of Wicker and John Wheaties, Rapist and Suffocator of Young Girls.' On Christmas Eve 1976, Berkowitz admitted shooting a dog named Rocket whose owner resided at 18 Wicker Street. Two days later, some neighbourhood children discovered 3 German Shepherds slain on an aqueduct adjacent to Wicker Street. In May 1977 Berkowitz firebombed the home of Rocket's master (no one was injured). Judy Placido was shot and wounded from canon-like blasts of a Bulldog 44 one borough away from her residence at 2208 Wickham Avenue.

The word 'wicker' has many denotations and connotations one of which is 'to bend' as in the 'bending' of reality. It is also connected to sorcery through its derivative, 'wicca', and to human sacrifice through the ancient British tradition of death by fire in a wicker effigy. In April, 1977 an obscure 1972 Scottish film entitled *The Wicker Man* was 'privately' screened not far from the Son of Sam murder scenes. [2] One of those murders took place at about the same time. A note was left at the crime location. Investigations into the exact

Peter Till

date of *The Wicker Man's* exclusive premier and the contents of the murderer's communication are continuing.

The movie is about the ritual murder and depicts the sacrifice of a policeman by fire. It is dedicated to an aristocrat who does not exist and the writer and director can't recall the author or title of the book upon which it is based. A few weeks after its limited NYC showing, David Berkowitz admits he firebombed Joachim Neto's home at 18 Wicker Street. While Berkowitz was incarcerated 3 more German Shepherds were slain. One had its ear

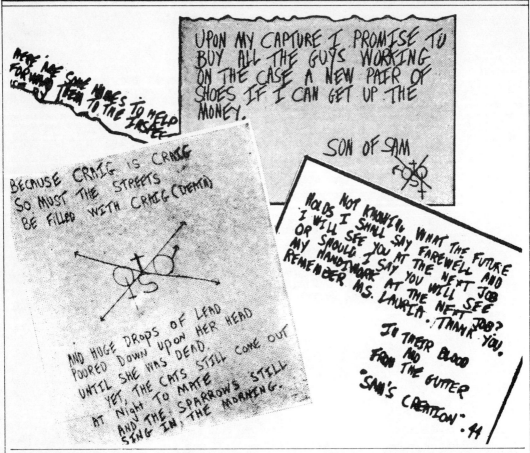

mutilated by a precision cut. Two had chains tied around their necks. They were found on the aqueduct near Wicker Street.

Another enigma is the 'John Wheaties' monniker. None of the .44 killer's victims were actually physically raped or strangled.

A neighbour of Berkowitz, Sam Carr, had a son (a son of Sam) who was a son of Uncle Sam as well, at the US Air Force base in Minot, North Dakota. It was there that he died of an 'apparently' self inflicted gunshot wound (through the mouth) six months after the apprehension of his father's neighbour. His name was John Wheat Carr. Several weeks after his demise a new TV program hit the national airwaves. It was called *SAM* about a dog whose name was Sam and who took commands from the police. John Wheat Carr's sister worked for the Yonkers Police Department and had a black dog Berkowitz claimed gave him orders to kill. He said it was Sam. Actually its name was Harvey. There was a stage play and Hollywood film by that name (Harvey), about a man who obeyed an invisible rabbit. At one point in our 'story' Berkowitz phoned the Yonkers Police and John Wheat Carr's sister answered.

While Canis Major rose to its highest point in the sky David Berkowitz was arrested, according to official reports, because his black and white Ford 'Galaxy' automobile had received a parking violation in the vicinity of the Stacy Moskowitz murder. One of the first statements Berkowitz made repeated his belief that he was a 'dog'.

During his trial he assaulted 5 cops, sending 3 to hospital and skipped into the courtroom packed to the rafters with maimed and disfigured survivors and their families and in American schoolyard sing-song told the mother of Stacy Moskowitz: 'Stacy was a hoo-wer! Stacy was a hoo-wer!' (Stacy was a whore). NY's 'seen everything' press corps described him that day as 'an awesome terror'.

Berkowitz has a steady engagement (315 years) at Attica State Prison where he now denies he ever practiced the Attic Arts. He's studying yoga and astral projection and offers standard psychiatric explanations for his acts. He has condemned his lawyers and court-appointed conservator as 'greedy sensationalists' for their attempts to put together a Son of Sam book deal with McGraw-Hill. A Greenwich village artists commune, the Middle of Silence Gallery, has been designated as 'my voice' by the convicted murderer. This group is attempting to arrange an exorcism and claims to have located a willing Catholic priest. Ex-Jesuit Malachi Martin *(Hostage to the Devil)* attempted the same thing but was foiled by NY Archdiocesan authorities.

I wonder if ritual murders like this one are a kind of inverted greening rite on behalf of a sentience which breathes plutonium and resides at 3 Mile Island? The stale blood and 'spiritual' fecal matter mentioned in the infamous letter remind this writer of a degraded version of the *kalas* present during magical operations. Of course the entire case is littered with the trappings of ceremonial murder. Is this in anyway sponsored by the US gov't? Terry Paterson, an Army buddy of Berkowitz, states that when he said he was the Son of Sam he was trying to say he was the son of Uncle Sam. Are the NYC police sticking to the 'lone nut' notion because their vision is limited, or because their lives will be if they offer contrary conclusions? There does seem to be a pattern of circumstances linking officials to ritual murders in Rochester, NY, the hillsides of LA and the state of Washington as well as Jonestown and John Wayne Gacy. Further research into FOP onamatology [3] and its connection to Scottish Rite bridge symbolism as well as Kenneth Grant's intriguing remarks about Saturnian 'sacred police' in *Cults of the Shadow* are in order.

Meanwhile some researchers believe that David Berkowitz was a hypno-patsy and that the authentic awesome terror, the one who doesn't like publicity and didn't get any, is, as he wrote in his missive to Jimmy Breslin, '...still here. Like a Spirit roaming the night. Thirsty, hungry, seldom stopping to rest...'

Michael Anthony Hoffman

NOTES
1) [Statement made by employees at the Westchester Animal Shelter, at Mamaroneck, who said Berkowitz's companion resembled one of the earlier sketches issued by the police. He did all the talking while Berkowitz patted dogs. *D.Express* 15 Aug; *D.Telegraph* 16 Aug 1977. Part of the NYPD 300-strong task-force were reassigned to look for this accomplice, but as far as we can tell there were no developments — Ed.]
2) [As I was about to start work on Michael Hoffman's manuscript my eyes fell upon a scrap of paper lying on a desk at the *Dark They Were* bookshop. It was notice of the formation of an appreciation society for *The Wicker Man*, to campaign for the general release of the 102 minute version in place of the grossly mutilated 87 minute version released in the US, by British Lion in 1973. Those interested, contact David J Lally: 75A Richbourne Terrace, London SW8. — Ed]
3) FOP is a 'lost chord' transposition in the esoteric onomatology employed by the western technological imperium whose hierarchy at one time consisted chiefly of masons. It is a sinister perversion of the Tantric concept of *sandhabhasa*.
If language is a kind of music we can state that FOP is intended to be performed in a key other than the one in which it was apparently written.
FOP has at least two meanings in this twilight language. It is the initials of the FRATERNAL ORDER OF POLICE (whose symbol is a pentagram) as well as a variation on the *Lakak Deror Pessah* theme of the 15th and 16th degrees of the Scottish Rite having to do with Bridge symbolism. The usual letters inscribed on the mystery bridge are LOP (for Liberty of Passage) and, infrequently, FOP (for Freedom of Passage). According to Dr. Syntax, the latter has greater currency in the rituals of Palladian masonry and among certain Scottish Rite circles with strong ties to the Ku Klux Klan.
4) [Sources: *NY Daily News* June 1977, 7-9 May 1978; *Cinefantastique* 6:3 (Cr: Rich Crowe); *Yonkers Herald Statesman* 26-28 Feb, 1 March 1979 (Cr: Eric Offerman); *Spotlight* 7 Nov 1977; *Salt Lake Tribune* 18 Aug 1977; *New York Post* 22 Feb 1978 (Cr: Mae Brussell); *Chicago Tribune* 11 April 1978 (Cr: Thoth); James Shelby Downard's notes on onomatology.]

Hardbacks

THE LEY HUNTER'S COMPANION: Aligned Ancient Sites: a new study with field guide and maps *by Paul Devereux and Ian Thomson (Thames & Hudson 1979; £6.50 hb, pp216, index, bib notes, maps, photos.)*

Ley hunters have been awaiting this book eagerly: their first impression on glancing through it will be that the authors have devoted an impressive amount of time and energy to researching and compiling it. Its 216 pages are divided into two main sections, the first of 80 pages being a general introduction to the subject of leys: Watkins and the discovery of leys; ley definitions; similar features elsewhere than Britain; statistical confirmation; archaeological ignorance; related subjects such as UFOs, cosmology, folklore, dowsing; and, not least important, a detailed description of how to undertake accurate ley-hunting mapwork and fieldwork.

Part 2 comprises 41 English leys studied in detail, with maps, diagrams, and many photographs of ley points. Ley fieldwork is not always easy, which is why so many 'leys' are actually nothing more than map alignments. But Devereux and Thomson have got out of their armchairs and walked these leys, often finding exciting confirmations of their presence. They have even surveyed some of the leys from the air, and aerial photographs add an extra dimension to their thorough documentation.

My only criticism, and that not a harsh one, concerns their effort to link UFOs with ley points. I am not against the idea that the two may be linked, indeed I think it likely, but I do not consider that the evidence so far put forward does other than present a vague suggestion that UFOs are not coincidentally sighted above or close to ley points. There have been thousands of UFO sightings in England, and there are many ley points. It is impossible that UFOs do not sometimes pass over ley points,

but that does not necessarily mean there is a link between the two. So for Devereux and Thomson to state, for example, 'The Malvern Hills have been the scene of some dramatic UFO sightings' and then briefly to describe two instances of UFOs seen in the area, with no specific linking to their Malvern ley, is misleading because similar instances repeated throughout the book will leave the reader with the impression that a definite link between UFOs and leys has been established. Whereas in fact there are few cases here of a UFO actually being sighted over a ley point. Also it is unfortunate that Devereux and Thomson make the claim 'Thus it was Stonehenge, symbolically, which provided the best visual evidence for the reality of UFOs.' The case to which they refer, a movie film taken in October 1977 and purporting to show UFOs, turned out to be highly controversial, and the opinion of investigators Peter Warrington and Jenny Randles (NUFON, June 1979, issue 61, p.3) is that 'the case is a result of possible observation of flares coupled with inconsistent witness testimony.' (A full report by Randles and Warrington appears in FSR vol. 24 no. 4.)

But the weakness of the UFO evidence in *THE LEY HUNTER'S COMPANION* does not detract from the book's other strengths, or the argument and proof put forward for leys. This book is the best champion leys have ever had. But even this is unlikely to stop archaeologists denigrating leys and ley-hunters. Listen to Aubrey Burl in his just-published book *Prehistoric Avebury:* 'Ley-liners draw impossibly accurate alignments from Avebury through Silbury Hill to a random barrow or church or mile-wide hill that God happened to place in the correct position.' (p.v) And: 'Ley-lines were first envisaged by Alfred Watkins, a brewery representative whose occupation may have contributed to the development of his ideas.' (p.201) A quite unnecessary slur on Watkins' character which seems rather weak ammunition against leys. Burl cannot resist other equally snide comments.

Let us hope that some archaeologists will be open minded enough to read *The Ley Hunter's Companion,* to note especially the material on statistical evidence, and the activities of the ongoing Dragon Project. Active and intending ley-hunters *must,* of course, read the book. *Janet Bord*

THE WEREWOLF DELUSION *by Ian Woodward (Paddington Press 1979; $15.50 hb pp256 index, bib, illos).*

A comprehensive look at the werewolf enigma, assembling a considerable amount of material, much of it drawn from earlier works by Baring-Gould, Summers and O'Donnell. One is a little surprised at this last conclusion as O'Donnell's *Werwolves* is, to put it politely, dubiously unreferenced. This criticism apart, *The Werewolf Delusion* is a beautifully produced and profusely illustrated examination of virtually all aspects of werewolfery, including both lycanthropic delusion and allegedly 'real' werewolves. And drawing from sources as diverse as science and theosophy, Woodward also looks at a variety of explanations for the phenomenon, including rabies, astral projection and sorcery, without ultimately committing himself to any of them. Also included are chapters on the grip that the werewolf myth has on literature, the cinema, etc. While not greatly advancing the field of werewolf studies, it is certainly an excellent introduction to a fascinating subject. *SM*

POLTERGEISTS An Annotated Bibliography of Works in English, circa 1880-1975 by *Michael Goss (Scarecrow Press, Metuchen, NJ USA 1979; $15.00 hb, pp351, indexes; distributed in Britain by Bailey Bros & Swinfen, Folkestone, Kent, £11.25).*

To most people an annotated bibliography might seem the driest and most uninteresting of books, but to anyone with an interest in that subject such a book can be a myriad of blessings, and even, as in this case, evoke a scholar's delight.

Michael Goss has taken 1111 citations of cases, descriptions, reports, reviews and books dealing specifically or mainly with poltergeist phenomena and their alleged human agents, and arranged them by title and author alphabetically, and cross-referenced them with two indexes, one of proper names and the other of geographical details. This allows greater flexibility in usage; for example you could follow the debate on a particular issue, case or theory through the original reports and later discussion to reviews of books in which the case is later cited. Or perhaps you want the titles of all the works on poltergeists by Nandor Fodor, or to see whether Harry Price ever commented on the famous slowly falling stones of the Grotten-dieck case of Indonesia — it's all here. Already in my own work this reference book has saved me considerable time on bibliographic questions. Goss annotates most of the entries with a summary of the item, and, in the case of the books or analytical articles, even lists the chapter titles and the cases cited. Valuable summaries of arguments expressed in critical letters and reviews are also given. Scarecrow are to be commended for publishing this work, sure to become an indispensible and mandatory reference book among poltergeist researchers, and all others interested in occult manifestations or psychic research.

RJMR.

MYSTERIOUS UNIVERSE: A Handbook of Astronomical Anomalies compiled by *William R. Corliss (The Sourcebook Project, Glen Arm, MD 21057, USA 1979; $15.95 hb, pp710, index, illos).*

The third volume of selections from the sourcebooks themselves, this one boasts over 500 articles and 120 illustrations on the subject of astronomical anomalies generally. For newcomers, or those living in the middle of the Gobi desert for the last four years, Corliss' Sourcebook has set itself the task of scavenging the extant publications for articles and data on topics, discoveries and phenomena on the fringes of known scientific knowledge. Corliss is a Fortean and has a particular eye for the sort of material that delights us. But his purpose is also serious, salvaging valuable, rare, pioneering and seminal work and descriptions that is normally difficult to locate or worse, becoming unavailable on microfilm 'because no one has ever asked for that volume, sir!', or actually disintegrating from old age.

While the looseleaf format of the Sourcebooks themselves (write to Corliss at the above address for details) are suitable for most researchers and allow for the on-going publication of additional material, there is a need on the general publications market, and for libraries, schools etc, for hardback editions — hence this volume joins the previous two thematic selections *Ancient Man,* and the *Handbook of Unusual Natural Phenomena.*

The chapters group the material under the following topics: the Sun; Vulcan, 'the lost intraMercurial planet'; Mercury; Venus; the environs of Earth; the Moon; meteors and meteorites; zodiacal light; Mars; Jupiter; Saturn; the planets beyond Saturn; enigmatic objects; comets; Bode's Law and other irregularities; stars, galaxies and cosmology. Most of the astronomical anomalies one can think of are represented here, and many others, including new discoveries by NASA and others. Recommended.

RJMR

SUNGODS IN EXILE by *Karyl Robin-Evans (Neville Spearman 1979; £ 3.75 hb, pp150, photos).*
THE PHILADELPHIA EXPERIMENT by *Charles Berlitz & William Moore (Souvenir Press 1979; £4.95 hb, pp186, photos).*

Two fantastical books which, despite assurances by their authors of gospel truth, leave one with the disagreeable suspicion of a clever hoax. These books claim to be authentic but are told in the slick style of modern detective or thriller fiction, complete with all the now familiar literary devices — in fact so familiar that *déjà vu* overwhelms the narratives.

The 'Philadelphia Experiment' is the allegation, cited in sensational occult and UFO books, that in 1943 the US Navy experimented with a device based on Einstein's work, which rendered a ship in the naval dockyard at Philadelphia totally invisible, and, some say, teleported it to Norfolk, Virginia, and back, with disastrous effects on the crew. The story originally came to light when a mysterious Carlos Allende sent an angrily annotated copy of an early UFO book back to its author Dr Morris Jessup. Jessup investigated the allegations with the Office of Naval Research, and later apparently committed suicide. Since then the story has been a staple of UFO and Fortean books, although I note the absence of its use by Lobsang Rampa in the 'Chronological Bibliography'. Berlitz and Moore chronicle the devious twists and turns in the unfolding myth until the point where

its complexity would collapse without material evidence and witnesses. As a result of years of research the authors claim to have interviewed several scientists, named by Allende, and uncovered a considerable amount of seemingly authentic corroborative evidence. As an exposition of the mystery I found the book a good read, but as usual with other modern books claiming to unveil vast governmental or military conspiracies, one is left with no tangible or unequivocal proof, only a series of impressions based on the authors' word. Interestingly, the authors themselves concur that if the 'Philadelphia Experiment' did not happen according to the legend, then *something* took place in the high security area of the Philadelphia Navy Yard in October 1943 that frightened a lot of scientists and military men into inventing this bizarre cover story. The issues are thus clarified but not resolved.

Another staple of UFO books and the 'Ancient Astronaut' enthusiasts is the story of the stone discs of Tibet which record, it's claimed, the forced landing of aliens who interbred with local tribesmen. This was effectively demolished by Gordon Creighton in *Flying Saucer Review* a few years back. *Sungods* claims to be a posthumous editing, by David Agamon, of the record of a secret expedition to Tibet in 1947 by the independently wealthy eccentric Oxford scholar Karyl Robin-Evans (already I'm suspicious). In an elegant and interesting if convoluted narrative, Agamon retells Robin-Evans' attempt to find the home of a mysterious metal plate, shown him by a Russian ethnologist who 'found' it while among the Dzopa tribe of Tibet. The disc tantalises us with a convenient conjunction of designs: a star (like the solar escutcheon of Churchward's *Mu*); a vessica shaped UFO; a dinosaur (?); a big-domed dwarf and two octopoid animals (or are they bugs?). Needless to say, our hero tracks down a whole set of plates in a secret temple, and comes away with the knowledge that the evolution of man on Earth was initiated by the original Dzopa, 'space-born rapists' from another world. Reads like Moorcock crossed with Von Daniken. *Caveat emptor.* *RJMR.*

UFOS AND RELATED SUBJECTS An Annotated Bibliography by *Lynn E Catoe (Gale Research Co., Detroit, Michigan 1978; pp410).*

First published in 1969 as a large-format paperback, this rich store of UFO sources has now been reissued in hard covers, with the addition of a short bibliography covering the later years up to 1976. As Leslie Shepard rightly says in his introduction to the new edition: 'This is the most comprehensive bibliography of Unidentified Flying Objects ever compiled.' The 1600+ items are arranged by subject, over 70 of them, ranging from Abductions to Selected Fiction, and including headings as diverse as Men in Black, Propulsion, Seductions, Solar System, and Hollow Earth Theory. The items are presented simply: author, title, place of publication, publisher, year, and number of pages; or in the case of articles: author, title, magazine, issue details, page numbers. Then follows a brief, but very useful, summary of the contents of the item.

Lynn Catoe is to be congratulated on her efforts in bringing together all the diverse material contained in this bibliography, which no serious UFO researcher should be without. It will lead him/her to much material he/she never knew existed.

Colin Bord

NIGHTMARE *by Sandra Shulman (David & Charles 1979; £6.50 hb, pp224, index, bib, lithographs).*

An entertaining and eclectic study of nightmares, vivid phantasies and the visions of delirium from the sleep of terrified children, convicted murderers, drug-addicted poets, nuns and monks, philosophers, drunks, archaic tribesfolk and modern man. Ms Shulman seems to have a Jungian bias while exploring, in a general way, the Freudian theory of dreaming related to stages of psychophysical growth, and interpreting the range of subjects (from sexual paranoia, murder and cannibalism to the more familiar but unspecified feelings of simple terror, anxiety and helplessness). Recommended, in spite of its generality, for the interesting sidelights it throws on the nature and content of hallucinatory experiences and their origins and effects. *RJMR*

ALIEN INTELLIGENCE *by Stuart Holroyd (David & Charles 1979; £5.95 hb, pp231, index, bib, photos).*

Perhaps the most disappointing of Holroyd's recent books. In the guise of a study of 'non-human intelligence' some very familiar material is warmed up and served with some elementary (or is it elemental?) mistakes. Hoping to shed light on the nature of human intelligence, which Holroyd expands to include spirituality, he gives us chapters on the intelligence of chimps, dolphins and other animals, computers and so-called 'artificial intelligence', the fairy beings (which Holroyd classes among

the 'physical' non-human intelligences), and then on to the meat of the book, the contacts with bizarre and paradoxical entities through spiritualism, mediumship and other 'inspirational' methods including 'beings' claiming to be spirits of the dead, visitors from other planets, other dimensions of being and even gods themselves. A purely 'phenomenal' book in that little attempt is made to distinguish cause from effect, and in this case some careless thought on Holroyd's part leaves one unconvinced that some of the 'contacts' are anything more than psychological aberrations or effects, and the consequences of this are ignored in his enthusiasm to reach the concluding chapters on philosophy and theology. *RJMR.*

SURGEON FROM ANOTHER WORLD *by George Chapman (WH Allen 1978; £5.50 hb, pp185, photos).*

Ghost written (sorry) by Roy Stemman, this is an informative, well written and researched biography of George Chapman, whose success and fame as a psychic healer is attributed to the guiding spirit of the Victorian surgeon William Lang. This is a spiritualist orientated book in which the spirit hypothesis is not critically examined, and evidence of the survival of the identity of Lang is presented *de facto.* *RJMR.*

FOLKLORE OF THE SEA *by Margaret Baker (David & Charles 1979; £4.95 hb, pp192, index, notes photos).*

A very worthwhile and interesting assembly of sea-faring myths and folklore by a well-read folklorist. Chapters on building and naming ships, ships at sea, phantom ships and sailors, talismans and taboos, naval and seafaring customs, weather gods and lore, and curiosities of sailors' language. There is also the expected, but competant, summary of the sea-serpent controversy. Much Forteana is omitted, or neglected, but the book is better value than many other similar collections. *RJMR.*

FOLKLORE, OLD CUSTOMS, AND SUPERSTITIONS IN SHAKESPERE LAND *by James H Bloom (Gale Research, Detroit, Michigan 1979; $11.00hb, pp167, index, notes).*

A reissue of Gale's 1973 edition, being a facsimile of Bloom's original of 1930. 20 chapters crammed with notes on the dress, customs, rhymes, antiquities and beliefs of Warwickshire regarding birth, marriage, baptism, building, death, the occult, fairs, work and the poor. *RJMR*

Paperbacks

INVENTORUM NATURA: (The Expedition Journal of Pliny the Elder) *by Una Woodruff (Paper Tiger 1979; £5.25, pp126, illustrated in full colour; introduction by John Michell).*

> *'All's fish they get*
> *That cometh to net.'*
> Thomas Tusser: *Hundred points of good husbandry.*

Pliny was born in AD 23, and was susceptible to somewhat more than the inevitable vagaries attendant upon such an auspicious birthdate.

He was a dragon-buff, a UFO spotter, an explorer, a naturalist, an unnaturalist, and a world historian — a kind of Latin H.G. Wells, and the discovery of an unknown manuscript from his hand is a choice event, if not blitz heaven.

Rooting through the muniment room of a Somerset manor house in a quest for the 'locked library' of Glastonbury Abbey (hidden from the world at the time of the dissolution of the monasteries, and rumoured to have contained the works of several ancient authors lost since classical times, as well as many Celtic texts and Druidical records) John Michell uncovered a mouldy volume replete with faded anatomical drawings: *Inventorum Natura*, the journal of a scientific expedition conducted by Pliny the Elder in search of material for his *Natural History.*

A carbon-dating test unfortunately destroyed a couple of pages of the mss., but established its authenticity. The owner subsequently declaring that he will from now on refuse to allow the mss. into any hands other than his own, and 'never to have modern flim-flam' near him again — an opinion which Mr. Michell has clearly respected by concealing as far as possible the exact whereabouts of the library. Indeed if news of the damage leaked too widely there would be little hope for those American scientists who wish to turn sections of the Shroud of Turin into charcoal.

However, the bulk of this extraordinary piece survives: *The Expedition Journal of Pliny the Elder*, translated from the Latin, and with the original illustrations redrawn by Una Woodruff with visionary zeal.

If you know nothing else of Pliny, you will probably have heard the expression *In vino veritas*, an abbreviated version of his proverb: Vulgogue veritas iam attributa vino est, 'now truth is commonly said to be in wine,' and reading this book you get the impression that either every member of the expedition was stoned out of his head , or else they were witnessing and recording a totally different state of play.

It is a study of fringe biology, an account of creatures, which, as John Michell puts it in his preface, 'seems to be hovering on the borderline between a real and a phenomenal existence,' and it makes Darwin's beagling seem as mundane as a visit to Tescos.

There are hybrids of fish and butterflies, and hybrids of lions and ants which Bartholomew Glanville later noted in the fifteenth century: 'while to other animals it is only an ant, to ants themselves it is as if it were a lion.' There are bees that make molten gold instead of honey; Mantichorae — gigantic red lions with stinging scorpion tales, and which the poet Skelton believed fed exclusively on human brains. There are Griffins that guard the Mountains of the moon, and birds much like flamingoes that are generated by reeds: mixtures between plant and animal, near the source of the Nile, not dissimilar perhaps to the barnacle goose tree of the Orkneys, and the tree-goose of Lancashire.

There are terrifying Basilisks, which Pliny observes 'turn the countryside into desert wherever they live,' (possibly from his account, and his maps, the Gobi desert) 'The venom of their stare is so powerful that they can split rocks and scorch grass with a glance...and who continue their generation by laying eggs which are hatched by toads at the time of the Dog Star.' Later author insisted that its cradle and swaddling bands consisted of warm dung, others however attempted to discredit the creature's existence altogether:

If the basilisk kills merely by being seen, then who has ever seen it?'
Jean Bodin, *Theatrum Naturae* (1596)

Fairly unanswerable unless Pliny had on board some Minerva's shield, some optical equipment which refracted the deadly glance. Doubtless he did, or else was immune. The basilisk, (also known as a cockatrice 'whose unavoided eye is murderous,') is perhaps an early incarnation of television. It's after all quite common to ask someone what they've just seen a moment ago on television, and for them to be quite incapable of recalling it. Pliny however was somehow able to remember without coming to any harm.

The expedition's first landfall was in Africa, from which, as Pliny remarked: *'Ex Africa semper aliquid nova',* there is always something new. There are of course Pygmies, and Giants, but also the Machlyes who are of dual sex — not entirely strange to behold in view of the recent

discovery of a Caribbean island that produces plethora of hermaphrodites who spontaneously become one sex or another at puberty.

The travellers also uncover a species of Anthropophagi, the Blemmyae, who have no heads, but faces in their chests, stemming from perhaps some dire gravitational quirk, and who feed on human flesh. Presumably the expedition felt uncomfortable in their presence since they shortly set sail for the coast of Arabia, sighting several sea monsters 'which we took at first to be small islands in the sea,' and dragons, as well as sea unicorns and sea spiders.

India yields an unusual snake plant: 'These,' Pliny reveals, 'bear white flowers which continually generate many thousands of small venomous snakes. The same plants caused the death of many men and horses during the expeditions of Alexander the Great.' There are Pegasi, of which little is known since they inhabit high mountainous regions; Unicorns, whose horns are sadly susceptible to the same superstitious vandalism as the rhinocerous nowadays; and double -headed serpents, the Amphisbaenae, of whom Pliny later drily commented in writing up these expedition notes in his *Natural History*, that it was 'as though one mouth were too little to discharge all its venom' and the name that he gave them has been retained by modern zoologists to describe a kind of legless tropical lizard, which can progress with either end foremost.

Pliny also inspired Aldrovandi in the Renaissance to make an extensive study of them which is included in his *History of Serpents and Dragons*, though he perhaps did them a disservice by anthropomorphising them. Aldrovandi compared the Amphisbaena to men of two minds, 'for,' he says, 'just as this abnormal snake having a head at each end used either end of its body for a tail, so the aforesaid men will follow the course most convenient for that.' The explanation of the Amphisbaena is simply perhaps that it persuaded its own DNA that two heads were better than one.

They then cross the Indian ocean to Malaya, and in the jungles there, 'filled with the fearful sound of hissing,' find that some of the creepers coiled around the trees are sinuously and sinisterly alive. There are also flesh eating plants that make John Wyndham's triffids seem as innocuous as daisies, and to whom the natives 'make human sacrifices so as to placate the spirits and gods of the forest.'

China is more prepossessing, and filled with dragons, which Pliny believed 'were bred in Aethyopia

where the Asachei inhabit...' It was (according to the *Hortus Sanitatis,* Book 2, Chapter 48) thought that dragon's flesh cooled those who ate it 'therefore the Ethiopians who dwell on that burning coast gladly eat of the flesh of dragons.' But clearly being used as ice-packs was a somewhat churlish waste of their resources and they were wont to abandon their breeding grounds for the more appreciative climes, such as China.

Pliny later described their method of travel in his *Natural History:* 'they are inwrapped foure or five of them one within another, like to a hurdle or lattise-worke, and thus passe the seas to find out better pasturage, cutting the waves and bearing their heads aloft, which serve them instead of sailes,' (Holland's translation, 1601) and then, somehow or other, on reaching China become a mite more transcendental, being ruled, Pliny notes in the *Expedition Journal,* 'by kings who are immortal, and who communicate with each other over great distances without the use of words...' and able to 'become invisible and visible at will. Some which do not possess wings, are yet able to fly. Others have no ears, but are able to hear with their horns.'

In the land called Hyperborea (the land beyond the North Wind which, from Pliny's map given here, approximates possibly to Japan or even Greenland) the expedition is diverted by a utopia where 'all sorrow is unknown.' None of the inhabitants die naturally, but choose their time of death, which they celebrate with banqueting and rejoicing, terminating their lives by leaping from a certain rock into the sea, (presumably when nepenthe is in short supply). Pliny observes these strange rocks, riddled with simulacra of the dead.

There are again dazzling mutants which Pliny describes in his pedegogical and sometimes quite off-hand manner: insects generated by plants, butterfly plants, moth plants, and dragonfly plants, and edible frogs (the two-headed variety apparently being more palatable and promoting luck and fertility).

In order to prepare their ship for the journey into the 'freezing ocean of the North,' they return briefly to the mainland of Asia, to be entertained by views of Perytons in Northern China: 'These creatures have the heads and legs of deer and the wings and bodies of birds. Most curious is the fact that they cast the shadows of men instead of their own bodies. It is thought that if one of them succeeds in killing a man its genuine shadow is returned by the gods.'

Doubtless feeling that to have his shade recycled by a Peryton was a rather uncongenial form of immortality, Gaius Plinius Secundus moved further north, spending time with the Hyppogriffs, and succumbing to the charms of wolf-women with double pupils — the shamans of these barren regions (Mongolia perhaps, or even Siberia).

Reaching Northern Scythia they encounter a race of Flying Men, who regard the travellers' earth-bound bodies as most unusual, and then, in the Baltic Sea, they come across one of their rarest finds, the Kraken, something of a mixture between a commissar and an oil-tanker. 'They have a terrifying appearance,' Pliny notes, 'with multiple heads and strong tentacles capable of encompassing the largest ships. They are in the habit of discharging a dark liquid which blackens and poisons the sea,' (and Una Woodruff's accompanying illustration is exquisitely grotesque).

In later literature, notably the studies of the oddly named German scholar Olaus Wormius, who referred to them as hafgufe, it was believed that it was impossible to find a carcase of the Kraken, for the good reason that these creatures were reputed to live until the end of the world and that no instrument was able to terminate the life of so monstrous a creature. But it was perhaps not entirely malign:

Bartholinus tells an amusing story of how the Bishop of Midaros, travelling home to his own country from foreign parts, found what he took to be an island, and upon it erected an altar and performed Mass. But the island was, in reality, a Kraken which respectfully waited until the ceremony was over, and the prelate had departed before slowly sinking beneath the waves.

Should the reader be irritated by such fables, it is interesting to note that Linnaeus, a naturalist of considerable repute, catalogued the Kraken in the first edition of his Systema Naturae as Sepia microcosmos, a cuttlefish that was an epitome of the world (though he curiously omitted it from later editions).

Pontoppidan, in his Natural History of Norway, reiterated accounts of the Kraken's monumental proportions, but tried to cut it down to size by explaining it as merely a cross between a cuttle-fish and a polyp, though this fits Pliny's description to some extent.

Pliny must have been overwhelmed by the sighting (although his style of writing is emotionally frugal to say the least) since he had been regaled with accounts of the Kraken's existence by his friend Trebius Niger. Niger had told him of a great monster with enormous arms which emerged from the sea each night to gorge itself

on the salted tuny in the curing ponds at Rocadillo in Spain. Understandably this annoyed the keepers of the fish ponds, and, as Pliny remarks in his chapter on the Kraken (in Holland's 1601 translation of his Natural History): 'in the end he gat himselfe the anger and displeasure of the masters of the said ponds and cisterns, with his continuall and immeasurable filching.' This predatory monster was finally set upon by savage dogs after a tremendous fight, it was killed, and its head taken to the local proconsul, Lucullus. The head was reported by Trebius Niger to be as big as a 90 gallon cask. The weight of the creature 700 pounds, and it had arms some 30 feet long. A shrimp however in comparison with Pliny's own sighting.

After relishing it, Pliny's ship, the Aelgaibus, moves on to the small islands off the coast of Northern Germany. Aelgaibus is a word for which I can find no translation, and no assistance is offered in the text.[...] is the closest to the prefix. The suffix 'gaibus,' (if dividing them thus is indeed the right clue) eludes me in both Latin and Greek. However, ailinos in Greek means a durge, and perhaps it is appropriate, the expedition being, let us hope, a requiem for man's cataracted resistance to true discovery.

> 'Sometimes he angers me
> with telling of the moldwarp
> and the ant.'
> Henry IV part I.

But this tale is not ill-told and would loosen the imaginative bowels of the most hardened rationalist.

Getting back on board Pliny's ship, 'duodecim servi fideles erant, qui propter fidum officium manumissi sunt.' (crewed by twelve trusted slaves who have become free men in respect of their loyal service), they find that the Germanic islands are inhabited by a tribe of fishermen called Auriti, or All Ears 'whose ears are of such abnormally large dimensions that they cover their whole bodies. As a consequence they have extremely sharp hearing, being able to hear even the fishes beneath the sea,' and Enid Blyton would turn in her grave at the sight of the accompanying plate, XLIII, which portrays them.

Witches abound, using mandrakes ('so deadly is their magic that trained dogs are employed to dig up the plants,') Dragonium, the sap of which is 'used as a substitute for genuine dragons' blood,' and Devil's Orchids. After doubtless ingesting some of these recondite fruits much in the manner of Vikings high on Amanita they then set sail for Britannia, and what they find there is too tasty to squander in a shallow review. Suffice it to say that the

Recording Angel would be insanely jealous of this prodigious saga as she stomps back to the typing pool. Una Woodruff's perspicuous paintings make Audubon look like Jackson Pollock, and she has reproduced the originals with auric glee. (Oddly, Synchronicity Studios have provided her with a similar name to Pliny's companion: Una Silyana, a possibly germinative detail, and certainly as Byron had it: 'A 'strange coincidence' to use a phrase / By which things are settled nowadays.')

> 'Eftsoones they saw
> a hideous hoast array'd
> Of huge sea monsters, such as living
> sence dismay'd.'
> Spenser, The Faerie Queene.

But these creatures expand the senses rather than dismay them. Is it true or is it false? I care not which trampoline delight chooses, but when pressed would fall back on St. Augustine: 'The important thing for us is to consider the significance of a fact, not to discuss its authenticity.'

Early zoos were exclusively priestly establishments. The strange animals kept in temples were vibrant gurus hinting at other modes of behaviour and development, and Pliny echoes this respectful awe. Later zoos became more secularised: 'It belongs to the position of the great,' wrote Matarazzo in the fifteenth century about regal Italian menageries, 'to keep horses, dogs, mules, falcons, and other birds, court jesters, singers, and foreign animals.' And such callous idiocy was becoming rife in Pliny's time; commenting on some forty elephants he'd sent from Rome, Caesar commented: 'They will, of course, be no use except to make a show.'

It is to his credit that Pliny, unlike later explorers who were simply big-game hunters who could flirt with a foot-note, resisted this attitude. This is not to argue that such creatures are mystically beyond understanding, but that lack of understanding of them has caused them considerable harm — witness an early guide-book published in 1774, entitled An Historical Description of the Tower of London and Its Curiosities (its Curiosities being the animals kept in the Tower which was the progenitor of the London Zoo — the royal menagerie being moved to Regent's Park from there in 1834).

'We cannot quit this subject,' writes the anonymous author, 'without lamenting the loss of a fine large ostrich which lately died here...The vulgar error that the ostrich can digest iron has been long since exploded; for in the year 1569 the Morocco Ambassador to the States General, among other rarities, having brought over to Holland an ostrich, as a present, it died in Amsterdam in a few days by swallowing iron nails which the poplace threw to it, upon a presumption that it could digest them like other food; but the ostrich being opened, about eighty nails were found entire in its stomach.'

Posterity should be grateful that Pliny refrained from feeding nails to any of the creatures who posed for his bestiary. Neither did he capture any of them, shoot them or eat them (though several of them might not have been averse to kebabing him), and thus perhaps they might have felt free to continue living, much as the Loch Ness monster, the coelacanth, the hairy man-like creatures of the mountains of the Himalayas and North America, and the giant birds, resembling the thunder birds of traditional Indian folk lore, that have been sighted in recent years over many of the United States, as Mr. Michell pertinently suggests in his preface.

Pliny was not entirely above a certain human chauvinism, believing for example that if you burnt the feathers of a vulture, the smell had an inhibiting effect upon venomous serpents (as well presumably upon the vulture's aeronautical skills) and he appropriately received his just deserts for this lapse by being singed and suffocated by poisonous fumes while making excessively close investigation of an eruption of the volcano Vesuvius, in AD 79.

But on the whole he conducts himself very tolerably — the David Attenborough of the Dark Ages — and occasionally takes a mischievous pleasure in the dominance of 'animal' over 'man'. In describing the remora, a versatile sucking fish which the Greeks called (echeneis) or 'stay-ship', of which he reported that 'if it settle and stick to the keele of a ship under water, it goweth the slower by that means; whereupon it was so called. (And for that cause also it hath but a bad name in matters of love, for inchanting as it were both men and women, and bereaving them of their heat and affection in that way...)', a creature which seemed to the Schoolmen to work in much the same fashion as a lodestone drawing iron. Pliny takes an inordinate joy in chronicling the indignation of the wretched Caligula whose royal barque was totally banjaxed by these magical, and perceptive limpets. According to Pliny, Caligula minced up and down the deck spluttering like a camp Ahab, furious that 'so small a thing as this should hold her back perforce,' (his camp ship),' and check the strength of all his warriors notwithstanding there were no fewer than 400 lustie men in his galley that laboured at the ore, all that ever they

could do to the contrary.'

Drawn towards more sympathetic hands however, the remore, whose virtue was accented by salt, could be persuaded, Niger informs Pliny, to 'draw up gold that is fallen into a pit or well, being never so deep, if it be let downe and come to touch it,' and happenchance the 'stay-ship' rewarded Pliny and Niger, its groupies, through its fiscal skills when in a beneficent mood.

Other contemporaries would not have been so privileged — here is Alexander Ross in his Arcana Microcosmi, in which he refutes Sir Thomas Browne's deflation of the phoenix, wherein the 'ancient sage', as he calls him, claims that the fabled bird is a conceit. Ross, in a chapter entitled Dr. Browne's 'Vulgar Errors' has a fine line, worthy of the Beast Liberation movement, after insisting that it is no wonder that the phoenix is so rarely seen, its instinct teaching it to keep away from man, the great enemy of all creatures.

'Had Heliogabalus, that Roman glutton, met with him, he had devoured him, though there were no more in the world!'
(London, 1651)

And the observation was based on the fact that the Roman Emperor was reputed to have given orders for the elusive bird to be captured and served up to him as a meal, since it was thought that a man would take on the attributes of what he ate; therefore, if he could only eat an immortal creature such as the phoenix he would as a result become immortal himself.

The phoenix has eluded butchers' shops, whose clients have had to make do with digesting, and reducing to their lowest common denominator, the qualities of pigs, chickens, sheep and cows, which fortunately do not guarantee longevity.

John Michell concludes: "Several of the human races, animals and plants, described here in Pliny's Journal and figured in Una Woodruff's reconstructions, have never since been recorded and must be considered, temporarily at least, to be extinct. Others have been sighted at various times up to the present day and may be due for future revival. This question is most properly left for the consideration of experts in fringe biology. It is hoped that their studies will be considerably advanced by the publication of this newly revealed manuscript, and that scholars, naturalists and all lovers of antique curiosities, will find pleasure and instruction in the unique glimpse of natural history in the ancient world here provided.

Pleasure indeed abounds, together with hyperspatial hints as to how to track down these paragons from

supernature.

"It is a sottish presumption to disdain and condemn that for false which unto us seemeth to bear no show of likelihood or truth."
Montaigne, Essays
but the penultimate word should be Pliny's — at the end of this stunning manuscript he declares: "Hail, Nature, mother of all creation, and mindful that I alone of the men of Rome have praised thee in thy manifestations, be gracious unto me." Mum's the word.

The leopard has changed his spots.

"Why," said the Dodo, in Alice, "the best way to explain it is to do it." And the only way to discover what Pliny and Una Silvana did and observed and explained is to walk into your nearest bookseller dressed as a Hydra and poultice 666 copies out of them, with 666 hot and scaly hands, before conducting such an expedition yourself.

Heathcote Williams

MESSENGERS OF DECEPTION: UFO Contacts and Cults
by Jacques Vallee (And/Or Press, Berkeley, California 1979; $6.95 pb, pp243, index, notes, photos — available in Dark They Were bookshop, London and others, £3.95).

Jacques Vallee's latest book, *Messengers of Deception,* is not so much about flying saucers as the effect that such phenomena have on society at large. His first two books, *Anatomy of a Phenomenon* and *Challenge to Science* objectively analyzed UFO reports and the history of the phenomenon. *Passport to Magonia,* widely acclaimed as a classic of UFOlogy, was published in 1969 and marked a radical departure for the researcher; a departure which led him to consider the similarities, and in some instances exact parallels, between flying saucer stories and the medieval tradition of fairies and little people. This venture into comparative mythology and folklore, combined with Carl Jung's book *Flying Saucers* and the writings of John Keel, helped pave the way to the current parapsychological approach taken by some modern-day researchers. The investigation into the psychological reality of the UFO experience was continued in *The Invisible College,* where Dr Vallee developed the thesis that paranormal phenomena, such as UFOs, sightings of the Blessed Virgin Mary, and encounters with unusual entities, represented part of a gigantic control system, through which human beliefs, ideals, and thought patterns were slowly being altered. If this is true, he argued with insight, we should be earnestly studying the subliminal and powerful effects that the UFO experience has on the percipient, society, and our general world-view.

Messengers of Deception, a continuation of this approach, is concerned with the negative and sinister aspects of the phenomenon, and how the UFO — religious symbol par excellence of popular culture — exerts its social influence through various media. *Messengers* is aimed at a large audience, and an audience it will surely find. It is well written, fast-paced, and carries considerable impact. And while all this is true, the book has its rough spots. . .

Carl Jung, the psychoanalyst, thought it highly significant that flying saucers should appear after two terrible world wars, when the traditional religions had lost much of their social-shaping influence. After the word 'flying saucer' entered the world vocabulary in 1947, the next interesting development to take place in the UFO arena was the appearance of the contactees: individuals who had claimed contact with the spaceships-upon-high, assorted and sundry Ascended Masters, the ever benevolent Space Brothers, and other types of astral excrement. There can be no doubt that the murky esotericism of the contactees represented a genuine, if sorely misguided, brand of religious impulse, and a large portion of Vallee's book is devoted to exploring the revolutionary motifs of this schizoid fringe.

Messengers is not on a par with Vallee's earlier writings, for, on the most basic level, the book is a warning against contactees and UFO cultism. Such a warning is more valid today than it has ever been, with the failure of orthodox science and religion to meet human needs, and the related proliferation of fringe groups and 'cults of unreason.' However, I found myself frequently wishing that Vallee would devote less space to the bleary-eyed devotees of the Saucer Religion, by fully developing the fascinating theoretical snippets that are dropped bombshell fashion throughout the course of the book.

Even more frustrating is Vallee's relationship with the mysterious 'Major Murphy,' a certain (anonymous), ex- US Intelligence official, which gives the book, in places, the flavour of a political espionage novel. In following up some of the Major's ideas, Vallee develops the hypothesis that belief in UFOs is being manipulated for political ends by certain human groups ....one of the few conspiracy theories *not* included in Wilson & Shea's *Illuminatus*! It is an interesting hypothesis, and the potential is certainly there, but I couldn't avoid feeling that the 'Major' had deceptive intentions of his own.

Despite these difficulties, *Messengers* is an important book; it is; without a doubt, the foremost work to appear on the sociology of UFO cultism and all the dangers implicit in giving one's mind over to 'higher intelligences.' Having demonstrated the demonic aspects of flying saucer cultism, Vallee refreshingly discusses, at the end of the book, the worthwhile result of man's confrontation with the UFO phenomenon. It is a personal theory, involving a variant of current physics, which transcends the Cartesian split between mind and matter, and points to fascinating relationships which may exist between consciousness and the physical world. It is here that Dr Vallee's brilliance shines through, and one can only hope that his next book is set against the background of this emerging paradigm, rather than the tragic delusions of the Space Brother religionists. *David Fideler*

EGYPTIAN RELIGION by E.A. Wallis Budge (RKP, 1979; £2.50, pp214, illus) EGYPTIAN MAGIC by E.A. Wallis Budge (RKP, 1979; £2.50, pp254, illus)

Two classic works, first published in 1899, now available in paperback. *Religion* deals largely in theory and belief, *Magic* in practice, both ceremonial and mundane; and though neither is indispensable to the other, they read better as a pair, taking *Religion* first, though *Magic* will probably be of more interest to Forteans. Both contain much interesting source material drawn from original Egyptian papyri, especially from the 'Book of the Dead', though the author translates and writes in a somewhat archaic style. His dating of the various dynasties should be treated with care, however; he places the First Dynasty at about 4,300 B.C.; more modern opinion at 3,100 B.C., and consequently compresses the following dynasties in turn. That apart, fascinating reading. *SM*

WORLDS BEYOND The Everlasting Frontier *edited by the New Dimensions Foundation (And/Or Press, Berkeley, California 1978; $6.95 pb, pp301, resource directory, illus).*

An introduction to the uninitiated into a variety of subjects including UFOs, space colonies, cryonics and life extension, as well as extraterrestrial life. The anthology is made up of 27 mini-chapters (or 'sequences') written by a myriad of space age popular culture heroes, some of the more well-known being Stewart Brand, Gerald O'Neil, Robert Anton Wilson, Buckminster Fuller, and even Timothy Leary. Writing within the realm of UFOlogy are Hynek, Stanton Friedman, Vallee and more. Unfortunately, the short length of the various 'sequences' make it impossible for the writers to develop any new, interesting arguments and the book is characterized by repetition of time-worn information. Also included is a resource directory, although we find no reference to *Flying Saucer Review* within the listing of UFO publications...even though Charles Bowen and Gordon Creighton are interviewed within the text! While being attractively produced, the book consists of light reading material aimed at the general public...Still, it might make a nice gift. *DRF*

PSYCHIC ARCHAEOLOGY by Jeffrey Goodman (Panther 1979; £1.50, pp256, bib.)

In 1971 Jeffrey Goodman, an archaeology student, had a vivid dream about excavating an important new site. In his book he recounts the story of finding this site at Flagstaff, Arizona, with the aid of Aron Abrahamson, a talented psychic. It is a fascinating story which shows an archaeologist finding confirmation of some astounding predictions about New World prehistory. This story alone makes *Psychic Archaeology* well worth reading. The author also includes chapters on pioneers in psychic archaeology (Bond, Cayce, and Ossowiecki), but he doesn't add very much to our understanding of them. Mr Goodman is on surer ground when he discusses his own particular interest, which is methods of training psychics to assist archaeologists, and ways of testing the accuracy of their predictions. It is to his credit that at all times he sympathises with the psychic and understands the strain imposed by his experiments.

This book is recommended to all archaeologists particularly in Britain where official resistance to psychic archaeology is strong. However, Forteans must wait a little longer for archaeologists to ask more interesting questions about the *nature* of psychic archaeology. What kind of information are psychics retrieving? Is Mr. Goodman's notion of the archaeologist training the psychic the wrong way round? It is tempting to picture excavations of the future with psychics as directors and archaeologists as shovels!

Valerie Thomas

STORIES ABOUT NOT BEING AFRAID OF GHOSTS *Compiled by the Institute of Literature of the Chinese Academy of Social Sciences (Foreign Languages Press, Beijing, 1979; 45p, pp92, illus)*

'There are no ghosts. Belief in ghosts is a backward idea, a superstition and a sign of cowardice.' Thus, preremptorily, begins the preface, and continues in the same hilariously doctrinal fashion for 16 pages! That out of the way, we have 35 short tales, arranged in chronological order, from Chinese literature of the 3rd to 19th centuries, all chosen on the theme of disbelief in, or defiance of, ghosts. A fascinating insight into the Chinese *conceptions* of ghosts, although the later stories are quite obviously fictional. The earlier ones are fair game for differing opinions. With numerous illustrations in the Chinese style.
SM.

THE DRAGON *by Francis Huxley (Thames & Hudson 1979; £2.95, pp96, bib, photos, illus).*

Yet another beautifully illustrated and worthwhile book in T&H's marvellous 'Art & Imagination' series. In this volume Huxley examines the dragon in all its forms as a symbol of 'the nature of spirit' and 'the spirit of nature', drawing on dragons in myths of all cultures, alchemical and dream symbolism and illustrated by photographs and drawings from manuscripts, frescos and paintings to embroidered robes, porcelain and sculpture. A delight.
RJMR.

UFOs *by Bob Rickard, illustrated by Geoff Taylor (Scimitar/ Archon Press 1979; 40p, pp32. Published in USA by Gloucester Press, NY; $1.00.)*

This beautifully illustrated children's book, besides introducing the reader to many aspects of the UFO puzzle, succeeds admirably in capturing the dream-like wonder of flying saucers. Included for the young reader are outlines of mystery airships, alien beings, UFO shapes, powers, and abductions, and even the sinister men-in-black. Many theories are examined, but the reader is encouraged to keep an open mind and think for himself. This would make a nice gift for youngsters who aren't easily frightened, as well as a fine addition to anyone's UFO collection. Recommended. *DRF*

Booklets

MYSTERY STALKS THE PRAIRIE *by Roberta Donovan & Keith Wolverton (THAR Institute, Raynesford, Montana 59469, USA 1976; price unknown, pp110, photos - available in UK from Suzanne Stebbing mail order).*
CATTLE MUTILATION: The Unthinkable Truth *by F Smith (Freedland Publishers, Cedaredge, RR1 Box 34, Cedar Mesa, Colorado 81413, USA 1976; price unknown, pp78 - available from Page Research mail order).*

Both these books tell the strange story of cattle mutilations (mutes) which have been taking place in over 20 American states during the past few years. There can be no doubt that the cattle *are* mutilated, not the victims of predators, and that the mutilations are expertly performed. This fact is made absolutely clear in *Mystery Stalks The Prairie*, by means of veterinarians' tesimony and a number of colour photographs, including close-ups of mutilations. In this book it is mainly the situation in Montana which is described, but it is representative of the situation throughout the mutilated states. As well as the actual wounds, other features of the phenomena are described: lack of tracks, even in ploughed fields and snow; the refusal of predators to eat corpses after mutilation; mysterious helicopters seen in the vicinity, also UFOs and big hairy creatures. The main theories are also discussed briefly, that is, religious or satanic cults, and UFOs — but the authors, and the law enforcement officers, are frankly baffled.

Not so F. Smith. He knows the answer, and sets out to tell us in *Cattle Mutilation, The Unthinkable Truth.* Whether we accept what he says depends on our attitude towards his 'evidence', but he is too dogmatic for me. I object to his continued reference to 'extraterrestrials', everyone who has thought about it at all must realise that we cannot be so sure where Ufos come from; his frequent references to Jesus to help make a point; his belief that 'out of respect for the human form, God's image, they'd never dissect human bodies no matter how much might be learned from that', and his implied belief that it's OK to dissect animals, a morality I find it impossible to accept. It's a pity his book had to degenerate into the rantings of a closed mind, because the first half is quite a useful rundown of the mutes situation, in which he makes some interesting points —that the mutilators obviously wish their handiwork to be discovered, so it probably has a message for us; that if UFOs are involved, all the weird aspects of mutes are acceptable if still not understood, for UFOs seem to be capable of anything.

Neither book has the answers, but both have plenty of facts, and both are instructive if somewhat gruesome reading on what appears to be yet another aspect of the multifarious UFO phenomenon. **JB.**

QUATERNION: A Textbook for Tomorrow (with the essay THE EATER OUT OF CHAOS) *by Dave Reissig (published by the author from: Hitheryon House, PO Box 452, Syracuse, NY 13201 USA, 1979; £1.75/$3.00 pb, refs, diags.)*

Quaternion is an integrative synthesis about the search for an inclusive and holistic world-view. It is based on the quaternity of Jung's psychological types, and the four corresponding levels of human expression — physical, emotional, mental, and spiritual. Included is an interesting section on Fortean phenomena, other portions being devoted to the author's thoughtful consideration of current-day social and political problems, which he traces to our particular mode of seeing reality.

The Eater Out Of Chaos is a fascinating, visionary essay about the Western cult of the ego, and the problematic dualism of non-existence and being. This book is full of stimulating ideas, and I recommend it highly. *DF.*

MASONIC ASSASSINATION *compiled by Michael Anthony Hoffman (Rialto Books, Box 343, Geneva, New York 14456, USA 1979; $5.99, airmail $2 extra, pp29, illos).*

A masterly piece of research and concise writing, presenting the known facts of the infamous assassinations in which the Freemason movement in America was directly and indirectly implicated. The victims were William Morgan, Joseph Smith (founder of the Mormon Church) and Edgar Allan Poe. Hoffman's portrait of the impotence of the Catholic Church is grim, its once vigorous resistance to Masonry now thoroughly undermined by the infiltration of high-ranking masons into the college of cardinals itself (the revised Mass goes under the title 'Novus Ordo' derived, it is argued, from the masonic motto 'Novus Ordo Seclorum') — and the only power on the world-stage capable of keeping the masons in check is the Mormon Church. Erudite appendices discuss 'Alchemy in Dallas', 'Masonic Jurisprudence' and the symbolism of beheading. *RJMR.*

Classified Exchanges

FORTEAN

CHAOS — a quarterly review devoted to Fort's cases and sources recommended to serious Forteans. Available for single issues or subscription at $2.00/£1.00 per issue. Published by Mr X's 'Res Bureaux': Box 1598, Kingston, Ontario K7L 5C8, Canada.

FATE — the oldest continuously published journal of articles on UFOs, psychic topics, mysteries and Forteana. Monthly by subscription or on newsstands: singles 40p/$1.00, or $10.00/yr (Overseas $11.00). Fate Magazine: 170 Future Way, Marion, CH 43302, USA.

FORTEANA — a very well produced Fortean newspaper, quarterly in Danish. Write for details. SCANFO: Classensgade 8, DK-2100, Kobenhavn 0, Denmark.

LANTERN — quarterly journal of the Borderline Science Investigation Group of East Anglia, covering the regional Forteana and antiquities. £1.00/yr (overseas rates on application). BSIG: 3 Dunwich Way, Lowestoft NR32 4RZ.

MICHIGAN ANOMALY RESEARCH — irregular (you know what we mean) report on current Michigan investigations. Available in return for services or equipment, or $5.00/4 issues. MAR: Box 1479, Grand Rapids, MI 49501, USA.

NESSLETTER — monthly newsletter on sightings, personalities and expeditions at Loch Ness. £1.75 $7.00 (other countries on application). Ness Information Service: Huntshieldford, St Johns Chapel, Bishop Aukland, Co Durham.

PURSUIT — another essential journal for any serious Fortean who considers himself informed. Published quarterly by the Society for the Investigation of the Unexplained, with in-depth, analytical, speculative and investigative articles on all modern Forteana. $10.00/yr (Overseas: $12.50 surface, $15.00 airmail). SITU: Membership Services, RFD 5, Gales Ferry, CT 06335, USA.

RES BUREAUX BULLETIN — a regular and frequent newsletter digest of Canadian and other Forteana, from Mr X, available on exchange or for clippings. Res Bureaux: Box 1598, Kingston Ontario K7L 5C8, Canada.

SCIENCE FRONTIERS — a brief digest of relevant articles in scientific literature, accompanying a list of mail-order Fortean books. The Sourcebook Project, Box 107, Glen Arm, MD 21057, USA.

SECOND LOOK — one of three professional mags who have the foresight to exchange with us. Published monthly; articles by 'big names' on UFOs, Sirius-type mysteries, space flight & colonization, and consciousness engineering. Singles $2.00; or $20.00/yr. Second Look: 10E Street SE, Washington DC 20003, USA.

SIS REVIEW — specialist journal devoted to scholarly discussion of cometary chaos, geological upheaval and chronological anomalies in antiquity, and other themes from the work of Velikovsky. Published quarterly by the Society for Interdisciplinary Studies; write for details. SIS: 6 Jersey House, Cotton Lane, Manchester M20 9GL.

SPECULA — quarterly journal of the American Association of Meta-science, covering frontline speculation on the new physics, psychotronic warfare, UFO energies and the physics of psychic healing. Write for details. AAMS: Box 1182, Huntsville, AL 35807, USA.

STIGMATA — report on Project Stigma, the continuing investigation into cattle mutilations and attendant mysteries; published one issue at a time at $1.00. Project Stigma: Box 1094, Paris, Texas 75460, USA.

TYCHONIAN SOCIETY BULLETIN — journal of a group of orthodox Christian scholars who uphold the belief in a geocentric isotropic universe. Write for details. Tychonian Society: 14813 Harris Rd, RR 1, Pitt Meadows, BC V0M 1P0, Canada.

VESTIGIA NEWSLETTER — quarterly journal of an active investigatory Fortean group in New Jersey. Write for details. Vestigia: RD 2 Brookwood Rd, Stanhope, NJ 07874, USA.

UFOS

APRO BULLETIN — monthly journal of the Aerial Phenomena Research Organisation, possibly USAs most respected and longest established UFO research body. Membership: $12.00 (Overseas $15.00 surface, $17.50 airmail). APRO 3910 E Kleindale Rd, Tucson, AZ 85712, USA.

AWARENESS — quarterly journal of Contact (UK), current investigations. Write for details. Contact (UK): 19 Cumnor Road, Boars Hill, nr Oxford, Oxon.

BUFORA JOURNAL — quarterly journal of the British UFO Research Association. Reports & investigations. Write for details. BUFORA: 30 Vermont Rd, Upper Norwood, London SE19 3SR.

CLYPEUS — a bimonthly journal of mysteries, in Italian, with a supplement *UFO & Fortean Phenomena* featuring translations into Italian of major articles in other languages. Write for details. Clypeus/Gianni Settimo: Casella postale 604, 10100 Torino, Italy.

EARTHLINK — quarterly journal of reports and investigation from Essex-based group. £2.50/yr (Overseas £4.00/4 issues). Earthlink: 16 Raydons Road, Dagenham RM9 5JR.

IL SENZATITOLO — a review journal in Italian. Write for details. Il Senzatitolo: Box 240, 42100 Reggio Emilia, Italy.

INFORESPACE — glossy bimonthly journal of reports, photo-analysis and investigations from the premier Belgian UFO group. Write for details. SOBEPS: Ave Paul Janson 74, 1070 Bruxelles, Belgium.

INTERNATIONAL UFO REPORTER — monthly review of cases reported to the Center for UFO Studies, edited by J Allen Hynek. $12.00/yr (Overseas: $15.00 surface, $22.00 airmail). IUFOR: 1609 Sherman Ave, Suite 207, Evanston, IL 60201, USA.

IRISH UFO NEWS — quarterly reports and investigations of Irish cases. £3.00/yr or for exchange. Irish UFO Research Center: 4 Copeland Drive, Comber, Co Down, N Ireland BT23 5JJ.

JOURNAL OF TRANSIENT AERIAL PHENOMENA — a new journal by the Research Dept of BUFORA, devoted to the technicalities of UFO research, data analysis and scientific studies. Inquire at the BUFORA address above.

LES EXTRATERRESTRES — glossy French journal of reports & investigation. Write for details. Les Extraterrestres: Saint Dennis Les Rebais, 77510 Rebais, France.

MUFOB — Britain's worldbeating quarterly of alternative UFOlogy — one more issue to go and then it reincarnates as *Magonia* with an even wider brief for the review and discussion of the paraphysical, psychological and mythological dimensions of UFOlogy. £1.75/yr (Overseas airmail $4.00). MUFOB: 64 Alric Ave, New Malden, Surrey KT3 4JW.

MAPIT SKYWATCH — quarterly review and reports journal of Manchester research group. Write for details. MAPIT: 92 Hillcrest Rd, Offerton, Stockport, Cheshire SK2 5SE.

NORTHERN UFOLOGY — monthly newsletter from affiliated groups in northern Britain with digests of their reports and investigations. Write for details. NUFON: 23 Sunningdale Drive, Irlam, Salford, M30 6NJ.

NOTIZIARIO UFOLOGICO ACOM — review journal in Italian. Write for details. Paolo Toselli: Spalto Borgoglio 45, 15100 Alessandria, Italy.

NYHETSBLAD — review journal of the Swedish archive group Arbetsgruppen For Ufologi, in Swedish. Write for details. AFU: Box 5046, 151 05 Sodertalje 5, Sweden.

TIJDSCHRIFT VOOR UFOLOGIE — review journal of the Dutch group NOVOBO, in Dutch. Write for details. NOVOBO: Lange Akker 28, 9982 HL Uithuizermeeden, Holland.

UFO NEWSCLIPPING SERVICE — 20 page monthly collection of that month's UFO reports from worldwide (mainly USA) papers plus some Forteana. For details and sample write UFONS: Route 1, Box 220, Plumerville, AR 72127, USA.

UFO OHIO journal and newsletter of Ohio and environs reports and investigations plus articles on UFOs and Forteana. $9.00/6 issues. Also publish the *UFO Ohio Yearbook 1979* featuring evidence on alleged UFOs and occupants in US military custody; $3.00. UFOIN: Box 5012, Rome, OH 44085, USA.

VIMANA — glossy Spanish journal on all subjects relating to UFOs, in Spanish. Write for details, or for exchange. CIOVE: Rualasal 22, Santander, Spain.

PSI
ALPHA — steadily improving newsstand bimonthly overview on UFOs, Psi, Earth Mysteries and Forteana, with some spiritualistic bias. £4.75/yr. Pendulum Pub. Co: 20 Regent Street, Fleet, Hants GU13 9NR.

EVP NEWS — monthly newsletter devoted to study of electronic voice phenomena. £1.20/yr (overseas airmail £4.50). Alan Cleaver: 12 Lime Tree Ave, Old Bilton, Rugby, Warks CV22 7QT.

PREMONITION TIMES — new monthly news and discussion journal and premonition bureau. $18.00/yr, single issue $1.75. Premonition Times: Box 82863, Lincoln, NB 68501, USA.

EARTH MYSTERIES
ANCIENT SKILLS AND WISDOM REVIEW — irregular journal of book and magazine reviews. Single issue 50p, or £2.00/yr. Paul Screeton: 5 Egton Drive, Seaton Carew, Hartlepool, Cleveland TS25 2AT.

ARCHAEOASTRONOMY — bulletin of the Center for Archaeoastronomy; reports, news, reviews, articles. Write for details. Center for Archaeoastronomy, Space Sciences Building, University of Maryland, College Park, MD 20742, USA.

CATASTROPHIST GEOLOGY — half-yearly review of work and study of discontinuities in Earth history and geology. $10.00/4 issues (add $3.00 for airmail). Johan B Kloosterman, Caixa Postal 41 003, Santa Teresa, Rio de Janeiro, Brazil.

IGNEWS — bimonthly newsletter of Manchester area cryptogeologists. 25p/copy, £2.10/6 issues. IGNews: BM Bulletin, London WC1V 6XX.

JOURNAL OF GEOMANCY — quarterly journal of the Institute of Geomantic Research. 60p/copy, £3.00/yr. IGR: 142 Pheasant Rise, Bar Hill, Cambridge CB3 8SD.

KADATH — glossy quarterly Belgian journal devoted to aspects of vanished civilizations, in French. Write for details. Kadath: 6 Boulevard Saint-Michel, B-1150 Bruxelles, Belgium.

THE LEY HUNTER — bimonthly journal of earth mysteries (soon to be quarterly), essential for keeping informed on ley and earth energy research. £3.00/yr (Overseas: £3.60 surface, $9.00 airmail). TLH: Box 152, London N10 2EF.

NEARA JOURNAL — quarterly journal of the New England Antiquities Research Association. $5.50/yr. NEARA: 11 Elizabeth Court, North Kensington, RI 02852, USA.

TERRESTRIAL ZODIACS NEWSLETTER — occasional. Free for donations, stamps or written contributions or exchange. Paul Screeton: 5 Egton Drive, Seaton Carew, Hartlepool, Cleveland TS25 2AT.

OTHERS
FANTASY MEDIA — news and reviews of fantasy films, tv, books, comix and magazines; apx 5 times a year. £3.00/yr (Overseas: $11.00 airmail). Fantasy Media: 194 Station Road, Kings Heath, Birmingham B14 7TE.

GNOME NEWS — newsletter of the Gnome Club of Great Britain; 3 times a year. Membership £2.50/yr (Overseas £3.50/yr). Gnome Club: West Putford, Devon EX22 7XE.

JOURNAL OF METEOROLOGY — monthly review and record of weather phenomena for UK, Europe and worldwide; much of interest to Forteans. £9.50/yr (Overseas: $22.00 surface, $28.00 airmail). Artetech Pub Co: Cockhill House, Trowbridge, Wiltshire BA14 9BG.

JUST MEASURE — newsletter of the anti-metrication lobby. Write for details. Anti-Metrication Board: Stroude Manor, Blackstroude Lane, Lightwater, Surrey.

KINGDOM VOICE — monthly newsletter on Biblical prophecy. £2.00/yr (Overseas: $5.00). Reginald Bradbury: Riverside Cottage, Bridgend, Harpford, Sidmouth, Devon EX10 0NG.

LIGHT TIMES — an enigmatic journal of iconoclasm with a side order of humour, spun off *Illuminatus!*. Write for details. Light Times: 615 Ocean Front Walk, Venice, CA 90291, USA.

NEUROLOG — occasional journal of The Network and the Corps of Reality Engineers. Much Fortean fun. Write for details. The Network: Box 317, Berkeley, CA 94701, USA.

Frogs Provençal

I must tell you a story that, although somewhat disappointing to begin with, has a highly instructive ending that would have delighted Charles Fort.

First the bad news: frogs did *not* fall out of the sky for three days at Chalon-sur-Saone in 1922. [See Fort p546] True, Fort's source — the front page of the *Daily News* of 5 September 1922 — said they did, but I have discovered that this was a journalistic fantasy.

Reasoning that the Paris correspondent of the *Daily News* must have picked the story up from a local newspaper, I wrote to the editor in Chalon-sur-Saone asking if he could look out the relevant back number and show it to me when I stayed in the town overnight en route to the south of France. He did better than that, publishing a paragraph about the impending arrival of a crazy English author, and asking if any of his readers could remember this improbable event.

When I met him, he gave me the telephone number of four or five people who had written or called as a result, and after talking to them, it seems clear that what had happened was a migratory plague of frogs crossing the roads. Observers remembered being unable to avoid squashing them as they bicycled. None had seen them dropping from the sky. And the original newspaper report, when I tracked it down in the local municipal library (magnificent — worth at least two stars in Michelin), mentioned only an 'infestation' of frogs observed on a single day.

However, I promise that what I am about to tell you is absolutely true, and provides the moral ending to the non-Fortean event at Chalon. I painstakingly copied out the original report, in French, from the local newspaper, and put it in the car with the other research papers. It vanished during the journey south. A couple of days later, one of my dowsing L-rods vanished from a securely fastened haversack. A day or so after that, the other L-rod vanished overnight from a locked car.

And when I recounted this sad story of the land-bound frogs to locals in the bar of the village where I was staying — Eygalieres in Provence — I was immediately told that frog falls in that area were widely known and accepted; and indeed, I met two impeccable witnesses who had seen it happen, once in the 1930's and once in c1945. Both men, independently, pointed to their thumb-nail to indicate the size of the frogs, which fell accompanied by rain, during thunderstorm conditions, but without debris. (Incidentally, a sceptical friend has suggested that the lack of debris in these cases may be because a whirlwind has lifted the frogs from a land surface, and that the dust would separate from the frogs at a higher altitude.) On both occasions, the frogs survived the impact of landing, and hopped about.

Francis Hitching. Twickenham, London

Cow's Elegy?

Several evenings ago some friends and I were walking on a local hilltop and we came upon the carcass of a dead cow lying in some long grass. I would estimate that the carcass had been there for a couple of days but due to the difficult terrain it had not been removed.

Later that same evening immediately after sunset all the cows and calves on the hilltop started to move urgently but silently along the fresh cowpath which led past the carcass. All the beasts without exception, young and old, gathered in a circle around the dead animal, their heads lowered and tails motionless. After several minutes, during which time the cowpath stragglers had caught up and joined the others, they started to slowly slip away into the dusk.

A strange and somewhat eerie sight and one which had quite an effect on all who witnessed it. Were the beasts responding to some telepathic herd instinct and saying goodnight to one of their kind or were they ruminating on the transient nature of their existence?

Alan Price. Lisvane, Cardiff

Towards a Fortean Classification System

Most of us in the 'strange phenomena' business, whether on a professional or dilettante basis, must maintain card-indexes or suchlike for the snippets of information which come our way: from which it must inevitably follow that we are all bugged by problems of classification.

I dare say most of us have solved this more or less to our own personal satisfactions, though for my own part I confess I am continually changing my mind and switching, say, bodily elongation from 'mystical' to 'physical' and so on. And of course the matter becomes even more awkward when it is a matter of interchange with other 'collectors'; though we share a common interest we do not necessarily share a common terminology.

I would like to suggest, therefore, that *Fortean Times* takes a lead towards establishing some kind of comprehensive classification system as a guide for us all. It would indeed be interesting to know if FT itself possesses a system in which it has sufficient confidence to publish it as a guide, or whether it, too, would welcome discussion leading to the establishment of a common classification system.

I am myself a librarian, and have had occasion to look into this matter of subject classification; and have come fairly definitely to the conclusion that the best solution is not a ready-made off-the-shelf solution, but a pragmatic one designed to fit the material rather than have the material forced to fit it.

Yet even if this is agreed as a basis, there are still many ways of subdividing the material, just as a chocolate bar or sheet of stamps can be divided this way or that. The most obvious method is a simple alphabetical list, but this is a cowardly dodging of the issue. On the other hand, the moment you start grouping phenomena you run the risk of begging questions — in particular, of making assumptions about them which can inhibit objective thinking about them. Is telekinesis a psychic or physical phenomenon? Does a poltergeist have objective reality? Could UFOs be mental projections, albeit with the power to affect radar?

I would be pleased to hear from other readers who may share my perplexity in this matter, or who believe they have solved the problem; similarly, I would be curious to hear what the Editor has to say on the matter.

Hilary Evans. Mary Evans Picture Library, Blackheath, London.

[Hilary Evans cogently pinpoints a fundamental problem for Forteans.

Having disregarded alphabetical and numerical lists based on existing library systems, and even Roget's Thesaurus, we are currently following a specific line of exploration. Fortean flexibility seems to be a function of the number of cross-references to other cases, events, subjects etc. Our other criterion is the phenomenon itself and not its hypothetical context; this leaves us free to deal with the reported effects, subjective AND objective, involved in 'UFO' or 'poltergeist' reports, for example, without subscribing to notions, implicit in those terms, of extraterrestrial beings, spirits of the dead, elementals, conspiracies, other dimensions or theology. Work is proceeding on experimental index of phenomenal effects with extensive cross-referencing. If it works, we will publish it for general comment and critical development. In the meantime, like Hilary Evans, we too would appreciate hearing from anyone with any ideas — RJMR.]

Two-Headed Oracle

We were recently in India with a French TV team making documentaries on Indian village life. On 5th April 1979 we visited a local festival of minstrels, at Sonamukhi in the district of Burdwan, West Bengal. It was attended by at least 200,000 people, and as is common at these events there was a funfair-cum-circus. It featured a twelve-year-old two-headed boy in a sideshow tent, lying on his back. He had one body, two necks and two heads, one physically and mentally more dominant than the other. They could speak independently of each other. The man in charge — who seemed to be a relative — asked various questions which the heads answered in turn. This was seen by seven members of the TV team.

It is still quite common at festivals in India to see exhibitions of prodigies.

Helen Coles and Bhaskar Bhattacharyya. London. [For more on recent freaks and prodigies turn to page 21. Ed]

Nessie the Elephant?

May I bring to the readers' attention a recent article in *New Scientist* (2 Aug) in which the authors claim to have solved the mystery of Loch Ness? After comparing photographs of Nessie with similar photographs from Burma they have identified Nessie as a swimming elephant. [See our 'Trends' section, this issue. Ed]

I dare say that the authors were not entirely convinced by their own explanation but they have overlooked an intriguing piece of evidence. The ancient Picts, it seems, were fond of carving pictures of animals on rocks. And pretty naturalistic pictures they were too — instantly recognisable as deer boar, golden eagle, salmon, or whatever — except for one animal which archeologists call 'the Pictish Beast' or 'swimming elephant'. [See illustrations.]

Mike Crowley. London.

Imperial Forteanism

Here are two possible references to an antique Chinese official known in T'ang times as the 'Inspector of Oddities'. Perhaps one of your readers who can read Chinese or has access to old star catalogues can take the matter further.

The first is a reference in Schlegel's *Uranographie Chinoise* (1879), to the Inspector's celestial counterpart, given as 'e602' Arietis. The problem here is which star is e602?

The second is a tentative identification with an official listed in Biot's French translation (1851) of the *'Rites of Chou'* (compiled 2nd cent. B.C.). Is this the inspector?

'The Inspector of Invading Oddities.

He is instructed in the ten effects of light, and his function is to observe extraordinary things and say if they are good or bad.

(Top) An assortment of naturalistic animal designs found on Pictish stones; the last design being the curiously stylized 'swimming elephant' motif, as seen (Below) on a stone at Meigle. See Mike Crowley's letter (Left) and notes on p29.

The first of the ten light effects is the invasion; the second the double sun; the third, the halo; the fourth, the hanging clouds; the fifth, the weakening of the light; the sixth, obscurities; the seventh, sky bands; the eighth, symmetrical arrangements of clouds; the ninth, (circular) rainbows; the tenth is called clouds that make you think.

He is in charge of calming people down, and getting them to hand over things which have fallen from the sky. He begins his work at the beginning of the year, and at the end of the year he analyses it.' (XXV, 30-32.)

John Cox London

Our Oriental Obscurities editor, Steve Moore, replies:

For those unfamiliar with Chinese literature, the Chou Li, an alleged description of the court ritual of the Chou dynasty (12th-5th centuries BC), is traditionally ascribed to the Duke of Chou (12th C. BC), although modern thought places its composition between the Warring States Period (5th-3rd C. BC) and the Former Han (1st C. BC) depending on whether one believes Liu Hsin of the Han found or forged the manuscript. Either way, it is very far removed from the T'ang (7th–10th C. AD); and official titles and the jobs attached to them were extremely prone to change; so a direct titular correspondence remains uncertain, though some such official doubtless existed throughout early Chinese history.

The T'ang official would presumably have been working under the Imperial Astronomical Board (or 'Ministry'), which itself changed its title several times during the T'ang, responsible for studying changes in the colour of the sun, the moon, constellations, winds, clouds and 'breaths'. The special department with which we are concerned seems to be the T'ung Hsuan yuan, 'Close for Communication with the Occult', whose personnel studied and prepared quarterly reports on the omens, forwarding them to the government ministries and historical archives. See Edward H. Schafer: Pacing the Void (University of California Press, 1977) p13.

Regarding the Chou official, we have found a reference to what may be another official with similar duties, from Alfred Forke: The World Conception of the Chinese (Probsthain, 1925) p5. Forke is again referring to Biot's Chou Li, but this time to chapter 26, where we find an official called the Pao-chang-shih (unfortunately my dictionary fails to make sense of this title). He too was on the astronomical 'staff': 'From the motions and changes of the planets and the stars, eclipses and parhelions, phases of the moon and the like they prognosticated lucky and unlucky auguries. The happiness of the empire depended on the gyrations of Jupiter, that of the feudal states on their special stars. The five kinds of clouds around the sun at the time of the solstices and equinoxes were indicative of imminent blessings or disasters, and so were the twelve varieties of winds. Green clouds meant insects, white meant death, red meant devastation by war, black, inundations, and yellow a rich harvest.'

Off-hand, I know of no complete English translation of the Chou Li.

Small Ads

TRUSS FUND
. . .in which Fortean Times acknowledges with grateful thanks the valuable donations sent by the following: Jim Brandon, David Dunthorn, Kevin McClure, Graham McEwan, John Peldyak, Roger Randle, Ted Schultz, Mike and Linda Ward, Roger Waddington, Nigel Watson, R Marty Wolf. Such heartening support helps us brave the slings and arrows of outrageous economic misfortune.

CLOSE ENCOUNTER UFO CASSETTES — Intriguing close sighting: contact: humanoid accounts. Witness excerpts. Narration by Norman Oliver FRAS. Send SAE for list NOW. Sample C60 £2.50. SKYQUEST, 95 Taunton Road, London SE12 8PA.

WARMINSTER — Ley and UFO Centre. Cottage now available to UFO researchers, skywatchers and ley hunters. Holidays or weekends. Sae details: UFO Services, 47 Belsize Square, London NW3.

THE OLD STONES OF LANDS END. This classic study of Cornish megaliths by John Michell, acclaimed essay on the nature of megalithic culture, is to be reprinted by Pentacle Books at £3.90, fully illustrated — third in a series of special reprints: No 1 being Alfred Watkins' seminal *The Ley Hunter's Manual* (£2.25), No 2, Eitel's oft-cited *Feng Shui* (£2.50). PENTACLE BOOKS, 6 Perry Rd, Bristol

ATTENTION UFO COLLECTORS! — Hundreds of new, used and rare books, magazines, newsletters and imported items for sale. Supply is limited, so act NOW! Send $2.00 for catalogue listing 24 pages long. Along with this you get a deluxe research newsletter sample. PAGE RESEARCH: PO Box 5012, ROME, OH 44085, USA.

FLYING SAUCERS, photos, newsletter, meetings, skywatches, research and investigation. SAE details: British UFO Society, 47 Belsize Square, London NW3.

UFO NEWSCLIPPING SERVICE — Want to keep up with the real 'close encounters'? One excellent way of doing so is with the UFO NEWSCLIPPING SERVICE, bringing you to UFO reports from the United States and around the world. Since 1969, our Service has obtained news-clippings from an international press clipping bureau, then reproduced them by photo-offset printing for our subscribers. Many fascinating UFO reports (photographs, landing and occupant cases, etc) are only published in smaller daily and weekly newspapers. Our Service provides these for you, along with wire-service items from Associated Press, United Press International, Reuters and other agencies.

Each monthly issue of the UFO NEWSCLIPPING SERVICE is a 20 page report containing the latest UFO reports from the US, England, Canada, Australia, South America and other countries. English translations of foreign language reports are also provided.

Let us keep you informed on world-wide UFO activity. For subscription information and sample pages from our Service issues, write today to:
UFO NEWSCLIPPING SERVICE
Lucius Farish,
Route 1 — Box 220
Plumerville, Arkansas 72127
USA

Next Issue

Scoop! For the first time in a Western publication, evidence for the **Chinese 'Bigfoot'**, presented by two anthropologists from the Academy of Sciences, Peking, no less! Part 1 of **David Fideler's** study of Fortean phenomena in the state of Michigan (postponed from this issue); **Michael Goss** on occult forces used to deadly effect in oriental fighting arts; a collection of engravings featuring death by ball lightning; and more Fortean notes.

In next and future issues, we'll continue our developments of style and content, opening our pages to more artists — with a variety of techniques from comix and cartoons to illustrations — inspired by our field's potential for humour as well as philosophy. These existential funnies will be under the creative editorship of our own inimitable Hunt Emerson. Steve Moore, Spirit of the Moon and chief of our Department of Oriental Obscurities, is cooking up a format in which to present Far Eastern Forteana in greater variety and quantity. And while we review our experiment with guest columns, we'd like to extend the invitation to any reader who feels strongly about any aspect of Forteana or FT. If you wish to air your opinion, on any relevant topic, and can keep it concise — about 500 words or less — the soap-box is yours. So stay with us — we've a lot more of what you want in the pipe-line.

PHENOMENA
A Book of Wonders

T-Shirt

Subscribe

The House of Lords UFO Debate.
Illustrated, Full Transcript with Preface by Lord Clancarty (Brinsley le Poer Trench) and Notes by John Michell.

The House of Lords UFO Debate.
Illustrated. Full Transcript with Preface
by Lord Clancarty (Brinsley le Poer Trench)
and Notes by John Michell.

"Is it not time that Her Majesty's Government informed our people of what they know about UFOs? I think it is time our people were told the truth." —Lord CLANCARTY.

The recent debate on unidentified flying objects (UFOs) in the House of Lords was the first to be held on this subject by any legislative body. The motion, calling upon the Government to promote international study of the rapidly growing UFO problem, was introduced to the Upper Chamber of the British Parliament by the Earl of Clancarty, better known as the pioneer UFO writer, Brinsley le Poer Trench.

Together with other speakers in the debate, notably the Earl of Kimberley, former Liberal spokesman on aerospace, Clancarty urges the Government to publish their secret files of UFO records and to reveal what is known about the phenomenon. His restrained, scholarly opening speech brings a variety of interesting responses from fellow peers. Contributions include charges of official UFO-news suppression, noble theories of UFO origins, accounts of members sightings and a theological intervention by the Bishop of Norwich. Marginal notes in this edition provide background information on the UFO cases and other matters referred to in this debate, and there are many relevant illustrations.

Published by *Open Head Press* and
Pentacle Books now available at £2.95 plus
30p post and packing from: *Open Head Press*,
2 Blenheim Crescent, London W11 1NN.

Trade enquiries apply to: *Pentacle Books*,
6 Perry Road, Bristol 1.

Also From FORTEAN TOMES ...

LAKE MONSTER TRADITIONS: A Cross-cultural Analysis

● By **Michel Meurger** with Claude Gagnon.
● The most significant contribution to the understanding of the phenomenology of water-monsters in 20 years. Challenges the prevailing dogmas of cryptozoologists, occultists, and sceptics by questioning the nature of the sightings themselves, taking in such diverse subjects as apparitions, witchcraft, UFOs, mermaids, mystery submarines, nature spirits, shamanic experiences, culturally conditioned misinterpretations of natural occurrences, monster images in art & fiction, & naturalization of the supernatural.
● Discusses material from North & South American, Scandinavian, Baltic, European, and many other countries. Cultural & historical sources include records of explorers, colonists, traders, Jesuits, ethnologists, whaling, fishing & hunting communities, Amerindian & other native cultures; includes unfamiliar material newly translated.
● Runner-up, Katherine Briggs Folklore Award 1989.
● "Well-argued, complex, bold, lavishly illustrated." – *Sunday Times*.

ISBN: 1 870021 00 2. 320 pages; 8 maps;   22 portraits; 31 photos; 141 line & tone illustrations;   notes and references in situ;   full bibliography & authority index; plus 3 other indexes. Paper **£12.95**. From good bookshops or by mail order from: **SKS, 20 Paul Street, Frome, Somerset BA11 1DX, UK,** enclosing a cheque for **£14.25 / $28.50.** (includes post & packing). Trade Inquiries to: **Chris Lloyd Sales, Box 327, Poole, Dorset BH15 2RG.**

MONSTRUM!   A Wizard's Tale.

In 1976, author **Doc Shiels** photographed Morgawr (the Cornish sea monster), and in 1977 he took his celebrated portrait of Nessie. Doc recalls this exciting time, when aided by sky-clad witches and the rituals of surrealchemy he forms an international group of magicians to raise up the monsters in lakes around the world with some success and some backlash. This is a paranormal adventure in an Alice-in-Wonderland landscape of enchanting coincidences made meaningful by Gaelic folklore, modern magic and Fortean phenomena. Doc crosses the tracks of the Little People, UFOs, the frightful Owlman, ancient celtic squids and the pookas and peistes of Irish belief.

Doc is the author of several books on stage magic, editor of *Nnidnid*, a magazine of surrealalchemy. He is also a playright, musician and busker, and well-known contributor to *Fortean Times*. Introduction by **Colin Wilson**.   Paper **£8.95**.

ISBN: 1 870021 04 5. 144 pages, 48 plates, photos & line illos, bibliography, index. From good bookshops or by mail order from: **SKS, 20 Paul Street, Frome, Somerset BA11 1DX, UK, enclosing a cheque for £9.75 / $20.00.** (including post & packing). Trade Inquiries to: **Chris Lloyd Sales, Box 327, Poole, Dorset BH15 2RG.**